CONTEMPORARY ISSUES IN FINANCE AND INSOLVENCY LAW VOLUME 1

There is increasing regulatory interdependence amongst Central, East and South East Asian, European and North American financial markets, and these markets account for over one-third of the world's population and global financial markets. As Asian markets become more integral to global financial economy, more cohesive, compatible and integrated insolvency and restructuring laws are essential. This two-volume work reviews why we should internationalise current cross-border insolvency and how we could restructure laws to address inadequacies.

The two volumes evaluate international regulatory reforms directed at detecting and managing cross-border insolvency and restructuring crises across the entire economy including financial markets. The authors call for schemes of arrangements and letters of comfort to be formally accepted as international legal tools. The work also assesses recent, but as yet largely unregulated developments in financial agreements, particularly the use of close-out netting provisions that serve as significant protective mechanisms prior to the declaration of an insolvency. It discusses international arbitration, data protection and artificial intelligence in cross-border insolvency and restructuring. Finally, the book seeks a meaningful balance between self-regulation through financial contracts and other party practices, and regulation imposed by governments and international financial regulators.

This extensive work will be a useful reference for legal practitioners, policy makers and scholars working on financial regulation and international financial laws.

Leon Trakman is UNSW Emeritus Professor and Former Dean of Law at the University of New South Wales in Sydney, Australia. He has held professorial appointments in the United States, at the University of Wisconsin, University of California (Davis) and Tulane; in Canada at McGill and Dalhousie; and in Australia at UNSW. He is author of ten books and over 150 journal articles, including on topics that are addressed in this book. A barrister and international commercial arbitrator, he serves on international commercial arbitration panels of global arbitration centres. A panellist under the NAFTA, he was regularly appointed by the US, Canadian and Mexican Governments to resolve trade and investment disputes. He currently serves on the remedies panel of the United States-Mexico-Canada Agreement (USMCA). He holds both master's and doctorate degrees from Harvard University.

Robert Walters is Senior Lecturer, Victoria University, Melbourne, Australia. Dr. Walters is also Adjunct Professor of Law, European Faculty of Law, New University, Slovenia, Europe, and admitted to practice law in Australia. In 2021 and 2022, he undertook a full Professorship at the European Faculty of Law. Dr. Walters is a Qualified International Arbitrator. He is a member of ASEAN Law Association – Singapore, Asia Pacific Scholar (Privacy/Data Protection) Network. His work on cross-border data flows in the new digital economy has been recognised globally, and in 2021 and 2022 he was engaged by national governments to undertake a project on determining data flows, data adequacy, data protection, cyber security and artificial intelligence across commonwealth countries. This work was commissioned to strengthen economic outcomes to a number of commonwealth countries in the digital economy and international trade. Dr. Walters specialises in transnational commercial and private law (data protection, cyber security, artificial intelligence, trade, cross-border insolvency/restructuring (netting arrangements), contracts, arbitration).

"Cross-border insolvency necessarily involves multiple jurisdictions. But, as this important new work demonstrates, it also routinely necessitates multiple perspectives – economic and legal, of course, but also social, political, and medical. A particular strength is the manner in which the book focuses on the digital economy, where data is a source of value but doesn't fall neatly into existing categories: Is it a good? Is it a service? Is it something else? At the same time, the authors ground their research in the practical and the pragmatic, offering concrete proposals in support of regulatory convergence and harmonisation that, they argue, will better enable the global economy to navigate increasingly choppy waters. For practitioners, scholars, and students it will be of great interest – and of great use."

Simon Chesterman, *Dean and Provost's Chair Professor of the National University of Singapore Faculty of Law and Senior Director of AI Governance at AI Singapore*

"In this innovative new book, Trakman and Walters make the case for urgent reform of cross-border corporate insolvency and restructuring law. Their account covers, but goes beyond, challenges with the existing enforcement and recognition regime, to call for 'internationalisation' of various legal tools and mechanisms, including several rarely discussed in a cross-border insolvency and restructuring context such as letters of comfort, data protection, and artificial intelligence. This impressive scope is matched by engagement with an impressive number of jurisdictions: Australia; India; Indonesia; China; Singapore; UK; US; and the European Union. The result is a book which deserves a place on the bookshelves of anyone interested in this important field."

Sarah Paterson, *Professor of Law, London School of Economics*

"As the world continues to grapple with the COVID-19 pandemic and economic downturn, this is a most timely and impressive study of cross-border insolvency. A particular strength is its extensive research. The authors cover not only technical substantive laws concerned with transnational insolvency, but also complicated private international law issues such as jurisdiction and international commercial arbitration, which are rarely discussed in the literature. It further identifies key emerging areas of international commercial law such as data protection and artificial intelligence that will form part of cross-border insolvency and restructuring. Specifically the book calls for nations to collaborate at internationalisation level for current and future economic shock. One of the finest works on cross-border insolvency, this book is essential reading for everyone interested in the insolvency law, international commercial law, private international law and international dispute resolution."

Weixia Gu, *Associate Professor, The University of Hong Kong Faculty of Law and Co-Chair, American Society of International Law Asia-Pacific Interest Group (2018–2021)*

"Throughout the COVID-19 pandemic the world has experienced various levels of financial stress, however in this context of global crisis some crucial aspects of financial infrastructural stress, such as cross-border insolvency and restructuring, have not often been spoken or written about. Against the backdrop of a period of growth, internationally, nevertheless a comparatively large number of entities have had to restructure or declare insolvency. With many entities based in multiple locations and in different countries, this book provides practitioners, scholars, and students with a highly sophisticated comparative legal analysis. The authors make an important point – that national and international regulators need to take a preventative approach, to ensure or minimise as far as possible future economic shocks, and ensure a high level of certainty. As the digital economy expands, the authors also highlight the importance of data and artificial intelligence technology to future cross-border restructuring and insolvency. In calling for greater internationalisation of these area of law and close-out netting provisions, the authors embrace the roles of international organisations such as UNCITRAL-UNICTAD which can have a positive effect. I highly recommend this book to anyone with an interest in cross-border insolvency or restructuring."

Michael Stuckey, *Professor and Dean of School of Law, University of Tasmania, Australia*

"Insolvency law and its practice sits within a country's legal system. The book explains how insolvency law and its various mechanisms – preventive and reconstructive, often 'multi-layered' – are applied to businesses under financial stress. The book's particular merit is its coverage of a broader range of insolvency laws and their intersections than we generally see, beyond the UNCITRAL Model Law and schemes of arrangement to close out and netting arrangements, keepwell agreements, arbitrations, data control and artificial intelligence. In comparing and contrasting different national approaches, this text makes a valuable and timely contribution to international insolvency law."

Michael Murray, *Principal at Murrays Legal, Sydney, Australia and Director, Australian Academy of Law*

CONTEMPORARY ISSUES IN FINANCE AND INSOLVENCY LAW

Volume 1

Leon Trakman and
Robert Walters

Routledge
Taylor & Francis Group
LONDON AND NEW YORK

First published 2023
by Routledge
4 Park Square, Milton Park, Abingdon, Oxon OX14 4RN

and by Routledge
605 Third Avenue, New York, NY 10158

Routledge is an imprint of the Taylor & Francis Group, an informa business

British Library Cataloguing-in-Publication Data
A catalogue record for this book is available from the British Library

Library of Congress Cataloging-in-Publication Data
A catalog record for this book has been requested

ISBN: 978-1-032-31884-4 (hbk)
ISBN: 978-1-032-31881-3 (pbk)
ISBN: 978-1-003-31187-4 (ebk)

DOI: 10.4324/9781003311874

Typeset in Bembo
by Apex CoVantage, LLC

CONTENTS

FIGURES

FOREWORD

Over the course of 2020 and 2021, the world was affected by, and attempted to come to terms with, the COVID-19 pandemic. The impact was very different from more recent economic and geopolitical shocks such as the 2008 global financial crisis (GFC). No nation was spared from the pandemic. It had an obvious and terrible effect on the lives of many people, not only in loss of life and ongoing medical problems but also on their jobs and livelihoods and the economies of the countries in which they lived. The movement of people ground to a halt nationally and internationally. Borders were closed, economic production stalled. Unlike the GFC, where economic production remained largely untouched, the pandemic forced millions of people out of work. There was a significant rise in cross-border insolvencies, offset to a degree by a rise in local and transnational restructuring. At the same time there was a decline in cross-border mergers and acquisitions as businesses responded to the pandemic by looking inwards, due to the uncertain global economic outlook.

In these circumstances, it is perhaps not a surprise that cross-border insolvency and restructuring are garnering more attention. A rise in transnational trade and investment preceded the pandemic and will be likely to rise again as the world learns to live with it. Companies are again looking at ways to maximise profits, while ensuring they operate with certainty, with the result that increasingly they are establishing offices and branches in other countries. This international growth has led to an increase in cross-border insolvency and restructuring and to international and national legal frameworks adapting to accommodate this activity. Such developments provide some legal certainty for entities under financial stress, as well as for their creditors and related parties. However, across borders the legal developments can be and are somewhat variable in nature and so not always amenable to consistent application in practice. The current international legal framework, coupled with domestic legislative, administrative and judicial regulatory measures, provides a foundation upon which to base and enhance global insolvency and reconstruction measures. However, there is scope to do more to harmonise cross-border insolvency and restructuring laws.

The lack of universal implementation or consistent application of the 1997 UNCITRAL Model Law on Cross-Border Insolvency has created challenges. Some states have not adopted the UNCITRAL Model Law while others have construed and applied it restrictively. In contrast, the jurisdictions that comprise the subject of discussion and comparative analysis in this book have generally adopted a universalist approach to cross-border insolvency and have implemented the UNCITRAL Model Law. In order to meet the needs of future development, consideration needs to be given to a convergence of approach by nation states by adopting a more universalist approach. While the authors of this book have only undertaken a limited comparison of the approaches of Australia, the European Union, China, Indonesia, India, Singapore, the United Kingdom and the United States, they have identified many similarities in the respective cross-border insolvency and restructuring legal regimes of those jurisdictions. But, more work can be done to achieve a higher level of legal convergence.

This book is timely. Its recommendations may strengthen the current international framework for cross-border insolvency and restructuring. The authors' analysis is thought provoking and demonstrates that the principles, concepts and tools available in private international law may not be sufficient to resolve the potential challenges and conflicts that are likely to arise in cross-border restructuring and insolvency in the future. Their proposals constitute a real contribution to the debate as to how to develop and entrench more effective mechanisms of cross-border insolvency.

The Honourable Justice Brigitte Markovic
Federal Court of Australia

PREFACE

Deglobalisation has been well underway for some time. The recent pandemic has, in the eyes of some international organisations, contributed to this. The World Economic Forum in 2020 summarised the current deglobalisation activity insightfully as follows:

> With coronavirus (COVID-19) raising concerns around globalization and world trade, global value chains are beginning to fray, as countries look inwards for economic growth, write two experts. Since the early 1990s until recently, the world had been witnessing an economic 'convergence', whereby poor countries were beginning to catch up with rich ones. Hyper-globalization drove the global export-to-GDP ratio from 15% to 25% over the two decades leading up to the 2008 global financial crisis. This export boom has fuelled rapid growth in developing countries. There is every reason to worry that a historic process of deglobalization is underway, threatening to scuttle the growth models of poor countries that previously used trade as a path to prosperity. Worst of all, this disturbing shift has been met by silence or even encouragement by those who should know better. The intellectual response to deglobalization and the reversal of the historic process of convergence has been a near-deafening silence. Very few academics or policymakers in advanced economies have spoken up in defense of an open global order on behalf of poorer countries. Cosmopolitan elites who previously had been loud and enthusiastic champions of globalization have sat on their hands.[1]

1 World Economic Forum, *How Deglobalisation Is Hurting the World's Emerging Economies*, https://www.weforum.org/agenda/2020/09/convergence-threatened-by-deglobalization-covid19/

However, in the new digital economy, the globalisation of commercial and personal data increases annually. Data, while often not thought of as an issue in cross-border insolvency, has continued to emerge as being challenging and problematic due to the fragmented approach of regulating cross-border data flows of personal data. While this book is not an explicit call to assist poorer countries directly, it defends the rules-based rule of law to assist emerging and developing countries, not only developed ones. In other words, by strengthening the global legal framework for transnational insolvency and restructuring, in our view, no one nation state should be disadvantaged, so long as the benefits in international economic growth are shared. We identify those benefits with the harmonisation and convergence of transnational law and policy governing cross-border restructuring and insolvency. The book does so by addressing the comparative and interdisciplinary research of the United Nations Commission on International Trade Law (UNCITRAL) Model Law on Cross-Border Insolvency and the International Institute for the Unification of Private Law (UNIDROIT) Principles on Close-Out Netting. Arguably these institutions have been instrumental in bringing together the nations of the world to establish a global framework that has sought to harmonise cross-border insolvency law. The book digresses slightly and aims to also address the emerging areas of law that challenge this, such as data protection and artificial intelligence.

This work is intended to make a significant step forward in promoting a global regulatory environment that provides a significant layer of certainty in regulating cross-border insolvency and corporate restructuring. However, there continues to be an urgent need to address immediate threats to global commerce, resulting from the pandemic, trade sanctions and other sources of international commercial disruption. Sustaining the harmonisation and convergence of divergent national laws is necessary going forward, however, in practice it is difficult to achieve. Promoting these developments is an essential mandate of both the UNCITRAL and UNIDROIT to undertake at the earliest possible time. This book is intended to advance these central goals in pursuing and attaining such harmonisation in relation to transnational insolvency and restructuring law. This is a priority for the international business community and governments to ensure the economy has another layer to shield itself for the next economic shock.

Professor, Dr. Leon Trakman
Dr. Robert Walters

ACKNOWLEDGEMENT

The authors extend particular thanks to Justice Brigitte Markovic, Federal Court of Australia, and Chair, United Nations Commission on International Trade Law – Coordinating Committee, for her valuable insight in reviewing draft Chapters 1, 2 and 3, and for her kind support and endorsement.

This book draws upon the work undertaken by global law firms that include but are not limited to Baker Mckenzie, Clifford Chance and Jones Day.

The authors thank Erazem Bohinc (Banking & Capital Markets, Frankfurt) from Clifford Chance for providing legal opinions contained in the firm's book on international swaps and derivatives. Thanks to Mr. Michael Murray, from Murray's Legal in Sydney, Australia, and to Neil Hammon for their work on domestic and cross-border insolvency and restructuring arrangements.

The book benefitted from the contributions of a number of academics. Among these, Professor Arne *Mavčič* of the European Faculty of Law, New University, Slovenia, Europe, was instrumental in connecting the authors with European experts in this field. Researchers in the field of finance and insolvency at Gujarat National Law University in India, notably Professor Dr. Mamata Biswal and Assistant Professor Harsha Rajwansh, provided valuable input on the law of insolvency in India. Associate Professor Sinta Dewi Rosadi at Universitas Padjadjaran, Indonesia, kindly verified information on Indonesia.

Importantly, the authors thank their respective partners for their support throughout the research and writing stages of this book. Leon Trakman is indebted to Lynne-Marie Wade for her caring and for kindly proofreading selected book chapters. Robert thanks his wife Catherine Tan for providing him with the time and space to complete the work.

1
PROBLEM DEFINITION

The world is facing significant economic, social, human health and geopolitical challenges. Since the Asian financial crisis in the 1990s, 2008 global financial crisis and the recent outbreak of COVID-19, trans-border economic activity has been severely impacted across the world. The book explores and compares alternative means of preparing for and regulating cross-border insolvency and restructuring. In proposing a pathway forward, the book will identify the nature and scope of global financial instability, emphasising the fragmentary nature of insolvency law. It will draw upon the work of the Organisation for Economic Co-operation and Development, which stresses the importance of insolvency and restructuring mechanisms to improve the overall health of the global economy.[1] In achieving these ends, the book will evaluate how the United Nations Commission on International Trade Law (UNCITRAL) and International Institute for the Unification of Private Law (UNIDROIT) in particular deal with cross-border insolvency and restructuring. The purpose will be to strengthen legal instruments that minimise the financial consequences of economic destabilisation upon discrete and collective international markets.

1.1 Introduction

The world of financial and insolvency law faces increased economic and geopolitical volatility. Volatility due to deficient and divergent financial regulations has 'immediate and prospective implications for banks that are actively engaged in

1 Müge Adalet McGowan, Dan Andrews, *Valentine Millot, Insolvency Regimes, Zombie Firms and Capital Reallocation Economics Department Working Papers No. 1399,* Organisation for Economic Co-operation and Development, ECO/WKP (2017), 31.

DOI: 10.4324/9781003311874-1

global financial service'.[2] Depending on their institutional structures and economic predilections, some banks will favour retrenchment; others will withdraw from foreign activities voluntarily; and yet others will withdraw by regulatory compulsion or economic necessity. Still others that choose to remain will grasp opportunities from those that exit to increase their market expansion into foreign markets.

The book briefly highlights the cumulative risk of replicating financial crises that leads to retrenchment in foreign banking as financial intermediation declines globally. Typically, the number of new foreign bank entries declined sharply in the years following the 2007–2009 financial crisis. The regulatory response of leading financial regulators has corroborated that such economic-financial crises are game-changer in governance measures adopted to normalise financial markets.[3] Since 2009, the world's leading economies have adopted ambitious agendas by which to regulate international financial markets. They have designed institutional systems to bolster international standards of financial compliance, to detect financial instability and to reinforce economic-financial surveillance.

Ferran, Moloney, Hill and Coffee highlight that financial regulators have proposed far-reaching financial reform measures to avoid local and foreign market breakdowns. The United States (US) has passed legislation to reinvigorate financial regulations.[4] The European Union (EU) has extended its pre-existing reform agenda on a measure-by-measure basis, rather than dealing with all financial regulatory measures in a single instrument. Australia, among other countries, has undertaken similar piecemeal financial reform measures.

However, despite concerted regulatory measures in specific jurisdictions, perceptible gaps in finance and insolvency laws remain in domestic, regional and international legal regimes.[5] Net foreign bank entry turned negative between 2010 and

2 Stijn Claessen, Neeltje van Horen, The Impact of the Global Financial Crisis on Banking Globalization, *IMF Economic Review*, Vol. 63, No. 4 (2015), International Monetary Fund, 878–882.

3 Eilís Ferran, Niamh Moloney, Jennifer G. Hill, John C. Coffee, The Regulatory Aftermath of the Global Financial Crisis, in *International Corporate Law and Financial Market Regulation*, Cambridge University Press, Cambridge (2012), Chapter 1.

4 Ibid.

5 Niamh Moloney, The European Securities and Markets Authority and Institutional Design for the EU Financial Market – A Tale of Two Competences: Part (1) Rule Making, *European Business Organization Law Review*, Vol. 12, No. 1 (March 2011), 41–86. In January 2011, the European Union established the European Securities and Markets Authority (ESMA). On the same day, two other sectoral European Supervisory Authorities (ESAs) were established (the European Banking Authority (EBA) and the European Insurance and Occupational Pensions Authority (EIOPA). So was the European Systemic Risk Board (ESRB) which has overall responsibility for monitoring systemic risk in the EU financial market and delivering related risk warnings. The ESAs replaced the network-based and unstable '3L3' committees (CESR (in the securities field), CEBS (in the banking field) and CEIOPS (insurance and occupational pensions)) which advised the Commission on the adoption of delegated rules and engaged in a range of supervisory coordination and convergence activities. The ESAs was further operationalised through the 2010 Omnibus Directive, which sets out the specific powers they will exercise under key EU financial market measures; a second Omnibus Directive is in preparation. It will be important to understand what if any institutional reform had taken place throughout the Asian countries discussed in this book during the same period.

2013, for the first time since 1995.[6] During that period of decline, the number of foreign banks active in international markets declined from 1,249 in 2007 to 1,229 in 2011.[7] Pertinently, too, only 19 foreign banks entered global markets in 2013, about one-sixth as many as the peak of 120 bank entrants in 2007.[8] Banks have also exited foreign banking markets through sales to other foreign banks or domestic banks, by acquisition or merger, or by complete closure.

The insolvency of businesses, including mega-global corporations, is a pivotal consequence of financial crises. Commencing in early 2020, COVID-19 has already heralded lasting financial shock waves, prospectively more devastating than the GFC of 2008. The full effects and financial impact of COVID-19 were far from settled at the time of concluding this book in 2021. Firstly, the GFC was confined to the banking and financial system. Secondly, the GFC did not lead to a disastrous decline in productivity or jobs. In contrast, the economic impact of COVID-19 is already demonstrating its potentially disastrous impact on the global economy. At the time of writing this book in mid-2020, millions of employees across the world are continuing to lose their jobs. The United National Labour Organisation estimates that the disruption to the world's economies caused by the COVID-19 pandemic will wipe out 6.7% of working hours globally in the second quarter of 2020 – the equivalent of 195 million jobs worldwide. The expected result is that workers in the informal sector that is not monitored by governments[9] – that account for 61% of the global workforce, or two billion people – will need income support just to survive and feed their families if their jobs disappear.[10] While these are only estimated numbers in grey employment markets, they are reflected in published data on unemployment in domestic jurisdictions. In Australia, since the pandemic was announced and government restrictions on the movement of people, there has been a geometric increase in unemployment.

Importantly, the financial crisis of 2007–2009 and the pandemic of 2020 both caused massive economic shocks, resulting in small and large businesses

6 Ibid. A comprehensive database on the entry and exit of banks in global markets became available in 1995.

7 Ibid.

8 Ibid.

9 International Labour Organization (ILO) Resolutions Concerning Statistics of Employment in the Informal Sector Adopted by the 15th International Conference of Labour Statisticians, January 1993, paragraph 5. The informal sector is broadly characterised as consisting of units engaged in the production of goods or services with the primary objective of generating employment and incomes to the persons concerned. These units typically operate at a low level of organisation, with little or no division between labour and capital as factors of production and on a small scale. Labour relations – where they exist – are based mostly on casual employment, kinship or personal and social relations rather than contractual arrangements with formal guarantees. Organisation of Economic Development and Cooperation, Statistics Portal, https://stats.oecd.org/glossary/detail.asp?ID=1350

10 The Guardian News, Covid-19 to Wipe Out Equivalent of 195m Jobs, Says UN Agency, https://www.theguardian.com/world/2020/apr/07/covid-19-expected-to-to-wipe-out-67-of-worlds-working-hours.

into insolvency. The evolving nature of the economic impact from COVID-19, reported by Laura Noonan in the *Financial Times* on 18 April 2020, was that lenders were expanding reserves in anticipation of mounting waves of defaults during the pandemic alone.[11] These estimates included loan loss charges at six big US banks reached $25.4 billion in the first quarter of 2020, a 350-per cent surge from a year earlier.[12] Noonan reported that these large US banks had clarified that they were battening down the hatches to deal with an expected surge in loan losses as the pandemic cast serious doubts over the capacity of consumers and companies to pay their debts. Bank of America's finance chief, Paul Donofrio, explained how lenders set their credit provisions after 'weighting a number of different scenarios, all of which assumed a recession of various depth and longevity'.[13] The result of these scenarios was a 'marked drop' in Gross Domestic Production (GDP) in the second quarter of 2020, and negative growth in GDP extending well into 2021.[14] Citigroup Chief Executive, Mike Corbat, indicated that Citibank had calculated its expected loan losses, using scenario-based modelled upon 'thousands of variables like GDP, unemployment, and many other stats' as well as 'the probability and severity of a recession'.[15] JPMorgan Chase assumed a 25% fall in US economic growth in the second quarter of 2020, and unemployment above 10%, 'followed by a solid recovery over the second half of the year'.[16]

In March 2020, these numbers climbed dramatically as many businesses shut down due to government regulations prohibiting employees from leaving their homes. It was estimated that unemployment for the second half of March in 2020 alone increased by a staggering 1.4 million to 2.4 million (16.8%) and underemployment increased by 374,000 to 1.52 million (10.6%).[17] While employment has risen in 2021 in significant parts of Asia, such as China, Australia, Singapore and Hong Kong, declines have continued in Europe, Latin America, and to a lesser extent, the United States. Regardless of these employment disparities arising in 2021, governments across the globe have responded to the pandemic by implementing large and comprehensive relief packages to support the unemployed and struggling businesses. The aviation sector has been one of the hardest impacted from COVID-19. In 2020, IATA estimates net losses for the Asian region to be $26.9 billion. IATA forecasts Europe to be the worst-hit global region in 2021 in

11 Laura Noonan, US Banks Brace for Surge in Loan Losses, New York, *Financial Times*, https://www.ft.com/content/87189e79-a442-44b9-a699-7bce47b5bc64. This marks a 350% surge in collective provisions across Bank of America, Citigroup, JP Morgan Chase, Wells Fargo, Goldman Sachs and Morgan Stanley versus a year earlier, as charges soared to levels not seen since the financial crisis.
12 Ibid.
13 Ibid.
14 Ibid.
15 Ibid.
16 Ibid.
17 Roy Morgan, *Extra 1.4 Million Australians Out of Work in Wake of COVID-19 Pandemic – 3.92 Million (27.4% of Workforce) Now Unemployed or Under-employed*, https://www.roymorgan.com/findings/8363-roy-morgan-unemployment-and-under-employment-march-2020-202004080900.

terms of airline losses, which are expected to decline by $11.9 billion.[18] An example of such losses in the transportation sector of the EU, is Lufthansa's reported loss of €6.7 billion.[19] The material effect from continuous lockdowns and restrictions in travel alone has been having a detrimental impact across the aviation sector and in-support sectors that rely on air travel. At the time of concluding this book in mid-2021, there were no updated figures for the aviation or other sectors. The result is that organisations will continue to experience financial stress, potentially leading to further cross-border insolvencies and restructuring.

The evidence also highlights that every time a country goes into a short lockdown, the economic impact can be significant. Lockdowns were associated with a 10–15% drop-in local economic activity, which is twice the reduction in local economic activity suffered by municipalities that were not under lockdown.[20] Across India, the aviation, tourism and hospitality industries have already sustained a high level of damage because of the COVID-19 outbreak, and after the lockdown, it was questionable to what extent they will be able to ride out this storm. The shutdown is bound to push India's fast-growing aviation industry into peril. The Centre for Asia Pacific Aviation (CAPA) has assessed that the Indian aviation industry will post staggering losses worth nearly $4 billion this year.[21] A similar story has been across the world in aviation and tourism sectors, which has experienced the biggest decline in activity, since the 9/11 terrorist attacks in New York.

An impending issue that has arisen is that, as financial stress continues in and across finance and banking sectors, small, medium and large-scale entities will explore different but also overlapping ways of managing loan defaults. A similar narrative of declining US financial markets, insolvencies, unemployment and loan defaults, is evolving in Australia, Asia, Europe and the UK. This book will highlight how not only insolvency, but also restructuring and schemes of arrangement(s) can be effective legal mechanisms to manage the ongoing debt crises, illustrated by banks facing often catastrophic loan defaults globally. This can also be illustrated further by the extensive restructuring that has been occurring during the pandemic, where the legal tools compared in this book play a pivotal role.

Banks are not alone in imposing massive risks on cross-border financing. A similar issue has unfolded in other areas of the financial market. As an important illustration, government lockdowns have had a staggering impact on derivative (over-the-counter) markets. The general method of serving default notices

18 KPMG, *The Aviation Industry Leaders Report 2021: Route to Recovery* (2021), 15, https://assets.kpmg/content/dam/kpmg/ie/pdf/2021/01/ie-aviation-industry-leaders-report-route-to-recovery.pdf.

19 Lufthansa Announces Record Loss, *DW News,* https://www.dw.com/en/lufthansa-announces-record-loss/av-56776101.

20 Kenzo Asahi, Eduardo Undurranga, Rodrigo Valdes, Rodrigo Wagner, The Effect of COVID-19 on the Economy: Evidence from an Early Adopter of Localised Lockdowns, *Journal of Global Health* (2021), doi: 10.7189/jogh.10.05002.

21 S. Mahendra Dev, Rajeswari Sengupta, *Covid-19: Impact on the Indian Economy, WP-2020–013,* http://www.igidr.ac.in/pdf/publication/WP-2020-013.pdf.

under an International Derivatives Swaps Association (ISDA) Master Agreement is through a standard derivative trading document that is transmitted by mail delivery, courier and facsimile.[22] In a lockdown, a counterparty may not be able to locate a courier or, even if they are able to do so, no one will be available at the delivery location to receive the default notice.[23] In contrast, under the 2008 GFC, delivering default notices in compliance with an ISDA Master Agreement was not impeded by a pervasive lockdown. This enabled counterparties to terminate derivative swaps.

Global economic shocks on the world's financial system and business sector cannot be decoupled from the economies of impacted states.[24] The functioning of the global financial system is inextricably linked to the daily functioning of modern regional and local economies. Both private and public actors fund their consumption and investment needs through bank loans or financial support provided by capital markets. These capital markets are also efficient means by which investors use market prices reliably to measure economic value when engaging in financial transactions. Financial institutions, in turn, engage in extended economic ventures well beyond their home states.[25] Some of Australia's leading banks, such as the Australia and New Zealand Banking Group Limited (ANZ) and the National Australia Bank (NAB), have established offices and services in third countries. For example, the ANZ has operations in more than thirty countries and employs approximately 38,000 people worldwide. American and Chinese banks have established branches across Europe, Asia and North America. Exemplars are the Bank of China, CITI Bank and the Hongkong and Shanghai Banking Corporation [HSBC].

The challenge ahead is how financial institutions can extend their activities beyond domestic markets, while recognising differences in regulatory mechanisms and their application in local, regional and global markets. A related task is to redress the limited development of laws and regulations governing such financial markets in multiple jurisdictions that nevertheless purport to apply them. A further hurdle, accentuated in the COVID-19 era, is that states, being wary of destabilised global financial markets, have retreated to domestic financial reform. The impact of COVID-19 upon derivative markets extends beyond delivering default notices to regulating the performance of derivative contracts. In issue, then, are the contractual requirements for a party to a financial transaction to secure performance relief due to COVID-19 and the legal regulation of relief provided for in force majeure clauses in finance contracts. Of note, the 2002 ISDA Master Agreement provides

22 *Impact of COVID-19 on Derivatives*, https://www.allens.com.au/insights-news/insights/2020/03/impact-of-covid-19-on-derivatives/. COVID-19 will have a range of impacts on over-the-counter derivative transactions. We set out some key documentation issues arising as a consequence of COVID-19 and our practical tips.

23 Ibid. Note however that, it is difficult to execute a Force Majeure Events under COVID-19.

24 Avgouleas Emilios, *Governance of Global Financial Markets: The Law, The Economics, The Politics*, Cambridge University Press (2012), 1–5.

25 Ibid, 10.

that a force majeure event occurs where it is 'impossible or impractical' for a party to perform so long as the force majeure or act of state is beyond that party's control and despite that party's reasonable efforts it cannot overcome such impossibility or impracticability.[26] In contrast, the 1992 ISDA Master Agreement does not refer to a force majeure event; however, parties to financing contracts often negotiate to include impossibility clauses in their derivative contracts which have a similar effect to the Master Agreement. As a result, ISDA Master Agreements have become significant in derivative contracting, an important issue that will be addressed with later in this chapter in relation to close-out netting provisions.

The retreat from globalisation in regulating financial transactions is counterproductive in failing to recognise significant deficiencies in the functioning of domestic financial regulations, coupled with both financial and human vulnerability in trans-border financial markets. The localisation of financial regulations, in the COVID-19 epoch, symbolises a geo-political regression to the pre-Bretton Woods era in which states maintain financial insularity on territorial grounds.[27] Domestic states, rather than seek interdependent financial markets globally, increasingly accentuate their financial isolation as a measure of their sovereignty and domestic public policy. Instead of opening local financial markets to an international regulatory order, they opt to insulate their local markets from that order. The incentive is to insulate themselves from global financial instability. Yet, in domesticating financial regulation on grounds of domestic public policy, they bypass their inescapable exposure to delocalised economic downturns and recessions. In effect, their regulatory insularity increases, rather than decreases, their precariousness in the face of global financial turbulence.

At issue is the need to evaluate the means of reconciling national and international regulatory reform through the lens of insolvency law. Concentrating on cross-border insolvency, this book will evaluate the effectiveness of industry and legal regulation in redressing destabilised financial markets in which once localised businesses progressively transact and secure finance. It will also compare how the respective jurisdictions under study deal with alternatives to insolvency, such as through restructuring and schemes of arrangements, amongst others. Similarly, it will highlight that differentiating between business solvency and insolvency often depends on defining insolvency in law in a manner that is compatible with the business environment in which that law is applied. Financial laws that disregard the law in financial markets to which their transactions apply are likely to render their

26 Ibid.

27 Michael D. Bordo, *The Operation and Demise of the Bretton Woods System; 1958 to 1971*. Rutgers University, National Bureau of Economic Research, and Hoover Institution, Stanford University Economics Working Paper 16116. The Bretton Woods system was established to avoid the perceived problems of the interwar period: protectionism (the devolution of international trade from multilateralism to bilateralism and autarky), beggar thy neighbour devaluations (currency wars), hot money flows and unstable exchange rate; and to provide a framework of monetary and financial stability to foster global economic growth and the growth of international trade.

financial dealings in those markets dysfunctional. Financial markets that operate in the absence of a stable regulatory framework variable in nature, inconsistent in operation, and tenuous in effectiveness.

The book will address deficiencies in existing regulatory models, and the need for the international community to consider expanding the current transnational framework for cross-border insolvency purposes and to expand the legal mechanisms used in restructuring. Additionally, the book will examine these tensions in regulating mergers and acquisitions, directed at stabilising financial markets. It will also scrutinise the divide between self and external governance of close-out netting provisions by which financial institutions terminate loans to limit their exposure to default.

1.1.1 Cross-Border Insolvency

Since the GFC, much has been written about international insolvency and the law. An ambitious feature in the reform of international insolvency law is to design corporate rescue proceedings to resuscitate debtor companies that are in financial distress.[28] The alternative is for debtor and creditor to restructure debts either voluntarily or through a freeze on legal proceedings by creditors. Illustrations of such schemes are deeds of arrangement between debtors and creditors in jurisdictions that draw from English law, such as Australia, Singapore and New Zealand.[29] These arrangements will be explored later in this chapter.

International insolvency proceedings ordinarily involve multiple parties, such as more than one debtor and multiple creditors with different financial interests in the devolution of funds. Insolvency determinations ordinarily also require the participation of multiple parties in the insolvency plan, through their collective approval of that plan, and sometimes their approval of a post-insolvency plan, such as reorganising the insolvent entity. Essential elements of insolvency to regulate in national law governing insolvency are: the orderly identification of the debtor's property; the verification of creditors' claims; the distribution of the debtor's divisible property to satisfy those claims; and the promotion of commercial morality.[30] Individual private rights of the parties to a liquidation, as Elina Moustaria argues, are transformed into their shared opportunity to participate in the collective approval and administration of a reorganisation plan.[31] Their shared plan to execute the reorganisation collectively, in effect, displaces their individual autonomy.[32]

28 Philip Wood, Principles of International Insolvency (Part 11), *International Insolvency Review*, Vol. 4 (1995), 109.

29 Ibid, 111.

30 Elina Moustaira, *International Insolvency Law, National Laws and International Texts*, Springer (2019), vii.

31 Ibid, 10.

32 Ibid.

Viewed in this way, the legal basis for domesticating insolvency law requires a more sustainable rationale than its formal jurisdictional predominance. In issue is the need for an international regime of insolvency law to be founded on a sustainable economic policy as the core underpinning of both the law governing finance and application across state borders. For example, the purpose of insolvency law in a modern free enterprise economy is to provide an equitable distribution of an insolvent debtor's assets to creditors that is consolidated in trans-border insolvency law.[33] The related purpose is to recognise that economic interdependence when an insolvent debtor trades, or has assets or creditors, in more than one jurisdiction.[34] Sefa Franken raises five theoretical considerations in the application of insolvency law and practice: (i) universalism; (ii) modified universalism; (iii) territorialism; (iv) cooperative territorialism; and (v) universal proceduralism.[35] She focuses on cross-border insolvency because commercial activities have become transnational since World War II. Financial services are no longer reliant on a single state. Asian, European, North American and African markets are intertwined. Geopolitical and economic shocks are felt in Asian, as in financial markets in North America and Europe.

Further legal complications arise in the application of insolvency law because the harmonisation of national laws have largely failed to encompass cross-border insolvency laws and regulations that are uniform in nature and application. Notwithstanding significant experience in the harmonisation of choice of forum and law rules, no international jurisdiction or applicable law of insolvency has eventuated. Nor is there cogent evidence that domestic insolvency laws and regulations are recognised or enforced internationally. As this book will demonstrate, this failure of domestic insolvency law to transcend that local jurisdiction is also a primary obstacle to developing an international insolvency case law, and jurisprudence.

Resistance to the internationalisation of insolvency law, arguably, is ascribed to the prevailing propertied conception of insolvency. A declaration of insolvency is identified with the jurisdiction in which the assets of the insolvent estate are located.[36] That historical conception is less pervasively applicable today. Businesses that operate across national boundaries often have assets at the places at which they operate their businesses, while their head offices remain historically determined, such as in the jurisdiction where the entity was founded, or where tax laws are perceived as being business friendly.[37]

Even more pertinently, if insolvency laws diverge substantially across domestic jurisdictions, it is reasonable to assume that the treatment of insolvent estates will

33 Neil Hannan, *Cross-Border Insolvency The Enactment and Interpretation of the UNCITRAL Model Law*, Springer (2017), 1.

34 Ibid, 2.

35 Sefa Franken, Cross-Border Insolvency Law: A Comparative Institutional Analysis, *Oxford Journal of Legal Studies*, Vol. 34, No. 1 (2014), 102–104.

36 Ibid.

37 Ibid.

be determined by the insolvency law in a discrete jurisdiction that diverges from the law elsewhere. The fact that businesses have assets in more than one jurisdiction is also a sound economic reason for insolvency regulations to transcend the law of one jurisdiction. Conversely stated, developing compatible insolvency laws across jurisdictions is a basis for promoting compatibility in their treatment of assets from any one of those states.[38]

The divergence of insolvency laws is also affected by local socio-economic circumstances within and across nation states. Notably, a global regulatory framework for insolvency law is impacted by trans-border poverty and unemployment. These growing, rather than receding, financial obstacles, not limited to the impact of COVID-19 upon global finance and insolvency, have limited the capacity of significant impoverished groups to finance their basic well-being. For Franken, cross-border insolvency law is important in determining (a) which court has jurisdiction over a cross-border insolvency case, (b) which substantive insolvency law applies to that case (based on choice-of-law rules), and (c) whether an insolvency judgement should be recognised by a foreign court and extended to the assets of an insolvent estate located there.

What accentuates the disparate regulations of finance and insolvency in cross-border transactions is the dichotomy between localised and globalised regulatory machinery and their socio-economic impact upon commerce, not limited to the transacting parties. There are two primary approaches in dealing with cross-border insolvency regulation, namely, territorialism and universalism. The territorial approach vests jurisdiction in each state in which the subject firm has assets. Each state will apply its own substantive insolvency laws to the administration of the firm's assets located in that state's jurisdiction.[39] In contrast, the universalist approach vests jurisdiction in that state at which the primary interests of the trans-border firm is located. The bankruptcy court has jurisdiction to initiate 'universal' insolvency proceedings, referred to as the 'main' proceedings.[40] We argue throughout that, it is this universalist approach that must be upheld and expanded upon.

Nonetheless, several issues arise in determining whether jurisdictions ought to adopt a territorial or a universal approach in regulating trans-border financial

38 Ibid.

39 Ibid. It also applies its own distributive rules to the division of the proceeds of the assets located in its jurisdiction. Creditors have to file their claims in each state in which an insolvency proceeding is opened. As a result, they will be confronted with a myriad of diverging distributive rules and policies. This territorial approach guarantees that each state can apply its own distributive rules and policies to assets located within its jurisdiction.

40 Ibid. The insolvency law of the state opening the main proceeding applies to the administration of the firm's assets wherever located. Likewise, the distributive rules of the state opening the main proceeding apply to the distribution of the proceeds of the assets wherever located.[13] Creditors have to file their claims only once with the main proceeding and they are confronted with a single set of distributive rules and policies. Under a universalist approach, states need to accept the application of foreign distributive rules and policies to assets located in their jurisdiction, if a court in a foreign state has opened a main insolvency proceeding.

insolvency. The first issue is whether the law of the jurisdiction in which the insolvency proceeding commences should govern the administration and distribution of the debtor's assets, wherever those assets are located.[41] The second issue is whether states should engage in cooperative territorialism in such regulation. In effect, each jurisdiction should deal with assets arising from insolvency within its jurisdiction. However, each should also allow foreign creditors to lodge insolvency claims in the jurisdiction in which proceedings commenced, although the claims of some local creditors may be prioritised over the claims of foreign creditors.[42] Importantly, too, the different insolvency administrators in each state would need to apply domestic law cooperatively with both domestic and cross-border regulatory regimes in insolvency proceedings.[43]

However, domestic financial regulators are not ordinarily faced with stark either-or choices. They are expected to mediate over the nature and application of domestic and cross-border regulatory proceedings. On the one side, sovereign states are relied upon to cooperate in mediating between a territorial and a universal approach in determining both the applicable jurisdiction, law governing insolvency proceedings, and the attachment of assets. On the other side, they require transnational, if not universal, measures to ensure the efficient and fair regulation of cross-border financing and insolvency. Such international regulatory mechanisms do exist. The overriding issues relate to their nature and operation, the certainty and predictability of their procedures, their consistency across jurisdictions, the legal consequences arising from adopting them, and whether they lead to the efficient and fair distribution of assets in consequence of insolvency and restructuring proceedings. The important correlative issue is how such international regulatory mechanisms are conceived and applied, whether they bind signatory states, and how they are applied and enforced. These issues will be discussed in relation to key institutions that purport to facilitate cross-border insolvency, commencing with the Model Law of the United National Commission on International Trade Law (UNCITRAL), directed at harmonising procedural rules to facilitate cross-border insolvency.

1.1.1.1 Transnational Insolvency (UNCITRAL Model Law)

The United Nations General Assembly endorsed the UNCITRAL Model Law on Cross-Border Insolvency on 15 December 1997.[44] The Model Law was designed by the UNCITRAL to assist countries in developing harmonised procedural rules of

41 See Sefa Franken, Cross-Border Insolvency Law: A Comparative Institutional Analysis, *Oxford Journal of Legal Studies*, Vol. 34, No. 1 (2014), 98.

42 Lynn M. LoPucki, Cooperation in International Bankruptcy: A Post-Universalist Approach, *Cornell Law Review*, Vol. 84, No. 696 (1999), 750. Cited in Neil Hannan, *Cross-Border Insolvency The Enactment and Interpretation of the UNCITRAL Model Law*, Springer (2017), 1.

43 Ibid.

44 Ibid.

coordination and assistance among jurisdictions in cross-border insolvency cases.[45] The Model Law extends to any foreign proceeding 'relating to insolvency'. The purpose of such proceedings is to reorganise and liquidate the assets of the insolvent debtor, subject to the following requirements. The proceedings are 'collective' (whether judicial or administrative). The assets and affairs of the debtor are subject to control or supervision by a judicial or other authority that is competent to control or supervise insolvency proceedings.[46] A cross-border purpose of the Model Law is to provide expedited and direct access by foreign representatives through an 'inbound request' made to the courts of the enacting State.[47]

This book argues for transitioning the Model Law to the status of Convention. While only recently enacted as a Model Law, it serves as a prospective blueprint for designing cross-border insolvency laws for adoption by nation states.[48] With the continued practice of companies establishing branch offices outside their states of origin, cross-border insolvency will continue to be important in transnational dealings. As Kevin Bickering has proposed, as 'transnational business activity [has] increased, procedural cross-border insolvency law must match this trend step-for-step by encouraging progression toward a more unified international bankruptcy regime'.[49]

On the backdrop of this context, the book will examine and compare the extent to which different jurisdictions have adopted and implemented the Model Law. It will also address gaps in both national and international insolvency law. **Chapter 2** will discuss the UNCITRAL Model Law on Cross-Border Insolvency in greater depth. At the outset, it is important to appreciate that the Model Law does not deal comprehensively with 'keepwell' agreements (letters of comfort) or with close-out netting provisions in commercial contracts. Both contract mechanisms have become important as means of self-regulation when a party has become financially exposed to insolvency risks.

In addition, the book proposes further harmonising the law governing the corporate restructuring across international borders and legal tools used to support this activity in addressing cross-border insolvency. It evaluates how international and

45 Fernando Locatelli, International Trade and Insolvency Law: Is the UNCITRAL Model Law on Cross-Border Insolvency an Answer for Brazil – An Economic Analysis of Its Benefits on International Trade, *Law and Business Review of the Americas*, Vol. 14, No. 313 (2008), 313.

46 Jenny Clift, UNCITRAL Model Law on Cross-Border Insolvency – A Legislative Framework to Facilitate Coordination and Cooperation in Cross-Border Insolvency, *Tulane Journal of International and Comparative Law*, Vol. 12, No. 307 (2004), 319–320.

47 United Nations Commission on International Trade Law, *UNCITRAL Model Law on Cross-Border Insolvency with Guide to Enactment and Interpretation (PDF)*, United Nations Publications (2014), Article 9.

48 Ishita Das, *The Need for Implementing a Cross-Border Insolvency Regime within the Insolvency and Bankruptcy Code 2016*, Vikalpa Sage (2020), https://doi.org/10.1177/0256090920946519.

49 Kevin Beckering, United States Cross-Border Corporate Insolvency: The Impact of Chapter 15 on Comity and the New Legal Environment, *Law and Business Review of the Americas*, Vol. 14, No. 281 (2008), 282.

regional organisations have sought to harmonise laws directed at restructuring 'in response to the rapid expansion of global economic activities in the latter part of the 20th Century', but have 'encountered significant difficulties in creating unified solutions and gaining wide acceptance of standards'.[50] The book will maintain that restructuring companies across international borders will therefore require the legal tools to respond to such 'difficulties' in arriving at harmonised solutions.

1.2 Restructuring

Restructuring is highly effective and regarded as an alternative to insolvency. Corporate debt restructuring can be an important component of economic adjustment programs supported by the International Monetary Fund (IMF).[51] Private debt restructuring is needed to revive medium term productivity and growth, thereby supporting a country's balance of payments adjustments.[52] This is particularly necessary, given that high levels of private debt can have a negative impact on public debt sustainability, potentially leading to the transfer of private debt to government balance sheets.[53] Due to the broad nature of debt restructuring, this book will only discuss schemes of arrangements, along with mergers and acquisitions.

Most of the world today is experiencing high levels of both public and private debt. Therefore, when pandemics and other geopolitical and global economic shocks occur, restructuring is a viable option, rather than relying wholly on insolvency proceedings. However, such restructuring comes with its own challenges. Thomas Laryea highlights how the restructuring process is complex and quite often difficult to achieve in times of economic decline.[54] He further stresses that unprecedented corporate, household and financial debt pressures evolve into sovereign debt pressures. Economic, social, human health (pandemic) and geopolitical shocks generally result in governments having less revenue. This leads to liquidity constraints and exchange rate pressures for governments, accompanied by financial constraints on corporations and households.[55]

Put another way and central to the response to financial stress are the costs that arise in corporations adopting formal or informal reorganisation procedures.[56] Brunassi and Saito highlight how the costs of financial distress can exceed any

50 Megan O'Flynn, The Scorecard so Far: Emerging Issues in Cross-Border Insolvencies under Chapter 15 of the U.S. Bankruptcy Code, *Northwestern Journal of International Law and Business*, Vol. 32, No. 391 (2012).

51 Thomas Laryea, *Approaches to Corporate Debt Restructuring in the Wake of Financial Crises*, International Monetary Fund (2010), 2.

52 Ibid.

53 Ibid, 4.

54 Ibid.

55 Ibid, 3.

56 Vinicius Augusto Brunassi Silva, Richard Saito, Corporate Financial Distress and Reorganization: A Survey of Theoretical and Empirical Contributions, Fundação Escola de Comércio Álvares Penteado – FECAP, Sao Paulo, Brazil, *RBGN São Paulo*, Vol. 22, Special Issue (2020), 403.

remaining firm value; leading to the dissolution of companies who sought to avoid by restructuring their debts.[57] They propose as an alternative the adoption of sustainable reorganisation plans that address this problem. Basically, the choice of restructuring is made according to the least-cost alternative.[58] They acknowledge that it is not easy to identify the choice that stakeholders view as the least expensive decision. Costs depend on the market tensions that are specific to the position of each company. To provide a solution for distress, they propose that companies raise money from outside investors and reorganise through debt restructuring and asset sales.[59] That view is comparable to the position similar in part to that adopted in this book, in highlighting the use of restructuring in law, institutional instruments and processes directed at facilitating transnational restructuring.

In developing laws that restructure debt clearly, comprehensively and efficiently, two preliminary steps require consideration: firstly, to determine the adequacy of the current legal frameworks within which states restructure debt; and secondly, to identify the forms of corporate debt restructuring that are available. Expressed expansively: 'corporate debt restructuring can take many forms directed at the debt and capital structure of a firm; it can include debt re-scheduling, interest rate reductions, debt-for-equity swaps and debt forgiveness'.[60] To be successful in securing longer term financial viability, corporations also need to restructure their debts operationally to render them more efficiently. These means include their resort to closures and reorganisation of their productive capacity.[61] Restructuring provides a level of early intervention and preventative measures, minimising the impact of the financial stress an entity is under. This book will not address government support programs that assist in corporate restructuring. However, it will examine whether and how states have recognised their foreign rehabilitation proceedings. It will also compare how differences in their respective legal frameworks effectively enable onshore restructuring. It will assess whether and how state courts regulate such corporate restructuring. The importance in identifying the nature and operation of these legal framework is in enabling regulators, scholars and practitioners to have up-to-date legal framework to facilitate the efficient management of financial markets, sectors and industries, and to prepare for ongoing and future financial shock waves.

1.2.1 Schemes of Arrangement

Another important, but not often discussed, mechanism for companies to restructure their financial management is through schemes of arrangements. They are also

57 Ibid.
58 Ibid.
59 Ibid.
60 Thomas Laryea, *Approaches to Corporate Debt Restructuring in the Wake of Financial Crises*, International Monetary Fund (2010), 7.
61 Ibid.

used in cross-border insolvency. Schemes of arrangement are especially valuable as flexible tools for reorganising a company's capital and debt.[62] They form the practical side of restructuring and has become very effective in cross-border corporate practice in response to financial challenges to individuals and entities throughout the COVID-19 pandemic.

There are further advantages to the use of schemes of arrangements that include, but are not limited to, providing certainty to the direct parties to these schemes particularly when the arrangement is completed.[63] Jason Harris emphasises that schemes of arrangement have been used to restructure companies for more than 160 years.[64] He reinforces Payne's observation that a scheme of arrangement is also used by creditors to address financial distress. These schemes have numerous advantages over other formal mechanisms, such as liquidation and voluntary administration, in applying to secured creditors, and in binding dissenting minorities of both secured and unsecured creditors. Harris is of the view that the ability to bind minorities within a specific class of creditors, referred to as a 'cram down', is efficient, too, to avoid delays in implementing the scheme of arrangement or in rendering its approval unduly uncertain. As Harris adds, if the scheme targets multiple classes of creditors, it must be approved by a majority of each class. If one class of creditors dissents, then the scheme fails. Resorting to schemes of arrangements is nevertheless problematic. One problem is that schemes vary across jurisdictions. Another is that a majority of classes of creditor can bind one or more dissenting classes, through cross-class cram down. These arrangements are also subject to criticism for being slow, costly, and cumbersome.[65] A difficulty in using such schemes to restructure debts is in requiring the composition of separate classes of creditors, obtaining approval from each class, and avoiding opportunities to greenmail lenders resulting in the diminution of the value of the debts owed to subordinate creditors. This problematic process contrasts with the less encumbered cross-class 'cram down' mechanism that is used in the United States to enable a court order to bind dissenting classes to a restructuring plan.[66]

The book will examine how the jurisdictions under study regulate schemes of arrangement in restructuring and securing the support of a majority of classes of creditors. It will discuss the classes of creditors that are engaged within such schemes of arrangement, as well as cross-border issues that have emerged in applying those schemes. It will also examine how such schemes vary across jurisdictions; the need for extensive consultation and negotiation among states to achieve a harmonised international approach; and the virtue of developing and testing a

62 Jennifer Payne, *Schemes of Arrangement: Theory, Structure and Operation*, Cambridge University Press (2014), 1.

63 Ibid.

64 Jason Harris, Class Warfare in Debt Restructuring: Does Australia Need Cross-Class Cram Down for Creditors' Schemes of Arrangement, *University of Queensland Law Journal* (2017), 73–74.

65 Ibid.

66 Ibid, 73.

number of different schemes to assess their operational sustainability in cross-border restructuring of debts.

1.2.2 Keepwell Agreements and Letters of Comfort

The importance of effectively managing the prospective insolvency or restructuring of parties to a cross-border financial arrangement cannot be underestimated, amounting to the loss of millions if not billions of dollars. The letter of comfort has become increasingly important in managing financial arrangements between a debtor and creditor prior to and during a restructure, or before insolvency has been declared. It has also become a useful tool in managing creditors as part of a company being placed into liquidation. Therefore, exploring some of the legal mechanisms available to manage and protect financial interests has become increasingly important in maintaining financial stability in already destabilised global financial markets. Keepwell agreements are mechanisms directed at achieving such sustainability. Referred to as letters of comfort in jurisdictions such as Australia and the UK, they are developed between a parent company and its subsidiary to ensure the solvency of both. To achieve this, the Keepwell agreements outline terms directed at ensuring that the subsidiary receives continuing financial support from the parent or its appointee.

The problem is that the jurisdictions that are scrutinised in this book have different conceptions of the nature and scope of keepwell agreements, including their application in law as in fact. This creates significant divergence in the criteria giving rise to the determination of insolvency, in the administration of insolvency proceedings, in the distribution of the insolvent's assets, and in enforcing insolvency decisions in relation to assets in other jurisdictions. These issues are dealt with directly later and in more detail later in the book.

Generally, keepwell agreements are not stand-alone documents in the US. They are rather read in conjunction with a credit agreement in which the parties agree to the terms of credit between them.[67] In the Beal Savings Bank case, the keepwell agreement was made in favour of the administrative agent, the lenders and their respective successors, transferees and assignees.[68] That case highlights the interconnectedness between the keepwell and the credit agreement. It further demonstrates that, unless otherwise expressly provided, the keep well agreement must be construed, administered and applied in accordance with the credit agreement. Determinative in the Beal Savings Bank case was how Article 8 of the credit agreement provided that:

> If any event of default shall occur for any reason, whether voluntary or involuntary, and be continuing, the Administrative Agent, upon the direction of

67 *Beal Savings Bank v. Sommer*, 8 N.Y.3d 318 (N.Y. 2007), [323].
68 Ibid, 322.

> the Required Lenders, shall by notice to the Borrower declare all or any portion of the outstanding principal amount of the loan and other obligations, to be due and payable of the commitments to be determined whereupon the borrower shall automatically and immediately be obliged to deposit with the Administrative Agent cash collateral in an amount equal to all Letter of Credit outstanding. Additionally, the foregoing, the Administrative Agent upon the direction of the Lenders may without further notice of default, presentment or demand for payment, protest or notice of non-payment or dishonour or other notices or demands of any kind.[69]

Thus, US courts read keepwell and credit agreements[70] in combination, so that the enforceability of those agreements becomes an important element in protecting the lender. However, letters of comfort are conceived of slightly differently from letters of credit in jurisdictions outside the US, such as Australia. Firstly, a keepwell agreement in Australia is referred to as a letters of comfort, namely, as a letter, usually written by a parent or holding company to a lender. Secondly, that letter gives comfort about a loan made to a subsidiary. In effect, the parent company acknowledges its liability for that loan. Thirdly, the letter is designed as a 'compromise between, on the one hand, a guarantee by the parent company of the debts of its subsidiary and, on the other hand, a placebo which gives no undertaking at all by the parent company'.[71] In effect, a keepwell agreement in the US is construed, administered and applied in accordance with the credit agreement. In contrast, a letter of comfort in Australia is a free-standing agreement by which a parent company agrees to some level of responsibility for the debts of its subsidiary. This is whether they are used as part of a restructure, insolvency or liquidation.

On the backdrop of this context, English courts act similarly to Australian courts.[72] They also distinguish between keepwell agreements as letters of comfort differently from the construction of keepwell agreements adopted in the US. The letter of comfort is designed primarily as a 'compromise between, on the one hand, a guarantee by the parent company of the debts of its subsidiary and, on the other hand, a placebo which gives no undertaking at all by the parent company'.[73]

The construction of a letter of comfort therefore differs in its legal nature from a keepwell agreement that prevails in the US. Unless the parties to a keepwell agreement provide otherwise, US courts construe the keepwell agreement in accordance

69 Ibid, 327.

70 *Lasalle Bank National Association v. Citicorp Real Estate Inc* 2003 US Dist LEXIS 12043, 18 July 2003.

71 *Chemco Leasing Spa v. Rediffusion plc* (19 July 1986, unreported, QBD); on appeal [1987] 1 FTLR 201.

72 *Australian European Finance Corporation Ltd. v. Sheahan* (1993) 60 SASR 187. In this case there was a subsidiary to the Duke Group Ltd. Duke Group had negotiated with Australian Finance Corporation to provide financial facilities to Duke Pacific. In resolving the loan arrangements, a letter of comfort was secured of the Duke Group.

73 *Chemco Leasing Spa v. Rediffusion plc* (19 July 1986, unreported, QBD); on appeal [1987] 1 FTLR 201.

with the applicable credit agreement. Reinforcing this difference, in the US a letter of comfort is used principally to encourage a lender to enter into a legally binding transaction with a subsidiary, while the parent company endeavours to avoid liability should the subsidiary fail to perform.

The expansive construction of a letter of wishes is illustrated by the US Federal District Court in *Lasalle Bank National Association v. Citicorp Real Estate Inc*[74] There, Brock Suite Greenville Inc. (Brock) operated a hotel under a franchise agreement with Marriott International Inc. (Marriott). Brock borrowed $6.76 million from LJ Melody & Company (Melody) in exchange for a promissory note and a mortgage on its hotel property. At Melody's request, Marriott issued a comfort letter in which it indicated the procedures it would follow if Brock defaulted on the franchise agreement, in particular that it would notify Melody of any breach. While not a liquidation or an insolvency matter, defaulting under a franchise agreement could result in a reorganisation of the entity. Melody sold the loan to Citicorp Real Estate (Citicorp) and assigned with it 'all rights, title and interest in, to and under the note, the mortgage and certain related loan documents'.[75] Citicorp, in turn, sold the loan under a Pooling and Services Agreement (PSA) to Lasalle Bank National Association (Lasalle). In the PSA, Citicorp made several representations and warranties, namely that 'there [was] no material default, breach or even of acceleration existing under the related Mortgage Note'.[76]

However, unbeknown to Citicorp, Marriott had already sent a notice of default to Brock's parent company. With regard to the enforceability of the letter of comfort, the Court considered a number of factors, such as the language of the instrument itself, for example, whether it was detailed and contained strong or operative language such as 'guarantee', 'contract' or other words of promise. It also evaluated the overall context in which the comfort letter was written including the sophistication of the parties; whether they sought legal advice as to the meaning and legal significance of the instrument; oral representations and previous dealings between the parties; the way in which the instrument was viewed in a particular trade, profession or business; the parties' reasons for issuing and accepting a comfort letter; and the role the instrument had in the transaction. Furthermore, the Court held that if and where the lender reasonably relied on the terms, express or implied, in the comfort letter, then the statements in the comfort letter, even if promissory language had been avoided, may be held enforceable under a theory of promissory estoppel or detrimental reliance, despite the parent company having had good reasons for wanting to avoid a formal guarantee.[77] The Court went onto demonstrate that, where a letter of comfort becomes legally binding, it will look at the broader

74 *Lasalle Bank National Association v. Citicorp Real Estate Inc.* 2003 US Dist LEXIS 12043, 18 July 2003.
75 Ibid, 4.
76 Ibid, 6.
77 Ibid, 5.

commercial transaction(s) that had been established, and the words specifically used in the letter.

More recently in 2018, an issue arose whether these legal mechanisms relating to letters of comfort and keep well agreements would be effective in being applied to China's bond market. Narae Kim and Lianting Tu observed that, with China's fast-growing US dollar bond market, China traditionally relied on a type of credit-protection pledge that is seldom used elsewhere. As a result of the exposure of Chinese investors to these agreements, they face a fresh test in finding out just what implications arise from keepwell agreements. Kim and Tu stress how these agreements, disproportionately used in the offshore Chinese debt market the past several years, are a sort of gentleman's agreement, namely a commitment to maintain an issuer's solvency that stops short of a payment guarantee from the parent company.[78] As an incipient adoption in the region, a keepwell agreement was established between China Energy Reserve & Chemicals Group and CEFC Shanghai International Group Ltd, due to the latter's default on their dollar notes in May 2018. The adoption of the keepwell mechanism had only a five-year gestation period in China as a means of assuaging the financial concerns of risk-conscious overseas investors. The result was that Chinese parties endorsed the offer of pledges by the parent of an issuer, alongside the issuance of bonds to enhance the creditworthiness of the issuer through its parent. Two years on, in March 2020, Ina Zhou and Rebecca Choong Wilkins,[79] identified the exacerbation of these instruments into default, in reporting that CEFC Shanghai had gone into liquidation, but that a court had yet to rule on the legal status of CEFC's keepwell bonds. China Energy Reserve is still negotiating a debt revamp with its offshore bondholders. This development in Chinese law is significant because entities emanating from jurisdictions outside China where keep well agreements (provisions) are commonplace, will need to be cognisant and vigilant that those provisions are accepted and enforceable in China. Until Chinese courts confirm whether and to what extent these provisions are recognised in China, the response to that concern remains uncertain.

The same caution applies to parties to infrastructure projects seeking to ensure that keepwell contract provisions in contracts are recognised and enforced in jurisdictions in which project operations are conducted and where the debtor has, or is likely to acquire, attachable assets. The book compares and discusses the acceptance, enforcement or otherwise, of increasingly important keepwell mechanisms within

78 Narae Kim, Lianting Tu, China Bondholders Set to Learn How Much a Promise Is Worth, *Financial Review* (2018), https://www.afr.com/markets/debt-markets/china-bondholders-set-to-learn-how-much-a-promise-is-worth-20180604-h10yfq. In 2018, Chinese issuers have a total about USD 100 billion of notes outstanding with keepwell agreements, accounting for about 80% of such dollar issued bonds globally.

79 Ina Zhou, Rebecca Choong Wilkins, How a 'Keepwell' Clause Protects China Bonds (or Not), *Washington Post* (March 2020), https://www.washingtonpost.com/business/how-a-keepwell-clause-protects-china-bonds-or-not/2020/05/14/bdae4d36-965b-11ea-87a3-22d324235636_story.html. This section and the following chapter on close-out netting provisions draw on the work undertaken by Robert Walters and Leon Trakman.

insolvency and restructuring agreements and in their legal application to infrastructure operations. The book will discuss the creditors engaged within such schemes of arrangement, as well as cross-border issues that have emerged. It argues the need to develop difference versions of letters of comfort as a means of structuring these legal instruments into a certain, predictable and as a user-adaptable international measure. In other words, due to their broad application and use, letters of comfort would need to be construed more restrictively to ensure that any nationalisation or internationalisation prescribed by principles of law or a model law pertain only to cross-border insolvency, restructure or liquidation proceedings. On this basis, the book proposes more comprehensive research to legitimate, stabilise and ultimately unify the international regulation of letters of comfort.

1.2.3 Mergers and Acquisitions

Mergers and acquisitions (MA) are fundamental yet complex transactions commonly used in the investment banking and private equities sectors.[80] Generally the terms 'mergers' and 'acquisitions' are used interchangeably in the literature.[81] Even though a conceptual distinction exits between mergers and acquisitions, and although some authors distinguish between them at all levels, most do not.[82] In general, an MA refers to all inter-firm linkages that lead to the integration of two entities. Such a combination can entail merging two roughly equally sized companies, as well as acquisitions in which one company obtains majority ownership of the other. Acquisitions are often presented in the economic press as mergers in order to avoid the pejorative conception of t the merger being perceived as a takeover. The result is to distinguish between the two terms: mergers referring to two entities of similar size, and acquisition in which one firm, generally the bigger one, acquires another firm of a smaller size. However, it is arguable that the words 'mergers' and 'acquisitions' can be used interchangeably to refer to the transactions entered into by a new economic unit that is founded on previously existing firms.[83] This book does not focus on whether and to what extent acquisitions are recast as mergers, other than to adopt the common usage of treating both under the same heading, as mergers and acquisitions.

The recent impact of COVID-19 has seen large and well-established entities enduring significant economic strain. Therefore, as COVID-19 continues to rapidly permeate our society and as financial markets struggle to maintain stability, a struggling entity can often manage social, economic and political shocks through

80 Paul Pignataro, *Mergers, Acquisitions, Divestitures, and Other Restructurings*, Wiley (2015), 1.

81 Noelia Gonzalo-Hevia, Marta Ortiz-de-Urbina-Criado, María Sacristán-Navarro, Megers and Acquisitions: Asystematic Review of the Literature from a Strategic Point of View, Universidad Rey Juan Carlos, Departamento de Economía de la Empresa, in Perrault, Etienne (ed), *Mergers and Acquisitions: Practices, Performance and Perspectives*, Nova Science Publishers (2013), 42–43.

82 Ibid, 43.

83 Ibid, 42.

an MA. In so restructuring, it can redress the loss of money and the risk of insolvency.[84] On the other hand, the MA pathway can be treacherous. Publicly announced MA are sometimes withdrawn after they are concluded or on re-evaluating them. These results can have a significant impact, not only for the MA parties, but upon spill over economic recoveries that extend beyond them.

MA can also lead to market instability, depending on their form and operation. Regarding their form, MA are generally horizontal or vertical in structure. A horizontal MA occurs between business entities operating within the same industry, leading to the new entity increasing its market share in that industry.[85] For example, an entity that produces motor vehicles in America increases its market share in purchasing an equivalent motor vehicle manufactured by a company in Australia. A vertical MA occurs between businesses operating in different capacities and at different levels within an industry supply chain. For instance, an entity may engage in a vertical MA in acquiring a business within its supply chain in the diverse oil and gas industry. Paul Pignataro believes that 'mergers are acquisitions constitute a level and form of restructuring because they both involve a level of reorganisation to improve business outcomes and profitability'.[86] In other words, this form of restructuring enables entities to renegotiate the pathway in improving their current economic viability.

In recent times, a potentially lucrative and increasingly popular MA strategy has emerged when large pools of private equity money are used to fund leveraged buyouts (LBOs).[87] An LBO is the buyout of a company with borrowed money in which the target company's assets serve as collateral. In industry parlance, the term 'leverage' refers to debt, and the borrowed money increases the buyer's purchasing power. In a private equity transaction, companies use their own money, in addition to debt, to finance the merger or acquisition of other companies.[88] In many cases, these private equity buyers restructure the target company and then sell their holdings when the value of the merged company has increased to a level at which the buyer can make a large profit. In short, 'private equity buyers with vast financial resources can have a major influence on merger activities'.[89]

Another factor influencing MA activity is the general trend towards corporate consolidation in certain industries, such as by technology companies during the frenzied boom of the 1990s. Consolidations are slightly different from acquisitions

84 Mara H. Rogers, Amelia Xu, Geetika Jerath, Norton Rose Fulbright US LLP, *COVID-19 Impact: Potential Risks and Problems in Signed M&A Deals*, Harvard Law School on Corporate Governance, 20 April 2020, https://corpgov.law.harvard.edu/2020/04/20/covid-19-impact-potential-risks-and-problems-in-signed-ma-deals/.

85 Paul Pignataro, *Mergers, Acquisitions, Divestitures, and Other Restructurings*, Wiley (2015), 5.

86 Ibid.

87 Business Reference Guide, *Mergers, Acquisitions & Financial Markets*, Salem Press, A Division of EBSCO Information Services, Inc, Editors of Salem Press. *Mergers, Acquisitions and Financial Markets, Vol. 2 Edition*, Salem Press (2017), 5.

88 Ibid.

89 Ibid.

in that the resulting company is a new entity.[90] In other words, under an acquisition the surviving entity takes responsibility for the liabilities, assets and functions of the acquired company. Under a consolidation, two or more entities combine into a single new entity while neither previous corporate entity exists.

Nonetheless, and despite the growth of MA and consolidations, 'worldwide foreign direct investment (FDI) has fallen significantly in recent years. Rising to approximately USD 1.76 trillion in 2015, these increasingly important global economic activities has declined in use since 2018'.[91] The Organisation for Economic Development (OECD) highlighted that, 'in the first half of 2019, global FDI flows decreased by 20% compared to the last half of 2018, to USD 572 billion. FDI flows dropped by 5% to USD 361 billion in Q1 2019 and by 42% to USD 210 billion in Q2 2019'.[92] This decrease in global flows was largely due to lower investments in the Netherlands and the United States and to disinvestments from Belgium and Ireland, both of whom are members of the European Union. MA have had a 'high failure rate in Europe of between 46% and 82% for some time, at variance with their anticipated outcomes'.[93] In addition, FDI flows from China to the US dropped from a peak of USD 16 billion in the second half of 2016, to less than 1.2 billion as Chinese companies invested less in the US and sold off some of their direct investments there.[94] This development has also contributed to negative FDI inflows and outflows between Hong Kong, China in Quarter 2 2019, even though Hong Kong is conceived as a global FDI gateway into and out of China.

A similar story has been played out in Australia.[95] While preceding COVID-19, a recent example was the 2018 sale by Wesfarmers of the UK DIY chain, Homebase, which was reportedly acquired by turnaround specialist Hilco Capital for just £1 (AUD 1.8). This acquisition took place after only two years of ownership of Homebase and the initial purchase price of £340 million.[96] Another example is Wesfarmers acquisition of Bunnings UK and Ireland which it then sold with reported write-downs of AUD 1 billion.[97] Wesfarmers, one of Australia's largest companies, and an experienced MA acquirer, has also been criticised for failing to understand the difference between DIY markets in Australia and the UK.[98] Referring to Wesfarmers' acquisition of Homebase in 2016, Craig Henshaw observes

90 Ibid.

91 Jing Yan, *Do Merger Laws Deter Cross-Border Mergers and Acquisitions?* University of Finance and Economics (2018), 376.

92 FDI in Figures, *Organisation for Economic Development* (2019), http://www.oecd.org/investment/FDI-in-Figures-October-2019.pdf

93 Agyenim Boateng, George Lordofos, Keith Glaister, Motives for European Mergers and Acquisitions, Analysis of Pre-merger Press Announcements and Post-merger Interviews, in Shlomo Tarba, Sir Cary Cooper, Riikka Sarala, Mohammad Ahammad (eds), *Mergers and Acquisitions in Practice: Vol. 1 Edition*, Routledge (2017), 6.

94 Ibid.

95 Craig Henshaw, *Seventy Per Cent of M&As Fail – Be One of the Thirty Per Cent* (2018), https://www.adviservoice.com.au/2018/10/seventy-per-cent-of-mas-fail-be-one-of-the-thirty-per-cent/.

96 Ibid.

97 Ibid.

98 Ibid.

that '[t]he investment has been disappointing, with the problems arising from poor execution post-acquisition being compounded by a deterioration in the macro environment and retail sector in the UK'.[99]

Given the threats flowing from MA mergers, and divergence in their regulation by states such as the UK and Australia, it is important to compare the law and rules pertaining to MA at a time of heightened geopolitical and economic tension. Used in conjunction with other restructuring mechanisms, the economic and legal impact of undertaking and MA can have enormous and sometimes negative impact upon entities and individuals. The essential need is for entities to be equipped to undertake cost effective and legally sustainable cross-border MA.

COVID-19 is also likely to accentuate the continued decline in FDI, until at least 2022. Predators may well secure greater control over not only private markets. Importantly, their actions may have a drastic impact upon national interests. Fearful of this impact, the Australian government has sought to redress predatory acquisitions since the advent of COVID-19. In March 2020, the Australian treasurer announced 'changes to Australia's foreign investment regulations, to reduce undue pressure on the Australian economy and Australian businesses'.[100] These responses have included changes made to the Australia's *Foreign Acquisitions and Takeovers Act 1975 (FATA)* for an initial period of six months that has yet to run its course.

This book will examine the effectiveness of such governmental measures and the extent to which states have responded comparably to the ongoing economic crisis and impact from COVID-19. MA and restructuring are the most important transactions an incorporated business can undertake, rivalled only by initial organisation or liquidation.[101] The combination of change on multiple dimensions with deliberation and financial significance, accords characteristic drama and complexity to these transactions. Their significance and complexity also make them challenging for corporate management and legal governance. Therefore, the book will

99 Ibid.

100 Chris Mitchell, Shane Bilardi, Chanel Mercurio, *Australian Government Increases Scrutiny on Foreign Investment as Part of Response to COVID-19* (2020), https://www.dlapiper.com/en/pr/insights/publications/2020/03/australian-government-increases-scrutiny-on-foreign-investment-as-part-of-response-to-covid-19/ The two key changes announced by the Treasurer, and which will be subject to new regulations to be released shortly, are: Effective from 10:30 pm (AEDT) on 29 March 2020, all proposed foreign investments which are subject to the *Foreign Acquisitions and Takeovers Act 1975 (FATA)* will require approval by the Treasurer, regardless of the value or the nature of the foreign investment. This change is to be achieved by reducing to $0 the monetary screening thresholds for all foreign investments under the FATA. The Australian Foreign Investment Review Board (FIRB), the body within the Australian Treasury established to advise the Treasurer and the Australian Government on Australia's Foreign Investment Policy and its administration, will be working with all existing and new applicants for foreign investment approvals to extend the review and approval timeframes from the current statutory 30-day period to up to six months.

101 John Coates IV, *Mergers, Acquisitions and Restructuring: Types, Regulation, and Patterns of Practice*, Harvard John M. Olin Discussion Paper Series Discussion Paper No. 781, July 2014, Oxford Handbook on Corporate Law and Governance, 1.

address regulatory gaps in responding to the economic and legal consequences of this pandemic. It will also evaluate the disproportionate impact of such consequences upon states, based on divergence in their economic and legal regimes, and in their disproportionate responses to that impact. Understanding divergence in the laws and rules of regulating cross-border financing transactions will provide individuals and entities with up-to-date knowledge and information on how, when and where to engage in FDI, including the costs and benefits of such investment. In addressing the overall regulatory gaps, the book will compare the rules applied by the Australian Foreign Investment Review Board to fill such gaps, and how regulatory bodies elsewhere do so, if that all.

Moreover, the book will extend its analysis beyond private MA arrangements, to states' support of such arrangements, including funding for commercial entities to acquire companies in other states. For instance, a state-backed authority in China may attempt to acquire, or secure an entity in Australia, or purchase a stake in it. The book will identify the relevant laws, rules and government organisations that are involved in both public and private acquisitions, notably through foreign investment laws that have attracted more scrutiny since the pandemic's outbreak. The book will compare how selected jurisdictions have tightened up their respective foreign investment laws, and the influence of these restrictions have had and will continue to have on current and future MA activities. It will do so in recognition of the financial fluidity that continues to follow the pandemic, accompanied by globalism's retreat into nationalism, and attenuated by trade and investment conflicts arising both regionally and globally.

Even as states turn inwards, companies will identify synergies and economic benefits in acquiring and merging with entities located primarily in other states. These financial benefits may take the form of increased debt capacity and consequential reductions in the cost of capital for the combined entity. In particular, large entities that are diversified can effectively correlate cash flow streams of subsidiaries and divisions acquired through MA. Such MA are also likely to 'reduce the cash flow volatility of the combined entity, thereby lowering the probability of bankruptcy'.[102] This increased debt capacity will give rise to two prospective consequences. Firstly, capital suppliers are likely to be willing to offer financial resources on better terms in order to reduce the firm's cost of capital. Secondly and more importantly, 'lower bankruptcy and insolvency risks are likely to increase the combined entity's leverage and enjoyment of greater tax savings without incurring the significant costs of financial distress'.[103] Therefore, MA can serve as a fundamental means of stabilising financial markets, particularly when experiencing national, regional and global economic, social, health and geopolitical shocks.

102 Ottorino Morresi, *Alberto Pezzi, Cross-Border Mergers and Acquisitions: Theory and Empirical Evidence*, Palgrave Macmillan (2014), 95.
103 Ibid.

1.3 Close-Out Netting

The book slightly diverges away from insolvency and restructuring to a legal tool that has become one of the most preventative measures every introduced into the international legal framework. This chapter will explore, in depth, the extent to which close-out netting is regulated internationally and domestically, stressing the enforceability of such provisions. It will discuss how close-out netting provisions impact upon international insolvency proceedings, in enabling parties to close out an agreed amount as part of an insolvent declaration. The book highlights the reasons for the growing importance of close-out netting over the last two decades and how such needs are met internationally, such as through the UNIDROIT Principles. It also evaluates the important, but often not discussed, UNIDROIT Principles on the Operation of Close-Out Netting Provisions, 2013,[104] that address the impact of insolvency upon cross-border commercial transactions.

The meaning and application of close-out netting is best considered in relation to evolving international financial practice. The globalisation and in some cases regionalisation of financial markets and institutions have grown significantly over the past five decades.[105] This development has increased the significance of providing for close-out netting in commercial contracts. The absence of such provisions in sub-prime financial markets materially exacerbated the GFC of 2007–2009.[106] Improper collateralisation of underlying trans-border commercial transactions was a main reason for the collapse of Lehman Brothers and its multiple counterparties.[107]

In response to these global disruptions, a close-out netting agreement can influence the collateral value of a transaction, by reducing or increasing the net amount one party owes the other.[108] Such close-out netting provisions within contracts are a 'relatively new addition to the finance regulatory framework'.[109] The current international definition of close-out netting is described as follows:

> Close-out netting provision' means a contractual provision on the basis of which, upon the occurrence of an event predefined in the provision in

104 *UNIDROIT Principles on the Operation of Close-out Netting Provisions*, 11 December 2013, https://www.unidroit.org/instruments/capital-markets/netting

105 Robert Walters, Leon Trakman, The Fragmented Approach toward Close-out Netting Provisions in Australia, Indonesia, Malaysia and Singapore Compared, *Journal of Banking Regulation*, Vol. 21 (2019), 1. https://doi.org/10.1057/s41261-019-00109-w. The discussion regarding close-out netting provisions draws on early work by the book authors.

106 Sylvie Durham, *Derivatives Deskbook: Close-out Netting, Risk Mitigation*, Litigation, 1–26, 27 (Keliann Kavanagh ed., 2nd ed., 2014); Arthur E. Wilmarth, Jr., The Dark Side of Universal Banking: Financial Conglomerates and the Origins of the Subprime Financial Crisis, *Connecticut Law Review*, Vol. 41, No. 963 (2009), 1044–1045 (discussing the subprime financial crisis that began in 2007), in Vincent R. Johnson, International Financial Law: The Case Against Close-out Netting, *Boston University International Law Journal*, Vol. 3. (2015), 102.

107 Ibid.

108 Ibid.

109 Robert Walters, Leon Trakman, The Fragmented Approach toward Close-Out Netting Provisions in Australia, Indonesia, Malaysia and Singapore Compared, *Journal of Banking Regulation* (2019), 1.

> relation to a party to the contract, the obligations owed by the parties to each other that are covered by the provision, whether or not they are at that time due and payable, are automatically or at the election of one of the parties reduced to or replaced by a single net obligation, whether by way of novation, termination or otherwise, representing the aggregate value of the combined obligations, which is thereupon due and payable by one party to the other.[110]

Importantly, close-out netting arrangements/agreements are important means of reducing risks in financial contracts, notably in relation to counterparty risks. Vincent Johnson identifies 'two related benefits that are attributed to close-out netting agreements. Firstly, such agreements allegedly mitigate counterparty risk on particular transactions' (i.e. 'credit risk').[111] Secondly, they redress systemic risk to the entire financial system'.[112] The perceived benefit, in both cases, is to minimise 'exposures on open contracts if one party should become insolvent or a like event occurs before the settlement date'.[113] However, Johnson argues against the use of close-out netting provisions. He points to five key areas where the netting provisions fall short. These include:

- **Excessive Externalization of Risk** – the strongest argument against close-out netting is that the process does little or nothing to minimize the risks that large-scale financial transactions create; rather, close-out netting merely shifts those risks to other persons who have no choice in the matter;[114]
- **Lack of Transparency** – there is a lack transparency. Thus, without any meaningful consent on their part, general creditors are forced to bear a larger share of the losses that occur soon after a party that is protected by a close-out agreement defaults, cashes in its chips, and leaves the table, even as its counterparty fails;[115]
- **Inconsistency and Opaqueness** – the problems with close-out netting agreements are not merely their lack of transparency and nondisclosure of material information. Far worse, close-out netting agreements are both deliberately opaque and unpredictable in operation. Parties to close-out netting agreements are given a great deal of freedom to define their terms by specifying, for example, what constitutes a default sufficient to trigger the closing-out process. While this flexible arrangement can be praised as consistent with the ideal of 'private ordering', it means that the operation of financial and

110 Principle 2, UNIDROIT Principles on the Operation of Close-out Netting Provisions, 11 December 2013 (emphasis in website).

111 V. Johnson, International Financial Law: The Case against Close-out Netting, *Boston University International Law Journal*, Vol. 33 (2015), 110–121.

112 Ibid.

113 Ibid.

114 Ibid, 116.

115 Ibid, 117.

insolvency law is far from predictable. In some instances, an adverse credit event affecting an affiliated entity is sufficient to justify termination and acceleration of mutual obligations; in other cases, it is not. There is no way for affected third parties to know much about when they are likely to be drawn into a maelstrom of close-out netting which, by accelerating obligations between the parties, may thrust one of those parties into bankruptcy[116];

- **Disparate Treatment** – close-out netting disproportionately favors large institutions. Banks are eligible to enter into close-out netting agreements in all 'netting friendly' jurisdictions. In many such places, so are insurance companies, investment firms, hedge funds, proprietary traders, pension funds, central banks, public authorities, [and] international financial institutions. In contrast, non-financial corporate entities are eligible only in certain cases. Even if small institutions qualify for the favored treatment of close-out netting under insolvency laws, the transactional costs are often so prohibitive as to effectively exclude them. Further, individual natural persons are generally only eligible under limited circumstances;[117] and
- **Accelerated Insolvency and Systemic Risk** – pose a great risk of thrusting some financial institutions prematurely into bankruptcy. This not only endangers specific institutions, but also creates a risk of precipitating an adverse domino effect of firm failures throughout financial systems. Despite these dangers, the law in netting-friendly jurisdictions insulates the financial institutions that assert their close-out rights from obligations under the law of insolvency. This is true regardless of the magnitude of the risks created by their activities and financial products. The special treatment accorded to credit derivatives by applicable insolvency laws may well increase systemic risk because it eliminates a possible curb on counter parties' rush to close out their contracts in the event of a wave of failure.[118]

While there is opposition to close-out netting based on these concerns, netting is viewed as an important contractual means of safeguarding against insolvency. Philipp Paech[119] argues that close-out netting is very similar to a process known as insolvency set-off. He elaborates that netting provides:

> a company goes into liquidation, an account must be taken of what is due from each party to the other in their mutual dealings. Secondly, the sums due from one party must be set off against the sums due from the other, even if the sums are not yet due, are contingent, or need to be ascertained.[120]

116 Ibid, 119.
117 Ibid, 120.
118 Ibid, 123.
119 Philipp Paech, Close-out Netting, Insolvency Law and Conflict-of-Laws, *Journal of Corporate Law Studies*, Vol. 14, No. 2 (2014), 419–452.
120 Ibid, 425.

Close-out netting achieves the same or a very similar result to insolvency set-off but is based on contract and therefore benefits from party autonomy, whereas the insolvency set-off rule is mandatory law.[121] Paech argues that close-out netting has the added advantage of reducing the exposure of the contracting parties to mandatory law, should one party become insolvent or should a like event occur.

This book will compare how close-out netting provisions operate in a world of competing goals and the continuing fragmentation of the legal landscape. The book will contrast the approaches taken by Australia, European Union, India, Indonesia, Singapore, United Kingdom and United States (New York), in regulating close-out netting provisions. In a narrower 2019 study, the authors noted that the current approach to regulating close-out netting provisions in Australia, Indonesia, Malaysia and Singapore was fragmented, even though the UNIDROIT had developed an internationally agreed definition. In responding to that fragmentation, the next sub-section and **Appendix 1** will discuss the Master Agreement adopted by the International Swaps and Derivatives Association (ISDA) and the use of that Master Agreement in close-out netting arrangements. The purpose will be to identify similarities in the purpose and function of derivative contracts and close-out netting provisions, particularly in protecting parties in economic crises.

1.3.1 Derivative Collateral Contracts (ISDA Master Agreement)

Dealing with the risk of default on a debt is important in maintaining financial stability in a modern economy, while derivative contracts are key means of promoting such security. This section, elaborated in **Appendix 1**, examines how derivatives balance liquidity and economic stability in cross-border finance agreements. A brief discussion of the Master Agreement of ISDA, addressing derivatives, is dealt with later.

Derivative contracts, once viewed as arcane and exotic financial instruments, have become commonplace tools utilised by companies of all sizes to hedge or otherwise reallocate market risks associated with their businesses. Mark Guinn and William Harvey maintain that a bank or other lender that extends credit to a company frequently takes account of the debtor's derivative commitments in determining its credit history and the risks in making loans to it.[122] However, given that 'collateral contracts are risk sharing mechanisms with limited commitment, it is difficult to make debtors repay debts by these means'.[123]

The ISDA Master Agreement serves as the contract under which over-the-counter (OTC) derivatives transactions between counterparties take place. The use of such master netting and credit support agreements between counterparties in the OTC derivatives market has become the most effective and widely used

121 Ibid.

122 Mark Guinn, William Harvey, Taking OTC Derivative Contracts as Collateral, *The Business Lawyer*, Vol. 57, No. 3 (May 2002), 1127–1128.

123 Weerachart T. Kilenthong, Collateral Premia and Risk Sharing under Limited Commitment, *Economic Theory* (2011), 475.

method of reducing credit risk. Nina Hval asserts that the 'importance of netting agreements in OTC Derivatives cannot be underestimated, as they permit counterparties to offset gains or losses relating to a number of transactions between them. Under a credit support agreement, securities can be pledged as collateral against the net credit exposure resulting from the mark-to-market valuation, accounting for the fair market value of all outstanding transactions'.[124] As a result, a party with net credit exposure may reduce or eliminate its credit risk against a counterparty by receiving an interest in securities, the value of which is equal to its net credit exposure. David Mengle argues that 'each transaction is not a separate contract but is instead incorporated by reference into a single netting agreement'.[125] He notes that there are 'two forms of netting within ISDA Master Agreements. Firstly, payment netting takes place during the normal business of a solvent firm. It involves combining offsetting cash flow obligations between two parties on a given day in a given currency into a single net payable or receivable. Determined in accordance with Section 2 of the ISDA Master Agreement 2002, payment netting is essentially the same as set-off'.[126] The second form of netting, Mengle contends, is close-out netting.[127]

Thus, in order to understand close-out netting provision, it is also important to understand the significance of over-the-counter derivative(s) contracts. Coupled with the need to understand the importance of netting are the UNIDROIT Principles on Close-Out Netting Provisions. These UNIDROIT Principles have played and continue to play a pivotal and key role in commercial law.[128] Still, there is an ever more pressing need for states and supranational polities to harmonise close-out netting agreements more effectively, including through wider participation of states operating both nationally and transnationally. These needs are discussed later.

1.4 The Need for Further International Reform

Underlying the rationale and call for the further internationlisation of cross-border insolvency and restructuring law, has in part, been part of the OECD's push for some time. This push by the OECD comes on the back of the increasing importance of these laws upon the overall health of the global economy. Horst Eidenmueller is of

124 Ibid.

125 David Mengle, *Close-out Netting and Risk Management in Over-the-Counter Derivatives,* International Swaps and Derivatives Association and Fordham University (2010), 1–4. (including reflection on ISDA 2002, Section 1, Appendix 1, discussed in Chapter 3).

126 Ibid, 2–3.

127 Ibid. The rationale for close-out netting is the nature of market risk management for over-the-counter derivatives and other financial contract, which involves maintaining a hedged, balanced portfolio by means of offsetting transactions with other counterparties. If a counterparty defaults, the portfolio is no longer balanced, so it is necessary either to replace the defaulted transactions or unwind the offsetting transactions. Failure to do so would, in effect, create open positions that are vulnerable to market fluctuations. Close-out netting makes it possible for intermediaries to manage risks following a default by facilitating the reestablishment of a balanced book.

128 UNIDROIT Principles on the Operation of Close-out Netting Pro- visions which were adopted by the UNIDROIT Governing Council at its 92nd session, Rome, 8–10 May 2013.

the view that insolvency laws in general, and corporate insolvency/restructuring regimes in particular, are economically important.[129] In an earlier study undertaken in 2016–2017, Müge McGowan and Dan Andrews make the point that there 'are significant differences in the designs of insolvency regimes amongst OECD member countries'.[130] Their study examined the period immediately following the 2008 GFC, and those entities categorized as 'zombie', namely, as being in considerable financial distress. In our view, distinct similarities exist between the need for government assistance by financially stressed 'zombie' companies then, and the recurrence of that need now as a consequence of the global pandemic.

McGowan and Andrews also affirm a pervasive argument in this book that, 'while there are differences amongst the insolvency and restructuring legal frameworks across the identified countries, domestic and global reform is direly needed. They elaborate that, reforms to insolvency regimes which reduce barriers to corporate restructuring and the personal costs of entrepreneurial failure also reduce the share of capital sunk into zombie firms. The benefits secured from reform measures are partly realised through the restructuring of weak firms, which in turn spurs the reallocation of capital to more productive firms'.[131] These findings carry strong policy implications, in demonstrating the scope for reform of insolvency regimes in many OECD countries to redress both the rising misallocation of capital and the increasing survival of low productivity firms that have contributed to the productivity slowdown. However, implementing such reform measures require considerable caution. While a 'reform can emerge as a potentially relevant tool to revive productivity growth, the available cross-country indicators of insolvency regimes have a number of drawbacks, particularly with respect to design features that are relevant for productivity outcomes'.[132] These drawbacks, in turn, make it difficult to identify potential growth dividends stemming from insolvency reform. McGowan and Andrews identify the baseline of global reform measures with the World Bank in which the costs of insolvency and restructuring are important means of promoting the overall health of the global economy. While the economic benefit of reformed insolvency and restructuring laws is only one contributing factor to the enhanced efficiency of the global economy, it is an area that reduces reliance on intrusive governmental intervention. While the authors do not call for the exhaustive internationalisation of insolvency or restructuring law, any additional or further internationalisation is arguably a factor in extending their economic benefits to the financial stability.

129 Horst Eidenmueller, *The Rise and Fall of Regulatory Competition in Corporate Insolvency Law in the European Union*, Law Working Paper N° 456/2019, University of Oxford and ECGI, 1–4.

130 Müge Adalet McGowan, Dan Andrews, Valentine Millot, *Insolvency Regimes*, Zombie Firms and Capital Reallocation Economics Department Working Papers No. 1399, Organisation for Economic Co-operation and Development (OECD), ECO/WKP (2017), 1.

131 Ibid, 16.

132 Ibid.

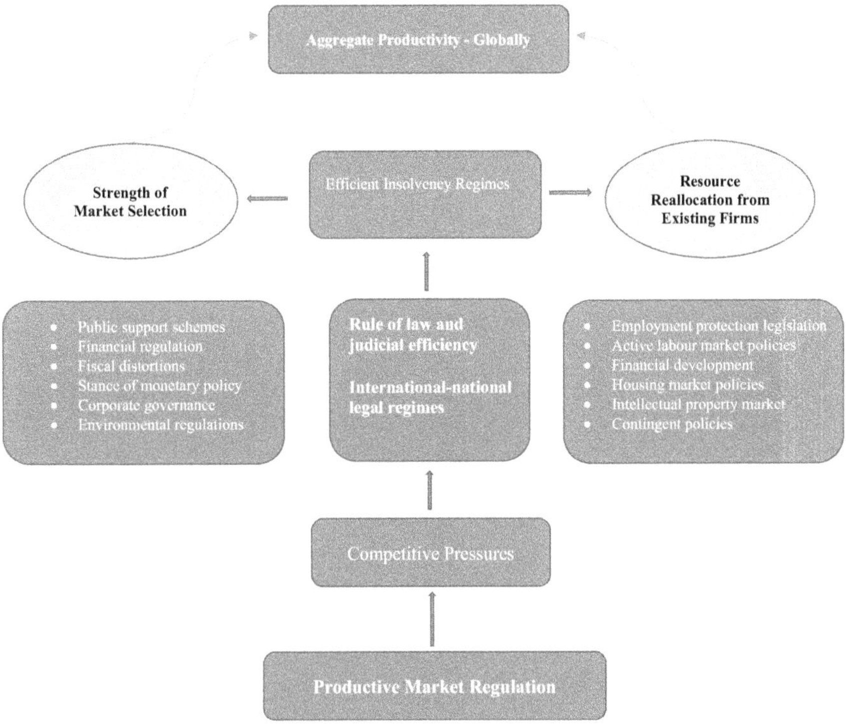

FIGURE 1.1 Policy and the law working together to underpin transnational insolvency and restructuring

Source: Adalet McGowan and Andrews (2016)[133]

Arguably, the diagram and the position taken by McGowan and Andrews underscores the overall need for further internationalisation of the international and national legal tools and mechanisms to promote 'Productive Market Regulation' across international financial sectors. They elaborate that: 'insolvency regimes are crucial due to market imperfections, such as coordination problems, incomplete contracts and information asymmetries, which make it difficult in practice for the private market to facilitate the exit of failing firms in an orderly fashion'.[134] When a debtor is suspected of being insolvent, creditors have an incentive to engage in a 'rush to the exit', rapidly enforcing their individual claims, even if it results in a reduction in the total value of recoverable assets. However, according to the McGowan and Andrews, in practice, 'it is difficult for debtors and creditors to write a complete private contract that ensures an optimal outcome ex ante due to the

133 Ibid, 31.
134 Ibid, 13.

high number of contingencies and the fact that the debtor can acquire new assets and liabilities after the initial contract. They state that:

> for these reasons, insolvency regimes that contain provisions to bring debtors and creditors to the table and thus deal in an orderly fashion with the financial distress of commercial entities (corporate insolvency regimes) and entrepreneurs who have either been trading as a sole proprietor or who are part of a closely-held private company (personal insolvency regimes) are crucial'.[135]

In furthering their argument, they maintain that:

> A strong rule of law and an efficient judicial system is crucial for the effectiveness and in turn the incentives for stakeholders to utilise – formal insolvency procedures, since: i) court involvement accounts for a large share of insolvency costs; ii) the efficient resolution of financial distress depends on courts' ability to verify information and enforce contracts; and iii) the ability of insolvency regimes to distinguish viable from non-viable firms will be reduced when courts are congested and judges lack the requisite expertise.[136]

More importantly, they highlight how insolvency regimes that do not unduly penalise entrepreneurial failures can spur firm creation, draw more talented individuals into entrepreneurship and incentivise radical innovation over conservative business strategies.

We propose a more preventative approach to minimise financially stressed entities having to declare insolvency. To achieve this, more extensive measures are needed to internationalise divergent domestic laws governing corporate restructuring. We argue that an even deeper level of legal harmonisation in financial and insolvency law is needed. Central to this way forward is the development of a Theory of Action[137] that can be used both by industry and regulators. Theories of Action have become particularly important in regulating scientific sectors such as

135 Ibid.

136 Ibid, 14. The authors note that there are other polices related to exit markets, such as, product market reforms that raise competitive pressures will strengthen market selection by making it more difficult for weak firms to survive and will increase the likelihood that the resources released by exiting firms will be reallocated to more productive uses. Third, even if product market regulations are well-designed, inefficient firms may still linger in the market due to policy weakness in other areas, including: inappropriate public support schemes, the 'evergreening' of loans to zombie firms by fragile banks and weak environmental regulations, which may enable laggard firms armed with obsolescent technologies to linger in the market. Fourth, the aggregate impact of policies that strengthen market selection will be enhanced by reallocation- friendly policies, particularly those that facilitate job turnover and labour mobility. Policies that facilitate the growth of productive firms will over time make it increasingly difficult for weak firms to survive, thus indirectly strengthening market selection and help channel the released resources to more productive uses.

137 Michael Jones, *'Action Regulation Theory' (2014). Faculty of Business – Papers (Archive)*, 405. https://ro.uow.edu.au/buspapers/405.

primary industries and food production. They have adaptable value in harmonising differences within and across families of law. The obstacle, in harmonising insolvency law is that domestic governments, regulators, practitioners, academics and the judiciary are largely unfamiliar with conceptual and interpretative divergence across families of law and how to accommodate those divergences. In contrast, comparative lawyers who are familiar with divergence in the substantive and procedural nature of domestic laws on insolvency and restructuring, are ordinarily better able to draft and interpret transnational laws that in order to reconcile those differences.[138]

A formal and functional problem is when the language used in drafting transnational laws to accommodate differences in domestic laws are abstract in nature and unable to reconcile the concrete divergence in the construction of domestic laws. As José Angelo Estrella Faria contended:

> It usually provides an opportunity for taking into account and solving possible problems of coordination or conflict with existing law either in the drafting of the new law or by amending the pre-existing law. That is not the case when a legal text is prepared at the international level for introduction into domestic legal systems. Those negotiating the legal text are usually experts in the area of law in question and are aware of the problems of coordination that may be encountered in many legal systems. However, the legal text is to a large extent drafted in the abstract, in a generic form that may have to be adapted to local circumstances. If it is done well, it will be drafted in clear language, will not use words with particular meanings in specific legal systems.[139]

Estrella Faria points out that there are 'difficulties in achieving international legal harmonisation, irrespective of the subject matter and form of the instruments used'.[140] One particular difficulty is that those who draft, interpret and apply domestic law often lack corresponding ability to understand international guides directed at construing those domestic laws, such as a convention on cross-border insolvency. To achieve a higher level of harmonisation across domestic laws, we argue for the development and adoption of transnational law guidelines, a model law and ideally, a convention to regulate crossborder insolvency. One such institution that has a role in the harmonisation of transnational commercial law is the UNCITRAL that, have adopted a number of legal tools and mechanism, such

138 José Angelo Estrella Faria, *Legal Harmonisation Through Model Laws: The Experience of the United Nations Commission on International Trade Law*, https://www.justice.gov.za/alraesa/conferences/2005sa/papers/s5_faria2.pdf.

139 Ibid, 9.

140 Ibid.

as Conventions,[141] model law(s),[142] Legislative Guidelines[143] and the UNCITRAL Rules, such as international commercial arbitration.[144]

Early forms of transnational commercial harmonisation date back to the 1920s. These include the Convention for the Unification of Certain Rules Relating to International Carriage by Air 1929 (The Warsaw Convention on Carriage by Air); and the International Convention for the Unification of Certain Rules of Law Relating to Bills of Lading 1924 (The Hague Rules on Bills of Lading). Choosing to establish a Convention has been used where the objective is to achieve a high degree of uniformity of law among signatory states, thus reducing the need for a party to undertake research of the law of another State party.[145] The advantages to having a Convention in place provides nation states with a set of rules that can be easily transposed into national laws. One of the drawbacks to this approach, however, is that it is also difficult to obtain the full agreement of all nation states to a convention, and amendments to a convention can, at time, be nearly impossible. Even though securing such agreement often arises in practice, the adoption of the convention for the International Sale of Goods (CISG) demonstrates that a convention need not be agreed to by all states in order to be successful. The CISG has not been adopted by all national sates, but is often used in transitional contract law, even by organisations in those states that have not ratified the instrument. In our view, such a convention provides a higher degree of legal certainty, in times of global uncertainty, not least of all uncertainty leading to instability across financial markets.

On the other hand, a model law has been viewed by UNCITRAL as providing a sound alternative to a convention in achieving further legal harmonisation. It provides nation states with an option to improve their national laws.[146] A model law is often chosen as the vehicle for harmonisation and improvement in view of the flexibility it provides nation states in preparing new laws.[147] The point is that the difference between a model law and a Convention comes down, in part,

141 *UNCITRAL United Nations Convention on Contracts for the International Sale of Goods* (1980), https://uncitral.un.org/sites/uncitral.un.org/files/media-documents/uncitral/en/19-09951_e_ebook.pdf.

142 UNCITRAL Model Law on International Commercial Arbitration (1985), Official Records of the General Assembly, Fortieth Session, Supplement No. 17 (U.N. document A/40/17) Annex I (reproduced in UNCITRAL Yearbook, vol. XVI:1985). The Model Law on International Commercial Arbitration assists Nation States to harmonise arbitration rules.

143 UNCITRAL Legislative Guide on Privately Financed Infrastructure Projects (U.N. document A/CN.9/SER.B/4).

144 UNCITRAL Arbitration Rules, https://uncitral.un.org/en/texts/arbitration/contractualtexts/arbitration. The UNCITRAL Arbitration Rules (revised 2010), 15 August 2010, deal with, amongst others, multiple-party arbitration and joinder, liability, and a procedure to object to experts appointed by the arbitral tribunal.

145 José Angelo Estrella Faria, *Legal Harmonisation through Model Laws: The Experience of the United Nations Commission on International Trade Law*, https://www.justice.gov.za/alraesa/conferences/2005sa/papers/s5_faria2.pdf.

146 International Commercial Arbitration, *UNCITRAL Secretariat Explanation of Model Law*, https://uncitral.un.org/en/texts/arbitration/modellaw/commercial_arbitration.

147 Ibid.

to the level of commitment a state takes in adopting the rules provided by each instrument. That is, and as outlined by the UNCITRAL, a Model Law is created as a suggested pattern for law-makers in national governments to consider adopting as part of their domestic legislation.[148] On the other hand, a convention is an instrument that is binding under international law on States and other entities with treaty-making capacity that choose to become a party to that instrument.[149] Therefore, any departure from a convention can only be achieved if the convention permits reservations to be taken to its provisions.[150] The challenge to establishing conventions on commercial law, is the level of uptake by nation states. Due to their inherent inflexible nature, they can, at times, be viewed as being an obstacle to ratification. Yet, they provide more benefits than obstacles over the longer term and in times of uncertainty, as business needs certainty.

The third level adopted by UNCITRAL has been the development of Guidelines[151] or Rules.[152] These are vast and varied that cover transnational arbitration and insolvency, amongst others. Guidelines and rules are very flexible in their approach and are used to clarify the application of a Model Law or Convention. They underpin the main objective, for example, the rules specified in transnational arbitral Model Law. A material benefit of Guidelines at the international level, is not different to such instruments being established at the national level. They assist individuals and entities in implementing the relevant law. They also provide specific information on the procedural and substantive aspects of the application of a Model Law or Convention. Therefore, while such Guidelines and Rules are viable options in addressing the issues raised in this book, we argue that they should be used, not only as rules of operation, but to assist in the development and implementation of a Model Law or Convention.

The UNIDROIT is an organisation with significant experience in preparing uniform laws on commercial and private law. Its uniform rules focus on developing unifying substantive laws, and only secondarily on the divergent nature of domestic laws.[153] As a result, the UNIDROIT seeks to establish uniform Principles for adoption in commercial law fields, such as transnational contracts[154] and

148 United Nations Commission on International Trade, https://uncitral.un.org/en/about/faq/texts.
149 Ibid.
150 Ibid.
151 UNCITRAL Legislative Guide on Privately Financed Infrastructure Projects (U.N. document A/CN.9/SER.B/4), United Nations sales publication No. E.01.V.4.
152 UNCITRAL Rules on Transparency in Treaty-Based Investor-State Arbitration 2014.
153 Ibid.
154 UNIDROIT Principles of international Commercial Contracts 2016. The main purpose of the new edition of the UNIDROIT Principles is to cover additional topics of interest to the international legal and business communities. https://www.jus.uio.no/lm/en/html/unidroit.contract.principles.note.html. Reproduced from the UNIDROIT Principles of International Commercial Contracts, published by the International Institute for the Unification of Private Law (UNIDROIT), Rome, Italy, Copyright UNIDROIT 1994, by permission of UNIDROIT. Readers are reminded that the official version of the UNIDROIT Principles of International Commercial Contracts also includes the Commentary thereto.

close-out netting. For instance, the UNIDROIT Principles on transnational contracts are intended to provide a system of rules tailored to the needs of transnational commercial transactions. While not yet generally adopted, the Principles strive to promote best practice leading to the best solutions, being certainty, predictability, fairness, transparency and efficiency.[155] Arguably, in seeking best practice, the UNIDROIT Principles affirm the United Nations Convention on Contracts for the International Sale of Goods 1980 (CISG). As the UNIDROIT Principles enunciate, only 'where the rule has been taken over more or less literally from the world wide accepted CISG is explicit reference made to its source'.[156] Moreover, and to the extent that both the UNIDROIT Principles and the CISG cover the same issues, the Principles adopt the CISG solutions, only with such adaptations as were considered appropriate to reflect the particular nature and scope of those Principles.[157]

The desirability of further harmonising commercial laws, for the current and any future pandemic alone, will go some-way to safeguard national and international economic activity in destabilised financial markets. A further argument for harmonisation is that a number of the legal instruments and tools that are identified in this book have already received a high level of international uniformity. For those tools that have not been formally endorsed internationally, such as letters of comfort and schemes of arrangement, they are still widely and commonly used, not only by the jurisdictions compared in this book, but also by most other nation states. These legal instruments are also not exclusive to one particular sector of commercial activity but are used across commerce, from banks to various public and private organisations. They are used as an individual or collective tool to manage financial risk across the public and private sectors. Whether those tools are drawn from UNCITRAL Convention on Cross-Border Insolvency, the UNIDROIT Principles on Close-out Netting Provisions, on schemes of arrangements, or on letters of comfort, they all seek to enable the public and private sector to manage various levels of financial risk. These instruments achieve such private and public ends through their adoption into domestic legal systems. There is every reason for them to apply more expansively to international commerce, notably to the regulation of trans-border insolvency and restructuring.

Accomplishing such ends also extends to restructuring schemes that assist in avoiding trans-border insolvencies. Such restructuring initiatives includes devising international law rules and a model law to regulate schemes of arrangement and letters of comfort. Corporate restructuring does not eliminate the devastating effect of insolvency upon multiple parties involved in commercial ventures that extend across national boundaries. It does assist in anticipating, preparing for and sometimes containing or avoiding the financial devastation caused by insolvency.

155 Ibid.
156 Ibid.
157 Ibid.

The book will demonstrate that the jurisdictions compared have adopted most of, if not all of the legal tools identified.

To underscore the importance of the earlier propositions greater uniformity and consistency is required in the global regulation of international trade and economic activity. In the words of the Chief Justice Sundaresh Menon of Singapore, one of the most powerful forces for globalisation is international trade,[158] and the international legal regime that now supports it. The global pandemic has extensively disrupted domestic, regional and global economic activity. The ascending trade 'challenges faced by states imposing tariffs or trade obstacles on each other, only heightens the need for greater harmonisation and legal convergence in financing trans-border commercial ventures'.[159] An indirect, but very important benefit of legal harmonisation is to reduce confusion and conflict over the contributory attributes of national legal regimes. Moreover, it is in the 'shared interests of nation states to adopt an international rules-based system and the rule of law, even if these rules are construed differently'.[160] The goal is to provide an efficient, but also a fair resolution of cross-border disputes, including disputes that relate to insolvency and restructuring.

The process of internationalising the law governing insolvency and restructuring is already supported in international law, albeit sometimes more impliedly than expressly. Current bilateral and multilateral trade and investment agreements stress free trade. They also highlight the importance of resolving disputes arising in trade and investment through internationally recognised conventions and codes. These include reliance on international laws to regulate finance and banking that facilitate economic trade across national borders, and laws that govern obstructions in those activities. Internationalising domestic laws that regulate finance, banking and insolvency through the harmonisation of those laws is central to achieving these ends. It is also the underlying motivation of this book.

Viewed functionally, nation states need to reduce, as far as is practical, their ongoing reliance upon regulatory competition if they are to reconcile divergent insolvency regimes efficiently. However, to achieve this end, as highlighted by McGowan and Andrews,[161] nation states need to respond to competition strategically, and not destructively. That includes them taking account of factors that militate in

158 Sundaresh Menon, Transnational Commercial Law: Realities, Challenges and a Call for Meaningful Convergence, *Singapore Journal of Legal Studies* (2013), 231–252.

159 Asif Afrat, Boosting Trade Through Legal Harmonisation, if Different Countries Have Similar Rules, the Legal Foundation for Cross-Border Transactions becomes Simpler and More Certain, and Costs of Transactions Can Be Lowered, *The Business Times* (2020), https://www.businesstimes.com.sg/opinion/boosting-trade-through-legal-harmonisation

160 David Stewart, *Promoting the Rule of Law and Economic Development through Private International Law*, https://www.oas.org/dil/esp/XXXVIII_Curso_Derecho_Internacional_David_Stewart_promoting_the_rule_of_law_and_econimic.pdf.

161 Müge Adalet McGowan, Dan Andrews, *Valentine Millot, Insolvency Regimes*, Zombie Firms and Capital Reallocation Economics Department Working Papers No. 1399, Organisation for Economic Co-operation and Development (OECD), ECO/WKP (2017), 3.

favour of regulatory competition, including: first, the diversity of legal rules that are 'on offer'; second, the 'incentives of states to compete with each other; and third, the feasibility of enabling market actors to make regulatory choices'.[162] However, these factors favouring regulatory competition are not sacrosanct. The EU has significantly harmonised the 'corporate restructuring and insolvency framework at the supranational level, paving the way for a more efficient, and speedier restructure and insolvency proceedings'.[163] By these means, it has radically reduced regulatory competition across member states of the EU.

While regulatory completion of insolvency and restructuring arrangements has been reduced across the EU, other jurisdictions discussed in this book have not followed this course. Long overdue, therefore, is the call for greater legal harmonisation of cross-border insolvency and restructuring laws. The global economic and social benefits include the expansion of current international and national frameworks. Some critics will argue that these benefits cannot be achieved because regulatory competition benefits states like Singapore, the UK and the US in establishing themselves as insolvency and restructuring hubs whose laws provide efficient transitional arrangements for entities under financial stress. This book presents qualified arguments to the contrary and without challenging the financial significance of these hubs. It maintains that reduced regulatory competition is especially necessary to protect the global economy from resurging global economic shock. Enabling cross-border parties to reorganise, such as by establishing a more standardised transnational regime for insolvency and restructuring, promotes greater economic stability in times of global instability. Enabling these parties to reorganise transnationally provides more predictability and more efficiency in corporate restructuring in a widely comprehended and accepted regulatory framework. The economic benefits of enabling entities to reorganise without being impeded by divergent state laws extends further, to the protection of jobs within a stable workforce. The beneficiaries of job protection encompass not only employees. Beneficiaries include employers, corporate networks, governments and consumers, as has become profoundly evident during the pandemic. What is needed is to further unify the regulatory structure that enables entities to reorganise and to do so as an economic and legal priority.

1.5 Research Purpose

The research will examine the UNCITRAL and the UNIDROIT as legal mechanisms that help facilitate cross-border insolvency and restructuring. Its purpose will

162 Horst Eidenmueller, *The Rise and Fall of Regulatory Competition in Corporate Insolvency Law in the European Union*, Law Working Paper N° 456/2019, University of Oxford and ECGI, 3. The phenomenon was initially studied with respect to the market for corporate charters in the US where Delaware enjoys a dominant.

163 Regulation (EU) 2015/848 of the European Parliament and of the Council of 20 May 2015 on insolvency proceedings (recast), O.J. L 141 of 5 June 2015, pp. 19 et seq. The recast EIR entered into force on 26 June 2017.

be to galvanise these and other international organisations and national governments/regulators, to strengthen the applicable legal framework and ensure that the current international rules-based system is not diluted but strengthened. It will do so by examining the national legal tools established to assist in facilitating the restructuring of financially stressed entities, to evaluate competing national regulations, and to assess their actual or prospective contributions to the transnational reform of corporate restructuring. The need for such reform measures is accentuated by international uncertainty over the impact of financial risk and the further economic risk of underestimating them in volatile markets. The further need is to maintain transparency in regulating cross-border insolvency and restructuring proceedings and to enhance the rule of law in resolving disputes between parties to such proceedings. The benefit is in providing another layer of trust in trading, investment and financial sectors. It also avoids divergent treatment accorded to parties in financial distress in discrete jurisdictions.

This book will accomplish these purposes by engaging in a comprehensive review the cross-border insolvency Model Law, close-out netting provisions contained in the UNIDROIT Principles, schemes of arrangement and letters of comfort. It will also focus on their respective capacities to unify the financial restructuring of cross-border investment internationally. For instance, it will consider whether the Model law on cross-border insolvency should be raised to the status of an international convention; and whether the UNIDROIT Principles on Close-out Netting Provisions should be boosted to a Model Law operating beyond the Model Law provided by the ISDA. It will examine whether schemes of arrangement that are widely used throughout an insolvency or restructure proceedings, should be accorded international status through either the UNIDROIT Principles or the UNCITRAL Model Law. So too, it will whether and how letters of comfort used in restructuring organisations ought to be reframed across national legal systems through the rubric of the UNIDROIT Principles.

Even as nation states turn inwards in regulating finance and banking, their need to accommodate the demands of global trade and investment remains encumbered by inconsistent national regulatory machinery. Furthermore, even though trade and investment agreements among states are primarily bilaterally and regionally, that serve multiple economic and political purposes. For example, the Regional Comprehensive Economic Partnership (RCEP),[164] which is a multilateral trade agreement, is purposed to provide a legal framework for the protection and enhancement of trade and investment internationally, not only regionally. This purpose embodies the intention of RCEP countries to prioritise an international

164 Regional Comprehensive Economic Partnership, about the Regional Comprehensive Economic Partnership (RCEP), https://www.dfat.gov.au/trade/agreements/not-yet-in-force/rcep. Free trade agreement between the Asia-Pacific nations of Australia, Brunei, Cambodia, China, Indonesia, Japan, Laos, Malaysia, Myanmar, New Zealand, the Philippines, Singapore, South Korea, Thailand, and Vietnam.

trade and investment framework, unlike the primarily regional framework adopted by the EU.

This book will also propose that emphasis be placed on unifying the rule of law in harmonising laws governing trans-border insolvency and restructuring. In proposing an enhanced regulatory framework to regulate cross-border insolvency and tools that apply to restructuring. It will advocate for a universal conception of the rule of law.[165] Grounded in ancient Greek philosophy, 'Church canons in the late Middle Ages and in the modern nation state in the Sixteenth Century, the rule of law remains imbedded in both national and international law, including commercial law'.[166] Inherent in the Magna Carta 'concluded against the backdrop of impending civil war within England and international conflict between England and France',[167] was the imbedding in the common law's rule of law. Significantly then and to the present day, Article 41 of the Magna Carta required that foreign merchants be safe and secure in entering, travelling in and leaving England. If they were detained because they came from an enemy state, they were to be properly treated and kept safe; and their treatment was owed reciprocally by their respective home states.[168]

The rule of law is reflected today in the internationalism of insolvency and, to a lesser extent, in restructuring law. In the UK case of *McGrath v. Riddell*[169] the House of Lords reiterated the unitary and universal principle in deciding upon the distribution of assets in England of Australian companies subject to liquidation under New South Wales law. The Court observed that the English and Australian laws on distribution differed, but not substantially. It held in favour of foreign rules of distribution applying to English assets, even if the result is that English creditors fail to obtain the full benefit of English law.[170] This form of internationalism reinforces the overall argument of this book, and indirectly acknowledges the extensive work undertaken across the international community to obtain a level of legal harmonisation and convergence in relation to cross-border insolvency disputes.

Arguably, the concept of the rule of law has significantly protected cross-border trade and investment for over a century. Robert McCorquodale asserts that 'the rule of law seeks to describe a set of principles of a system that does not yet exist fully in any location, but which is sought to be attained'.[171] He

165 Simon Chesterman, An International Rule of Law? *The American Journal of Comparative Law*, Vol. 56, No. 2 (2008), 331–332.

166 Adriaan Bedner, An Elementary Approach to the Rule of Law, *Hague Journal on the Rule of Law* (2010), 48.

167 Christopher Greenwood, *MAGNA CARTA and the Development of Modern International Law*, Lionel Cohen Lecture 2015, Jerusalem (2015), 444–445.

168 Ibid, 445.

169 [2008] UKHL 21, [2008] 1 W.L.R. 852.

170 Ibid.

171 Robert McCorquodale, Defining the International Rule of Law: Defying Gravity? *International and Comparative Law Quarterly*, Vol. 65, No. 2 (2016), 277–278.

contends that the rule of law is often dismissed internationally, primarily in lacking force in imposing compliance requirements. In referring to the 2012 United Nations (UN) Declaration on the Rule of Lawat the National and International Levels, McCorquodale highlights that there is 'broad acceptance of an international rule of law'.[172] He maintains that the 'limitation in its application continues to be the lack of a definition of an international rule of law, and its frequent use in undermining the existence of a legitimate international legal system'.[173] In referring to Martti Koskenmiemi, McCorquodale makes the point that the 'conception of an international rule of law is heavily influenced by politics, and subject to subjective desires, passions and prejudices which, in combination, lead to international anarchy'.[174] He recognises that a measure of politics is 'inevitable in construing the rule of law, and that rule is best consolidated on the basis of non-political rules of law'.[175] An even more challenging conception of the rule of law, is Richard Fallon's proposition that 'it is contestable, and that its true meaning depends on the resolution of significantly contestable normative issues and disagreements'.[176]

However, and even with the absence of a fully coherent definition of the rule of law adopted internationally and applied in international commercial disputes, it promotes legal harmonisation and convergence. Today, parties to commercial restricting arrangements rely on various international legal instruments that have significantly promoted legal harmonisation and convergence. The UNCITRAL has established international legal rules for the conduct of arbitration[177], mediation[178], the sale of goods[179], procurement[180] and public-private partnerships.[181] It has addressed micro, small and medium sized enterprises, electronic commerce, insolvency, security interests, online disputes resolution, international payments

172 Ibid, Declaration on the Rule of Law at the National and International Levels 2012 made at the High-Level Meeting on the Rule of Law at the National and International Levels (n 1).

173 Ibid.

174 Ibid. Martti Koskenniemi, *The Politics of International Law*, Hart (2011), 36.

175 Ibid.

176 Richard Fallon, The Rule of Law' as a Concept in Constitutional Discourse, *Columbia Law Review*, Vol. 97, No. 1 (2007), 6, quoted in J. Waldron, Is the Rule of Law an Essentially Contested Concept (in Florida), *Law and Philosophy*, Vol. 21 (2001).

177 UNCITRAL Model Law on International Commercial Arbitration (1985), with amendments as adopted in 2006, https://uncitral.un.org/en/texts/arbitration/modellaw/commercial_arbitration.

178 UNCITRAL Model Law on International Commercial Mediation and International Settlement Agreements Resulting from Mediation (2018), https://uncitral.un.org/en/texts/mediation/modellaw/commercial_conciliation.

179 International Sale of Goods, https://uncitral.un.org/en/texts/salegoods.

180 UNCITRAL Model Law on Public Procurement (2011), https://uncitral.un.org/en/texts/procurement/modellaw/public_procurement.

181 UNCITRAL Model Legislative Provisions on Public-Private Partnerships (2019), https://uncitral.un.org/en/texts/procurement/modellaw/public_procurement.

and transport of goods.[182] The UNCITRAL is also increasingly accepted in cross-border commercial contracts based on internationalised legal norms, concepts and rules, construed in the best interest of the impacted nation states, not one at the expense of the others. More recently, in 2018, the position adopted in this book was reinforced by the Secretary General Mr Guterres of the United Nations who called 'for a renewed commitment to a rules-based system'.[183]

This book acknowledges the challenges in maintaining a rules-based system and to adapt it to changing global dynamics, notably restructuring and insolvency in the pandemic epoch. For example, the long-standing commitment of the UK to the maintenance and enhancement of an international rules-based system since WWII needs to be adopted due to its entry into Brexit in late 2020.[184] Should other member states of the European Union follow the UK, there will further fragment the agreement of states to further advance transnational law reform.

The EU's interests in doing so, as before, are to maintain predictability and stability between states as sovereign actors and to rejuvenate its economic partnerships, primarily outside the EU.[185] Nicholas Wright envisages this rejuvenation internationally as encompassing reliance on three main institutional and rule-based sources: '(i) formal structures and institutions such as the United Nations, International Monetary Fund, World Trade Organisation, along with regional organisations such as the European Union, Association of South East Nation, and North Atlantic Treaty Organisation; (ii) rules, treaties and international law; the UN Convention on the Law of the Sea, UN Refugee Convention, or the Treaty on the Non-Proliferation of Nuclear Weapons; and (iii) the norms and values that have developed around and through these organs to support and promotion of democracy, equality, and human rights'.[186] While none of these institutions and the laws that underpin their operation are perfect, they have significantly stabilised the world economy, over many decades.

The UNCITRAL and the UNIDROIT, along with organs such as the International Swaps and Derivatives Association (ISDA), Basel Committee on Bank

182 United Nations Commission on International Trade Law, https://uncitral.un.org/en/texts UNCITRAL formulates modern, fair, and harmonized rules on commercial transactions. These include conventions, model laws and rules which are acceptable worldwide, legal and legislative guides and recommendations of great practical value, updated information on case law and enactments of uniform commercial law, technical assistance in law reform projects, regional and national seminars on uniform commercial law.

183 United Nations, *Secretary-General Calls for Renewed Commitment to Rules-Based Order, Reformed, Reinvigorated, Strengthened Multilateralism System, as General Debate Opens* (2018), https://www.un.org/press/en/2018/ga12062.doc.htm.

184 Nicholas Wright, *The UK and the International Rules-Based System*, The Foreign Policy Centre (2018), https://fpc.org.uk/the-uk-and-the-international-rules-based-system/. As a middle-rank power with ambitions to maintain global reach, the UK today still possesses the capacity to exercise significant international influence, not least through its membership of key international institutions.

185 Ibid.

186 Ibid.

Supervision, International Bar Association, amongst many others, have particular roles in transnational commercial dealings. However, culture, ideology and differences between legal families influence the acceptance and adoption of international commercial laws. For these reasons, some nation states have not fully embraced the trans-nationalisation of commercial laws and institutions. Where they have done so, they have adopted such internationalisation only in part into their national laws. Thus, on the backdrop of this context, this book will argue that the international harmonisation and convergence of commercial laws, including, cross-border insolvency and restructuring, close-out netting provisions, amongst others, goes some way to stabilising the international economy. In a time of increased international uncertainty, there is an urgent need to better support transnational commercial activity.

1.6 Research Challenges

There are both points of focus and limitations in conducting this research. The first is the shifting landscape of the global pandemic (COVID-19). The second is Brexit in which the United Kingdom ceased to be a member state that left the European Union. Thus, one of the impediments to undertaking this research was the shifting global financial situation faced by the world resulting from repeated lockdowns arising from COVID-19 and trade conflicts between states. Another challenge was is that there are parts of this book that were written before the UK-EU Brexit agreement in December 2020. Thus, the book discusses some issues without differentiating between the EU and UK. The book also acknowledges that, even though Brexit was approved, the EU, and particularly the UK, have significant work ahead in both adopting and implementing laws relating to insolvency and reconstitution. The book addresses both pre- and post-Brexit developments until August 2021.

Given the breadth and depth of the laws examined, some chapters will compare selected aspects of the internationalisation of insolvency and restructuring laws in the jurisdictions that are otherwise studied in the book. The book also underscores the complexity of accurately comparing jurisdictions, countries and cultures in their treatment of cross-border insolvency and in restructuring through national and supranational legal frameworks. Moreover, it highlights that the subject-matter in some chapters is broad in scope, leading to gaps in comparing legal frameworks adopted in and across national jurisdictions. These frameworks are interrelated, especially in being applied to insolvency and restructuring arrangements. Furthermore, the book stresses that the legal tools employed, such as schemes of arrangement and letters of comfort, will play an important role in underpinning the law governing corporate restructuring and insolvency. Yet, given the distinctive use of such schemes and letters, such instruments are only effectively dealt with through separate research studies. More pervasively, the book proposes further study on whether and how emerging economies adopt and use the legal tools and instruments that are studied in the book, such as in choosing whether and how to implement the UNCITRAL Model Law on Cross-Border Insolvency.

A further focus of this book is to address the current geopolitical overlay that is changing the way governments around the world view current and future trade law. There are cultural values and ideological differences emerging between states and regions of the world that the book cannot fully explore due to the fluid nature of the landscape that changes daily, weekly and monthly. This is especially evident in relation to how states in the jurisdictions studied have responded to the pandemic by adopting divergent trade policies and tightening their foreign investment rules. The book concentrates on the legal rules governing foreign investment and trade law, not on the political stances of states adopting, or rejecting, them.

In addition to the foregoing, this book compares the legal frameworks and the law of the respective jurisdictions identified. It does not comment on political or policy related issues. While it argues for greater harmonisation of cross-border insolvency law, it concentrates on the laws of insolvency and restructuring in the selected states, including the interpretation and application of those laws by domestic courts and by international commercial arbitrators. The analysis is informed by international consulting and law firms and by country specific experts.

Finally, the book refers to the law of the EU and compares how the EU has regulated and applied the law of cross-border insolvency, close-out netting provisions, schemes of arrangements and letters of comfort. It does not address nor compare the EU restructuring framework, except where applicable such as schemes of arrangement.

1.6.1 Referencing

Referencing accords with the Australia Legal Citation Convention. Divergence from that citation convention is limited to citations to domestic legislation, courts and scholarship in select states. The purpose is primarily to enable the reader to readily identify national and international sources of law.

1.7 Structure

This book contains two volumes. Where so indicated, some chapters are divided into different sub-parts, due to the need for intensive comparisons to be undertaken. **Chapter 1** highlights the problem definition, structure and methodology of the book. It identifies economic, social, human health and geopolitical challenges in global financing. This analysis includes the Asian financial crisis in the 1990s, the 2008 GFC and COVID-19, all having a significant effect on financial markets. These disruptions of financial markets have highlighted how each crisis has centred around the financial sector. However, COVID-19 has also resulted in a production decline. The economic impact has been significant and increasingly throughout 2020–2021, during which companies either declared insolvent or engaged in restructuring. The chapter evaluates how the jurisdictions studied can play greater roles in supporting and broadening the functions of international organisations, such as the UNCITRAL and the UNIDROIT. It calls for further internationalisation of cross-border insolvency and restructuring law(s), and the legal tools and mechanisms that support these functions.

Chapter 2 is divided into two parts. Part 1 examines the development of cross-border insolvency. It also explores the transition from territorialism to the internationalisation of insolvency and the development of the UNCITRAL Model Law on Cross-Border Insolvency. It then examines important provisions in the Model Law that states need to consider in order to implement more homogeneous and functional national insolvency laws. Part 2 discusses the domestic implementation of the UNCITRAL Model law and its regional application in the EU, Australia, Singapore and India. It touches on the impact that Brexit is likely to have on cross-border insolvency.

Chapter 3 examines one of the most widely used legal tools, **schemes of arrangement,** to assist in facilitating the restructuring of companies, whether domestically or internationally. The flexibility of such schemes is a formidable contributor to the restructuring process and a viable alternative to often costly and cumbersome insolvency proceedings. Multilayered in nature, schemes of arrangement are effective tools by which states can effectively manage the restructuring of financial arrangements with creditors, through mergers, demergers, takeovers and acquisitions. The chapter is divided into two parts. Part 1 compares the law of Australia, European Union, United Kingdom and United States. Part 2 examines the law governing such schemes in Singapore, India, Indonesia and China. The chapter identifies different terminology used to describe schemes of arrangement and reorganisation plans in these different jurisdictions and the need to reconcile them in order to maintain efficient cross-border proceedings. Importantly, the chapter provides a strong justification for reconstituting the UNCITRAL and UNIDROIT into principles or a model law that sets out the specific requirements and content of an international scheme of arrangement.

Chapter 4 explores the current day use of **letters of comfort** (LC). Apart from schemes of arrangements, comfort letters can assist in facilitating corporate restructuring as a further alternative to insolvency. Letters of comfort can be used to regulate such issues as the security of the debtor or creditor guarantees. They can also be effectively used by lawyers, liquidators, administrators, accountants or auditors in managing restructuring arrangements. Regulators can also use them to inform entities that no further regulatory action will be undertaken. The chapter's primary purpose is to propose the internationalisation of LC. The means is through a comprehensive evaluation of LC by the UNCITRAL or UNIDROIT to determine the value of incorporating them into UNCITRAL or a Model Law.

Chapter 5 examines a further alternative to cross-border insolvency, namely, **mergers and acquisitions** (MA). The chapter is divided into two parts. Part 1 demonstrates the link between MA law and foreign investment rules. It identifies how foreign investment rules have emerged as a major influence upon MA activity, notably in 2020–2021 following the outbreak of COVID-19. The chapter highlights how nation states have tightened their foreign investment rules in response to the pandemic. Part 1 compares Australia, EU and United Kingdom.

Part 2 compares the laws governing mergers and acquisitions in the US, Singapore and India. It highlights challenges for MA in responding to competing policies, to promote trans-border investment, while also protecting state sovereignty such as through national security measures. The chapter stresses the challenges posed by M&A going forward, given the present time at which states are becoming increasingly territorial, while continuing to compete for foreign investment.

Close-out netting provisions, while not on the radar of many legal scholars, are widely used by practitioners. They have emerged as an important preventative legal tool, protecting millions of dollars in international transactions prior to an insolvency. They are not a tool that is used during or as part of a restructure. The remaining chapters in this book arecontained in volume II. **Chapter 6** examines the 2013 UNIDROIT Principles on Close-out netting that were designed to be adopted and applied by national legal systems. However, nearly a decade later, the question is whether the UNIDROIT Principles remain current. Chapter 6 examines the development of those Principles and the key areas in which netting lacks harmonisation across national legal systems. Chapter 6 is divided into three parts. Part 1 examines the development of the 2013 UNIDROIT Principles and the key areas in which netting lacks harmonisation. Part 2 explores whether and how the EU, UK, China and the US have adopted close-out netting provisions. Part 3 compares the treatment of close-out netting in Australia, Indonesia, Singapore and India. The chapter proposes that close-out netting provisions be further internationalised; and that the UNIDROIT Principles be raised to the status of an UNCITRAL Model Law.

The remaining chapters in this book are contained in Volume II

Chapter 7 explores the benefits of **international commercial arbitration** (ICA) to resolve cross-border insolvency. ICA is a central means of resolving international trade and investment disputes. With the implementation of the UNCITRAL Model Law on Cross-Border Insolvency in 1997, ICA is perceived as an efficient institution through which to resolve cross-border insolvency disputes. The perceived benefit of resorting to ICA to resolve cross-border insolvency disputes are similar to those attributed to transnational contract disputes: the perception of greater neutrality, confidentially, expediency and reduced expense compared to judicial proceedings. In contrast, there remains a high level of tension in applying ICA to cross-border insolvency. This chapter explores some of those tensions, particularly between the insolvency obligations of parties negotiated prior to the commencement of arbitration and their obligations arising from the insolvency. The chapter also examine the further tension between how the judicial and arbitral resolution of cross-border insolvency disputes.

Chapter 8 extends the main theme of the book to exploring the role of **personal data** in cross-border insolvency. The need to protect personal data is not ordinarily contemplated in cross-border insolvency and restructuring proceedings. However, corporations acting through their legal and executive officers, are increasingly required to manage corporate activities to limit the risks of violating personal data rights including in insolvency proceedings. This chapter identifies the fragmentary regulation of personal data across domestic legal systems, focusing on Australia, the European Union, China and the United States. It demonstrates the differences in how they define personal data, construe consent to the use of personal data, and apply those conceptions to an entity that is subject to insolvency, restructuring or merger-acquisition. The protection accorded to personal data is most evident when data subjects have not consented to their personal data being transferred or sold to a third party, leading in legal and reputational damage caused by the corporation deemed responsible for such action and its legal consequences.

Chapter 9 further extends the book's main theme by exploring how **artificial intelligence (AI)** has emerged as a challenge to both data protection and cross-border insolvency, but as a benefit in cross-border insolvency disputes. The chapter explores how technology is used to change the manner in which the law is developed, administered and applied across multiple economic sectors, varying from manufacturing and industry maintenance, to professional services provided to the medical and legal professions. The chapter will also identify how technology that is currently available is being used to predict a company's level of financial stress, the prospects of its insolvency, and the potential for it to be restructured.

Chapter 10 brings the book together. It demonstrates the importance of further internationalisation of the complex but important areas of law discussed in the foregoing chapters. It stresses that a combination of the preventative measures discussed in the foregoing chapters can avoid forcing individuals and entities into insolvency on experiencing financial stress. It highlights the fundamentally importance of reorganisation as a preventative measure, in limiting the likelihood of insolvency.

The chapter also demonstrates how a multi-layered approach to redress financial risk can facilitate coherence, consistency and transparency in cross-border restructuring and insolvency. Close-out netting provisions can be used to close out a contract payment of a financially stressed entity that might otherwise require its restructuring or be subject to insolvency. Schemes of arrangement can act as multi-purpose legal tools in merger, demerger, takeover, creditor and debtor management. Letters of comfort can reduce the risk of loss arising from threats of insolvency, while also facilitating the restructure of a financially stressed entity.

Yet, these preventative measures are adopted inconsistently, if at all, by nation states and the jurisdictions compared throughout this book. They are applied diversely by domestic courts, with reverberating impact upon parties operating beyond domestic borders. They are also limitedly developed internationally. However, the virtue of developing a regulatory framework to govern trans-border insolvency and restructuring is increasingly recognised in international laws, codes and conventions. The diversity of legal tools that are available in regulating financial transactions and schemes, coupled with their increasingly global use, underpins the central argument of this book: that further internationalisation of cross-border insolvency and restructuring law should be undertaken. The COVID-19 outbreak is evidence of a global event that has and will continue to dilute the ability of finance parties to engage in cross-border restructuring through mergers and acquisitions. It underscores the central position of the book, that the UNCITRAL and UNIDROIT need to strengthen the universalist approach to cross-border insolvency and restructuring. The book therefore argues for the need to further develop and reform the law governing cross-border insolvency, to minimise the impact of global shocks on the financial stability worldwide; and to offer a Theory of Action in going forward.

1.8 Conclusion

History suggests that the world is increasingly experiencing interrelated economic, human health, political and social upheavals. From the recent COVID-19 to the protests in Hong Kong, the war and conflict in the Middle East, Yemen and Syria, trade wars between states and price disruptions in key industries such as oil, they are all having an impact on global financial markets. The digital economy is emerging with comparable volatility and subject to the similar challenges as these traditional sectors. The cross-border flow of personal data, while explored later in the book, will be an important addition to cross-border insolvency and restructuring.

This chapter has demonstrated that there are various legal mechanisms that states can utilise to stabilise financial markets. One such mechanism is to redress legal fragmentation in the law regulating those markets and to respond to the lack of understanding of regulatory divergence across states. An essential further response is to reconcile those regulatory disparities that lead to market instability. That market instability is evident, not only in domestic financial markets, but in global hubs that service parties from domestic markets. In an era of global financial instability, the fallout arising from divergent regulations of global corporate collapses, is felt both domestically and internationally.

In the absence of uniform laws governing the securing of debt, its repayment, and insolvency arising from debt, the legal consequences extend to international finance markets. At risk are financial hubs that service the transactions of corporate entities located in multiple jurisdictions with diffuse regulatory regimes including laws regulating insolvency Global financial hubs are part of, not exceptions to, such regulatory divergence. Even if they are insulated by domestic laws that seek to protect them, global hubs are vulnerable to financial instability arising from unpaid loans and accumulated debts that are shielded by out-of-state domestic laws. These risks extend to long-standing global financial hubs in the UK, EU and US, Singapore and Australia. Yet, this risk is not restricted to financial markets, it also has implications for the investment sector in which companies engage in mergers and acquisitions, because any long-term increase in financial stress across the economy, reduces the level of money that is available, other than through government stimulus packages. It further impacts upon global trade in undermining the efficient operation of the international legal framework in which enable financial stressed among trans-border entities leads to financial instability and shortfalls in global markets. Notably, these shortfalls include financial hubs that have emerged in China and are emerging in India and Indonesia. With populations that exceed 2.5 billion, these hubs represent the global financial centres of the future, but also centres of future financial risk.

In addressing the regulation of trans-border corporate entities and financial hubs, the book will provide legal scholars, industry, legal practitioners and students with a comprehensive approach to examining key areas of the applicable laws and regulations. The book will focus selectively on insolvency laws and practices, including close-out netting and keepwell agreements. It will examine restructuring through schemes of arrangements, and mergers and acquisitions. Importantly, too, it will evaluate and propose reform in global financial markets within an ever more interdependent international legal framework. Its overriding purpose will be to promote regulatory convergence and further harmonisation in the interests of financial stability.

The book will not present a typecast model of financial regulation based on the crippling financial impact of COVID-19. Nor will it treat the disaster as more than a bizarre moment in time and history, which society will transcend in the immediate future. However, the book will contend that epidemics and pandemics, along with other economic, human health, social and political shocks, are becoming ever more frequent. Nor have innovative methods of protecting public health and stabilising financial markets such as through fiscal bailouts, offset these global human, political and financial disasters. Contending otherwise is to ignore a modern history of economic and political precipitation, and to rely on piecemeal and selective regulation of financial markets within a multifaceted global community.

In promoting these ends, the book will highlight the saliency of greater cooperation across jurisdictions, to stimulate legal convergence in regulating financial markets. It will stress the need for regulating states to cooperate to ensure that their respective legal frameworks satisfy, not only their sovereign needs, but also provide economic stability across an interdependent international community. In accomplishing these ends, the book will recommend greater acceptance of key international organisations that can and do respond to, but also transcend the disparate financial systems, of signatory states. Among the international institutions studied will be the UNCITRAL and UNIDROIT. The pervasive purpose will be to propagate appropriate legal mechanisms that minimise the impact of future, national, regional and global economic shocks.

The recommendation underlying the chapters in the book are progressive, but still rules-based in concentration. Their rallying call of one-for-all extends beyond a collective cry for the unification of a disjointed financial regulatory framework.[187] It is also a call for the application of a rule of law that is rounded in rules that are applicable to the international commercial order and financing in particular. The book will argue that the comprehensive review of the laws, legal principles and concepts discussed throughout this book is now urgently needed for sustaining cross-border insolvency law in a fluid global climate that includes novel modalities. Not least among these are IT developments that facilitate, but also impinge upon,

187 Leon Trakman, Aligning State Sovereignty and Public Policy, Regulating Foreign Investment, *Tulane Law Review*, Vol. 207 (2018–2019), 62.

global financing and investment, leading to ever more threatening hazards such as corporate malfunctioning due to violations of personal data.

A further call in this book is for the reduction of regulatory competition among states in cross-border insolvency and restructuring. Doing so, will benefit states and the international business community by providing a further layer of stability and legal certainty in engaging in commercial activities. On the other hand, the cliché 'one-for-all' is for rule-based regulatory consistency that will incentivise even states that seek to profit as regulatory hubs for insolvency and restructuring proceedings. The attendant rationale is for states to achieve these ends by concentrating on the collective pursuit of fundamental principles of justice, under the well-established rules-based rule of law framework. That rationale is applicable to states that subject investors to confusing and inconsistent laws in the jurisdictions in which they invest, especially in a time of heightened geopolitical, economic, human health and social tensions.[188]

Cybersecurity risks arising from both state and non-state intrusions will be further risks of financial instability. Yet, this is not explored in this book, and is an area of further research.

188 Ibid.

2

TRANSNATIONAL INSOLVENCY PART 1

Transitional trade and investment have grown significantly over the last 50 years. Territorialism is less viable as a policy that can survive the constant market shocks, in an otherwise global financial and trading market. The universalist approach has an ever more cogent rationale today. This is because the economic reality of a financially interdependent world order and expanding reliance on that order to sustain cross-border traffic and thought it, domestic economic development.

This chapter is divided into two Parts. Part 1 examines the development of cross-border insolvency and briefly the 2019 addition of UNCITRAL Model Law on Enterprise Group Insolvency. It also explores the evolving transition from territorialism to the internationalisation of insolvency and the progress of the UNCITRAL Model Law on Cross-Border Insolvency. Part 2 discusses the domestic implementation of the UNCITRAL Model law and its regional application in the European Union (EU).

The ensuing chapters make the case for the UNCITRAL Model Law on Cross-Border Insolvency to be revised to a Convention. Such a Convention can provide a comprehensive framework through which to regulate trans-border financial dealing, and facilitate stability in the face of ever growing social, economic, human health, environmental and political volatility, globally. A convention can also provide a legal structure within which entities can regulate their own trans-border dealings in goods and services, including in providing financial services.

2.1 Introduction

The globalisation of trade and investment has resulted in companies being ever less confined to a single nation state. Such globalisation in a time of heightened

DOI: 10.4324/9781003311874-2

de-globalisation by some states and a stronger push for regionalisation by others.[1] With a steady shift towards internationalisation of banking and finance, greater harmonisation and convergence across states. It also led to countervailing political and economic tension over the perceived loss of autonomy of states over both inbound and outbound investment.

The ensuring harmonisation and convergence of insolvency law is accentuated by greater independence among states, contrasted against the commitment of other states to de-globalisation. Confronted by ongoing threats to human health and trade standoffs among states, geopolitical and economic divergence along economic and political lines remains high, accentuated by the localisation of trade and investment and the re-emergence of fragmentary domestic laws governing cross-border finance. Such fragmentation has threatened to unravel the gains acquired from legal harmonisation. It is highlighted in the localised governance of cross-border finance, illustrated by the insularity of domestic banks engaged in global financing from international regulation. That insularity played a critical role historically, in accentuating currency crises in Great Depression of the 1930s. It plays a similarly critical role in the global economic order of the 2020s.[2]

Governments have reacted to unstable financial markets, not only by reverting to domestic legal regulation, but also by reconstituting trans-border banking regulations.[3] Moving forward, during the 1990s, regulators throughout East Asia, in many Latin American countries, and Russia, reacted to the vulnerability of poorly developed accounting systems, corruption and the intrusion of politics through regulatory scrutiny and the imposition of penalties.[4] In responding to these periods of financial instability, regulators responded by providing legal and financial support. In some cases national laws were significantly revised, to minimize any future economic shock. Whether they did so timeously and adequately is more contentious, despite their cognizant of the risks of inertia[5].

These financial shocks and events resulted in countries accelerating their regulatory responses to ensure that trade and investment sectors had greater levels of certainty and stability including financially. The result was a resurgence in the

1 Kenneth Rogoff, *Deglobalisation Will Hurt Growth Everywhere,* https://www.theguardian.com/business/2020/jun/04/deglobalisation-will-hurt-growth-everywhere.

2 Harold James, *The End of Globalisation: Lessons from the Great Depression*, Harvard University Press (2001), 98. James notes in the final chapter that, there is a paradox about the rapid shift of the last ten years towards market economies. The integrated world economy is shaken by crises – stock exchange upsets, debt crises, Mexico's 'tequila effect', the 'Asian flu', contagion in Russia and South America. The dramas lead to more and more unease about 'globalization' – or alternately, as its critics call the process, 'neoliberalism', 'turbocapitalism', 'casino capitalism', 'disordered capitalism', 'capitalism pure', and 'Anglo-Saxon economics'. With every crisis, the new events spell the end of a particular model of liberal economics, the so-called Washington consensus. But despite the shocks and the shrieks, there is no interruption. On the contrary, the drive to the market becomes faster; and its former critics are converted into proselytes.

3 Ibid, 98.

4 Ibid.

5 Ibid.

collaboration between states to resolve cross-border legal and policy issues, leading to higher levels of stability and economic growth. Economic rationality, in our view, confirms that any retreat from support for the current international rules-based framework underlying financial and banking laws, will undermine the gains achieved by states and international institutions charged with developing finance laws and regulations collaboratively, not in mutual isolation. The fluidity of cross-border trade and investment requires nothing less.

The writings of Harold James on de-globalisation throughout the early 2000s reinforce this view. He highlighted how the 'political implications of the new world order are anti-elitist; and renders increasingly untenable any defence of the privileges of the entrenched elite through state control of economic activity'.[6] He elaborated that this 'elite group neither deserves much sympathy, nor is it likely to preserve the doctrines that made it powerful. Indeed, its main vestige lies in lawlessness – the phenomenon of nomenklatura privatisation whereby, in the anarchy of the transformation process, the old elite builds up its propertied position for the future. The entrenchment of the defence of elitism could pose a threat in and from former and current socialist states. The result could be elite-sponsored and challenged chaos. It could also disrupt progress in establishing a more consistent legal framework for cross-border banking and finance, typified by greater cohesion in the domestic support for alternatives to insolvency, such as restructuring, along with mergers and acquisitions'.[7] Such localisation could also decouple the interconnected cross-border regulation of financial markets in favour of the regulatory protection of domestic elites. An ancillary result of the planned reversion to localisation could be to reverse globalised new technologies to their domestic regulation of trans-border banking and finance.

There are a number of highly successful UNCITRAL model laws, as identified earlier in this book, and conventions that have facilitated and coordinated cross-border trade and investment, such as the sale of goods. These models serve as responses to economic disruptions, such as the 2008 global financial crisis and attendant business failures. The 2020–2021 COVID-19 pandemic also poses a devastating threat to the global economy and a source of local, regional and global business insolvency. Each global shock has had ripple effects, varying from political instability to social unrest. Each has given rise to the need for international legal responses, such as the governance framework provided by the UNCITRAL to redress cross-border insolvency.

Omnipresent today is the pervasive need to strengthen the current day international regulatory regime to redress global financial shocks that has ripped across multiple financial and banking sectors and is unprecedented in its reach and duration. Put another way, the foundations for a more robust international insolvency legal framework has been evolving for more than a decade. This book argues that

6 Ibid.
7 Ibid.

it is time to strengthen this framework, by expanding its conceptual and functional application to cross-border insolvency. Therefore, now is also a judicious time for the international community to consider and begin working on the development of an international cross-border insolvency convention. This convention can be supported by a Model Law that provides further clarification in applying it to specific areas of insolvency. It can be facilitated through the UNCITRAL, by strengthening its existing model directed at facilitating the governance of cross-border insolvency.

2.2 The Evolution of Insolvency

Insolvency is a consequence of an entity not being able to pay its debts as they fall due, and is derived from the Latin word *solver.*[8] From inception, not being able to pay debts was a factual condition and, not a determinant of a legal duty arising that condition. In primitive societies, there were no laws regulating the debtor's insolvency,[9] nor stipulating for payment of debts to creditors because there were no debtors and creditors.[10] Credit did not exist. According to Louise Levinthal, 'credit that evolved subsequently was based on the trust that a person puts on someone else's good faith. Prior to that, undertaking to pay a debt in good faith was an unknown concept'.[11] It was the economic need for subsistence and to improve one's life conditions that forged the practice of loans. However, the 'emergence and expansion of the duty to repay a loan in good faith was treated as a regulatory response to an economic abnormality and subject to punishment. Indebtedness was, from the very beginning, the target of severe sanctions, both religious (excommunication) and legal (death and slavery); and directed at preventing debtor default and discouraging borrowing'.[12] These sanctions were 'entrenched in law since the recorded history of commerce and trade, spanning the Middle Eastern and Roman worlds'.[13] During this early period the notion of insolvency was primitive when compared to the treatment of insolvency, particularly in financial hubs, today.

Insolvency law is therefore 'rooted in both commercial and financial law. It determines which party is under a duty to pay when there is insufficient money to compensate all who sustain financial losses'.[14] So conceived, the law cannot avoid

8 Philip Wood, *The Law and Practice of International Finance Series, Vol 1: Principles of International Insolvency*, Sweet and Maxwell, 3rd ed. (2019), 25.

9 Louise Levinthal, The Early History of Bankruptcy Law, *University of Pennsylvania Law Review*, Vol. 66 (1918), 223, in Catarina Frade, *Bankruptcy, Stigma and Rehabilitation*, ERA Forum (2012), 46.

10 Catarina Frade, *Bankruptcy, Stigma and Rehabilitation*, ERA Forum (2012), 46.

11 Bo Carlsson, David Hoff, Dealing with Insolvency and Indebted Individuals in Respect to Law and Morality, *Social & Legal Studies*, Vol. 9, No. 2 (2000), 293–317, in Catarina Frade, *Bankruptcy, Stigma and Rehabilitation*, ERA Forum (2012), 46.

12 Ibid.

13 Paul Omar, *On the Origins and Challenges of Court-to-Court Communications in International Insolvency Law*, International Insolvency Institute, at 1, https://www.iiiglobal.org/sites/default/files/originsandchallengesofcourttocourtcommunicationsininternationalinsolvency.pdf.

14 Philip Wood, *Principles of International Insolvency*, Part 1, Allen & Avery (1995), 94.

choosing who is to bear the risk of financial loss, so that there is a legal winner and a loser.[15] Is the current legal framework wrong to choose between, or to nominate a winner or loser? In our view the answer is 'no' and therefore someone has to determine who is to bare the risk of loss. The law is also responsible to nominate the person who is to carry the largest portion of the risk. Put another way, the creditor lending money to a party bares the risk that the debtor may not fully repay the loaned money. However, the creditor should not bare all the risk. Therefore, the legal framework for allocating ensuing losses, including the law of insolvency, was established to balance the level of loss borne by each party.

The establishment of that legal framework was gradual. From 480 AD until the 12th century, there is little evidence of formal insolvency law evolving from Roman law. The early renaissance heralded a resurgence in the exchange of goods across Europe. Universities evolved, as did the study of law. Roman law was adapted to meet the needs of a modern age. Merchants travelled from then distant places like Lombardy in Northern Italy across Europe to trade and set up offices for the exchange of goods and sale of commodities en route and at destination ports and mercantile markets.[16]

Yet, long before the Roman Empire, a legal procedure had emerged to regulate the relationship between creditors and insolvent debtors.[17] A basic feature of this regulatory system was that the life and property of an insolvent debtor was owed to his creditors.[18] This position has not changed and is still central to insolvency law today. Initially, the debtor as a person was the main target of the creditor. As a result, the execution of the debt initially entailed the physical execution of person owing that debt. Thereafter, the debt was executed through the property, or tangible assets, of that debtor.

This shift from the execution of the person to the execution of the tangible assets of that person continued for several centuries, evolving over at least two distinctive phases: '(i) the proceedings in the older Roman law according to the Twelve Tables and (ii) a weakening of the creditors' power through lex Poetelia and lex Julia'.[19] In the next stage, according to Gratzer's study, 'creditors were given instant access to the debtor's property on the non-payment of that debt. Through the *lex Poetelia (326 B.C.),* the debtor's failure to fulfil his duty to pay the debt became a criminal offence'.[20] However, the creditor's unlimited rights to the life, property and family of the debtor were restricted. Among other things, the *lex Poetelia* abolished the right to ill-treat, kill or sell the debtor and his family as slaves. The debtor was still

15 Ibid.

16 Ibid.

17 Karl Gratzer, Default and Imprisonment for Debt in Sweden: From the Lost Chances of a Ruined Life to the Lost Capital of a Bankrupt Company, in Karl Gratzer, Dieter Stiefel (eds), *History of Insolvency and Bankruptcy from an International Perspective*, Södertörns högskola (2008), 18–20.

18 Ibid, 18–19.

19 Ibid, 19.

20 Ibid.

forced to stay in the creditor's private prison in a kind of debtor's servitude, but he regained his freedom if the debt was settled. Only if the debtor was suspected of trying to escape, was the creditor allowed to put him in chains.[21] A debtor who went into hiding could be subjected to a bankruptcy process (*missio in bona*) in which the creditor received a letter of attorney (*missio*) from the receiver (praetor) to dispose of the debtor's property (*bona*). As a result, the debtor also lost his civil rights (*infamia*). No consideration was taken of whether he had become insolvent by accident, or whether he was responsible for his insolvency. The sanctions on the debtor remained harsh. Even the temporary inability to pay a due debt led to the loss of both the debtor's property and liberty.[22] Thus, the early development of the law of insolvency can best be described as brutal. The debtor was subject to horrendous treatment for not being able to service the creditor, even when that inability was due to circumstances beyond the debtor's control.

Following the collapse of the Roman Empire, Germanic law rose to the forefront, including in the regulation of debt.[23] Gratzer asserts that 'according to old Germanic law, an insolvent debtor was subjected to just as severe a treatment as in old Rome. Default was in itself seen as a crime'.[24] In the ensuing centuries, with the development of the embryonic nation state in the Sixteenth Centuries, the law regulating debt was primarily inward looking, focusing on the responsibility of the debtor to creditors in the jurisdiction for failure to repay the debt. However, domestic law still needed to regulate the consequence of debtors absconding by fleeing the jurisdiction. As a result, some of the first bankruptcy statutes, such as the Statute of Bankrupts of Henry VIII in 1542 in England and the French Insolvency Ordinances of the 1560s provided for such eventualities. The bankruptcy statute of Henry VIII sought to prevent debtors from leaving the jurisdiction, including by ensuring their physically containment by domestic courts.[25] The French Ordinances took a slightly different route. It concentrated on finding the absconded debtor and bringing him back to the jurisdiction. Even today, many 'modern insolvency systems incorporate elements of these two styles of dealing with debtors leaving the jurisdiction'.[26] Thus, it can be seen that, throughout history, the underlying principles of insolvency have not changed, notably, in involving essentially two parties, a creditor and debtor. What has changed is the number of creditors that are engaged in insolvency proceedings, the complexity of those proceedings, the involvement of creditors from multiple jurisdictions and the need to engage in trans-border insolvency proceedings.

21 Ibid, 20.
22 Ibid.
23 Karl Gratzer, Default and Imprisonment for Debt in Sweden: From the Lost Chances of a Ruined Life to the Lost Capital of a Bankrupt Company, in Karl Gratzer, Dieter Stiefel (eds), *History of Insolvency and Bankruptcy from an International Perspective*, Södertörns högskola (2008), 21.
24 Ibid.
25 Ibid.
26 Ibid.

Still, changes have occurred. From 1706, a regulation under the English law of bankruptcy provided that a bankrupt person could be released from liability for a debt contracted before the act of bankruptcy and could start anew. In contrast, an insolvent debtor was not given this option. He could not be discharged from his old debts but remained responsible for them for the rest of his life, including the likelihood of imprisonment.[27] This distinction between 'with the increase of economic activities and the emergence of new occupations, the definition of who was a trader and who was not became more and more controversial and the distinctions became increasingly blurred'.[28] For Margrit Schulte Beerbühl, the 'process of bankruptcy was a rather simple procedure. It started with the denial of payment by the debtor. Any further proceeding rested with the creditor because a debtor could not declare himself bankrupt until 1825'.[29] The process for commencing legal proceedings rested with the creditor who was responsible for initiating proceedings with a petition to the Lord Chancellor in Chancery Lane for a commission of bankruptcy.

What can be demonstrated from this early period is that the creditor had responsibility for commencing legal action against the debtor. The creditor as the source of that action remains today. The creditor ordinarily initiates proceedings to claw back the money owed by the debtor. What has changed over the centuries relate, first, to the powers of creditors to proceed against debtors; and second, to the social and legal reasons for the debtor being held liable for unpaid debts.

As this book will demonstrate, the powers of creditors today diverge starkly from their powers historically. Insolvency today is not determined by the creditor, but by declaration of the insolvent and/or by order of court. The debtor's liability is limited to property, not life. The debtor is civilly, not criminally liable for debts.[30] What has changed across the insolvency landscape is how more attention has been provided to developing legal tools to assist in managing financially stressed companies before they declare insolvency.

What has not changed is that the law is still directed primarily at protecting the creditor. While the creditor cannot declare the debtor insolvent, the creditor has standing to apply to a court for an order of insolvency. The creditor is also legally empowered to seek multiple civil remedies against the debtor either in conjunction with, or separately from insolvency proceedings.[31]

What has also evolved are the social reasons for, and legal responses to, the debtor's liability for being unable to repay debts. This very notion of insolvency has changed from societal stigma that discouraged debt and sanctioned insolvency, to a legislative framework directed at individuals and entities being able to rehabilitate.

27 Margrit Schulte Beerbühl, The Risk of Bankruptcy among German Merchants in Eighteenth-century England, in Karl Gratzer, Dieter Stiefel (eds), *History of Insolvency and Bankruptcy from an International Perspective*, Södertörns högskola (2008), 67.

28 Ibid.

29 Ibid.

30 Ibid.

31 Ibid.

This shift is based, in part, on the perceived need to provide stability across financial sectors in which bankruptcy disrupts the flow of investment. Catarina Frade identifies how regulating bankruptcy has emerged as legal requirement to facilitate economic progress in cross-border trade.[32] Fade further notes that:

> [The] absence of a regulatory framework in primitive societies with no conception of debt was displaced over time with the legal acknowledgement of a collective debt execution process that was available to everyone who, for personal or business reasons, was unable to pay debts. Earlier stages in this regulatory acknowledgement was a deeply negative and stigmatizing cultural and religious reprobation of insolvent debtors.[33]

Liability for debt was historically directed at the public humiliation and shame of the debtor and his family. The intention was to retaliate against, and punish, the debtor for assuming debts that he did not, or could not, repay. Over time, this retaliatory animus and punitive measure directed at the debtor gave way to the principle of compensation for the benefit of the creditor. While liability for debt today, it is probably not as overt in public humiliation as it was all those years ago, it nevertheless, still exists. Entities in financial stress, other than listed companies, can declare insolvency or restructure without having to disclose, in part, their initiation and conduct of insolvency. Such proceedings, arguably, are conducted behind closed doors. However, a stigma is still attached to the end result, namely, that a company has fallen into financial stress and had to restructure or declare insolvency. It some cases, insolvency proceedings have a knock-on effect because an individual who has to declare bankruptcy, may be obliged disclose that status such as in applying for jobs. The identification of bankruptcy with traders also acquired greater social acceptance. The execution of bankruptcy against the debtor-trader was also progressively replaced by the execution against his assets.[34]

The cruelty and degradation associated with bankruptcy over a number of centuries and among several civilisations, also abated, but not completely.[35] The persistent attitude of rejection shown to those who, for any reason, 'did not honour the binding pacts to pay their debts, identified with *pacta sunt servanda* in Roman Law, persisted from India to Western Europe and the United States'.[36] The stigma borne by the debtor and the punitive social response to regulatory attempts to rehabilitate the debtor, continues today. As highlighted by Frade, the social stigma associated with insolvency continues to depicts the debtor's failure in the financial management of his life or business, and condemns him as being too ambitious and

32 Catarina Frade, *Bankruptcy, Stigma and Rehabilitation*, ERA Forum (2012), 48–49.

33 Ibid.

34 Ibid.

35 Rafael Efrat, The Evolution of Bankruptcy Stigma, *Theoretical Inquiries in Law*, Vol. 7, No. 2 (2006), 365–393, in Catarina Frade, *Bankruptcy, Stigma and Rehabilitation*, ERA Forum (2012), 48–49.

36 Ibid, 48–49.

taking out loans instead of relying to his resources.[37] This stigma remains a source of public reprobation, humiliation, or at least, embarrassment in contemporary society. Arguably, no matter what is one's culture, race, creed, nationality or where one resides, debtors would not want the world at large to know their personal or professional financial standing.

However, the level of stigma was not limited to punishment or subjecting the debtor to social retribution through bankruptcy proceedings. The level of stigma was more pronounced if the insolvency was the product, in whole or part, of the criminal activity of fraud, or if the unpaid debt disrupted social services. Thus, the ripple effect of corporate insolvency cannot be underestimated. It is exemplified by mass unemployment, social disruption, economic hardship and possibly poverty. It can impoverish and degrade targeted debtors. It can rebound on financial markets, perpetuating the circle of economic decline.[38]

Government regulators have responded to the commercial disruption caused by corporate insolvency by developing different models of rehabilitation following insolvency. One pervasive model is the fresh start model of new opportunities adopted in North America and related common law jurisdictions.[39] The other main model in the continental Europe is the model of re-education and rehabilitation.[40] While by no means all encompassing, both models encourage and reward appropriate risk-taking and focus on creating value.[41] The common law model seeks these ends primarily by provided legal mechanisms that allow entities to take such a risk. The Continent European model concentrates on rehabilitation to provide a sustainable environment for credit. The purpose is for EU member states to have a robust harmonised legal framework, while maintaining a level of independence and sovereignty from the EU system at large.[42] The common denominator is to avoid expanding credit to the extent that corporate entities are so indebted that minor geopolitical, social, human health or economic shocks to impede them from repaying their debts.

Central to the practice of insolvency today, is the threat of transnational insolvency receding from core element of the global economic and legal order to a source of its decline. In essence, the global economic system is based on a principal-agent relationship between entrepreneurs (who need investment funds) and investors

37 Ibid.

38 Ibid.

39 United States Supreme Court, within the *Local Loan Co v. Hunt* [292 US 234, 244 (1934)], in Catarina Frade, *Bankruptcy, Stigma and Rehabilitation*, ERA Forum (2012), 53.

40 Jason, Kilborn, *Foundations of Forgiveness in Islamic Bankruptcy Law: Sources, Methodology, Diversity* (11 August 2011), in Catarina Frade, *Bankruptcy, Stigma and Rehabilitation*, ERA Forum (2012), 53.

41 James H.M. Sprayregen, Annual Banquet Acceptance Remarks of James Sprayregen, Lifetime Achievement Award International Insolvency: From Punitive Regimes toward Rescue Culture, *Emory Bankruptcy Developments Journal*, Vol. 36, No. 1 (2020), 6–10.

42 Paolo Manganelli, The Modernization of European Insolvency Law: An Ongoing Process, *Journal of Business & Technology Law*, Vol. 11, No. 153 (2016), 153.

(who provide the investment funds).[43] Maintaining an economically viable principal-agent relationship is necessary to promote secure international trade, financial and investment markets. They depend on a high level of stability. Insolvency, and to a lesser extent restructuring, underpins the need for this stability. Therefore, establishing viable insolvency laws is equally necessary to avoid financial chaos arising from the growing internationalisation of insolvencies involving large financial, banking and other entities that trade and invest in multiple states. Here, the law of insolvency is essential as a legal mechanism to reduce transactional costs to provide creditors and debtors with rights and remedies arising from business failures.

Laws of insolvency that destabilise such rights and jeopardise such remedies raise, rather than reduce, these transaction costs by producing economic inefficiencies. Firstly, inefficient liquidation may limit credit recoverability. Secondly, the continued operation of a company with irreversible debt can cause further losses which rapid liquidation could have avoided

These inefficiencies are most pronounced in distinguishing between the historical but still commonly used conception of 'default' and the modern-day conception of 'insolvency' and 'bankruptcy'. 'Default' essentially entails two related elements: the debtor has not paid his debt, and the debtor is unwilling or unable to do so. In effect, he is in default when his liabilities exceed his assets and unwilling or unable to redress that imbalance.[44] Insolvency is the result of a legal determination that his/her total liabilities exceed the total assets, and that determination is reached in accordance with the applicable law and procedure governing the insolvency. That is, the home country. The problem is that domestic, regional and international laws of insolvency diverge. That divergence is especially germane in cross-border insolvencies and challenging in establishing insolvency rules and procedures that transnational in nature and cohesive in operation. That divergence adds an addition layer of regulatory burden, whereby a party in one state that becomes insolvent needs to understand the laws of the other state. The more divergence, arguably, the higher the cost of governing and managing a cross-border insolvency. The next section discusses the internationalisation of insolvency law.

43 Elazar Berkovitch, Ronen Israel, Optimal Bankruptcy Laws across Different Economic Systems, *The Review of Financial Studies*, Vol. 12 (1999), 347, 348. In Fernando Locatelli, International Trade and Insolvency Law: Is the UNCITRAL Model Law on Cross-Border Insolvency an Answer for Brazil – An Economic Analysis of Its Benefits on International Trade, *Law and Business Review of the Americas,* Vol. 14, No. 313 (2008), 320–321.

44 Karl Gratzer, Default and Imprisonment for Debt in Sweden: From the Lost Chances of a Ruined Life to the Lost Capital of a Bankrupt Company, in Karl Gratzer, Dieter Stiefel (eds), *History of Insolvency and Bankruptcy from an International Perspective*, Södertörns högskola (2008), 15–16. Bankruptcy is a legal finding that imposes court supervision over the financial affairs of those who are insolvent or in default. In modern legislation, insolvency is often a necessary but not sufficient condition for bankruptcy. For the latter to exist, one needs a bankruptcy law. Insolvency and bankruptcy laws can be seen as part of an authority's determination to protect property rights.

2.3 Internationalisation of Insolvency Law

The internationalisation of banking, finance, investment and trade practice has resulted in entities being located in multiple jurisdictions. The result is that 'international insolvency law (or cross-border insolvency) has developed as a *sui generis* system of private international law for transnational insolvency, directed at regulating cross-border insolvency efficiently'.[45] Predominantly based on the norm of modified universalism, the purpose of a cross-border insolvency system is to prescribe efficient levels of centralised proceedings that are both recognised and facilitated by foreign authorities. The aim of the cross-border system is to maximise value and enable business rescue by taking account of all relevant stakeholders wherever they are located.[46] Such modified universalism is prefaced on these related principles. Firstly, the debtor's estate includes the totality of its worldwide assets. Secondly, the claims of all worldwide creditors are dealt with in one insolvency proceeding. Third, that proceeding is governed by the law of the place that is most closely connected to the debtor. That place, in widely endorsed regulatory models, is 'the place of the main proceedings'.[47]

The remodelling of trans-border insolvency and to a lesser extent restructuring laws has expanded since the Asian financial crisis in the late 1990s. International institutions such as the International Monetary Fund (IMF), the World Bank, and UNCITRAL have actively promoted reforms that provide formal rehabilitation alternatives to a contractual workout (an agreement between an individual borrower and a licensee for the repayment of an outstanding and unpaid indebtedness), or to a liquidation. These institutions, by and large, have incorporated features such as stay on creditor enforcement to prevent runs on the debtor's assets and avoid the use of unauthorised mechanisms for post-commencement financing. The institutions also require judicial approval of formal reorganisation plans, and for converting rehabilitation to liquidation proceedings, should the debtor fail to have a reorganisation plan confirmed.[48] These international institutions also endorse a broader spectrum of formal and informal debt resolution procedures to promote access to affordable credit and financial stability.

45 Irit Mevorach, Adrian Walters, The Characterization of Pre-insolvency Proceedings in Private International Law, *European Business Organisation Law Review*, Vol. 21 (2020), 855–894.

46 Ibid.

47 Neil Hannan, *Cross-Border Insolvency The Enactment and Interpretation of the UNCITRAL Model Law*, Springer (2017), 2. See also, Robert K. Rasmussen, Where are All the Transnational Bankruptcies? The Puzzling Case for Universalism, *Brookland Journal of International Law*, Vol. 32 (2007), 983; Rosalind Mason, Local Proceedings in a Multi-State Liquidation: Issues of Jurisdiction, *Melbourne University Law Review*, Vol. 30 (2006), 145, Jay Lawrence Westbrook, A Global Solution to Multinational Default, *Michigan Law Review*, Vol. 98 (2000), 2276; Alexander M. Kipnis, Beyond UNCITRAL: Alternatives to Universality in Transnational Insolvency, *Denver Journal of International Law and Policy*, Vol. 36 (2008), 155; Jay Lawrence Westbrook et al. (eds), *A Global View of Business Insolvency Systems*, Martinus Nijhoff (2010), 230–231.

48 Ibid, see also – UNCITRAL Legislative Guide on Insolvency Law, Part Two (United Nations 2005), 83–103, 113–119, 209–238.

Arguably, this relatively new international framework for regulating insolvency provides greater certainty and stability to local and trans-border economies. It limits the scope of punitive legal measures by allowing debtors to take a step back, review their operations and make changes to ensure, as far as possible, their survival. For instance, the success of a Chapter 11 Bankruptcy under the US Bankruptcy Code has, in part, elevated it to a global template or standard for the formal reorganisation of insolvency law. However, sustainable international standards need to be designed flexibly to accommodate different legal systems at varying stages of economic development.[49]

The internationalisation of insolvency law to date reflects a universal, albeit early stage, approach to cross-border insolvency. Such universalism is buttressed by modified mechanisms construed as 'modified universalism';[50] 'secondary insolvency'; and 'contractualism' and 'territorialism'.[51] An important further challenge for the international legal and financial community is to use these mechanisms to achieve modified universalism in restructuring. Restructuring, in our view is a subset of cross-border insolvency. The difference is that restructuring can commence before a full declaration of insolvency. As a preventative approach, restructuring also has far more benefits than insolvency which, arguably, should be invoked only as a last resort measure.[52]

Meng Seng Wee argues that 'there are merits for both universalism and territorialism'.[53] He points out that the judiciary in Singapore, while adopting the universalist approach, has rendered it slightly more flexible to facilitate cooperation between Singapore and foreign liquidators. This approach implements UNCITRAL Model Law on Cross-Border Insolvency. It also reflects that jurisdictions like the EU have also used the UNCITRAL Model Law to promote cooperation between states and especially between, their courts.

Expanded conceptions of universalism have also been endorsed by international institutions, notably by United Nations General Assembly's endorsement of the Model Law on Cross-Border Insolvency [CBI] on 15 December 1997. The history of the UN Model Law is significant. Initiated at the first Judicial Colloquium on

49 Ibid.

50 Meng Seng Wee, Lessons for the Development of Singapore's International Insolvency Law, *Singapore Academy of Law Journal*, Vol. 23 (2011), 938. Wee also refers to: Jay Westbrook, A Global Solution to Multinational Default, *Michigan Law Review*, Vol. 98 (2000), 2276; Lynn M. LoPucki, The Case for Cooperative Territoriality in International Bankruptcy, *Michigan Law Review*, Vol. 98 (2000), 2216; Frederick Tung, Is International Bankruptcy Possible? *Michigan Journal of International Law*, Vol. 23 (2001), 31; Lynn M. LoPucki, Universalism Unravels, *American Bankruptcy Law Journal*, Vol. 79 (2005), 143.

51 Lynn M. LoPucki, Cooperation in International Bankruptcy: A Post-Universalist Approach, *Cornell Law Review*, Vol. 84 (1999), 696.

52 Meng Seng Wee, Lessons for the Development of Singapore's International Insolvency Law, *Singapore Academy of Law Journal*, Vol. 23 (2011), 938.

53 Ibid.

Cross- border Insolvency in Canada on 22 March 1995, the Model Law responded to growing concerns by the UNCITRAL, national governments and the legal profession, about the perceived lack of transnational harmonisation on cross-border insolvency.[54] The perceived problems were attributed to diverse and inconsistent legal approaches to cross-border insolvency arising from disparate laws across and within legal systems. The idealised response to such legal divergence was for a universal insolvency law to provide legitimate legal avenues to resolve financial obstacles arising from compounding debt that extended across national boundaries. In the absence of an international insolvency law that harmonises domestic law, regulation was left to the disparate domestic statutes and divergent judicial practices of states.

This disparate nature and application of insolvency law has jeopardised the implementation of liquidation or reorganisation plans across national borders. It has also impeded maximising the value of the debtor's assets and maintaining employment. Such deficiencies in insolvency law set the scene for the international community, most pronouncedly the General Assembly of the United Nations, to come together to resolve legal fragmentation at the national level.[55] The intended benefit of doing so is to bolster legal mechanisms in the international legal toolbox, and to stabilise financial markets locally, regionally and transnationally.

In the ensuing twenty years, the United Nations further progressed the internationalisation of insolvency law. In 2018, it implemented the Model Law on Recognition and Enforcement of Insolvency-Related Judgments (MLREIJ).[56] Moreover, since the implementation of the Model Law on Cross-Border Insolvency in 1997, several global institutions have recommended the adoption of the Model Law.[57] However, has been considerable debate over how to develop the Model Law further. Notably, at its 48th Session, the UNCITRAL Commission referred to the 47th Session of 2014 in which it gave Working Group V (Insolvency Law) a mandate to develop a model law or legislative provisions for the recognition and enforcement of insolvency-related judgements.[58] The UNCITRAL has also made some progress in implementing a model law on bankruptcy. In 1992 it proposed

54 United Nations General Assembly, Cross-Border Insolvency, Report on UNCITRAL – INSOL Judicial Colloquium on Cross-Border Insolvency, A/CN.9/413, March 1995.

55 United Nations General Assembly, Cross-Border Insolvency, Possible Issues relating to judicial cooperation and access and recognition in cases of cross-border insolvency, A/CN.9/WG/WP.42, September 1995.

56 United Nations Commission on International Trade Law, Model Law on Recognition and Enforcement of Insolvency-Related Judgments, https://uncitral.un.org/en/texts/insolvency/modellaw/mlij

57 Chandra Mohan, Cross-Border Insolvency Problems: Is the UNCITRAL Model Law the Answer? *International Insolvency Review*, Vol. 21, No. 3 (2012), 199–223.

58 UNCITRAL Working Group V report on cross-border recognition and enforcement of insolvency-related judgments delivered at 48th session, A/CN.9/WG.V/WP.135.

that the Commission evaluate the international aspects of bankruptcy, and more specifically cross-border insolvency.[59]

Notwithstanding the slow progress in developing a regulatory regime for cross-border insolvency, the international community has recognised the value of a universal legal framework. The Group of 22, comprising Finance Ministers and Central Bank Governors of the twenty two most significant national economies reacted to the 1997 Asian financial crisis by encouraging the wider use of the UNCITRAL Model Law on CBI or the adoption of similar mechanisms to facilitate the efficient resolution of cross-border insolvencies.[60] The IMF, in 1999, recommended the adoption of the Model Law as an 'effective means' of facilitating 'the recognition of foreign proceedings and the cooperation and coordination among courts and administrators of different countries'.[61] The Asian Development Bank acted similarly in 2000, in adopting its 'Good Practice Standards'.[62] Fifteen years after the implementation of the Model Law, the American Law Institute released its Global Principles for Cooperation in International Insolvency Cases.[63] Its 2012 version sought to complement the UNCITRAL Model Law on CBI by coordinating the administration of international insolvency cases involving the same debtor. In particular, the American Law Institute aimed to promote (i) the orderly, effective, efficient and timely administration of insolvency proceedings; and (ii) the identification, preservation and maximisation of the value of the debtor's assets, including the debtor's business, on a global basis.[64]

59 United Nations Commission on International Trade Law, Cross-Border Insolvency, 1994, A/CN.9/398 - Cross-border insolvency: Report on UNCITRAL - INSOL Colloquium on Cross-Border Insolvency, https://undocs.org/en/A/CN.9/398

60 Chandra Mohan, Cross-Border Insolvency Problems: Is the UNCITRAL Model Law the Answer? *International Insolvency Review*, Vol. 21, No. 3 (2012), 199–223.

61 Ibid.

62 Ibid. In 2000, ADB published two reports that examined the issues: 'Insolvency Law Reforms in the Asian and Pacific Region' and 'Secured Transactions Law Reform in Asia: Unleashing the Potential of Collateral' (Volumes I and II of Law and Policy Reform at the Asian Development Bank). The first report established 16 good practice standards for an acceptable insolvency law regime. The regime could serve as a tool for DMCs to assess their own insolvency law regimes and assist in identifying and developing appropriate standards, at 36. https://www.adb.org/sites/default/files/institutional-document/31331/ar2000.pdf.

63 The American Law Institute for Discussion at the Eighty-Ninth Annual Meeting on May 21, 22, and 23 2012, and 2016, Transnational Insolvency: Global Principles for Cooperation in International Insolvency Cases Global Guidelines for Court-to-Court Communications in International Insolvency Cases, Global Rules on Conflict-of-Laws Matters in International Insolvency Cases. https://onlinelibrary.wiley.com/doi/epdf/10.1002/iir.1228. The texts, which are reproduced subsequently, are the concrete ('black-letter') formulations embodied in the Final Report of the Transnational Insolvency Project conducted between 2005 and 2012 on behalf of the American Law Institute and the International Insolvency Institute. The Joint Reporters for the project were Professor Ian Fletcher and Professor Bob Wessels, working with the support of eminent experts from more than 30 different states across Europe, North and South America, India, South-East Asia, China, Japan, Australia, and South Africa and from the OHADA organization (2017).

64 Ibid, Principle 2, 222.

While it is out of the scope of this chapter to examine the 2012 Global Principles in their entirety, Principle 13 is pertinent because it provides for international jurisdiction over trans-border insolvency. It stipulates that the courts or other authorities of a state should have jurisdiction to open an insolvency case in respect of a debtor when either (i) the debtor's centre of main interests is situated within that state's territory or (ii) the debtor has an establishment within that state's territory. In contrast, Principle 36 provides that 'a plan of reorganisation should be final and binding upon the debtor and the creditors who participate in the main proceeding when (i) that plan is adopted in a main proceeding pending in a court with international jurisdiction with respect to the debtor under Global Principle 13.1, and (ii) there is no parallel proceeding pending with respect to the debtor'.[65] Promoting and encouraging court-to-court cooperation further strengthens the use and outcome of transnational insolvency. Such soft law instruments assist in preserving high valued assets by ensuring that both creditors and debtors effectively manage the financial stress. The result of such management is to minimise the economic impact both upon themselves and upon the broader economy. What is not understood is how far these Global Principles extend, given that not all states have accepted important elements of soft law to help facilitate court-to-court dialogue and cooperation. This is an area of further research to better understand these positives and negatives attributed to soft law instruments, but is outside the scope of this Book.

Notwithstanding this, domestic courts have highlighted the importance of the Global Principles along with the Global Guidelines, notwithstanding that the Principles constitute 'soft' law. In 2012, the UK Supreme Court joined appeals in (i) *Rubin SA & Ors* and (ii) *New Cap Reinsurance Corp Ltd & Anor v. Grant and others*. The Court supported the 2012 Global Principles specifying that the jurisdiction with international competence over insolvency proceedings is that of the country of the centre of main interests of the debtor.[66] In August 2013, the US Court of Appeals for the Third Circuit, in *Re ABC Learning Centers*, identified that the overriding objective of Global Principle 1 was to:

> enable courts and insolvency administrators to operate effectively and efficiently in international insolvency cases with goals of maximizing the value of the debtor's global assets, preserving where appropriate the debtors' business, and furthering the just administration of the proceeding.[67]

65 ALI-III Global Principles for Cooperation in International Insolvency Cases 2012, Principle 13, https://www.iiiglobal.org/sites/default/files/ALI-III%20Global%20Principles%20booklet_0.pdf

66 [2012] UKSC 46 (24). In Bob Wessels, Bert Van Goon, *Cross-Border Insolvency Law: International Instruments and Commentary*, Wolters Kluwer (2015), Chapter 4, paragraph 21.

67 *RE: ABC Learning Centres Limited, n/k/a ZYX Learning Centres Limited; A.B.C. USA Holdings Pty Ltd, Debtors in Foreign Proceedings RCS Capital Development, LLC*, Appellant. No. 12–2808. United States Court of Appeals, Third Circuit. Decided: 27 August 2013.

Citing another part of the Global Principles, the Court noted further that:

> [t]he emphasis must be on ensuring that the insolvency administrator, appointed in that proceeding is accorded every possible assistance to take control of assets of the debtor that are located in other jurisdictions.[68]

In issue going forward will be whether the Global Principles and accompanying Guidelines are accepted by states compared in this book, among others, in order to build on the modified universalist approach to cross-border insolvency. The direction adopted by the global community towards uniformity in insolvency law remains disparate. The World Bank's Revised Principles for Effective Insolvency and Creditor/Debtor Regimes in 2016 reinforces a risk management approach for the banking and finance sectors, including to incorporate updates to UNCITRAL's Legislative Guide on Insolvency Law.[69] Numerical support for the Model Law currently stands at 51 jurisdictions, as of June 2020.[70] Arguably, there is considerable work to do for the remaining two thirds of nation states to adopt the UNCITRAL Model Law on CBI. The lack of take up by states should not be viewed as a significant obstacle to further transnational insolvency and restructuring reforms across the international arena, so long as states leading international financial markets support such developments.

The UNCITRAL Model Law on CBI, notably, applies to any foreign insolvency proceeding. Ian Fletcher highlights that the Model Law is based on access, recognition, relief and cooperation.[71] Neil Hannan emphasises further, that the 'Model Law has three core objectives (i) to provide for expedited control of the debtors' local assets and their protection from unilateral actions by creditors, (ii) to give the local court considerable discretion to grant various kinds of relief to an administrator from a foreign main proceeding and (iii) to provide that this discretion is supported by a statutory mandate to cooperate, subject to ensuring that the debtor and its creditors are adequately protected'.[72]

68 Ibid. Global Principle 24.

69 Revised Principles for Effective Insolvency and Creditor/Debtor Rights Systems (2016), http://siteresources.worldbank.org/INTGILD/Resources/Proposed_amendment_to_Principles.pdf. The Bank has also benefited from an ongoing collaboration with the International Association of Insolvency Regulators (IAIR) to survey the regulatory practices of IAIR member countries and develop recommendations for strengthening regulatory capacity and frameworks for insolvency systems. A similar collaboration with INSOL International has provided feedback and input in the areas of director and officer liability and informal workout systems.

70 Ibid.

71 Ian Fletcher, *Insolvency in Private International Law, National and International Approaches,* Oxford University Press, 2nd ed. (2005), 444–451, in Neil Hannan, *Cross-Border Insolvency: The Enactment and Interpretation of the UNCITRAL Model Law*, Springer (2017), 2.

72 Neil Hannan, *Cross-Border Insolvency: The Enactment and Interpretation of the UNCITRAL Model Law*, Springer (2017), 10–11.

The UNCITRAL Model Law identifies that the purpose of insolvency proceedings is to reorganise and liquidate the assets of the insolvent debtor according to specified requirements. Firstly, the proceedings are designed to be collective, whether judicial or administrative. Secondly, the 'assets and business affairs of the debtor are subject to control or supervision by a judicial or other regulator who have sufficient authority to exercise control over insolvency proceedings'.[73] Thirdly, the 'Model Law's purpose is to provide expedited and direct access of foreign representatives to insolvency proceedings through an 'inbound request' made to the courts of the enacting state'.[74] Still, the Model Law 'does not provide complete uniformity'.[75] The following section briefly examines the UNCITRAL Model Law on Cross-Border Insolvency.

2.4 UNCITRAL Model Law on Cross-Border Insolvency (Model Law)

The Model Law comprises 32 Articles. It focuses on access of foreign representatives and creditors to courts in the enacting state,[76] recognition of a foreign proceeding and relief,[77] cooperation with foreign courts and foreign representative,[78] and concurrent proceedings.[79] While it is out of scope of this book to examine the

73 Jenny Clift, UNCITRAL Model Law on Cross-Border Insolvency – A Legislative Framework to Facilitate Coordination and Cooperation in Cross-Border Insolvency, *Tulane Journal of International and Comparative Law*, Vol. 12, No. 307 (2004), 319–320. This section draws upon the work of Robert Walters, Cross Border Insolvency and the 2022 Australia-India Comprehensive Economic Cooperation Agreement? Business Law Review, Wolterskluwer, forthcoming 2022.

74 United Nations Commission on International Trade Law. UNCITRAL Model Law on Cross-Border Insolvency with Guide to Enactment and Interpretation (PDF). United Nations Publications, 2014, Article 9. Signatories as at 2020 are: Australia 2008, Bahrain 2018, Benin, 2015 (b), Burkina Faso 2015 (b), Cameroon 2015 (b), Canada 2005, Central African Republic 2015 (b), Chad 2015 (b), Chile 2013, Colombia 2006, Comoros 2015 (b), Congo 2015 (b), Côte d'Ivoire 2015 (b), Democratic Republic of the Congo 2015 (b), Dominican Republic 2015, Equatorial Guinea 2015 (b), Gabon 2015 (b), Greece 2010, Guinea 2015 (b), Guinea-Bissau 2015 (b), Israel 2018, Japan 2000, Kenya 2015, Malawi 2015, Mali 2015 (b), Mauritius 2009, Mexico 2000, Montenegro 2002, Myanmar 2020, New Zealand 2006, Niger 2015 (b), Panama 2016, Philippines 2010, Poland 2003, Republic of Korea 2006, Romania 2002, Senegal 2015 (b), Serbia 2004, Seychelles 2013, Singapore 2017, Slovenia 2007, South Africa 2000, Togo 2015 (b), Uganda 201, United Arab Emirates, Dubai International Financial Centre 2019, United Kingdom of Great Britain, Great Britain 2006, British Virgin Islands 2003 (a), Gibraltar 2014 (a), United States of America 2005, Vanuatu 2013, Zimbabwe 2018.

75 Gerard McCormack, Anil Hargovan, Australia and the International Insolvency Paradigm, *Sydney Law Review 18*, Vol. 37, No. 3 (2015), 389.

76 United Nations Commission on International Trade Law, Model Law on Cross-Border Insolvency, https://uncitral.un.org/sites/uncitral.un.org/files/media-documents/uncitral/en/1997-model-law-insol-2013-guide-enactment-e.pdf

77 Ibid, chapter ii.

78 Ibid, chapter iii.

79 Ibid, chapter iv.

entire Model Law in detail, some of its most important chapters include, but are not limited to, international obligations of the state;[80] competent court or authority;[81] interpretation;[82] participation of a foreign representative;[83] and access of foreign creditors.[84] The book will examine the important elements and obligations that states should take up to strengthen legal convergence in cross-border insolvency.

A significant feature that makes the Model Law particularly important internationally is the way in which it provides and promotes access to insolvency proceedings in different jurisdictions. As identified in Chapters 1 and 2 of the Model Law, foreign representatives have the right of access to the domestic courts in each state engaged in concurrent proceedings. Without conceding jurisdiction to the courts of those states, the Model Law proposes that they have the right to participate in domestic insolvency proceedings.[85] Were the Model Law to have denied such access transnationally, the parties would be inhibited from resolving insolvency issues expeditiously. The result would be to prolong and exacerbate instability in insolvency proceedings and to destabilise business dealings in the impacted financial market.

This section addresses the access of inbound and outbound to different aspects of cross-border insolvency. Firstly, in relation to outbound aspects, Article 5 authorises the person or body administering a reorganisation or liquidation under the law of the enacting state (referred to as the insolvency representative)[86] to act in a foreign state in furtherance of local proceedings.[87] In terms of inbound requests, a

80 Ibid, Article 3. International obligations of this State: To the extent that this Law conflicts with an obligation of this State arising out of any treaty or other form of agreement to which it is a party with one or more other States, the requirements of the treaty or agreement prevail.

81 Ibid, Article 4. Competent court or authority: The functions referred to in this Law relating to recognition of foreign proceedings and cooperation with foreign courts shall be performed by [specify the court, courts, authority or authorities competent to perform those functions in the enacting State].

82 Ibid, Article 8. Interpretation: In the interpretation of this Law, regard is to be had to its international origin and to the need to promote uniformity in its application and the observance of good faith.

83 Ibid, Article 12. Participation of a foreign representative in a proceeding under [identify laws of the enacting State relating to insolvency] Upon recognition of a foreign proceeding, the foreign representative is entitled to participate in a proceeding regarding the debtor under [identify laws of the enacting State relating to insolvency].

84 Ibid, Article 13. Access of foreign creditors to a proceeding under [identify laws of the enacting State relating to insolvency] 1. Subject to paragraph 2 of this article, foreign creditors have the same rights regarding the commencement of, and participation in, a proceeding under [identify laws of the enacting State relating to insolvency] as creditors in this State.

85 Ibid, and Article 14.

86 This terminology reflects the language used in article 5 of the Model Law and is used for consistency with the UNCITRAL Legislative Guide on Insolvency Law, which explains that an 'insolvency representative' is 'a person or body, including one appointed on an interim basis, authorized in insolvency proceedings to administer the reorganization or liquidation of the insolvency estate': Introduction, para. 12 (v), In UNCITRAL Model Law on Cross-Border Insolvency with Guide to Enactment and Interpretation, 25–26, https://uncitral.un.org/sites/uncitral.un.org/files/media-documents/uncitral/en/1997-model-law-insol-2013-guide-enactment-e.pdf.

87 Ibid, Article 5.

'foreign representative applying for access to and participation in proceedings in the enacting state has the following rights: of direct access to the courts of the enacting state;[88] to apply to commence a local proceeding in the enacting state subject to the legal conditions applicable in that state;[89] and to apply for recognition of the foreign proceedings in which they were appointed to represent'.[90] Upon recognition, 'a foreign representative is entitled to participate in insolvency-related proceedings conducted in the enacting state under the law of that state'.[91] Those 'access and related rights do not subject the foreign representative or the foreign assets and affairs of the debtor to the jurisdiction of the enacting state for any purpose other than that application'.[92] Additionally, Articles 13 and 14 provide that foreign creditors have equal rights to domestic creditors before domestic courts.

Chapter 3 of the Model Law addresses, in our view, some of the most important articles in the model law. Article 15 underpins the justification for the development of the Model Law. It plays an important role in harmonising the national laws in the application for recognition of a foreign proceeding. In recognition of a foreign proceeding, Article 17 encourages states to implement provisions within their national law, directed at acceptance of foreign proceedings in accordance with the 2018 UNCITRAL Model Law on Recognition and Enforcement of Insolvency-Related Judgments Judgements (REIRJ). It is out of scope to discuss the REIRJ in detail. However, incorporating a provision like Article 17 into the domestic law of signatory states would not prevent modification or termination of recognition of foreign judgements if it is shown that the requisite grounds for granting enforcement were wholly or partially lacking, or had ceased to exist.[93] A further note of caution is required. The Model Law is not intended to accord recognition to all foreign insolvency proceedings. Subject to Article 6, Article 17 specifies that the Court in the enacting state should recognise the foreign proceeding without further requirement once the requisites specified in Article 2, concerning the nature of the foreign proceeding, are met. These requirements include provision for collective proceedings,[94] participation of the foreign representative, and that evidence required by Article 15 has been provided.

The process of application and recognition of foreign proceedings is aided by the presumptions contained in Article 16 that enable the Court in the enacting State to presume the authenticity and validity of the certificates and documents,

88 Ibid, Article 9.
89 Ibid, Article 11.
90 Ibid, Article 15.
91 Ibid, Article 12.
92 Ibid, Article 10.
93 Ibid, Article 17.
94 These requirements are that the foreign proceeding is, as a matter of course, a collective proceeding for the purposes of liquidation or reorganization under the control or supervision of the court. See UNCITRAL Model Law on Cross-Border Insolvency with Guide to Enactment and Interpretation (2013), 26–29.

originating in the foreign State, that are required by Article 15.[95] Article 6 allows such recognition to be refused where it would be 'manifestly contrary to the public policy' of the State in which recognition is sought. These ordinarily are preliminary issues to be considered when an application for recognition of foreign proceedings is made.[96] However, the UNCITRAL notes that no definition of what constitutes public policy is attempted, as notions vary from State to State. Nevertheless, the intention is that the public policy exception should be interpreted restrictively, and that Article 6 should be used only in exceptional and limited circumstances.[97] Differences in insolvency schemes do not themselves justify a finding that enforcing one State's laws would violate the public policy of another State. The largely untested issue is the extent to which states adopt a sovereigntist conception of public policy and purport to give it a broader construction, notably on grounds of protecting domestic economic stability.

Articles 19, 20 and 22, underpin the need for the recognition and application of foreign proceedings and judgements. Attempts at legal harmonisation would be fruitless in their absence. Typically, a transnational insolvency proceeding involving an Australian and Singapore entity with offices and branches in the US and UK, where those proceedings could commence, should also be recognised in Australia and Singapore. In other words, Article 19 authorises the Court in the enacting state to grant the type of relief that is usually available only in collective insolvency proceedings (when relief is available under Article 21), as opposed to 'individual' relief that may be granted before the commencement of insolvency proceedings under rules of civil procedure.[98] That is, the rules of civil procedure of the jurisdiction where the proceeding is being undertaken will apply. However, it must be noted that the discretionary 'collective' relief under Article 19 is somewhat narrower in scope than the relief under Article 21.[99]

Accordingly, Articles 20 and 21 encourage states to recognise a foreign main proceeding, and that any relief provided is to be granted upon recognition of a foreign proceeding. Article 22 undertakes to ensure that bankruptcy protection is provided to creditors and other interested persons. In relation to Article 22,

95 Ibid.
96 Ibid.
97 United Nations Commission on International Trade Law, Model Law on Cross-Border Insolvency, https://uncitral.un.org/sites/uncitral.un.org/files/media-documents/uncitral/en/insolvency-e.pdf. Article 6. Explanatory note states: As the notion of public policy is grounded in national law and may differ from State to State, no uniform definition of that notion is attempted in article 6. In some States the expression "public policy" may be given a broad meaning in that it might relate in principle to any mandatory rule of national law. In many States, however, the public policy exception is construed as being restricted to fundamental principles of law, in particular constitutional guarantees; in those States, public policy would only be used to refuse the application of foreign law, or the recognition of a foreign judicial decision or arbitral award, when that would contravene those fundamental principles.
98 Ibid, 80.
99 Ibid.

Andrew Dawson makes the point the 'Model Law provides that an ancillary court may grant additional relief to the foreign representative'.[100] This discretionary relief includes 'expanding the bankruptcy stay, assisting with discovery efforts within the ancillary jurisdiction and entrusting local assets to be administered or distributed in the foreign full proceeding'.[101] Dawson goes onto say that, to be eligible for discretionary relief, there are two principal restrictions applicable to foreign non-main proceedings. Firstly, the foreign proceeding must either be a foreign main proceeding or a foreign nonmain proceeding. In the parlance of the Model Law, the foreign representative can only obtain discretionary relief if a foreign full bankruptcy application was filed and where the debtor has at least an establishment. Secondly, Dawson states there are substantive restrictions designed to protect creditors. Those protections depend on the type of relief sought and on the type of foreign proceeding. The baseline substantive protection for creditors is found in Article 22(a); 'whereby the Court must be satisfied that the interests of the creditors and other interested persons, including the debtor, are adequately protected'.[102] That said, and as highlighted by Dawson, national courts are permitted to place conditions on any discretionary relief. Further, the Model Law provides additional restrictions when the foreign representative asks the ancillary court to turn over local assets to be distributed in the foreign proceeding. Therefore, the Model Law directs the Court specifically to examine the interests of local creditors. However, before granting relief to a foreign non-main proceeding, namely, 'where the debtor has an establishment but not its centre of main interests, there is one more requirement'.[103] The court may issue 'orders as to passing on and distributing local assets only when it is satisfied under the local choice of law rules, that its orders will be administered appropriately by a foreign court. Thus, the court may issue discovery orders only if satisfied that it relates to information required in that foreign non-main proceeding'.[104] Put another way, discovery orders can be used to obtain the necessary information identified in Article 21, such as, to confirm assets, affairs, rights and obligations or liabilities of the debtor. However, this will differ for third party discovery; and to date, courts will generally not extend discovery to broad financial information.[105] Viewed this way, discovery is somewhat limited,

100 Andrew Dawson, Modularity in Cross-Border Insolvency, *The Chicago-Kent Law Review*, Vol. 98 (2018), 687–694.

101 Ibid.

102 Ibid.

103 Ibid, 687.

104 Ibid.

105 *United States*: Petroforte Brasiliero de Petroleo Ltda., 542 B.R. 899, 903 (S.D. Fla 2015), CLOUT 1625, *United States*: Platinum Partners Value Arbitrage Fund L.P., 583 B.R. 803 (Bankr. S.D.N.Y. 2018), *United States*: Millennium Global Emerging Credit Master Fund Ltd., 471 B.R. 342 (Bankr. S.D.N.Y. 2012); United States Bankruptcy Code, 11 U.S.C. sect. 1507 (enacting art. 7, MLCBI), gives effect to the principle of art. 7 of the MLCBI. In UNCITRAL Digest of Case Law on the UNCITRAL Model Law on Cross-Border Insolvency, 2021, https://uncitral.un.org/sites/uncitral.un.org/files/media-documents/uncitral/en/20-06293_uncitral_mlcbi_digest_e.pdf, 67–68.

not unlike prevails in domestic insolvency proceedings across jurisdictions. The critical issue is that, in comparing the insolvency laws in the states whose laws are examined in this book, it will become evident how the right to discovery proceedings differ. That difference will also enable practitioners to identify and respond to disparate legal proceedings, and formalities, across jurisdictions.

Article 23 discourages the conduct of proceedings that are detrimental to creditors. Thus, intervention by a 'foreign representative in insolvency proceedings can be undertaken where the debtor is a party'.[106] Central to Article 23 is its elaboration of Article 17, providing for the recognition of the foreign proceeding. This accords a foreign representative standing to initiate actions under the law of the enacting State. Article 21 expressly affirms that this 'standing avoids or renders ineffective other legal acts that are detrimental to creditors'.[107] However, it does not address the right of a foreign representative to bring such an action in the enacting State under the law of the State in which the foreign proceeding is taking place. Therefore, the effect of Article 17 is that 'a foreign representative is not prevented from initiating an action by the sole fact that the foreign representative is not the foreign representative appointed in the enacting State'.[108]

Chapters 4 and 5 of the Model Law provide for another important concept of transnational communication, namely, to allow for cooperation and communication between foreign courts and foreign representatives under Article 25 of the Model Law. Drawing on that Article, John Pottow, argues that the Model Law's limited provisions on transnational communication can be clustered into two broad areas, administrative and substantial. The first cluster, administrative provisions, might be divided further into two subsidiary categories: firstly, provisions related to international cooperation and communication, and, secondly, antidiscrimination rules. The first category includes, for example, Articles 25 to 30, in which the Model Law codifies a series of rules built from the fledgling precedents of ad hoc sovereign cooperation and international protocols. Moreover, Article 25, in providing for cooperation and direct communication between a court of this [nation] state and foreign courts or foreign representatives, mandates the court cooperate 'to the maximum extent possible'.[109] Article 25 also makes explicit the domestic court's entitlement to 'communicate directly with, or to request information or assistance directly from, foreign courts.'[110] These changes are especially important in civil law jurisdictions in which such power may not be readily inferred from inherent judicial authority. On the other hand, under the common law, there is an increasingly aspirational approach

106 UNCITRAL Model Law on Cross-Border Insolvency with Guide to Enactment and Interpretation (2013), 26–29, Article 24.

107 Ibid, 92.

108 Ibid.

109 John Pottow, Procedural Incrementalism: A Model for International Bankruptcy, *Virginia Journal of International Law* (2006), 961–962.

110 Ibid.

to international cooperation.[111] Arguably, Articles 25 to 27 can be considered as central provisions of the Model law because they strengthen cross-border approaches towards cooperation. Without cooperation across international borders, the Model Law would be ineffective. Furthermore, Articles 25 and 26 promote the idea that an insolvency representative is to maximise upon such cooperation.

The recognition of foreign main proceedings does not prevent the commencement of local proceedings in the enacting State. Nor does the commencement of local proceedings in that State terminate recognition already accorded to foreign proceedings or prevent recognition of foreign proceedings.[112] Article 29 addresses adjustments in the relief available where there are concurrent proceedings.[113] The basic principle is that, for the grant of relief in foreign proceedings to be recognised, that relief should be consistent with the relief granted in local proceedings, irrespective of whether the foreign proceeding was recognised before or after the commencement of the local proceeding. For example, where local proceedings have already commenced at the time the application for recognition is made, relief granted in the foreign proceeding must be consistent with the provision for and conditions or relief in local proceedings. If the foreign proceeding is recognised as a main proceeding, the automatic relief available on recognition of that proceeding under Article 20 will not apply.[114] However, the recognition of such relief has little to no relevance in limiting the jurisdiction of the Court to commence or continue insolvency proceedings. Article 28 must be read in conjunction with Article 29, which, as stated earlier, is to provide that recognition of a foreign main proceeding will not prevent the commencement of a local insolvency proceeding concerning the same debtor, as long as the debtor has assets in the State.

On the other hand, Articles 31 and 32 concentrate on reconciling and encouraging greater coordination in the recognition of foreign insolvency proceedings. Article 31 establishes a presumption that recognition of a foreign proceeding is proof that the debtor is insolvent where insolvency is required for the commencement of a local proceeding.[115] Article 32 is precautionary in nature. It establishes a rule to avoid situations in which a creditor might make claims and be paid in multiple insolvency proceedings in different jurisdictions, thereby potentially obtaining more favourable treatment than other creditors.[116]

Notwithstanding the objective of promoting consistency in enforcing cross-border insolvency decisions, the enforcement approach taken by courts in most common and civil law jurisdictions has been inconsistent from inception. Generally, the Model Law on cross-border insolvency proceeding 'does not specifically

111 Ibid.

112 UNCITRAL Model Law on Cross-Border Insolvency with Guide to Enactment and Interpretation (2013), 26–29, Article 28.

113 Ibid, 31.

114 Ibid.

115 Ibid, 32.

116 Ibid.

address the enforcement of foreign cross-border insolvency judgments within local jurisdictions'.[117] Consequently, over the last decade the enforcement of foreign insolvency judgments in the UK, Australia, and the US has been inconsistent and largely unpredictable.[118] UK courts have refused to enforce some foreign insolvency judgments, contrary to judicial precedent and significantly narrowing the application of the Model Law. Australian courts have also declined enforcement of foreign insolvency judgments in disregard of the Model Law.[119] American courts have similarly disregarded the objectives of the Model Law by continuously expanding Chapter 15's limited exceptions to enforcement.[120] These divergences from the Model Law ignore that, for cross-border insolvency proceedings to be effective, legal harmonisation is needed to ensure that domestic courts promote cooperation and direct communication of a person or body administering a reorganisation or liquidation, with foreign courts or foreign representatives.[121] These divergences across jurisdictions and the need for ensuring greater cooperation in administering a reorganisation or liquidation, is explored further in Part 2 of this chapter.

In summary, the Model Law establishes a 'procedural structure as the foundation for a cross-border system, which extends beyond a set of international standards'.[122] However, significant gaps remain in harmonising cross-border insolvency law. The Model Law does not expressly address choice of law issues, and only impliedly considers outbound insolvency issues through rules on international jurisdiction.[123] Addressing these gaps through a convention on insolvency law, extended Model Law rules and judicial determinations can make the transnational insolvency regime more complete and less prone to territorial bias. It may also help streamline insolvency proceedings, such as to facilitate enforcement, by removing excessive territorial protections and ensuring general consistency in proceedings across jurisdictions.[124] Making such revisions should be informed by, refer to and rely on norms of modified universalism. They should be guided by a principled and consistent approach directed at promoting the widespread application of these norms. In the following Section we propose a review of the authority and scope of the Model Law and for its status to be raised to the level of a convention.

117 Lia Metreveli, Toward Standardized Enforcement of Cross-Border Insolvency Decisions: Encouraging the United States to Adopt UNCITRAL's Recent Amendment to its Model Law on Cross-Border Insolvency, *Columbia Journal of Law and Social Problems* (2017), 327–328.

118 Ibid.

119 Ibid.

120 Ibid.

121 UNCITRAL Model Law on Cross-Border Insolvency with Guide to Enactment and Interpretation (2013), Article 26.

122 Jay Lawrence Westbrook, Interpretation Internationale, *Temple Law Review*, Vol. 87 (2015), 739–754.

123 Irit Mevorach, *The Future of Cross-Border Insolvency: Overcoming Biases and Closing Gaps*, Oxford University Press (2018), 255–256.

124 Ibid.

2.5 Time for the Model Law to be Raised to Convention Status

Earlier in this chapter, it was briefly argued that a convention on insolvency would render the law governing trans-border proceedings more cohesive, less contradictory and clearer in its application and enforcement. It is our view that, after 20 years since its implementation, it is time to straddle the gap between a cursory review of the UNCITRAL Model Law on CBI and the more expansive and detailed reviews giving rise to conventions on private international law (PIL):[125]

> At the time when the Model Law was developed, a global agreement on jurisdictional rules to govern insolvency proceedings and choice of law rules was rejected by the participating states. The understandable concern then was to avoid substantive dissension among states over the nature and application of cross-border insolvency laws and proceedings.[126] In our view, while the Model Law has achieved exceptional results, given its limited objectives, its status as an unenforceable law is ill-suited to current global demands. What is required now is greater coherence within an interdependent global environment dominated by virtually instantaneous access to debt and, sometimes, precipitation into insolvency. This requirement is recognized by international commentators, including judges, who highlight that, despite the expansion of cross-border trade, more uniformity is needed to deal with the insolvency of both state and non-state actors.[127] Illustrating this perception during the Global Financial Crisis, Bob Wessels contended that an insolvency convention: 'should act as an aid for judges to navigate in uncharted waters, should ensure that all stakeholders in a restructuring or insolvency have the information they need to make informed decisions and should adopt procedural safeguards to ensure the integrity of all judgments given[128]

125 Susan Block-Lieb, Terence C. Halliday, Less is More in International Private Law, *NIBLeJ* Vol. 3, No. 43 (2015), 50–55.

126 Ibid, 55.

127 Mohan S. Chandra, Cross-Border Insolvency Problems: Is the UNCITRAL Model Law the Answer? *International Insolvency Review*, Vol. 21, No. 3 (2012), 199–223. Research Collection School of Law, also see – Sir Nicholas Browne-Wilkinson VC in Re Bank of Credit and Commerce International (No. 3) [1992] BCC 83 at 89; Sir Donald Nicolls VC in Re Paramount Airways Ltd [1993] 3 All E.R.1 at 11; Hoffman J in Re Maxwell Communications Corp plc (No. 2) [1992] BCC 757 at 766. For a fuller discussion see Sir Peter Millet, Cross-Border Insolvency: The Judicial Approach, *International Insolvency Review*, Vol. 6 (1997), 99–11.

128 Bob Wessels, *Judicial Coordination of Cross-Border Insolvency Cases*, Kluwer, Deventer (2008), 45. Wessels' quote continues 'Beautiful words, which seem a distant echo from recent history, but Working Group V (Insolvency Law) of UNCITRAL has agreed to progress on the idea with a study that will consider a range of possible issues. Such issues include 'world-wide convention' matters, such as the time and cost required to negotiate a convention and for it to enter into force, reciprocity, interpretation, alignment with existing treaties in certain areas, an inventory to the matters that make States shy or reluctant to follow the Model Law, as well as an assessment into States' support for an international insolvency convention'

However, the UNCITRAL Working Group maintained that the Model Law was not sufficiently developed to secure blanket international harmonisation, It deferred instead to national laws (e.g. on questions of priority debts) to achieve agreement on insolvency procedures and to facilitate the efficient and effective resolution of cross-border insolvency disputes.[129] Articles 6 and 7 reinforced this view, by bestowed upon enacting States, a wide discretion in the choice of insolvency principles and procedures that would be followed.[130]

However, there are several highly successful UNCITRAL models that can be replicated to strengthen the current governance framework in cross-border insolvency. One such model is the Convention on the International Sale of Goods (CISG) 1980. While not every state has adopted the CISG, it has been applauded for transcending the boundaries between the common and civil law regulation of the sale of goods. Luca Castellani maintains that the 'CISG has provided a uniform regime for the settlement of disputes related to the international sale of goods. Its carefully balanced system of contractual remedies facilitates interaction between a buyer and a seller in curing deficiencies in performance'.[131] These mechanisms are usually not available under national law, which typically contains provisions designed for short-range transactions. Castellani also highlights the importance of the CISG in providing greater legal predictability and stability in times of constant geopolitical and economic upheaval. He also maintains that the application of the CISG has led to a reduction in transaction costs, in the form of lower prices for imported and exported goods. The CISG is also supported by UNIDROIT Principles of International Commercial Contracts that fill gaps in the CISG. Chapter 1 has highlighted the OECD's emphasis on insolvency, restructuring and the rule of law in supporting global economic stability and security. The book will reinforce that rationale throughout the ensuing chapters.

2.6 Conclusion

A highly integrated regional and world economy demands a well-functioning insolvency and restructuring international legal framework. To achieve this, this book makes the case to further harmonise the current cross-border and restructuring legal regimes. This chapter has demonstrated that this process of internationalisation is already underway. The 1997 UNCITRAL Model law on Cross-Border Insolvency has been instrumental in shaping how states and their courts regulate cross-border insolvency. The Guide to the Interpretation of the UNCITRAL

129 Arjya B. Majumdar, The UNCITRAL Model Law on Cross-Border Insolvency, *India Law Journal*, Vol. 2, No. I (2009).

130 Ibid.

131 Luca Castellani, *The Adoption of the CISG in Portugal: Benefits and Perspectives: A adoção da CISG em Portugal: benefícios e perspetivas*, Legal Officer, UNCITRAL Secretariat Outubro (2013).

Model Law also recognises the growing need to respond to the changing global landscape surrounding insolvency:

> [The] increasing incidence of cross-border insolvencies reflects the continuing global expansion of trade and investment. However, national insolvency laws have by and large not kept pace with the trend, and they are often ill-equipped to deal with cases of a cross-border nature. This frequently results in inadequate and inharmonious legal approaches, which hamper the rescue of financially troubled businesses, are not conducive to a fair and efficient administration of cross-border insolvencies, impede the protection of the assets of the insolvent debtor against dissipation, and hinder the maximisation of the value of those assets. Moreover, the absence of predictability in the handling of cross-border insolvency cases impedes capital flow and is a disincentive to cross-border investment.[132]

In responding to these deficiencies, advocates for the UNCITRAL Model law on cross-border Insolvency have proposed a universalist approach for adoption by member states. They have reinforced the need for rehabilitating and restructuring the law of insolvency, rather than punishing companies under financial stress to face the precipitously threat of insolvency proceedings. However, this universal idealism has hardly been achieved to date. States have largely retained their territorial responses to cross-border insolvency, although some have embraced the Model Law in their national laws.

On the positive side, the Model Law has provided a pathway to strengthen the legal convergence and harmonisation of legal procedures regulating transnational insolvency in a time of global economic uncertainty. On the other side, the Model Law does not adequately address choice of law issues in which legal divergence prevails over legal convergence. The Model Law also focuses on outbound insolvency proceedings; and its application is subject to territorial biases. Rather than continuing down the pathway of allowing states to embrace territorial habits, the international community needs to strengthen universalism in trans-border insolvency proceedings.

The Model Law has two interrelated purposes directed at developing international insolvency and restructuring law. The first purpose is to assist states in further developing their national insolvency laws and procedures. The second purpose is to promote a harmonised and fair framework to redress the difficulties of debtors experiencing severe financial distress and insolvency. The Model law responds to these purposes by establishing a functional framework in which the debtor has assets in more than one jurisdiction, or the creditors of the debtor are not located in the same state. Central to the Model Law is that the debtor's centre of main interest assumes principal responsibility for managing the insolvency of the debtor, regardless of the number of States in which the debtor has assets and creditors, but subject to appropriate coordination procedures to accommodate local needs.

132 UNCITRAL Model Law on Cross-Border Insolvency with Guide to Enactment and Interpretation (2013), 20–21.

In issue for the Model law was and remains to establish a functional balance between state territoriality directed at protecting localised economies and de-localising those proceedings to protect debtors, creditors and states outside of that localised economy. That balance was sought by reconciling trans-border procedures governing insolvency proceedings, without negating procedural differences among states, nor seeking the substantive unification of insolvency law. In pursuing this functional balance, the Model Law promotes a uniform but distinctly procedural approach to resolving cross-border insolvency disputes.

The Model Law has allowed adopting countries to determine their own substantive law, while at the same time, provided the framework for foreign representatives 'equal, simple, and fast access' to their law. More pervasively, it has provided a tool for authorising and encouraging cooperation and coordination between jurisdictions in building this framework. Its four key building blocks are: access, recognition, relief (assistance), and cooperation. It is argued that the time is now right for the Model Law to be reviewed to ensure further harmonisation to ensure business efficacy within a global economic order in which financial stress is a core impediment.

The most important motivator for an international convention on insolvency, as proposed in this Book, are procedural deficiencies and uncertainties in the Model Law and inconsistencies in its application in trans-border insolvency proceedings. The existing UNCITRAL, UNIDROIT and other models identified in this chapter offer institutional and structural guidelines in developing, facilitating and coordinating a convention on trans-border insolvency. Principles like the UNIDROIT Principles potentially strengthen the trans-border application of that convention. Recognition of the economic need for those Principles and overcoming political objections to them, are the hurdles that lie ahead.

Adopting a trans-border insolvency convention will confirm and strengthen the already extensive regulatory measures. Enabling early intervention and prevention measures will address financial strain before it regresses into irreversible insolvency. The initiation and conduct of timely insolvency proceedings will potentially enable a financially debilitated entity to be restructured and remain viable. Establishing and elaborating upon such a regulatory framework will also provide greater confidence in business entities that depend on loan financing to maintain operations. Preserving their markets will also ensure greater market certainty for their creditors, customers, and employees. In addition, doing so at a macro-legal level will stabilise economies. It will reduce governments having to respond to expanding national debts through costly fiscal and related stimulus measures. It will go some way in retaining high levels of liquidity in the financial system that face destabilisation. Importantly, these economic measures are increasingly priorities for states in general in times of economic and political tumult in a somewhat borderless global economy.

As highlighted earlier in this book, even with the protectionist policies being implemented by governments, the rise of a multi-polar global economic order is likely to evolve away from predominantly bilateral economic agreements between states to multilateral treaties that require a legal framework that states can share. Accomplishing this shift in trans-border insolvency law requires a robust international legal framework to overcome two seemingly intransigent pathways to global economic stability. Centrally in issue is not only the virtue of decoupling an unduly entrenched alignment between localised business interests and domestic government policy. In contention is the virtue of building legal convergence and harmonisation across state boundaries to offset and over-exuberant territorialism that fragments and damages trans-border commerce. The global economy needs less emphasis on transitory political victories that are stained by pervasive economic losses.

An area for further research in facilitating this transition is the UNCITRAL Model Law on Enterprise Group Insolvency released in 2019.[133] Its purpose is to promote cooperation between national courts and insolvency representatives. Furthermore, it aims to develop group insolvency solutions, fair and efficient administration, the protection of assets, the facilitation of rehabilitation and the protection creditors.[134] It has all the hallmarks of adding another layer to the internationalisation of cross-border insolvency and restructuring for further development.

133 UNCITRAL Model Law on Enterprise Group Insolvency, https://uncitral.un.org/en/texts/insolvency.

134 Ibid, Preamble.

2

JURISDICTIONS APPROACH TOWARDS CROSS-BORDER INSOLVENCY PART 2

This chapter follows from the previous chapter that discussed the internationalisation and universalism of cross-border insolvency in principle. This chapter demonstrates how specific jurisdictions, not limited to those that have adopted the Model Law, have embraced this universalist approach, while continuing to rely on elements of territorialism. The chapter will compare developments in the European Union, Australia, Singapore, United Kingdom (UK) and India. It will highlight some of the likely challenges to be faced by UK companies as a result from Brexit.

2.1 Introduction

The choice of the law to regulate insolvency often involves a trade-off between a law that promotes increased economic activities and another law that has the opposite effect. On the one side, law enables the parties to efficiently resolve a financial dispute, to minimise the debtor's financial stress, protect creditors and facilitate trans-border financing. On the other side, is law that protracts financial stress, benefits creditors selectively and undermines confidence in trans-border financing.[1] Further, exacerbated debtor stress will often have a contagion effect. Not only will it accelerate financial stress by denying the restructuring of debts that could otherwise limit economic harm to the debtor and creditors involved in insolvency proceedings. It will potentially disrupt trans-border financing beyond the economic loss to both.

1 Sefra Frankin, Cross-Border Insolvency Law: A Comparative Institutional Analysis, *Oxford Journal of Legal Studies*, Vol. 34, No. 1 (2014), 97–99.

DOI: 10.4324/9781003311874-3

The discussion in this chapter on the restructuring of debt demonstrates the benefit of a harmonised legal framework to limit inconsistency and incongruence in cross-border insolvency proceedings and to highlight the efficiency of centralised control over insolvency and restructuring proceedings. Ensuing sections will evaluate the approach taken by the jurisdictions compared in relation to insolvency proceedings conducted at the 'centre of main interests' of the debtor, namely, in the main state (COMI), as distinct from proceedings in any other state in which debtor has an 'establishment' being a non-main or secondary state (COMI2).

The central focus of this chapter will be on the contagion effect of the law of insolvency of a dominant state, not limited to the main state upon the insolvency law in another or other states, not limited to a non-main state. Under scrutiny will be how this dependence between states can impact upon the harmonisation of insolvency and restructuring law, notably when insolvency proceedings are conducted in more than one state. Attention will be given to the significance of the UNCITRAL Model Law on Cross-Border Insolvency Regulation 2006 (CBIR). Further analysis will be devoted to the development of cross-border insolvency law in the EU; the prospective divergence from EU Law in pre- and post-Brexit UK; and further legal divergence in jurisdictions like Australia, the US and Singapore.

More pervasively, it will explore universal and territorial approaches that states adopt towards trans-border insolvency, and more often, their choice of variable blends of universalism and territorialism. It will consider how such variability leads to the inconsistent treatment of creditors and debtors according to the law prevailing in different states at which insolvency proceedings are initiated and conducted. Some emphasis will also be given to the significance of variability in cross-border insolvency laws in times of global economic and political disruption, such as in the wake of COVID-19 and its sequelae.

A pervasive question posed throughout the chapter is in examining the extent to which the Model Law on Cross-Border Insolvency is applied restrictively or expansively in specific domestic jurisdictions. The specific issue will be whether and how domestic states have developed, and their courts have applied, universal procedural rules to govern trans-border insolvency. It will illustrate that, while some states such as Australia and Singapore are seeking to do so, the EU and UK post-Brexit, face more formidable obstacles in progressing such universal rules of procedure domestically. This is because competition in the market itself will direct how the UK respond, and how far they may deviate from the EU model. Therefore, this and the following chapter, will highlight the opportunity for further work to be undertaken, in collaboration with UNCITRAL, to promote the universalist approach proposed by this book.

2.2 European Union

The EU has not fully implemented the UNCITRAL Model Law on Cross-Border Insolvency Regulation 2006 (CBIR). The insolvency law of the EU traces back the 1995 European Convention on Insolvency Proceedings which was not fully adopted and never came into effect.[2] It took another five years before the EU adopted preliminary legislation on a framework for insolvency. However, European states did enact insolvency laws before the formation of the EU. These laws were designed largely to liquidate company assets and distribute to creditors the proceeds of an insolvency based on the legal ranking of their claims.[3] Their insolvency laws were primarily designed to punish a delinquent debtor, rather than aid in its rehabilitation or reorganisation:[4] '[a]n entrepreneur who failed to succeed in business was considered as a social threat'.'[5] The problem was that these insolvency regulations were not consistently adopted across European states, nor effectively addressed on the formation of the EU. To remedy this lack of a EU wide insolvency law, the Council of the European Union established its first insolvency law by Council Regulation No. 1346/2000. However, that Law has not provided common rules to 'regulate European insolvency proceedings, but rather focused on coordinating insolvency proceedings as they existed and continue to exist under the national laws of Member States'.[6]

Still, the EU has provided a viable framework in developing a universal model for the regulation of insolvency, notwithstanding the absence of such a model in the EU itself. In 2000, the EU adopted the European Insolvency Regulation (EIR).[7] That Regulation favoured a universalist approach, permitting the initiation of secondary in addition to the main proceeding.[8] In coming into effect in 2002, it sought to enable cross-border proceeding to operate efficiently, providing measures for coordinating the handling of debtors' assets, and to avoid forum shopping.[9] It also sought to streamline cross-border insolvency proceedings, introduce rules for improving the coordination of debtor's assets, and prevent forum shopping. It stipulated that the courts of the Member State at which the debtor's centre of main interest (COMI) was situated, identified before as the 'main state', shall have jurisdiction to open insolvency proceedings and having the same effect, without further formalities, in any other Member State.[10] In contrast the courts of Member States

2 European Union Council, *Convention on Insolvency* (1995), http://aei.pitt.edu/2840/1/2840.pdf.

3 Ibid, Article 3. Also see Paolo Manganelli, The Evolution of the Italian and U.S. Bankruptcy Systems – A Comparative Analysis, *Journal of Business and Technology*. Vol. 5 (2010), 237–238.

4 Ibid, 237.

5 Ibid, 238.

6 Paolo Manganelli, The Modernization of European Insolvency Law: An Ongoing Process, *Journal of Business and Technology*, Vol. 11 (2016), 152–154.

7 Council Regulation 1346/2000 of 29 May 2000 on Insolvency Proceedings 2000 O.J. (L 160), 1, Article 26.

8 Nora Wouters, Alla Raykin, Corporate Group Cross-Border Insolvency Between the United States and European Union: Legal & Economic Developments, *Emory Bankruptcy Developments Journal*, Vol. 29 (2013), 394–396.

9 Ibid, also see Bob Wessels, *EU Insolvency and Its Impact on European Business*, CESIFO DICE Report, January 2006, at 16, 17.

10 Paolo Manganelli, The Modernization of European Insolvency Law: An Ongoing Process, *Journal of Business & Technology Law*, Vol. 11 (2016), 157.

were accorded jurisdiction only if the debtor possessed an establishment within the territory of an other Member State. These proceedings, referred to as 'secondary proceedings', only related to the assets of the debtor situated in the territory of the Member State where the secondary proceedings commenced, and could only consist of 'winding-up proceedings' (liquidation).[11] In addition to this, the Regulation went some way to addressing the applicable law, determining when a proceeding commenced within a Member State. It further provided for creditors of the insolvent debtor to lodge their claims in either main proceedings or secondary proceedings. It also provided for the right of recognition of insolvency proceedings among Member States.[12]

The framework for regulating insolvency within the EU was initially significantly restricted in its scope of operation. Specifically, the European Commission's Regulation of 2000 established a cross-border insolvency regime within the EU for cases where the debtor has its COMI in an EU Member State.[13] The Regulation did not deal with cross-border insolvency matters that extended beyond an EU Member State to third countries.

In contrast, the UNCITRAL Model took into account a number of international conventions, treaties and regulations. These included: the negotiations leading to the Council Regulation No. 1346/2000 of 29 May 2000[14] on insolvency proceedings; the European Convention on Certain International Aspects of Bankruptcy (1990);[15] the Montevideo Treaties on International Commercial Law (1889 and 1940); the Convention regarding Bankruptcy between Nordic States (1933); and the Convention on Private International Law (Bustamante Code) (1928).[16] The UNCITRAL Model Law also offered EU Member States a complementary regime of considerable practical value to address the many cases of cross-border cooperation that were not covered by the EU Insolvency Regulation.[17]

More than a decade since the enactment of 1346/2020 EU Insolvency Regulation, 'the European Parliament approved the revised European Regulation on insolvency proceedings, Regulation 2015/848'.[18] This Regulation repealed Regulation 1346/2000. Yet, from the outset and central to the operation of 2000 Regulation, was the need to determine the location of the state at the centre of the debtor's main interests [COMI]. This jurisdictional issue was considered by a series

11 Ibid.
12 European Union Council, *Convention on Insolvency* (1995), http://aei.pitt.edu/2840/1/2840.pdf, Article 16, 17 25.
13 Council Regulation (EC) No 1346/2000 of 29 May 2000 on insolvency proceedings O.J. L 160.
14 Ibid.
15 UNCITRAL Model Law on Cross-Border Insolvency with Guide to Enactment and Interpretation (2013), 22.
16 Ibid.
17 Ibid.
18 Regulation (EU) 2015/848 of the European Parliament and of the Council of 20 May 2015 on insolvency proceedings, O.J. L 141.

of EU Courts in often complex but material jurisdictional proceedings. One such case involved the insolvency of Eurofood IFSC Ltd.

On 2 May 2006, the European Court of Justice rendered a landmark decision in *Eurofood IFSC Ltd.*[19] It decided that the presumed location of the COMI can be rebutted based only on factors which were both objective and ascertainable by third parties. On 10 February 2004, an application was lodged before the Tribunale Civile e Penale di Parma (District Court, Parma) (Italy) for a declaration that Eurofood was insolvent. The date of the hearing was fixed for 17 February 2004. On 20 February 2004, the District Court in Parma held that Eurofood's COMI was situated in Italy, and that it had international jurisdiction to determine whether Eurofood was located in a state of insolvency.[20] By 23 March 2004, the High Court decided that, according to Irish law, the insolvency proceedings in respect of Eurofood had been opened in Ireland on the date on which the application was submitted by the Bank of America, namely 27 January 2004. Taking the view that the COMI of Eurofood was in Ireland, it was held that the proceedings opened in Ireland were the main ones.[21] The Court argued:

> The scope of that concept is highlighted by the 13th recital of the Regulation, which states that 'the centre of main interests' should correspond to the place where the debtor conducts the administration of his interests on a regular basis and is therefore ascertainable by third parties.[22]

The court went onto rule:

> Where a debtor is a subsidiary company whose registered office and that of its parent company are situated in two different Member States, the presumption laid down in the second sentence of Article 3(1) of Council Regulation (EC) No 1346/2000 of 29 May 2000 on insolvency proceedings, whereby the centre of main interests of that subsidiary is situated in the Member State where its registered office is situated, can be rebutted only if factors which are both objective and ascertainable by third parties enable it to be established that an actual situation exists which is different from that which location at that registered office is deemed to reflect.[23]

The position adopted in *Eurofood* had been upheld by the European Court of Justice in *Interedil Srl (in liquidation)*.[24] Noting that the *Corte suprema di cassazione*

19 Case C-341/04, *Eurofood IFSC Ltd (Grand Chamber) ECLI:EU:C:2006:281.*
20 Ibid, 22.
21 Ibid.
22 Ibid, 32.
23 Ibid.
24 *Interedil Srl (in liquidation) v. Fallimento Interedil Srl & another [2011] EUECJ C-396/09.*

had adjudicated by means of order on the preliminary issue of jurisdiction, it held that the Italian court had jurisdiction. It maintained that the presumption in the second sentence of Article 3(1) of the Regulation that the COMI corresponded to the place of the registered office, could be rebutted under various circumstances. Evidence in support of Italy as the main centre of interest included: the presence of immovable property in Italy owned by Interedil; the existence of a lease agreement in respect of two hotel complexes and a contract concluded with a banking institution; and the fact that the Bari register of companies had not been notified of the transfer of Interedil's registered office.[25] The European Court of Justice ruled on Article 3(1) of the Regulation that:

> [A] debtor company's main centre of interests must be determined by attaching greater importance to the place of the company's central administration, as may be established by objective factors which are ascertainable by third parties. Where a company's central administration is not in the same place as its registered office, the presence of company assets and the existence of contracts for the financial exploitation of those assets in a Member State other than that in which the registered office is situated cannot be regarded as sufficient factors to rebut the presumption unless a comprehensive assessment of all the relevant factors makes it possible to establish, in a manner that is ascertainable by third parties, that the company's actual centre of management and supervision and of the management of its interests is located in that other Member State.[26]

This decision reinforced the determination reached by the courts in *Eurofood*. However, as a practical matter, courts will consider various options to determine the centre of main interests. These include but are not limited to, the location of debtor's business premises and bank accounts used to pay creditors; the place of work of the debtor's employees; and the choice of law agreed upon in creditor contracts.

Notwithstanding the judicial interpretations of Regulation 1346/2000, culminating before the European Court of Justice, the earlier EU Insolvency Regulation 2015/848 places greater stress on harmonising insolvency law relating to entities in EU states. Regulation 2015 accords a wider scope to rules regulating pre-insolvency and hybrid insolvency proceedings within the EU.[27] Secondly, it provides for new rules in relation to secondary proceedings. Thirdly, it goes some way to addressing the location of the COMI in the EU. Fourthly, it provides that secondary proceedings can be opened in Member State other than where the debtor's COMI was

25 Ibid.
26 Ibid, [59].
27 Paolo Manganelli, The Modernization of European Insolvency Law: An Ongoing Process, *Journal of Business & Technology Law*, Vol. 11 (2016), 162–166.

located, provided that the debtor has an 'establishment' in that jurisdiction. Thus, a central theme underlying Regulation 2015/848 is to limit its territorial scope to the location of the COMI within the territory of a Member State.

In addition, the 2015 Regulation established a new instrument to improve upon access to information for creditors, interested party, and courts.[28] Its purpose was to prevent the opening of parallel insolvency proceedings, leading it to create a central European database that was linked with a national electronically searchable database.[29] Notably, it specified that certain essential information must be published immediately after the commencement of the relevant proceedings, including:

a. date of the opening of insolvency proceedings;
b. relevant court;
c. type of insolvency proceedings;
d. whether the proceedings are main or secondary proceedings;
e. debtor's name, its registered office, and number;
f. name and contact details of the insolvency practitioner appointed in the proceedings; and
g. time limit for lodging claims, or a reference to the criteria for calculating that time limit.[30]

The Regulation also sought to standardise the procedure for filing and lodging claims to promote the idea of group insolvency proceedings; and to prevent forum shopping. However, the only reference to the UNCITRAL Model Law is at Preamble 48 which states:

> [I]nsolvency practitioners and courts should take into account best practices for cooperation in cross-border insolvency cases, as set out in principles and guidelines on communication and cooperation adopted by European and international organisations active in the area of insolvency law, and in particular the relevant guidelines prepared by the UNCITRAL.[31]

Nonetheless, and rather than developing new EU law to overcome the issues surrounding court communication and cooperation in cross-border insolvency proceedings, the EU established two initiatives: The Cross-Border Insolvency Court-to-Court Cooperation Principles (JudgeCo Principles') and the EU Cross-Border Insolvency Court-to-Court Communications Guidelines (JudgeCo Guidelines').[32] The EU JudgeCo Principles strengthen the efficient and effective

28 Ibid.
29 Ibid.
30 Ibid.
31 Ibid.
32 Prof. Dr. Bob Wessels Emeritus Professor International Insolvency Law Leiden University, *EU Cross-Border Insolvency Court-to-Court Cooperation Principles* (2015). Generally, these Principles follow those of the Global Principles, Guidelines and Rules are the product of a report entitled

communication between courts in EU Member States in cross-border insolvency cases. The EU Cross-Border Insolvency Court-to-Court Cooperation Principles promotes international cooperation in insolvency cases.[33] These Cooperation Principles encompass: the non-binding status and objectives; the case management of courts; the equal treatment of creditors; and principles about the judicial decisions itself, its reasoning and proceedings such as on providing a stay or moratorium.[34] Several further Principles relate to the conduct of the proceedings, such as notifications and the authentication of documents. They also address the outcome of judicial cooperation, such as cross-border sales, assistance in a re-organisation, and rules for binding creditors to an international re-organisation plan.[35] The EU JudgeCo Principles have the pervasive aim of overcoming obstacles faced by the courts of EU Member States such as formalistic and detailed national procedural laws, concerns about judicial impartiality, unease with the use of certain legal concepts and terms, and evidently language.

The EU framework for insolvency largely replicates the framework established by the UNCITRAL Principle. However, the EU framework of insolvency procedures, to date, has neglected third countries cooperation with member states. In contrast, third party states, like Australia, have adopted legislation which provides for court-to-court cooperation beyond the EU JudgeCo Principles of cooperation that apply only to member states. In our view, it is time for the EU to expand its current legal framework regulating cross-border insolvency in order to be more fully integrated into the international community, and to provide greater economic stability within both EU and non-EU markets. The EU can accomplish such integration, in part, by expanding its adoption of the UNCITRAL Model Law. However, this proposed expansion is not without obstacles, as are addressed later.

Notable differences between the EU and non-member states have emerged over the nature and application of principles of cooperation and consolidation of insolvency proceedings. For example, in the US, corporate groups can have a single consolidated proceeding; but there is no such mechanism for EU corporate groups. The European Insolvency Regulation (EIR), which dictates how its signees treat intra-EU insolvencies, does not explicitly address corporate groups.[36] While a single, efficient proceeding is possible under the EIR, it is not legally prescribed. The difficulty of achieving a single efficient proceeding involving EU and non-EU insolvency proceedings is exacerbated when a cross-border EU-US firm is required to coordinate insolvency proceedings under the EIR and the US Bankruptcy Code (US Code). These complications are expounded by divergent EU and

---

'Transnational Insolvency: Global Principles for Cooperation in International Insolvency cases' (ALI-III Global Principles Report) presented to the ALI and III in 2012.

33 Ibid.

34 Ibid.

35 Ibid.

36 Nora Wouters, Alla Raykin, Corporate Group Cross-Border Insolvencies Between the United States and European Union: Legal & Economic Developments, *Emory Bankruptcy Development Journal* (2013), 388–391.

non-EU institutional structures, such as judicial structures. For example, unlike the US, the EU has no specific courts that deal with cross-border insolvency.[37] Moreover, the EIR grants its member states far more autonomy to apply local law in insolvency proceedings than the US Code grants its states. With the finalisation of Brexit in December 2020, this divergence poses potential challenges for UK companies with branch offices in mainland Europe.

A particular concern for UK and EU businesses is whether the current legal framework governing insolvency in the UK will diverge from the EU following Brexit. Arguably, this framework is likely to be reversed. Brexit Therefore, the question arises: What are the challenges facing the business community from Brexit and its impact on cross-border insolvency? The next section briefly examines the UK's approach to cross-border insolvency and what, if any, issues relating to the regulation of cross-border insolvency will arise post Brexit.

2.3 United Kingdom

At the time of writing this book the UK was a Member State of the EU, and during the final stages of completing this book it had left the Union. Therefore, this Section will highlight insolvency law pre-and-post its exiting from the Union. First, it will be demonstrated how the UK had fully embraced the EU insolvency laws. Second, and upon vacating membership of the EU, it will be demonstrated how the UK today has adopted an independent pathway and no longer use EU law in cross-border insolvency as its benchmark. Thus, since 1 January 2021, future cross-border insolvency proceedings have been subject to the post Brexit-UK legal regime. What remains unclear, however, is the manner in and extent to which the UK will diverge the EU insolvency law in adopting this new direction. At the time of writing, for example, there is no clear indication how the UK will reframe its insolvency law, if at all. If the UK does not do so, it is also unclear how differently UK courts will construe its insolvency law than they did before Brexit. Complicating this issue is the fact that EU insolvency law embraces the UNCITRAL Model Law, that the Model law is universalist in its focus, and that the UK is likely to favour such universalism to preserve its status as a global financial hub. Reinforcing such UK leanings are the issues addressed next.

Whilst a member of the EU, the UK had embraced key elements of EU Council Insolvency Regulation 2015/848, the UK Cross-Border Insolvency Regulations (2006/1030) and the UNCITRAL Model Law on Cross-Border Insolvency. The UK incorporated the Model Law into its regulatory framework and the implications of its actions upon cross-border UK-EU insolvency proceedings following of Brexit. However, at least until August 2021, the UK has not established a framework outside the UK by which to regulate cross-border insolvency and restructuring.

37 Ibid.

As introduced in the previous Section, the UK's adoption of the Model Law came into effect through the Cross-Border Insolvency Regulations 2006 (UKIR).[38] The UK was one of only a handful of member states that has embraced the Model Law, along with Slovenia, Greece, Poland and Romania at that time.[39] Regulations also gave effect to the EU Council Insolvency Regulation/2015/848 (Recast Regulation) being an update to Regulation 1346/2000.[40] The Recast Regulation sought to ensure the efficient administration of insolvency proceedings involving an individual or business with business activities or financial interests in an EU state, other than the one in which that individual or business was usually based. The Recast Regulation also had direct application within each EU Member State (apart from Denmark that opted-out), without the need for separate state enactments.

Section 1 of the UKIR highlights the importance of the Model Law to the overall regulatory framework governing cross-border insolvency in the UK. The UKIR provides that, in accordance with Article 21, 'relief application' means an application for relief submitted to the UK court by a foreign representative under Article 21(1) or (2) of the Model Law. It also recognises that EU law is followed in any territorial proceedings that fall within Articles 3(2) and 3(4) of the EIR and within the definition of insolvency proceedings in Article 2(a) of the EIR. The UKIR also provides that the definitions adopted in the Model Law have the same meaning when they are used in the Schedule of the UKIR.

Additionally, the UKIR provides that a main proceeding in the UK is subject to Article 3(1) of the EIR and falls within the definition of insolvency proceedings in Article 2(a) of the EIR. Specifically, 'Member State Liquidator' means a person falling within the definition of liquidator in Article 2(b) of the EIR who is appointed in proceedings in a member state other than the UK. A 'modification or termination order means an order by the UK court pursuant to its powers under the Model Law to modify or terminate recognition of a foreign proceeding, to 'stay' and 'suspend' proceedings referred to in Article 20(1), or to any other relief granted under Article 19 or 21 of the Model Law'.[41] The Model Law means the UNCITRAL Model Law as set out in Schedule 1 to the UKIR.

These provisions demonstrate the UKIR's endorsement, application and use of the Model Law. This proposition is reinforced by Section 14 of the Insolvency

38 Cross-Border Insolvency Regulations 2006, SI 2006/1030, United Kingdom. Insolvency Act 2000 c39 s 14(1), provided the overall power for the Regulations to be established. The Insolvency Act 1986 also deals with the issue of cross-border insolvency and allows a court to take action to assist a foreign court in a designated country. See Part 1, in relation to the reference to EC

39 Status: UNCITRAL Model Law on Cross-Border Insolvency (1997), https://uncitral.un.org/en/texts/insolvency/modellaw/cross-border_insolvency/status.

40 Council Regulation 1346/2000 of 29 May 2000 on Insolvency Proceedings 2000 O.J. (L 160), 1, Recast by Regulation (EU) 2015/848 of the European Parliament and of the Council of 20 May 2015 on insolvency proceedings, O.J. L 141.

41 Ibid, Section 1.

Act 2000[42] which allows the Secretary of the relevant government department to provide for regulation under the UNCITRAL Model Law, as extended to England and Wales.[43] However, problems can arise when there is a conflict between the UNCITRAL Model Law and the UKIR, and between the UKIR and the EIR. Where the conflict is between the UKIR and the UNCITRAL Model Law, the Model Law prevails. Where a conflict arises between the UKIR and the EIR, the EIR ordinarily prevails. These rules for resolving conflicts, particularly between the UKIR and EIR become complex when multiple cross-border insolvency issues arise within and outside the EU. These issues can be divided into three areas. First, matters that traverse internal borders within the UK. Second, matters that transcend the UK border, but remain within the EU border (until Brexit). Third, matters that only apply to jurisdictions outside the EU, such as, Australia, India, Singapore and the US. To reinforce this, the EIR prevailed while the UK remained an EU member and the insolvency involved UK parties within the EU. On the other hand, the UNCITRAL Cross-Border Model Law applies in the UK, for instance, when a UK court seeks cooperation with a foreign court outside the EU.

An important consideration for UK legislators is how to respond to these cross-border insolvency issues following Brexit. For example, should they adopt and apply the UNCITRAL Model law to all cross-border insolvency issues, or resolve otherwise? Answering this question raises a further consideration relating to whether courts in England and Wales choose to accept the jurisdiction of the foreign court and, once having done so, whether they will have foregone their jurisdiction to decide that matter.[44] Article 3 of Schedule 1 of the UKIR, implementing the Model Law in the UK, makes it clear that the EIR prevails over the Model Law where a case of a conflict arises.[45] Article 7 of the UKIR, following the text of the UNCITRAL Model Law, provides that nothing in the UKIR limits the power of a court or insolvency office holder from providing additional assistance under other laws of Great Britain. This would include providing assistance under Section 426 of the UK Insolvency Act.[46] Furthermore, Article 8 of the UKIR, also following the Model Law on the approach to interpretation, provides that regard be made to the international origin of the Model Law and the need to promote uniformity in

42 Insolvency Act 2000, Section 14, In this Section – 'foreign proceedings' has the same meaning as I the model law on cross-border insolvency, 'insolvency law' has the same meaning as in Section 426(10)(a) and (b) of the Insolvency Act 1986, 'the model law on cross-border insolvency' means the model law contained in Annex I of the report of the 30th session of UNCITRAL.

43 *Government of India v Taylor* [1955] AC 491, HL. Insolvency Act 1986 Sections 14, 426.

44 Insolvency Act 1986, Section 235, 291, 312, 333, 208, 354, 279(3), 426, *Hughes v Hannover Rückversicherungs AG* [1997] 1 BCLC 497 CA, *Re HIH Insurance Ltd (HL(E))* [2008] 1 WLR.

45 Howard P. Morris, Gabriel Moss, Federico M. Mucciarelli, Christoph G. Paulus, *Cross-Border Insolvencies after Brexit: Views from the United Kingdom and Continental Europe,* Brexit: The International Legal Implications, Paper No. 17 (2018), 4–6.

46 Council Regulation 1346/2000 of 29 May 2000 on Insolvency Proceedings 2000 O.J. (L 160), 1, Recast by Regulation (EU) 2015/848 of the European Parliament and of the Council of 20 May 2015 on insolvency proceedings, O.J. L 141, Section 426.

its application.[47] According to Morris et al, the Model Law should be interpreted in the same way in every state that adopts it. Given that terms of the COMI were borrowed from the draft Convention that became the EIR, the COMI should be interpreted in the same way as the interpretation laid down by the CJEU for the EIR.[48]

In further reconciling foreign proceedings, Article 17 of the UKIR provides that the foreign proceeding 'shall' be recognised, encompassing recognition of a foreign main proceeding located at the COMI, or where an establishment is located in a jurisdiction of secondary proceedings: that is, the establishment is located in a jurisdiction outside of the UK. Accordingly, Article 17 of the UKIR mirrors the system of main and secondary proceedings. The spirit of the English maxim 'justice delayed is justice denied', is also reflected in the UKIR. Article 17(3) requires that the 'application for recognition be decided 'at the earliest possible time'.[49]

Furthermore, Article 20 of the UKIR provides that, upon recognition of a foreign main proceeding, there is to be a stay of secondary proceeding,[50] insofar as these are material to the resolution of the main interests. This is not unlike the stay in winding up proceedings under the UK Insolvency Act 1986.[51] Arising from this issue is whether the courts of England and Wales have the power to lift that stay.[52] The prevailing view in the EU, in treaties and conventions varying from trade and insolvency to family law, is that judgements in enforcing states must be consistent with decisions reached in the state in which the judgement was made. In the case of *Hoffmann v. Krieg*[53] the Court reasoned that courts of state parties to the EC Convention on Jurisdiction and the Enforcement of Judgements in Civil and Commercial Matters, Brussels 1968 (Full Faith and Credit Convention) must 'seek . . . to facilitate as far as possible the free movement of judgments, and should be interpreted in this spirit'.[54] Recognition and enforcement must therefore 'have the result of conferring on judgments the authority and effectiveness accorded to them in the State in which they were given'.[55] In effect, the Court reasoned that

47 Howard P. Morris, Gabriel Moss, Federico M. Mucciarelli, Christoph G. Paulus, *Cross-Border Insolvencies after Brexit: Views from the United Kingdom and Continental Europe*, Brexit: The International Legal Implications | Paper No. 17 (2018), 4–6.

48 Ibid.

49 Ibid.

50 Council Regulation 1346/2000 of 29 May 2000 on Insolvency Proceedings 2000 O.J. (L 160), 1, Recast by Regulation (EU) 2015/848 of the European Parliament and of the Council of 20 May 2015 on insolvency proceedings, O.J. L 141.

51 Insolvency Act 1986.

52 Ibid.

53 C-145/86, *Hoffmann v Krieg* [1988] ECR I-00645.

54 Ibid, paragraph 10, *Qenard Report on the Convention on Jurisdiction and the Enforcement of Judgments in Civil and Commercial Matters*, Official Journal 1979, C 59, 42–43.

55 Ibid.

decisions reached in the state in which the judgement was made are enforceable in other signatory states:

> A foreign judgment which has been recognized by virtue of Article 26 of the Convention must in principle have the same effects in the State in which enforcement is sought as it does in the State in which the judgment was given; (2) A foreign judgment whose enforcement has been ordered in a Contracting State pursuant to Article 31 of the Convention and which remains enforceable in the State in which it was given must not continue to be enforced in the State where enforcement is sought when, under the law of the latter State, it ceases to be enforceable for reasons which lie outside the scope of the Convention.[56]

The Court directed further that:

> Article 36 of the Convention must be interpreted as meaning that a party who has not appealed against the enforcement order referred to in that provision is thereafter precluded, at the stage of the execution of the judgment, from relying on a valid ground which he could have pleaded in such an appeal against the enforcement order, and that that rule must be applied of their own motion by the courts of the State in which enforcement is sought. However, that rule does not apply when it has the result of obliging the national court to make the effects of a national judgment which lies outside the scope of the Convention conditional on its recognition in the State in which the foreign judgment whose enforcement is at issue was given.[57]

As a result, recognition of a judgement is somewhat restricted to where the law of one country gives direct effect to the law in another country.[58] In reinforcing this, the EIR establishes the mandatory rules related to jurisdiction, according to the opening of the main and secondary proceedings between EU member states, and in compliance with mandatory choice of law rules and mandatory recognition and enforcement of insolvency proceedings. Viewed this way, these mandatory rules apply where the COMI of the debtor is located there or in another member state. Once the main proceeding is opened in the debtor's 'home country',' all other countries where the debtor has assets are subject to the laws of the main proceeding country.[59] Therefore, EU member states, including the UK at the time of writing, must recognise that the main proceedings, and the local law in the country of those main proceedings, dictate the liquidator's powers.

56 Ibid, 671.
57 Ibid.
58 Ibid.
59 Samuel Bufford, International Insolvency Case Venue in the European Union: The Parmalat and Daisytek Controversies, *Columbia Journal of European Law*, Vol. 12 (2006), 394.

However, challenges have arisen in recognising and enforcing cross-border insolvency judgements and over whether that enforcement can be undertaken in the UK under domestic private international law rules. In *Rubin v. Eurofinance,*[60] the UK Supreme Court sought to resolve whether enforcement may be affected through the international assistance provisions of the UNCITRAL Model Law, implemented by the Cross-Border Insolvency Regulations 2006 (SI 2006/1030) that are generally applicable. Alternatively, it considered whether such enforcement was determined by the assistance provisions in Section 426 of the Insolvency Act 1986, which applies to a limited number of countries, including Australia. Importantly, the Court reinforced the current legal framework and how cross-border issues are to be construed as follows:

> Apart from the EIR, none of these instruments deals expressly with the enforcement of judgments in insolvency proceedings. First, section 426 of the Insolvency Act 1986 provides a statutory power to assist corporate as well as personal insolvency proceedings in countries specified in the Act or designated for that purpose by the Secretary of State. All the countries to which it currently applies are common law countries or countries sharing a common legal tradition with England. Second, the EC Insolvency Regulation applies to insolvency proceedings in respect of debtors with their centres of main interests within the European Union (excluding Denmark). Third, the CBIR implements the Model Law. The CBIR supplements the common law, but do not supersede it. Article 7 of the Model Law provides: 'Nothing in this Law limits the power of a court or British insolvency officeholder to provide additional assistance to a foreign representative under other laws of Great Britain.[61]

In reconciling the court's approach to the application of the common law and co-operating with a foreign jurisdiction, the Supreme Court argued:

> [A]t common law the court has power to recognise and grant assistance to foreign insolvency proceedings. The common law principle is that assistance may be given to foreign officeholders in insolvencies with an international element. The underlying principle has been stated in different ways: 'recognition . . . carries with it the active assistance of the court': In *re African Farms Ltd* [1906] TS 373, 377; 'This court . . . will do its utmost to co-operate with the United States Bankruptcy Court and avoid any action which might disturb the orderly administration of [the company] in Texas under ch 11': *Banque Indosuez SA v. Ferromet Resources Inc* [1993] BCLC 112, 117.[62]

60 [2012] UKSC 46.
61 Ibid, 24–25.
62 Ibid, 29.

The Court went further by referring to *Credit Suisse Fides Trust v. Cuoghi*,[63] whereby Millett LJ stated:

> In other areas of law, such as cross-border insolvency, commercial necessity has encouraged national courts to provide assistance to each other without waiting for such co-operation to be sanctioned by international convention . . . It is becoming widely accepted that comity between the courts of different countries requires mutual respect for the territorial integrity of each other's jurisdiction, but that this should not inhibit a court in one jurisdiction from rendering whatever assistance it properly can to a court in another in respect of assets located or persons resident within the territory of the former.[64]

This case demonstrates that the current legal framework for cross-border cooperation in insolvency proceedings is well grounded in EU and UK judicial practice. Importantly, the framework provides a balance between cross-border insolvency cooperation and the expeditious resolution of disputes based on commercial necessity. It promotes mutual respect in regional and international insolvency proceedings and offsets the fragmentation of cross-border insolvency proceedings in a destabilised global economic order.

More recently in 2017, High Court of England and Wales was required to apply the UK Cross-Border Insolvency Regulations (2006) in *Re International Bank of Azerbaijan*.[65] This involved an application by a foreign representative of the indebted OJSC International Bank of Azerbaijan, for an order recognising the restructuring procedure of the Azerbaijan bank in a foreign main proceedings under Article 17, Schedule 1 to the Regulations 2006.[66] Secondary proceedings were brought in the UK because a number of the bank's transactions were governed by English law and contain English jurisdiction and arbitration clauses. The Court of Justice maintained that:

> Article 17 of schedule 1 to the Regulations, pursuant to which this application is brought, requires the court to recognise the foreign insolvency proceedings if certain criteria are satisfied. First, the debtor must be subject to a foreign proceeding, as defined by Article 2 of schedule 1 to the Regulations. Second, the applicant for recognition should be a foreign representative, as also defined by Article 2 of schedule 1, and, third, the application must satisfy a number of evidential requirements in Article 15 of schedule 1. Then, recognition follows, subject only to an exception under Article 6 of the Regulations where it would be manifestly inappropriate in relation to the public

63 [1998] QB 818, 827.
64 Ibid, 30.
65 *Re International Bank of Azerbaijan Case* No: CR-2017–003973 [2017] EWHC 2075.
66 Ibid, 1–5.

> policy of Great Britain or any part of it for the court to grant recognition. I should say that there is nothing in the evidence to which Mr Perkins has drawn my attention pursuant to the obligation of full and frank disclosure to which such applications as this are clearly subject, which would be a candidate for any such public policy exception in this case.[67]

Therefore, and prior to Brexit, the UK framework for insolvency effectively provided for four ways in which to manage foreign insolvency proceedings. As stated in *Moris etal*,[68] these four distinct processes include: (i) the EIR; (ii) Section 426 of the Insolvency Act 1986 applying to Commonwealth countries, Hong Kong and Ireland; (iii) the UNCITRAL Model Law within the UK Cross-Border Insolvency Regulations 2006; and (iv) the common law of England and Wales.

Nonetheless, UK courts have reaffirmed the importance of the *Gibbs* Rule of 1890 even though this Rule diverges from the Model Law and Regulation 2006. The Rule in *Antony Gibbs* provided that liquidation of the debtor company, engaged in copper exchanges in the UK, was subject to English Law because its contracts with the creditors in France were subject to the rules and regulations of the *London Metal Exchange in Gunel.*[69] The Court of Appeals affirmed that: 'it is common ground that this court is bound, as was the judge, by a rule of English private international law which is often referred to as "the *Gibbs* rule" or "the rule in *Antony Gibbs*"'.[70] However, and while embraced, the *Gibbs* Rule has been criticised as an outdated relic from an era when international cooperation in insolvency matters was in its infancy, and where a parochial outlook tended to prevail.[71] The key criticism is that the *Gibbs* Rule is increasingly anachronistic in a world in which the principle of modified universalism has inspired cross-border cooperation in insolvency matters, including the UNCITRAL Model Law. In addition,

67 Ibid, 9.

68 Howard P. Morris, Gabriel Moss, Federico M. Mucciarelli, Christoph G. Paulus, *Cross-Border Insolvencies after Brexit: Views from the United Kingdom and Continental Europe,* Brexit: The International Legal Implications | Paper No. 17 (2018), 2.

69 *Gunel Bakhshiyeva (Azerbaijan) and Sberbank of Russia Neutral Citation Number:* [2018] EWCA Civ 2802.

70 Ibid, [23] ('The rule takes its name from the decision of this court (Lord Esher MR, sitting with Lindley and Lopes LJJ) in *Antony Gibbs & Sons v. La Société Industrielle et Commerciale des Métaux (1890) LR 25 QBD 399.* The defendant was a French company which entered into contracts with the plaintiffs, who were merchants carrying on business in London, for the purchase of consignments of copper, to be delivered and paid for in England. The contracts were subject to the rules and regulations of the London Metal Exchange. After the contracts were made, but before the due dates for delivery of much of the copper, the defendant went into liquidation in France, and refused to accept delivery of the copper. In its defence to an action brought by the plaintiffs for non-acceptance of the goods, the defendant argued that the French liquidation operated as a discharge from liability on the contracts under French law. This argument was rejected by the trial judge, who gave judgment for the plaintiffs for the loss sustained on resale in respect of all the copper, including that of which delivery was not due until after the liquidation.

71 Ibid, 29.

common law courts have recognised the UNCITRAL as part of the common law.[72] In taking account of these criticism, Court in *Gunel Bakshiyeva* argued against the Gibbs Rule being applied to circumvent the requirements of the Model Law and the Regulations. However, it concluded that there is nothing in Article 21 of the Model Law to maintain that the procedural power to grant a stay could properly be used to circumvent the *Gibbs* rule. Thus, and while the Court criticised the Gibbs rule, it did however apply it. Accordingly, it concluded that it:

> would be wrong in principle to use the powers contained in Article 21(1)(a) and (b), or any other provisions of the Model Law as incorporated in the UK Insolvency Regulations, to circumvent the English law rights of the English creditors under the *Gibbs* Rule.[73]

Therefore, and based on this recent decision, a court in the UK is still willing to apply the *Gibbs* rule, in order to interpret and apply both the Model Law and the UKIR. Whether this will change post Brexit is open to speculation.

The EIR arguably favours a universalist approach. Not only does it permit the opening of secondary proceeding in addition to the main proceeding, it protects creditors' property rights and expectations in secondary proceedings on grounds that those proceedings are sometimes necessary to protect those creditor rights.[74] This raises an important question over how the UK will respond to this universalist approach post-Brexit. The lessons learnt from Brexit will provide an overview of the issues that are likely to arise following it.

2.3.1 Brexit

A Deal Brexit was reached on 31 December 2020. However, it is worthwhile to briefly understand the debate that arose from a No Deal Brexit and a post-Brexit period. That is, it was initially thought that under a No Deal Brexit there would be a reduction in the number of ways in which cross-border insolvency can proceed. This proposition was based on the prospect of reducing the current four processes to three due to the inapplicability of the EIR post-Brexit. This would raise immediate issues about the application of cross-border insolvency regulations to UK companies with branches and offices in both the EU and the UK.

A No Deal Brexit would have posed significant challenges for entities operating within the UK and the EU, rendering the future regulation of cross-border

72 Ibid.

73 Ibid, 95.

74 Nora Wouters, Alla Raykin, Corporate Group Cross-Border Insolvencies Between the United States and European Union: Legal & Economic Developments, *Emory Bankruptcy Development Journal* (2013), 393.

insolvency proceedings uncertain.[75] The UK would have ceased to enjoy the benefits of the Recast EIR, including automatic recognition of UK insolvency proceedings and insolvency practitioners' powers across the EU, irrespective of whether the Recast EIR was incorporated into UK law through the Withdrawal Act.[76] It would also have wound the clock back many years whereby legal challenges to the regulatory framework would revert to fragmentation and threaten harmonisation. The result of a no-deal Brexit, in the absence of any alternative overarching instrument, is that recognition of UK initiated insolvency proceedings would have been subject to the private international law of individual Member States.[77] In addition, those proceedings would have been subject to more local law restrictions, and in some cases, even protections, than was the case before Brexit. A no-agreement post-Brexit withdrawal would also likely have impeded the rescue from insolvency of UK companies with branches and offices in both the EU and UK. It would also have led creditors to sustain considerable financial loss, particularly relating to the returns available to them.[78] The dangers of a no-deal Brexit appear to have been well understood, such as in written responses in the House of Commons on 5 April 2018, in response to the Secretary of State for Business, Energy and Industrial Strategy. The postulation was that the UK and EU would likely need to negotiate specifically to reach a cooperation agreement directed at resolving cross-border insolvency disputes. The UK House of Commons noted:

> The exact future relationship between the EU and UK on civil judicial cooperation, including the recognition of insolvency and restructuring procedures, judgments and Insolvency Practitioner qualifications is subject to negotiations with our EU partners. It is in the interests of the UK and the EU that there continues to be an effective, and fit for purpose, framework for resolving cross-border legal disputes. The Government has made clear that an effective framework of civil judicial cooperation is an important part of the deep and special partnership we want to establish with the EU.[79]

However, even with this understanding and the advent of Brexit in September 2020, the UK Government continued to take a hard line in developing new legislation to override aspects of the Brexit withdrawal agreement. The UK's

75 Chris Umfreville, Paul Omar, Heike Lücke, Irene Lynch Fannon, Michael Veder, Laura Carballo Piñeiro, Recognition of UK Insolvency Proceedings Post-Brexit: The Impact of a 'No Deal' Scenario, *International Insolvency Review*, Vol. 27 (2018), 442–444.

76 Ibid, 442.

77 Ibid, 443.

78 Ibid, 444.

79 Ibid, 441. House of Commons Deb 5 April 2018 C134602 W (Answer provided by Andrew Griffiths MP, Parliamentary Under Secretary, Department for Business, Energy and Industrial Strategy).

proposed legislation was even more problematic in being potentially contrary to international law,[80] in departing from the original exit agreement and placing in jeopardy state aid and the Northern Ireland customs framework. A particularly challenging case was therefore likely to have arisen when proceedings under the COMI was within an EU member state, when that EU state had not implemented the Model Law and when the UK was no longer subject the EIR. A further complexity was whether a foreign court would have the discretion to permit foreign 'officeholders to carry out any act in an EU member state. However, the court would still have retained the discretion to supervise the office holder in the exercise of his functions and may have decided not to accord him automatic recognition of all his acts. The challenge was whether the judgement would automatically be recognised and applied.[81]

The further concern extended beyond the UK post-Brexit. It related to, and still relates to the need to determine the applicability of the COMI under the Brexit arrangements in which a member state had not implemented the Model Law. Even though there might not have been a bilateral agreement between the UK and that EU member state, it may not be adequately addressed in cross-border insolvency.[82] Therefore, the law of insolvency in the member state might need to be relied upon to govern the COMI, such as when that COMI is within the territory of the UK. As a result, there are a number of issues for states exiting the EU to resolve under their insolvency laws to manage insolvency with EU member states, among others, following the implementation of an exit agreement, such as Brexit. Therefore, these matters would need to be considered by any member state wanting to leave the EU in the future, beyond the UK.

Importantly and central to the UK's pathway out of the EU was the establishment of the European Union (Withdrawal Agreement) Act 2020 (EUA).[83] The EUA, gave legal effect to the overall UK-EU Withdrawal Agreement (WA) that had been established on 17 October 2019.[84] Both the WA and EUA enable the EIR to continue to apply to insolvency matters, provided the proceeding was implemented before 31 December 2020. In facilitating this process pursuant to Article 50 Treaty on the European Union, in conjunction with Article 106a of

80 Baker McKenzie, UK Plan to Undermine Withdrawal Treaty Puts Brexit Talks at Risk, *Daily Briefing* (7 September 2020), https://www.lexology.com/library/detail.aspx?g=78d50689-7970-4ed7-a973-75069235469d, The agreement is an international treaty, the EU could bring proceedings against the UK, under the dispute resolution mechanism of the agreement,' said Catherine Barnard, a European law professor at Cambridge University.

81 Chris Umfreville, Paul Omar, Heike Lücke, Irene Lynch Fannon, Michael Veder, Laura Carballo Piñeiro, Recognition of UK Insolvency Proceedings Post-Brexit: The Impact of a 'No Deal' Scenario, *International Insolvency Review,* Vol. 27 (2018), 431.

82 Ibid.

83 European Union (Withdrawal Agreement) Act 2020, https://www.legislation.gov.uk/ukpga/2020/1/contents/enacted.

84 United Kingdom Government Brexit, New Withdrawal Agreement and Political Declaration, https://www.gov.uk/government/publications/new-withdrawal-agreement-and-political-declaration.

the Euratom Treaty, and subject to the arrangements laid down in this Agreement, the law of the Union and of Euratom in its entirety ceases to apply to the United Kingdom from the date of entry into force of this Agreement.[85]

The legal effect of the process in transitioning from a Member State to a non-member of the Union is fundamentally important to the overall stability of financial and investment markets. Arguably, the EU has prided itself on the single market concept for some decades. This has provided a level of stability across the EU economy. However, with increasing fractious relationships amongst EU members, Brexit may not be the last exit by a Member State. Therefore, any withdrawal agreement has to provide a framework to minimise any disruption and provide as much legal certainty as possible. Nonetheless, and while the EIR has, to date, remained part of UK insolvency law, it has little impact or influence beyond 1 January 2021. The resulting effect is that insolvency in the UK, and even though the Model Law has been adopted into national law, will revert back to the common law, rather than rely on the more specific codified provisions in the EIR.

On this backdrop, Brexit what is also uncertain is whether the UK will formulate laws to regulate trans-border insolvency that are distinct from both the EIR and the UNCITRAL Model Law on Cross-Border Insolvency; or whether they will adapt these laws selectively to suit domestic needs. As the UK has already incorporated the Model Law into its national framework, it is in our view that it will increasingly apply the universalist approach attributed to the Model law, to extend the global reach of its already substantial financial markets. What is also likely is that the UK will diverge from the EIR, given the focus of its insolvency law on protecting UK creditors compared to some EU states like Italy that focus more on protecting debtors. Uncertain, too, is whether the UK would subscribe to an international convention on trans-border insolvency. However, that uncertainty applies equally to other states faced with that choice.

2.4 Australia

Australia adopted the UNCITRAL Model Law on Cross-Border Insolvency as an annex to Schedule 1 of its Cross-Border Insolvency Act 2008 (Cth) (CBI Act).[86] Yet, until recently, Australia's laws in relation to cross-border insolvency derived from the bankruptcy laws of the United Kingdom. More recently, Australia has implemented much, if not all, of the Model Law. Sandeep Gopalan and Michael Guihot maintain that, by adopting the Model Law, Australia has become a

85 Agreement on the withdrawal of the United Kingdom of Great Britain and Northern Ireland from the European Union and the European Atomic Energy Community, 19 October 2019, Presented to Parliament pursuant to Section 1 of the European Union (Withdrawal) Act (No. 2) 2019 and Section 13 of the European Union (Withdrawal) Act 2018, 3.

86 Cross-Border Insolvency Act 2008, Act No. 33. This section draws upon the work of Robert Walters, Cross Border Insolvency and the 2022 Australia-India Comprehensive Economic Cooperation Agreement? Business Law Review, WoltersKluwer, forthcoming 2022.

significant country in the field of cross-border insolvency, along with some of the world's most economically powerful nations.[87] However, they attribute an inherent flaw in the adoption of the Model Law in that, the longer it takes for the Model Law to be adopted globally, the greater the probability that its adoption will lead to its inconsistent application and interpretation. This concern applies to Australia as to other countries. Australia's adoption of the UNCITRAL Model Law in its ACBI Act reflects its intention to facilitate cross-border trade and investment.[88] However, states that adopt the Model Law at different times are likely to diverge over its terms and their application, and notably in how their courts apply that law to promote trade and investment. That is one reason to promote an international convention on trans-border insolvency in which state signatories adopt the convention as a whole, subject to expressly qualified exceptions.

Australia's CBI Act relates entirely to international and not domestic insolvency. It relies on UNCITRAL Model Law Cross-Border,[89] and it applies it to both corporate and personal insolvency. The Act consists of only 23 sections and is considerably shorter than most legislative Acts regulating the various elements of insolvency. However, it does diverge from the UNCITRAL Model Law in some respects. Article 21 of the Model Law allows a foreign representative to conduct examinations. In contrast, Sections 596A–596F of Australia's Corporations Act 2001 (Cth) and the Supreme Court[90] and Federal Court Corporations Rules[91] are incorporated into the CBI Act, which prescribe the procedures for the conduct of an examination. These procedures are not provided for in the Model Law. Australia's CBI Act also provides the requirements for interpreting the Model Law. Section 6 incorporates the Model Law. Section 8 extends the scope of Section 6, by providing that the Model Law has force in Australia as if it was incorporated into Australia's *Bankruptcy Act 1966*; Chapter 5 (other than Parts 5.2 and 5.4A), Section 601CL, and Schedule 2 of the *Corporations Act 2001*. However, not all entities associated with insolvency proceedings are included as being subject to the Act. Section 9, notably, excludes specifically authorised deposit-taking institutions[92] in accordance with the *Banking Act 1959* and the *Life Insurance Act 1995*.[93]

87 Sandeep Gopalan, Michael Guihot, Recognition and Enforcement in Cross-Border Insolvency Law: A Proposal for Judicial Gap-Filling, *Vanderbilt Journal of Transnational Law*, Vol. 48 (2015), 1272–1273.

88 Gerard McCormack, Anil Hargovan, Australia and the International Insolvency Paradigm, *Sydney Law Review*, Vol. 37, No. 3 (2015), 389.

89 Cross-Border Insolvency Act 2008, Act No. 33, defines the Model Law to mean the Model Law on Cross-Border Insolvency of the United Nations Commission on International Trade Law, set out in the Annex to United Nations General Assembly Resolution A/RES/52/158 (1997).

90 Commonwealth – *Federal Court (Corporations) Rules 20,* Australian Capital Territory – *Court Procedures Rules 20,* New South Wales – *Supreme Court (Corporations) Rules 1999*, Northern Territory – *Corporations Law Rules*, Queensland – *Uniform Civil Procedure Rules 1999,* South Australia – *Corporations Rules 2003* and *Corporations Supplementary Rules 2015*, – *Supreme Court (Corporations) Rules 2008*, Victoria – *Supreme Court (Corporations) Rules 2013*, Western Australia – *Supreme Court (Corporations) (WA) Rules 2004*.

91 Federal Court of Australia, https://www.fedcourt.gov.au/forms-and-fees/forms/corporations-rules.

92 *Cross-Border Insolvency Regulations 2008*, Select Legislative Instrument 2008 No. 12

93 *Banking Act 1959, Life Insurance Act 1995*.

For the UNCITRAL Model Law to be fully applied in Australia, however, is for its state and federal courts to determine. Section 10 of the CBI Act addresses this by ensuring that both the Federal Court of Australia and the Supreme Courts of the states and territories can perform functions identified in the Model Law that relate to the recognition of foreign proceedings and cooperation with foreign courts. Importantly, the Act provides for the functions of key participants in cross-border insolvency matters. Sections 11, 12 and 13 apply to the 'functions of trustees, foreign creditors and the recognition of foreign proceedings. More broadly, they provide that the Model Law has the force of law in Australia in relation to the function of trustees in bankruptcy proceedings,[94] and registered liquidators in corporate insolvencies'.[95] Section 12 allows access of foreign creditors to Australian insolvency proceedings. It specifies that the claims of foreign creditors, other than concerning tax and social security obligations, must not be ranked lower than the unsecured claims of other creditors solely because the creditor concerned is a foreign creditor. In addition, Section 14 largely replicates the scope of Article 18 of the Model law.[96] It expands its scope to ensure that the relevant national laws, such as the *Bankruptcy Act 1966* and *Corporations Act 2001*, encompass a foreign representative informing the Court promptly of any other foreign proceeding.

A key feature is how Section 16 of the CBI Act replicates Section 2 of Article 20 of the UNCITRAL Model Law, in determining how it will affect the recognition of a foreign main proceeding. Likewise, Sections 17 and 18 implement Paragraph 1 of Article 23 and Subparagraph (f) of Article 27 of the Model Law in relation to avoiding actions that are detrimental to creditors and applicable forms of cooperation. While Section 19 specifies that Article 7 of the Model Law is applicable nationally, it also extends the type of additional or appropriate relief to each state and territory in Australia. That said, the Model Law is operational across Australia's states and territories, such as in Victoria and New South Wales.

Most noteworthy is how Australian judicial decisions illustrate these developments in cross-border insolvency law. In *Chow Cho Poon,*[97] an entity under Singapore law, appointed a liquidator under compulsory liquidation, using the Australian Bank of WestPac. The liquidator sent Westpac a copy of the Singapore Court's order of 28 February 2008 and asked Westpac to 'render the accounts operative' according to the joint signatures of any of two of several persons whose names and specimen signatures were set out in the liquidator's covering letter. In response, Westpac stated that it was not in a position to render the accounts operational as the appointment of a liquidator must be recognised by courts within Australia.[98] The Supreme Court of New South Wales noted the national laws empowered an Australian court to request that a court of an external Territory, or of a country other than Australia which has jurisdiction in external administration matters, act

94 *Bankruptcy Act 1966,* subsection 5(1).
95 *Corporations Act 2001,* Section 9.
96 *Cross-Border Insolvency Act 2008*, Act No. 33, Section 14.
97 *Re Chow Cho Poon (Private) Limited* [2011] NSWSC 300 (15 April 2011), 7–9.
98 Ibid.

in aid of, and be auxiliary to, it in an external administration matter.[99] Moreover, the Supreme Court maintained that the Explanatory Memorandum to the Bill, that became the Cross-Border Insolvency Act, made it clear that Section 22 of that Act includes conflicts between Section 581 of the Corporations Act and Article 25 of the Model Law adopted by Australia.[100] The Court referred to the importance of the Model Law and the obligations it places on jurisdictions that adopt it. It stated that:

> The Model Law imposes a mandatory obligation on the court to cooperate with courts or representatives of foreign jurisdictions. The words 'shall cooperate' are used in the relevant part of the Model Law [article 25]. In contrast, section 29 of the Bankruptcy Act imposes a mandatory obligation on the court to assist only the courts of prescribed countries (subsection 29(5) of the Bankruptcy Act states what prescribed countries are) but permits the court to exercise its discretion as to whether it should assist other foreign courts.[101]

However, the Court held that, should there be an inconsistency between the Corporations Act 2001 and the UNCITRAL Model Law as it was adopted in Australia, the Court was required to apply the Model Law. Specifically, it held that Division 9 of Part 5.6 of the Corporations Act 2001, or Part 5.7 of the Corporations Act 2001, were in conflict with the Model law adopted in the Annex to the CBI Act.[102] The case highlighted the importance of national law, in incorporating the relevant Model Law provisions. It further illustrated how Australia, not only embraced the international legal framework, giving it full effect by replicating it in Schedule 1 of the CBI Act. The scope attributed by legislation and the Australia judiciary to the Model Law is comparable to the adoption of the Model Law in other countries, including the UK. What is different is that Australia adopted the Model Law in its earlier inception in 2008. Centrally in issue is whether countries, including but not limited to Australia now, and the UK post-Brexit, are likely to adopt universal rules governing trans-border insolvency. Alternatively, are they more likely to revert to a regional, bilateral or otherwise shared construction such as in construing insolvency such as insolvency legislation and/or the UNCITRAL Model Law. For example, courts within the British Commonwealth that embrace the common law. In contradistinction to such a shared common law approach, states that adopt a civil law approach may accept or reject, whether in whole or part, the common law approach adopted by legislatures and courts in common law Commonwealth jurisdictions. A collateral view arises in assessing common

99 Ibid.
100 Ibid, 29.
101 Ibid, 43.
102 Ibid, [24].

law interpretations of shared laws, such as the UNCITRAL Model Law compared to civil or customary law interpretations.

In the case of the UK, any evolution towards universal rules on trans-border insolvency is likely to be fast-tracked post-Brexit, attributable in part to an inward-looking approach adopted by UK courts in the past and perceived gaps in the Model Law. As the English Court of Appeal contended in 2013 in *Rubin v. Eurofinance SA*,[103] the Model Law was limited in not providing for the recognition of foreign insolvency judgments.[104] However, since that case was decided in 2013, UNCITRAL has done considerable work to remedy this inward-looking approach to the recognition of trans-border insolvency judgements. Most notably is its establishment in 2018 of the UNCITRAL Model Law on the Recognition and Enforcement of Insolvency-Related Judgments.[105] Even though the 2018 Model Law did redress some of these inward-looking issues, its impact upon the domestic implementation of universal rules of insolvency remain largely untested. So too, while Australia incorporated the Model Law on Trans Border Insolvency in 2008, a decade before the establishment of the Model Law on the Enforcement of Insolvency-Related Judgements, the Australian Trans-Border Insolvency Act had already advanced significantly in adopting a universalist approach to trans-border insolvency.

Arguably, Australian courts have sought to fill gaps in trans-border insolvency disputes under the UNCITRAL Model Law on Trans-Border Insolvency, as adopted into Schedule 1 of Australian Act. In *Zetta v. Linkage Access* in 2018,[106] and notably in 2019,[107] the applicant sought an injunction in the 2018 case, and then in 2019, a freezing order in accordance with Article 21 of the Model Law, to prevent the removal of a ship from Australian waters. The Federal Court of Appeal maintained that, as a process under the Model Law, there were no issues related to the freezing order. It added that significant fraud was 'not a particularly powerful reason for refusing relief under the Model Law, and certainly not one which would justify the deployment of the potentially expensive tools of discovery.'[108] Both the 2018 and 2019 cases highlighted how the procedural aspects of the Model Law are likely

103 [2013] 1 AC 236.

104 Ibid. In Rubin, judgment in default was given by a US Bankruptcy Court against a company in Chapter 11 rehabilitation proceedings. The Applicant Receivers were unsuccessful in applying for enforcement of the judgment in England. The judgment would not have been enforceable under English domestic law. Article 21 of the UK Insolvency Act, in referring to 'any appropriate relief' after recognition of foreign main proceedings, did not extend to recognition and enforcement of a foreign court's judgments in circumstances in which domestic law would not otherwise grant recognition.

105 2018 of the UNCITRAL Model Law on the Recognition and Enforcement of Insolvency-Related Judgments, 2019, https://uncitral.un.org/sites/uncitral.un.org/files/media-documents/uncitral/en/ml_recognition_gte_e.pdf.

106 *King (Trustee), in the matter of Zetta Jet Pte Ltd v Linkage Access Limited* [2018] FCA 1979.

107 *King (Trustee), in the matter of Zetta Jet Pte Ltd v Linkage Access Limited (Discovery)* [2019] FCA 1408.

108 Ibid, 25.

to be embraced by Australian courts, and to provide the parties with the procedural tools by which to resolve complex transnational insolvency disputes.

Interestingly, the *Zetta* case has not been finalised, and at the time of writing this book there were outstanding matters on insolvency yet to be finalised by the Court. Yet, the applicant filed an interlocutory application in the Recognition Proceeding which sought urgent injunctive relief under Article 19 of the Model Law, as contained in Schedule of the Cross-Border CBI Act 2008.[109] On the same day, the Court granted an interim injunction under Article 19, restraining Linkage Access from removing the Dragon Pearl from Australian waters until 6 pm on 25 July 2018. It further extended the injunction to 5 pm on 31 July 2018. On 31 July 2018, the Court dismissed the application for the injunction with costs. The Court went onto consider the procedural aspects of Article 23, which provides that a foreign representative has standing to commence a claim. However, it held that Article 23 does not enable a cause of action by which that representative can enforce the claim, if and where, the domestic law does not so permit. This, notably, impacts upon the applicability of 23 of the Model Law to the process of decision-making, here, the enforceability of a claim.

A year later, in the matter of *Zetta,*[110] the Federal Court of Appeal re-examined the orders that was issued to stop the movement of a ship (the Dragon Pearl) from leaving an Australian port. The Court highlighted how Mr King had sought freezing orders under Art 21 of the UNCITRAL Model Law to prevent that removal. It held that the original trial judge was correct in declining to grant the injunction sought by Mr King on *res judicata* but referred the case back to the trial court to consider whether the sale of vessel was a voidable transaction. While the result of that determination was not yet known at the time of writing, it is evident that both the 2018 and 2019 *Zetta* cases highlighted how the courts embraced the procedural aspects of the Model Law and endorsed its use by parties in resolving complex transnational insolvency disputes.

Noteworthy, whilst these proceedings were progressing through the Australian courts, Mr King filed an action in the United States Bankruptcy Court for the Central District of California, Los Angeles Division. The claim sought relief from a number of defendants, including Linkage, relating, inter alia, to orders to unwind the allegedly fraudulent conveyance of the *Dragon Pearl* to a Mr Cassidy through the alleged use of the misappropriated funds of Zetta Jet. On 23 January 2019, Mr King obtained default orders against Linkage in that advisory proceeding.[111] The Court maintained that, as the Proceedings were guided by the Model Law, no issues related to the freezing order had arisen. It further noted that a breach by Mr King of the implied undertaking in doing his level best 'to reverse

109 That application was made under Article 19 of the Australian Trans Border Act because at that time the US Insolvency Proceeding had not been recognised.

110 *King (Trustee), in the matter of Zetta Jet Pte Ltd v. Linkage Access Limited (Discovery)* [2019] FCA 1408.

111 Ibid, 3.

the consequences of what appears to be a significant fraud does not strike me as a particularly powerful reason for refusing relief under the Model Law, and certainly not one which would justify the deployment of the potentially expensive tools of discovery'.[112] This determination in the US case further affirms the procedural grounds to grant, or refuse to grant, relief under the Model Law.

Further common law cases affirm the authority of a court to impose a default judgement on a party who fails to appear or otherwise submit to the jurisdiction of a court in foreign insolvency proceedings. The Court in *Zetta* referred to the enforcement by a UK court of the judgment of the US Federal Bankruptcy Court for the Southern District of New York (the US Bankruptcy Court) for approximately USD 10 million rendered in default of appearance under State and Federal law in respect of fraudulent conveyances and transfers.[113] In the UK Supreme Court case of *New Cap*, a default judgment of the New South Wales Supreme Court, Equity Division, was issued for approximately USD 8 million in respect of unfair preferences under Australian law was enforced under the UK Foreign Judgments (Reciprocal Enforcement) Act 1933 ('the 1933 Act'), and, alternatively, pursuant to powers under Section 426 of the UK Insolvency Act 1986.[114] In each of the appeals, the Courts accepted or found that the party against whom orders were made or judgements were entered were neither present (nor, for the purposes of the 1933 Act, 'resident') in the foreign country, nor submitted to its jurisdiction (which are the relevant conditions for enforceability at common law and under the 1933 Act); but that those conditions did not apply to judgments or orders in foreign insolvency proceedings.[115] The Court, in referring to Dicey[116] highlighted the position that Rule 43 which states: a court of a foreign country outside the UK has jurisdiction to give a judgment that is capable of enforcement in the UK. In so doing, and following Dicey, the Court maintained that Rule 43 applies in four key areas:

> 1), where, the person against whom the judgment was given was, at the time the proceedings were instituted, present in the foreign country. 2), if the person against whom the judgment was given was claimant, or counterclaimed, in the proceedings in the foreign court. 3), where, the person against whom the judgment was given submitted to the jurisdiction of that court by voluntarily appearing in the proceedings. 4) Furthermore, if the person against whom the judgment was given had before the commencement of

112 Ibid, 25.

113 Ibid, 2.

114 *Rubin SA & Ors* and (2) *New Cap Reinsurance Corp Ltd & Anor v. Grant and others*, [2012] UKSC 46 (joinder of actions in *Rubin* and *New Cap*)

115 Ibid.

116 Ibid, Dicey, Morris & Collins, *Conflict of Laws* (14th ed., 2006); Dicey, Morris and Collins, *Conflict of Laws*, 15th ed., 2012, 14R-054.

> the proceedings agreed, in respect of the subject matter of the proceedings, to submit to the jurisdiction of that court or of the courts of that country.[117]

In summary, the Australian Cross-Border Insolvency Act and judicial decisions have applied the Model Law on Trans-Border Insolvency expansively. They have progressed significantly in closing the gaps in establishing and applying universal procedural rules to govern trans-border insolvency. Nonetheless, compared to the UK and the EU, Australia's approach to cross-border Insolvency is relatively straightforward. Its trans-border insolvency Act provides a strong basis for how other states can establish similar insolvency laws that embody the Model Law. Arguably, the UK post-Brexit could consider a similar model to that of Australia, or Singapore as will be discussed later. On the other hand, the diversity in national insolvency laws evidences the extent to which each state designs its insolvency laws to suit its unique circumstances and policy preferences.

In a further shift towards universalism, the 2018 UNCITRAL Model Law on the Enforcement of Insolvency-Related Judgements is likely to facilitate greater uniformity in resolving divergence among states and courts in resolving trans-border insolvency claims; but it is too early to so decide with confidence.

2.4.1 The Gibbs Rule

Evidence that the Australian law of trans-border insolvency has progressed beyond the Insolvency Regulation in the UK is readily illustrated by the divergence of Australian law from the 1890 *Gibbs* case in English law.[118] The Rule, applicable in English Law, denies recognition to a foreign insolvency restructuring, such as a scheme of arrangement, to the extent that it seeks to discharge debts that arose pursuant to a contract governed by English law. The Rule in *Gibbs* case is controversial and has been subject to both judicial and academic criticism, but English courts have not abandoned it. While it is persistently affirmed in the UK, recent Australian cases rejected it. In 2020, the New South Wales Supreme Court in *Wollongong Coal Limited and Jindal Steel & Coal Australia Ltd*[119] considered whether the Rule should be applied in Australia.[120] It maintained:

> Nor is it necessary to consider whether the rule in Gibbs case, assuming it applies in Australia, gives rise to a need for dual schemes of arrangement for Australian scheme companies whose debt obligations are governed by foreign law, accepting that an Australian court has power to approve a

117 Ibid.
118 *Antony Gibbs & Sons v La Société Industrielle et Commerciale des Métaux* (1890) LR 25 QBD 399.
119 [2020] NSWSC 73.
120 Ibid, 62.

> scheme even if the effect will be to modify or discharge obligations under a contract which stipulates that it is to be governed by the law of another forum.[121]

On that basis, it appears that the Gibbs Rule in Australia, as in the US, is all but dead. It is viewed critically as being antiquated, as preserving territorialism rather than enhancing the universalist approach to insolvency. In summary, Australia has structured its insolvency laws to give some protection to the blameless in insolvency matters. This protection extends to both creditors and non-creditors located within or outside Australia. American jurists have maintained, somewhat comparably, that Chapter 11 of the US Bankruptcy Code is designed to protect as many non-creditors as possible.[122] Both Australian and American law apply such protection as a general principle, but not as an absolute rule.

2.5 Singapore

Cross-border insolvency law in Singapore resided in the Companies Act 2006 until 2020. In July 2020, the Insolvency, Restructuring and Dissolution Act (IRDA) was implemented. The IRDA replaces the Bankruptcy Act and the corporate insolvency and restructuring provisions in the Companies Act. Part 11, Section 251 of IRDA refers directly to the UNCITRAL Model Law. Section 252 goes onto to provide that the Model Law (with certain modifications to adapt it for application in Singapore) as set out in the Third Schedule, has the force of law in Singapore. In the interpretation of any provision of the Third Schedule, the following documents are relevant for the purposes of Section 9A(3)(f) of the Interpretation Act (Cap. 1): '(a) any document relating to the Model Law that is issued by, or that forms part of the record on the preparation of the Model Law maintained by, the United Nations Commission on International Trade Law and its working group for the preparation of the Model Law; and (b) the Guide to Enactment of the UNCITRAL Model Law on Cross-Border Insolvency (UN document A/CN.9/442)'.[123]

The Third Schedule in the IRDA is the starting point in understanding the application of the Model Law in Singapore. By replicating most of Article 1 of the Model Law, the IRDA extends its scope of application to where a foreign court or a foreign representative seeks assistance in Singapore in connection with a foreign proceeding. That assistance is sought in proceedings in a foreign State that are

121 Ibid, 63.

122 Sandeep Gopalan, Michael Guihot, Recognition and Enforcement in Cross-Border Insolvency Law: A Proposal for Judicial Gap-Filling, *Vanderbilt Journal of Transnational Law*, Vol. 48 (2015), 1228–1235.

123 Insolvency, Restructuring and Dissolution Act 2020, Third Schedule.

connected to the proceeding under Singapore insolvency law in which both proceedings are taking place concurrently with the same debtor. Such recognition of foreign insolvency proceedings or requests for assistance also arise where creditors or other interested persons in that foreign State have an interest in requesting the commencement of, or participating in, a proceeding under Singapore insolvency law.

However, there are specific obligations whereby the Singapore Court cannot grant any relief, or modify relief already granted, or provide any cooperation or coordination. That denial of the right to grant or modify a grant of relief arises by virtue of any of the provisions in the Singapore IRDA, 'if and to the extent that such relief or modified relief or cooperation or coordination would, in the case of a proceeding under Singapore insolvency law if and to the extent that such relief or modified relief or cooperation or coordination would, in the case of a proceeding under Singapore insolvency law, be prohibited'.[124] The IRDA also enables the relevant minister to limit application of the IRDA by order in the Gazette. Additionally, the IRDA will not apply to a foreign proceeding regarding a debtor who has been insured under the provisions, for example, of the Third Parties (Rights against Insurers) Act or the Motor Vehicles (Third-Party Risks and Compensation) Act). The IRDA does not apply to a relief, stay or suspension under Article 19 or 21. Its application is further limited by Sections 46 and 47 of the Land Titles Act 1993.

In a similar way to that of Australia, Singapore has generally replicated the relevant Articles of the Model Law in the IRDA. Article 3 specifies the international obligations of Singapore that, in the event of any conflict or conflicts with an obligation of Singapore arising from any treaty or agreement to which it is a party with one or more other States, the requirements of the treaty or agreement will prevail. While it is out of scope to examine what, if any, treaties or agreements are impacted by Article 3, that Article by and large priorities that treaty or agreement over the IRDA.

As a result, the importance of the IRDA in regulating cross-border insolvency in Singapore is significant, but also constrained by international laws and conventions to which Singapore is a signatory. On the one side, the IRDA recognises foreign proceedings and more importantly cooperation with foreign courts, creditors and representatives.[125] On the other side, Article 4 of the IRDA limits such duties to

124 Ibid, Section 3. The Court must not grant any relief, or modify any relief already granted, or provide any cooperation or coordination, under or by virtue of any of the provisions of this Law if and to the extent that such relief or modified relief or cooperation or coordination would, in the case of a proceeding under Singapore insolvency law, be prohibited under or by virtue of – (a) this Act; (b) Part VII or Section 61, 62 or 76A of the Banking Act; (c) Section 27(2) or 52(2) of the Deposit Insurance and Policy Owners' Protection Schemes Act; (d) Part IIIAA of the Insurance Act; (e) the International Interests in Aircraft Equipment Act; (f) Part IVA or IVB or Section 178 of the Monetary Authority of Singapore Act; (g) the Payment and Settlement Systems (Finality and Netting) Act; (h) Division 4 of Part III, or Part IIIAA, of the Securities and Futures Act; or (i) any other written law that the Minister may, by order in the Gazette, prescribe.

125 Ibid, Article 4.

determinations by the High Court in Singapore. No such limitation exists within the Model Law or the other jurisdiction examined in this book that has adopted the Model Law. In effect, the IRDA enables office holders responsible for insolvency matters under Singapore to act in a foreign state,[126] including to act on behalf of an entity in a foreign state under Singapore insolvency law. Yet, this authorisation is often achieved effectively only when the foreign state supports such foreign participation in judicial proceedings in Singapore, such as by foreign court releasing documents to Singapore courts and enforcing Singapore judicial decisions.[127] In addition to this restrictive measure on the inclusion of foreign participation, the foreign representative has limited admissibility in Singapore proceedings, other than in relation to the application to proceed itself.[128] This leads to a tension under Singapore law. On the one side, Article 11 of the IRDA provides that a foreign representative can apply to commence a proceeding under Singapore insolvency law. That foreign representative can also, upon recognition of such a foreign proceeding, participate in proceedings involving the debtor under Singapore insolvency law.[129] This position also works in reverse, insofar as Article 13 provides foreign creditors with access to a proceeding under Singapore insolvency law. On the other hand, Article 15, one of the most important provisions related to cross-border insolvency, establishes procedures with which a foreign representative must comply in applying to the Court for recognition of the foreign proceeding.[130]

A further issue relates to the practical steps that are needed for foreign proceedings to be recognised by a Singapore Court. Article 17 of the IRDA[131] provides for such steps to be undertaken, but subject to a number of exemptions and other considerations. Firstly, the recognition of foreign proceedings is subject to Article 6, which provides considerable flexibility to admit or exclude such proceedings based on the broad public policy considerations of Singapore. For the foreign

126 Ibid, Article 5.

127 Ibid. The Court has the power to appoint any other person or persons to act in a foreign State on behalf of a proceeding under Singapore insolvency law, as permitted by the applicable foreign law.

128 Ibid, Article 10.

129 Ibid, Article 12.

130 Ibid, Article 15, Note the procedural steps to achieve this. An application for recognition must be accompanied by (a) a certified copy of the decision commencing the foreign proceeding and appointing the foreign representative; (b) a certificate from the foreign court affirming the existence of the foreign proceeding and of the appointment of the foreign representative; or (c) in the absence of evidence mentioned in sub-paragraphs (a) and (b), any other evidence acceptable to the Court of the existence of the foreign proceeding and of the appointment of the foreign representative. An application for recognition must also be accompanied by a statement identifying all foreign proceedings and proceedings under Singapore insolvency law in respect of the debtor that are known to the foreign representative. The foreign representative must provide the Court with a translation into English of documents supplied in support of the application for recognition.

131 Ibid. Further exceptions and consideration need to be taken into account in relation to (a) it is a foreign proceeding within the meaning of Article 2(h); (b) the person or body applying for recognition is a foreign representative within the meaning of Article 2(i); (c) the application meets the requirements of Article 15(2) and (3); and (d) the application has been submitted to the Court mentioned in Article 4.

proceeding to be recognised in accordance with Article 17, it must take place in the state in which the debtor has its COMI. Nevertheless, the Court has the discretion to modify or terminate such recognition under Articles 15, 16, and 18. In addition to Article 17, Article 19 grants relief in limited circumstances, namely, upon application of a foreign proceeding, for property that requires urgent protection of the debtor, or to protect the interests of the creditor. Furthermore, relief may also be granted when a foreign proceeding has been granted, to protect the property of the debtor or the interests of the creditor.[132]

Notwithstanding this, the effect of a foreign main proceeding in Singapore can include a stay for debtor's property, rights, obligations or liabilities. It can also apply to when the transfer, encumbering, or other disposal of any property of the debtor is to be suspended.[133] Likewise, protection is afforded to creditors and interested persons including through provisions to avoid acts that would be detrimental to creditors and intervention by a foreign proceeding[134] in Singapore. One of the key aims of the Model Law was to help facilitate cooperation amongst courts located in different states. Chapter 4, Article 25 of the IRDA, achieves this by promoting cooperation and direct communication between a court of Singapore and foreign courts or foreign representatives. To reinforce this point, Gerard McCormack and Wai Yee Wan make the point that the 'Model law promotes cooperation between states in both hard and soft law form'.[135] They argue, the 'Model Law adopts a modified version of the universalist approach, by allowing for the opening of more than one set of insolvency proceedings, particularly in States where the debtor has a business presence'.[136] They go onto say that 'the state extending cooperation or assistance may simply be recognising the authority of a foreign insolvency representative to speak for the debtor or giving the insolvency representative standing before the domestic courts'.[137] Secondly, the use of orders relating to insolvency becomes important when they are at the request of a foreign representative. Thirdly, consistency in the recognition of foreign insolvency proceedings and in granting relief faciliates greater uniformity in the enforcement of foreign orders.[138] Nonetheless, to underpin Article 25, Article 26 goes a step further by providing cooperation and direct communication between the Singapore insolvency officeholder

132 Ibid, Article 21.

133 Ibid, Article 20.

134 Ibid, Articles 22, 23, 24.

135 Gerard McCormack, Wai Yee Wan, Model Law on Cross-Border Insolvency Comes of Age: New Times or New Paradigms, *Texas International Law Journal*, Vol. 54, No. 2 (2019), 273–304.

136 Ibid.

137 Ibid.

138 Ibid. The Model Law addresses the first two levels of cooperation between States and partially addresses the third level. When the Model Law was first conceived, its aim was to provide a framework for countries to adopt so as to obtain consistency in the recognition of foreign insolvency proceedings and granting relief in aid of the foreign courts, giving foreign creditors or foreign representatives access to local courts and cooperation between courts in countries where the debtor's assets are located. Thus, the Model Law facilitates, to the maximum extent possible, the optimal management of cross-border insolvency so as to benefit debtors, creditors and other stakeholders as well as the economies in which these stakeholders function.

and foreign courts or foreign representatives. However, this approval is limited to the appointment of a person to act at the direction of the Singapore court: 'to communicate information by any means considered appropriate by the Court; to coordinate the administration and supervision of the debtor's property and affairs; to approve or implementation by courts of agreements concerning the coordination of proceedings; and to coordinate concurrent proceedings regarding the same debtor'.[139] Additionally, Article 30 of the IRDA ensures that more than one insolvency proceeding can be coordinated at any one time. In effect, this permits coordination of more than one foreign proceeding with proceedings in Singapore. In adopting the universalist approach, Meng Seng Wee argues that 'universalism enhances the prospects of corporate or business rescue'.[140] He goes onto say that:

> The rescue of a financially distressed multinational company requires a high level of co-operation to administer. It is impossible to achieve this if the courts involved adopt an essentially territorialist approach. Without a more or less unified international approach, the business of the insolvent company will become fragmented and asset values will be quickly destroyed. The simultaneous administration of Maxwell Communications Corp plc in England and Chapter 11 proceeding in New York was only possible because of the high degree of co-operation between court Justices.[141]

Arguably, the position taken by Wee has been embraced by the other jurisdictions examined in this book. To fully implement a universalist, or as we argue, an international approach to cross-border insolvency or restructuring, requires deep trust and cooperation between courts in different jurisdictions. On the other hand, Wee argues that the Model Law can be adopted by any legal system without requiring major or even any change in domestic law.[142] The Guide to its enactment acknowledges that the scope of the Model Law is limited to some procedural aspects arising in cross-border insolvency cases, and that it is intended to operate as an integral part of the existing insolvency law in the enacting state.

While the Model Law has been adopted in Singapore for some time, Singaporean courts have not engaged in discussion of the IRDA since its implementation and the writing of this book. However, when the Model Law provisions were incorporated into Singapore's Corporations Act 2006, the Court in *Re: Zetta Jet Pte. Ltd. and others*[143] noted that the UNCITRAL Model Law on Cross-Border Insolvency 1997 had the force of law in Singapore pursuant to s 354B of Singapore's

139 Insolvency, Restructuring and Dissolution Act 2020, Article 27.

140 Meng Seng Wee, Lessons for the Development of Singapore's International Insolvency Law, *Singapore Academy of Law Journal*, Vol. 23 (2011), 940.

141 Ibid.

142 Meng Seng Wee, The Belt and Road Initiative, China's Cross-Border Insolvency Law and the UNCITRAL Model Law on Cross-Border Insolvency, *Chinese Journal of Comparative Law*, Vol. 8 No. 1 (2020), 116–142.

143 *Re: Zetta Jet Pte Ltd and others (Asia Aviation Holdings Pte Ltd, intervener)* [2019] SGHC 53.

Companies Act.[144] This was enacted under the Tenth Schedule of that Act 'the Singapore Model Law'.[145] Moreover, the Court argued that public policy also required it to have regard to the international basis of the Model Law and the promotion of its uniform application, as required under Article 8 of the Singapore Model Law.[146] More pervasively, the Court compared elements of the Model Law implemented in Singapore to elements of the law of Australia, the US, and the EU while the UK was still part of the EU. Similar to Australia and the other jurisdictions that have adopted the UNCITRAL Model Law on Cross-Border Insolvency, Singapore has shifted from a moderately territorialist approach towards cross-border insolvency to the modified universalist approach as envisaged by the Model Law. As a result, Singapore is more likely to fully implement the Model Law.[147] The case confirmed how Singapore continues to embrace the globalisation of commercial law. The island state generally embraces the idea of implementing the international rules-based system and the rule of law. Doing so has provided it with a platform to enable business to thrive and not be overburdened by unnecessary transnational regulations.

2.5.1 The Gibbs Rule

The Gibbs rule was rejected in Singapore. In *Pacific Andes Resources Development Ltd,*[148] the High Court noted that, when a contractual obligation is governed by English law, a further rule should be developed. That rule should provide that, if one of the contract parties is the subject of insolvency proceedings in a jurisdiction with which he has an established connection based on residence or ties of business, it should be recognised that the parties reasonably expected the possibility of such proceedings in entering into their relationship, and in furnishing a ground for the discharge to take effect under the applicable law.

The inference arising from *Pacific Resources* is that the principle in *Gibbs* does not create an obstacle to the exercise of jurisdiction. If there is sufficient connection between the subject matter in dispute, the assets in contention and the state warranting the exercise of jurisdiction, debts that are not governed by Singapore law, may be legitimately compromised within a scheme proposed under s 210.[149] In a similar way to Australia and the US, Singapore courts have declined to endorse the Gibbs rule. Such is the debate amongst scholars in Singapore that, in 2017, Kannan Ramesh contended that the '*Gibbs* principle is a creature of antiquity that should now be consigned to the scrapyard of history because it is out of touch with

144 Cap 50, 2006 Rev Ed ('Companies Act').
145 Ibid, 1.
146 Ibid, 17.
147 Wai Yee Wan, Gerard McCormack, Implementing Strategies for the Model Law on Cross-Border Insolvency: The Divergence in Asia-Pacific and Lessons for UNCITRAL, *Emory Bankruptcy Developments Journal*, Vol. 36 (2020), 60–62.
148 [2016] SGHC 210, 48.
149 Ibid, 52.

modern business practices and the push toward legal convergence'.[150] Ramesh further argues that 'there is little sense in anchoring oneself obstinately to a principle that has little basis in principle and even less in relevance. He believes, the courts should play an active role in modernising cross-border insolvency law by scouring the common law for these relics of legal history and purging them uniformly and decisively'.[151]

Singapore, consistent with its broader policy of being hospitable to foreign business, has adopted an international rules-based system of law. This broad policy directive is embodied in Singapore's promotion of international trade and investment law, including the UNCITRAL Model Law on Cross-Border Insolvency. Not unlike Australian, Singapore's recent legislative reform has reflected the Model law's focus on unifying cross-border insolvency proceedings. It has also demonstrated a commitment to transnational cooperation and communication between its courts and foreign courts in insolvency proceedings. Singapore's adoption of the Model Law has also reflected its long-standing commitment to legal certainty, including but not limited to resolving cross-border insolvency disputes. The limitation in Singapore's cooperation with foreign courts is that the reach of judicial cooperation and the extent of relief granted is restricted to Singapore's High Court.[152] As a pervasive preference, for many decades Singapore has sought to serve as an economic global trade and investment hub in South East Asia, and as a commercial bridge between East and West. As businesses continues to become increasingly global, Singapore's decision to adopt the Model Law reflects its support for the global evolution of cross-border insolvency law.[153] Singapore's further purpose is for the Model Law to boost its slowing economy to encourage further investments there.

2.6 India

India had, at the time of writing this book, not adopted the Model Law on cross-border insolvency. India, similar to the other jurisdictions examined in this chapter, have followed the common law. It is a developing country and emerging economic powerhouse in the Asia region. Therefore, understanding the current framework for cross-border insolvency is an important step for India, future transnational trade, investment for the country and its many businesses.[154]

150 Kannan Ramesh, The Gibbs Principle: A Tether on the Feet of Good Forum Shopping, *Singapore Academy of Law Journal* (2017), 73–74. This section draws upon the work of Robert Walters, Cross Border Insolvency and the 2022 Australia-India Comprehensive Economic Cooperation Agreement? Business Law Review, WoltersKluwer, forthcoming 2022.

151 Ibid.

152 Ibid.

153 Ryan Halimi, *An Analysis of the Three Major Cross-Border Insolvency Regimes,* International Immersion Program Papers (2017), 47.

154 Priya Misra, Cross-Border Corporate Insolvency Law in India: Dealing with Insolvency in Multinational Group Companies-Determining Jurisdiction for Group Insolvencies, *VIKALPA, The Journal for Decision Makers*, Vol. 45, No. 2 (2020), 93–103.

Even though India has not adopted the Model Law, cross-border insolvency can be traced back to the case of *Macfadyen* in 1908.[155] The proceedings involved the liquidation of an Anglo-Indian partnership, after the death of one of the partners. The London and Madras trustees came to an agreement, confirmed by courts in both England and India, on admitted claims and promised that surplus sums would be remitted for a global distribution.[156] When the agreement was challenged, the English Court stated that the agreement was 'clearly a proper and common-sense business arrangement' and that it was 'manifestly for the benefit of all parties interested'.[157] This long held adoption and alignment of Indian commercial law to that of the UK is not new, given that Indian law has well established legal underpinnings in English Law and in the UK's commercial law framework.

Shukla and Jayram, maintain that the Law Relating to Insolvency and Winding up of Companies (May 2000) (Eradi Committee Report), took account of the sweeping changes that globalised trade had in opening up of the Indian economy and raised the importance of cross-border insolvency.[158] It also recommended that the Model Law be implemented in India, by amending Part VII of the Companies Act 1956.[159] In the following year, the Advisory Group on Bankruptcy Law (Mitra Committee) stated that the Indian law (as it existed then) 'is not comparable to the standard set in international legal requirement and as such stands apart and alone and has not taken into consideration of any cross-border relation'.[160] Even though the 2000 Eradi and 2001 Mitra Committee Reports, both acknowledged the need for a cross-border insolvency law and recommended the adoption of the Model Law, India has yet to do so.

Shukla and Jayram elaborate on the value of India adopting the recommendations of the Eradi and Mitra Committees, in incorporating the Model Law, and in revamping its inward domestic insolvency and bankruptcy laws. Should India implement the Model Law, it would better equip its commercial sector to expand trade and investment throughout Asia as well as to other regions of the world.

While India lags somewhat behind Australia and Singapore in supporting universalism in cross-border insolvency law, its 2016 Insolvency and Bankruptcy Code[161] (IB Code) has strengthened India's cross-border insolvency regime, albeit raising complex implementation issues. Section 234 of the 'the IB Code 'introduced an enabling mechanism for enforcing the provisions of the Code. It provides for

155 *In re P. Macfadyen & Co. Exparte Vizanagram co., Ltd* [1908] 1 K.B. 67.

156 Sudhaker Shukla, Kokila Jayaram, *Cross-Border Insolvency, A Case to Cross the Border Beyond the UNCITRAL*, https://ibbi.gov.in/uploads/resources/c3593c9f41984c6f31f278974de3cf37.pdf.

157 Ibid.

158 Ibid.

159 Ibid, Report of the Justice Eradi Committee on Law Relating to Insolvency of Companies, Company Law Cases, 2000, Vol. XII, 1297–1334.

160 Ibid, Standing Committee on International Financial Standards and Codes: Report of the Advisory Group on Bankruptcy Law (2001), Reserve Bank of India, May.

161 Insolvency and Bankruptcy Code 2016, http://www.mca.gov.in/Ministry/pdf/TheInsolvencyandBankruptcyofIndia.pdf

bilateral agreements (as well as multilateral agreements) to be entered by the Central Government of India with other countries as a means to tackling issues related to cross-border insolvency.[162] Problematic though, when compared to the other jurisdictions discussed in this book, is the limitation of Section 234. It requires the Indian government to have established a bilateral agreement with a third country before any cross-border insolvency can commence. More problematic, but outside scope of this book, establishing, framing and sustaining bilateral arrangement can be a cumbersome. Moreover, the fact that India's bilateral treaty partners may negotiate to incorporate different provisions in their bilateral instruments, is likely to lead to the fragmentation of India's cross-border insolvency regime. Should this risk materialise, the efficiency sought by the Model Law would be significantly diminished.

Further, Section 235 of India's IB Code provides for a mechanism that can be adopted by the Adjudicating Authority to seek assistance from foreign countries with which a reciprocal arrangement has been reached for enforcing the provisions of the IB Code.[163] An obstacle that can arise from the processes established under the Code is that cross-border insolvency agreements based on bilateral treaties take time to implement.[164] The IB Code also stops short of fully adopting the Model Law. To date, the Code has limited the application of the Model Law to two specific sections, that is, to Sections 234 and 235 that deal with agreements entered into with foreign countries. The Code provides that the Indian government may enter into an agreement with the government of another country to enforce provisions of the Code.[165] The Indian government may direct that the IB Code apply in regard to the assets of the corporate debtor or debtor located in a country outside India with which reciprocal arrangements have been made, shall be subject to the conditions as stipulated.[166] That said, Das further notes that Section 235 of the Code provides for letters of request to be made to countries that are located outside the territory of India. While limited, the current provisions provide that:

> If during the pendency of the insolvency resolution process, or liquidation, or bankruptcy proceeding, the resolution professional, liquidator, or bankruptcy trustee feels that the assets of the corporate debtor or debtor are located in a country outside India with which reciprocal arrangements have been made, he may apply to the Adjudicating Authority (National Company Law Tribunal) under the Code regarding the procurement of evidence or

162 Kushal Bansal, *Jet-Airways and Cross-Border Insolvency – Interplay*, https://www.amicusservices.in/docs/Jet-Airways-and-Cross-Border-Insolvency-Interplay-May-14-2020.pdf.

163 Ibid.

164 Ibid.

165 Ishita Das, The Need for Implementing a Cross-Border Insolvency Regime within the Insolvency and Bankruptcy Code 2016, *The Journal for Decision Makers*, Vol. 45 (2020), https://doi.org/10.1177/0256090920946519.

166 Ibid, Section 234.

> initiation of action in relation to such assets. The Adjudicating Authority, upon the receipt of such application, may issue a letter of request to a court or a competent authority to deal with the request on being satisfied that evidence or action with regard to the foreign assets is required in connection with the insolvency resolution process, or liquidation, or bankruptcy proceeding.[167]

The case for India to do more, in our view, is particularly urgent at this time. The both limited and complex nature of cross-border insolvency, and more broadly restructuring, when operating outside the scope of the UNCITRAL Model Law could be increasingly dilatory and add costs to the parties involved. In reinforcing the 2016 Code and its application to cross-border insolvency, the collapse of the Indian Jet Airways airline in 2019, is a stark reminder of the complexity of these cases. The company, registered in Mumbai with a base it had established in Amsterdam, was placed into bankruptcy in the Netherlands.[168] The Indian National Company Law Tribunal ruled the Dutch judgement on the bankruptcy was void because Sections 234 and 235 of the IB Code had not come into force in India, at the time of this case. The case then turned to the development of a cross-border insolvency protocol (CIP),[169] whereby the clauses within this document laid out, similar to a contract, the administrative and governance processes for restructuring to occur, in and across, different jurisdictions. The CIP stated that:

> The application made by the Dutch Trustee, appealing the 20 June 2019 order of the NCLT before the Hon'ble National Company Law Appellate Tribunal, New Delhi ('NCLAT'), the NCLAT, by its orders dated 12 July 2019 and 21 August 2019 ('NCLAT Order'), inter alia, directed the RP, in consultation with the CoC (creditors of the company), to consider the prospect of co- operating with the Dutch Trustee so as to have joint 'corporate insolvency resolution process of the Company' and further vide its order dated 04 September 2019 directed the RP under the Indian Proceedings to reach an arrangement/agreement with the Dutch Trustee to extend such cooperation to each other, further allowing the CoC to guide the RP to enable him to prepare an agreement in reaching the terms of arrangement of cooperation with the Dutch Trustee in the best interest of the Company and all its stakeholders ('Proposed Cooperation').[170]

167 Ibid.

168 *State Bank of India v. Jet Airways (India) Ltd.* & Ors., CP 2205 (IB)/MB/2019, *Jet Airways (India) Ltd. (Offshore Regional Hub) v. State Bank of India & Anr., Company Appeal* (AT) (Insolvency) No. 707 of 2019.

169 National Company Law Appellate Tribunal New Delhi, Company Appeal (AT) (Insolvency) No. 707 of 2019, https://ibbi.gov.in/uploads/order/b7bbd5ba93be73bb4602dfe25f25cdd4.pdf.

170 Ibid, 3.

More broadly, the CIP went further, expressing the need for cross-border cooperation and facilitation to ensure prompt action was taken to restructure the company. It further stated that:

> The Parties acknowledge that while the Indian Proceedings is one that is focused on the revival/resolution of insolvency of the Company and the maximization of the value of its assets for the benefit of all its stakeholders, the main objective of the Dutch Proceedings is to deal with the liquidation of the assets of the Company located in the Netherlands and therefore, agree: (a) this Protocol represents a statement of intentions and guidelines designed to minimize the costs and maximize value of assets/recoveries for all creditors of the Proceedings, by promoting the sharing of relevant information among the Parties and the international coordination of related activities in the Proceedings, while respecting the separate interests of creditors and other interested parties to the Proceeding, and the independence, sovereignty, and authority of the NCLT/NCLAT and Dutch Bankruptcy Court.[171]

The CIP arguably represents the beginnings in applying elements of the UNCITRAL Model Law in India. More importantly, the CIP is a demonstration of how national legal instruments can be utilised to enhance cross-border insolvency and restructuring, by adopting elements of the international framework. While there is considerable work for India to undertake, at the time of writing this book, the Centre for Corporate and Insolvency Law at Gujarat National Law University informed us in March 2021 that India is moving towards adopting the Model Law in 2021–2022.[172] The concluding section argues briefly why the Model Law should be reconsidered.

2.7 Conclusion

Cross-border insolvency issues are here to stay, at least for the foreseeable future. Nonetheless, a relatively limited number of states have embraced a universal approach towards cross-border insolvency. A few states, as illustrated by Australia and Singapore, have adopted and implemented the UNCITRAL Model Law on Cross-Border Insolvency. There remains a long way to go before that Model Law is adopted by a multiplicity of other states.

The purpose and effect of the key provisions of the Model Law and Cross-Border Insolvency Regulations 2006 (CBIR) is to provide for a greater level of

171 Ibid, 2.1.1.

172 Professor Mamata Biswal, Centre for Corporate & Insolvency Law at Gujarat National Law University, Gujarat India.

access,[173] recognition and relief,[174] along with cooperation and coordination.[175] This is illustrated in the modelling of the EU's Cross-Border Insolvency Regulations 2006 (CBIR) upon the Model Law; and how, by these means, the CBIR achieves greater coordination among insolvency proceedings in multiple states. The reconciliation between localised and multi-localised insolvency laws goes to the very heart of universalism, namely, promoting the implementation of shared, but not perfectly symmetrical, domestic insolvency laws. The recognition of foreign entities, representatives, and judicial proceedings at the COMI, however ideal, needs to accommodate the local interests of states in the uniform application of the Model Law.

Perfect symmetry in the adoption and construction of the Model Law is unrealistic among purportedly sovereign states. Resolving trans-border insolvency disputes in a consistent and transparent manner, is realistic. Recognising foreign insolvency entities and proceedings can minimise the time-consuming and costly management of transnational insolvency issues. That recognition can lead to greater recognition of insolvency orders, such as relate to relief, beyond courts of the states making those orders. Importantly, too, the judicial adoption of widely recognised rules of recognition of foreign proceedings and interested parties can fill time and space gaps that otherwise would impede trans-border insolvency proceedings. Even if such uniformity is accomplished imperfectly in countries like Australia, those accomplishments can assist other countries like the UK in constructing the Model Law should a 'no-deal Brexit' have prevailed Brexit.

The quest, therefore, is for a balance between competing interests, such as between the COMI and secondary interests in insolvency proceedings. This balance is illustrated when a court grants an application for interim relief at its discretion early in insolvency proceedings, while determining that application later in light of foreign proceedings and evidence from foreign representatives. This balance is further illustrated when a court grants an automatic stay of proceedings upon recognition of main proceedings, and relief in main or secondary proceedings following that recognition.[176]

Central to the importance of the future to regulating cross-border insolvency and restructuring activities is the fact that nation states, on the one hand, encourage international trade, investment and finance. On the other hand, there is a need to recognise that such encouragement often spills over into transnational insolvencies when entities fall into financial stress of their own making or national or international economic shocks that are out of the control of companies. The case for states adopting consistent and uniform laws on insolvency is a further

173 Chapter II, Article 9, United Nations Commission on International Trade, Model Law on Cross-Border Insolvency, https://uncitral.un.org/sites/uncitral.un.org/files/media-documents/uncitral/en/1997-model-law-insol-2013-guide-enactment-e.pdf

174 Ibid, Chapter III.

175 Ibid, Chapter IV.

176 Ibid, Article 19–21.

by-product of the reality that corporate entities function in multiple states. The challenge ahead is the extent to which universalism in transnational insolvency law is attainable. No state can reasonably be relied upon to implement a wholly borderless regime of cross-border insolvency law. That contradiction in terms requires international regulators such as UNCITRAL drafters, state legislatures and courts to weigh the economic and social benefits of trans-border insolvency proceedings in light of divergence in implementation among states that pursue both ideologically and functionally disparate public policies. The reality is that states that adopt protectionist insolvency laws on ideological grounds are incentivised to rationalise those grounds economically as well. Conversely, states that pursue cross-border policies on economic grounds legitimate their action ideologically through expansive, even if not universalist, theories of cooperation among states and their subjects.

The UNCITRAL Model Law on Cross-Border Insolvency, understandably, underscores the particular economic and social value of multilateral insolvency law. It promotes the idea of granting foreign entities relief by providing an adoptable and consistent framework across states in which to obtain recognition of foreign insolvency proceedings. It encourages cooperation between courts that allow foreign creditors and foreign representatives to access local courts at which the debtor's assets are located. It also provides a platform to promote financial rehabilitation and corporate restructuring to achieve beneficial economic outcomes for local, regional and global economies. A 'winner take some' rather than 'all' approach, arguably, can often limit the economic disruption stemming from corporate failures and functional threats to in industrial sectors. That 'winner take some' advantage, while contestable, is accentuated in times of global recessions and economic dislocation of trade and investment. As highlighted in this chapter, this dislocation is visible across much of the services industry, particularly tourism.

Seeking a sustainable balance between nationalism and transnationalism in cross-border insolvency law will continue to be a moving target. States will sometimes, unavoidably, respond to that moving target differently. In supporting primarily trans-regionalism, the EU has largely adopted the principles of the UNCITRAL Model law. However, it has left it to member states to deal with cross-border insolvency matters that arise in third countries. This chapter has demonstrated that courts in Singapore and Australia have been receptive to universalist principles in the management of international insolvencies, albeit differently, than has the UK to date. Those who seek to preserve state territorialism in regulating cross-border insolvency proceedings are likely to criticise the more universalist approaches adopted by Australia and Singapore. Conversely, those who strive for universalism are likely to challenge those who support what is conceived as being state parochialism and regulatory isolationism. While there are diverging approaches amongst the jurisdictions compared in this chapter, Australia, Singapore and India have adopted the UK common law. In part, a universalist approach had begun across common law countries, without the Model Law. The EU is a notable exception.

Forthcoming chapters further demonstrate that the differences among states that incorporate the Model Law on Cross-Border Insolvency are seemingly minor; yet, on other occasions. These differences pose further challenges in cross-border insolvency outcomes when judgements by local courts are coherent but inconsistent. Illustratively, common law countries that have largely embraced the Gibbs rule, notably in England and Wales, diverge from other common law jurisdictions like the US and Australia that reject that Rule. The challenge, post-Brexit, is that the continuity of the Gibbs Rule will render English and Welsh insolvency proceedings more exclusionary.

The next chapter will examine the nature and application of close-out netting provisions to promote greater certainty and also efficiency in banking in a technologically advancing era. The chapter will also explore how close-out netting can facilitate greater uniformity across states in regulating, and streamlining, cross-border insolvency. Subsequent chapters will further assess legislative and administrative tools and judicial challenges across jurisdictions that are directed at rendering their insolvency regimes more transparent in operation. These tools can also facilitate restructuring proceedings.

3

RESTRUCTURING: SCHEMES OF ARRANGEMENTS PART 1

Both recognising and regulating insolvency is important in maintaining stability across the global economy. However, an alternative and just as important to the sometimes costly and cumbersome process of insolvency, is for a company to restructure. In achieving any restructure or reorganisation, the modern-day legal framework supports the process through specific legal mechanisms and tools. One important legal tool that is the scheme of arrangement. Schemes of arrangement, to date, fall within national laws and facilitate ongoing commercial activity. As a legal instrument, it is now used for multiple purposes in managing creditors, mergers, demerges, takeover(s) and acquisitions. This chapter poses the question – is it time to internationalise this legal tool? The chapter argues that it is a fitting time for UNCITRAL, ideally in collaboration with the UNIDROIT, to undertake a formal review in assessing how this tool could function internationally. The purpose is to develop an internationally agreed scheme of arrangement through Principles embodied in a Model law.

This chapter is divided into two parts. Part 1 examines the use of schemes of arrangement in Australia, European Union, United Kingdom and United States. Part 2 builds on Part 1 and compares developments in Singapore, Indonesia, India and China. The chapter highlights that, while these jurisdictions use different terminology to describe schemes of arrangement. These differences can be reconciled in establishing a uniform regime to regulate them.

3.1 Introduction

An alternative to the sometimes costly and cumbersome process of insolvency, is to restructure the company. Any restructure could involve cross-border arrangements whereby an entity has multiple branches spread out and located in various countries. This chapter explores schemes of arrangement (SA), which have been a

DOI: 10.4324/9781003311874-4

successful legal tool to assist in corporate restructuring, notably in restructing debt. As introduced in chapter 1, SAs often constitute binding agreements reached by shareholders and approved by courts of law. SAs arguably serve a 'useful economic function because they lessen the difficulty and costs for a company to rearrange its relationship with its shareholders or creditors for the purposes of facilitating, amongst other things, changes to capital structure'.[1] They have also been useful to corporate reorganisations such as 'mergers and takeovers, dispute settlement, and the restructuring of an organisation that is otherwise in the early stages of significant financial stress'.[2] This chapter expands on the overall theme of the book by comparing the jurisdictions of Australia, China, European Union (EU), India, Indonesia, United Kingdom (UK) and the United States (US). It has been divided into two Parts. Part 1 examines Australia, the EU, UK and US. Building upon Part 1, Part 2 compares Singapore, Indonesia, India and China.

This chapter will demonstrate whether these jurisdictions have embraced schemes of arrangement. It will also identify a pathway forward, to ensure commercial entities have such an important legal tool available to them in the future, and how it can be improved. The chapter will argue, comparably to its proposal for close-out netting provisions, that either the UNIDROIT or UNCITRAL, or both, should undertake a formal review of SAs. The goal should be to develop an internationally agreed scheme of arrangement and embody it in uniform Principles and a Model law.

It is our view that, in promoting a universal approach in cross-border insolvency, more needs to be done to assist in corporation restructuring and reorganisation. The rationale is that strengthening the legal tools to enhance the implementation of the universalist approach to restructuring and reorganisation will add another layer of legal stability and legal certainty to the international economy. The importance of restructuring entities cannot be underestimated. On their inception, some scholars considered SAs as 'the ugly child of the corporate restructuring framework'.[3] SAs are now considered the restructuring vehicle or tool of choice for large companies and larger corporates to manage

1 *Re Cheung Kong (Holdings) Ltd.* [2015] 2 HKLRD 512. See also Mohan Goplan, Creditors Schemes of Arrangement and Dissenting Creditor Protection, *SAcLJ*, Vol. 30 (2018), 903–905.

2 Charles Zhen Qu, Stefan H. C. Lo, Schemes of Arrangement: Economic Analysis of three issues relating to Classification of Claims, *UNSW Law Journal*, Vol. 40, No. 4 (2017), 1440–1441. Schemes facilitate collective decision-making in that, absent this procedure, a proposed arrangement or compromise would not be binding unless there is unanimous consent, which can be costly to obtain. See also, *Re Aston Resources Ltd [2012] FCA 229; Re Kumarina Resources Ltd [2013] FCA 549; Re SABMiller Plc [2017] 2 WLR 837;* Jennifer Payne, *Schemes of Arrangement: Theory, Structure and Operation*, Cambridge University Press (2014), Chapters 3–4.

3 Gerald McCormack, Jennifer Payne, *Schemes of Arrangement, Theory, Structure and Operation*, Cambridge University Press, Cambridge (2014), x1vii and 409 pp., ISBN: 9781107016408, *The European Business Organization Law Review*, Vol. 16 (2015), 167–171.

debt.[4] In some cases, SAs have provided states with the ability to transform themselves into financial hubs to which they attract business from across global and regional markets. The UK, typically, has served for some years as both a European and an international hub for the provision and regulation of financial services. These services include a globally recognised framework to facilitate clear and efficient restructuring procedures.

SAs serve as valuable and flexible tools in reorganising a company's capital.[5] Therefore, the chapter will trace the steps in the development of SAs. It will examine the applicability or otherwise of SAs in cross-border restructuring-reorganisation activities.

Notwithstanding this, central to the overall advantages of SAs is the idea that it can be used by companies, creditors and members to reach agreement on a wide range of reorganisations or alterations in relation to the company's capital, provided that the agreement is subsequently sanctioned by the court. They offer a way forward to assist companies to reorganise their debt and/or equity capital effectively. A further benefit is their flexibility.[6] They can be used either as an alternative to, or alongside, more traditional legal and practical mechanisms for reorganising a company's capital. A completed SA also provides the parties with a level of certainty and finality. This is reflected in an agreement that the parties negotiate and if sanctioned by a court, is binding upon them. In practice, SAs are court-sanctioned compromises between a debtor company and one or more classes of creditors.[7] Once the negotiated agreement or 'scheme' has been approved by members and creditors and sanctioned by a court, it will be set aside subsequently in very limited circumstances. In general, this will only occur where 'consent of the members and/or creditors has been obtained by fraud, although in some cases the Court will refuse to set aside the scheme even where fraud has occurred'.[8] Such 'schemes of arrangement' provide further certainty in enabling the majority of the members or creditors to reach a scheme by agreement that also binds minorities. Arguably, that result limits the risk of schemes of arrangement failing due to dissension or recalcitrance among a minority of the parties, unless the Court requires their agreement at some level. Throughout this chapter schemes of arrangement will be referred to in full or by reference to schemes or SA.

4 Ibid.

5 Jennifer Payne, *Schemes of Arrangement: Theory, Structure and Operation*, Cambridge University Press (2014), 1–2.

6 Ibid, 3.

7 Adam Gallagher, The Growth of Schemes of Arrangement as the Tool of Choice in Complex Restructurings, *American Bankruptcy Institute Journal* (October 2010), 36.

8 Jennifer Payne, *Schemes of Arrangement: Theory, Structure and Operation*, Cambridge University Press (2014), 3. See also Christian Pilkington, Kevin Heverin, Schemes of Arrangement in Cross-Border Restructuring- Issue of Jurisdiction and Recognition, *White & Case, ChaseCambria*, Vol. 8 (2001), 1.

There are disadvantages in the use of SAs. They have been viewed as 'complex, cumbersome and expensive'.[9] By and large, this has been a result of significant court supervision required in some cases. On the other hand, this will differ depending on the jurisdiction. Furthermore, SAs were often used to separate groups of members and creditors into classes to consider and vote on the scheme. This requirement creates logistical and classificatory difficulties, and is undoubtedly one of the most complex issues for a company wishing to make use of this legal mechanism.[10]

A further issue that has also arisen is whether there is enough legal convergence amongst states to both nationalize and internationalize them.

This chapter will demonstrate that SAs are regularly adopted and widely used in practice. Supporting the case for globalising SAs through an international convention, is the destabilisation of global economies arising from COVID-19, and the accompanying financial stress faced by business entities engaged in cross-border transactions. The significance of such financial stress was discussed in Chapter 1. In addressing these issues, the UNIDROIT Principles on Close-out Netting Provisions, to be discussed in Chapter 6, has demonstrated that the unification of netting laws globally can assist in advancing international financial stability. Further accentuating economic stabilisation globally is the Convention on the International Sale of Goods (CISG), even though it has not been adopted by all states Arguably, the internationalisation of schemes of arrangements can assist further in stabilising trans-border financial transactions. This chapter argues that incorporating these schemes into a set of uniform legal principles or within a model law on restructuring/insolvency can lead to a better understanding of their use and value in global business.

A preliminary issue is to determine the current manner and scope of SAs in international law and practice. Firstly, a question arises as to the level of impact the UNCITRAL Model Law on Cross-Border Insolvency has had on SAs. While not specifically stated in the 1997 UNCITRAL Cross-Border Insolvency Model Law, SAs are mentioned in the later 2004 UNCITRAL Legislative Guide to Insolvency. It states 'that not all debtors that falter or experience serious financial difficulty in a competitive marketplace should necessarily be liquidated; a debtor with a reasonable prospect of survival (such as one that has a potentially profitable business) should be given that opportunity where it can be demonstrated that there is greater value (and, by deduction, greater benefit for creditors in the long term) in keeping the essential business and

9 Jennifer Payne, *Schemes of Arrangement: Theory, Structure and Operation*, Cambridge University Press (2014), 5.

10 Ibid, 6.

other component parts of the debtor together'.[11] It goes onto say that 'reorganization does not imply that all of the stakeholders must be wholly protected or that they should be restored to the financial or commercial position that would have obtained had the event of insolvency not occurred'.[12] In referring to reorganisation, the UNCITRAL, arguably, has the same meaning as restructuring an entity. As a result, the use of a scheme to reorganise an entity, as conceived under the UNCITRAL, achieves a comparable result as under a restructure. More specifically, the reorganisation or restructure does not imply that the debtor will be completely restored, or that its creditors will be paid in full, or that ownership and management of an insolvent debtor will continue to preserve their pre-existing positions. Management of the debtor entity may be changed, and therefore, the interests of equity holders may be reduced, employees may be retrenched and the source of a market for suppliers may disappear. In general, the restructure does imply that whatever form of plan, (scheme or arrangement) is agreed, the creditors will eventually receive more than if the debtor were to be liquidated.[13] However, it is our view that there could be a rise in the perceived value and use of SAs, as the economic conditions resulting from the global pandemic in 2019–2022, continue to reshape and impact the economy placing ever more businesses into financial stress. To manage whatever level of financial stress a business is enduring, one option is the use of a restructuring program, via a scheme of arrangement.

Nonetheless, the ensuing part briefly examine SAs as they relate to ISDA Master Agreements and Netting Arrangements. It briefly explores close-out netting provisions were compared, as they relate to ISDA Master agreements.

3.1.1 Schemes of Arrangement: ISDA Master Agreements and Netting Arrangements

ISDA Master Agreements have emerged as a contractual mechanism of choice adopted by most states to govern large amounts of money transfers and transactions around the world. A more challenging example is the interrelationship between SAs and ISDA Master Agreements (along with close-out netting provisions). ISDA Master Agreements have become important as they also incorporate close-out netting provisions (see Appendix 1). While out of scope of this section to examine every jurisdiction, using the UK as an example, a non-defaulting party will generally have sufficient time, following notice of the meeting of creditors, to consider a scheme, to exercise its rights under

11 The United Nations Commission on International Trade Law (UNCITRAL), Legislative Guide on Insolvency Law, 2005, 27–29. Note this Guide came after the UNCITRAL 1997 Model Law on Cross-Border Insolvency was implemented.

12 Ibid, 27–29.

13 Ibid.

the close-out netting provisions of the ISDA Master Agreement, and to do so before the scheme is approved. The scheme itself will still require approval from a specified majority of the creditors (or relevant class of creditors) and to be sanctioned by the Court in accordance with the requirements of the Companies Act 2006. It will then become binding on all creditors, at least where the non-defaulting party has a credit monitoring process in place.[14] However, there are some circumstances in which it may be advantageous for a non-defaulting party not to close-out its position prior to a scheme of arrangement being sanctioned by the court.[15] Notably, under a SA, a non-defaulting party will generally have sufficient time, following notice of the meeting of creditors, to consider the company voluntary arrangement and to exercise its rights under the close-out netting provisions of the ISDA Master Agreement. Using the UK as an example, this process can be undertaken before the scheme is approved by the specified majority of the creditors as required under the UK Insolvency Act 1986, at least where the non-defaulting party has a credit monitoring process in place.[16] Centrally, what has emerged in the UK is the multiple roles and scenarios that netting arrangements and SAs have in supporting the management of contracts that govern large amounts of money.

In another example from Singapore, it is demonstrates how the interconnectedness between ISDA Master Agreements and schemes of arrangements were used by Lehman Brothers as part of managing a restructuring process. Firstly, the 2018 SA between Lehman Brothers International and the Scheme of Creditors,[17] was established to 'manage matters of restructuring'.[18] The facts were that, on 15 September 2008, an application of the company itself was placed into administration pursuant to Schedule B1 to the Insolvency Act.[19] The SA referred directly to both the 1992 ISDA Master Agreement, 1992 version of the Master Agreement (Multicurrency Cross-Border) and the 2002 ISDA Master Agreement. It provided that the 'Company shall determine the High Case Scheme Distribution; determine the Adequate Reserves in accordance with Clause determine the Net Available Funds; and publish a Scheme Outcome Statement'.[20] In most circumstances, an ISDA Master Agreement is likely to also contain close-out netting arrangements. Thus, while limited, an indirect connection existed among the ISDA Master Agreement,

14 Memorandum of Law for the International Swaps and Derivatives Association Inc, Validity and Enforceability under English Law of Close-out Netting under the 2002, 1992 and 1987 ISDA Master Agreements, https://www.isda.org/a/LHtEE/englandwalesnettblackline2015.pdf.

15 Ibid.

16 Ibid.

17 In the High Court of Justice Chancery Division Companies Court In the matter of Lehman Brothers International, CR-2018–003713, https://www.pwc.co.uk/business-recovery/administrations/lehman/draft-scheme-document-2-may-2018-sealed.pdf.

18 Ibid, 5.

19 Ibid.

20 Ibid, 30.

SAs and netting provisions, they cumulatively had a role in protecting an entity either prior to, during or through the execution of the restructure.

In a further example of these challenges, on 2 October 2012, a Restructuring Agreement, similar to a scheme of arrangement, was prepared between Torm Singapore and Nordea Bank.[21] It was developed to restore Torm following it entering into financial difficulty. The 2012 Agreement referred directly to both the 1992 and 2002 ISDA Master Agreements. As a stage in the restructuring process, 'it was acknowledged and agreed that the close out of any Hedging Agreement in accordance with paragraph 15 (*Notice of Hedging Termination*) and paragraph 22 (*Termination of Hedging Exposures*) of the Implementation Plan shall not be capable of being unwound following the Termination Date and/or Longstop Date in the event that such close out has already occurred, and accordingly, this Clause 5.4 shall not apply to the close out of any Hedging Agreements'.[22] Additionally, the agreement made special mention of a scheme of arrangement. It stated that:

> [T]o the best knowledge of the Original Obligors, having made all reasonable enquiries, no order has been made, petition presented or resolution passed for (i) the winding up, dissolution, bankruptcy, administration or reorganisation of any Group Member (by way of voluntary arrangement, scheme of arrangement or otherwise); or (ii) the appointment of a liquidator, receiver, administrative receiver, administrator, compulsory manager or other similar officer in respect of any Group Member or any analogous procedure has been commenced in any jurisdiction.[23]

Given these developments, the restructuring agreement that made reference to close-out netting arrangements formed part of a Hedging Agreement. The SA went further, identifying the relevant law by which the agreement was to be governed. It stated:

> This Scheme shall be governed by, and construed in accordance with, English law and the Scheme Parties hereby severally agree that the courts of England shall (save as otherwise provided in the Dispute Resolution Procedure set out at Part VI of this Scheme) have exclusive jurisdiction to hear and

21 Reorganisation Agreement between Torm A/S Torm Singapore Pte Ltd. The Financial Institutions named herein, as Original Lenders The Companies and Institutions named herein, as Original Time-Charter Owners, The companies and institutions named herein as Original Bareboat Owners The Existing Security Agents The Facility Representatives The Financial Institutions named herein as Underwriting Super Senior Providers The Hedging Banks Danske Bank A/S acting as Co-ordinator Danske Bank A/A acting as proposed Administrative Agent and Nordea Bank Danmark A/S acting as proposed security.

22 Ibid, 5.4.

23 Ibid, 23.7.

> determine any dispute or Proceedings arising out of or in connection with the Explanatory Statement or this Scheme, or the operation of this Scheme, and the Scheme Parties hereby severally submit to the exclusive jurisdiction of the courts of England for such purposes. The Scheme Parties also waive any objections to Proceedings in the courts of England that are based on the grounds of venue or that the Proceedings have been brought in an inconvenient forum.[24]

Arguably, the SA achieves multiple ends. First, it draws on the obligations set out in the ISDA Master Agreement and any close-out netting arrangements, to constitute all or part of any restructure program. Secondly, similar to commercial contracts, a clause specifying the governing law to resolve a dispute arising, provides the parties with an agreed way forward. Third, the agreement can provide the parties with an option to resolve a dispute arising from the SA by resort to international commercial arbitration.[25] Such a provision is also common in transnational commercial trade and investment contracts. Fourth, it is clear from the earlier example that schemes are viewed widely as a tool that can have multiple functions through a restructuring procedure. Fifth, SAs can serve to manage debt, manage creditors, facilitate a reorganisation/restructure, amongst others.

The multiple ways in which schemes can be used highlights how valuable they are, and can be, as a facilitative legal tool. However, a question arises as to whether their flexibility would be an obstacle to the potential internationalisation of schemes of arrangement. A further potential impediment, is whether court sanctioned schemes would be difficult to achieved? The next section examines and compares SAs as they apply in Australia, EU, UK and the US. It limits that examination to whether schemes of arrangements are regulated by these jurisdictions. It evaluates only schemes of arrangements as they are applied in restructuring and does not address acquisitions.

3.2 Australia

SAs are widely used as a restructuring tool for entities in Australia.[26]. In the Australian context, a scheme of arrangement is a shareholder and court-approved statutory arrangement between a company and its shareholders that becomes binding on all shareholders by operation of Part 5.1 of the Corporations Act 2001 (CA). The scheme structure can be used to reconstruct a company's share capital, assets or liabilities. It can also be used to affect a compromise between a company and its creditors (which includes option holders). They can also serve specific purposes that

24 Ibid, 37.1.

25 Ibid, 1.1.

26 Tony Damian, Andrew Rich, *Schemes, Takeovers and Himalayan Peaks: The Use of Schemes of Arrangement to Effect Change of Control Transactions*, Centre of Commercial, Corporate and Taxation Law, University of Sydney (2013), 12.

include de-mergers, reverse takeovers, eliminating minority shareholders, interposing a non-operating holding company, demutualisation, restructurings, amalgamations and creditor comprises.[27] A further application of SAs in Australia is where they can be used for the restructuring of an entity in accordance with s 411 of the Corporations Act, which appears in Pt 5.1 of Chapter 5 – External Administration. A scheme can only be used by a 'Part 5.1 body', which is defined as a company or a registrable body that is registered under Division 1 or 2 of Part 5B.2 of the CA.[28] They are limited to companies and body corporates that are registered under the CA. Schemes also do not apply to smaller businesses, even though they may engage in cross-border commercial activities.

In addition to this, the *Corporation Regulations 2001* (the Regulations) underpin the CA and provide for the administrative arrangements for schemes and their development.[29] Yet, in practice, Schedule 8 sets out the required information that must 'accompany information' related to an agreement. However, this does not deal with the transfer to a trustee according to Part 4 of Schedule 8. The resulting effect requires an explanatory statement of the following information that includes:

- the expected dividend that would be available to scheme creditors if the company were to be wound up within 6 months after the date of the hearing of the application to the Court for an order under subsections 411 (1) and (1A) of the Act;[30] and
- if a composition of debts is proposed the expected dividend that would be paid to scheme creditors if the Scheme were put into effect as proposed; and
- a list of the names of all known scheme creditors and the debts owed to those creditors; and
- if a scheme creditor is known to be a guaranteed creditor the name of the creditor and the amount of the debt owed; and
- if a scheme creditor is known to be an internal creditor the name of the creditor and the amount of the debt owed.[31]

27 Corporations Act 2001, Part 5.1 – Arrangements and Restructurings.
28 Ibid.
29 Corporations Regulations 2001, schedule 8, under Part 5.1 of the Corporations Act 2001.
30 Corporations Act, Section 411 Administration of compromises etc. (1) Where a compromise or arrangement is proposed between a Part 5.1 body and its creditors or any class of them or between a Part 5.1 body and its members or any class of them, the Court may, on the application in a summary way of the body or of any creditor or member of the body, or, in the case of a body being wound up, of the liquidator, order a meeting or meetings of the creditors or class of creditors or of the members of the body or class of members to be convened in such manner, and to be held in such place or places (in this jurisdiction or elsewhere), as the Court directs and, where the Court makes such an order, the Court may approve the explanatory statement required by paragraph 412(1)(a) to accompany notices of the meeting or meetings.
31 Corporations Regulations 2001, schedule 8, 8201.

Central to the 'accompanied information' required, are the additional requirements set out in section 411. Notably, section 411(1A) of the CA requires that where an 'arrangement is proposed, the court is to be satisfied of the holding company or of a creditor of the holding company; or the holding company is being wound up – of the liquidator'.[32] Therefore, the Court can order a 'meeting, on a consolidated basis, of the creditors of the holding company and of each of the subsidiaries or of such class or classes of those creditors as the court determines and, where the court makes such an order, the court may approve the explanatory statement required by paragraph 412(1)(a) to accompany notices of the meeting or meetings'.[33] Importantly it will be argued that, national courts play an important role in approving and governing schemes of arrangement. The court must also be satisfied that the number of creditor meetings that would be required are not so onerous as to result in a significant impediment to the timely and effective consideration by those creditors of the terms of the compromises or arrangements.

Moreover, in further administering a scheme of arrangement, 'a statement must contain a statement that a court order under section 411 (1) and (1A) of the Act is not an endorsement of, or any other expression of opinion on, the scheme'.[34] The statement must contain a report on the financial position of the company along with a copy, certified by a director or by a secretary of the company, stipulating that all financial statements have been lodged with the Australian Securities and Investment Commission (ASIC), the. the statutory regulatory authority in Australia. The statement must 'also confirm or otherwise whether the company is a trustee'.[35] Based on this, the Court can only make an order where 14 days of notice has been provided for a hearing on such an application. Additionally, the regulator ASIC has had the opportunity to examine the arrangement and explanatory statement. Thus, for a scheme to be effective and considered by the Court and regulator, it must be accompanied by an explanatory statement. The scheme must outline and explain the arrangement, setting out information related to but not limited to whether a meeting is be held outside of Australia. Then, the Court must have regard to the residence of the creditors or members, or the creditors or members included in the class concerned. Upon satisfying these requirements, the scheme becomes binding on the creditors, or on a class of creditors, or on members or on a class of members. On the other hand, this process is limited to

> 'a meeting convened in accordance with an order of the court where the arrangement is agreed to by a majority in number of the creditors, with at

32 Corporations Act 2001, Section 411(1A).
33 Ibid.
34 Corporations Regulations 2001, schedule 8. 8202.
35 Ibid, 8203.

> least 75% of the total amount of the debts and claims of the creditors present and voting in person'.[36]

The percentage of 75% has emerged as a similar percentage across most jurisdictions' schemes of arrangements, with variants along the way.

Nevertheless, central to any scheme, is the contents and information required for it to be complete. Apart from the accompanying information outlined earlier, the statement must also include information as to whether the 'company is being wound up, or the director accepts or otherwise the scheme and any reasons as to why or why not that acceptance was granted'.[37] It must identify whether a director is not available to consider the scheme and the reason for not being available, or if the relevant directors decide not to recommend including the reasons for that decision.

On the one side, and in the case of winding up the entity, or under official management, the above information must also be included in the statement, along with whether the scheme has been generally accepted by the liquidator or administrator.[38] The statement will also need to:

> include further relevant information that takes into consideration the number, description and amount of marketable securities of the company and for each director of the company by whom or on whose behalf shares in that company are held, whether the director intends to vote in favour of, or against, the scheme; or the director has not made a decision.[39]

The SA will need to confirm whether the other party to the restructuring holds any marketable securities and what amount of these securities are being held. Further, it needs to outline the particulars of payment,[40] and whether the directors had knowledge of liquidation or management of the financial position of the entity before the annual general meeting. Centrally, where the other party to the restructuring under the scheme of arrangement is an entity or director, the statement must outline that the proposal is in the best interests of the entity's members. Where there are two or more reports on the establishment of the scheme, they must be attached to the explanatory statement.[41]

36 Corporations Act 2001, Section 411.
37 Corporations Regulations 2001, schedule 8, 8301.
38 Ibid.
39 Ibid, 8302.
40 Ibid, note further requirements set out in 8302. Additionally, Sections 314 or 317 Corporations Act 2001 need to be met in relation to financial reporting and financial reports to be tabled at the annual general meeting.
41 Ibid, 8303–8304.

Additionally, valuing the company profits, assets and shareholdings at the time of an SA has a further direct importance in providing a level of economic stability. This information must also form part of the accompanying explanatory statement. It is intended to enable, both creditors and the market to determine the viability of the entity. To these ends, the company should provide a forecast of profits along with the value of assets, and highlight 'who has a shareholding of less than 30%'.[42] This step in the process highlights who has the majority control over the entity. What is not clear is the reason why the figure of 30% was chosen. That is an area in need of further research and exploration.

Nonetheless, where marketable securities have been issued, an outline of the formula used to calculate that offer to members is also to be provided.[43] Marketable securities are to be granted an official quotation to the securities exchange, and are required to be registered with ASIC.[44] A further requirement is the need to obtain a quotation of securities for more than one exchange in a three-month period, before being lodged for registration. The regulatory process requires a number of procedural steps to be followed for a scheme to be effective in different circumstances. In a case where the securities have not provided a quotation, the statement must set out all the information required of a director, liquidator or official manager about the company that is the subject of the scheme. Furthermore, the explanatory statement must set out the 'particulars of the intentions of the directors in relation to continuing the business, any major changes to the company and information on the future employment of employees'.[45] Importantly, throughout this process, there is not only regulatory oversight and obligations to be met, but also the specified role of the Court in setting relevant orders. The oversight from the judiciary is a central theme that has emerged for the governance of an SA. It is arguably a powerful step in requiring scrutiny of a scheme from the outset. This requirement is distinguished from contracts between parties that ordinarily do not lead to court intervention until one party has breached the contract and the other party seeks the Court to intervene and decide on the loss incurred.

In summarising the important elements of a scheme in Australia, the scheme of arrangement must be accompanied by an explanatory statement, to be provided to the creditors. An application to the Court must be made so that its permission can be granted for meetings to be convened with relevant creditors. The permission of the Court allows the creditors vote on the proposed scheme of arrangement. As a

42 Ibid, 8305–8306.
43 Ibid, 8307.
44 Ibid, 8308.
45 Ibid, 8309–8310.

result, ASIC, not just the Court, has an oversight role.[46] In particular, ASIC is to be provided with a prior notice and the opportunity to comment on the explanatory statement. Once court approval has been obtained, the statement can be distributed to classes of creditors, and they must approve the scheme, by a majority which must represent 75%. There needs to be a forecast of profits and value of assets and an outline of who holds less than highlight 30% of the overall shareholding. Upon approval by the court, the scheme of arrangement can be implemented.

In reinforcing these important procedural steps, the New South Wales Supreme Court of Australia, in *Re Boart Longyear Ltd.*,[47] highlighted how the overall position adopted by this book to the universalist approach towards cross-border restructuring. The facts in that case were that, by the Originating Process filed on 24 April 2017 the Plaintiffs, Boart Longyear Limited ('BLY') and several associated entities, the creditors sought orders under ss. 411 and 1319 of the *Corporations Act 2001* (CPA) to convene meetings of creditors to consider and, if the Court thinks fit, approve two schemes of arrangement. In so doing, orders were sought to

> restrain any further proceedings in accordance with section 411(6) of the CA. Orders were also sought where one of the directors of the companies was resident in the US be authorised to act as a 'foreign representative' for the purposes of making an application to the United States Bankruptcy Court for recognition of the Australian proceeding (approval of the schemes), under Chapter 15 of the United States Bankruptcy Code.[48]

Noteworthy too, was that the application for orders pursuant to s 411(16) was brought prior to the application for an order to convene the scheme meetings. The Court noted that:

> The creditors who supported the schemes comprised a significant proportion of the total debt held by secured creditors (77.9%). It was likely that the companies would shortly become insolvent absent any moratorium with their creditors. If approved, the schemes had the potential to result in a better return to creditors than a winding up.[49]

Despite this, and apart from the Court confirming the process required under section 411 of the CPA and the Regulations, the Court went further reaffirming

46 Australian Securities and Investment Commission, Schemes of Arrangement or Reconstruction, https://asic.gov.au/for-finance-professionals/registered-liquidators/your-ongoing-obligations-as-a-registered-liquidator/external-administration-controller-appointments-and-schemes-of-arrangement-most-commonly-lodged-forms/flowchart-13-scheme-of-arrangement-or-restructuring/.
47 [2017] NSWSC 537. https://www.caselaw.nsw.gov.au/decision/590a717be4b0e71e17f5942f.
48 Ibid.
49 Ibid.

that the 75% threshold not only had to be met, but it was to be exceeded in this case.

Furthermore, the Court held that 'in relation to making of an order under section 411, the reference to "further proceedings" in s 411(16) is not limited to proceedings presently in existence, but includes those proceedings not yet commenced'.[50] This is conducive to the orderly and efficient consideration of the proposed schemes. It is also consistent with the trend in modern international insolvency practice to recognise the risks of multiple proceedings which do not involve any form of collective resolution of claims against a company in financial difficulty. The Court also stated that:

> For a compromise or arrangement to be 'proposed' for the purposes of s411(16), it does not require that all steps of the scheme be completed. It is likely to be sufficient that the substantial features of the scheme have been identified and made known to creditors. In this case, a proposal existed because a detailed announcement was made to the ASX at an early stage which set out the substance of the proposed schemes and detailed explanatory memoranda were provided to ASIC, including draft expert reports. In exercising its discretion under s411(16), the Court would also have regard to the risk that individual steps taken by creditors (as was present in this case) could give rise to a preference or seek to frustrate the procedure in s411(16), which could potentially force a company into voluntary administration or liquidation.[51]

In regard to appointing the director as a foreign representative, Black J held that:

> The same reasons that support an order under s 411(16) in order to preserve the opportunity for a restructuring of the companies may well support the grant of a stay of proceedings in the US. Although no foreign proceeding yet existed in the US, this application fell within the ambit of Article 1 because it was made in respect of potential US proceedings in connection with the Australian s411 proceeding seeking approval of the schemes. The fact that there could be potential proceedings in the US was enough to enliven the Court's jurisdiction to co-operate with the US Courts in order to avoid acts detrimental to creditors under Article 23 of the Model Law.[52]

The second and equally important consideration arising from Article 23 of the Model Law on Cross-Border Insolvency was how the Court confirmed the

50 Ibid.
51 Ibid, 9–12.
52 Ibid, 3–19.

jurisdiction of appointed foreign representatives. In particular, the Court acknowledged the complex question of its jurisdiction to appoint a foreign representative. It noted that, under the Australian Cross-Border Insolvency Act implementing the Article 25 of the Model Law, the Court would 'co-operate to the maximum extent possible with foreign courts or foreign proceedings, in matters referred to in Article 1.'[53] It noted further that Article 1, extends to 'assistance sought in this State by a foreign court or a foreign representative in connection with a foreign proceeding'.[54] Black J. maintained that, this provision does not apply strictly. However, he held that, because the application was made in respect of potential US proceedings in connection with s 411 of the Corporations Act 2001, this was sufficient to satisfy the requirements of Article 1. As a result, he found that the Court had jurisdiction to co-operate under Article 23 of the Model Law.[55] Central to the overall successful application of the Model Law has been its ability to facilitate cooperation and assistance between national courts located in different nation states. The Court noted the orders sought were for circumstances that:

> many creditors will not have had formal notice of this application, it is appropriate to reserve liberty to any interested party, including any creditor of the Plaintiffs and the Australian Securities and Investments Commission to apply on one business days' notice, which would permit such a creditor to seek to set aside or vary these orders if so advised.[56] Thus, the order was made.

Chapter 15 of the US Bankruptcy Code broadly corresponds to the UNCITRAL Model Law on Cross-Border Insolvency, which is set out in Schedule 1 of the Cross-Border Insolvency Act 2008 (Cth). Furthermore, Article 1 of the Model Law states that it applies in circumstances where assistance is sought by a foreign court or foreign representative in connection with a foreign proceeding, or in a foreign state in connection with a proceeding under Australian insolvency law (amongst other factors). The case confirmed the fundamental elements of the Australian Corporations Act 2001 and Regulations that need to be met for a court to grant an order. It demonstrated that, these requirements extended to cross-border insolvency-restructuring. It established further that Australia, in adopting the Model Law through the Cross-Border Insolvency Act 2008, can not only harmonise insolvency law, but can also, where required, support a restructuring procedure through schemes of arrangement in a third country. While the case did not call for the internationalisation of schemes of arrangement, it can be argued, from the analysis and confirmation of the universalist approach in Australia, that developing

53 Ibid, 19–20.
54 Ibid.
55 Ibid, 20.
56 Ibid.

an international scheme of arrangement beyond national laws is a viable option. The next section evaluates the use of schemes of arrangement in the EU and UK respectively.

3.3 European Union

The EU has for some time been working on a proposal to establish a centralised SA (to meet its supranational needs), which would largely be modelled on the UK SA. In 2019, the European Commission released a Directive on preventive restructuring[57] (Restructuring Directive), which is largely based on the UK schemes of arrangement.[58] However, the role of the EU framework did not specify the operational requirements of SAs. Rather it left that to Directive 2017/1132[59], which became effective in July 2021. The Directive sets the minimum standards that are required in developing a restructuring plan (RP).

The nature of a restructuring plan is therefore similar in both the UK and US schemes of arrangement,[60] even though the terminology and title of the scheme diverges across jurisdictions. The purpose of SAs, in each case, is to enable financially stressed organisations to restructure. What is unclear, is whether SAs are similar to the Australian equivalent version and only pertaining to corporations that are registered by the states, under national laws. Nonetheless, and while elements are left to member states national laws, the restructuring plan would need to highlight the separation between secured and unsecured creditors.[61]

Moreover, the EU Restructuring Directive provides that the overall 'restructuring framework should be available to debtors, including legal entities and, where so provided under national law, natural persons and groups of companies, to enable them to address their financial difficulties at an early stage, when it appears likely that their insolvency can be prevented and the viability of the business can be ensured'.[62]

57 Directive (EU) 2019/1023 of the European Parliament and of the Council of 20 June 2019 on preventive restructuring frameworks, on discharge of debt and disqualifications, and on measures to increase the efficiency of procedures concerning restructuring, insolvency and discharge of debt, and amending Directive (EU) 2017/1132 (Directive on restructuring and insolvency), O.J. L 172.

58 Matti Engelberg, The Proposed EU Framework for Preventive Restructuring and the English Schemes of Arrangement Regime – Seeking the Best Preventive Model for Each Member State, *Capital Markets Law Journal*, Vol. 14, No. 2 (108), 1–3.

59 Directive (EU) 2017/1132 of the European Parliament and of the Council of 14 June 2017 relating to certain aspects of company law O.J. L 169, 30.6.2017, 46–12.

60 Mathew Thorn, Manhal Zaman, *And, More Keeping Up with the Joneses: The New EU Restructuring Directive and Reforms in the United Kingdom*, Norton Rose Fulbright (2019).

61 Directive (EU) 2019/1023 of the European Parliament and of the Council of 20 June 2019 on preventive restructuring frameworks, on discharge of debt and disqualifications, and on measures to increase the efficiency of procedures concerning restructuring, insolvency and discharge of debt, and amending Directive (EU) 2017/1132 (Directive on restructuring and insolvency), O.J. L 172, 26.6.2019, Preamble (44).

62 Ibid, preamble 24.

Importantly, the EU Directive provides that the restructuring framework should be available

> before a debtor becomes insolvent under national law, before the debtor fulfils the conditions under national law for entering collective insolvency proceedings, which normally entail a total divestment of the debtor and the appointment of a liquidator. In order to avoid restructuring frameworks being misused, the financial difficulties of the debtor should indicate a likelihood of insolvency. Additionally, the restructuring plan should be capable of preventing the insolvency of the debtor and ensuring the viability of the business.[63]

Reinforcing the approach, the EU has established a preventative framework that is aimed at minimising economic impacts to the EU economy.

A further application of the process, similar to that of other jurisdictions is that the restructuring plan must also be confirmed by means of a cross-class 'cram-down' in which all classes of creditors and minority objections are 'crammed down' in order to ensure that the restructuring plan passes.[64] A central feature of the restructuring plan is to include measures affecting the rights of workers, whereby the debtor or its management who has acted in a criminal, fraudulent, or detrimental manner in business relations are identified.[65]

Based on these requirements, the EU Restructuring Directive not only reflects the schemes of arrangement of the UK and US, but also that of the Australia and Singapore. In our view, the UK and US have arguably set the benchmark for schemes of arrangement and their structure, format and any accompanying plans or forms. As a result, a level of internationalisation in resort to SAs has, whether by accident or design, been achieved. This has been largely achieved on the backdrop of jurisdictions looking to other jurisdictions who have well-established legal mechanisms in place. Such a cross-jurisdictional comparison is not novel, and is attributable to many other areas of commercial law. On the one side, nation states establish a legal framework that places them at the forefront of governing commercial arrangement, nationally and internationally. On the other side, other nation states adopt those laws, such as data protection and cyber security. The result is a variable level of internationalisation that now includes schemes of arrangement.

In enhancing such the aforementioned, a fundamental element in restructuring is the appointment of a relevant practitioner. To achieve this the EU Directive provides that

> member states should allow for the appointment of a practitioner in the field of restructuring where a judicial or administrative authority grants the debtor

63 Ibid.
64 Ibid, Article 11.
65 Ibid, preamble 30.

> a general stay of individual enforcement actions, provided that in such case a practitioner is needed to safeguard the interests of the parties within the RP. Similar to the other jurisdictions compared in this chapter, the RP needs to be confirmed by a judicial or administrative authority.[66]

Furthermore, the judiciary has a role in ensuring the any new finance, or the current workforce, is appropriately considered. Therefore, confirmation from the applicable judicial or administrative authority is necessary to ensure that the reduction of the rights of creditors or interests of equity holders is proportionate to the benefits of the restructuring; and that these impacted parties have access to an effective remedy.[67] Centrally, the EU takes a step further by describing what member states need to confirm that, 'not limited to whether there are dissenting affected parties; the restructuring plan contains provisions on new financing; or the plan involves a loss of more than 25 % of the work force'.[68] This procedural step is important. It ensures that the parties carry out the obligations set out in the plan. It also allows for the debtor to bring an enforcement action that, depending on the member states, is obtained for a period of 12 months.[69] Without such a level of enforcement oversight, certainty and confidence in schemes of arrangements would be significantly diluted.

Nor can the role of the judiciary be underestimated in ensuring the right of parties to decline the restructuring plan.[70] The role of the judiciary in restructuring, again, resembles the role of the courts have in schemes of arrangement in the UK and Australia. Specifically, the purpose is to enable the cycle of the plan to have full and comprehensive effect in protecting or minimising significant economic disruption to the economy:

> [M]ember states should ensure that a judicial or administrative authority is able to reject a plan where it has been established that it reduces the rights of dissenting creditors or equity holders either to a level below what they could reasonably expect to receive in the event of the liquidation of the debtor's business, whether by piecemeal liquidation or by a sale as a going concern, depending on the particular circumstances of each debtor, or to a level below what they could reasonably expect in the event of the next-best-alternative scenario where the restructuring plan is not confirmed.[71]

66 Ibid.
67 Ibid, 48. Article 10, 12.
68 Ibid.
69 Ibid, 32.
70 Ibid, Article 15, 16.
71 Ibid, 49. However, where the plan is confirmed through a cross-class cram-down, reference should be made to the protection mechanism used in such scenario. Where Member States opt to carry out a valuation of the debtor as a going concern, the going-concern value should take into account the debtor's business in the longer term, as opposed to the liquidation value. The going-concern value is, as a rule, higher than the liquidation value because it is based on the assumption that the business

Any plan needs also to take into account the contractual rights of the debtor that have been provided for in accordance with ipso facto clauses. Typically, supply contracts that contain *ipso factor* clauses enable the contract to be terminated on grounds of insolvency. The plan may also be used when a debtor applies for preventive restructuring measures. Conversely, creditors, workers, and equity holders, where permitted under national law, have a right to vote on the adoption of a restructuring plan.[72] Additionally, where the plan has been challenged on grounds of not complying with the best-interests-of-creditors, further conditions can be established by member states to protect equity holder(s).[73] Yet, any such additional conditions regarding *ex officio* participation, can be refused by the judiciary and should not prevent insolvency of the debtor or ensuring the viability of the business.[74] Arguably, these additional conditions assist in supporting the economic integrity and stability of the Union and commercial activities taking place in its member states. Nevertheless, the question arises as to the requisite contents of a plan. Article 8 directs member states to ensure a minimum standard is used. It states that a restructuring plan is to confirm:

- the identity of the debtor;
- the debtor's assets and liabilities at the time of submission of the restructuring plan, including a value for the assets, a description of the economic situation of the debtor and the position of workers, and a description of the causes and the extent of the difficulties of the debtor;
- the affected parties, whether named individually or described by categories of debt in accordance with national law, as well as their claims or interests covered by the restructuring plan;
- where applicable, the classes into which the affected parties have been grouped, for the purpose of adopting the restructuring plan, and the respective values of claims and interests in each class;
- where applicable, the parties, whether named individually or described by categories of debt in accordance with national law, which are not affected by the restructuring plan, together with a description of the reasons why it is proposed not to affect them;
- where applicable, the identity of the practitioner in the field of restructuring; and the terms of the restructuring plan, including, in particular
- any proposed restructuring measures as referred to in point (1) of Article 2(1);[75]

continues its activity with the minimum of disruption, has the confidence of financial creditors, shareholders and clients, continues to generate revenues, and limits the impact on workers.

72 Ibid, (43). Member States should be able to provide for limited exceptions to this rule. Parties unaffected by the restructuring plan should have no voting rights in relation to the plan, nor should their support be required for the approval of any plan.

73 Ibid.

74 Ibid, (50).

75 Ibid, Article 8, (ii) where applicable, the proposed duration of any proposed restructuring measures; (iii) the arrangements with regard to informing and consulting the employees' representatives in accordance with Union and national law; (iv) where applicable, overall consequences as regards

- a statement of reasons which explains why the restructuring plan has a reasonable prospect of preventing the insolvency of the debtor and ensuring the viability of the business, including the necessary pre-conditions for the success of the plan.[76]

The contents of any plan, in our view, is one of the most important components to any restructuring, specifically protecting current and future financing. From a policy perspective, the protection of new financing and new creditors is necessarily at the forefront of any restructure. It will, in part, protect not only creditors and debtors, but also the legal mechanisms of the Plan that are directed at providing broader protection to the overall economy. To achieve these protections, Article 17, requires that new and interim finance be safeguarded. However, Article 18, goes further. It requires that,

> without prejudice to Article 17, Member States shall ensure that, in the event of any subsequent insolvency of a debtor, transactions that are reasonable and immediately necessary for the negotiation of a restructuring plan are not declared void, voidable or unenforceable on the ground that such transactions are detrimental to the general body of creditors, unless other additional grounds laid down by national law are present.[77]

The remaining Articles of the Restructuring Directive address the directors' duties and judicial procedure, which are both out of scope of this chapter.

In essence, the EU Directive, while given a different name to schemes of arrangements, has arguably embraced the universalist approach attributable to such schemes. In large part, the EU project of legal harmonisation and convergence has forced the establishment of this Directive, to enhance and strengthen the EU's single market. Without it, the EU would have faced fragmented national laws that would undermine the objective of ensuring the strength and stability of the Union's economy including in times of financial stress. Arguably, adopting the Union approach, as supported by its regional framework, it is a step towards the internationalisation of schemes of arrangement and restructuring plans. Following the EU

---

employment such as dismissals, short-time working arrangements or similar; (v) the estimated financial flows of the debtor, if provided for by national law; and (vi) any new financing anticipated as part of the restructuring plan, and the reasons why the new financing is necessary to implement that plan.

76 Ibid. Member States may require that that statement of reasons be made or validated either by an external expert or by the practitioner in the field of restructuring if such a practitioner is appointed. Member States shall make available online a comprehensive check-list for restructuring plans, adapted to the needs of SMEs. The check-list shall include practical guidelines on how the restructuring plan has to be drafted under national law. The check-list shall be made available in the official language or languages of the Member State. Member States shall consider making the check-list available in at least one other language, in particular in a language used in international business.

77 Ibid, Article 17–18.

restructuring model could be a starting point in establishing specific schemes at the international level.

3.3.1 United Kingdom

The UK has arguably established itself as a business-friendly hub in the northern hemisphere, for some time. It has assisted to promote SAs as sustainable alternatives to insolvency proceedings. The English law scheme of arrangement is, like its counterparts in other jurisdictions compared in this book, a court approved compromise or arrangement between a company and its shareholders or creditors that can be used to maintain solvency of a financially distressed debtor. Its increased importance as a tool for restructuring to prevent or reduce the risk of insolvency is readily reflected in the diversification of financing sources sought over the past decade since the 2009 financial crisis. However, following the recasting of the European Insolvency Regulation (EIR)[78] in 2017, the European Restructuring Directive (ERD)[79] in 2019, and Brexit in 2020–2021, could impact upon regulatory competition and the market for corporate restructuring throughout the EU.[80] Horst Eidenmüller is of the view that there will be less regulatory competition and that the UK will almost certainly lose its dominant market position.[81] This prospective loss of UK dominance over SAs is even more likely after the adoption of Brexit, from whence the EU's dominance is likely to expand.

Eidenmüller argues that the UK has been losing its appeal as a restructuring tool in cross-border settings since 2016. He believes the key issue that has arisen is with respect to regulatory competition in corporate insolvency (law) that contains possible externalities in the choices available to dominant market actors. More importantly, the EU has directed attention to establishing a legal framework that focuses on preventing insolvency, giving the debtor benefit of the restructure. This preventative approach also aims to protect the overall financial economy from entities that find themselves in economic difficulty. The EIR, according to Eidenmüller, sought to achieve this to discourage parties from engaging in forum shopping for alternative jurisdictions and laws. However, the UK has remained an attractive jurisdiction for corporate restructuring, notably from its Scheme of Arrangement, a procedure that is not contained directly in the EIR.

Arguably, the 2017 recast of the 2017 EIR did not reverse such forum shopping in corporate restructuring. However, the 2019 ERD to be implemented in 2021,

78 Council Regulation (EC) No. 1346/2000, European Insolvency Regulation, of 29 May 2000 on insolvency proceedings [2000] OJL 160/1–18.

79 Directive (EU) 2019/1023, European Restructuring Directive of the European Parliament and of the Council of 20 June 2019 on preventive restructuring frameworks [2019] OLJ 172/18–55.

80 Horst Eidenmüller, The Rise and Fall of Regulatory Competition in Corporate Insolvency in the European Union, *The European Business Organization Law Review*, Vol. 20 (2009), 547–566.

81 Ibid.

is likely to reduce such forum shopping.[82] Whether it will substantially reverse the dominance of the UK in the European restructuring market is uncertain. The EU's approach has nevertheless advanced in adopting an early interventionist approach to insolvency by providing for the restructuring of debt. Whether this framework has been fully effective post Brexit, was to early to determine in 2022. For instance, entities located in the EU may turn to the UK, if their respective legal frameworks remain corporate friendly, to establish the main office-branch in the UK, rather than in the Union. The far-reaching issue of insufficient harmony in international business extends beyond Brexit. In issue is the overarching need for greater consistency in corporate restructuring and less emphasis on competition among regulatory states. This issue extends beyond whether the regulatory states in issue is the EU or the UK, to the manner of such regulation, and to the extent to which it diverges between them as well as from regulatory states elsewhere. In the eyes of Eidenmüller, the

> European law-maker still struggles to find a consistent approach to the fundamental issue of harmonisation versus regulatory competition – in corporate (insolvency) law as elsewhere. In corporate insolvency law, for example, the recast EIR now explicitly acknowledges that forum shopping and the associated regulatory competition may be a good thing. On the other hand, European lawmakers continue to harmonise member states' pre-insolvency restructuring frameworks, edging out differences and reducing the incentive to *forum shop*.[83]

Using related arguments, Eidenmüller maintains that the ERD is inefficient and harmful legislation and should be repealed.[84]

In effect, harmonisation in corporate restructuring as conceived in the EU, and SAs in the UK is more salient, from the perspective of trans-border economic stability than the stature of a dominant state whose restructuring or SA regime transcends regulatory regimes in other states. In issue is whether Brexit could have a detrimental impact to restructuring of UK entities that are located in the EU, and vice versa. On the one side, following the implementation of the 2002 EIR, corporate entities opted to seek restructuring under the UK's scheme of arrangement with its hub in London. This was due, in part, to the adoption of an SA scheme there, but also to the UK offering a professional restructuring services. This included the ability of corporate debtors and their creditors to adopt SAs in the UK both flexibly and effectively and both before and after insolvency.

What will be fascinating to observe, over time, is whether UK legislators undertakes a reform program to make insolvency more efficient and effective, not only

82 Ibid.
83 Ibid.
84 Ibid.

for UK entities vis-à-vis EU creditors in London, but also in recognition of UK creditors operating in the EU. Viewed negatively, if competition between the EU and UK to attract international business becomes more intensive, a regulatory war could eventuate. Viewed positively, a regulatory regime that minimalises red tape in corporate restructuring would enhance both EU-UK and global financial dealings.

In 2020, the UK adopted the Corporate Insolvency and Governance Act (the Act), shortly before the Brexit-Deal was finalised.[85] Schedule 9 of the Act made provision for arrangements and restructuring for companies in financial difficulty. The Act reinforced developing UK law in which scheme of arrangement entails three functional steps. First, it requires that a 'compromise or arrangement' be proposed between the company and its members or creditors. That scheme will often be proposed by the board on the company's behalf. The proposal was followed by a judicial application under section 896 of the Companies Act 2006 for an order summoning the parties to a meeting or meetings. Second, the meeting(s) of the members and/or creditors will be held to seek the approval of the scheme by the appropriate majorities. Third, the scheme requires judicial sanction, and that judicial order sanctioning the scheme be delivered to the Registrar of Companies.[86] Again, under this regulatory scheme, UK courts have an important role in overseeing the governance of these schemes of arrangements. Finally, at the time of concluding this book in late 2021, a negotiated Deal Brexit had been established, however, there was no information available as to whether the UK will develop new restructuring laws or otherwise depart from the framework identified earlier.

Notwithstanding these developments, earlier UK judicial decisions when the UK was well entrenched in the EU, reflect the UK's long-standing position on schemes of arrangement. This, in our view, is unlikely to change significantly on account of Brexit. The UK is likely to strive to minimalize further changes in order to distinguish its governance of SAs from the EU. It is also likely that the UK will provide additional means of streamlining the process underlying schemes of arrangement to further develop, apply, implement and oversee those arrangements. That said, it is out of scope to conjecture over what, if any, reform might be undertaken in the near term.

What is clear is that English courts have regulated the different stages of SA proceedings to ensure that they comply with equitable standards of fairness, notably in arriving at arrangements with the participation of impacted parties. A central issue, however, is whether English courts are willing to enforce arrangements reached by creditors that are divided into different classes. In *Re Hawk Insurance Co. Ltd*.[87] the Court considered whether to sanction the scheme of arrangements reached in which the liquidators divided the insurance creditors into different classes. While the Court did not provide consistent guidance on the criteria it required to sanction

85 Corporate Insolvency and Governance Act 2020, (legislation.gov.uk).
86 Companies Act 2006.
87 [2001] EWCA Civ 241; [2002] BCC 300, 12.

the scheme, Chadwick L.J. highlighted the importance of procedural fairness in the formation and operation of such schemes. In considering the scope and application of section 425 of the Companies Act (1985), he stated:

> It can be seen that each of those stages serves a distinct purpose. At the first stage the court directs how the meeting or meetings are to be summoned. It is concerned, at that stage, to ensure that those who are to be affected by the compromise or arrangement proposed have a proper opportunity of being present (in person or by proxy) at the meeting or meetings at which the proposals are to be considered and voted upon. The second stage ensures that the proposals are acceptable to at least a majority in number, representing three-fourths in value, of those who take the opportunity of being present (in person or by proxy) at the meeting or meetings. At the third stage the court is concerned (i) to ensure that the meeting or meetings have been summoned and held in accordance with its previous order, (ii) to ensure that the proposals have been approved by the requisite majority of those present at the meeting or meetings and (iii) to ensure that the views and interests of those who have not approved the proposals at the meeting or meetings (either because they were not present or, being present, did not vote in favour of the proposals) receive impartial consideration.[88]

The facts of this case were, Hawk was a small motor insurance company that, for several years, had underwritten a non-life book including liability insurance. The entity had experienced financial stress, leading to the appointment in 1976 of Chris Hughes and Philip Singer from PricewaterhouseCoopers as provisional liquidators.[89] The scheme of arrangement developed for Hawk was an valuation scheme providing estimation of liabilities that did not accurately reflect overall balances in order to achieve an early resolution. This case went on appeal in which the Court of Appeal determined whether the differing treatment of creditors' claims ultimately gave creditors different rights which put them in different classes. In an appeal from Arden J. in the Court of first instance, the Court of Appeal held that all insurance creditors should be treated as one class. The inference underlying its decision appears to be that, unless the rights of creditors diverge material, a court should not sanction the division of creditors into different classes. An underlying purpose of treating creditors as being members of one class is to safeguard their right to consult one another, and that their division into classes undermines that capacity to consult, unless classes of creditors have materially different interests.

The Companies Act (2006) has elaborated on the subscribers and other persons who agree to become members and whose names are on the company's register

88 Ibid.
89 Ibid.

of members in accordance with Sections 112.3, and 895(1).[90] These provisions reflect recognition of the multiple uses of SAs, and their importance in facilitating a valuation scheme providing an overall estimation of the debtor company's liabilities. Adopting this approach under the Companies Act provides a platform for an organisation to determine whether the management of liabilities will affect their future operations.

Further reinforcing elements of the application and importance of schemes of arrangement in restructuring under the UK model, is the High Court's decision in *Re Columbus Energy Resources plc*[91] It provides insight into the essential elements of an SA. There, an application was made by Columbus Energy Resources plc, quoted oil and gas producer, to sanction a scheme of arrangement (the Scheme) under Part 26 of the Companies Act 2006. The purpose of that scheme was to affect a takeover of the company by Bahamas Petroleum Co plc (BPC). The terms of the scheme were straightforward in that the shareholders will transfer their shares in the Company to BPC in exchange for ordinary shares in BPC. Under the scheme, the exchange price represented a premium to shareholders of 11% based on the closing price on 10 June. Importantly, the scheme was approved by the statutory majorities at a meeting of scheme shareholders held on 27 July 2020. The meeting was convened pursuant to an order made by Jones J. on 29 June 2020.[92] It was this proposed meeting that was in issue. A complicating issue was that during June 2020 the world was gripped by COVID-19, and that many countries had very strict conditions in place that restricted the movement of people. This extended to those meetings that were required to vote of schemes and their contents. The restrictions meant that shareholders could not convene in person to vote.

This inability of creditors to vole in person was a significant regulatory impediment to the application of the scheme. Therefore, Judge Jones ordered that it was not possible for the shareholders to consult with each other at the proposed meeting itself, although they will have the ability to make their views known by exercising their proxy voting rights.[93] More noteworthy, is that the Corporate Governance and Insolvency Bill 2020 was passed in December 2020, coming into effect in March 2021. It addresses the issues of having to hold a meeting at a particular place, which traditionally meant in person. Schedule 14, section 3(3) now provides that need not be held at any particular place. Section 3(4) goes further

90 Companies Act 2006, The definition of 'creditor' for the purposes of a scheme is dealt with in Section 5.2. 4 However, an application for an order giving directions for meetings to approve a scheme can be made by any creditor or member, or by a liquidator or administrator: Companies Act 2006, s. 896(2). See Section 2.2.1. 5 Companies Act 2006, s. 899(1) and (4).

91 *Re Columbus Energy Resources plc* [2020] EWHC 2452 (Ch), [2020] 8 WLUK 20.

92 Ibid, 1–3.

93 Ibid, paragraph 16. At the date of this witness statement, the Corporate Governance and Insolvency Bill 2020 is in the final stages of its passage through Parliament. The proposed practical arrangements set out in the Scheme Document reflect the current draft of the Bill which restricts shareholders' rights to do anything other than vote at meetings. It is likely that by the time of the Proposed Meeting, the Bill will have been passed into law, although this is not certain.

and allows for a meeting to be held, and any votes may be permitted to be cast by electronic means or any other means.[94] Arguably, in the modern world in which technology has shifted many commercial operations online, these meetings under UK law can now be undertaken online. Moreover, Trower J. held that:

> The provisions of Schedule 14 of the *Corporate Insolvency and Governance Act 2020* (on the ability of companies to hold meetings during the Covid-19 pandemic) applied to meetings of members under Part 26 of the Companies Act 2006. On 5 August 2020, Trower J sanctioned a scheme of arrangement (the 'Scheme') effecting the takeover of Columbus Energy Resources plc ('Columbus') by Bahamas Petroleum Company plc ('BPC'). The takeover was effected by way of a transfer scheme of arrangement pursuant to Part 26 of the Companies Act 2006, under which the holders of Columbus' ordinary shares of 0.05p each surrendered their shares to BPC in exchange for newly issued shares in BPC.[95]

Trower J. elaborated that:

> the proposed scheme of arrangement under Part 26 CA 2006 must be approved at a court convened meeting of creditors or members, as the case may be, or any class thereof. This process obviously addresses the EU law in requiring a member state to have judicial oversight of schemes of arrangement. Trower J went further stating that in relation to voting majorities, it was established that the votes in favour of the scheme constituted 89.15 per cent by number of Scheme shareholders present and voting in person or by proxy (74 out of 83) comprising 98.05 per cent by value.[96] Slightly more than 238 million of the 243 million scheme shares which were voted at the meeting voted in favour of the scheme. The total turnout of 26 per cent of all scheme shares was, relatively speaking, a high turnout for meetings of members of the Company.[97]

Trower J. went onto say that:

> The first of those issues is that the Scheme includes provision for the treatment of fractional entitlements which have the effect of giving some shareholders a marginally more favourable treatment than others. The second issue is that some shareholders gave irrevocable undertakings to vote in favour of the Scheme. In these circumstances and applying the long-established test of

94 Corporate Governance and Insolvency Act 2020, schedule 14, 3(3)(4).
95 Ibid, 1–5.
96 Ibid.
97 Ibid.

> whether the rights of Scheme shareholders are not so dissimilar as to make it impossible for them to consult together with a view to their common interest, the single class was appropriate.[98]

In conclusion, Trower J. was satisfied that CGIA 2020 meant that what had occurred in connection with this scheme was indeed a 'meeting' for the purposes of Part 26 of the Companies Act 2006. The case raises the question how the Brexit Deal might influence UK legislatures to diverge in regulating SAs from EU Law on a restructuring plan (being the EU equivalent to an SA). It further reinforced the approach generally taken by the Court that a full explanation to the Court is required over how shareholders had communicated the implementation and development of the restructuring plan. For the practitioner, and operationalising the law, these communications could involve the sharing of documents, videos, and the exchange of questions and answers. The purpose would be to ascertain whether the majority shareholders supported a proposed scheme through the exercise of a right to vote.

The issues for the UK post Brexit will be whether the UK wishes to retain the rights of shareholders involved in such reorganisations, in order retain its status as a restructuring hub in Europe, but also in recognition of competition from other global hubs such as New York and Singapore. In our view, the current process is unlikely to change, at least in the short term. The UK will likely want to build on its reputation as being open for SA business, in the face of a highly competitive but also congested global financial markets. Lawyers in London and on the Continent have generally agreed that, for comparable reasons, the UK will achieve these ends and be unlikely to face contrary consequences as a result of Brexit.[99] What is less clear is whether and if so, when and how the UKs dominance as a European locus for SAs will be challenged by modified competition elsewhere as other states seek a greater share of the global financial markets. Such potential competition is also a sound reason, as this book argues, to establish a more uniform global regime to regulate SAs, to promote consistency in the nature and scope of schemes of arrangement. That need for certainty is all the more salient given that debtors and creditors are often located in multiple jurisdictions.

Nonetheless, the UK has already adopted measures to retain and grow its finance markets in recognition of potential competition for market share by the EU and other states elsewhere. Specifically, in response to COVID-19, the UK had engaged in significant reforms of its insolvency and restructuring law. The Corporate Governance and Insolvency Act 2020 (UK CGIA Act), apart from addressing

98 Ibid, 10–13.

99 Franklin Jimmie, Schemes of Arrangement Have Bigger Problems Than Brexit, *International Financial Law Review* (2019). 'The UK will still be an interesting hub for companies worldwide to restructure their businesses via the English scheme of arrangement,' he said. 'Scheme proceedings never specifically benefited from automatic recognition in Europe, and from a more academic point of view, even in a no-deal Brexit situation, the UK scheme could still be applicable.

online meetings of parties engaged in such schemes, introduced requirements for free standing moratoriums and restrictions on termination of contracts for the supply of goods and services. Most noteworthy, was its introduction of a restructuring plan that generally resembles schemes of arrangement.[100] As a sign of the economic impact of COVID-19, the first Restructuring Plan under the new laws was prepared to manage Virgin Atlantic Airways solvent recapitalisation, which expected, at the time of writing, to raise £1.2bn.[101] An important and as yet untested feature of the UK's new Restructuring Plan process, is the possibility of 'cross-class cram-down' directed at binding whole dissenting classes of creditors. Whether or not Virgin's Restructuring Plan will involve the use of a 'cross-class cram down' will only become clear after creditors have voted on the proposals.[102] Arguably, the signs from the UK are that, its 2020 CGIA Act will further maintain its global stranding as a pre-eminent finance hub.

In Re *gategroup Guarantee Limited*,[103] not more than two months following the UK's formal exit from the EU, the High Court on 11 February 2021 ordered the convening of two meetings of creditors of gategroup Guarantee Limited to consider and, approve a restructuring plan under Section 901C of the Companies Act 2006.[104] At issue was whether it was a restructuring plan or a plan of compromise. The Plan Company was incorporated on 8 December 2020[105], and in a sign of possible things to come as a result of the global pandemic, the Court highlighted that COVID-19 was starting to hit sectors, such as the airline and other passenger carriers that rely on catering. The Court further noted the extent of business the Group had before the pandemic had been declared, in 2019. Specifically, the Group had served over 700 million passengers and provided catering for more than 5 million flights. Even though the extent of decline in its customer base and overall business due to flights was not available, the Group was nevertheless confident that it retained a strong core business. It therefore maintained that it could survive the global pandemic and continue as a viable entity as and when flight and passenger

100 Corporate Insolvency and Governance Act 2020. David Ampaw, David Manson, *The New UK Restructuring Plan – The 'Super Scheme'*, https://www.dlapiper.com/en/uk/insights/publications/2020/10/restructuring-global-insight/restructuring-plan/. Drawing some inspiration from a Scheme of Arrangement under Part 26 of the Companies Act 2006 (Scheme), the new Restructuring Plan is a powerful and flexible new court supervised restructuring process that will likely find favour for companies with a connection to the jurisdiction or English law governed credit agreements or contracts to bind stakeholders to a rescue plan. Unlike a Scheme, the new Act permits a Restructuring Plan to be imposed on a dissenting class of creditors, a so called 'cross-class cram-down' which we evaluate in detail later.

101 ASHUST, *Virgin Atlantic First to Launch UK's Restructuring Plan*, https://www.ashurst.com/en/news-and-insights/legal-updates/virgin-atlantic-first-to-launch-uks-new-restructuring-plan/

102 Ibid.

103 Re *gategroup* Guarantee Limited [2021] EWHC 304.

104 Ibid, 1.

105 Ibid, 3.

numbers increased.[106] Importantly, the Plan was only one part of a wider proposed restructuring scheme by which it would address the problems created by the pandemic. The Court, in referring to the legal framework for schemes of arrangement, stated that:

> Section 901C is within the new Part 26A of the 2006 Act, implemented by the Corporate Governance and Insolvency Act 2020 ('CGIA 2020'). The new procedure under Part 26A is intended to draw on the practice and principles applied by the court in sanctioning schemes of arrangement under Part 26 of the 2006 Act. Part 26, the court may sanction a scheme only if both (i) a majority in number (ii) representing 75% by value of the creditors or class of creditors (or members) approve the scheme. In contrast, under Part 26A there is no numerosity requirement: a plan may be sanctioned under section 901F provided that creditors (or members) representing 75% by value of the creditors or class of creditors (or members) approve it. Part 26 applies irrespective of the financial state of the company. By section 901A, however, Part 26A applies only if the following two conditions are satisfied: <u>Threshold Condition A</u>: 'the company has encountered, or is likely to encounter, financial difficulties that are affecting, or will or may affect, its ability to carry on business as a going concern'; and <u>Threshold Condition B</u>: 'the purpose of the compromise or arrangement is to eliminate, reduce or prevent, or mitigate the effect of, any of the financial difficulties mentioned in [Threshold Condition A]'.[107]

Further, the Court pointed out that 'it is a feature of most schemes and plans that the court is required to reach a determination on matters such as jurisdiction without the benefit of full adversarial argument on the point'.[108] On the issue of jurisdiction as part of a cross-border restructuring process, the Court maintained that:

> One of the discretionary factors in relation to a cross-border scheme is whether it will be effective in the relevant foreign jurisdictions. That is of particular relevance, given the artificiality of the structure adopted in order to compromise Plan Creditors' claims, against other Group companies. The Plan Company has adduced evidence from experts in both Swiss law and Luxembourg law. Both experts are of the opinion that the Plan, and its compromise of claims by Plan Creditors against other obligors in the Group, would be recognised and enforced in their respective jurisdiction, notwithstanding that they conclude that it is to be regarded as an insolvency proceeding and thus

106 Ibid, 5–7.
107 Ibid, 35–36–38.
108 Ibid, 71.

> within the bankruptcy exclusion in the Lugano Convention. Both experts place reliance on the fact that the Plan Company is incorporated in, and has its COMI in, England and the fact that the Issuer has moved its COMI to England. This expert evidence (including the steps taken to shift COMI) falls to be considered more thoroughly at the sanction hearing.[109]

Similar to a cross-border insolvency dispute, issues of jurisdiction will continue to arise where branches of a company are located in different states. This will be further complicated where the COMI has been determined to be in one state, and the issuer of the Plan has either moved or resides in another state. The complicating issue of jurisdiction in this case highlighted that, when a member state leaves a supranational polity, the flow on effects, while perceived to be minor, are significant in law. This is because, by moving the COMI from the EU to the UK, the EU is now a third country, and the law of the EU is no longer relevant where it had been identified under the Withdrawal Agreement (see Chapter 3). Finally, the Court in Re *gategroup,* concluded that its jurisdiction applied, that it could sanction the Plan, and that the Plan constituted a compromise or an arrangement implemented in accordance with Part 26A of the Corporate Governance and Insolvency Act 2020 (CGIA) (as stated earlier, section 901C is within the new Part 26A of the 2006 Act implemented under the CGIA Act).

While this case is significant to the overall discussion regarding schemes of arrangement, the subtle but important differences between the cases of *Re gateway* and *Re Columbus* is the reference to a scheme of arrangement versus a restructuring plan. Arguably they could be one in the same mechanism. However, according to the UK Government, the introduction of the *Corporate and Insolvency Governance Act 2020* went further by introducing a new mechanism for a 'compromise or arrangement', widely referred to as a 'restructuring plan'.[110] While the new mechanism has been developed to better manage creditors, similar to a scheme, a restructuring plan provides that:

- a 'debtor in possession' process – there is no insolvency practitioner required to be appointed to administer, supervise or monitor, albeit specialist restructuring advisors will be closely involved in its preparation and implementation, and is subject to court oversight and sanction;
- members and/or creditors are divided into appropriate classes, depending on how their rights are to be affected;
- creditor approval with voting thresholds of 75% by value in each class (Schemes have an additional requirement of 75% in number, which does not apply to the Plan); and

109 Ibid, 211–212.

110 The Gazette, *The UK Restructuring Plan: An Overview*, https://www.thegazette.co.uk/insolvency/content/103936.

- where sanctioned, binds both unsecured and secured creditors (unlike a company voluntary arrangement).[111]

The benefit of adopting this new legal tool that goes beyond schemes of arrangement is that it does not allow creditors to disrupt a proposal that would result in the company in retaining a level of financial stability. Therefore, the question arises whether the new compromise plan intrudes upon internationalising schemes of arrangement. In our view, it does not. First, there can be more than one international scheme of arrangement or plan. Second, however the scheme or plan is named, it is arguable that any legal tool that has been endorsed by national legislation can be internationalised. Finally, the new process implements a similar process to US Chapter 11 being a cross-class 'cram down'. The next section explores how the US has approached schemes of arrangement.

3.4 United States

The US, similar to its counterpart across the Atlantic Ocean, the UK, has also established itself as restructuring friendly. Chapter 11 of the US Bankruptcy Code enables entities to undertake a 'restructure or re-organisation when in financial difficulties'.[112] In regulating cross-border restructuring or re-organisation,[113] Chapter 15 of the Code requires further issues to be addressed. Such scrutiny reinforces that 'schemes of arrangement . . . are continually viewed as an important legal mechanism providing for the estimation and liquidation of a debtor's liabilities'.[114]

The section below will focus on the process and reorganisation or restructuring plan and identify what, if any, oversight is required by US courts or regulators. Chapter 11 provides that both a creditor and a debtor can file a plan to commence insolvency proceedings. Central to the operation of Chapter 11 is to understand the subtle difference between what the debtor and creditor are statutory entitled to do during this first step. For the debtor, filing a plan can be undertaken with a petition that commence a voluntary case, or at any time in either a voluntary or

111 Ibid.

112 Bankruptcy Code, TITLE 11 – BANKRUPTCY. This title was enacted by Pub. L. 95–598, title I, §101, 6 November 1978, 92 Stat. 2549, https://www.govinfo.gov/content/pkg/USCODE-2011-title11/pdf/USCODE-2011-title11.pdf.

113 Ibid, '(23) 'foreign proceeding' means proceeding, whether judicial or administrative and whether or not under bankruptcy law, in a foreign country in which the debtor's domicile, residence, principal place of business, or principal assets were located at the commencement of such proceeding, for the purpose of liquidating an estate, adjusting debts by composition, extension, or discharge, or effecting a reorganization.'

114 Jennifer Morton, Recognition of Cross-Border Insolvency Proceedings: An Evaluation of Solvent Schemes of Arrangement and Part VII Transfers under U.S. Chapter 15, *Fordham International Law Journal*, Vol. 29 (2006), 1312–1313.

involuntary case. Only the debtor may file a plan until after 120 days following the date of the order for relief under Chapter 11.[115] Yet, for the

> 'security holders committee, a creditor, an equity security holder, or any indenture trustee, may file a plan if and only if a trustee has been appointed under this chapter; the debtor has not filed a plan before 120 days after the date of the order for relief under this chapter; or the debtor has not filed a plan that has been accepted, before 180 days after the date of the order for relief under this chapter, by each class of claims or interests that is impaired under the plan'.[116]

Significant too, the 120-day period may not be extended to a date that is more than 18 months after the date of the order for relief. In addition, the 180-day period may not be extended beyond a date that is 20 months after the date of the order. The plan is slightly different for small businesses. Chapter 11 enables the

> debtor (only) to file a plan until after 180 days after the date of the order for relief. Yet, this can be extended by notice and a hearing; or the court. Moreover, for small business, the plan can be accompanied by a disclosure statement and filed no later than 300 days following the date of the order for relief.[117]

This extended timeframe for smaller business, arguably, provides more time for those entities to plan a way forward, where they otherwise would have less capital and other financial resources to fund complex insolvency proceedings.

A further and complex requirement is the statutory obligations to classify claims within the restructuring plan itself. Section 1122 provides that 'a plan may place a claim or an interest in a particular class only if such claim or interest is substantially similar to the other claims or interests of such class'.[118] It is important to note that this is subject to whether 'a plan designates a separate class of claim that consists of every unsecured claim that is less than or reduced to an amount that the court approves as reasonable and necessary for administrative convenience'.[119] Notwithstanding this, a restructuring plan can be filed in court, to determine the minimum

115 Bankruptcy Code, TITLE 11 – BANKRUPTCY. This title was enacted by Pub. L. 95–598, title I, §101, 6 November 1978, 92 Stat. 2549, Ibid, §1121. (c) Any party in interest, including the debtor, the trustee, a creditors' committee, an equity.

116 Ibid.

117 Ibid, (3) the time periods specified in paragraphs (1) and (2), and the time fixed in Section 1129(e) within which the plan shall be confirmed, may be extended only if – (A) the debtor, after providing notice to parties in interest (including the United States trustee), demonstrates by a preponderance of the evidence that it is more likely than not that the Court will confirm a plan within a reasonable period of time; (B) a new deadline is imposed at the time the extension is granted; and (C) the order extending time is signed before the existing deadline has expired.

118 Ibid, Section 1122.

119 Ibid.

level of information that is required for such a plan. The answer is severalfold. Firstly, §1128(a) requires the Court to conduct a hearing on any plan of reorganisation proposed by the trustee or any other party. Secondly, §1123 sets out the minimum required contents of plan. That said, the restructuring plan is to:

- designate, classes of claims, other than claims;[120]
- specify any class of claims or interests that is not impaired under the plan;
- specify the treatment of any class of claims or interests that is impaired under the plan;
- provide the same treatment for each claim or interest of a particular class, unless the holder of a particular claim or interest agrees to a less favourable treatment of such particular claim or interest;
- provide adequate means for the plan's implementation,

(1) retention by the debtor of all or any part of the property of the estate;
(2) transfer of all or any part of the property of the estate to one or more entities, whether organized before or after the confirmation of such plan;
(3) merger or consolidation of the debtor with one or more persons;
(4) sale of all or any part of the property of the estate, either subject to or free of any lien, or the distribution of all or any part of the property of the estate among those having an interest in such property of the estate;
(5) satisfaction or modification of any lien;
(6) cancellation or modification of any indenture or similar instrument;
(7) curing or waiving of any default;
(8) extension of a maturity date or a change in an interest rate or other term of outstanding securities;
(9) amendment of the debtor's charter; or
(10) issuance of securities of the debtor.[121]

These measures pertaining to a class of claims and other interests, could be impaired by the plan unless the plan specifically categorises and details the legal, equitable, and contractual rights that should not be impacted.[122] Additionally, this impairment will also extend to where the plan provides for any contractual provision that allows the claim holder to either demand or receive an accelerated payment following a default. A further impairment will arise where the plan establishes a process to resolve a default that occurred before or after the commencement of an insolvency. Such an impairment will also apply to where the plan attempts to reinstate the

120 Ibid, subject to §1122 of this title, classes of claims, other than claims of a kind specified in Section 507(a)(2), 507(a)(3), or 507(a)(8) of this title, and classes of interests.

121 Ibid, §1123, or of any entity referred to in subparagraph (B) or (C) of this paragraph, for cash, for property, for existing securities, or in exchange for claims or interests, or for any other appropriate purpose.

122 Ibid, §1124.

maturity of the claim, and compensate the holder, and does not otherwise alter the legal, equitable, or contractual rights of the claim.

Nonetheless, and central to the process of filing, is the fact that the plan for reorganisation and restructure can either be accepted or rejected on the grounds of good faith. On the one side, the acceptance or rejection of a plan cannot be achieved following the commencement of an insolvency case. Therefore, the acceptance of a plan can occur where a written disclosure statement has been approved, following notice and a hearing by the court that determines whether the plan contains adequate information. The court may approve a disclosure statement without a valuation of the debtor or an appraisal of the debtor's assets.[123] This is in contrast to other states, as discussed earlier, that require such a statement to provide an evaluation of the assets. When using a disclosure statement, the plan can be provided to each holder of a claim or interest of a particular class. The plan can also be in different forms and apply to each class outlining specific information regarding amount, detail and other information relevant to them. On the other side, the regulator having oversight of disclosure statements can, not only enforce the statement, but also require a review or an order of approval.

A further distinguishing process is the need to comply with the requirements for large and small entities. For instance, because the US has provided different requirements for small business, the court may determine that the plan itself provides adequate information and that a separate disclosure statement is not necessary.[124] In contrast, larger entities should have a disclosure statement attached to the plan. However, §1125 does not provide a threshold of what constitutes a large or a small entity. Furthermore, a court can either approve the disclosure statement in both cases. On the other side, the acceptance or rejection of the plan can occur where the debtor provides adequate information to support its position. Yet, once conditionally approved, the disclosure statement is to be forwarded to the relevant party no later than 25 days before the hearing or confirmation of the restructuring plan.[125] The disclosure statement can be combined with the hearing on confirmation of a plan. The statement is similar to that of Australia's explanatory statement. It provides information supporting the plan, and in the case of Australia, the scheme of arrangement.

A further component in accepting the plan can be found in §1126. It specifies that, following acceptance or rejection of the plan by the creditor or security holder, the Secretary of Treasury has the discretion to accept or reject the plan. However, where acceptance or rejection occurred before the commencement of the insolvency, the plan may be deemed to have been automatically accepted or

123 Ibid, §1125.

124 Ibid.

125 Ibid, **(g)** Notwithstanding subsection (b), an acceptance or rejection of the plan may be solicited from a holder of a claim or interest if such solicitation complies with applicable non-bankruptcy law and if such holder was solicited before the commencement of the case in a manner complying with applicable non-bankruptcy law.

rejected when the solicitation complied with any applicable non-bankruptcy law, rule, or regulation.[126] A class of claimants can only accept the plan upon approval by the creditors. Any class claim acceptance or rejection of the plan can only be achieved where there are at least two-thirds more than one-half of such a class of creditors.[127] Also, on the request of a party, and following notice and a hearing, the court may designate any entity whose acceptance or rejection of such plan was not in good faith, was not solicited or procured in good faith or in accordance with the provisions of this title.

Nonetheless, as with any plan to reorganise or restructure an entity, large or small, there must be provision for the plan to be modified to ensure it is either current and/or meets the needs of the parties, when circumstances change. Thus, in accordance with §1126, a plan can be amended at any time. However, this is subject to the requirements of §1122 (classification of interests) and §1123[128](contents of the plan). A plan that has been modified and meets the requirements of §1122 and §1123, will come into effect following modification once the Court confirms the plan. Such judicial oversight is consistent with the requirement in the other jurisdictions examined in this chapter. On the other side, where the debtor is an individual, the US trustee can modify the plan at any time, following confirmation of the debt. It can increase or reduce the amount of payments, extend or reduce the time period of payments or alter the amount of the distribution to a creditor.[129]

Apart from the overall obligations for the parties to follow Chapter 11, the US court is also responsible for holding a hearing to not only confirm the plan but also ensure a party be provided with the opportunity to confirm the plan.[130] Therefore, in approving the plan in accordance with §1129, the court is responsible to ensure that the requirements of Chapter 11. However, the proponent of the plan is obliged to disclose the identity and affiliations of any individual proposed to be appointed and to serve as an officer. Disclosure is also required of the identity of any inside employee. The relevant regulator has to approve the rates of the debtor and any rate changes.

126 Bankruptcy Code, TITLE 11 – BANKRUPTCY. This title was enacted by Pub. L. 95–598, title I, §101, 6 November 1978, 92 Stat. 2549, §1126 (2) if there is not any such law, rule, or regulation, such acceptance or rejection was solicited after disclosure to such holder of adequate information, as defined in §1125(a) of this title.

127 Ibid, **(f)** Notwithstanding any other provision of this Section, a class that is not impaired under a plan, and each holder of a claim or interest of such class, are conclusively presumed to have accepted the plan, and solicitation of acceptances with respect to such class from the holders of claims or interests of such class is not required. **(g)** Notwithstanding any other provision of this Section, a class is deemed not to have accepted a plan if such plan provides that the claims or interests of such class do not entitle the holders of such claims or interests to receive or retain any property under the plan on account of such claims or interests.

128 Ibid, §1122 and §1123.

129 Ibid.

130 Ibid, §1128.

A further important element in the management of a class of claims, is that each class has to accept the plan or receive and retain the claim or interest in property which are not to be impaired under the plan.[131] Where the holder has agreed to the claim being different to the treatment accorded to others, the plan is to reflect such treatment. In other words, if the claim is something other than property or remuneration, it is to be highlighted within the plan.[132] For acceptance of the plan, it must be undertaken to ensure a class is not impaired. However, a class could accept the plan while impaired, as long as no insider has accepted the plan. However, any confirmation of the plan is not likely to be followed by liquidation,[133] or the need for further financial reorganisation, unless the liquidation or reorganisation is proposed in the plan. Therefore, for a plan to be confirmed under liquidation proceedings would need to have concluded. The process in confirming a plan in the US is similar to the procedural requirements in Australia, the EU and the UK.

In a sign that cross-border recognition of the restructuring and application of schemes of arrangement is growing, is the recent US decision to enforce a scheme of arrangement sanctioned in the UK. In *re Avanti Communs. Grp PLC*,[134] the Court was required to determine whether it could recognise and enforce a scheme of arrangement that had already been sanctioned by the courts in the UK. The judgement highlighted the growing recognition and enforcement of schemes of arrangement sanctioned by UK courts becoming recognised in the US. The case dealt with a 'debtor under the laws of England and Wales, with subsidiaries incorporated in England, Isle of Man, Germany, Sweden, Turkey, Cyprus, Kenya, Nigeria, Tanzania and South Africa'.[135] The debtor's headquarters and primary place of residence was in London. Avanti was a satellite operator providing fixed satellite services in Europe, the Middle East and Africa through its fleet of Kaband satellites. The debtor's satellites were positioned in orbital slots that had been recorded by the International Union Master International Frequency Register. Avanti provides for sale satellite data communications services on a wholesale basis to a range of service providers who supply four key end markets, broadband, government, enterprise and backhaul.[136] The case reaffirmed that issues presented by third-party releases under Chapter 15, which received different treatment to Chapter 11 cases and that focus primarily on the foreign court's authority to grant such relief.[137] A central issue in the Chapter 15 case is whether a court should recognise and enforce the foreign court order based on the principle of comity. Well settled case law in the UK expressly authorises third-party releases in schemes proceedings, particularly

131 Ibid, 8.

132 Ibid, 9.

133 Ibid, 10, note the additional administrative requirements under this Section.

134 *In Re Avanti Communs. Grp. PLC* No. 18–10458, 2018 Bankr. LEXIS 1078 (Bankr. S.D.N.Y. 9 April 2018). https://casetext.com/case/in-re-avanti-commcns-grp-plc-1

135 Ibid, 606–608.

136 Ibid.

137 Ibid, 607.

the release of affiliate-guarantees under Chapter 15. The US District Court sanctioned the Avanti scheme, and concluded the:

> Avanti scheme should be recognized and enforced in the US. In regards, to the requirements for Recognition of a Foreign Proceeding, the court noted that §1517(a) of the Bankruptcy Code provides that the court shall, after notice and a hearing, enter an order recognizing a foreign main proceeding if: (1) such foreign proceeding for which recognition is sought is a foreign main proceeding . . . within the meaning of section 1502; (2) the foreign representative applying for recognition is a person or body; and (3) the petition meets the requirements of §1515.[138]

Accordingly, the Court made the point that the foreign main proceeding 'shall be recognized . . . if it is pending in the country where the debtor has the centre of its main interests, § 1517(b)(1)'. The Bankruptcy Code presumes that '[i]n the absence of evidence to the contrary, the debtor's registered office . . . is presumed to be the center of the debtor's main interests § 1516(c)'.[139] The Court went further maintaining that:

> The Bankruptcy Code further provides that a recognition order shall be entered if the foreign representative applying for the recognition is a person or body and that the petition meets the requirements of section 151 Chapter 11 USC §1517(a)(2)-(3). Section 1515 requires presentation of (1) a certified copy of the decision commencing the foreign proceeding and appointing the foreign representative; 92) a certificate from the foreign court affirming the existence of the proceeding and appointment of the foreign representative; or (3) in the absence of (1) or (2), evidence which the court deems sufficient to confirm the existence of the foreign proceeding and appointment of the foreign representative. §1515(b) The petition must also be accompanied by a statement identifying all known foreign proceedings with respect to the debtor, Chapter 11 USC §1515(c), and if applicable, a translation of the evidentiary materials into English, §1515(d).[140]

The Court concluded that by:

> recognising the UK Proceeding (including the Scheme and Sanction Order) and enforcing the Release of claims against the Debtor and its non-debtor subsidiaries will assist the orderly administration of the scheme of arrangement

138 Ibid, 612. U.S.C §1517(a). While not explicit in this Section, the foreign proceeding and the foreign representative must meet the definitional requirements set out in Sections 101(23) and 101(24).

139 Ibid, 611.

140 Ibid, 612.

> by the UK court and help the implementation of the scheme for the debtor and granted the recognition and enforcement of the plan (SA).[141]

Additionally, the Court made a separate order granting relief that had been entered into the pleadings. Arguably, between the common law systems of the UK and the US, a settled position has emerged in which restructuring legal mechanisms, such as schemes of arrangement, will be recognised by each other's court. In our view, legislation and court decisions in both states underscore the overall position and argument embodied in this book that it is time to internationalise cross-border restructuring legal mechanisms. These commonalities are increasingly justified, as this chapter illustrates, in internationalising schemes of arrangement.

The internationalisation of schemes of arrangement is reinforced by courts that apply principles of private international law to resolve cross-border disputes. In *Re Stripes US Holdings Inc*,[142] the Court was asked to 'sanction a scheme in relation to a Delaware company, Stripes US Holdings Inc. (SUSHI). SUSHI's parent was Steinhoff Europe AG (part of the South African based global retail group), and its only significant asset was shares in Mattress Firm Holding Corp (the leading retailer of mattresses in the US)'.[143] Prior to the launch of the scheme in the UK, the Mattress Firm subsidiaries filed for protection under Chapter 11 of the US Bankruptcy Code with the intention of consummating a sale in a short timeframe to take advantage of Black Friday sales.[144] However, in order for Mattress Firm to raise new debt, SUSHI needed to be cleansed of its existing indebtedness, including a USD 200 million credit facility governed by English law. The scheme proposed to swap the debt of SUSHI for new instruments issued by its parent, Steinhoff. The scheme was approved by all lenders under the credit facility that were present and voting at the scheme meeting (representing by value 92.46% and by number 61.29% of all entitled creditors). The Court was asked to sanction the scheme on this basis.[145] SUSHI was a foreign unregistered company and therefore eligible to be wound up in England. The Court then turned to the question of jurisdiction over the scheme creditors, certain of which were incorporated in an EU member state other than the UK. It referred to law and jurisprudence of the EU on the position of jurisdiction, as the UK was at the time a member of the EU. Smith J. ruled that:

> So I come to the final point, which is the question of sufficient connection with this jurisdiction and the effectiveness of any order I might make. As I pointed out early on in this ruling, in this case the relevant agreement which is the subject of the Scheme has a governing law which is English law.

141 Ibid, 19.
142 [2018] EWHC 3098, https://www.bailii.org/ew/cases/EWHC/Ch/2018/3098.html.
143 Ibid, 2–5.
144 Ibid, 9–10.
145 Ibid, 17.

> Generally speaking, that is enough to establish a sufficient connection. The view is that under generally accepted principles of private international law, a variation or discharge of contractual rights in accordance with the governing law of the contract should be done by the court of that law and will be given effect to in other third-party countries. So, it seems to me that this is a case where simply by reason of the applicable law, there is a sufficient connection. Related to this, however, is the question of efficacy. I would want to be quite cautious in terms of exercising my discretion in relation to sanctioning the Scheme were it to be the case that this is something that would affront comity with courts in the United States or in some way cut cross the jurisdiction under Chapter 15 of the US Bankruptcy Code. I am satisfied, however, that is not the case.[146]

Smith J. further ruled that the scheme of arrangement should be sanctioned. The case, while before UK courts, noted that in cross-border issues, the rules of private international law still apply in relation to confirming jurisdiction. The case further highlighted and reaffirmed that the universalist approach to schemes or arrangement has, by and large, been accepted in both the UK and the US. The proliferation of schemes of arrangement, and the growing acceptance of the schemes by courts in cross-border restructuring processes, underscore the argument that the schemes need to be harmonised internationally. While there was no call by the Court to raise the status of schemes of arrangement to an international level, based on the analysis of these cases, both the US and UK have arguably endorsed the need for schemes of arrangement to play a major role in restructuring. In our view, schemes of arrangement are and will increasingly be fundamental to the ongoing rules-based system and rule of law. They will provide the very foundation for efficient and effective resolution of cross-border insolvency matters. More importantly, diverging from these well-established rules will undermine the social and economic fabric underpinning western democracy including its emphasis upon procedural fairness.

3.5 Conclusion

Cross-border insolvency has a very important role to play in maintaining financial stability within the current day global economy. It provides individuals and entities with a process by which to terminate contractual obligations and finalise debt arrangements. However, an alternative and increasingly important alternative to insolvency is the ability for an entity to restructure, whether domestically or transnationally.

Arguably, one of the most important legal tools to have emerged to assist in facilitating cross-border restructuring is schemes of arrangement. They have been,

146 Ibid, 63–66.

in most jurisdictions, supported by national laws. While they have added another layer of law to an already crowded legal framework governing insolvency, the role and responsibility they now play in stabilising broader economic activity should not be underestimated. Without SAs, the ability for a company under financial stress to restructure would be significantly limited, if not non-existent. In most cases, the company would automatically fall into insolvency.

Viewed this way, without the legislative or regulatory backing and the ability for a court to oversee the development of schemes (their content and protection accorded to either party), SAs would have little legal relevance. This court-sanctioned approach to preventative cross-border insolvency measures, benefits both debtors and creditors. It also benefits the overall world economy, particularly in a time of a pandemic and related economic and political shock. Given these developments, it is our view that strengthening and enhancing the preventative approach to cross-border insolvency, as well as internationalising schemes or arrangement and other plans, are to be viewed as assisting most concerned parties, not limited to debtors and creditors. Therefore, in reverting to the questions posed at the beginning of this chapter, the answer is that the flexibility of such plans and differences in their judicial oversight would not inhibit their internationalisation. As a result, cross-border cases concerning SAs are also subject to principles of private international law. Here, the parties adopted a choice of law in their contracts that provide for schemes of arrangement, that refer disputes to national, not only international law is unlikely to displace the application of national law to them. Cross-border parties are expected to continue to provide SAs in their contracts and to adopt national choices to resolve disputes that relate to such SAs. Nor would SAs inhibit the global development of a broader legal framework that provides another layer of legal certainty to cross-border commercial operations. On the contrary, schemes would become a legal priority in calming troubled international financial waters. Drafted clearly through choice of forum and choice of law clauses, court sanctioned schemes that diverge across jurisdictions should not pose overarching difficulties.

By expanding on the already preventative approach to insolvency at the national level and raising it to the international sphere, the benefits of having transnational schemes of arrangement, outweigh their limitations. Adopting a preventive approach to schemes of arrangement that is comparable to the approach to cross-border insolvency, in our view, would enable a debtor to retain possession of the company during the life of the scheme of arrangement. The resulting benefit is in allowing a financially stressed company to retain its management and knowledge base, while restructuring to obtain an improved financial position. Internationalising that approach also provides greater certainty to debtors and creditors that operate businesses in multiple jurisdictions.

The central question in this chapter is whether it is time to internationalise schemes of arrangement. In our view, the answer to this question is a categorical – yes. Based on this chapter alone, reinforced by the next chapter, the value of internationalising schemes of arrangement, restructuring and reorganisation is highlighted first generally and then specifically under the laws of Australia, the EU, UK and US. The statutory and case law adopt similar approaches, although they brand the conceptual bases differently.

Yet, the 2020 introduction of a compromise plan in the UK follows the US in favouring a compromise plan, while adopting a preventative approach to insolvency, outside of a scheme. This process is considered more rigid because it cannot be used to disrupt a proposal that can save a company. Still, this compromise plan does demonstrate a movement towards transnational uniformity, through its adaption in two states that serve as hubs for international finance transactions. It also reinforces the process by which leading trade and investor states continue to look to each other to internationalise systems and processes through their national laws. More importantly, these progressive steps required in adopting and enforcing a compromise plan extends further to protect debtor companies and their creditors by providing an option to precede, and potentially displace, the debtor declaring insolvency. It also adds further to the stability of the economy, particularly in times of global economic and financial stress, including but not limited to the pandemic. However, further research is needed to determine the manner in, and extent to which, other states have adopted similar steps in using compromise plan, even though they refer to them differently.

The chapter does not envisage perfect harmony in the law and practice relating to schemes of arrangement. States that compete for international business and seek to preserve their sovereignty as independent nations, are unlikely to fully forego their control over such arrangements. What is envisaged is the emergence of greater uniformity in the nature and application of such schemes, in acquiring comparable functional properties and being capable of application in cross-border trade and investment. Different nomenclature in describing such schemes is not critical in practice. As noted in the chapter, some states refer to such schemes as schemes of arrangements, while others refer to them as restructuring plans. These differences need to be taken into consideration, but without disregarding their similar purposes and application. Their adoption as legal mechanisms also need to reinforce their function as important alternative legal tools that assist in sustaining companies that are in financial stress. Still, these differences should not undermine the growth of an international regime in which such plans and schemes are capable of being reconciled.

Accordingly, the chapter stresses the virtue of a wider study on the regulation of such plans and schemes within states, beyond their adoption by the states studied in this chapter. Also required is a further examination of the economic benefits derived from such plans or schemes, both in general or in particular cases, to underscore their saliency in the growth of a sustainable global economy.

While there were no national figures at the time of writing this book on the extent of the use of schemes of arrangement, throughout the COVID-19 pandemic, or shortly after its declaration, they are likely to remain in place. In some states, as demonstrated in the chapter, procedures are provided for national courts to approve them, providing a further layer of certainty and security over the process for their legal adoption and use. More noteworthy, is how they have emerged as tools with multiple functions, such as managing creditors, mergers, demerges, takeovers and acquisitions.

The chapter argues that it is time for the UNCITRAL or UNIDROIT, or both, to begin further investigating the benefits of schemes of arrangement for the purpose of internationalising them. Any uniform proposal should replicate the UNIDROIT Principles on close-out netting provisions. Alternatively, either the UNCITRAL or UNIDROIT, or both, should consider the possibility of developing a Model Law specifically for schemes of arrangement. While the arrangements outlined in this chapter generally apply to local restructuring processes, adopting a transnational approach to internationalise schemes of arrangement will strengthen alternative arrangements to the current UNCITRAL Model Law on Cross-Border Insolvency.

Achieving this will have significant benefits in providing the commercial sector with further confidence that internationalising such arrangements will provide both a robust and transnational approach to cross-border insolvency. Importantly, it will further underpin the importance these international organisations have in supporting and developing long standing harmonisation and legal convergence. Part 2 of this chapter examines Singapore, Indonesia, India and China's approach to schemes of arrangement.

3

RESTRUCTURING: SCHEMES OF ARRANGEMENTS PART 2

3.1 Singapore

The importance of schemes of arrangement cannot be underestimated in Singapore. For a number of decades, it has demonstrated that it is one of the top-performing and business friendly economies in the region and the world. To retain that status, the island state has to continue to innovate and develop its legal framework in order to provide businesses with practical ways of managing any restructuring process.

Throughout 2020, Singapore undertook a law reform exercise to consolidate its insolvency laws. On 30 July 2020, the Insolvency, Restructuring and Dissolution Act 2018 (IRDA) came into effect.[1] The IRDA consolidated all of Singapore's insolvency and restructuring laws into a single piece of legislation. Prior to the IRDA, the procedures for a scheme of arrangement were set out in Section 210 and 211 of the Companies Act (Cap. 50). In 2017, the Companies Act was amended to significantly enhance the scheme of arrangement regime, introducing improved statutory moratoriums and pre-pack schemes, amongst other innovations.

In Singapore, the procedure for schemes of arrangement was created by the Companies Act, and its interpretation and application is largely driven by judicial interpretation.[2] This section will not examine the legislation that preceded 2017, but rather focus on the current framework of the IRDA. The IRDA is viewed as introducing a process that is more efficient than the complex arrangements under the law for mergers and acquisitions of takeovers.[3]

1 Insolvency, Restructuring and Dissolution Act 2018, (No. 40).
2 Wan Wan Yee, Casey Watters, Gerard McCormack, Schemes of Arrangement in Singapore: Comparative and Empirical Analysis, *American Bankruptcy Law Journal* (2020), 1–4.
3 Sarah Paterson, Rethinking Corporate Bankruptcy Theory in the Twenty-First Century, *Oxford Journal of Legal Studies*, Vol. 36 (2016), 697.

DOI: 10.4324/9781003311874-5

With the implementation of the IRDA, Part 5 provides for schemes of arrangement. It applies only to cases that involve a compromise or an arrangement between a company and its creditors or any class of those creditors.[4] Similar to Australia and the UK, Section 64 requires that 'a court can restrain proceedings where a company proposes, or intends to propose, a compromise or an arrangement between the company and its creditors or any class of those creditors'.[5] The court's role in this process is:

> the ability to issue an order to restraining the appointment of a receiver or manager over any property, restraining the commencement or continuation of any proceedings, the commencement, continuation or levying of any execution, distress or other legal process against any property of the company, taking of any step to enforce any security over any property of the company, or to repossess any goods held by the company or the enforcement of any right of re-entry or forfeiture under any lease in respect of any premises occupied by the company.[6]

Arguably, the Singapore legislation, and its judicial interpretation, reflects the law in the UK and other common law jurisdictions, in relation to SAs as to other areas of commercial law. In applying to the Court for a SA in Singapore, a company must undertake to ensure that there has been no order or resolution passed to wind up the company, or required under section 210(1) of the Companies Act 1967.[7] Similar to the other jurisdictions compared, the Court plays an important role in the application and implementation of a scheme of arrangement. Section 10 deals with transparency requirements imposed on the parties to a SA, specifically, with the power of the debtor to compromise with creditors, members and holders of units of shares. This power is limited in requiring the debtor company to

> publish the application in the Gazette in at least one English local daily newspaper, and send a copy of the notice published in the Gazette to the Registrar of Companies. In making an application to the court, the debtor company is also required to provide information that the company's creditors will support the proposed SA.[8]

4 Insolvency, Restructuring and Dissolution Act 2018, (No. 40), Section 63. (2) Except as provided in Sections 69, 70 and 71, this Part does not derogate from Sections 210 and 211 of the Companies Act.

5 Ibid, Section 64, (a) an order restraining the passing of a resolution for the winding up of the company.

6 Ibid.

7 Companies Act 1967, Section 210(1). Power to compromise with creditors, members and holders of units of shares. Where a compromise or an arrangement is proposed between, a company and its creditors or any class of them; a company and its members or any class of them; a company and holders of units of shares of the company or any class of them the Court may, on the application in a summary way of any person referred to in subsection (2), order a meeting of the creditors, the members of the company, the holders of units of shares of the company, or a class of such persons, to be summoned in such manner as the Court directs.

8 Insolvency, Restructuring and Dissolution Act 2018, Section 64.

Additionally, where the company has not proposed the use of an SA to the creditors or class of creditors, its application to court must be accompanied by an outline of the SA.[9] This requirement for the debtor to provide the Court with a statement of explanation is comparable to that requirement in the UK and Australia. As a further requirement, the statement of explanation must include information as to why the creditors or class of creditors were not informed of the proposed SA.

In addition to this, the company is also 'required to inform the court of a full list of every secured creditor, along with a list of unsecured creditors who are related to the company, where there are 20 or more unsecured creditors'.[10] However, the Court has the ability to require that any act undertaken in accordance with the order is to be performed within Singapore. The court has the concomitant obligation to the debtor company to submit information regarding its financial position so that creditors can assess its financial stability and that of its proposed SA. The court has the ability then to 'evaluate the report to determine the company's assets and further determine whether the company can acquire or dispose of property, grant securities no later than 14 days following the acquisition disposal or grant of a security'.[11] The court can also require the debtor company to submit periodic financial reports,[12] outlining any forecasts of potential profitability and cash flow from the operations and, where required, extending the period for which any order applies'.[13] Arguably, the Court has a significant role in assisting to protect debtor companies from declaring insolvency. The court's role further strengthens the universalist approach that Singapore has taken towards rehabilitation and restructuring.

Central to the overall process of establishing a scheme of arrangement in Singapore are two steps. On the one hand, it can impose a moratorium,[14] providing that an application for an SA be made within 12 months of the application being filed with the court.[15] On the other hand, the Court can impose an automatic moratorium, in which no order is made for the passing of a resolution for the winding up of the company, or to restrain the appointment of a receiver or manager.[16] Furthermore, where an automatic moratorium applies, no execution, action based on distress or other legal process can commence. Nor can any steps be taken to enforce any security of property or repossession of goods under any chattels leasing agreement or hire-purchase agreement.[17] Nonetheless, the 'company

9 Ibid, Section 211.
10 Ibid.
11 Ibid, Section 64(6)(b).
12 Ibid, Section 64(6)(c).
13 Ibid, Section 64(6)(d).
14 Ibid, Section 64(8).
15 Ibid, Section 64(9).
16 Ibid, (c) no proceedings (other than proceedings under Section 210 or 212 of the Companies Act, or this Section or Section 66, 69 or 70) may be commenced or continued against the company, except with the leave of the Court and subject to such terms as the Court imposes.
17 Insolvency, Restructuring and Dissolution Act 2018, (No. 40 of 2018), Section 64(8). (f) despite Sections 18 and 18A of the Conveyancing and Law of Property Act, no right of re-entry or forfeiture under any lease in respect of any premises occupied by the company may be enforced, except with the leave of the Court and subject to such terms as the Court imposes.

is obliged to within 14 days from when the order' is made, to lodge the order with the Registrar of Companies.[18]

Notwithstanding this, Section 65 goes onto provide:

> the court with the power and ability to restrain certain proceedings that have been afforded under section 64(1), above. Thus, section 65 allows the court to make an order restraining the passing of a resolution for the winding up of the company or restrain the appointment of a receiver. It can also restrain the commencement or continuation of any proceedings against the related company, except with the leave of the Court. However, the court can further impose further restraints on the commencement, continuation or levying of any execution, distress or other legal process against any property.[19]

A further restraint can be applied to stop the enforcement of securities in relation to property and any right of re-entry. However, any application for restraint can only be achieved when no order has been made, an order under section 64(1) is currently being enforced, or the company has a significant role in the SA.[20] Additional requirements can also be imposed during the moratorium period in relation to the disposition of property.[21] Therefore, the Court can impose a moratorium where the creditor has submitted an application to restrain the company from disposing of property, transferring shares or altering the rights of company members. However, this is not a mandatory process of the Court.

In *Re IM Skaugen SE and other matters*[22] these considerations relating to a moratorium were considered by the High Court of Singapore:

> IMSPL Pte. Ltd., an entity in the Skaugen Group of companies, filed an application for a moratorium order pursuant to Section 211B of the Companies Act. At the time, IMSPL had yet to propose a scheme to its creditors, but had stated its intention to do so. On the other hand, MAN Energy Solutions SE opposed the moratorium application. At issues was that the scheme under normal circumstances would not be approved, which amounted to 76% of IMSPL's unsecured debt. In seeking a moratorium, the Court granted

18 Ibid, an order made under subsection (1), (7) or (10).

19 Ibid, (other than Section 210 or 212 of the Companies Act or this Section or Section 66, 69 or 70).

20 Ibid, Section 65, (d) the compromise or arrangement mentioned in paragraph (c) will be frustrated if one or more of the actions that may be restrained by an order under subsection (1) are taken against the related company; (e) the Court is satisfied that the creditors of the related company will not be unfairly prejudiced by the making of an order under subsection (1). (3) When the related company makes the application under subsection (1) to the Court (a) the related company must publish a notice of the application in the Gazette and in at least one English local daily newspaper, and send a copy of the notice published in the Gazette to the Registrar of Companies.

21 Ibid, Section 66.

22 *Re IM Skaugen SE and other matters* [2018] SGHC 259.

> IMSPL's application, based on the restructuring process that Skaugen had undertaken and creditors did not object to IMSPL's application.[23]

Three important but overlapping issues emerged from this case. First, the case was the requirement that the moratorium application be made in accordance with the Companies Act. Second, was the recognition of schemes of arrangement. Third, the Court was required to determine whether the restructuring approach fell within the international legal framework established by the UNCITRAL Model Law on Cross-Border Insolvency.

The Court ruled that 'MAN SE's objections were not fatal to the moratorium application because a scheme had yet to be proposed, thus leaving the door open for the scheme to address this and any other issues that arise'.[24] However, the Court evaluated the test by which to confirm the level of evidence required for a scheme of arrangement to be operational. It held that the test was 'whether on a broad assessment, there was sufficient evidence for the court to determine that there was a reasonable prospect of the compromise or arrangement working and being acceptable to the general run of creditors.'[10] In reconciling the Singapore approach towards insolvency and schemes of arrangement, the Court held that the scheme:

> as originally designed was not intended as an insolvency regime, but a means of facilitating the adjustment of shareholders' rights, or creditors' rights, without the need for unanimity from the shareholders or creditors as the case may be. It allowed for a statutory cram-down of contractual rights, provided that minimum thresholds of support had been obtained. It was a hybrid mechanism that allowed the implementation of debt restructuring arrangements, without being seen as making an insolvency application, under a process that involved a layer of judicial oversight to ensure that the rights of minority creditors were not unfairly or oppressively subjugated. As such, it fell short of formal insolvency proceedings.[25]

On the other side, and while the IRDA had not yet been implemented, the Court noted that the statutory regime surrounding schemes of arrangement would change from the earlier rights-based debt restructuring program to what the Court defined as a debtor-in-possession regime.[26] The decision further clarified the threshold required for companies to apply to the former section 211B moratorium, now section 66 under IRDA. The Court held that 'it lacked a level of protection in relation to moratoriums, when compare with liquidation and judicial management

23 Ibid, 1.
24 Ibid.
25 Ibid, 30.
26 Ibid, 31.

under the Act'.[27] Most noteworthy, was the acceptance and reaffirmation of the overall universalist approach that Singapore has taken to cross-border insolvency and restructuring. The Court stated that:

> 'The changes brought about by the s 211B, which was only recently introduced via the Companies (Amendment) Act 2017 (No 15 of 2017) ('the Amendment Act'), were undertaken in an attempt to enhance Singapore's restructuring framework and to further Singapore's capabilities in managing cross-border insolvencies. The key changes related to the framework for schemes of arrangement and judicial management, rescue financing, pre-package schemes, and cram-down provisions as well as the adoption of the UNCITRAL Model Law on Cross-Border Insolvency.[28]

The Court concluded and granted the moratorium orders on the terms that were sought. The case, while not calling for the internationalisation of schemes of arrangement, demonstrated that cross-border restructuring is as important, and quite possibly more important, in the contemporary world than ever before.

In a further case related to a moratorium concerning restructuring was *Hyflux Ltd. v. SM Investments Pte. Ltd.*[29] The Court noted that, during the course of 2018, the plaintiff and defendant entered into negotiations, which led to the conclusion of the Restructuring Agreement. The application for a Restructuring Plan stemmed from an agreement between the parties relating to an investment by the defendant in the plaintiff, Hyflux (Restructuring Agreement). The plaintiff was at material times, and at the time of this judgment, in the midst of a restructuring effort. The plaintiff was covered by a moratorium under s 211B of the Companies Act (Cap 50, 2006 Rev Ed) ('CA') which has been extended by the Court several times since 2018. The moratorium was imposed to allow the plaintiff to eventually propose a scheme of arrangement to its creditors.[30]

Under the Restructuring Agreement, the defendant would invest in the plaintiff by, inter alia, subscribing for shares in the plaintiff. Various conditions were specified in the Restructuring Agreement. Clause 5.1(e)(i), stipulated that the consent of the Public Utilities Board ('PUB') for the change in control of Tuaspring Pte.

27 Ibid, 32. At para 33 and 35, the Court went further in identifying two weaknesses in the moratorium for a scheme of arrangement. First, that the moratorium for a scheme of arrangement was not available upon filing and only on application, unlike the automatic moratorium which applied upon filing for judicial management pursuant to s 227C of the Act, a non-debtor-in-possession insolvency regime. The second weakness that was identified was the precondition that a moratorium might only be ordered under s 210(10) if a compromise or arrangement 'had been proposed' between the company and its creditors. In other words, a compromise had to be first proposed before an application under s 210(10) could be made.

28 Ibid, [29].

29 Hyflux Ltd v. SM Investments Pte Ltd [2019] SGHC 236, https://www.supremecourt.gov.sg/docs/default-source/module-document/judgement/hyflux-v-smi-gd-final-pdf.pdf.

30 Ibid, 2.

Ltd. ('Tuaspring'), a subsidiary of the plaintiff which ran a desalination plant, was to be obtained. The Court ruled that:

> Under [former] s 211B of the CA, an automatic moratorium is triggered when an application is made. Prior to the expiry of the automatic moratorium period, the applicant may apply for an extension, the granting of which is at the discretion of the court and grounded in the provisions of s 211B of the CA. It is clear from the statutory provisions that the court's discretion is wide enough to allow for the imposition of various conditions, and carve outs may be allowed for certain claims by creditors.[31]

The Court went onto say that:

> While there does not appear to be any mention of an exception for counterclaims in any of the Parliamentary debates relating to the enactment of s 211B of the CA, I do not find that the intention was manifested to require leave to be obtained for counterclaims. Clearer language would have been expected to be used had that been the intention. It follows that a counterclaim made in respect of a claim brought by a company undergoing s 211B restructuring would not require leave of court, but only in so far as it operates to extinguish or negate the claim, without affecting the position of the other creditors. Thus, any part of a counterclaim that goes beyond operating as a defence, such as a claim for damages or property, would require the leave of court.[32]

Since the implementation of the IRDA, the moratorium process provides further time for parties to adjust their respective claims and counterclaims, in order for an entity to continue in another form, at a later point in time. Since the implementation of IRDA and at the time of writing this book, there had been no further consideration given by the courts to section 66. What this process also informs, is the commitment that Singapore has made to provide for a string of preventative regulatory approaches that minimise the impact of the restructuring of corporate debt upon the economy and overall community.

The IRDA addressed in its implementation measures, is how rescue financing is to be undertaken. According to section 67,

> where an order has been applied for under the aforementioned section 64(1), the court can impose further orders on the company that if the company is wound up, the debt arising from any rescue financing obtained, or to be obtained, by the company is to be treated as if it were part of the costs, and

31 Ibid, 11–12.
32 Ibid, 221–223.

> the debt arising from any rescue financing obtained is to have priority over all the preferential debts that have been specified.[33]

Yet, any rescue financing is to be secured by security interest. The security interest that is subject to an 'existing security interest has priority where the company would not have been able to obtain the rescue financing and there is adequate protection for the interests of the holder'.[34] Upon such an application under section 67, a notice must be forwarded to each creditor. However, the 'reversal or modification on appeal of an order under subsection (1)(c) or (d) does not affect the validity of any debt incurred'.[35] Interestingly, the Act does not provide specifically for the content of an SA, unlike some of the other jurisdictions compared that either specify the contents of the scheme, reorganisation or restructuring plan. That is something that Singapore might consider in the future.

Nevertheless, in accordance with section 68 of the IRDA,

> where it is ordered by the court under section 210(1) of the Companies Act a meeting of the creditors, or a class of creditors, the company is required to state in every notice mentioned in section 211(1) of that Act, the manner in which a creditor is to file a proof of debt with the company; and the period within which the proof is to be filed. Moreover, at section 69, the court can order a re-vote, and under section 70, the court has the power to cram down provided it applies to a compromise or a scheme.[36]

This test for establishing a scheme is that at least a majority in number of creditors in each class votes in favour of a scheme. That means that a group of dissenting creditors who whose claims are comparatively small in value will not have their votes substantially diluted because the value of their claims is comparatively small to one or more large creditors. That is,

> single creditor with a claim whose value exceeds 75 per cent of the total value of creditor claims may satisfy the value test on its own, but will still only be able to push through a scheme if a majority in number of creditors, including other creditors who may have smaller claims, also vote in favour of the scheme.[37]

With the oversight of the Court approving the SA and where the voting thresholds have been met, the Court will need to be satisfied, before so approving,

33 Insolvency, Restructuring and Dissolution Act 2018, (No. 40 of 2018), Section 67.
34 Ibid.
35 Ibid.
36 Ibid, Section 68.
37 Mohan Gopalan, Creditor Schemes of Arrangement and dissenting Creditor Protection, *SAcLJ*, Vol. 30, No. 2 (2018), 902.

that those who attended the meeting fairly represented the class of creditors.[38] Additionally, the Court must determine whether the scheme would be approved.[39]

The newly implemented framework imposes the views of majority creditors on the dissenting minority, while the traditional scheme process has certain built in protections to prevent dissenting creditors from being unfairly prejudiced. These protections strike a balance between the policy objectives of promoting restructurings, on the one hand, and the protection of dissenting creditors' rights from being unfairly varied, on the other.[40] The benefit of the judicial management of an SA is most material when the debtor and creditors cannot reach agreement on a restructuring process.

Most noteworthy too, are the judicial management attributes contained in the IRDA.[41] Section 89(1) is material to schemes of arrangement because it provides that the judicial manager of a company must perform certain functions when implementing the overall judicial management.[42] These functions translate into ensuring that, in accordance with any judicial management program, the judicial manager must take steps to ensure the survival of the company, in whole or in part, and that there is approval according to section 210 of the CA or section 71 of a compromise or an arrangement. The judicial manager is also responsible for the realisation of a company's assets or property on a winding up. Managers appointed by the Court have wide powers and responsibilities, as they assume the role of sitting directors. In other words, they have the responsibility to retain the company assets or property rather than proceed summarily to winding it up. Importantly, too, the judicial manager is required to act in the interest of the creditors. Based on this, any judicial order issued generally is valid for a period of 180 days to facilitate responsible management, unless the Court extends the initial order. While there are similarities between schemes and judicial management, they do achieve different outcomes. Judicial management is valuable as a further tool in restructuring and preventing full insolvency of a company. Indirectly, judicial managers are responsible for schemes of arrangement because they have a major role to ensure that the entity survives.

The introduction of the IRDA has, in our view, gone a long way to expanding the overall process to promote and support cross-border insolvency and restructuring. It provides that foreign companies, not specifically incorporated in Singapore, apply for and use a Singapore scheme of arrangement. In other words, an incorporated entity in Australia undertaking business in Singapore, today, can access the

38 Ibid.
39 Ibid.
40 Ibid.
41 Insolvency, Restructuring and Dissolution Act 2018, Section 89. judicial manager', in relation to a company, means a person appointed under this Part to manage the company and its affairs, business and property, but does not, unless a contrary intention appears, include an interim judicial manager.
42 Ibid, Section 89(1).

framework for its scheme of arrangement. Of note, and when contrasted against the UK and US insolvency regimes, Singapore's framework is closer to the UK and Australia than to the US. However, it does vary from the UK framework. Yee, Watters and McCormack believe the English scheme of arrangement is a model for 'early stage' restructuring procedures. They elaborate that Singapore's scheme functions as a de-facto debtor-in-possession restructuring regime, but that it does not have the stigma of a bankruptcy or insolvency because it is a procedure based on company rather than insolvency law.[43] It is activated by the filing of documents with the Court and by an application to the Court to convene meetings of relevant creditors in order for it to approve the scheme.

The value of the process adopted in Singapore for the approval of schemes of arrangement is demonstrated by comparing it to schemes in other jurisdictions such as the UK and US. As a further comparator, the UK model of SAs differs from Chapter 11 of the US Bankruptcy Code.[44] Under Chapter 11, a debtor remains in the control of the debtor company. It allows for the cram-down of entire classes of creditors (not only within classes). It has a robust automatic stay procedure, and sophisticated tools to deal with pre-packs and super-priority financing. Chapter 11 also applies a sophisticated method to deal with valuation of the enterprise.[45] Having an efficient and effective regime in place enables businesses to continue to operate, whilst they are reorganising their affairs. As highlighted in Chapter 1 of this book, this benefits not only debtors and creditors. It also protects jobs and ensures the continuity of economic activity. Importantly, the US framework places the debtor in control of the entity while the process of restructuring or insolvency is underway. The benefit of doing so is in enabling the debtor entity to continue to operate, subject to compliance with judicial requirements established under Chapter 11.

The manner in which courts in Singapore regulate schemes of arrangement is addressed in case law there. Courts have held that they may discount the votes of creditors as those creditor interests (as distinct from rights)[46] may differ from 'ordinary, independent and objective creditors of the same class.'[47] In the *SK Engineering* case, two Scheme Companies sought, among other things, the Court's sanction of two schemes of arrangement that had been approved by their respective creditors in accordance with s 210(3AB) of the Companies Act.[48] The two Scheme Companies then proposed the Schemes to their respective creditors. The material terms of the Schemes were identical, except for the quantum of the failsafe payment provided

43 Wan Wan Yee, Casey Watters and Gerard McCormack, Schemes of Arrangement in Singapore: Comparative and Empirical Analysis, *American Bankruptcy Law Journal* (2020), 1–3.

44 Ibid.

45 Ibid.

46 Ibid.

47 *SK Engineering & Construction v. Conchubar Aromatics* SGCA 51 (2017).

48 Ibid, 3.

for in each scheme, and JAC R&M's acceptance of the JEI Restructuring Proposal within 30 days after the JEI Restructuring Proposal is implemented. The agreement between the parties to that scheme provided that:

> [T]he Company [*ie*, Conchubar in the case of the Conchubar Scheme, and UVM in the case of the UVM Scheme] hereby agrees to sell its entire interest (whether direct or indirect) and/or shareholding in JAC (the 'Company's JAC Interest') to JEI, and JEI hereby undertakes and agrees to purchase the Company's JAC Interest subject to the obtaining of the appropriate waivers and consents in respect of the transaction; and JEI hereby agrees and undertakes that such purchase shall be made by the issuance to the Company of shares or convertible bonds in JEI ('JEI New Shares/Bonds') of equal or greater value to the Company's JAC Interest to be determined by way of a third-party valuation. Within 30 days after the transactions in Clause 2.1 are completed, the Company hereby agrees and undertakes to distribute the JEI New Shares/Bonds to the Eligible Creditors *pari passu* according to their share of the Approved Outstandings (the 'Effective Date'). Within 30 days of the earlier of (i) one (1) year from the date of this Scheme and (ii) the date that the Company receives notice from JEI that the JEI Restructuring Proposal has been rejected by [JAC's R&M] ('the Expiry Date'), the Company shall give notice to the Eligible Creditors as to whether it intends to propose a new Scheme. If the Company intends to propose a new Scheme, it shall have the liberty to convene an Eligible Creditors' Meeting for the Eligible Creditors to vote on the new Scheme within 60 days thereby superseding this Scheme if accepted.[49]

The agreement, provides details of the nature of the two schemes' agreements and the debtor company's obligations, including to provide eligible creditors with notice on whether it intends to propose a new scheme. On the question of whether the assignments of some of the two Scheme Companies' debts were made for the purpose of circumventing the headcount test in s 210(3AB)(*a*), the Court took the

> view that a critical issue arising in these Appeals is whether the assignments to Universal and Estanil of part of the receivables due to Chemicals from Conchubar and the assignment to Emirates of part of the receivables due to MacNair from UVM were assignments which were made for the purpose of circumventing the headcount test in s 210(3AB)(*a*) of the Companies Act, rather than genuine assignments.[50] Without these assignments, the schemes could not have been approved because the headcount test would not have

49 Ibid, 28.
50 Ibid, 68.

> been satisfied: there would have been only one creditor voting against each of the Schemes (*viz*, SKEC) and one creditor voting in favour (*viz*, Chemicals in the case of the Conchubar Scheme, and MacNair in the case of the UVM Scheme).[51]

Central to the case was the notion of vote splitting.[52] Here, the Court undertook its own inquiry and concluded that the Schemes were unworkable.[53] The case highlights the arrangements set out under section 210 of the Singapore Companies Act, and how two scheme creditors and vote-splitting are likely to complicate the approval of those schemes.

Nonetheless, Singapore, by adopting elements of both the UK and US Chapter 11, has retained its position as a regional restructuring hub. Similarly, the implementation of the IRDA has strengthened the application, use and oversight of schemes of arrangement and judicial management there. Its implementation through Singapore law has furthered the universalist approach to cross-border insolvency and the applicability of the UNCITRAL Model Law on Cross-Border Insolvency.

Singapore's approach to SAs is consistent with their overall approach to its broader policy objective of being an international business hub. It reflects the need for insolvent entities to engage in a restructure efficiently. Singapore courts, as in other jurisdictions compared in this chapter, have a major role in overseeing SAs. Their functions extend to being satisfied that the relevant provisions of the IRDA and Companies Act have been complied with, notably that attendees of the meeting are representative of a class of creditors. However, unlike the UK and Australia that require details of the content of an SA to be attached to a scheme when it is submitted to the Court for approval, Singapore does not so provide. In our view, this disparity should be addressed to establish a consistent set of rules to be applied to the contents and governance of schemes that applies transnationally. Wee Meng and Seng Hans Tjio have recently noted that deglobalisation has commenced, even though Singapore is developing 'itself into an international centre for debt restructuring as part of its strategy to export its services and for this purpose embarked on an ambitious project to reform both its domestic and cross-border insolvency laws'.[54] The authors refer to the first Prime Minister of Singapore, Lee Kuan Yew, who was influenced by Arnold J. Toynbee's *A Study of History* who believed that civilisations that succeeded were those that were constantly challenged.[55] 'Creative minorities' maintained engagement and were never self-satisfied. The alternative was stagnation, decline and the eventual disintegration of those states. Singapore

51 Ibid.
52 Ibid, 80–84.
53 Ibid, 98–101.
54 Wee Meng, Seng Hans Tjio, *Singapore As International Debt Restructuring Center: Aspiration and Challenges*, NUS Law Working Paper 2021/004, EW Barker Centre for Law & Business Working Paper 21/02, 1.
55 Ibid, see also Michael D. Barr, *Lee Kuan Yew, The Beliefs Behind the Man,* Curzon, Richmond (2000).

has so survived and thrived economically against the backdrop of de-globalisation, and the continued financial deluge caused by the pandemic upon international trade and investment. Given its success in attracting business globally to it as a financial hub, Singapore is likely to play a significant role in the globalisation of schemes of arrangement. The next section examines Indonesia's development of an alternative to schemes of arrangement.

3.2 Indonesia

Indonesia, as commented earlier in this book, is a civil law jurisdiction. Rather than provide for schemes of arrangement, it has adopted restructuring or reorganisation plans. This enables a financially stressed entity to suspend payments to allay that stress.[56] This section will compare the Law of the Republic of Indonesia No 37 2004 on Bankruptcy and Suspension of Obligation for Payment of Debts (Indonesian Law on Bankruptcy) with equivalent legislations in other jurisdictions identified in this book. It will examine whether reform is needed in Indonesia to achieve greater consistency and to fill gaps in its restructuring laws according to current world practice.

Section 1 of the Indonesian Law on Bankruptcy provides that an entity cannot repay its debt can request that the debt repayments be suspended.[57] Conversely, a creditor that estimates that a debtor is unable to fulfil repayment obligations may also request a suspension of payment of that debt. The purpose, if the request is granted, is to enable the parties to propose a composition plan that must outline a payment offer for the debtor to pay in full or part thereof of the debt to unsecured debts. This composition plan equips the creditor with additional measures by which to secure repayment of debt, while the debtor can only make the request for suspension of its payments. However, Article 223 provides a public interest option for large institutions, such as banks and security companies, to file for a suspension of their obligations on grounds that doing so would be in the 'public interest'. It so provides: 'where the debtor is a bank, security company, stock exchanges, clearing and custodian institutions, central securities depository institutions, insurance companies, reinsurance companies, pension funds, and state-owned companies active in public interests'.[58] That 'public interest' would generally include economic grounds to ensure these institutions have the option to also file for a suspension of obligation for payment of debt.

The law provides that the petition for suspension of the obligation to pay a debt be filed with the Court.[59] It is to be signed by an attorney. If the debtor

56 Law of the Republic of Indonesia No 37 2004 on Bankruptcy and Suspension of Obligation for Payment of Debts, Chapter III. This section has been verified by Associate Professor Dr. Sinta Dewi, University of Padjadjaran, Bandung, Indonesia.

57 Ibid, Article 222.

58 Ibid, Article 223, those that can file petition for a suspension of obligation for payment of debt shall be institutions as referred to in Article 2 paragraphs (3), (4) and (5).

59 Ibid, Article 224.

entity files that request, its petition must be accompanied by a list outlining the amount it owes as well as its accounts receivables. If the creditor so petitions, the Court has the power to summons the debtor within seven days prior to the hearing date to provide an account of the debt. Article 222 also permits the debtor to present a copy of the composition plan in which it proposes to its creditors a plan to restructure its debts and reorganise its business operations, the Plan's purpose is to provide a way in which the debtor can pay its outstanding debts, whether in whole or in part.[60]

For the composition plan to be adopted, the debtor is required to attach it to the petition, for consideration and approval by the Commercial Court. However, unlike in UK and Australian law, the Indonesian Bankruptcy law does not require the debtor to provide details of the composition plan. The law provides for a PKPU (Penundaan Kewajiban Pembayaran Utang) procedure to be conducted before the relevant commercial court for the resolution of unpaid debts. It establishes further that the Court is required to issue a bankruptcy judgment against the debtor 'for a maximum of 270 calendar days after the Commercial Court issues a PKPU court order'.[61] For the composition plan to be effective, it must be approved at the creditors meeting by the affirmative votes of more than half of the concurrent creditors (or their proxies) that are present at the composition the meeting; and by concurrent creditors that hold at least two-thirds of all accepted or provisionally accepted unsecured claims held by the concurrent creditors present in the meeting.[62] The petition is also required, under Article 224, to be made available to the Registrar Office to provide public access to it,[63] Article 225 provides that, when the debtor files the petition, the Court must determine whether to grant a temporary suspension of the obligation to pay the debt within three days of the petition being registered. Further provision is made for the management of the composition plan, including that a judge be appointed, along with one or more administrators, to oversee the management of the debtor's assets.[64]

The procedures when a creditor files a petition for the suspension of obligations for payment of debt are comparable but not identical to those that apply when the debtor so petition. The suspension must be granted within 20 days of its registration. Should the petition be granted, a supervisory judge and at least one administrator is to be appointed who are jointly responsible for managing the debt (assets) going forward.[65]

60 Ibid, the provisions referred to in Article 6 paragraphs (1), (2), (3), (4), and (5) shall apply on mutatis mutandis basis as the procedure(s) for filing a petition for a suspension of obligation for payment of debt as referred to in paragraph (1).

61 Ibid.

62 Allen & Overy, *Restructuring across Borders*, Bankruptcy and Suspension of Payment Proceedings (September 2020), 10.

63 Law of the Republic of Indonesia No 37 2004 on Bankruptcy and Suspension of Obligation for Payment of Debts, Chapter III, Article 244.

64 Ibid.

65 Ibid.

Following the decision under Article 225 on the temporary suspension of debt payment, the Commercial Court through the relevant administrator must summon the debtor and any known creditors to appear before a session that is to be held within 45 days following the Court's decision.[66] Therefore, if the debtor fails to fulfil the requirements to appear before the hearing, any temporary suspension of debt payment awarded can itself be suspended. In so doing, the Court can take the issue a step further by declaring the entity in debt is bankrupt. The composition plan, similar to schemes of arrangement in the common law countries of Australia, Singapore, the US and the UK, allows the debtor to restructure. The composition plan details how outstanding debts are to be restructured and typically provides, among other things, for rescheduled and extended payment terms, perhaps with a grace period, reduced interest rates and a waiver of penalties and overdue interest.[67] However, the contents of the plan are not proscribed, unlike in the common law jurisdictions of Australia and the UK.

In addition to the obligations of the Court, the administrator must immediately announce the temporary suspension of obligation for payment of debt in the State Gazette and for at least in 2 daily newspapers designated by the supervisory judge.[68] Such an announcement requires an invitation to attend a hearing before a judge and set out the date, venue, and time of the said session, the name of the supervisory judge(s) and the name and address of the administrator. There is, however, an additional option available, whereby a reconciliation proposal, a settlement plan (otherwise known as a composition plan), is to be established. It provides the opportunity for an offer to be made, for the remaining debt to be paid out, or for the debtor be discharged from its obligations. Where this option has been taken up, and upon a temporary suspension of obligation for payment of debt exists, the announcement on the temporary suspension is to be made within 21 days before the proposed date of the session with the judge. The temporary suspension of the obligation for payment of the debt will only be effective from the time it has been approved.[69]

Viewed this way, Article 228 refers to the 'obligations of the parties and the court at the session. It allows the court to hear from the debtor, supervisory judge, administrator and creditors who are present or their representatives or Attorneys-in-fact appointed by virtue of power of attorney'.[70] It sets out that the Court will consider all the facts presented by the individuals representing these groups to determine a pathway forward. Moreover, the creditor has the right to present

66 Ibid, Article 225.

67 Dewi Savitri Reni, Dimas Indartono, *Recent Developments in Bankruptcy Law and Suspension of Debt Payments in Indonesia*, https://www.ssek.com/blog/recent-developments-in-bankruptcy-law-and-suspension-of-debt-payments-in-indonesia

68 Law of the Republic of Indonesia No 37 2004 on Bankruptcy and Suspension of Obligation for Payment of Debts, Chapter III, Article 226.

69 Ibid, Article 227.

70 Ibid, Article 228.

relevant information even if it not summoned to do so. On the other side, where the composition plan is attached to the petition, it can be voted upon, provided the requirements of Article 267 have been satisfied. Article 267 requires that 'before absolute decision on composition ratification by the court, the composition plan is to be forfeited'.[71] Nevertheless, 'failure to meet these requirements or the unsecured creditors have not voted on the composition, at the request of the debtor, the creditors shall decide to grant or refuse a permanent suspension of obligation for payment of debt'.[72] Centrally, where the Court decides to permanently suspend the obligation for the payment of debt under Article 225, the debtor is obliged to declare bankruptcy. Any permanent suspension cannot exceed 270 days following the original temporary suspension. Central to any suspension, for a permanent suspension of an obligation for the payment of debt to be granted under Article 229,[73] the Court is to 'ensure that approval has been obtained from more than half of unsecured creditors who are present, and who represent a minimum of two thirds of all claims admitted or temporarily admitted of unsecured creditors'.[74]

Any dispute arising between the administrator and creditor in relation to voting rights is to be decided by the supervisory judge. However, where the 'declaration of bankruptcy and suspension of obligation for payment of debt are heard at the same time, the suspension of debt payment' is to be decided upon prior to determining further issues.[75] These considerations are subject to the qualification that,

> where there has been a temporary suspension of the obligation for payment of debt is terminated because the unsecured Creditors do not agree to the granting of a permanent suspension of obligation for payment of debt or an extension, on the final day the administrator is to inform the court to declare the debtor bankrupt.[76]

Additionally, where there is no agreement on the composition plan, then on the final day of the hearing, the administrator shall so inform the Court, and the Court shall declare the debtor bankrupt no later than on the next day. A creditors committee can be formed and appointed by the Court, where the 'petition for the suspension of obligation for payment of debt includes debts of a complex nature or numerous creditors'.[77]

71 Ibid, Article 267.

72 Ibid.

73 Ibid, Article 229 ('b. the approval or more than 1/2 (a half) of unsecured Creditors whose accounts receivables are guaranteed by lien, fiduciary security, security right, mortgage, or other collateral rights on property, which are present and represent at least 2/3 (two-thirds) of all claims of the unsecured Creditors or their Attorney-in-fact who present in the session'.)

74 Ibid, Article 229.

75 Ibid, 'In order that the petition for suspension of obligation for payment of debt shall be adjudicated first, after the Debtor files the petition for declaration of bankruptcy, the petition for suspension of obligation for payment of debts shall be filed in the first hearing of the bankruptcy declaration'.

76 Ibid.

77 Ibid, Article 231.

Notwithstanding this, the Court has the additional responsibility to instruct the registrar to 'prepare a list outlining each suspension obligation of payment, the date when the temporary payment was granted and permanent suspension along with any extensions'.[78] It should also outline any court decisions on the suspension of payments, the name of the judge or judges and administrators. Importantly, the Supreme Court has the responsibility to outline further provisions on the form and content of the list, which enables it to exercise its discretion in reaching a determination. The remainder of Chapter III pertains to the administration of both temporary and permanent suspension of payments, for example, where there are married couples involved. It is out of scope to examine these provisions further.

Following the 1997 Asian financial crisis, with a notable impact upon Indonesia, the comparative stability of the New Order ended there when President Suharto was forced to resign in May 1998, after 32 years in office.[79] This led to state reforms that drastically changed numerous aspects of the economic and legal order. Furthermore, outdated government rules and regulations (e.g. company law) were gradually replaced with laws which were more suitable for the country's rapidly globalising economy. Subsequently, Indonesia implemented two bankruptcy policy reforms. The first was its issuance of Law No. 4 of 1998. The second was its issuance of Law No. 37 of 2004. These are examined in more detail earlier.[80]

Shubhan asserts that both laws have progressively changed the basic concepts, philosophies, and principles of previously applied bankruptcy laws.[81] Despite this, Law No. 37/2004 still contains two basic insolvency approaches that extend back to the Dutch law origins of the Indonesian legal framework, notably liquidation in bankruptcy and a weak voluntary debt compromise procedure. Thus, the question for the Indonesian Government is whether it wishes to establish a similar regulatory framework for schemes of arrangement that has been adopted in the other jurisdictions examined earlier. Such modifications would go some way, not only to modernise its legal framework, but also to provide an additional level of protection and stability for Indonesian entities. Problematic though is that there is no clear indication of the centre of main interest (COMI) under Indonesian Law. While Indonesia does adopt a multi-layered approach through a petition, composition plan or reconciliation proposal, it varies significantly from other states, particularly those with common law regimes. On the other hand, Indonesian courts have significant roles, acting through the registrar and the judge, to oversee the supervision of the debt repayments. In this case, its regulatory regime is comparable to those in the other jurisdictions. Given the fragmented approach that has emerged, Indonesian entities operating within and with entities from Australia and Singapore would

78 Ibid, Article 232.
79 Hadi Shubhan, The Effects of Reforming Regulation in Resolving Insolvency towards EODB Rank Improvement: Evidence from Indonesia, *International Insolvency Review* (2020), https://doi.org/10.1002/iir.1372
80 Ibid.
81 Ibid.

benefit from being able to rely on a more comprehensive arrangement process. In issue is the sectorial approach to commercial and other laws in Indonesia that has emerged over many decades. This has notable significance for banks where insolvency proceedings conducted through the dissolution and liquidation procedures are based on Law No. 40 of 2007 on Limited Liability Companies (Company Law).

In a more recent development, Andi Kadir observed that the Chairman of the Supreme Court had just issued a decree on judicial guidelines for bankruptcy and court supervised restructuring (PKPU) processes (Supreme Court Decree) which sets out how Commercial Court judges are to manage bankruptcy and PKPU cases.[82] In Kadir's view, the resulting effect was that the Court established Decree No. 3/KMA/SK/I/2020, which only allowed unsecured creditors to file a PKPU petition against the debtor. Kadir maintains that this allows secured creditors to commence PKPU proceedings that forces the debtor into debt-restructuring. The risk in this process is that, if the debtor fails to restructure its debt during that PKPU process, it will be declared bankrupt.

A multi-layered approach to restructuring debt in Indonesia, arguably, would serve both its domestic and its transnational objectives, not least of all in establishing an inward and outward restructuring regime that is both sustainable and efficient. These objectives would be more readily accomplished were Indonesia to embrace and realise the benefits of it adopting SAs, comparable to its neighbours Australia and Singapore. Given that Indonesia, like the EU, is a civil law jurisdiction, it also has the advantage of adopting elements within the EU's approach. The next section will explore how India has adopted schemes of arrangement.

3.3 India

Schemes of arrangement, comparable to the UK, the US, Australia and Singapore, have also formed part of the universalist approach to restructuring adopted in India. Arguably, India, similarly to Singapore and Australia, has followed the UK model closely in its commercial law generally. India is also emerging as an important trading partner of the states compared in this book and across the Asia Pacific Region. Therefore, and given India's large financial presence in international trade and investment market, understanding its approach to SAs is likely to enhance trans-border financial dealings between entities within its own and in partner states.

The Indian regime of restructuring of stressed assets is governed by the Companies Act 2013 and the Insolvency Bankruptcy Code 2016. Both were introduced, in part, to address chronic delays and dismal debt recoveries that were rampant in

82 Andi Kadir, Indonesia: Supreme Court Reintroduces the Right of Secured Creditors to File a Petition for Court Supervised Restructuring (PKPU), *Baker Mackenzie* (May 2020), https://www.lexology.com/library/detail.aspx?g=f910c373-144f-4f97-86a5-1eb3a31396a0.

the financial system.[83] A central motivating purpose was to implement a clear, coherent and time-bound liquidation process and to limit gaps and loopholes in its structure and operation. As a result, the Indian Companies Act 2013 provides the basis for schemes of arrangement to be applied across India. The law provides for court-approved schemes for the reorganisation of failing entities, including their undergoing liquidation.[84] Central to such reorganisations are schemes of arrangement that constitute a compromise or an arrangement between the debtor company and its creditors or between the debtor company and its members.[85] The regime includes the reorganisation of the company's share capital through consolidation of shares of different classes, or the division of shares into shares of different classes, or upon both methods.

An example of restructuring under the Indian Companies Act is provision for a scheme of arrangement that is used as part of a demerger. Reinforcing the application of the Companies Act is the presentation of a scheme of arrangement between Future Retail Limited and Bharti Retail Limited and their Respective Shareholders and Creditors.[86] It stipulates:

> Sections 391 to 394 read with Sections 100 to 104 of the Companies Act, 1956 and Section 52 of the Companies Act, 2013 and other applicable provisions of the Companies Act, 1956 / Companies Act, 2013 for i) Reorganisation of paid up equity share capital of BRL pursuant to the relevant provisions of the Companies Act, 1956 / Companies Act, 2013, as may be applicable; ii) Demerger of the Retail Business Undertaking *(defined hereinafter)* of Future Retail Limited ('FRL') into Bharti Retail Limited ('BRL') pursuant to the relevant provisions of the Companies Act, 1956 / Companies Act, 2013, as may be applicable; and iii) Demerger of the Retail Infrastructure Business Undertaking *(defined hereinafter)* of BRL into FRL pursuant to the relevant provisions of the Companies Act, 1956 / Companies Act, 2013, as may be applicable. This Scheme also provides for various other matters consequential or otherwise integrally connected therewith.[87]

Based on this, the scheme highlights the provisions of the Companies Act 2013 that are material in facilitating and managing the reorganisation of an entity. It is

83 L. Viswanathan, *Schemes of Arrangement: A Second Chance at Resolution for Indian Companies in Liquidation,* http://www.chasecambria.com/site/journal/article.php?id=1277 also see Insolvency Bankruptcy Code 2016, https://www.indiacode.nic.in/bitstream/123456789/2154/1/A2016__31.pdf.

84 Ibid.

85 Gaurav Tiwaris, *India: Binding Nature of Scheme of Arrangement or Compromise,* https://www.mondaq.com/india/shareholders/772784/binding-nature-of-scheme-of-arrangement-or-compromise.

86 Composite Scheme of Arrangement between Future Retail Limited and Bharti Retail Limited and Their Respective Shareholders and Creditors, (Under Sections 391 to 394 read with Sections 100–104 of the Companies Act, 1956 and Section 52 of the Companies Act, 2013, as amended), https://www.felindia.in/Announcements/Approved/Scheme_FRL_BRL.pdf.

87 Ibid.

another example of how versatile and adaptable schemes have become, and, in this case, extended to facilitate a demerger. While demergers are not often discussed, they are equally supported by the legal regimes in most other countries compared in this book. It is out of the book's scope to compare the full breadth of law pertaining to demergers. However, the 2018 case of *Pipeline Infrastructure Private Limited*[88] illustrates the benefit of mergers in facilitating the restructuring of failing companies. Here, The Mumbai National Company Law Tribunal (NCTL), as recently as 2018, highlighted that the 'scheme of arrangement is between East West Pipeline Limited (EWPL – Gujarat based company) and Pipeline Infrastructure for the purpose of merging an undertaking of Demerged Company (EWPL) into the Resulting Company (Applicant in this application with an arrangement of payment'.[89] In reinforcing the current arrangements for SAs under the Companies Act 2013, the NCLT argued that in 'view thereof, the appointed date is hereby decided as the date on which the demerged undertaking has been valued'.[90] Counsel for the Applicant argued that:

> [S]ince the NCLT, which dealt with the scheme of demerged company, has approved the scheme leaving it open to the company to decide appointed date in future cannot become ratio to toe the same line by this Bench, because it is against the mandate given in Section 232 (6) of the Companies Act 2013.[91]

This determination was reaffirmed in 2020, where Counsel pointed out that:

> The demerger will enable the Demerged Company to concentrate its resources on its upstream business undertaking comprising pipeline, integral to the petroleum and natural gas fields, which is a regulated business, leading to better administration and efficiency of operations and the Scheme will optimise the capital structure and profitability for the Demerged Company by way of reduced cost.[92]

To facilitate such a demerger, the Court held that the use of a scheme of arrangement is in the best interests of the shareholders, employees and the creditors of the Demerged Company and the Resulting Company.[93] It also provided for meetings of Equity Shareholders of the Applicant Company to be held as aforesaid, 'a notice convening the said meeting, at the place, date and time of the aforesaid and stating

88 Connected cases *Pipeline Infrastructure Private Limited C.A.* CA (CAA) CSA NO. 719 OF 2018, No. 4097/MB.IV/2019, CP (CAA) No. 906/MB.IV/2020.
89 Ibid.
90 Ibid, CP (CAA) No. 906/MB.IV/2020, paragraph 6.
91 Ibid, No. 4097/MB.IV/2019, paragraph 35.
92 Ibid, CP (CAA) No. 906/MB.IV/2020, paragraph 6 (v).
93 Ibid.

that copies of the scheme of arrangement and the statement required to be furnished pursuant to section 230(3) of the Companies Act 2013'.[94] The Court further directed the Applicant Company to:

> serve notice to the Central Government, concerned Income Tax Authority, Petroleum and Natural Gas Regulatory Board and Registrar of Companies along with a copy of the notice of meeting of equity shareholders, Statement under Section 230(3) of the Companies Act 2013 and Scheme of Arrangement with a direction that the authorities shall submit their representations, if any, within a period of 30 days From the date of receipt of such notice to the Tribunal and copy of such representations shall simultaneously be sent to the Applicant Company and in case no representations is received within the stated period of 30 days by the Tribunal, it shall be presumed that the authorities have no representation to make on the proposed Scheme of Arrangement.[95]

The case reflects a common theme that is emerging in the jurisdictions studied in which shareholders are managed through a restructure, a scheme of arrangement or plan that differ, limitedly, across jurisdictions. The case also demonstrates how India has placed a time limit within which the Court is to review an application, consistent with time limits imposed in most other jurisdictions compared.

Following considerable debate as to whether the scheme was valid throughout 2018 and 2019, the Court in this case, concluded in 2020 that: (i) the scheme does not violate any of the provisions of the law;[96] (ii) it is to be legally sanctioned, (iii) a copy of the scheme and Order of the Court is to be filed with the Registrar of companies, and (iv) all concerned regulatory authorities are to act on a copy of this Order along with Scheme duly certified by the Deputy/Assistant Registrar of this Tribunal.[97]

Central to these determinations is Chapter XV of the Indian Company Act 2013 (CA). That Act establishes the framework for compromises, arrangements and amalgamations, similar to other states compared in this chapter. More specifically, the regulation of SAs commences with Section 230. It provides the power for an arrangement to be established between the parties, creditors and members. Any proposed arrangement between a company and its creditors or class of creditors must be affirmed by a Tribunal that issues an order requiring a meeting of creditors. However, that Tribunal will not sanction an SA unless a certificate from the company's auditor accompanies the SA, confirming that the accounting standards

94 Ibid, No. 4097/MB.IV/2019, paragraph 6.
95 Ibid, paragraph 36.
96 Ibid, CP (CAA) No. 906/MB.IV/2020, paragraph 16.
97 Ibid, paragraph 18, 19, 21.

of the company conform with the arrangements set out in Section 133. That Section prescribes that

> the Central Government may prescribe the standards of accounting or any addendum thereto, as recommended by the Institute of Chartered Accountants of India, constituted under section 3 of the Chartered Accountants Act, 1949 (38 of 1949), in consultation with and after examination of the recommendations made by the National Financial Reporting Authority.[98]

Given these developments, the application for an SA to the Court under Section 230 must be accompanied by an affidavit in accordance with subsection 2. In other jurisdictions, the information accompanying an SA assumes various forms such, as an explanatory statement or some other mechanism or tool. In Indian, the Affidavit serves an important role in requiring that additional information regarding the company be made available to the Tribunal, here outlining the

> facts of the company, most recent financial position, auditors report regarding accounts, any reduction in share capital, and debt restructuring consented to by not less than 75%, of the secured creditors in value. Additionally, it must also include creditor's responsibility, auditor report of debt restructuring will conform to liquidity test.[99]

While most of this information appears in SAs or in explanatory statements in the other jurisdictions compared, an issue for India is whether to follow suit in establishing consistency in the cross-border recognition of schemes.

Nonetheless, where a meeting is required by Order of a Tribunal, a notice is to be forwarded to creditors or class of creditors and to all the members or class of members.[100] Additionally, where a meeting is proposed to be called pursuant to an order of the Tribunal, a notice is to be sent to all the creditors or class of creditors, explaining its effect to them. As a further procedural step, the notice must be placed on the company's website, and forwarded to the Securities and Exchange Board and stock exchange where the securities of the companies are listed. The notice can be issued by advertisement; however, it must clearly articulate the time when the SA will be available.[101] The same notice must also be provided to any person who will have a voting right directly or through their proxy(ies). However, where there is an objection to the SA, it can be made by persons holding less than 10%

98 Company Act, 2013, Section 133.

99 Ibid, Section 230(2), '(iv) where the company proposes to adopt the corporate debt restructuring guidelines specified by the Reserve Bank of India, a statement to that effect; and (v) a valuation report in respect of the shares and the property and all assets, tangible and intangible, movable and immovable, of the company by a registered valuer'.

100 Ibid, Section 230 (3).

101 Ibid.

of the shareholding or having any outstanding debt that is not less than 5%.[102] The notice and any accompanying documents must also be forwarded to the Central Government, the income-tax authorities, the Reserve Bank of India, the Securities and Exchange Board, the Registrar, the respective stock exchanges, the Official Liquidator, and the Competition Commission of India.[103] Any SA that has been sanctioned by a Tribunal will be binding on creditors and class creditors where three-quarters of the majority of persons representing the value of the creditors, or class of creditors, have so agreed at the appointed meeting. Cases from 2018 to 2020 demonstrate how the validity of a scheme can emerge under national laws. It further highlights the flexibility that such schemes provide in restructuring a company, and offer examples of how such schemes are used in demergers.[104]

Schemes are also effectively used in India to facilitate the amalgamation of creditors and takeover offers. In *Miheer H. Mafatlal Mafatlal Industries Ltd.*,[105] in addressing issues related to a scheme, the Supreme Court highlighted the process and treatment of creditors and class creditors in any amalgamation under the CA. The facts were that:

> [T]he respondent-company MIL which was the petitioner before the learned Single Judge has its registered office at Ahmedabad in Gujarat State. It was incorporated on 20th January 1913 under the name 'The New Shorrock Spinning & Manufacturing Co. Limited 'and its name was subsequently changed to 'Mafatlal Industries Limited 'as per the fresh Certificates of Incorporation dated 24th January 1974 consequent upon change of name, as sanctioned by the Registrar of Companies, Gujarat, Ahmedabad. The Authorised Share Capital of respondent- company was Rs. 100,00,000/- (Rupees on hundred crores only) divided into 30,05,500 equity shares of each and 69,94,500 unclassified shares of Rs. 100/- each. The Subscribed Share Capital of the respondent-company as on 31st March 1993 was Rs. 26.30 crores (Rupees twenty-six crores thirty lacs only) divided into 26,90,000 equity shares of Rs. 100/- each.[106]

The Supreme Court confirmed that 'a compromise is offered to a sub-class of a class of creditors or shareholders otherwise equally circumscribed by the class [so that] no separate meeting of such sub-class of the main class of members or creditors is required to be convened'.[107] In doing so, the Supreme Court further confirmed the 'scheme of compromise and arrangement is neither unfair nor unreasonable to

102 Ibid.
103 Ibid, Section 230 (5).
104 See the cases discussed directly.
105 (1996) 87 Comp. Cas. 792 (SC).
106 Ibid.
107 Ibid, 5.

the minority shareholders represented by the appellant',[108] provided that the SA is established according to the process set out in the approved scheme. As a result, the Court dismissed the appeal on grounds that it was not justified in the 'interests of justice'.[109]

In addition to this, the Tribunal, when making an

> order for the purposes of Section 230(6), is to ensure the 'SA provides for the conversion of preference shares into equity shares, protect[s] [the] class of creditors and where the SA results in the variation of the shareholders rights in accordance with section 48'.[110]

Section 48 provides for variations in shareholder rights. The order is also to be filed with the Registrar by the company within 30 days of receipt of the order.

The Court has flexibility is regulating meetings of creditors to vote on SAs. It can dispense with a meeting where 90% of creditors or class of creditors have agreed to the SA. On the one hand, the Tribunal cannot approve an SA on the basis of a buy back. To achieve a buy back, a company may purchase its own shares or other specified securities in accordance with Section 68. It is out of scope to discuss Section 68 comprehensively, other than to note that an SA can include a takeover offer. On the other hand, a takeover is subject to any party appealing to a Tribunal, and the Tribunal has the power to grant the application via an order.[111]

A further question arises over the Tribunal's authority to intervene by issuing an order that requires the parties to engage in specific actions. For example, Section 231 provides that the 'Tribunal has the power to supervise the implementation of the SA. It has the power to direct the parties to make any necessary modifications to the SA to ensure it can be implemented effectively'.[112] On the other hand, where the company cannot fulfil its payment of debt under the SA, the Tribunal has the power to issue a further order to ensure the winding up of the company.

Thus, the Tribunal has important powers of oversight in the implementation of the order and to ensure that the SA conforms with the legislative requirements. Its

108 Ibid, 9(3).

109 *Miheer H. Mafatlal v. Mafatlal Industries Ltd.* (1996) 87 Comp. Cas. 792 (SC).

110 Ibid, Section 230 (6–7), (d) if the compromise or arrangement is agreed to by the creditors under sub-section (6), any proceedings pending before the Board for Industrial and Financial Restructuring established under Section 4 of the Sick Industrial Companies (Special Provisions) Act, 1985 (1 of 1986) shall abate; (e) such other matters including exit offer to dissenting shareholders, if any, as are in the opinion of the Tribunal necessary to effectively implement the terms of the compromise or arrangement: Provided that no compromise or arrangement shall be sanctioned by the Tribunal unless a certificate by the company's auditor has been filed with the Tribunal to the effect that the accounting treatment, if any, proposed in the scheme of compromise or arrangement is in conformity with the accounting standards prescribed under Section 133.

111 Ibid.

112 Ibid, Section 231.

powers to enforce and implement the SA are comparable to most of the other jurisdictions studied. In each case, the exercise of these powers is intended to provide a level of certainty in maintaining business continuity; and to stabilise the economic fallout arising from financial stress upon the commercial sector and public at large.

SAs have a wide scope in India, in being able to be used for mergers and demergers with other entities within and outside of India. While it is out of scope of this Section to discuss these arrangements, when it comes to the transfer of shares under an SA, the transfer can be undertaken, 'provided that every circular containing the offer by the directors is accompanied a statement outlining the money available'.[113] Arguably, the circular is the notice of information regarding the shares. It is to be submitted to the Registrar, and the Registrar can refuse the circular. However, where the registrar has declined the circular, an appeal can be made to the Tribunal.

In summary, the legal regulation of SAs in India are similar to the UK, and also comparable to the Australian and Singapore. Yet, Indian law does diverge slightly. In India, the SA process begins with the board of directors of a debtor company proposing a compromise or arrangement between itself and its creditors or shareholders.[114] Varottil, in confirming this, emphasises that to 'operationalise such a compromise or arrangement, the company makes an application to the High Court to convene meetings of the respective classes of creditors. One issue that has exercised the minds of Indian courts relates to the classification of creditors'.[115] This is because the requisite majority of each class of creditors must approve the scheme separately. Indian courts have generally followed the English jurisprudence relating to classification, in that a class 'must be confined to those persons whose rights are not so dissimilar as to make it impossible for them to consult each together with a view to their common interest'.[116] Indian courts have found it is 'obvious that unless a separate and different type of Scheme of Compromise is offered to a sub-class of a class of creditors or shareholders otherwise equally circumscribed by the class no separate meeting of such sub-class of the main class of members or creditors is required to be convened.'[117] Therefore, for Varottil, while Indian courts place considerable emphasis on classification of creditors, they are not swayed by minute differences among creditors that result in artificial distinctions among creditors.

For India, the SA offers several advantages in debt restructuring. The first advantage is its wide scope. The 'courts have generally interpreted the terms

113 Ibid, Sections 238–239.

114 Umakanth Varottil, *The Scheme of Arrangement as a Debt Restructuring Tool in India: Problems and Prospects*, NUS Working Paper 2017/005, NUS Centre for Law & Business Working Paper 17/02, 6.

115 Ibid, 6–7.

116 Ibid.

117 Ibid.

'compromise' and 'arrangement' broadly to encompass various types of transactions that include financial restructuring, as well as corporate restructuring that might involve the sale of assets or business of the debtor company or its amalgamation with another company'.[118] Secondly, the SA can be utilised in the context of both solvent and insolvent companies. By enabling an early restructuring of a company's debts, an SA can help to insolvency. An SA can also protect against potential cross-defaults that might render the company's financial situation even graver. Varottil is of the view that, the reasons for the benefits of SAs in India is largely no different to that of the other jurisdictions compared. SAs, are significant legal mechanisms that provide an alternative to insolvency. The binding effect that an SA has on the company and its parties, once approved by the Court, has, in our view, is one of the most important instruments underpinning the reliability in implementing these arrangements. The Indian experience also highlights their emergence as an effective tool to manage de-mergers. Finally, India has provided a legal framework in which the debtor company can continue to operate. Such an approach benefits not only the entity in question but provides further and broader benefits to the economy. The next section examines how China deals with reorganisation plans that are comparable to schemes of arrangement.

3.4 China

China's resort to a reorganisation plan (RP) under its Enterprise Bankruptcy Law (EBL)[119] is similar to the EU's restructuring plan. China's RP is also comparable to schemes of arrangement adopted by the common law jurisdictions examined in this book. Specifically, China's EBL was established as a statutory-based reorganisation plan and process designed as a mechanism by which to resurrect corporate entities caught in financial malaises, particularly during financial crises.[120] To date, the EBL and the RP have operated efficiently, as was demonstrated in their application to the high number of enterprises that plunged into bankruptcy throughout the 2008 GFC. Emily Lee noted that:

> during the global financial crisis, the EBL served its intended purpose – the prevention of a greater number of small-and medium-sized enterprises in temporary financial difficulties from premature corporate bankruptcy; but

118 Ibid.

119 The Enterprise Bankruptcy Law of the People's Republic of China (EBL), adopted at the 23rd Meeting of the Standing Committee of the Tenth National People's Congress of the People's Republic of China on 27 August 2006, is hereby promulgated and shall go into effect as of 1 June 2007, Chapter VIII Reorganization, https://www.ilo.org/dyn/natlex/docs/ELECTRONIC/74665/108007/F161827255/CHN74665%20Eng2.pdf.

120 Emily Lee, The Reorganization Process under China's Corporate Bankruptcy System, *The International Lawyer*, Vol. 45, No. 4 (2011), 939.

> the implementation of the EBL and, by extension, China's corporate bankruptcy system was less than ideal.[121]

A central feature of the EBL is the development, approval and implementation of a Reorganization Plan. More specifically, Section 2 in Chapter VIII provides for the development and approval of an RP. The judiciary's role in the RP is confined in the first instance to Article 79. It provides that a debtor or administrator shall, within six months from the date when the people's court rules that the debtor should undergo reorganisation, submit a draft plan for reorganisation to the people's court and the creditors' meeting at the same time. Similar to the other jurisdictions compared, Article 79 also provides for the Court's role in directing, approving and curtailing the RP. Importantly, the Court can rule on the procedure for the reorganisation and determine when the RP should be terminated for failure to submit a draft plan for reorganisation on schedule. A period of three months extension can be provided for the RP to be submitted to the Court. However, Article 79 does not clarify the grounds on which such an extension may be granted.[122] Therefore, any extension request would need to be clarified by a local practitioner before applying this process.

Central to the development and application of any RP is its contents. Article 81 sets the minimum requirements for the content of an RP. These include:

- the debtor's plan for business operations;
- classification of the creditors' claims;
- the plan for the adjustment of the claims;
- the plan for payment of the claims;
- the period of time for implementing the reorganization plan;
- the period of time for supervising the implementation of the reorganization plan; and
- other plans conducive to the debtor's reorganization.[123]

Notably, the EBR does not require premiums to be reported in an RP.[124] Once the RP has been developed, the process requires the draft form to be put to the creditors, through a creditors' meeting, whereupon it can be subject to a vote. Centrally, Article 82 allows for the 'creditors holding the following categories of the claims

121 Ibid.

122 Ibid, Article 79. Note, Article 80, 'Where it is the debtor who manages his own property and business operations, a draft plan for reorganization shall be formulated by the debtor'.

123 Ibid, Article 81.

124 Ibid, Article 83. 'The creditor involved in the said ones shall not take part in the voting of the draft plan for reorganization'.

to attend the creditors' meeting at which the draft plan for reorganization is to be discussed'.[125] Specifically, any 'vote

> can only be undertaken according to the secured claims on the debtor's specific property or, the wages, subsidies for medical treatment, injuries and disability and the pensions for the disabled and the families of the deceased which the debtor owes, the basic old-age insurance premiums and the basic medical insurance premiums which he owes and fails to enter in the employees' personal accounts, and the compensations which should be paid to the employees'.[126]

A vote can also be extended to taxes the debtor fails to pay and to common claims. The notion of common claims is not specific in the Article and would also require further clarification in proceeding under the EBL.

The Chinese reorganisation plan emerged in a somewhat similar manner to other jurisdictions. Its purpose is, to protect creditors and prevent insolvency. That is evident, too, in proceedings relating to procedures governing creditors voting on the RP and the Court approving it. Article 84 stipulates that the Court shall, within 30 days from the date when it receives a draft plan for reorganisation, convene a creditors' meeting for a vote on the draft.[127] Article 84 provides further that the debtors or administrators are obliged to explain the contents of the plan and make themselves available to answer any questions at the meeting where the vote is to take place. Article 86 requires that the draft RP be approved when more than two-thirds vote on the plan. It provides further that, when 'all relevant groups have agreed to the plan, it is deemed to have been fully adopted'.[128]

The final step for approval requires either the debtor or administrator to table the final plan in court within 10 days of it being adopted. The court has '30 days to either approve or otherwise of the plan. Similar to the other jurisdictions compared in this chapter, the court in China has a significant role in approving a reorganization plan'.[129]

Judicial oversight in authorising, supervising and approving the RP cannot be underestimated. It not only protects the debtor and creditors, as other interested parties such as workers. It also provides oversight and accountability, to avoid the ripple effect upon other businesses that are associated or otherwise connected,

125 Ibid, Article 82.

126 Ibid.

127 Ibid, Article 84. See also Article 85: 'Representatives of the capital contributors of a debtor may, as non-voting participants, attend the creditors' meeting to discuss a draft plan for reorganization. Where a draft plan for reorganization involves the adjustment of the rights and interests of capital contributors, a group of capital contributors shall be formed to vote on the matter'.

128 Ibid, Article 86.

129 Ibid.

directly or otherwise, with the entity under financial distress. The overall economic benefit of the RP is to promote stability across the economy, particularly in markets facing regional or global financial disruptions.

A lingering question under the RP relates to what will occur if the creditors vote to reject the RP. Provision is made for a further vote following a further consultation process.[130] If the second vote rejects the RP, the following will be implemented:

- compensation will be paid;[131]
- claims will be paid or the group has voted to accept the RP;[132]
- any repayment will not be lower than that allotted under the procedure for bankruptcy;[133]
- the rights and interests of capital contributors are adjusted in a fair and impartial manner;[134]
- members of the same voting group are treated fairly; and
- the debtor's plan for business operations is feasible.[135]

As procedural steps, Article 88 requires that, if a draft plan for reorganisation is not adopted and is not approved according to the provisions of Article 87, 'the people's court shall rule that the procedure for reorganization should be terminated and shall declare the debtor bankrupt'[136]. This important step provides considerable power to the Court to not only approve, but also to terminate the RP. This considerable oversight can be viewed as a very positive step in preventing entities from entering into insolvency. What is less clear is whether the People's Court will approve or terminate a reorganisation plan for a cross-border restructure. However, comparable uncertainty is likely to arise in foreign state courts as well.

130 Ibid, Article 87.

131 Ibid, '(1) according to the draft plan for reorganization, the claims as specified in Subparagraph (1) under the first paragraph of Article 82 of this Law will be paid in full as far as the specific property is concerned, the losses caused by postponed payment will be compensated for in a fair manner, and the secured interests will not be substantially impaired, or the voting groups concerned have adopted the draft plan for reorganization'.

132 Ibid, '(2) according to the draft plan for reorganization, the claims as specified in Subparagraphs (2) and (3) under the first paragraph of Article 82 of this Law will be paid in full, or the voting groups concerned have adopted the draft plan for reorganization'.

133 Ibid, '(3) according to the draft plan for reorganization, the proportion for repayment of the common claims will not be lower than that as allotted under the procedures for bankruptcy liquidation at the time when the draft plan is submitted for approval, or the voting groups concerned have adopted the draft plan'.

134 Ibid, '(4) in the draft plan for reorganization, the rights and interests of capital contributors are adjusted in a fair and impartial manner, or the group of capital contributors has adopted the draft plan'.

135 Ibid, '(5) in the draft plan for reorganization, members of the same voting group are treated fairly, and the order arranged therein for payment of the claims does not contravene the provisions of Article 113 of this Law'.

136 Ibid, Article 87–88.

Central to the establishment of any RP in China is its implementation. The responsibility for implementing the RP rests with the debtor and administrator, following approval from the Court.[137] Furthermore, according to Article 92,

> upon approval by the court, the RP becomes binding on the parties – the creditor and debtor. On the other hand, where the creditor fails to declare his claims according to the provisions of this Law, he shall not exercise his right when the reorganization plan is being implemented; however, when the implementation of the plan is concluded, the creditor may exercise his right in compliance with the conditions for payment of claims of the same category as specified in the reorganization plan.[138]

Article 92 elaborates that the right enjoyed by a creditor against the debtor's guarantor and all the joint-and-several debtors shall not be affected by the reorganisation plan. Additionally, where the debtor cannot or fails to implement the plan, the Court can terminate the plan and declare the debtor bankrupt.[139] Finally, under Article 94, upon full implementation of the RP and implementation of all conditions, the debt is either paid in full or exempted, rendering the debtor no longer liable. In effect, this means that the RP has been deemed finalised.

In the matter of *ST Canghua Cangzhou Chemical Industrial Co. Ltd.* (ST Canghua) of June 1996, ST Canghua made its initial public offering, and its shares were publicly traded on the Shanghai Stock Exchange (SHSE). Having experienced losses for two consecutive accounting years in 2005 and 2006, the SHSC invoked its Stock Listing Rules 13.1.3 and 13.2.1 with 'ST' to warn investors of its delisting risk.[140] ST Canghua had been subject to significant financial stress; and by 2005 its overall operations deteriorated due to the misappropriation of its operational cash

137 Ibid, Article 89 and 90. Article 91: 'At the expiration of the period when being supervised, the administrator shall submit a report on supervision to the people's court. From the date when the report on supervision is submitted, the administrator's duty of supervision is terminated. Any interested party to the reorganization plan shall have the right to consult the report on supervision submitted by the administrator to the people's court. Upon application by the administrator, the people's court may decide to extend the period for supervision over the implementation of a reorganization plan'.

138 Ibid, Article 92.

139 Ibid, 'Where the people's court decides to terminate the implementation of a reorganization plan, the commitment taken by the creditors on adjustment of the claims in the plan shall be invalidated. However, the repayment received by the creditors due to implementation of the plan shall remain effective, and the part of the claims for which no repayment has been paid shall be regarded as bankruptcy claims. The creditors as specified in the preceding paragraph may continue to join the distribution, only when the other creditors in the same sequential order receive the same proportion of repayment. Under the circumstances as specified in the first paragraph of this Article, the guaranty provided for implementation of the reorganization plan shall continue to be effective'.

140 See (临*2007–006)* 河北宝硕股份有限公司重大事项公告 *(Announcement of Hebei Baoshuo Co. Ltd on Some Major Event)*, 126 (26 January 2007), in Zhao Huimiao, Bankruptcy Reorganization of Listed Companies with Chinese Characteristics, *American Bankruptcy Law Journal*, Vol. 90, No. 4 (2016), 5–6.

flow (RMB 365 million to construct a PVC resin project). As elaborated upon in Zhao Huimiao's article,[141] notwithstanding St Canghua's 60,000 tons of production line [it] was also forced to stop because of its failure to remove possible defaults for safe production. Further to the aforementioned, ST Canghua provided a guarantee to a number of listed companies for over RMB 2.6 billion. This guarantee included RMB 867 million for Baoshuo for which Canghua had undertaken joint and several liabilities for Baoshuo's debts. In January 2007, Baoshuo entered bankruptcy. As a result of its guarantee, ST Canghua was unable to maintain its normal operation due to many such credit claims arising from its liability for Baoshuo's debt.[142] In 2007, ST Canghua filed a reorganisation application to the Court which came into effect in 12 June 2007, following the coming into effect of the EBL on that same month. The purpose of the reorganisation was to rescue Banghua from its debt.

The Court ruled that:

> ST Canghua [had] entered [into] reorganization proceedings and designated the liquidation group as the administrator. Yet, with the support of the Canghua local government the state-owned business was still not accepted by the court without the approval of [the] Cangzhou municipal government, to ensure [the] protection of state-owned assets and maintaining social stability.[143]

Huimiao elaborates that the principle or concept of social stability is a key policy objective of the national and local Chinese governments. Therefore, a bankruptcy proceeding is likely to raise sensitive political issues for the regulating authorities, whether arising at the commencement or during its development of the reorganisation, and whether relating to the approval or implementation of an RP. These sensitive policy issues are further heightened where state-owned enterprises are involved.

The implications of this case are that, only when the state-owned authority signed an agreement requiring that they will maintain social cohesion and stability, will the Court approve the RP. Thus, a cautionary note for any entity developing an RP in China is to demonstrate how it will meet these policy objectives. Moreover, these policy objectives are required to be identified in the RP itself. In global tension between universalism on the one hand and greater protectionist and de-globalisation, China is demonstrably on the pathway towards universalism in reorganization plans, conceived in common law jurisdictions as schemes of arrangements. China is also highlighting demergers in its RPs, with the prospect of demergers expanding in significance beyond mergers and acquisitions in

141 Ibid.
142 Ibid.
143 Ibid.

restructuring. In this regard, China has accepted a model of legal transplantation that is comparable to the UK's Australian, Singaporean and Indian model of schemes of arrangement and to a lesser extent the US model. Emily Lee maintains that that China has adopted a corporate rescue system that is a 'hybrid of the systems used in the US and the UK, the former refers to 'debtor-in-possession' and the latter, 'administrator replacement'.[144] Lee notes that under the

> US system, the debtor company's management is permitted to stay and continue to run the business as a going concern; under the UK system, the management would be replaced by an independent administrator who would run the business during the reorganization process. Although, under the Chinese system, the administrators must be appointed by the People's Court from the roster system, kept and operated by the said court.[145]

More pervasively, Lee argues that China's reorganisation planning system is the most innovative feature of the EBL, because of its applicability to all enterprise legal persons. However, it is understood that any reorganisation can take a long time and be expensive. That said, and as highlighted in the aforementioned,

> a 'reorganization requires the submission of numerous plans: 1) the business plan of the debtor company; 2) the classification of debt claims; 3) the plan for claims adjustment; 4) the plan for claims repayment; 5) the time limit for implementing the reorganization plan; 6) the time limit for supervision over the implementation of the reorganization plan; and 7) other plans favourable to the debtor company's reorganization'.[146]

China's focus, is to avoid cumbersome and drawn-out insolvency proceedings that accentuate financial stress across the economy, whether arising from geopolitical, economic and health shock, among other disasters. China's preventative approach to economic destabilisation domestically also demonstrates its endorsement of a harmonised international perspective towards restructuring.

The EBL has posed, and continues to pose, challenges, notably in relation to the concept of residence. Article 3 of the EBL provides that bankruptcy cases shall be under the jurisdiction of the People's Court of the place at which the debtor resides. The concern that Emily Lee expressed in 2011 was that China's judges would be reluctant to accept bankruptcy or reorganisation applications. This posed threats of evocation over the utility of the EBL, and that some judges would be

144 Emily Lee, The Reorganization Process under China's Corporate Bankruptcy System, *The International Lawyer*, Vol. 45, No. 4 (2011), 942.

145 Ibid, 942–943.

146 Ibid.

unwilling to accept applications for reorganisation until they ascertained the predisposition of local interests.[147] Lee identified how Article 3 of the EBL is the source of the denial of jurisdiction other than that of the People's Court at the place where the debtor resides. In her view, Article 3 is overly restrictive, given that China is a vast country, that creditors and debtor assets may be located throughout the country and the creditors may not be aware of the debtor's principal place of business.[148] She maintains that the 'domicile' issue can, but should not bar the Court from accepting bankruptcy petitions.

The most viable alternative, in maintaining viability internationally, is for Chinese regulators to consider tempering the domicile requirement to enhance the likelihood of preserving the debtor's enterprise as a going concern. In light of this, Article 3 of the EBL might be amended to temper the residency requirement, subject to exploration for sustainable alternative measures. Inherent in that exploration is an assessment of the impact of these measures upon resident and non-resident entities. Centrally in issue, but difficult to resolve, is the dilemma for entities operating in China that are subject to the overarching reach of local governments. In issue is the risk of local courts denying financially distressed listed companies access to reorganisation primarily in response to local interests. However, that issue ought not to discount local courts denying reorganisation due to the lack of feasible plans such as to resettle workers, or to avoid potential threat to social stability locally. The balance for the local People's Court is to evaluate the claims of local governments in light of standards for commencing and sustaining restructuring under the 2006 EBL.[149] In practice, this is a matter for China to resolve.

3.5 Conclusion

Parts 1 and 2 of this chapter reinforce the case for further internationalisation of cross-border restructuring laws and legal mechanisms. While there are differences in approach taken by the respective jurisdictions compared, by and large there are sufficient similarities among them to warrant scaling up schemes of arrangement from national to transnational laws. Schemes of arrangement and restructuring plans that are more consistently framed and regulated across jurisdictions can provide greater certainty to debtors and creditors facing financial stress at different stages in their trans-border operations. Even marginal divergences in the rules of rescue across states can impact substantially upon the treatment of debtors and creditors, such as when domestic laws prioritise jurisdiction over national schemes and plans differently.

147 Ibid, 951.
148 Ibid.
149 Zhao Huimiao, Bankruptcy Reorganization of Listed Companies with Chinese Characteristics, *American Bankruptcy Law Journal*, Vol. 90, No. 4 (2016), 5–6.

The chapter maintains that the universalist approach to insolvency, while already widely adopted, should be extended further to facilitate restructuring. International legal mechanisms have been used to rebalance economic, political, social and environmental volatility particularly since WWII. That case is especially germane today in which financial volatility is omnipresent and has led to the exponential grow in corporate insolvency in trans-border trade and investment. Importantly, schemes or arrangements, efficiently developed and applied, are important measures in redressing the financial threats arising from such volatility. They provide a high level of protection to creditors, while enabling the debtor to retain full control of the financially stressed enterprise while it is being restructured. The overall benefit of a successful restructuring is a return to financial viability of the financially stressed enterprise.

An attenuating benefit of restructuring schemes is not only in allowing a sufficient level of oversight and approval by an authorised tribunal, but also by reducing the burden to perform pre-exiting contractual obligations that are no longer economic sustainable. More pervasively, what has emerged from the study is that most of the earlier-mentioned states, including the EU, have left the debtor in possession of the company throughout the restructuring process. This has considerable benefits in maintaining the continuity of the company's dealings by a debtor that remains competent to conduct business efficiently notwithstanding the financial stress that led to the restructuring.

The multilayered approach adopted in the jurisdictions studied also demonstrates the effectiveness of the often comparable measures they have used to manage creditors, mergers, demerges, takeovers and acquisitions. It is arguable that what has emerged are measures that are more than restructuring tools, but formidable and widely accepted legal mechanisms that warrant further development. Their emergence as multilayered measures should also not constitute obstacles to their internationalisation. Nor should their multidimensional features undermine their value in meeting the needs of parties operating across jurisdictions. The commonalities of such schemes also serve as a much needed foundation upon which to devise an international legal regime for preserving, as far as practicable, the viability of business enterprises in the face of intruding financial obstacles. Arguably, that legal foundation would enhance cross-border business enterprise, its adoption by the international business community and its recognition by legislatures and courts in multiple jurisdictions. These accomplishments in the global village of industry and trade are most achievable through their institutionalisation. Central to achieving that end is the capability of the UNCITRAL and UNIDROIT to develop a set of Principles, and ideally a Model Law, that sets out the specific requirements and content of an international scheme of arrangement. Such institutionalisation does not necessarily envisage identical nomenclature, such as in the nature and wording of schemes of arrangement or reorganisation plans. Nor does it envisage the adoption of identical layers of machinery upon which schemes and plans must operate in all signatory jurisdictions. What it does envisage is a consistent body of with principles that are capable of incorporation into domestic jurisdictions to suit both domestic and trans-border industry needs, including but not limited to those of the immediate parties. The common denominator sought is an efficient and fair legal regime that reconciles their domestic with their shared international interests. Doing so is not intended to achieve perfect universalism, but a uniform system of principles, incorporated into a model law, that is capable of adaptability in implementation and consistency in operation, locally, regionally and globally.

4

RESTRUCTURING: LETTERS OF COMFORT

Insolvency and restructuring can come in different forms and sizes.[1] Letters of Comfort (LC) are otherwise commonly known or referred to as 'keepwell' letters or comfort letters. They can be used for various purposes such as security for the debtor or creditor debtor guarantees, or through the negotiations of an insolvency or restructure. They are, and can be used by, lawyers, liquidators, administrators, accountants, or auditors. It is out of scope of this chapter to examine all the possibilities of their use, and by whom. Rather, the chapter focuses on the use of LCs for either COVID-19 purposes or restructuring an entity that may be subject to insolvency. The chapter will examine and compare the respective approaches taken by Australia, the European Union, the United Kingdom (UK), Singapore, India, Indonesia, the United States (US) and China. It will demonstrate that there are many similarities in the approaches taken by the respective jurisdictions. On the other hand, this chapter proposes that broader research is needed to confirm whether LCs should fall under a national or an international framework.

4.1 Introduction

The development and practice of commercial law – trade and commerce – dates back centuries. Daniel Defoe's analysis of the vagaries of trade and commerce at the beginning of the 18th century provides some insight into the ever-evolving character of mercantile practice:

> Trade is a Mystery, which will never be completely discovered or understood; it has its Critical Junctures and Seasons, when acted by no visible

1 Thanks to Michael Murray from Murray Legal, Sydney, Australia, for looking over and advising on this chapter.

DOI: 10.4324/9781003311874-6

> Causes, it suffers Convulsion Fit[t]s, hysterical Disorders, and most unaccountable Emotions – Sometimes it is acted by the evil Spirit of general Vogue, and like a mere Possession 'tis hurried out of all manner of common Measures; today it obeys the Course of things, and submits to Causes and Consequences; tomorrow it suffers Violence from the Storms and Vapours of Human Fancy, operated by exotic Projects, and then all runs counter, the Motions are eccentric, unnatural and unaccountable – A sort of Lunacy in Trade attends all its Circumstances, and no Man can give a rational Account of it.[2]

Since this early period, commercial, trade and investment law has grown into multibillion-trillion-dollar economic activity. This chapter examines the application of letters of comfort, which are also referred to as comfort letters or keepwell letters. This different nomenclature will be used interchangeable throughout the chapter, however their meaning will be the same. The chapter will explore the nature and significance of LC during times of a pandemic and elsewhere. It will view them as another legal mechanism or legal tool that is seldom discussed in the reorganisation-restructuring of entities. It will also explore their use by banks or other financial institutions in response to financial stress or an impending insolvency of a debtor.[3] As highlighted by Lang Thai, 'over the years, banking lawyers and academics have accepted that a comfort letter may contain one or more of the following three terms'.[4] The first is an undertaking by a parent company to maintain its shareholding or other financial commitment in the subsidiary. A second form of comfort letter is an undertaking by a parent company to use its influence to see that the subsidiary meets its obligation under the primary contract. The third and the weakest form of comfort letter is a '*mere* confirmation that the parent company is aware of the loan agreement with the subsidiary, but without any express term that the parent company is prepared to take any responsibility for the primary obligation of the subsidiary'.[5] LCs are extensively used in numerous fields of business, law and finance in these different forms. LCs are also recognised in national legal systems, such as Australia, EU, Indonesia, India, Singapore, United Kingdom, United States and China.

2 J. G. A. Pocock, *The Machiavellian Moment,* Princeton University Press, Princeton (1975), 452–453.

3 *Viuda de José Tolra v. Société de développement regional du Languedoc Roussillion* – decision of the *Cour de Cassation (Chambre Commerciale)* 21 December 1987. See also *Lordex v. La Rhénane* – decision of the Cour de Cassation (Chambre Commerciale) dated 9 July 2002, *Askea v. Société Générale* decision of the *Cour de Cassation (Chambre Commerciale)* dated 19 April 2005.

4 Lang Thai, Letters of Comfort: A Comparative Evaluation of Australian, United States and English Jurisdictions, *Current Commercial Law*, Vol. 7, No. 1 (2000), 1–12. J. Lipton, *Good Faith and Letters of Comfort* (Unpublished July 1998); W. Weerasooria, *Bank Lending and Securities in Australia,* Butterworths (1998), 276–277.

5 Ibid.

Generally, a comfort letter is an instrument written by a third party and is designed to encourage the creation of an agreement between two other parties.[6] They are, in some circumstances considered a gentleman's agreements. This is because the drafter of the letter, by making a unilateral statement, does not become a party to any agreement and also does not make any promise or otherwise assume any legal obligation. They are perceived as providing an assurance such as that a debt will be paid, without guaranteeing that result in law. However, in using affirmative language of assurance, courts can conceive them as being binding. Moreover, depending on how a comfort letter is framed, it can involve the drafting party in subsequent legal action, as when a holding company becomes involved in legal proceedings brought against its subsidiary. Despite the holding company's endeavour not to assume legal obligations, it will often become embroiled in them.[7] Typically, a parent company that wants to avoid being a guarantor will often issue a comfort letter to a lending institution contemplating the extension of credit to a subsidiary of the parent company. The letter may nevertheless involve the parent company in enforcement proceedings.[8]

In connecting letters of comfort to cross-border insolvency or restructuring, a starting point is the 2012 report by the Basel Committee on Banking Supervision which examined the use of intra-group support measures (tools) available to banks, insurers and securities firms in managing financial negotiations.[9] Prioritisation of the claim in insolvency depends on the loan's seniority. Typically, intra-group senior loans are generally ranked *pari passu* with other senior loans of the same debtor. Similarly, intra-group subordinated loans are generally ranked *pari passu* with other subordinated loans of the same debtor.[10] Central to the facilitation of these ranking and related activities is the use of letters of comfort, as a tool usually applicable to sustain business operations during periods of actual or potential financial stress.[11] The 2012 Report recognises that, while comfort letters are not the principal tools in regulating such financial stress, they are widely used to manage liquidity and to provide working capital financing to support continuing business operations.[12] The Report also notes that comfort letters, often involving non-complex letters, can be prepared and delivered expeditiously, such as to secure a creditor's position in an insolvency. In addition, they can address the impact of a cross-border reorganisation-restructure on access to finance.[13]

6 Herbert Bernstein, Joachim Zekoll, The Gentleman's Agreement in Legal Theory and in Modern Practice: United States, *The American Journal of Comparative Law*, Vol. 48 (1998), 98–99.

7 Ibid.

8 Ibid.

9 Basel Committee on Banking Supervision, *The Joint Forum: Report on Intra-group Measures*, Bank for International Settlements (2012). 1.

10 Ibid, 17.

11 Ibid, 10.

12 Ibid.

13 GuidetoCross-BorderTransactionsDeloitteLegal(2013),https://www2.deloitte.com/content/dam/Deloitte/global/Documents/Legal/dttl-legal-international-guide-to-secured-transactions-2014.

Importantly, the 2013 Report of Deloitte Legal highlights that the most common use of comfort letters in an insolvency or restructure is to provide security to creditors.[14] They are often used in a restructure to secure shares and the financial standing of a subsidiary for the future funding of a business and its operations.[15] While letters of comfort are not ordinarily central to a restructuring, they are often important in a debtor negotiating to secure capital and finance prior to or during a restructure, or prior to declaring insolvency. In support of LCs is the risk of jeopardising millions of dollars in failing to use them. It is worth noting, at the outset, that letters of comfort perform a different function from letter of request that constitute a non-binding request such as for information relating to a debt.

Comfort letters are described and used differently. Firstly, they can be referred to as comfort letters, letters of comfort, keepwell agreements, support letters, letters of awareness and commitment letter, amongst others. Secondly, a court can construe them as guarantees, depending on the context. Thirdly, even though LCs are distinguishable from letters of awareness that are binding, courts in states that still recognise and enforce them. This can occur when the LC is detailed, or where the Court construes the language of assurance expansively as indicative of an intent to contract.[16]

Extensively used since the 1980s, LCs are often drafted by a parent company to encourage a lending institution to issue credit to a subsidiary.[17] Bernstein and Zekoll note that in 1998, 'the enforceability of a comfort letter depended on factors such as the language of the instrument itself. Secondly, the intent on the part of the drafter to be bound as guarantor is likely to be found if the instrument, despite the fact that it calls itself a 'comfort letter', contains operative language such as 'guaranty, contract or other words of promise'.[18]

Accentuating the diverse construction of comfort letters, including a court treating them as binding and enforceable, is the legal effect that courts attribute

pdf, 10. Loan restructuring and domiciles of holding security dynamics. Similarly, in cases of loan restructuring or insolvency procedures, consider that the dynamics thereof could be significantly affected by, the holding company whose shares are pledged being incorporated in one jurisdiction or the other. Therefore, such issues are best considered in advance, at the transaction structuring stage.

14 Ibid, 53, 57, 63, 67, 73, 99.

15 The Wolf Thesis Guide to Restructuring Loans and Enforcement of Security in Central, Eastern & Southeastern Europe, WOLF THEISS Rechtsanwälte GmbH & Co KG. 2020, 13, https://www.wolftheiss.com/fileadmin/content/focus_topics/SpecialSits/WT_restloans_romania.pdf. Comfort letters and similar documents encompass a promise to maintain ownership of shares, financial standing of a subsidiary or provision of necessary funding for a business or project do not typically amount to guarantees, but the parties' intent and proper construction of the document may alter this position.

16 Ibid.

17 Herbert Bernstein, Joachim Zekoll, The Gentleman's Agreement in Legal Theory and in Modern Practice: United States, *The American Journal of Comparative Law*, Vol. 48 (1998), 98–99.

18 Ibid, 99–100.

to the letter's language.[19] The general assumption is that the company providing a comfort to the lender is intended to make, or not demand repayment of, the loan, while not providing any legally binding guarantee to the lender. The holding company, illustratively, uses language in the LC that fall short of committing itself to any legal liability should the subsidiary default on a formal contract of debt to which the letter of comfort is addressed. Thai asserts, first, that 'the language of these letters is often worded in such a way that one may describe these as having a bipolar nature: a) language intended to enhance the parent company's own image and profile through products and services provided by its subsidiary; and b) disclaimer of liability language'.[20] An example of this is where a parent company undertakes to maintain its shareholding or other financial interests in the subsidiary until the loan is fully repaid by the subsidiary. Here the parent company would have gained some benefits from its indirect association with the subsidiary, without being liable for repayment of the loan.[21]

Second, Thai maintains that the parent company may issue a comfort letter with the primary objective of avoiding contingent liability on its balance sheet, where the parent company is concerned that the disclosure of a guarantee on its financial statements may affect its own ability to borrow. Third, Thai contents that the terms of a parent company's existing credit agreements may 'prohibit it from providing guarantees or limit the amount of guarantees which it can provide'. Fourth, in some jurisdictions, 'a guarantee may attract unfavourable tax and other foreign exchange consequences and thus on this basis, the parent company may wish to avoid those liabilities by issuing a comfort letter instead.'[22] Fifth, for all their perceived benefits, LCs are subject to caution and criticism, including a reluctance to use them.[23] At issue is the responsibility and obligations that come when the parent company also deals with a subsidiary. Thus, the letter of comfort may impede any expedient restructure or insolvency. Viewed this way, managers are reluctant to tie the hands of their successors by even a moral commitment, without good reason.[24]

Company officers considering issuing comfort letters must themselves 'be comforted' that their company is not exposed to legal, or any reputational risks. They must also take account of the risk of being held accountable for acting outside their powers as company directors, making contractual promises that harm the company's standing and exposes it to legal action. The most immediate of these risks is

19 Lang Thai, Letters of Comfort: A Comparative Evaluation of Australian, United States and English Jurisdictions, *Current Commercial Law*, Vol. 7, No. 1 (2000), 1–12.

20 Ibid, 2.

21 Ibid.

22 Ibid.

23 Briefing note, *Letters of Comfort: A Practical Guide*, The Association of Corporate Treasurers. The Association of Corporate Treasurers (ACT) sets the benchmark for international treasury excellence (2013; https://www.treasurers.org/ACTmedia/loc.pdf).

24 Ibid, 11.

that a court may construe the comfort letter as legally enforceable, as when LC is discovered in judicial proceedings as being reported internally to the company as a *de facto* guarantee.[25]

Coupled with these established risks associated with the use of comfort letters, is scepticism about the benefits of using them as assurances in times of economic fragility. Thus, the risk of uncertainty over the nature, duration and depth of an economic disruption, such as arose from the pandemic, that induces vulnerable companies to adopt make-shift measures to sustain their financial stability. Such measures include the use of letters of comfort. Used as instruments of survivorship, they are tested, and retested through the second, third or fourth waves of the virus and through the sequelae of trans-border threats to financial stability globally. In issue is the unprecedented economic risks to large- and small-scale corporate enterprises, including strong incentives to declare insolvency unless they can restructure their businesses expeditiously. Such accelerating financial stress can encourage vulnerable debtors, and their holding companies, to seek compromises with creditors collaboratively, where possible, but without guarantees in an unstable financial climate. Such corporate action can also precede regulatory responses to COVID-19, including in governing the use of letters of comfort to subvert ethical business practice, by providing 'almost' guarantees that are not legally actionable.

Letters of comfort can nevertheless solidify and strengthen businesses and redress their economic vulnerabilities in the face of continuing COVID-19 disruptions. Apart from a full restructure of the organisation, as was discussed in Chapter 3 on schemes of arrangements, letters of comfort can assist in managing the short-term options available to a vulnerable company, or its holding or otherwise affiliated companies. Illustratively, a letter of comfort can help to provide temporary relief through financial support to a financial stressed subsidiary company.[26] However, the use of LCs does not detract from such vulnerable entities subsequently entering into schemes of arrangement or restructuring. This temporary arrangements that support the use of comfort letters, arguably, 'can also be extended and are highly relevant where a debtor is supported by a sponsor, parent company, or major shareholder that is willing to financially support the debtor and guarantee the performance of its obligations to its creditor'.[27] For sponsored relationships to be effectively maintained, therefore, a LC serves as an important tool in enabling a parent company, sponsor, or shareholder to facilitate the injection of third party capital into the debtor company (such as through subordinated debt or equity); to cure defaults as they arise over a pre-determined period; and to otherwise support the debtor while it works through its financial distress. In further support of the debtor is the use of related instruments, such as the express subordination, postponement

25 Ibid.

26 Lisa Hiebert, Ryan Laity, Borden Ladner, Gervais LLP, *Managing COVID-19 and its Fallout*, Association of Corporate Counsels (May 2020), https://www.lexology.com/library/detail.aspx?g=8c73c643-a485-420d-bf0c-5eec2d32d266.

27 Ibid.

and standstill by a parent company, sponsor or shareholder of its advances to the debtor in favour of senior creditors; and the creditor's reservation of all rights to repayment of the obligations.[28]

Central to the impact from the outbreak of COVID-19, has been the EU reinstituting letters of comfort for the first time in 20 years, following an extended period of hibernation. The European Commission published its first comfort letter in nearly 20 years on April 29, 2020, as discussed in the EU sub-section. The reason behind reverting back to this legal tool, was to foster cooperation among businesses during the 2020 coronavirus pandemic.[29] While this strategic reinstatement was not directed at insolvency or restructuring, it demonstrates the broad use of these instruments.

The expanding resort to legal mechanisms such as LCs during times of heightened financial stress, in our view, will play a major functional role in providing another layer in stabilising financial markets and fostering cooperation between businesses. Even though LCs have not been nationalised in domestic laws that would not prevent them from being adopted internationally. The challenge, as with schemes of arrangement, is the extent to which LCs will be elevated to the international legal landscape with the support of states, in the absence of ancillary domestic laws. If these letters receive international recognition including a formalised but adaptable template for their use, it will provide a stabilising legal tool to be used especially, but not exclusively, in times of international uncertainty. The starting point could be to provide a framework for the regulation of LCs in relation to restructuring and/or insolvency.

Notwithstanding their largely unregulated development and use, letters of comfort have been categorised similarly across the common and civil law divide. In the UK for example, letters of comfort cover three important objectives. This includes being a statement of awareness of financing; a commitment to maintain ownership interests; and support for creditors.[30] Additionally, LCs generally contain an acknowledgment of a parent company's awareness of the provision of financial accommodation to his subsidiary; and a statement by the parent company of the support required by the lender.[31] Australian scholars have given LCs a different focus, placing them into categories of strong, medium or weak, according them different levels of recognition and on occasion, legal enforceability.[32] In civil law

28 Ibid.

29 Morgan Lewis, *COVID-19: The Return of the Comfort Letter 2020*, https://www.jdsupra.com/legalnews/covid-19-the-return-of-the-comfort-13092/.

30 Phillip Wood, *International Loans, Bonds, Guarantees, Legal Opinions*, Sweet and Maxwell, London (2007), 401. in Anton Trichardt, *Letters of Comfort: A Trans-System Analysis*, International Banking and Finance Law series, Wolters Kluwer (2012).

31 G. D. Cooper, J. G. Fox, Commercial Morality – Enforceability of Letters of Comfort, *Journal of Banking and Finance Law and Practice* (1990), 66, in Anton Trichardt, *Letters of Comfort: A Trans-System Analysis*, International Banking and Finance Law series, Wolters Kluwer (2012).

32 J. Kelly, *Comfort Letters in Australian Banking Practice – A Moral Obligation or Contract?* (unpublished thesis Macquarie University Sydney) (1990), 16–20, in Anton Trichardt, *Letters of Comfort: A Trans-System Analysis*, International Banking and Finance Law series, Wolters Kluwer (2012).

jurisdictions, LCs have generally been categorised as credit agreements; an agreement of the parent company with its subsidiary; a tool to manage the subsidiary; and a tool to demonstrate the financial structure of the subsidiary. A further category that has emerged in the civil law adheres to the French model of categorising LCs. Civil law also construes LCs as a declaration of commitment between parent and subsidiary; and a financial assurance given by the parent to the creditor in the event of the subsidiary defaulting on its obligations, such as are owed to a bank.[33]

Anton Trichardt elaborates that 'these types of letters fall into categories purely based on their content and the degree of comfort or enforceable promise made therein. They are classified according to their "strength" or "weakness" according to the bank'.[34] In 2010, Trichardt called for a more useful framework to 'define three classes of letters of comfort according to the extent of commitment entered into by the parent company; namely, letters of comfort properly so called, medium strength letters or comfort, and strong comfort letters'.[35] However, it is time to take these legal mechanisms one step further, and develop an international framework. Such an approach could be comparable to the regulatory framework developed to accommodate close-out netting provisions. Applying this framework to insolvency and restructure can significantly offset disadvantages in doing so. Illustratively, the framework can allow flexibility to companies authoring and relying on LCs, based on the discrete corporate context including the nature of the financial stress and the intended scope of the LC assurance. So devised, LCs are capable of being regulated internationally but still being versatile in operation. They can be used to satisfy a range of economic needs, particularly in serving as preventative tools in restructuring. The next section examines Australia's approach to letters of comfort.

4.2 Australia

In Australia, a letter of comfort falls within the legal framework of the common law. That is, there is a limited statutory base for letters of comfort. LCs may instead be embodied in commercial legislation, such as Australia's Corporations Act 2001. Australia has a lengthy history of the use of letters of comfort for various reasons. In *Banque Brussels Lambert SA v. Australian National Industries Limited,*[36] the defendant company applied for a line of credit, for which the bank required a reassurance from the principal shareholder of the company. The subsidiary company defaulted on its loan and the bank bought proceedings against the parent company based on the letter of comfort provided by the principal shareholder. The defendant (Australian National Industries) held 45% of the issued capital of the holding company

33 Anton Trichardt, *Letters of Comfort: A Trans-System Analysis*, International Banking and Finance Law series, Wolters Kluwer (2012), 54–56.

34 Ibid, 58–60.

35 Ibid.

36 *Banque Brussels Lambert SA v. Australian National Industries Ltd.* (1989) 21 NSWLR 502.

that owned 100% of the subsidiary lender.[37] The bank required the letter of comfort, in a form satisfactory to it, as a condition of the loan. The defendant refused to provide a guarantee. The result was a dispute over the letter of comfort which had been negotiated as a compromise. Importantly, the letter itself contained three paragraphs from which the Court sought a clarification. First was a confirmation of awareness paragraph. Both parties agreed that this paragraph had no promissory effect. The central dispute arose from the second and third paragraphs. In the second part, the defendant had stated that 'it would not be their intention to reduce their shareholding in the borrower. In the second part, it had stated that 'they would provide the bank 90 days-notice of any decision to dispose of any shareholding'.[38] Moreover, these two paragraphs expressed that

> we take this opportunity to confirm that it is our practice to ensure our affiliate [the borrower] will at all times be in a position to meet its financial obligations as they fall due. These financial obligations include repayment of all outstanding loans with 30 days.[39]

The Court then examined the language in the letter itself, to identify the nature and level of intention of the drafter, specifically to decide whether it demonstrated an intention to be bound in contract. The Court ruled the 'letter of comfort from the shareholder contained an undertaking of a contractual obligation that could be enforced by the bank'.[40] The Court held that the letters' of comfort purpose was mainly to induce the bank to extend the line of credit to the subsidiary company. The language of the letter is therefore of paramount importance and may be construed by courts as having a binding effect.

In one of the most prominent cases, *Re Ansett Australia,*[41] the administrators were appointed to manage the financial affairs of the airline Ansett Australia. The case related to the restructure of companies before one company had declared insolvency. Comfort letters were used to manage and negotiate the administration by appointed administrators.[42] On 12 and 14 September 2001, Messrs Peter Hedge, Greg Hall and Allan Watson were appointed administrators of Ansett Australia Limited (and the other companies in accordance) with the provisions of Pt 5.3A Corporations Act 2001 (Cth).[43] This entailed management of a group of companies referred to as the 'Ansett Group', consisting of Ansett Australia and Air New

37 Ibid.

38 Ibid. Also see Alan Tyree, the Bank of Brussels Case, http://www2.austlii.edu.au/~alan/comfort.html.

39 Ibid, 2.

40 Ibid.

41 *Re Ansett Australia Ltd and Mentha* (2001) 19 ACLC 1,678.

42 Ibid, 1.

43 Ibid.

Zealand Engineering Services Limited.[44] The appointment of these administrators resulted in resolutions of the Ansett group on 12 and 14 September 2001. The first administrators caused the airline operations of the Ansett group to cease at 2:00 am on Friday 14 September 2001.[45] However, three days later, on 17 September 2001, the Court ordered new administrators, Mark Francis Xavier Mentha and Mark Anthony Korda, to be appointed jointly and severally as administrators of the Ansett group. The Court excluded Hazelton Air Charter Pty Limited, Hazelton Airlines Limited, Hazelton Air Services Pty. Ltd., appointing Michael James Humphris as administrator with effect from the time at which Messrs Hedge, Hall and Watson gave notice in writing of their resignation as administrators of the Ansett group.[46] However, on 17 September 2001 Messrs Hedge, Hall and Watson resigned as administrators of the Ansett group and they were replaced by Mr. Humphris. On 4 October 2001, the administrators of the Ansett Group were appointed administrators of Air New Zealand Engineering Services Limited pursuant to the provisions of Pt 5.3A of the Act.[47]

Given these developments, the initial issues surrounding the appointment of administrators were resolved. On 5 October 2001, the administrators filed an application in the Court, in accordance with Sections 447A and 447D of the Act.[48] Centrally, the administrators sought orders for the

> Approval of the Agreement entitled Memorandum of Understanding (MOU) between the Ansett Group and the Air New Zealand Group and others ('the Agreement'). Further or alternatively to paragraph 2 hereof, that the Plaintiffs may properly perform and give effect to the Agreement.[49]

Three days later, on 8 October 2001, the Hazelton administrator filed an application in substantially the same terms seeking orders that the Court approve the agreement, or alternatively an order to properly perform and give effect to the agreement. A Memorandum of Understanding was also established, setting out the companies and administrators.[50] Following the administrators being formally appointed, enquiries were made in relation to the financial position of Air New Zealand, whereby the Ansett group sought financial assistance from Air New Zealand. Interestingly, Air New Zealand was financially stressed at the time and had at the time written down its investment in the Ansett Group by $NZ1.32 billion.[51]

44 Ibid.
45 Ibid.
46 Ibid, 2.
47 Ibid.
48 Ibid, 3.
49 Ibid.
50 Ibid, 4.
51 Ibid, 25.

Of concern to the administrators was that the proceedings might lead to Air New Zealand being placed into insolvency administration under New Zealand law.[52]

However, three months prior, in August 2001, Air New Zealand, wrote a letter of comfort to the directors Ansett Holdings Limited, Ansett International Limited and Ansett Australia Limited stating the following:

Dear Sirs,

Letter of Comfort

In its capacity as the ultimate parent company and sole beneficial shareholder of the Companies, Air New Zealand Limited ('ANZ') hereby confirms to you that it is its current policy to take such steps from time to time as are necessary to ensure that its wholly owned subsidiaries (including the Companies) are able to meet their debts as they fall due.

We will advise you promptly in the event of any change in this policy.

The previous paragraphs set out our bona fide intention in respect of the matters mentioned, but shall not create any contract between us and any of you, nor a guarantee nor indemnity in respect of our obligations hereunder, enforceable at law or in equity.

Notwithstanding the previous paragraph, we will make available to you on request in writing from time to time advances for the sole purpose of enabling you to pay working capital liabilities incurred by you in respect of property or services purchased or sold in the ordinary course of your business, subject to the following conditions:

a) the maximum aggregate amount of all such advances (whether or not they remain outstanding at any particular time) shall not exceed the equivalent of A$400 m;
b) such advances will continue to be available to you until withdrawn and such withdrawal has been notified in writing to you by Air New Zealand (provided that such withdrawal shall not take effect earlier than 4 weeks after the date that notification is given); and
c) in making a request for an advance you will be deemed to represent, warrant and undertake to us that the advance is required, and will be applied, to pay working capital liabilities of yourself incurred in respect of property or services purchased or sold in the ordinary course of your business.

This Letter of Comfort is governed by New Zealand law.[53]

52 Ibid.
53 Ibid, 23.

The Court highlighted that, central to the issues which led to the execution of the Memorandum of Understanding, were claims under the Letter of Comfort and the identification of claims which might be made against Air New Zealand Ltd and the directors and officers of companies in the Air New Zealand group and the Ansett Group.[54] At issue, was concern that, if the Ansett Group received any payment from Air New Zealand, and subsequently became insolvent, the administrators might be required to disgorge the payments made to creditors with preferential rights.[55] The administrators, therefore, required that either the payment be made by the New Zealand Government, or that the New Zealand Government give the administrators an appropriate indemnity. On 3 October 2001, the New Zealand Government agreed to give the administrators the indemnity. A further concern was expressed by the administrators stating: 'It is always safer and prudent for an insolvency practitioner not to settle claims without a thorough investigation'.[56] The Court, in reconciling whether to use of the memorandum of understanding or the letter of comfort, noted that the:

> administrators have formed a considered commercial decision that it is in the interests, and for the benefit, of the Ansett group and its creditors that they enter into the Memorandum of Understanding which involves, in particular, the receipt of $150 million, the giving up of any further claims under the Letter of Comfort and the giving up of certain claims which the Ansett group might have against Air New Zealand and the Directors.[57]

The Court also stressed the further issue of how to discern the benefits and disadvantages in relation to Part 5.3A of the Corporations Act. It noted that the administrators have taken the position that:

> When balancing all of the advantages and disadvantages and having regard to the objects of Part 5.3A of the Corporations Act, namely to try and keep Ansett's business in existence if it is at all possible to do so, or if not, to maximise the return to creditors that it is in the interests of all Ansett stakeholders for this transaction to proceed.[58]

The Court's position, in the early stages of the case, highlighted the importance of maintaining business activity. More importantly, by analysing the law, it was arguably attempting to maintain the operations of the Ansett Group, to minimise the loss of employment and economic activity that the airline generated across Australia.

54 Ibid, 24.
55 Ibid, 32.
56 Ibid.
57 Ibid, 33.
58 Ibid, 75–77.

The Court then reverted to the construction of the LC, stating that the proper construction of the LC related to the amount the three Ansett companies were entitled to claim.[59] The Court concluded that the obligations under the LC, and the competing claims of Air New Zealand's did not need to be considered. Therefore, the Court ordered that, according to Section 447D of the Act, the MOU was given effect.[60]

Despite the Court not deciding the case based solely on any obligations or otherwise arising from the letter of comfort, the case highlighted the connection between these letters and the parties negotiating pre-insolvency matters. The inference was that the LC plays an important role in enabling the parties to negotiate for a level of security and financial stability in restructuring. In this case, the letter of comfort provided the basis for managing the ongoing relationship between the parent company and its shareholder. Furthermore, it provided the basis for the management of the Ansett Group's working capital liabilities in regard to the managed property and services; it specified a maximum aggregate amount to be advanced; and it established how it could be withdrawn. Thus, a letter of comfort can be quite broad in its scope. It can manage multiple issues, comparable to a scheme of arrangement and to a contract of administration more generally. It can provide clarity, but also extend the scope and application of the applicable law to LC, albeit on a case-by-case basis. A residuary question is whether to rely on courts to continue to regulate LCs piecemeal, and to provide the parties with flexibility in their use, subject to a judicial determination as to their legal standing. Alternatively, would legislation provide greater clarity and more consistency in the regulation of LC?

More than 15 years after the Bank of Brussels case, in *Newtronics Pty. Ltd. (in liq) v. Atco Controls Pty. Ltd.*,[61] the plaintiff, 'Newtronics sued its parent company, the first defendant Atco on its contractual obligation to provide financial support and not to call on secured debts to the detriment of unsecured creditors. While the case centred around securing debt as part of a liquidation, it was brought under the banner of liquidation consisting of a winding up process in which the Court declares the entity solvent or insolvent. Newtronics also sued the second defendants, along with Atco, in conversion. As the parent company of Newtronics, Atco held a mortgage debenture in its favour ('the mortgage debenture') as security for loans it had made to Newtronics'.[62] A fundamental aspect of Newtronics' contractual claim against Atco was a series of 'letters of support' written to Newtronics' auditors between 1994 and 2001. The written submissions asserted by Newtronics that the

59 Ibid. The outcome of any proceeding against the Directors in respect of the causes of action which have been released is incapable of any realistic assessment at the present time. What is relevant for present purposes, is that extensive investigations would be required before any decision could be made whether any proceedings against the Directors should be launched. Even if they were, the outcome would remain uncertain for a considerable period of time.

60 Ibid, 88.

61 [2008] VSC 566 69 ACSR 317 26 ACLC 1576 [2010] ALMD 2962.

62 Ibid.

case 'does not concern a letter designed to provide comfort to a bank' in 'the original classic context of a "letter of comfort"', and that '[n]o generalised or simplistic proposition about 'letters of comfort' should be relied on'.[63] Newtronics relied instead upon the existence of a contract between it and its parent company, maintaining that the terms of the obligations critical to the dispute were contained the letters of support.[64] The issue of the enforceability of those LCs turned on whether the words used in them were 'promissory and not merely representational'.[65] A further issue was whether the letter of comfort placed obligations on the provider to assume a level of legal responsibility, or merely a moral responsibility towards the beneficiary.

The Court elaborated that the question of obligations arising from LCs are resolved differently in different cases. Additionally, it debated, in response to the assertion by Newtronics in their written closing submissions, that the case did not concern a letter designed to provide comfort to a bank in 'the original classic context' of a 'letter of comfort'; they asserted in the alternative that '[n]o generalised or simplistic proposition about 'letters of comfort' should be relied on.'[66] Nonetheless, it was arguable that these letters did more than merely provide non-binding comfort to Newtronics' auditors or, even to Newtronics' directors, in that they contained the essential terms of an agreement between Atco and Newtronics. Those terms 'known to both', and were 'intended to be relied upon and which [were] relied upon'.[67] Moreover, in referring to *Gate Gourmet Australia Pty. Ltd. (In Liq) v. Gate Gourmet Holding AG*,[68] which was broadly similar to the current case, Einstein J. held that 'the terms of letters of comfort clearly indicated 'a promissory intent to be bound in terms of legal relations'.[69]

The Court concluded that, 'when regard was had to the implications for directors of the parent company of contravention of the insolvent trading provisions of the Corporations Law, the objective intention of the letter was to convey a contractual promise'.[70] Similarly, in referring to the case of *Banque Brussels*,[71] Rogers C.J. held that a letter from the principal shareholder of a company to its bankers had contractual force. However, in earlier Australia cases this position was not decided upon authoritatively. That Court nevertheless did draw upon *Australian European Finance Corporation Ltd. v. Sheahan*,[72] in which it was established that the plaintiff had earlier been advised by its solicitors that there was considerable doubt about the contractual enforceability of letters of comfort. Accordingly, the Court concluded

63 Ibid.
64 Ibid, 2.
65 Ibid, 7.
66 Ibid, 6.
67 Ibid, 12.
68 *Gate Gourmet Australia Pty. Ltd. (In Liq) v. Gate Gourmet Holding AG* [2004] NSWSC 149.
69 Ibid.
70 Ibid.
71 *Banque Brussels Lambert SA v. Australian National Industries Ltd.* (1989) 21 NSWLR 502.
72 (1993) 60 SASR 187

that the letter of comfort was not and could not have been intended to be a legally enforceable contract of security, but at most contained a non-promissory statement of intention. Generally, however, LCs should be considered as statements of commercial intent rather than as promises which are capable of being legally enforced.

However, when courts hold that comfort letters are ambiguous and the parties' intention are uncertain, English and possibly American courts lean to a finding of unenforceability. Accordingly, the Court in *Neutronics*[73] was not persuaded that the parties intended that the letter would amount to a legally enforceable security. At most it contained a non-promissory statement of intention, and not a settled position on enforceability. What adds some legal certainty is to understand the intention of the party providing and the reasonably construction, and reliance upon it, by the other party. While flexible in nature, and used for different purposes, the contents of LCs in relation to insolvency and the protection of the creditor and debtor remains variable and somewhat indeterminable. What is needed, as is illustrated in the *Neutronics* case, is the value of a more coherent regulatory response and guidance in constructing and interpreting LC.

Later in *Commissioner of Taxation v. BHP Billiton Finance Ltd.,*[74] the Court considered the extent to which letters of comfort serve as the backdrop of a scheme to manage and reduce tax. At issue, amongst others, was whether the

> steps in the scheme identified by the Commissioner, comprising Finance's acquiescence in the revocation of BHPB's letter of comfort, the entry into the deed of support, calling for payment of the debt owed by TM and the write off of the TM debt gave rise to a tax benefit or whether, as the primary judge found, the steps in the scheme did not alter the fact that the TM debt was bad and was a debt that Finance was entitled to write off as bad whether the steps in the scheme identified by the Commissioner were taken or were not taken.[75]

The facts were that the taxpayer (TP) was one of a group of companies incorporated to borrow money to lend to companies in the group. It borrowed from lenders within and outside the group at commercial rates of interest and lent to group companies at higher rates. TP earned taxable income.[76] TP was the vehicle through which financed group companies were selected by the ultimate parent (BHPB) as vehicles through which the group's investment decisions were executed. Borrowing and lending was TP's only business. TP had no equity, direct or indirect, in the companies to which it lent. As to background, TP had been incorporated in 1975. Since then, TP had successfully carried its business on a regular and systematic basis. It had lent to companies in the group, namely to DRI and to TM. The loans

73 [2008] VSC 566 69 ACSR 317 26 ACLC 1576 [2010] ALMD 2962.
74 [2010] FCAFC 25.
75 Ibid.
76 Ibid, 1–2.

were made consistently with TP's ordinary course of business. Each loan was for a project requiring capital expenditure.[77] Following TPs use of four letters of comfort to manage the ongoing tax reduction scheme, the Court argued that:

> In order to commence these formal arrangements, it is necessary to revoke the Letter of Comfort and enter into the Deed of Support. However, BHP Finance submitted that but for the scheme alleged by the Commissioner, the debt would still have been bad and thus capable of being written off. In particular, Finance pointed to the letters of comfort that were issued for the purpose of directors being able to sign the accounts for the year or years to which the letter related. They gave the directors of TM undoubted comfort for that purpose, they were not intended to create legally enforceable rights and obligations as between TM and BHPB, and that, in particular, TM provided no consideration to BHPB for the grant of such rights.[78]

The Court maintained further that:

> The Commissioner concedes that his Pt IVA case has a narrow compass. It only arises if by reason of the 1999 comfort letter it could reasonably be expected that the BHPTM loan was recoverable by Finance. For the reasons set out above, even if the terms of the comfort letters are equivalent to a guarantee between BHPB and BHPTM, none of the letters (including the 1999 comfort letter) created third party rights in favour of Finance. Moreover, even if the 1999 comfort letter had not been revoked, it could not reasonably be expected that BHPB would honour the undertaking made in the 1999 comfort letter to BHPTM and its directors. Although the letters of comfort conferred no rights on Finance, Finance (acting reasonably) could have pressed TM to enforce TM's contractual rights against BHPB (if necessary) by having TM wound up and funding a liquidator to bring proceedings against BHPB. A liquidator of TM would have been duty bound to have sort to enforce the 1999 letter of comfort for the benefit of TM's creditors.[79]

From this recent case, it can be demonstrated that letters of comfort can be used for multiple purposes. On the one hand, they are questioned over the contractual rights they afford to a direct or third party. On the other hand, they created binding obligations that are enforceable by creditors. In this case, the LCs were viewed in part as providing a clear benefit to creditors in managing the tax reduction. The Court maintained that the Australian stance was distinctive, that it demonstrated

77 Ibid.
78 Ibid, 62–64.
79 Ibid, 53.

the diminished influence of English law, and was aptly encapsulated in the Court's reference to Ross Buckley that:

> It is the right of British jurists to give absolute primacy to technical legal rules. However, such an approach is at odds with the resurgence of equitable principles recognised in a string of recent decisions in the High Court of Australia and will ill serve the orderly development of Australian commerce.[80]

Australian courts, arguably, place primary importance on the purpose of comfort letters, in seeking to induce reliance by actual or prospective creditors. That approach, which is different from the approach of English courts, evidences in some ways the trend of 'commercial morality'.[81] This moral trend allegedly establishes a link between the letter of comfort, the Court's methodology, and the standard of interpretation it uses in construing the LC. Australian courts, predominantly, also take a subjective view in construing the meaning of an LC, focusing on the behaviour of the parties. They also adopt standards of good faith and fair dealing in establishing a connection between the LC and the commercial relationship. The resulting approach has many similarities to that of contract law, whereby the courts generally look to the terms of the contract and to the behaviour of the parties to determine the nature of their intention.

Demonstrating this, the Court in *Gate Gourmet Australia Pty. Ltd. (in liquidation) v. Gate Gourmet Holding AG*[82] highlighted that:

> Gourmet Gate Australia Pty Ltd (in liquidation) (GGA) was part of the Gourmet Gate Group (Group). At all material times, GGA, the Australian trading company of the Group, was a wholly-owned subsidiary of a non-trading Australian holding company, Gourmet Gate (Holdings) Pty Ltd (GGH), which was, in turn, a wholly-owned subsidiary of Gourmet Gate Holding AG (GGAG), the holding company of the Group. GGA was not only undercapitalised, but the sole basis on which it was permitted to operate was wholly dependent upon borrowings organised within the Group, including

80 Ibid.

81 Ibid. 'On 17 September 2001, I ordered that Mark Francis Xavier Mentha and Mark Anthony Korda ('the administrators') be appointed joint and several administrators of the Ansett group other than Hazelton Air Charter Pty Limited, Hazelton Airlines Limited, Hazelton Air Services Pty Ltd ('the Hazelton companies'), and that Michael James Humphris be appointed administrator of the Hazelton companies with effect from the time that Messrs Hedge, Hall and Watson gave notice in writing of their resignation as administrators of the Ansett group. On 17 September 2001 Messrs Hedge, Hall and Watson resigned as administrators of the Ansett group and thereupon the administrators were appointed administrators of the companies in the Ansett group and Mr Humphris ('the Hazelton administrator') was appointed administrator of the Hazelton companies. On 4 October 2001, the administrators were appointed administrators of Air New Zealand Engineering Services Limited pursuant to the provisions of Pt 5.3A of the Act'.

82 [2004] NSWSC 149. Not able to obtain actual case from NWSC. In Law institute Victoria, https://www.liv.asn.au/LIV-Home/Practice-Resources/Law-Institute-Journal/Archived-Issues/LIJ-November-2004/The-comfort-letter-trap#fnB80.

> external borrowings, always underpinned by arrangements made higher up in the Group. GGA's borrowings were supported by two comfort letters.[83]

The first comfort letter read as follows:

> This is to confirm that the parent entity, Gate Gourmet International AG, will provide the financial support that may be necessary to enable Gate Gourmet (Holdings) Pty Limited and its controlled entities to meet its financial commitments as and when they fall due. This guarantee will not be withdrawn before Gate Gourmet (Holdings) Pty Limited and its controlled entities have sufficient means to meet their obligations without the support of the parent entity.[84]

The second comfort letter was similar to the first one, except that (a) it was addressed to GGH; (b) it was provided by GGAG; (c) it referred to GGAG as the parent entity; and (d) the words 'Letter of support' were substituted for the word 'guarantee' in the second sentence.[85] On the basis of this letter, GGA prosecuted a number of claims against GGAG, GGH and the individuals who signed the comfort letter. The following questions arose: (i) On a proper construction, did the second letter of comfort provide an obligation? (ii) Did the second comfort letter form a contract giving rise to further obligations? On the first point, the Court, in referring to the *Bank of Brussels* case, adopted a similar position in regard to obligations arising from the obligations arising from the letter of comfort. On the second question, the Court confirmed that the letter of comfort constituted a binding contract. This case reinforced earlier Australian decisions that, where a letter of comfort provides a level or promissory obligation, it will have contractual attributes. Furthermore, the courts will invariably look to the intention of the parties attributed to the letter in order to better understand the level of obligation provided.

Notwithstanding this, the decisions also confirm what legal scholars have long argued, as outlined earlier in this chapter, that letters of comfort provide a flexible approach to many different business transactions and are widely used in practice. They can be used in diverse contexts to facilitate negotiations relating to finance, amongst other functions, during a restructure, insolvency or as part of a winding up process. The next section examines the approach taken in the EU.

4.3 European Union and United Kingdom

The application of letters of comfort in both the EU and UK varies. This section discusses their use within these two jurisdictions. As stated in the introduction to this chapter, the terminology used to describe LCs across members states is subtly different due to localised linguistic and legal differences, and divergence in their

83 Ibid, 1–2.
84 Ibid, 47.
85 Ibid.

historical application. For instance, LCs are categorised in Germany under 7 different categories. That categorisation includes a distinction drawn between:

> Declarations or statements (a) providing information about the parent company's participation in the subsidiary; (b) stipulating a prohibition against asset stripping; (c) pertaining to changes in the parent company's participation in the subsidiary; (d) containing moral obligations only; (e) pursuant to which the parent company undertakes to exercise its influence over its subsidiary so that the latter meets its obligations; (f) whereby the parent company undertakes to maintain its subsidiary's solvency; and (g) pursuant to which the parent company commits itself to ensure that the subsidiary will be managed and financially supported to enable the subsidiary to meet its obligations.[86]

There is also evidence that, France has categorsied four different types of LCs. These are: first, those containing declarations or statements confirming the parent company's approval of the operations of its subsidiary; second, letters in which the parent company commits itself to maintaining its participation in the subsidiary until the financial facility granted to the subsidiary has been paid back in full; third, the parent company provides an assurance that it will ensure that the subsidiary is able to satisfy its obligations to the bank or person or entity granting credit; fourth, the parent company undertakes to substitute itself for the subsidiary in the event of the latter defaulting in its obligations to the bank or other financing institution. There are further differences in the nature and scope of LCs across the 27 members of the EU. However, discussing them in beyond the scope of this book.

As a response to COVID-19, the EU has evaluated over some years the alleged lack of effective application of letters of comfort. According to the European Commission, since the entry into force of Council Regulation (EC) No 1/2003[87], parties making undertakings can no longer notify their agreements to the Commission in order to receive an individual exemption from Article 101 of that Regulation. Instead, consistent with the 2012 Treaty on the Functioning of the European Union (TFEU),[88] those parties are responsible to assess, themselves, whether their agreements and practices are valid.

86 [2004] NSWSC 149. Not able to obtain actual case from NSWSC. In Law institute Victoria, https://www.liv.asn.au/LIV-Home/Practice-Resources/Law-Institute-Journal/Archived-Issues/LIJ-November-2004/The-comfort-letter-trap#fnB80, 47.

87 Council Regulation (EC) No 1/2003 of 16 December 2002 on the implementation of the rules on competition laid down in Articles 81 and 82 of the Treaty (Text with EEA relevance) O.J. L 1.

88 26 October 2012 Official EN Journal of the European Union C 326/49, https://eur-lex.europa.eu/legal-content/EN/TXT/PDF/?uri=CELEX:12012E/TXT.

In view of the unprecedented challenges arising from challenges to such agreements and practices arising since COVID-19, the EU decided to

> exceptionally provide undertakings with ad hoc feedback or comfort on the legality of cooperation initiatives that need to be swiftly implemented in order to effectively tackle the COVID-19 pandemic; Communication from the Commission of 8 April 2020, Communication on a Temporary Framework for assessing antitrust issues related to business cooperation in response to urgency situations stemming from the current COVID-19 outbreak.[89]

Even though the purpose of letters of comfort were to secure such essentials as medicines required during the pandemic, the EU highlighted the need to also establish an association among generic pharmaceutical manufacturers. It also stressed the importance of them cooperating in responding timeously and effectively to a shortage in essential medicines required for COVID-19 patients.[90]

Nevertheless, this comfort letter is best described, in our view, as a mechanism to counter competition within the EU the manufacture and distribution of COVID-19 medicines outside the framework established by agreement among associated pharmaceutical manufacturers. The TFEU specifies that 'this comfort letter does not cover any discussion of prices or any other possible coordination on issues which are not strictly necessary for effectively achieving the aims set out above'.[91] The comfort letter is also subject to participating undertakings; not to unduly increase prices beyond what is justified by possible increases in costs; and to acceptance of those increases. The TFEU confirms that the EU will not tolerate conduct amounting to opportunism in seeking to exploit the COVID-19 crisis as a 'cover' for non-essential collusion or other anticompetitive behaviour.[92] While this regulatory response was not traditionally applied to debt relief between entities and financial institution in their responses to a financial stressed debtor, the Regulation is prospectively versatile in its application, and able to be extended to letters of comfort.

The question arises, is this the start of the further use and acceptance of comfort letters across the EU? A further accentuating question is whether a new form of comfort letter will now become common place, outside of the traditional letter that is commonly viewed in contract terms? Only time will confirm whether they will formally be extended to broader business and commercial dealings across the EU.

89 Communication from the Commission Temporary Framework for assessing antitrust issues related to business cooperation in response to situations of urgency stemming from the current COVID-19 outbreak 2020/C 116 I/02, C/2020/3200OJ C 116I, (2020), 7–10.

90 Ibid.

91 Ibid.

92 Ibid.

Nonetheless, more than 20 years ago, the EU Court of Justice considered letters of comfort in light of purchasing agreements. In *Langnese-Iglo GmbH v. Commission of the European Communities,*[93] the Court noted that

> by virtue of Article 168a of the Treaty and the first paragraph of Article 51 of the Statute of the Court of Justice, an appeal from the Court of First Instance may be based only on grounds relating to the infringement of rules of law, to the exclusion of any appraisal of the facts.[94]

The letter of comfort formed one of the bases of the appeal. This section will only deal with what the Court commented and decided on, in relation to the letter of comfort. The facts were that Langnese-Iglo GmbH, a company incorporated under German law, established in Hamburg (Germany), represented by Martin Heidenhain, Bernhard M. Maassen and Horst Satzky, Rechtsanwälte, Frankfurt am Main, with an address for service in Luxembourg at the chambers of Jean Hoss, 2 Place Winston Churchill. The appellant, appeal against the judgment of the Court of First Instance of the European Communities (Second Chamber, Extended Composition) of 8 June 1995 in *Langnese Iglo v. Commission.* The parties were seeking to have that judgment set aside.[95] Furthermore, by application lodged at the Registry of the Court of Justice on 18 August 1995, Langnese-Iglo GmbH brought an appeal, pursuant to Article 49 of the EC Statute of the Court of Justice, against the judgment of the Court of First Instance of 8 June 1995 in *Langnese-Iglo v. Commission* (hereinafter 'the contested judgment') in which that Court dismissed in part its application for the annulment of Commission Decision 93/406/EEC of 23 December 1992 relating to a proceeding pursuant to Article 85 of the EEC Treaty against Langnese-Iglo GmbH (hereinafter 'the contested decision').[96] On the issue and nature of the letter of comfort, the Court further noted that:

> Having regard to the legal nature of comfort letters, the sending of such a letter, in which the Commission has reserved the right to re-open the procedure in the event of there being any appreciable change affecting certain matters of law or of fact on which its assessment had been based, cannot entail the consequence that the Commission, when actually re-opening the procedure, would no longer be entitled to take account of a factual situation which existed before the comfort letter was sent but was brought to its notice only later, particularly in connection with a complaint lodged at a later stage. In referring the court of Frist Instance, the COJ noted that Langnese-Iglo

93 Case C-279/95, *Langnese-Iglo GmbH v Commission of the European* Communities, Judgment of the Court (Fifth Chamber) of 1 October 1998. Celex No. 61995CJ0279.

94 Ibid.

95 Ibid.

96 Ibid, 1.

> submitted that the Commission was bound by the assessment it made in its comfort letter in view of the fact that it was not in a position to show that that letter had been obtained on the basis of incorrect or incomplete information or that the legal or factual situation prevailing in the ice-cream market had undergone any appreciable change since the letter was sent (paragraphs 28 to 30 of the contested judgment).[97]

The Court further highlighted:

> Langnese-Iglo also maintained that even though the comfort letter had been addressed to Schöller, the Commission and the participants – including Langnese-Iglo – in the procedure initiated in response to the Association's letter of 6 December 1984 nevertheless agreed that the notification by Schöller in May 1985 concerning the ice-cream supply agreements which it had concluded and the request made at that time for the issue of a negative clearance were also valid for all the members of the Association. The comfort letter covered all the exclusive agreements existing in the ice-cream market, and that it was a communication informing the undertaking concerned. The comfort letter itself, provided for the procedure to be reopened, where there was any appreciable change affecting certain matters of law.[98]

Viewed this way, the Court held that a comfort letter cannot mean that it is no longer entitled to take account of a factual situation which existed before the letter was sent but was brought to its notice only later, particularly in connection with a complaint lodged at a later stage.[99] On this basis, the Court ruled that on the first ground of the appeal, partly inadmissible and subsequently rejected. This is another demonstration of how a letter of comfort has emerged as a widely used tool that is flexible in its reach. From a policy perspective, and particularly in relation to a pandemic, the ability to use comfort letters, has undoubtedly provided a further layer of flexibility, but more importantly, certainty in the market.

4.4 United Kingdom

Traditionally, letters of comfort in the UK are different from those in the Continental Europe where they are widey regarded as having binding effect. In the UK, there are cases which make it clear that there is a certain amount of uncertainty over the nature and scope of LCs. There has obviously been a 'reluctance of some companies to give a guarantee because it counts their borrowing limits and things

97 Ibid, 18–25.
98 Ibid.
99 Ibid, 30.

of that sort, which problems we do not have'.[100] As they have no legislative backing, letters of comfort have continued to be applied as though there was no legal reform required for their application.

In the UK letters of comfort have been an important legal tool for a number of decades. In *Kleinwort*[101] the defendants, a public limited company incorporated in Malaysia, which was formed as a wholly owned subsidiary and incorporated in England to operate as a ring dealing members of London Metal Exchange. In granting an acceptance credit/multi-currency cash loan facility to the subsidiary for its trading, the plaintiffs, who were merchant bankers, relied on a letter of comfort, to ensure the business was in a position to meet its liabilities.[102] More specifically, the letter of comfort stated that: 'it was the defendants policy to ensure that the business of Metals was at all times in a position to meet Its liabilities to the plaintiffs'.[103] The Court questioned the level of undertaking or obligation the words that the letter of comfort had provided. Thus, in February 1989, the matter was on Appeal, from September 1987, whereby Kleinwort obtained damages for breach of warranty.[104] In 1985 the tin market had collapsed when the international Tin Council announced that it was unable to meet its liabilities, which ran into hundreds of millions of British pounds. Consequently, the plaintiffs sought repayment of outstanding moneys. However, no repayments were made and Metals went into liquidation.[105] The Court, came back to the central issue of the case, whether the words in the letter of comfort were to be treated as a warranty or a promise.[106] The Court went onto point out that the absence of express words of warranty as to the present facts, or the absence of present words of a promise as to the future conduct, does not conclusively exclude a statement from being a warranty or promise.[107] In conclusion, the Court argued that no contractual promise had ensured. Rather it set out a level of moral obligation between the parties. Based on the moral obligation expressed in the letter of comfort, the Court concluded it was used with the intention of securing finance.[108] The case demonstrated that, letters of comfort have become a valuable negotiation tool. This early case highlighted that the Court will look at whether there are contractual promises expressed in the letter of comfort, or, there is merely a moral obligation. Where it is determined that a moral obligation exists,

100 D.K. Avgitidis, *Groups of Companies: The Liability of the Parent Company for the Debts of Its Subsidiary*, Ant. N. Sakkoulas Publishers, Athens (1996), 304. In Anton Trichardt, *Letters of Comfort: A Trans-System Analysis*, International Banking and Finance Law series, Wolters Kluwer (2012), 79–82.
101 *Kleinwort Benson Ltd v Malaysia Mining Corp Bhd* [1989] 1 W.L.R. 379.
102 Ibid, C-D, 379.
103 Ibid, d, 380.
104 Ibid, E-G, 379–380.
105 Ibid.
106 Ibid, E-F, 390.
107 Ibid, F, 390.
108 Ibid, F, 394.

that there is no specific contractual promise, and therefore, in this circumstance, enforce the obligation of the letter of comfort.

In a more recent case of *Etihad Airways PJSC v. Prof Dr. Lucas Flöther,*[109] the facts were that 'an application by the Defendant (Insolvency Administrator), on behalf of Air Berlin plc (AB) for declaratory relief and a stay of proceedings commenced by the Claimant (Etihad) on 22 January 2019'.

> Air Berlin disputed the jurisdiction of the English court on the basis that the jurisdiction clause contained in a Facility Agreement concluded between Etihad and Air Berlin, and which provides for the jurisdiction of the English court, has no application to the claims which have given rise to the present proceedings.[110]

'Those claims are made by Air Berlin in proceedings commenced by the Insolvency Administrator of Air Berlin against Etihad in the Regional Court of Berlin on 24 July 2018'.[111] The claims made in the German proceedings related to a letter dated 28 April 2017 from Mr James Hogan, the then President and CEO of Etihad Aviation Group PJSC, to the directors of Air Berlin (the 'Comfort Letter'), which provided as follows:

> For the purposes of the finalisation of the financial statements of Air Berlin plc for the year ended 31 December 2016, having had sight of your forecasts for the two years ending 31 December 2018, we confirm our intention to continue to provide the necessary support to Air Berlin to enable it to meet its financial obligations as they fall due for payment for the foreseeable future and in any event for 18 months from the date of this letter. Our commitment is evidenced by our historic support through loans and obtaining financing for Air Berlin.[112]

In the German proceedings, Air Berlin advances two alternative claims against Etihad under German Law:

i) A claim for breach of the Comfort Letter on the basis that the Comfort Letter is legally binding.
ii) Alternatively, if the Comfort Letter is not legally binding, a pre contractual claim in *culpa in contrahendo*, on the basis that Etihad used its negotiating power during the negotiations between the parties to avoid providing a clearly

109 [2019] EWHC 3107 (Comm), 2019 WL 06134056.
110 Ibid.
111 Ibid, 1.
112 Ibid, 2.

binding statement whilst, at the same time, inspiring the trust of Air Berlin that it would adhere to the commitment in the Comfort Letter.[113]

At issue was that 'within the German proceedings, Air Berlin advances two alternative claims against Etihad under German Law:

> i) a claim for breach of the Comfort Letter on the basis that the Comfort Letter is legally binding, and ii) alternatively, if the Comfort Letter is not legally binding, a pre contractual claim in *culpa in contrahendo*, on the basis that Etihad used its negotiating power during the negotiations between the parties to avoid providing a clearly binding statement whilst, at the same time, inspiring the trust of Air Berlin that it would adhere to the commitment in the Comfort Letter.[114]

Noteworthy too, the letter of comfort did not contain a jurisdiction clause.[115] Additionally, Etihad alleged the:

> comfort letter and any contractual claim in connection therewith are subject to English law on the true construction of the governing law clause in the Facility Agreement and pursuant to the EU regulations, Rome 1 and Rome 2. In paragraph 7, Etihad alleges that the comfort letter does not amount to a legally binding promise to provide financial support.[116]

The Court ruled that, the letter and the related claims in the German proceedings had to be determined by reference to English law. It based that determination on the jurisdiction clause that was contained in the facility agreement which was expressly governed by English law and which it extended to claims in respect of the letter and the related claims in the German proceedings. There was no reason why the jurisdiction clause should not extend to disputes arising in relation to the letter.[117] On the point as to where the jurisdiction clause was inapplicable under EU law, the Court noted the letter was not a binding contractual commitment but a statement of intention ancillary to the facility agreement. Neither party could reasonably be surprised by the referral of disputes under the letter to the English court, considering not only the letter's close connection to the facility agreement but also the English law and jurisdiction clauses in the agreements in the support package to which Etihad and AB were party. AB could not argue that the dispute relating to the letter originated in a relationship other than in connection with which

113 Ibid, 3.
114 Ibid, 18.
115 Ibid.
116 Ibid, 35.
117 Ibid.

the agreement conferring jurisdiction was concluded. It therefore concluded that the requirements of Article 25 were satisfied. Thus, and while there were separate documents (comfort letter – facility agreement), the jurisdictional clause in the agreement did extend to the letter because of the legal relationship with Regulation 1215/2012, Article 25. Rather than relying on EU law to specify a level of the contents of a comfort letter, the Court confirmed how such correspondence provides a level of enforceable obligation, which can be derived from EU law.

A decade earlier in the case of *Associated British Ports v. Ferryways,*[118] the Court determined that:

> [A] side letter of agreement constituted a comfort letter. The facts of this case were on appeal from the 2008 judgement of Field J, Ferryways a Belgian company which was formed in order to operate a roll-on, roll-off ferry service between Ostend and Ipswich. Its 'share capital was owned as to 40% by the state-owned Belgian investment company Gimvindus (acting through another company); as to 40% by an associated company of MSC Belgium (MSCB), which is in turn indirectly controlled by Mediterranean Shipping Company (SA) Geneva Group, the second largest liner container shipping company in the world; and as to 20% by Mast(GB) Limited, a company owned by the businessmen whose idea had given rise to the project. In furtherance of the project, Ferryways entered into a series of agreements with Associated British Ports (ABP).[119]

By agreement dated 5 January 2000 (the First Agreement) between ABP and Ferryways, ABP guaranteed a five-hour turnaround of 160 units at its port at Ipswich at designated slot times and at specified rates. The agreement was to run for five years. From time-to-time, variations in relation to charging rates were agreed by letter and by an addendum dated 16 June 2001. Ferryways guaranteed an annual throughput of 25,000 units through Ipswich from 7 February 2001 to 6 February 2005. Initially, the business expanded rapidly. However, there were problems with the linkspan across which the trailers traversed at Ipswich. Ferryways wanted ABP to improve it, but this required an estimated investment of £6.1 million by ABP, which naturally wanted to secure a long-term commitment from Ferryways. Negotiations led to a new agreement between Ferryways and ABP dated 1 September 2003 (the Second Agreement) which replaced the First (Letter) Agreement. The Second (Letter) Agreement was expressed to run from 1 September 2003 to 31 December 2024. It made provision for priority use of appropriate berths by Ferryways, for turnaround time and for the construction of a new linkspan. There was further provision for index-linked charges. Volume was dealt with by way of

118 [2009] EWCA Civ 189.
119 Ibid, 1.

an annual minimum throughput obligation which also required Ferryways to compensate ABP in the event of a shortfall. The Kay J. ruled that:

> [T]he Letter Agreement was a letter of comfort. In one sense it is surprising, verging on surreal, for a promisee in the position of ABP – the would-be comfortee – to assert that a document is a letter of comfort. More usually, such a contention would be expected to come from a promisor – or would-be comforter. However, surprise recedes a little when it is submitted that the document is not just a letter of comfort but a legally binding letter of comfort.[120]

Viewed this way, the case highlighted how the Court has determined that the use of different and varying language to describe a letter of agreement as a letter of comfort. The Court, in referring to earlier judgements, reinforced that a letter of agreement will form a comfort letter – where such correspondence has a level of promissory obligation(s), and those obligations can be enforced. It is this promissory obligation that has become the commonality from state to state and jurisdiction to jurisdiction. What confuses practitioners and scholars is the varying titles that have been given to letters of comfort. This challenge should not be viewed as a challenge or obstacle, whether they are defined as a letter of comfort or some other instrument, they have emerged as achieving similar things.

As highlighted throughout this book, Brexit is challenging many areas of economic activity, and industries and the legal ramifications are broad. Comfort letters are no exception. In reinforcing the aforementioned case of *Etihad Airways,*[121] it highlighted further challenges facing entities in financial stress and proceedings commencing in the EU. Etihad Airways PJSC (Etihad) was a significant shareholder in Air Berlin plc (Air Berlin) in April 2017. One of the 'major Facility Agreements was for EUR 350 million. The proceedings began in Germany as a result of the conditions of the comfort letter being breached'.[122] However,

> Etihad issued its proceedings in the UK arguing they were not liable, and that the both jurisdiction and proceedings fall within the UK court. At issue was the scope of English law, and Article 25 of EU Regulation No 1215/2012 (Brussels Recast).[123]

120 Ibid, 16.
121 [2019] EWHC 3107 (Comm), 2019 WL 06134056.
122 Ibid.
123 Ibid, 5.

Noteworthy too, is that now in early 2021, other airlines find themselves in a position of having to either restructure, declare insolvency or obtain government subsidies, as a result of the ongoing response and transnational flight restrictions from COVID-19.

Etihad acquired a 2.99% stake in Air Berlin in August 2011 and, in December 2011, increased its shareholding to 29.21% by subscribing for 31.57 million new shares for a subscription price of €72.9 million pursuant to an agreement dated 19 December 2011.[124]

The Facility Agreement, which was drafted in English, was expressed to be governed by English law and contained an exclusive jurisdiction clause in favour of the English courts. Justice Jacobs was of the view that the parties had intended disputes arising under the Comfort Letter to fall within the jurisdiction clause contained in the Facility Agreement. The jurisdiction clause in the Facility Agreement was formulated as what is commonly called an asymmetric jurisdiction clause, where only one party (usually, as in this case, the borrower) agrees that a particular court has exclusive jurisdiction while the other party (usually the lender) has discretion to bring proceedings before any other court with jurisdiction.[125] Air Berlin argued that:

> This asymmetry precluded the jurisdiction clause from being determined to confer exclusive jurisdiction under Article 25 such that Article 31(2) was not engaged. Jacobs J in referring to the case of Commerzbank v. Liquimar[126], reaffirmed that the English courts position that asymmetric jurisdiction clauses fall within the scope of Article 25. Importantly, the court looks at, and addresses the obligations of the parties set out in the agreements and comfort letter(s), forming part of an overall contract. In this case the however there were contractual obligations to the borrower. On the other hand, in relation to insolvency the court noted that the value of the assets (measured at the higher of the going concern value and the liquidation value) of the borrower is less than its liabilities, and there is no positive going-concern prognosis, such test to be applied in accordance with Section 19 para. 2 of German Insolvency Code.[127]

The Court declined to support Air Berlin's position for the proceedings to fall within UK jurisdiction. On the other hand, it was not clear what, if any, changes would arise to letters of comfort. It is our view that based on their operation and not being formally recognised within relevant national legal frameworks, comfort

124 Ibid.
125 Ibid.
126 Ibid, [2017] EWHC 161 (Comm).
127 Ibid, 17.

letters will continue to be used, where required, post Brexit. While they are used generally, the courts will turn to the obligations specified to determine whether there is a contract. The comfort letter is often used to provide a starting point to for parties to negotiate commercial outcomes. The play a beneficial role in restructuring of organisations, and will be construed in cross-border matters according to their terms. To overcome any potential issues, in cross-border matters, it is advised that any comfort letter or other agreements be drafted with specific and clear provisions. The next section examines Singapore's approach to letters of comfort.

4.5 Singapore

Singapore is considered a legal hub for Southeast Asia. They, along with the UK, are viewed as being insolvency and restructuring/reorganising friendly. Singapore has established a legal framework that replicates in many ways that of the UK. For comfort letters this is no different. In *Hongkong and Shanghai Banking Corporation Ltd.,* the plaintiffs claimed for the sum of $8,843,545.55, plus interest and costs.[128] The case considered three letters of comfort, or as the case highlighted letters of awareness. What has emerged is that countries are referring to letters of comfort in different ways. In Singapore the use of the phrase letter of awareness can also constitute a comfort letter. The Court noted that letters of awareness (comfort letters) are commonly issued by a parent company to the lender giving comfort to the lender for a loan made to a subsidiary company.[129] The three letters of comfort were issued that outlined how ownership, amongst other things, would continue of the borrower Jurong Engineering. The Court noted that the letter of awareness constituted:

> 'We confirm that we are aware that you have offered to grant/continue banking facilities to Huge Corporation (S) Pte. Ltd. ('the borrower') for SGD26,000,000 as per your Letter of Offer dated 3 August 1994 and approve the terms and conditions of such banking facilities. We also confirm that, so long as any amount is outstanding to you under such banking facilities:
>
> - We will continue to maintain our (50%) 51% ownership of the borrower and hereby undertake to advise you forthwith in the event of any decision being taken to dispose of the whole or part of our shareholding in the borrower.

128 *Hongkong and Shanghai Banking Corporation Ltd v Jurong Engineering Ltd* [2000] SGHC 20, https://www.supremecourt.gov.sg/docs/default-source/module-document/judgement/2000-sghc-20.pdf. Letters of Awareness, or comfort letters, are commonly issued by a parent company to the lender giving comfort to the lender for a loan made to a subsidiary company.

129 Ibid.

- We will cause the borrower to be operated and maintained in such a way as to be in a financial position to meet all its obligations from time to time to you. If the borrower is unable for any reason to meet its obligations, we [shall] will endeavour to either:
- make funds available to the borrower sufficient to meet its obligations, or
- have funds made available to the borrower by others in amounts sufficient to enable the borrower to meet its obligations.
- We will not take any action which will result in the borrower being unable to carry on its business or otherwise being unable to meet all its obligations from time to time to you and hereby undertake to advise you forthwith of any circumstances which may affect the continuing operation of the borrower.
- We will furnish you with our consolidated annual audited financial statements and accounts and will procure that the borrower will furnish you with annual audited financial statements and accounts together with such additional financial information as may be reasonably required.
- This letter is to be interpreted according to Singapore Laws.[130]

The Court dismissed HSBC's claim and held that the letters in question did not give rise to legally enforceable obligations. In considering the extent of the use of the letters, the Court pointed to a feature of the law and process within Singapore. It highlighted that the Business Instruction Manual Graded Letters of Awareness (Comfort) in the following manner:

> Grade 1 indicated 'a very strong letter of awareness containing covenants regarding financial assistance, management control and retention of shareholding'; Grade 2 indicated 'a less strong Letter of Awareness which may include only two out of the three conditions in a Grade 1 Letter'; Grade 3 indicated 'all other Letters of Awareness which are effectively no more than an acknowledgement that the facility had been granted'. Each time the plaintiffs forwarded a draft Letter of Awareness to the first defendants, they always sent a draft which complied with the sample 'Grade 1' Letter of Awareness in their Business Instruction Manual. The first defendants then made changes to the original drafts and the plaintiffs' internal memoranda showed that after the changes, the first Letter of Awareness could no longer be classified as a 'Grade 1' Letter of Awareness. Instead, the plaintiffs classified it internally as a 'Grade 2' Letter. Similarly, after the amendments made by the first defendants, the second and third Letters of Awareness were also

130 Ibid.

> considered to be 'Grade 2' Letters of Awareness by the plaintiffs. Clearly, although the first defendants only changed one or two words in the plaintiffs' original drafts, these changes actually cut down the plaintiffs' legal rights as interpreted by the latter's internal guidelines. Yet, the plaintiffs accepted the 'Grade 2' Letters of Awareness without protest.[131]

Based on this, it was HSBC that had, through its own internal procedures, graded the letters in this way, as part of their daily operations. It must also be noted that other entities may not grade letters of comfort in this way. Thus, it is up to the organisation as to how they manage and classify such letters. Viewed this way, the Court took the view that the letters of comfort or letters of awareness were themselves drafted in a way that the language was specific. The letters formed part of the overall negotiations of the parties. The Court also argued that they represented a gentleman's agreement, and that this agreement only went as far as specifying or confirming the moral obligations of the parties, rather than any further specific obligations.[132] Nevertheless, and consistent with the other jurisdictions compared, the enforceability of letters of comfort in Singapore is based on the legal relationship and any promissory statements/obligations or otherwise contained in the letters. It must be noted that this was only a brief look at Singapore's approach and a much wider examination is needed. Nonetheless, they will be viewed as to their contractual obligations in a similar way to that of Australia and UK. The next section examines the US approach to letters of comfort.

4.6 United States [US]

The US generally refers to comfort letters as keepwell agreements. In the same way as the other jurisdictions compared in this chapter, comfort letters are enforceable in the US. However, in the US, they are often tied to accounting standards, similar to Singapore. It is out of scope of this chapter to examine the respective accounting standards and their impact to comfort letters.

In *Lasalle Bank National Association v. Citicorp Real Estate Inc.* of December 1997,[133] Brock Suite Greenville, Inc borrowed USD 6.75 million from LJ Melody Company (LJM), a mortgage loan provider secured by a mortgage on a hotel that Brock Suit styled as a Residence Inn by Marriott.[134] LJM sold the loan to Citicorp and subsequently assigned all rights title and interest in, to and under the note, the mortgage and certain related loan documents. In response to a request by

131 Ibid.
132 Ibid.
133 *Lasalle Bank National Association v Citicorp Real Estate Inc,* 02 Civ. 7868 (HB).
134 Ibid, 17.

LJM, 'Marriott sent a comfort letter to LJM in the same month, dated 18 December 1997 detailing what procedures Marriott would follow if Brock were in default under its franchise agreement'. Five years later, on 28 March 2003, Citicorp filed a third-party complaint against Marriott for failure to notify Citicorp of Brock Suite's default despite Marriott's undertaking of this obligation in the letter to LJM and against Criimi and Orix for failure to timely notify Citicorp of Brock Suite's default as required by PSA, §2.05(d). In regards to letters of comfort, the Court argued that:

> They are common devices in business, there is relatively little case law on the extent to which courts will give them any legal effect. They are an instrument written by a third party and is designed to encourage the creation of an agreement between two other parties. [S]ometimes a comfort letter leads to the subsequent involvement of the drafting party in the agreement itself, despite that party's original intent that the letter not create any obligations, comfort letters are often drafted by a parent company and are aimed at encouraging a lending institution to issue credit to a subsidiary.[135]

The drafter of the instrument needs to avoid incurring liability on the parent company's part for the non-performance of the potential debtor, the subsidiary. Yet, at the same time, if the parent company wished to encourage the potential creditor, the financial institution would want to enter into a legally binding transaction. In other words, a comfort letter of this type is aimed at being something more than a letter of introduction, but something less than a guaranty or suretyship commitment.[136] Nevertheless, in relation to their enforceability, these letters will be evaluated on their contents and intent of the parties. That is, the Court took the additional position that:

> [T]he enforceability of a comfort letter depends on a number of factors, the first being the language of the instrument itself. An intent on the part of the drafter to be bound as guarantor is likely to be found if the instrument, despite the fact that it calls itself a 'comfort letter', contains operative language such as 'guaranty', 'contract' or other words of promise. The more detailed the instrument, the more likely a court will be to find it indicative of an intent to contract.[137]

In the US, although comfort letters generally do not give rise to legally binding obligations, courts will enforce them in accordance with a contract or

135 Ibid, 17–19.
136 Ibid.
137 Ibid.

promissory obligations. A general theme that has emerged across the various jurisdictions examined in this chapter is that these letters will be examined and based on their contents and extent to which they provide for a level of promissory obligation. Both sides argued the comfort letter that support their respective contentions. For example, Marriott noted that the letter was addressed to LJM and the letter itself stated that Marriott would issue a substantially similar replacement letter if requested to do so but only to certain specified successors.[138] The Court held that 'as a sophisticated commercial entity, Citicorp should have known that the promises contained in a letter of comfort do not bind the promisor'.[139] On the other hand, Citicorp pointed to the specific language used in the letter, for example, whereby, 'Marriott stated that the following are the producers that Marriott will follow and referred to its promises contained in the letter as obligations'.[140] Moreover, Marriott argued that obligations would remain in effect while both the franchise agreement and LJM's note remained in effect. Because of the fact-specific nature of the inquiry, the Court did not dismiss Citicorp's claim as they had alleged that it received the comfort letter and relied on the obligations set out in the letter. The Court permitted the opportunity to develop sufficient facts to show that they had relied on the obligations set out in the letter.

The case highlighted a similar approach that has been adopted by other common law countries towards the extent of enforceability of comfort letters. The US, have assisted entities in managing debt once they find themselves in financial stress, restructuring their operations, or providing greater equity. Therefore, these letters are enforceable where there is a clear intention and promissory obligations imposed on the parties. In other words, the courts, similar to a contract, will look carefully at the contents of the letter to confirm or otherwise to determine whether a level of promissory obligation exists. The next section examines the approach taken by India for letters of comfort.

4.7 India

The Indian experience with letters of comfort continues to be an unsettled compromise between the application, use and enforceable or non-enforceable obligations they create. Veena Sivaramakrishnan, is of the view that:

> India considers them to hold a mystifying position in the financing spectrum. While some interpret it as an enforceable obligation on the issuer, some merely see it as an unenforceable representation of a fact. In common

138 Ibid.
139 Ibid.
140 Ibid.

> parlance, letters of comfort are a letter issued by a parent company or other related party/affiliate which has a controlling stake or power over another entity, to the lenders of the Obligor.[141]

Sivaramakrishnan argues that:

> Letters of comfort are intended to provide some form of comfort to the lenders in relation to the obligations and performance of the obligor. The level of comfort will be integrally linked to the nature of statements made by the issuer in the letters of comfort. These statements generally relate to assurance of financial soundness of the obligor to repay its debt and perform its obligations and also at times provide comfort as regards the issuer itself.[142]

Firstly, in the 2009 case of *Lucent,*[143] the Delhi High Court considered a letter of comfort. At issue was the whether the letter provided a guarantee. The Court noted that the 'letter of comfort' merely stated that the plaintiff would issue the proposed guarantee in future at the time of the proposed facility of Rs.484 crores being finalised 'subject to the terms and conditions stated in the term sheet and satisfactory documentation'.[144] Secondly, in referring to the Australian Bank of Brussels case, the Court stated that:

> There should be no room in the proper flow of commerce for some purgatory where statements made by business men, after hard bargaining and made to induce another business person to enter into a business transaction would, without any express statement to that effect, reside in a twilight zone of merely honourable engagement. The whole thrust of the law today is to attempt to give proper effect to commercial transactions. . . . If these statements are appropriately promissory in character, courts should enforce them when they are uttered in the course of business, and there is no clear indication that they are not intended to be legally enforceable.[145]

141 Veena Sivaramakrishnan, *India: Letter of Comfort: Enforceable Guarantee of Moral Obligation*, https://www.mondaq.com/india/contracts-and-commercial-law/549604/letter-of-comfort-enforceable-guarantee-or-moral-obligation.

142 Ibid.

143 *Lucent Technologies Inc. vs. ICICI Bank Ltd. & Ors.* [2009], https://indiankanoon.org/doc/55650626/.

144 Ibid, 53–54.

145 Ibid, 77.

So far as the letter of comfort is concerned, the Court laid down the following principles that were outlined in the Australian case of *Bank of Brussels,*[146] which gave valuable guidance on the subject. The Chief Justice of Australia held that:

> In determining whether a letter of comfort gives rise to contractual obligations a) the ordinary rules of construction and interpretation relating to contracts apply; b) the overriding test is that of the intention of the parties as deduced from the document as a whole, seen against the background of the practices of the particular trade or industry and in the events surrounding its inception; c) the prima facie presumption that in respect of commercial transactions there is an intention to create legal relations applies, and the onus of proving the absence of such intention rests with the party who asserts that no legal effect is intended. In the circumstances, and taking into account the negotiations leading to the final version of the letter of comfort, and a close textual analysis of its terms, the letter of comfort contained 2 enforceable contractual promises, breach of which gave rise to a liability in damages where the shares. . . . were sold without the plaintiff being given 90 days' notice. The Australian court was of the view that it would be inimical to the effective administration of justice in commercial disputes, that a court should use a finely tuned linguistic fork.[147]

Again, and similar to the other jurisdictions examined in this chapter, at issue is whether the letter of comfort created a binding – promissory obligations, and whether those obligations can be enforced. The Court was of a view that:

> The circumstances and documents do not indicate that the parties intended to create any legal relations. The very terms of the letter dated 13th September, 2000, the term sheet enclosed therewith and the response of the plaintiff as contained in letters of comfort dated 27th September, 2000 and 30th November, 2000 are a strong indicator in this regard. Both use phrases and concepts having clear technical legal significance and do not manifest any intent that a final and concluded contract had been entered into. In view of the above discussion, it, therefore, has to be held that the communications placed before this court do not contain the kind of assent required to make for a binding contract.[148]

Central to this was how the issuer was not under any financial obligation to pay any amount under the agreement between the borrower and the bank. While the

146 Ibid, *Banque Brussels Lambert SA v. Australian National Industries Ltd.* (1989) 21 NSWLR 502.
147 Ibid.
148 Ibid, 114.

case did not specifically rule on the letters, the Court reinforced the UK approach, which is consistent with most of India's commercial laws. Moreover, the case further demonstrated and reinforced that a comfort letter that holds a party or parties to a promissory obligation comes with a level of consequences that are no different from performing a contract. Three years later in 2012, in the case of *United Breweries (Holding) Ltd*:[149]

> The respondent No.1 herein sanctioned a loan of Rs.70.00 lakhs in favour of respondent No.2 herein. The loan agreement dated 6.3.1996 was executed by respondent No.2 and respondent No.1. The third and fourth respondents herein executed a surety agreement dated 6.3.1006 giving collateral security of schedule I and II properties. The appellant executed a letter of comfort dated 2.3.1996 as per Ex-P14. Respondent No.2 committed default and did not repay the amount as agreed. Hence, respondent No.1 invoked surety agreement dated 6.3.1996 given by respondent Nos.3 and 4 by issuing notice dated 16.9.1998. Respondent Nos.3 and 4 did not pay the amount despite the notice.[150]

The Karnataka High Court argued:

> Sri. K.G. Raghavan, learned Senior Advocate appearing on behalf of the appellant submits that Ex-P14-the 'letter of comfort' is wrongly interpreted and treated as 'letter of guarantee' by the Court below and the same has resulted in mis-carriage of justice. Further Ex-P14 nowhere mandates the appellant that he should repay the dues of respondent No. 2, in case, respondent No. 2 or the guarantors i.e., respondent Nos. 3 and 4 fail to repay the loan amount to respondent No. 1. In other words, accordingly, Ex-P14 is not a letter of guarantee, but, is mere a letter of comfort. Said submissions are opposed by Sri. D.S. Joshi, learned counsel appearing on behalf of respondent No. 1. It was contended that Ex-P14 though titled as 'letter of comfort' is clearly a 'letter of guarantees', inasmuch as, the wordings used in the said document amply reveal that the appellant has undertaken to repay the loan of respondent No. 2, in case of non-payment of loan by respondent No. 2 or respondent Nos. 3 and 4 herein. M/S United Breweries (Holding) Ltd, Bangalore v. Karnataka State Industrial Investment and Development Corporation Limited, Bangalore & Others.[151]

149 *United Breweries (Holding) Ltd v State Industrial Investment & Development Corporation Limited* [AIR 2012 Kar 65], https://www.legitquest.com/case/ms-united-breweries-holding-ltd-bangalore-v-karnataka-state-industrial-investment-and-development-corporation-limited-bangalore/dd859.

150 Ibid.

151 Ibid, 126.

The Court went onto say that the:

> letter of comfort nowhere reveals that the appellant stood as guarantor for the loan disbursed by respondent No. 1 in favour of respondent No. 2. The letter merely stated that the 'associate company (debtor company) will meet the financial and contractual obligations and that the appellant herein undertaken all reasonable steps to ensure that the debtor company conducts its operations efficiently to meet its obligations in the usual course of business. The comfort letter is more in the nature of recommendatory letter.[152]

However, the Court went further and argued that in this context, we may usefully refer to the definition of 'letter of comfort', as found in *P. Ramanatha Aiyar's Advanced Law Lexicon*, 'A document that indicates one party's intention to try to ensure that another party complies with the terms of a financial transaction without guaranteeing performance in the event of default'.[153] From the material on record, it is clear that the letter of comfort merely indicates the appellant's assurance that the respondent No. 2 would comply with the 'terms of a financial transaction without guaranteeing performance in the event of default'.[154] The case was a further illustration that, where a guarantor is liable, they will only be liable for their guarantee and no other. There will be no additional liability, and based on the comfort letter was only to inject funds into the other party and not discharge a debt. Based on this, the comfort letter would amount to a guarantee if the terms fall within Section 126 of the Contracts Act. Yet, and central to the position on letters of comfort have in India, where the provisions of the Contract Act have not been met, the comfort letter cannot amount to a guarantee and the matter was dismissed.

Central to contract law in India is the Contract Act 1872, and more specifically Section 126 relate to letters of comfort. Thus, Section 126 of the Indian Contracts Act, and the relevance of those provisions to the contents of a letter of comfort, were further considered by the Court. Section 126 states that a contract of guarantee, surety, principal debtor and creditor – a contract of guarantee is a contract to perform the promise, or discharge the liability, of a third person in case of his default. The individual or entity who provides the guarantee is called the surety; the person in respect of whose default the guarantee is given is called the principal debtor, and the person to whom the

152 Ibid, 376.

153 Ibid, P. Ramanatha Aiyar, Shakil Ahmad Khan, P. Ramanatha Aiyar's *Advanced Law Lexicon – The Encyclopaedic Law Dictionary with Words & Phrases, Legal Maxims & Latin Terms (Set of 4 Volumes) Hardcover*, LexisNexis, India (23 December 2016).

154 Ibid.

guarantee is given is called the creditor'.[155] In 2020, the notion of a guarantee being provided within a letter of comfort was considered in *Yes Bank Limited.*[156] Essel group company Living Entertainment Ltd (LEL) borrowed $50 million from Yes Bank in 2016 to buy shares in its unit, Veria International. Promoter Goenka had provided guarantees for the loan. Separately, LEL entered into a put option agreement with another group firm, ATL Media. Under the put option, if the promoter stake in Zee fell below 30%, ATL must buy up to a 64.38% stake that LEL held in Veria International, and also repay the loan.[157] Nevertheless, between 2016 to 2019, there were a number of developments that formed part of the ongoing negotiations in relation to the structure and organisation of the business.[158] Firstly, in March 2016, a comfort letter was issued outlining the support of ATL for the need to inject equity-debt, so as to meet the ongoing capital and debt requirements. Secondly, it also included an outline of the proposal regarding the expansion of its business by honouring any put options and guarantees, and called for its operations outside the country to hold a minimum of 51% shares.[159] Thirdly, the Court ruled that a letter of comfort can constitute a guarantee only if its terms meet the conditions set out in Section 126 of the Indian Contract Act 1872. A guarantee may be either oral or written. Such an approach is no different to the other common law countries compared in this chapter.

At issue, and as outlined in the aforementioned, was the construction and contents of the comfort letter, and whether the guarantee formed an ongoing contractual obligation. In confirming the essential elements of the comfort letter, the Court concluded that, Zee had an obligation under the Put Option Agreement, and there was no requirement to repay debt owed by LEL to Yes Bank.[160] The Court further noted that all other correspondence was clearly understood by the parties as to who did what and when, regarding funding arrangements.[161] The case reinforced that under Indian law, unlike that of its

155 Ibid.

156 *Yes Bank Limited v. Zee Entertainment Enterprises & Ors., LD-VC-IA NO. 01 of 2020* IN LD-VC-SUIT NO. 120 of 2020.

157 Ibid, 5–17.

158 Ibid.

159 Ibid, 19–25.

160 Ibid.

161 Ibid, 46. In referring to Australian common law, the court noted that in Banque Brussels, the defendant, Australian National Industries or ANI was the corporate parent of Spedley Securities Ltd. Spedley went to Banque Brussels for a loan. ANI issued a Letter of Comfort saying it would not dilute its shareholding in Spedley below 45% without 90 days' prior notice Banque Brussels. It also said that it was its practice to ensure that its affiliate Spedley would at all times be in a position to meet its financial obligations when they fell due, including repayment of all loans made by the bank under the arrangements mentioned in that LC. For a substantial amount, ANI divested its equity in Spedley. It did so without notice to the bank. Spedley defaulted in repayment of the bank's loan. Banque Brussels sued – but in damages for breach of ANI's commitment not to divest

common law counterparts such as Australia who does not have specific contracts legislation, a guarantee will amount an obligation that is a contractual obligation. Therefore, any comfort letters containing these obligations will be enforceable.

The importance of these recent decisions for comfort letters cannot be underestimated in the Indian context. They, in our view, need to be clearly worded to ensure that the intent of the letter is not ambiguous. As highlighted throughout this chapter the common law countries, such letters have to create a level of intention followed by an obligation. Only when this has been established will the courts determine whether any contractual arrangements exist. On the other hand, in the case of India, there is no specific obligation established by a comfort letter, the Court may award damages, and they are increasingly becoming an instrument that provide a level of security and accountability to parties. The next section examines whether Indonesia uses letters of comfort.

4.8 Indonesia

Indonesia differs from the other jurisdictions compared in this chapter. Indonesia do not formally use or recognise letters of comfort. Such letters cannot be used as security of debt or property arrangements.[162] Even though they have not been accepted in Indonesia, the courts have discussed and considered their use. However, from time to time, be used by the banking sector, although it is not common practice. The Indonesia courts have briefly discussed the application of letters of comfort. While it did not rule on the contents of the letter, it highlighted that they pervade the civil law, in managing debt. In the 2017 case of The Indonesia Overseas Bank,[163] (Indover),

> by summons of 26 November 2014, the trustees appealed the judgments of the Amsterdam District Court of 12 May 2010, 24 August 2011, and 27 August 2014, rendered under the above-mentioned case/cause list numbers between BI (Bank of Indonesia) as claimant in the main verification action,

---

its stake in Spedley. Indeed, even in Banque Brussels, the Court held that the LoC in question was not a guarantee. ANI was held not to be liable for the repayment of the loan on Spedley's default.

162 Verified by Sinta Dewi, Associate Professor at Faculty of Law University of Padjadjaran, Bandung, Indonesia.

163 *Antonie VAN HEES and Catharina Maria HARMSEN v. Bank of Indonesia, Court of Appeal Amsterdam, Case no: 200.169.606/01 Case/cause list no Amsterdam District Court: C/13/449889 / HA ZA 10–380,* https://www.stibbe.com/~/media/03%20news/publications/indover/2017/08a%20judgment%20amsterdam%20court%20of%20appeal%2014%20november%202017%20unofficial%20translation.pdf.

> defendant in the counterclaim, and the trustees as defendants in the main verification action and claimants in the counterclaim.[164]

On appeal to the:

> [T]he trustees moved that the Court of Appeal, by immediately enforceable judgment as far as the law allows, (i) overturns the judgment of 27 August 2014; (ii) dismisses BI's claims; (iii) allows the trustees' claims; (iv) orders BI to repay the trustees what the latter paid to BI in compliance with the aforementioned judgment; and (v) orders BI to pay the costs of the proceedings in both instances. BI further moved that the Court of Appeal, by immediately enforceable judgment as far as the law allows, upholds the judgment of 27 August 2014, as the Court of Appeal understands it to the extent that its claims were allowed and the claims of the trustees were dismissed, and orders the trustees to pay the costs of the proceedings.[165]

Nevertheless, in the cross appeal, BI moved that the Court of Appeal, by immediately enforceable judgment as far as the law allows, the judgment of 27 August 2014 to the extent that its claims were dismissed. BI further moved that:

> [T]he Court of Appeal rules '(i) that BI's claim in the bankruptcy of Indover has immunity, being the property of a central bank, or state property intended for public use, and as such may not be attached or used for setting off, or for any other form of execution; (ii) that the prejudgment attachment is null and void; and (iii) that any new attachment of BI's claim in the bankruptcy of Indover or of other property of BI is null and void by operation of law.[166]

BI additionally claimed in the cross appeal that the:

> trustees be prohibited from attaching property of BI again, subject to a penalty, and that it be declared that the trustees have no cause of action with their alternative claim brought on behalf of the joint creditors based on unlawful act/tort, and that the trustees be ordered to pay the costs of the proceedings. Further, as part of the cross appeal, the trustees moved that the grounds for appeal be dismissed and that BI be ordered to pay the costs of the proceedings.[167]

164 Ibid, 1.
165 Ibid.
166 Ibid.
167 Ibid.

However, the Court did not recognise a letter of comfort. It stated that:

> A major part of the funding is currently provided by the parent company, Bank Indonesia ('BI'). As agreed with BI, Indover is obliged to repay part of this funding every month. However, Indover is hardly able to independently attract (long-term) funding at a commercial rate, so that the mandatory repayments to BI translate directly into a further diminishing in value of the credit portfolio. It is expected that a Letter of Comfort from BI, as issued in the past as well, might help Indover attract external funding. We understand that you are still negotiating such Letter of Comfort with BI.[168]

It must be noted that the aforementioned was presided over in the courts of the Netherlands and not a court in Indonesia. The Court went onto confirm the importance of the Indonesian civil code in relation to an agreement being formally binding. The Court argued that:

> Pursuant to Article 1320, preamble, and at (1), Indonesian Civil Code, an agreement may only exist if those who bind themselves to it consent. Material in this instance – also because the trustees based their principal claim on it – is whether, by issuing the press release of 16 February 1998 and sending its letter to DNB dated 9 March 1998, BI must be deemed to have consented to the alleged obligations. The circumstances of the case must also be considered in this assessment.[169]

While not an expanded examination of the Indonesian landscape pertaining to comfort letters, the resulting effect saw the Court dismiss the appeal. A key feature under the Indonesian model is how the Court declared that BI's claim in the bankruptcy has a level of immunity. Therefore, letters of comfort are far from settled.[170] They have been somewhat rejected by the courts. While it is a decision for Indonesia, it is recommended that they look more broadly at the benefits of letters of comfort to their economy. The final Section examines the state of China.

4.9 China

In China, comfort letters can be best described as tools to manage the intent and expectation(s) of parties in commercial dealings. Increasingly, they have been used to also determine the obligation, in a similar way to common law countries of UK,

168 Ibid, 2.4.
169 Ibid, 3.5.3.
170 Confirmed by Sinta Dewi, Associate Professor at Faculty of Law University of Padjadjaran, Bandung, Indonesia.

US and Australia. However, they are often referred to as commitment letters. In *Foshan Municipal People's Government*,[171] the Court highlighted that in May 1994, the Fishan Municipal Government issued to the Bank of Communications the commitment letter No. 030 of the Foshan Municipal Government. It stated that:

> Zhonogya Enterprises Limited Company is an enterprise of this municipality stationed in Hong Kong. In order to further develop the foreign trade of this company, this company has specifically applied to your bank for US$10 million of credit. The application for credit quota was approved by the government. The letter went onto say that this government hopes that your bank will be able to give support in light of the actual demands for the business development of this company. The government would like to urge this company to practically perform the repayment liability and to repay the principal and interest of loans to your bank on schedule. If this company does not repay the principle or interest of loans or defaults in the repayment of principal or interests of loans, this government will take charge of it and not let your bank suffer any economic loss.[172]

Clearly the letter outlined the terms of the agreement to loan the company money, and where those conditions were or would not be fulfilled, the government could step in. In October of the same year, two further letters were issued outlining the arrangements for additional repayment of money borrowed. While not specifically referred to as a comfort letter, the letter performed the same functions as comfort letters in other jurisdictions. The People's Republic of China Supreme People's Court held that the commitment letter has no guarantee obligations as the government was responsible only for resolving the problem. The Court took the position that this can never be interpreted as taking liability as the guarantee.[173].

These letters have also emerged in a similar way to comfort letters. In the case of *Bank of Communications*,[174] the Supreme People's Court found that there was no enforceable guarantee provided by the Liaoning provincial government in accordance with the terms of the letter (comfort letter), which was issued by the Hong Kong bank that provided a letter of credit. The contents of the letter stated that:

> We (Liaoning provincial government) are aware that you (the HK Bank) have agreed to provide, or continue providing, a banking facility to the borrower: a general letter of credit facility in an aggregate amount of HK$50 MILLION.

171 Foshan Municipal People's Government vs. Bank of Communications (Hong Kong Branch) Re: Guarantee Dispute [2005], http://www.lawinfochina.com/display.aspx?lib=case&id=383.

172 Ibid.

173 Anton Trichardt, *Letters of Comfort: A Trans-System Analysis*, International Banking and Finance Law series, Wolters Kluwer (2012), 24.

174 *Bank of Communications (Hong Kong Branch) v. Ganjyun Company Limited, Yunfu Municipal People's Government and Others Re: Dispute over Loan Guarantee Contract* (Appeal) [2015].

> We hereby undertake as follows: we agree to the above financing arrangements being provided, or to continue to be provided, by you to the borrower; we will use our best endeavours to maintain the existence and normal operations of the borrower, we will use our best efforts to ensure that the borrower performs its responsibilities and obligations in respect of the facility utilized by it; and if the borrower becomes unable to pay any of its obligations under the facility as required by you, we will provide assistance in dealing with the debts owed by the borrower to you such that you do not suffer any economic loss'.[175]

The Court ruled that:

> this letter and its guarantee, or conditions was not enforceable because the terms of the letter only proved that the letter only required the government to provide assistance in dealing with the defaulted debts, without expressing any intent to discharge those debts on behalf of the borrower, and the HK Bank did not request the government to discharge the defaulted debt.[176]

The bank only required the government to perform its undertaking outlined in the letter. Against this backdrop, as can be seen from this brief overview in China, comfort letters are far from being fully accepted by the judiciary. While China and Indonesia have many similarities regarding the adoption of the civil law, their respective approach to comfort letters has emerged albeit quite differently and they are far from being fully accepted by the courts. Indonesia though, has not formally adopted comfort letters. However, China has embraced different forms of comfort letters. They function in the same way as common and other civil law jurisdictions, provided they provide a level of contractual obligation.

4.10 Conclusion

Letters of comfort have served the commercial sector well for a number of years. For example, in common law countries, they have been utilised with effectiveness and efficiency in managing restructuring of corporate entities. On the other side, they are relatively new addition to most civil law jurisdictions. And, in the case of Indonesia there is no clear settled position on their use. First, they can be defined in different terms such as comfort letters, letters of comfort, keepwell agreements, support letters, letters of awareness, commitment letter, amongst others. Second, they can also amount to a guarantee. Third, and while subtly different from letters of awareness once they have a level of contractual obligation(s), their enforceability

175 Ibid.
176 Ibid.

is more or less assured by the courts. Fourth, and more pervasively, they have been used widely and been described as contracts, agreements or purchasing agreement. Comfort letters have also been described as providing relief through financial support, foster cooperation, provide a benefit to creditors and cut across the common and civil law divide. Moreover, they can be used as part of a restructure, insolvency or winding up of an entity, and are a valuable tool to commence negotiations between parties.

Courts will also consider other elements of these letters and whether they provide for guarantees. Some jurisdictions, for instance Australia and UK, compared to the others jurisdictions take a strict approach.

The decisive point is that letters of comfort, being a practical legal tool, are an effective and efficient mechanism for entities having to reorganise their current arrangements with creditors. This is fundamentally important to ensure financial stability of both the entity experiencing financial stress and the broader market. They have the ability to be flexible and there are no limits on the amount of comfort letters that can be used. Comfort letters can either be guarantees or opinions, and where they are guarantees, they will be treated by the courts differently to opinions.

For practitioners, these letters need to be carefully drafted, particularly when dealing with entities that are located and based in two different jurisdictions. Central in delineating the use and application of comfort letters is, they extend further than merely providing a level of comfort to parties and the directors of companies. In some situations, such a letter can act as a significant circuit breaker where the company is heading for insolvency. However, where an individual or responsible office within and entity obtains a comfort letter prior to any knowledge of insolvency, the resulting effect can protect, the responsible offer(s). Drafted correctly, they can serve as a defence.

Therefore, they have become important documents, and, from and practice management perspective, those responsible for the letters need to ensure they are drafted appropriately for the circumstances that they are to serve. Moreover, even between common law jurisdictions, the adoption and application of comfort letters vary, and largely the law is underdeveloped in this area – across the jurisdictions examined. Arguably, it is our view that this underdevelopment of the law surrounding comfort letters also extend to other mature and emerging economic and financial hubs.

In turning back to the central question of this chapter – is there an opportunity for comfort letters to be properly regulated? That is, should they, in a similar way to schemes of arrangement, be specified in national legislation? A further accentuating question, and even in the face of countries turning inward and globalisation rapidly diluting, is it time to internationalise these instruments? Doing so, is likely to cause a significant level of legal and policy debate. However, in our view, the timing is right to internationalise comfort letters and bring them into line with close-out netting provisions. Yet, in considering this approach, any internationalisation or national regulation of these tool should be narrowed to only deal with restructuring, insolvency and winding up. This is likely to accelerate their harmonisation. A first step, would be to introduce the contents of a letter as a set of Principles.

Adopting this approach would not diminish their use. Rather, it would bring other countries that rarely use them along and further integrate cross-border insolvency and restructuring processes. Furthermore, the broader benefit for establishing such an approach, is another layer available to stabilising finance markets, in a time of heightened international uncertainty. Therefore, a more comprehensive study needs to be undertaken by UNCITRAL or UNIDROIT to confirm or otherwise of the need to internationalise comfort letters.

5

RESTRUCTURING: MERGERS AND ACQUISITIONS PART 1

Mergers and acquisitions (MA) act as another alternative to insolvency. This chapter only examines some of the key laws of Australia, the European Union (EU), India, Singapore, the United Kingdom (UK) and the United States (US) that pertain to cross-border mergers and acquisitions. This chapter has been separated in to two parts. Part 1 will examine Australia, the EU and the UK. Part 2 will only examine the US, Singapore and India. This chapter does not discuss Indonesia or China. At issue are the foreign investment rules that have been established by the respective jurisdictions and the impact these rules have on MA. More pervasively, the chapter demonstrates the balance between restructuring, cross-border insolvency and anti-competition behaviour in a time when technology is pervading the economy. This chapter further highlights the complex issues related to calling for the internationalisation of foreign investment rules. Some governments have responded to COVID-19 by amending their respective foreign investment rules. In some cases, the rules have been significantly tightened to curtail predatory behaviour from foreign entities, semi-government and government organisations. The pandemic has, in part, highlighted the changing and evolving nature of economic activity and foreign investment across the world.

5.1 Introduction

Mergers and Acquisitions are not new and can be traced back to the 19th century. They are alternative to insolvency, and a form of restructuring or re-organisation, when an entity experiences financial stress. MA also create competition for corporate control, motivated by both private economy and regulatory incentives. Private incentives include imperfections and asymmetries in domestic product and capital markets, creating a competitive environment of the market and differences in tax

DOI: 10.4324/9781003311874-7

systems.[1] Regulatory incentives also include variations in corporate governance, and policy frameworks towards foreign investment. Management that acts in its own interest may cause financial losses to shareholders, which provides a potential for other firms to intervene. The liberalisation of foreign entry and ownership has, for a number of decades, opened up more opportunities for a cross-border MA activity.[2] Nonetheless, *mergers* and *acquisitions* are two terms used by many interchangeably in spite of the fact that they do not relate to same types of operations.[3] On the one hand, a merger occurs when two (or more) companies agree to merge into a new single company rather than remain separated for creating business synergies. On the other hand, an acquisition is the purchase of existing shares issued by another company for increasing ownership or control level by the acquiring company.[4] Central to any MA activity is the rules and laws governments and regulators impose on foreign entities. Foreign investment is a significant part of international business and of the global economy.

Companies that invest in third countries can expand to new marketplaces; shift their production facilities across national boundaries; and secure more advanced technologies, products, skills, and modes of financing.[5] Foreign companies can provide host countries and their domestic economies with the infusion of capital, updated technologies, improved and more efficient production processes, organisational capacities, management skills, market networks, improved job prospects and employment.[6]

Moreover, the international rules pertaining to foreign investment date back to 1948. Between 1948 to 1994, the General Agreement on Tariffs and Trade (GATT) provided the rules for much of the world trade.[7] In addition, the OECD has been promoting the liberalisation of capital account operations among its members since the early 1960s. Even so, the code of liberalisation covering cross-border services

1 Ashoka Mody, Shoko Negishi, *The Role of Cross-Border Mergers and Acquisitions in Asian Restructuring*, World Bank (2000), 6. See also, Richard Caves, International Corporations: The Industrial Economics of Foreign Investment, *Economica*, Vol. 38 (1971), 1–27. See also Charles Kindleberger, *American Business Abroad: Six Lectures on Direct Investment,* Yale University Press, New Haven, CT (1969). See also Kenneth Froot, Jeremy Stein, Exchange Rates and Foreign Direct Investment: An Imperfect Capital Market Approach, *Quarterly Journal of Economics*, Vol. 106 (1991), 1191–1217.

2 Ibid.

3 Organisation for Economic Co-operation and Development Mergers and Acquisitions (M&A) Type Transactions as a Part of FDI Statistics, https://www.oecd-ilibrary.org/docserver/9789264045743-19-en.pdf?expires=1609809541&id=id&accname=guest&checksum=4AE5506FDE6AE6FCC0CD E9BF05C4EF00.

4 Ibid.

5 Leon Trakman, Nicola Ranieri, Foreign Direct Investment: An Overview, in Trakman, Ranieri (eds), *Regionalism in International Investment Law*, Oxford University Press (2013), 1.

6 Ibid.

7 Nicolas Coeurdacier, Roberto A. de Santis, Antonin Aviat, *Cross-Border Mergers and Acquisitions and European Integration*, Economic Policy, Oxford University Press (2009), 60.

has not yet been agreed.[8] Coeurdacier, de Santis and Aviat make the point that the General Agreement on Trade in Services (GATS) was the only agreement at the international level that regulates and liberalises trade in financial services as well as investment of financial services providers. The GATS agreement was negotiated in the Uruguay Round (1986–94). Members (self) committed to launch successive rounds of services negotiations with a view to achieving a progressively higher level of liberalisation. They go onto say that the 'first such round was to begin no later than 5 years from the date of entry into force of the Agreement and, accordingly, started in 2000'.[9] Within the time frame of the overall negotiating deadline of 1 January 2005, the Doha Development Agenda establishes that 'participants shall submit initial requests for specific commitments by 30 June 2002 and initial offers by 31 March 2003'.[10] Since then there has been continued fluctuations across the economy in MA activity, largely influenced by economic conditions, national policy objectives by nation states and transnational trade in goods and services.

Leon Trakman and Nicola Ranieri identify three categories of foreign investment. Firstly, 'equity capital is the value of the multinational corporation's (MNC) investment in shares of an enterprise in a foreign country. An equity capital stake of 10 per cent or more of the ordinary shares or voting power in an incorporated enterprise, or its equivalent in an unincorporated enterprise, is normally considered as a threshold for the control of assets'.[11] Trakman and Ranieri make the point that this category includes both MA and Greenfield investments (the creation of new facilities). MA are important sources of foreign investment for developed countries, although the relative importance varies considerably. Secondly, reinvested earnings are the MNC's share of affiliate earnings not distributed as dividends or remitted to the MNC. Such retained profits by affiliates are assumed to be reinvested in the affiliate. This can be present in MA restructuring as a result of cross-border insolvency. The third category refers to other capital, short- or long-term borrowing and lending of funds.

Against this backdrop, MA are not sharply defined, instead referring to fuzzy set of similar transactions.[12] As commonly understood by practitioners, the core of MA is a deliberate transfer of control and ownership of a business organised in one or more corporations. Restructuring has been viewed as a deliberate, significant and unusual alteration in the organisation and operations of a business, commonly in times of financial or operational distress, typically accompanied by changes in

8 Ibid.
9 Ibid.
10 Ibid.
11 Leon Trakman, Nicola Ranieri, Foreign Direct Investment: An Overview, in Trakman, Ranieri (eds), *Regionalism in International Investment Law*, Oxford University Press (2013), 2.
12 John Coates, *Merges, Acquisitions and Restructuring: Types, Regulation, and Patterns of Practice,* Oxford Handbook on Corporate Law and Governance Discussion Paper No. 781 (2014).

ownership or finance, as when a company merges two divisions or sells off a business unit. Nonetheless, MA and restructuring commonly occur together.

Apart from MA being another alternative to insolvency and restructuring, the theory behind why entities choose to either merge or acquire another entity is multilayered. It can take place for a number of reasons. Firstly, it could be as a result of two companies having compatible market opportunities, scope, technical skill and assets.[13] Secondly, there is financial compatibility between entities that afford a lower capital cost enabling new products to be bought to market. Third, some companies seek to 'obtain strategic realignment that has been imposed by regulation or technology and therefore it enables the entity to acquire capabilities to adapt more rapidly to environmental changes than could be achieved if developed internally'.[14] Fourth, hubris has been adopted as a theory of practice as a result of 'managerial confidence, whereby, those acquiring the entity believe the valuation is accurate exceeding the market position, usually resulting in the overestimation and payment of the entity'.[15] Conversely, a fifth theory is when individuals seek out undervalued companies to acquire their asset and build them up to be a formidable market player. Sixth, one of the most desired positions for any company to achieve, is to be the only player in the market.[16] However, this is viewed by a number of governments as problematic, due to the monopolistic environment it creates, forcing or inhibiting others to either retain their position or enter a market. Generally, companies will seek out competitors to acquire or merge with, so as to create a monopoly. On the other side, other theories that have emerged include managerialism (increasing the size of the company), tax (obtain unused net operating losses and tax credits), and from time-to-time misevaluation.

MA activity has for some time been in decline, even before the outbreak of COVID-19. As noted by Accenture, the level of MA, at least in the short term while writing this book had significantly contracted in the United States (US) alone.[17] That is:

> Deal volume in the first half of 2020 dropped 49%, with deal value down 22% from the year before. Many deals have fallen by the wayside. Marathon Petroleum's sale of its Speedway convenience stores fell through after the oil price collapse. Xerox Holdings called off its pursuit of HP, while SoftBank Group Corp. backed away from its planned bailout of WeWork. The only mega-deals greater than US$5 billion are being struck in industries that have been largely unaffected by the crisis, a notable example being the

13 Dinald DePamphillis, *Mergers, Acquisitions, and other Restructuring Activities: An Integrated Approach to Process, Tools, Cases, and Solutions,* Elsevier (2017), 6.

14 Ibid.

15 Ibid.

16 Ibid.

17 COVID-19: Rebalance for Resilience with M&A, https://www.accenture.com/_acnmedia/PDF-122/Accenture-COVID-19-Rebalance-for-Resilience-Mergers-and-Acquisitions.pdf.

announcement of the acquisition of GrubHub by Dutch food delivery company Just Eat Takeaway, for US$7.3 billion.[18]

They go onto say that the 'significant drop is not unexpected and is consistent with other economic shocks, where the dip in deal value has approached 50%'.[19] More pervasively, liquidity is held at a premium, valuations fluctuate, credit tightens, and companies focus inwardly. However, the drop is historically most pronounced with mega-deals, whereas smaller deals continue as companies shed assets and distressed businesses seek MA solutions to solvency.[20] Arguably, the same or similar scenario is being played out in and across other nation states, particularly those hardest hit by COVID-19.

The resulting impact from COVID-19 on the economy has been profound. Because people's movements were restricted, productivity in some sectors all but stopped. The economic impact was still be felt in 2021–2022, and not fully understood. Yet, the rise in financially stressed companies was significant, even with government support. Importantly, a consequential effect from this loss of productivity is that, MA could be not only a viable option to restructure a business. Arguably, the current strategy has been to utilise MA as a preventative process to manage financial stress and a company becoming insolvent. However, as a response, some states such as Australia have amended their foreign investment rules, which could impact on the level of MA activities in that country.

Across the Asia region, a similar story had emerged, whereby COVID-19 also played havoc with MA transactions in 2020–2021.[21] Even before the coronavirus pandemic, the easy period of economic expansion in the Asia-Pacific (APAC) region was coming to an end. That will also be further accentuated if a prolonged correction in equity markets further reduces asset prices from their recent highs. Thus, the aggregate 'value of APAC-target transactions declined in the region in by 21% between 2017 and 2019'.[22] Another report released by Baker McKenzie estimated in 'October 2019, before COVID-19 was formally announced to the world that MA transactions declined by up to 25%'.[23] Nonetheless, as at the conclusion of 2020, the global MA market experienced its slowest first two months of a year since 2005. Despite this, the value of global deal-making sank to a six-year low to 1 March 2020. There was $119.2 billion worth of deals announced in the first two months of the year, a 49% fall compared with the same period last year, according

18 Ibid, 3.

19 Ibid.

20 Ibid.

21 Rohit Ramesh, Jens Kengelbach, Timo Schmid, Victor Chen, *The Asia-Pacific M&A Report: Deal-making in Turbulent Times*, https://www.bcg.com/about/people/experts/rohit-ramesh. Overall, the pace of cross-border outbound transactions in which an APAC buyer acquires a target in another market continued to slow.

22 Ibid.

23 Baker McKenzie, *M&A to Drop 25% in 2020 in the Face of an Uncertain Global Economic Landscape*, https://www.bakermckenzie.com/en/newsroom/2019/10/global-transactions-forecast-2020.

to Refinitiv.[24] Therefore, as a result of COVID-19 pandemic, many transactions were put on hold, and the true extent of the number of MA as a result of financial stress or insolvency would not be fully realised until late 2021 and even into 2022.

More noteworthy too is, MA are often thought of as being domestically driven, yet, cross-border MA have been very effective. In other words, Donald DePamphillis makes the point that, similar to domestic mergers, cross-border mergers vary between industry clusters.[25] He believes that both are triggered by similar factors; but unlike domestic MA waves, deals completed later in the cross-border MA cycle tend to show significantly higher abnormal acquirer returns. Also, they tend to be much higher than transactions completed out-side of waves.[26] Post-merger operating performance is also better for within-wave cross-border deals. This superior performance is even greater if the target country is different from the acquirer's country in terms of such things as culture, economic development, geographic location, capital market maturity and legal system. DePamphillis further believes that empirical evidence supports the notion of superior performance whereby firms are likely to undertake cross-border deals in the same country if they observe positive stock price reactions to previous comparable deals. However, cross-border deals often have a higher level of risk than domestic transactions due to a greater number of unknowns. This includes, but not limited to, stock market reaction to past deals that either confirms (or rejects) the wisdom of a takeover.[27] In more recent times, that uncertainty has been further heightened by governments' response to protecting business from predatory behaviour through COVID-19.

On the other hand, cross-border acquisitions can be structured in different ways according to the commercial objectives of the acquirer, and these can have major implications on the subsequent integration program. Business deals can be structured as either asset deals, where specific assets and liabilities are purchased, or stock deals, where the owners' shares of the legal entity are traded. Andrew Scola makes the point that there are two core components to a cross-border transaction. The first is the asset:

> deal that allows for the seller to retain the legal entity and the acquirer purchases specific tangible or intangible assets such as manufacturing facilities, equipment, licenses, contracts, intellectual property, brand rights, or inventory. Asset sales can provide specific tax benefits and increase cash ow, while

24 Financier Worldwide, *Outlook for Global M&A,* https://www.financierworldwide.com/outlook-for-global-ma#.X9Me4i2r00p.

25 Donald DePamphillis, *Mergers, Acquisitions, and other Restructuring Activities: An Integrated Approach to Process, Tools, Cases, and Solutions,* Elsevier (2017), 13.

26 Ibid. The superior performance of cross-border acquirers who do deals later in the cycle may reflect their ability to learn from prior deals made by industry peers in the target country. Earlier deals within the industry establish comparable transaction values that may be used for valuation of the target firm thereby limiting the acquirer's risk of overpaying. If in these prior deals investors have rewarded acquirers by bidding up their share prices, investors are more likely to applaud similar deals in the future, as long as the acquirer does not overpay.

27 Ibid, 13.

minimizing liabilities transferring with the sale. Secondly, the stock deal that allows the acquirer to purchase the stock directly, obtaining partial or full ownership of the seller's legal entity itself. All assets and liabilities, 'contracts, and permits held by the entity at the time of the sale are retained by it and come with the deal'.[28]

A similar outcome can also exist with mergers. Therefore, the rationale and the law pertaining cross-border MA is complex and varies from state to state. Viewed this way, to facilitate cross-border MA transactions having a robust and strong legal and institutional environment in the target country, increases the transaction cost for cross-border deals.[29] It provides a platform for the transfer of knowledge, skills, corporate governance and practices along with benefits of investments transnationally. However, Feito-Ruiz and Menéndez-Requejo counter this view and believe that transferring better corporate practices from the target to the bidder firms does not work well. The issue coincides with regulatory 'changes in countries with a strong legal and institutional environment, which may make access to markets for firms from countries with weak legal and institutional environments more difficult'.[30] Arguably, during and post COVID-19, this will be a significant factor for those developing countries that have a weak and significantly less mature legal and institutional framework to support and facilitate MA.

Moreover the recent work undertaken by Michael Christofi et al in 2019, which states that 'prior to the pandemic, who argue that in support of the above, there is considerable evidence that many acquirers fail to gain value from cross-border'.[31] Central to this position is how various studies have argued that strategic and financial variables are non-significant in explaining post-MA performance and that technology needs to develop further to enhance the predictability of the success or otherwise of a cross-border MA. Yet, and on the contrary, stable institutions and an open policy to trade can contribute significantly to attracting more inward FDI, through MA. This suggests that policies should focus more on long-term fundamentals, rather than short-term reform policies. Also, financial market development seems to be crucial to foreign investment, especially to cross-border MA. Since policy makers in most countries aim to improve both inward and outward FDI, the specific determinants of cross-border MA should be taken into account as important policy makers.[32] Thus, it is conceivable that the theory behind why

28 Andrew Scola, Legal, Financial, Social and political Interdependencies with Cross-Border Integration, in Scott Whitaker (ed), *Cross-Border Mergers and Acquisitions,* John Wiley and Sons (2016), 69.

29 Isabel Feito-Ruiz, Susana Menéndez-Requejo, Cross-Border Mergers and Acquisitions in Different Legal Environments, *International Review of Law and Economics*, Vol. 31 (2011), 169–187.

30 Ibid, 185.

31 Michael Christofi, Demetris Vrontis, Alkis Thrassou, S.M. Riad Shams, Triggering Technological Innovation through Cross-Border Mergers and Acquisitions: A Micro-foundational Perspective, *Technological Forecasting & Social Change*, Vol. 146 (2019), 148–166.

32 Paula Neto, António Brandão, António Cerqueira, The Macroeconomic Determinants of Cross-Border Mergers and Acquisitions and Greenfield Investments, *IUP Journal of Business* (2010), 28.

MA occur and whether they are successful is not settled. Nevertheless, MA result in competing legal outcomes. MA can further support and underpin domestic investment. They can assist in the transfer of liquidity and economic activity transnationally, create competition while at the same time establish monopolistic outcomes, whereby a company can dominate the market. These competing legal and policy outcomes are something that governments around the world are constantly grappling with.

Part 1 of this chapter will examine the regulatory approach required to undertake a merger-acquisition in Australia, EU and the UK. Part 2 of this chapter compares India, Singapore and the US. While the comparison is limited to these states, it will only highlight briefly the respective jurisdictions' laws pertaining to MA. Rather, this chapter will focus on the foreign investment rules that have a significant impact on cross-border MA activities. These rules have become increasingly important, whereby some states have since the outbreak of COVID-19 tightened them up. This chapter does not address the antitrust, tax and financial control-reporting issues that arise from MA.

5.2 Australia

The position in Australia regarding MA is regulated by the Corporations Act 2001, and the Australian Competition and Consumer Act 2010 (CCA). Australia's merger control framework is dominated by Section 50 of the CCA. The CCA is supported by the Australian Competition and Consumer Commission 2008 Guidelines.[33] Mergers in Australia, whether domestic or cross-border, are driven by assessments that have been developed with an increased emphasis on competitive theories of harm and the effect of constraints, which facilitates a more integrated analysis.[34] Thus, the current-day Australian framework is largely based on anti-competition needs, to ensure there is no single monopoly or a single merger that creates a lack of competition in the market place.

Section 50 limits the extent of investment by a merger that would have the effect, or be likely to have the effect, of substantially lessening competition in a market. Moreover, Section 50 applies to a wide variety of mergers and acquisitions.[35] A merger involves the shareholders of two companies becoming the shareholders of a new merged company. An acquisition occurs when one company acquires a shareholding in, or the assets of, another company. Generally, when assessing its impact on competition, little turns on whether a transaction is, strictly speaking, a merger or an acquisition.[36] In addition, there are a large number of

33 Australian Competition and Consumer Commission Merger Guidelines 2008 (amended 2017), https://www.accc.gov.au/system/files/Merger%20guidelines%20-%20Final.PDF.

34 Ibid, 1.

35 Ibid, 4.

36 Ibid.

considerations that need to be taken into account when the regulator assesses the viability or otherwise of a proposed merger. These include:

a. the actual and potential level of import competition in the market;
b. the height of barriers to entry to the market;
c. the level of concentration in the market;
d. the degree of countervailing power in the market;
e. the likelihood that the acquisition would result in the acquirer being able to significantly and sustainably increase prices or profit margins;
f. the extent to which substitutes are available in the market or are likely to be available in the market;
g. the dynamic characteristics of the market, including growth, innovation and product differentiation;
h. the likelihood that the acquisition would result in the removal from the market of a vigorous and effective competitor; and
i. the nature and extent of vertical integration in the market.[37]

Based on the aforementioned, where an acquisition is proposed, Section 50(4) provides where 'a person has entered into a contract to acquire shares in the capital of a body corporate or assets of a person'.[38] It further provides that:

> the contract is subject to a condition that the provisions of the contract relating to the acquisition will not come into force unless and until the person has been granted an authorization to acquire the shares or assets; and the person applied for the grant of such an authorization before the expiration of 14 days after the contract was entered into.[39]

Therefore, 'the acquisition of the shares or assets shall not be regarded for the purposes of this Act as having taken place in pursuance of the contract before the application for the authorization is disposed of or the contract ceases to be subject to the condition; whichever first happens'.[40] Central to the overall requirements set out in Section 50, there are a number of threshold tests that the regulator will also consider such as,

> notification, competition (restraints, nature-monopolistic), the number of failing entities, products that are substitutes and regions they are located, discrimination of customers, horizontal and non-horizontal/vertical mergers, and barriers a merger or acquisition may broadly have in the market.[41]

37 Competition and Consumer Act 2010, Section 50(3).
38 Ibid, Section 50(4).
39 Ibid.
40 Ibid.
41 Ibid, 15–38.

This test reinforces Australia's approach to monitor competition and monopolies being established from an acquisition or merger. In part, it acts as a level of protection of local companies.

In the case of *ACCC v. Pacific National*[42] the Court was concerned the proposed sale of the Acacia Ridge Terminal (ART) by entities within the Aurizon group of companies (Aurizon) to entities within the Pacific National group of companies (Pacific National) pursuant to a Business Sale Agreement executed on 28 July 2017. Pursuant to:

> clause 5.1 of the Business Sale Agreement, completion of the sale was conditional on, amongst other things, the parties receiving competition law clearance for the sale in one of three ways: 1) written confirmation from the ACCC that it did not propose to intervene in the acquisition pursuant to Section 50 of the *Competition and Consumer Act 2010*; 2) authorisation of the acquisition by the Australian Competition Tribunal under Part VII of the Act; or 3) the Federal Court declaring or making orders to the effect that the acquisition would not contravene s 50 of the Act.[43]

At issue was whether:

> the ACCC did not provide the parties clearance to proceed. On 18 July 2018, it commenced a proceeding in the Federal Court alleging, amongst other things, that the sale of the ART pursuant to the Business Sale Agreement would contravene s 50 of the Act and sought orders restraining the parties from completing the sale. At the time of trial, the ACCC's allegation was that the acquisition of the ART by Pacific National would be likely to have the effect of substantially lessening competition in markets.[44]

In *Australian Competition and Consumer Commission v. Pacific National Pty Limited,*[45] the Court ruled that 'accepting an undertaking proffered by Pacific National relating to the future conduct of the ART (the Undertaking), the proposed sale of the ART by Aurizon to Pacific National would not contravene Section 50 of the Corporations Act 2001'.[46] The Court went to considerable length to explain the important principles supporting decisions surrounding acquisitions in Australia, namely that of the competition and market. It argued that the principal concept in Section 50, competition within a market, has been the subject of

42 *Australian Competition and Consumer Commission v Pacific National Pty Limited* [2020] FCAFC 77.
43 Ibid, 2.
44 Ibid, 3.
45 *Australian Competition and Consumer Commission v Pacific National Pty Limited* (No 2) [2019] FCA 669, paragraph 1611.
46 Ibid, 4.

considerable judicial analysis and is well understood. In referring to the 1976 case of *Re Queensland*,[47] it noted that:

> Competition may be valued for many reasons as serving economic, social and political goals. But in identifying the existence of competition in particular industries or markets, we must focus upon its economic role as a device for controlling the disposition of society's resources. Thus, we think of competition as a mechanism for discovery of market information and for enforcement of business decisions in the light of this information. It is a mechanism, first, for firms discovering the kinds of goods and services the community wants and the manner in which these may be supplied in the cheapest possible way. Prices and profits are the signals which register the play of these forces of demand and supply. At the same time, competition is a mechanism of enforcement: firms disregard these signals at their peril, being fully aware that there are other firms, either currently in existence or as yet unborn, which would be only too willing to encroach upon their market share and ultimately supplant them. This does not mean that we view competition as a series of passive, mechanical responses to impersonal market forces. Competition expresses itself as rivalrous market behaviour.[48]

The Court further considered that:

> A market is the area of close competition between firms or, putting it a little differently, the field of rivalry between them (if there is no close competition there is of course a monopolistic market). A market is the field of actual and potential transactions between buyers and sellers amongst whom there can be strong substitution, at least in the long run, if given a sufficient price incentive. Let us suppose that the price of one supplier goes up. Then on the demand side buyers may switch their patronage from this firm's product to another, or from this geographic source of supply to another. As well, on the supply side, sellers can adjust their production plans, substituting one product for another in their output mix, or substituting one geographic source of supply for another. Whether such substitution is feasible or likely depends ultimately on customer attitudes, technology, distance, and cost and price incentives.[49]

47 Ibid, *Re Queensland Co-operative Milling Association Ltd* (1976) FLR 169 (QCMA), paragraph 1870189.

48 Ibid, 100.

49 Ibid, 101.

The Court ruled, taking the same position as the 2019 case, 'that in light of it that there was no apprehended contravention of s 50(1) and therefore to dismiss the ACCC's proceeding in its entirety'.[50] Pacific National is to be released from its undertaking. If costs cannot be agreed, there should be a further hearing on the papers to resolve that issue. The case highlighted that, within Australia, competition is one of the most problematic issues arising from an acquisition or merger. The law itself is constantly competing and working with itself. On the one side, competition as a principle serves to ensure there is a level of equitable and fairness playing field, so as no single entity obtains dominance. On the other side, it competes with the broader market of actual and potential transactions between buyers and sellers. Thus, while they are at time in tension, at other times they serve to complement each other. Overall, the case reinforced Australia's key position and the law in such transactions, and the fine line in balancing economic outcomes that benefit companies and the community.

On the other hand, Chapter 6 of the Corporations Act 2001 regulates for the acquisition or takeover of an existing entity. Section 602 provides for certain controls over an acquisition that include the voting shares in a listed company or an unlisted company with more than 50 members; or voting shares in a listed body; or voting interests in a listed managed investment scheme- takes place in an efficient, competitive and informed market.[51] The threshold test in Chapter 6 limits the acquisitions of relevant interests in voting shares, whereby an individual cannot acquire a relevant interest in issued voting shares in a company where the company is a listed company; or an unlisted company with more than 50 members. This limitation in Section 606 is further extended to where:

> a person acquiring the interest does so through a transaction in relation to securities entered into by or on behalf of the person; and because of the transaction, that person's or someone else's voting power in the company increases i) from 20% or below to more than 20%; or ii) from a starting point that is above 20% and below 90%.[52]

These criteria also apply to a person who must not acquire a legal or equitable interest in securities of a body corporate. While the threshold for a takeover has been to establish a framework that supports the Australian government's policy settings to ensure the right types and balance of mergers and acquisitions exist through the state, there are exemptions. They are 'acquisitions of relevant interests in a company's voting shares that are exempt from the prohibition in Section 606(1); and acquisitions of relevant interests in a company's voting shares resulting from acquisitions of legal or equitable interests in securities of a body corporate that

50 Ibid, 440.
51 Corporations Act 2001, Section 602.
52 Ibid, Section 606.

are exempt from the prohibition in Section 606(2)'.[53] This is provided that the acquisition is a result from the acceptance of an offer under a takeover bid. It also applies where a bid is provided by a class of securities that are as a result from an on-market transaction. However, this is only achieved where the acquisition is by or on behalf of the bidder under a takeover bid, and it occurs during the timeframe for which the period of the bid has not expired. Further, in achieving an acquisition can be undertaken also has a bid for all the voting shares in the bid class; and the bid is unconditional; or conditional according to Section 652C(1) or (2).[54] There are up to 19 exemptions under Section 611 related to acquisitions that are takeovers. They include:

> on-market purchase of convertible securities during bid period, acceptance of scrip offered as takeover consideration, nature consideration, approval by resolution of target, target newly formed, manner of acquisition 3% creep in 6 months, rights issues, dividend reinvestment, initial public offering, underwriting of fundraising, acquisition through listed company, wills, forfeiture of shares, compromise, arrangement, liquidation, or buy-back.[55]

It is out of scope to examine Chapter 6 of the Corporations Act, although there are a number of procedural steps to be undertaken pre, during and post a takeover. Nonetheless, underpinning the regulatory framework for MA is the national foreign policy and rules for foreign ownership in Australia. Furthermore, schemes of arrangement within the Corporations Act 2001, can also be used to assist in the facilitation of cross-border mergers, particularly acquisitions (takeovers). The next section briefly examines Australia's current rules pertaining to foreign purchases of specific commercial assets in Australia. The importance of understanding the foreign investment rules comes at a time of heightened uncertainty, and a higher level of restrictions are being imposed by states. Australia is no exception.

5.2.1 Foreign Purchasing Rule

Foreign investment, particularly during the time of COVID-19, became quite political in Australia. There was increasing concern in the community that companies that had been financially stressed by the impact of the pandemic were being taken advantage of by international investors. As a result, the Australian government, for the first time in a number of decades, undertook a significant review. Consequently, the *Foreign Acquisitions and Takeovers Act 1975* (FATA) was amended

53 Ibid, Section 611.
54 Ibid, Section 652C(1)-(2) relates to returning securities as part of election.
55 Ibid, section 611.

by the Australian Parliament in December 2020.[56] The reform process requires as of 1 January 2021, for investors (foreign persons)[57] to;

- Seek approval for all investments in sensitive national security land or businesses (including starting such a business), regardless of value.[58]
- Be subject to enhanced monitoring and investigation powers, as well as stronger and more flexible enforcement options and penalties.[59]
- Continue to bear the costs of administering the foreign investment regime, under a reformed fee framework that will be fairer and simpler for foreign investors.[60]

Central to this, Section 67 becomes very important as to the Treasurer's power to approve and monitor current and new foreign investments. The resulting effect is that the Treasurer can prohibit what has been determined as a significant action (i.e. investment) from entering into an agreement with an Australian business, terminating a significant agreement with an Australian business, and acquiring an Australian land. One of the most sensitive areas in 2020 was the acquisition of land, particularly for the purposes of agriculture production. That is, the threshold also includes the requirement to limit the acquisition of agribusiness. Section 67(3) provides that: to acquire a direct interest in an Australian entity that is an agribusiness, or an interest in securities in an entity directing a specified foreign person (whether alone or with specified associate or class of associates) not to:

a. increase the proportion of the total voting power, or the total potential voting power, in the entity that the person is in a position to control (or increase that proportion beyond a specified proportion); or
b. increase the proportion of interests in issued securities in the entity that the person holds (or increase that proportion beyond a specified proportion).[61]

56 Treasurer of the commonwealth of Australia, Major reforms to Australia's foreign investment framework pass the parliament, https://ministers.treasury.gov.au/ministers/josh-frydenberg-2018/media-releases/major-reforms-australias-foreign-investment-0, *Foreign Acquisitions and Takeovers Act 1975* No. 92, 1975

57 Ibid, Section 4, 'foreign person means (a) an individual not ordinarily resident in Australia; or (b) a corporation in which an individual not ordinarily resident in Australia, a foreign corporation or a foreign government holds a substantial interest; or (c) a corporation in which 2 or more persons, each of whom is an individual not ordinarily resident in Australia, a foreign corporation or a foreign government, hold an aggregate substantial interest; or (d) the trustee of a trust in which an individual not ordinarily resident in Australia, a foreign corporation or a foreign government holds a substantial interest; or (e) the trustee of a trust in which 2 or more persons, each of whom is an individual not ordinarily resident in Australia, a foreign corporation or a foreign government, hold an aggregate substantial interest; or (f) a foreign government; or (g) any other person, or any other person that meets the conditions, prescribed by the regulations'.

58 Ibid, Section 4.

59 Ibid.

60 Ibid.

61 Ibid, Section 67(3).

Similarly, there are limits in relation to acquiring land, whereby a 'foreign person will be directed (a) not to acquire any interests in the land or other thing concerned; or (b) to acquire any such interests only to a specified extent'.[62] Moreover, there is power under Section 69 assets to be disposed of by the Treasurer for most of what is stated in Section 67. Importantly, the overall responsibility of decisions rests with the treasurer and not the broader Australian Government. On the one side, in practice, there appears that nothing would stop a Minister or the Prime Minister from recommending to the Treasurer to invoke the rules and requirements set out earlier. Nevertheless, in order to invoke the earlier significant actions, the overall threshold test is underpinned by: Section 40 – entities; Section 41 – business; Section 42 – agribusiness; and Section 43 – land. On the other side, under Section 44, there is the power to make additional regulations for other sectors that are deemed to be significant actions and require additional protections and controls from foreign investment. It is out of scope of this chapter to examine the regulations.

Notwithstanding this, Section 46 provides for one of the most important elements of the law because it determines where and what a notifiable action constitutes. That is, a notifiable action is a proposed action by a 'foreign person: (i) to acquire a direct interest in an Australian entity or Australian business that is an agribusiness; (ii) to acquire a substantial interest in an Australian entity; or (iii) to acquire an interest in Australian land'.[63] Thus, a notifiable action will only become notifiable when it meets one of the threshold tests outlined earlier. However, and unlike for a significant action, there does not need to be a change in control for actions relating to entities and businesses to be notifiable actions. Therefore, the question arises what the threshold test is. This can be found at Section 50. It provides for a serious threshold tests to be considered. First, is the fact that neither threshold test places an economic or dollar value on the acquisition of an entity, business or land. It provides '(i) a person acquiring a direct interest in an Australian entity or Australian business that is an agribusiness and with regard to the value of the consideration for the acquisition; (ii) the total value of the other interests held by the person, alone or together with one or more associates in the entity

62 Ibid.

63 Ibid, Section 46. Section 47 prescribes four levels of conditions of a notifiable action. The first condition is that the action is any of the following: (i) to acquire a direct interest in an Australian entity or Australian business that is an agribusiness; (ii) to acquire a substantial interest in an Australian entity; (iii) to acquire an interest in Australian land.

Note: For the definition of acquire a direct interest or a substantial interest, see Section 20. Second condition – threshold 3) The second condition is that the threshold test is met in relation to the entity, business or land (see Subdivision B of Division 4). Third condition – kinds of entities covered (4) If paragraph (2)(a) or (b) applies, the third condition is that the entity is: a) an Australian corporation that carries on an Australian business, whether alone or together with one or more other persons; or b) an Australian unit trust; or c) an Australian entity that is the holding entity of an entity mentioned in paragraph (a) or (b). Last condition – action taken by a foreign person (5) The last condition (whether paragraph (2)(a), (b) or (c) applies) is that the action is or is to be taken by a foreign person.

or business; or (iii) previously acquired from the entity or business'.[64] Put simply, any person who acquires and interest in an agribusiness or any Australian owned business, can do so, however, the acquisition will be subject to the level of value-ownership proposed by the individual or entity. Second, is acquiring interests in securities in an entity, or issuing securities in an entity whereby the overall value is measured by the higher of the total asset value for the entity, or the total issued securities value for the entity.[65] The third element is where there is an agreement mentioned in paragraph 40(2)(d) in relation to an entity, or altering a constituent document of an entity as mentioned in paragraph 40(2)(e).[66] In this circumstance the whole of the value of the asset is assessed. The fourth element, is acquiring interests in the assets of an Australian business, whereby the value of the consideration for the acquisition is measured. The fifth element constitutes entering or terminating a significant agreement with an Australian business, and the total value of the assets of the business will be assessed.[67] This threshold is clearly directed at protecting business that put into the wrong hands, which would have a significant impact over the long term to local jobs and investment. It minimises foreign entities linked to foreign governments from entering the market.

A further threshold test corresponds to land whereby Section 52 provides that land is of a kind that is prescribed by the regulations for the purposes of this subsection. Yet, for agricultural land where total value of interests is above the threshold value; the threshold test will be met if the land is agricultural land and all interests in agricultural land are held by the foreign person, alone or together with one or more associates, along with the consideration for the acquisition of the interest in the land.[68] Noteworthy too, there is no set dollar or economic value that has been attached to the threshold test for land. There could be a number of reasons for this approach. Australia is a large continent and for instance the value of agricultural land in dollar terms varies significantly. The price per hectare along coastal regions is significantly higher than that in central Australia. Apart from protecting sectors such as agriculture, it ensures that only a manageable level of land falls into the hands of foreign entities linked to foreign governments. This new approach taken by Australia ensures that certain land types are protected from external investment that could harm the sovereignty of the nation. The dichotomy for Australia has been to attract solid investment from international sources. Yet, when analysed closely, the reciprocal rights of land ownership for Australian individuals' or entities in many foreign countries is highly restricted. That is, for an Australian to own land in certain countries in Asia, is all but impossible. Further, what is not apparent is the reach of the foreign investment laws, to minimize ownership through

64 Ibid, Section 51.
65 Ibid.
66 Ibid, Section 40(2)(e)(d), meaning of significant action.
67 Ibid, Section 51.
68 Ibid, Section 52, (3) The threshold test is met in relation to land if both of the following apply: (a) the land is not land prescribed for the purposes of subsection (1) or agricultural land; (b) the value of the interest in the land is more than the value prescribed for the purposes of this paragraph.

partnerships between citizens. . It is out of scope of this chapter to fully explore the legal and policy differences, due to the many variables involved.

The Australian framework, similar to the others examined throughout this chapter, aims to balance the need for MA activities with that of other competing legal and policy objectives such as creating anti-competitive sectors. However, this has not always been the case. From the 1980s to 2020, Australia had adopted an approach which had been premised on the liberal assumption that the national economy is fully enmeshed in the global system and should harness resources regardless of their origin.[69] It has now transformed into an investment framework that is focussed on national security, while maintaining a liberal approach to foreign investment. David Hundt makes the point that central to this alignment towards 'national security has been greater scrutiny of the economic aspects of national security. He further notes that in early 2019, the US, the UK and other countries made significant reforms to their foreign investment regimes, particularly in respect of national security issues, reporting that he had travelled to the United States to learn more about their changes first hand'.[70] Rather than Australia being an outlier among capitalist economies by its extensive review of proposals for foreign investment, David Uren argues, 'Australia is being used as a template by other countries looking to place additional controls on incoming investment'.[71] The resulting effect has seen the foreign Investment Review Board (FIRB), transformed from an economic focus, identifying benefits to Australia from foreign investment and monopolistic behaviour. The FIRB today has a central role 'in the shaping and execution of the economic components of national security policy'.[72] How the role of the FIRB will evolve in the future is unknown. It is our view that their scope of investment considerations should now include national security, environmental matters, money laundering, and illegal migration. It could and should be also tied to ethic development, deployment and use of current and future artificial intelligence, biohazards, pests and diseases.

Notwithstanding this, Australia has been influenced by the US antitrust jurisprudence. The former Australian Attorney-General, Lionel Murphy QC, was largely responsible for the pivot in Australian policy on legal affairs to the US as a role model.[73] Attorney-General Murphy was of the view that, like the *Sherman Act 1890* (US), the law should be drafted in broad terms, leaving it to the courts to develop the law to suit Australian requirements. He argued that:

> Provisions, particularly those describing the prohibited restrictive trade practices, have been drafted along general lines using, wherever possible, well

69 David Hundt, The Changing Role of the FIRB and the Politics of Foreign Investment in Australia, *Journal of Political Science*, Vol. 55, No. 3 (2020), 328–343.

70 Ibid, 328–335.

71 Ibid, 328–340.

72 Ibid.

73 Russel Miller, What if Australia Took More Notice of the EU Competition Law? *Australian Journal of Competition and Consumer Law*, Vol. 28 (2020), 1–10, 305.

> understood expressions. . . . The Courts will be afforded an opportunity to apply the law in a realistic manner in the exercise of their traditional judicial role.[74]

With the establishment of the CCA, Australia has, in part, allows for the courts to have a significant role in determining MA practices and behaviours, ensuring that monopolies are not created. In 2020, Lionel Murphy QC called on Australia to undertake a review of the existing framework and questioned whether Australia should consider the EU approach (to competition), which would have a flow on effect to cross-border mergers and acquisitions.[75] For a transaction that may be subject to an FIRB approval under the FATA, it is crucial that the entire deal is genuinely conditional upon the grant of such approval and this is expressly stated in the transaction documentation.[76] If the signed transaction documentation does not have such conditionality, it may be in breach of the FATA. Moreover, other national laws will need to be considered such as privacy (data protection), amongst others. Australia has for an extensive period been a foreign investment friendly country. It has welcomed foreign investment from all corners of the globe. Yet, it is a good example of when the investment landscape changes internationally, how a country can respond and significantly shift the focus of who and what can invest in both publicly and privately. It remains to be seen whether post COVID-19 Australia's approach to foreign investment returns to its pre-COVID-19 position.

5.3 European Union

While not specifically providing for mergers and acquisitions, starting point within the EU is the anti-competitive provisions that were established under the Treaty establishing the European Economic Community (Treaty of Rome of 1957).[77] The removal of barriers to trade between the member states and the establishment of a common market, have proven to be formidable achievements from the implementation of European Economic Community. Additionally, the Treaty on the Functioning of the European Union (TFEU), which was introduced by the Treaty of Lisbon in 2007 and came into force in 2009, provides in Article 3.1 (b) that the

74 Ibid, 1–2.

75 Ibid.

76 Tatiana Stack, Mergers & Acquisitions Structuring, *Macquarie Journal of Business Law*, Vol. 8, No. 243 (2011), 256.

77 Treaty of Rome, https://eur-lex.europa.eu/legal-content/EN/TXT/?uri=LEGISSUM%3Axy0023 See also Tania Pantazi, The Legal Framework for Mergers and Acquisitions in the European Union and the United States, in A. Bitzenis (ed), *Mergers and Acquisitions as the Pillar of Foreign Direct Investment,* Springer (2012), Chapter 11.

establishing of the competition rules necessary for the functioning of the internal market is one of the areas where the EU has exclusive competence.[78]

Viewed this way, the core provisions of EU Competition Law are articles 101 and 102 of TFEU, formerly articles 81 and 82 of the Treaty establishing the European Community (TEC). Article 101 deals with 'decisions, agreements, and concerted practices that may affect the prevention, restriction, or distortion of competition within the internal market, while article 102 regulates the abuse of a dominant position'.[79] More specifically, Council Regulation (EC) No 139/2004 on the control of concentrations between undertakings,[80] establishes the relevant controls for merges across the EU. Regulation no. 139/2004 sets the rules for controlling the transactions with community dimension, in order to avoid a negative impact towards society.[81]

Underpinning the implementation of Regulation (EC) No 139/2004, Commission Regulation (EC) No 802/2004 on the control of concentrations between undertakings was established to enable the Commission to carry out a proper assessment of commitments offered by the notifying parties with a view to rendering the concentration compatible with the common market, and to ensure due consultation with other parties involved, with third parties and with the authorities of the Member States as provided for in Regulation (EC) No 139/2004.[82] Regulation (EC) No 802/2004 sets out further procedural steps that are to be undertaken, but they do not need to be examined in this chapter. Article 3 of Regulation (EC) 139/2004 arguably established one of the most important features of the regulation. It defines the notion of concentration, stating that a 'concentration constitutes an anti-competitive action by an entity, and includes control on a lasting basis resulting from the merger of two or more previously independent undertakings or parts of undertakings, or the acquisition, by one or more persons already controlling at least one undertaking, or by one or more undertakings, whether by purchase of

78 European Parliament resolution of 16 February 2017 on improving the functioning of the European Union building on the potential of the Lisbon Treaty (2014/2249-INI) (O.J. C 252, 18.7.2018, p. 215).

79 Treaty on the Functioning of the European Union, Official Journal of the European Union C326/47.

80 Council Regulation (EC) No 139/2004 of 20 January 2004 *on the control of concentrations between undertakings* (the EC Merger Regulation) (Text with EEA relevance) *O.J. L 24, 29.1.2004, Preamble 17.*

81 George Marian Aevoae, Roxana Dicu, Daniela Mardiros, *How Do the Foreign Direct Investments Flow? The Case of the Cross-Border M&As in the European Union,* 65, in Proceedings of the 13th International Conference Accounting and Management Information Systems AMIS 2018, June 13–14, 2018, The Bucharest University of Economic Studies 6, Piața Romană, 1st district, Bucharest, 010374 Romania.

82 Commission Regulation (EC) No 802/2004 of 7 April 2004 implementing Council Regulation (EC) No 139/2004 on the control of concentrations between undertakings (Text with EEA relevance) *O.J. L 133, 30.4.2004, 1–39.*

securities or assets, by contract or by any other means, of direct or indirect control of the whole or parts of one or more other undertakings'.[83]

Article 3(2) extends the notion of concentration to a level of control by rights or a person. Firstly, control by a person constitutes:

> rights, contracts or any other means which, either separately or in combination and having regard to the considerations of fact or law involved, confer the possibility of exercising decisive influence on an undertaking, in particular by ownership or the right to use all or part of the assets of an undertaking, rights or contracts which confer decisive influence on the composition, voting or decisions of the organs of an under-taking.[84]

Secondly, control can be acquired by persons or undertakings which 'are holders of the rights or entitled to rights under the contracts concerned; or . . . while not being holders of such rights or entitled to rights under such contracts, have the power to exercise the rights deriving therefrom'.[85] Against this backdrop, the threshold test for a concentration is or has a broader community dimension which can be found in Article 1 that provides, the:

> combined aggregate worldwide turnover of all the undertakings concerned is more than EUR 5,000 million; and the aggregate Community-wide turnover of each of at least two of the undertakings concerned is more than EUR 250 million, unless each of the undertakings concerned achieves more than two-thirds of its aggregate Community-wide turnover within one and the same Member State.[86]

Furthermore, this threshold will not be met where a combined aggregate worldwide turnover of all the undertakings concerned is more than EUR 2,500 million. Additionally, where at least three Member States, the combined aggregate turnover of all the undertakings concerned is more than EUR 100 million. On the other hand, where in each of at least three Member States included for the purpose of point (b), the aggregate turnover of each of at least two of the undertakings concerned is more than EUR 25 million; and the aggregate community-wide turnover of each of at least two of the undertakings concerned is more than EUR 100 million.[87]

However, and provided that each undertaking achieves more than two-thirds of its aggregate community-wide turnover within one and the same Member State,

83 Council Regulation (EC) No 139/2004, Article 3(1).
84 Ibid, Article 3(2).
85 Ibid, Article 3(3).
86 Ibid, Article 1(2).
87 Ibid, Article 1(3).

then this threshold is no longer applicable. The remainder of Regulation (EC) 139/2004 sets out the procedural steps for review and further oversight by a Member State and the EU Commission. These provisions are outside the scope of this comparative analysis.

Central to cross-border acquisition is Directive 2004/25/EC.[88] It coordinates certain safeguards which, for the protection of the interests of members and others, Member States require companies governed by the law of a Member State the securities of which are admitted to trading on a regulated market in a Member State, with a view to making such safeguards equivalent throughout the Community. Furthermore, it is necessary to protect the interests of holders of the securities of companies governed by the law of a Member State when those companies are the subject of takeover bids or of changes of control and at least some of their securities are admitted to trading on a regulated market in a Member State.[89] While out of scope to fully examine this directive, it establishes measure for the protection of minority shareholders,[90] and a threshold for squeezing out[91] and the right to sell out,[92] amongst other procedural things. Nonetheless, this is subject to the overall principles and rules established by the EU for screening foreign investment.

5.3.1 Foreign Purchasing Rule

The EU Regulation 2019/452 establishing a framework for the screening of foreign direct investments into the Union[93] on the grounds of security and public order came into force as of 11 October 2020. The Regulation, first adopted in March 2019, seeks to protect the EU by facilitating Member States and the Commission to collectively assess potential cross-border threats posed by specific foreign direct investments. It provides the framework for 'the screening of foreign direct investments and for cooperation should provide Member States and the Commission with the means to address risks to security or public order in a comprehensive manner, and to adapt to changing circumstances, while maintaining the necessary flexibility for Member States to screen foreign direct investments on grounds of security and public order taking into account their individual situations and national specificities'.[94]

88 Directive 2004/25/EC of the European Parliament and of the Council of 21 April 2004 on takeover bids (Text with EEA relevance) *O.J. L 142, 30.4.2004, 12–23.*

89 Ibid, Preamble 1&2.

90 Ibid, Article 5.

91 Ibid, Article 15.

92 Ibid, Article 16.

93 Regulation (EU) 2019/452 of the European Parliament and of the Council of 19 March 2019, establishing a framework for the screening of foreign direct investments into the Union Official Journal of the European Union L 79 I/1.

94 Ibid, Preamble 8.

Similar to Australia, the EU has directed its member states to consider the broader security threats to themselves and the Union. An added dimension to the EU criteria is public order. In other words:

> In determining whether a foreign direct investment may affect security or public order, it should be possible for Member States and the Commission to consider all relevant factors, including the effects on critical infrastructure, technologies (including key enabling technologies) and inputs which are essential for security or the maintenance of public order, the disruption, failure, loss or destruction of which would have a significant impact in a Member State or in the Union. In that regard, it should also be possible for Member States and the Commission to take into account the context and circumstances of the foreign direct investment, in particular whether a foreign investor is controlled directly or indirectly, for example through significant funding, including subsidies, by the government of a third country or is pursuing State-led outward projects or programmes.[95]

Against this backdrop, Article 2 defines 'foreign direct investment' to mean:

> an investment of any kind by a foreign investor aiming to establish or to maintain lasting and direct links between the foreign investor and the entrepreneur to whom or the undertaking to which the capital is made available in order to carry on an economic activity in a Member State, including investments which enable effective participation in the management or control of a company carrying out an economic activity.

Similar to the other jurisdictions compared in this chapter, a 'foreign investor' includes a natural person of a third country or an undertaking of a third country, intending to make or having made a foreign direct investment'.[96] Most noteworthy, is how the EU has incorporated security into the framework by relying on the Treaty on European Union and the Treaty on Functioning of the European Union. In other words, the common framework is without prejudice to sole responsibility of Member States for safeguarding their national security, as provided for in Article 4(2) TEU.[97] It is also without prejudice to the protection of their essential security

95 Ibid, Preamble 13.

96 Ibid, Article 2.

97 Treaty on European Union, Official Journal of the European Union C326/13, Article 4(2), 2. The Union shall respect the equality of Member States before the Treaties as well as their national identities, inherent in their fundamental structures, political and constitutional, inclusive of regional and local self-government. It shall respect their essential State functions, including ensuring the territorial integrity of the State, maintaining law and order and safeguarding national security. In particular, national security remains the sole responsibility of each Member State.

interests in accordance with Article 346 TFEU.[98] Cleary, the definition responds to both the economic and social needs of the Union. It includes a private entity located in the third country, and an organisation that is backed by a government, such as a state-owned enterprise. Nonetheless, structured very differently to the other jurisdictions, the EU has chosen to be more descriptive in what they consider to be important elements for protecting and limiting foreign investment. Thus, Article 4 provides that member states and the Commission are to consider the following specific sectors:

> critical infrastructure, whether physical or virtual, including energy, transport, water, health, communications, media, data processing or storage, aerospace, defence, electoral or financial infrastructure, and sensitive facilities, as well as land and real estate crucial for the use of such infrastructure and critical technologies including artificial intelligence, robotics, semiconductors, cybersecurity, aerospace, defence, energy storage, quantum and nuclear technologies as well as nanotechnologies and biotechnologies.[99]

In addition to this, the highest level of protection on security and public order grounds is also afforded to energy or raw materials, food security, sensitive information (including personal data, or the ability to control such information) or the freedom and pluralism of the media.[100] Viewed this way, the threshold test for determining whether any of these sectors could be subject to a security or public order test is determined by:

> a) whether the foreign investor is directly or indirectly controlled by the government, including state bodies or armed forces, of a third country, including through ownership structure or significant funding; b) whether the foreign investor has already been involved in activities affecting security or public order in a Member State; or c) whether there is a serious risk that the foreign investor engages in illegal or criminal activities.[101]

98 Treaty on Functioning of European Union, Official Journal of the European Union, C 326/194, Article 346 (ex Article 296 TEC), The provisions of the Treaties shall not preclude the application of the following rules:

no Member State shall be obliged to supply information the disclosure of which it considers contrary to the essential interests of its security; any Member State may take such measures as it considers necessary for the protection of the essential interests of its security which are connected with the production of or trade in arms, munitions and war material; such measures shall not adversely affect the conditions of competition in the internal market regarding products which are not intended for specifically military purposes.

99 Ibid, Article 4. Note that technology also includes those technologies that have a dual use items as defined in point 1 of Article 2 of Council Regulation (EC) No 428/2009 of 5 May 2009 setting up a community regime for the control of exports, transfer, brokering and transit of dual-use items (O.J. L 134, 29.5.2009, p. 1).

100 Ibid, Article 4.

101 Ibid, Article 4.2.

When compared to the threshold test of other jurisdictions, the EU arguably takes a broader scope than that of Australia.

As a procedural step to ensure continuity across the EU and its member states, Article 6 requires that 'a member state is to notify not only the Commission but also other member states of any foreign investment that will be subject to a screening (assessment) process'.[102] To strengthen cooperation amongst member states, there is a requirement in accordance with Article 7:

> that a foreign direct investment planned or completed in another Member State which is not undergoing screening in that Member State is likely to affect its security or public order, or has relevant information in relation to that foreign direct investment, it may provide comments to that other Member State. The Member State providing comments shall send those comments to the Commission simultaneously.[103]

Moreover, there are further control mechanisms in place to protect the Union-wide security and public order interests. In accordance with Article 8, where the:

> Commission considers that a foreign direct investment is likely to affect projects or programmes of Union interest on grounds of security or public order, the Commission may issue an opinion addressed to the Member State where the foreign direct investment is planned or has been completed.[104]

Arguably, and understandably, the EU has had to take a broader view to foreign investment rules, security protection and public order interests of its member states than that of other jurisdictions. The current threshold test is similar to other states compared in this chapter, that does not provide for an economic or monetary threshold.

Rather, the Union has identified key sectors, in the same way as Australia, for example, although the sectors are different. The framework underpins the

102 Ibid, Article 6.

103 Ibid, Article 7.

104 Ibid, Article 8. 2. (a) (b) (c) The procedures set out in Articles 6 and 7 shall apply mutatis mutandis, subject to the following modifications: as part of the notification referred to in Article 6(1) or the comments referred to in Articles 6(2) and 7(1), a Member State may indicate whether it considers that a foreign direct investment is likely to affect projects and programmes of Union interest; the opinion of the Commission shall be sent to the other Member States; the Member State where the foreign direct investment is planned or has been completed shall take utmost account of the Commission's opinion and provide an explanation to the Commission if its opinion is not followed. The list of programs that fall within Article 8(3) include: European GNSS programmes (Galileo & EGNOS): Copernicus: Horizon 2020: Trans-European Networks for Transport (TEN-T): Trans-European Networks for Energy (TEN-E): Trans-European Networks for Telecommunications: European Defence Industrial Development Programme: Permanent structured cooperation (PESCO).

common market concept that has been a hallmark of Union law and policy since the establishment of the Coal and Steel Treaty post World War II. The framework promotes efficiencies and in part protects consumers.[105] However, when compared to other jurisdictions, there is a clear distinction with the terminology used such as concentration and dominance, whereas as other refer to competition. Nonetheless, the same thing and achieve very similar results. In balancing the beneficial economic outcomes of the single market with competition for the market, John Kettle is of the view that, 'both competition in the market and competition for the market are continuing works in progress'.[106] He calls for a wider study if the benefit that digital technologies could play in this area of the law. Kettle further calls for a broader and comprehensive re-evaluation of the process of market definition, market power and measuring competitive harm. For Kettle, in achieving this an assessment of whether firms with 'market power should be subject to additional regulatory obligations',[107] further complicate the need for balancing investment, economic activity with antitrust laws that provide for a level of economic equality.

On the other side, the complex and interwoven legal framework of the EU also requires additional EU law to be considered more broadly when evaluating competitive advantages as a result of an MA.[108] Arguably, advancements in technology and the ability for them to change so rapidly annually will further complicate how technology can play a role in MA, while ensuring competition in and for

105 Tania Pantazi, The Legal Framework for Mergers and Acquisitions in the European union and the United States, in A. Bitzenis (ed), *Mergers and Acquisitions as the Pillar of Foreign Direct Investment*, Springer (2012), Chapter 11.

106 John Kettle, Competition and Consumer Law, EU Antitrust Policy Leads the Way on Digital Platforms, *ALJ*, Vol. 94, No. 99 (2020), 105–106.

107 Ibid, 106.

108 Regulation (EU) 2016/679 of the European Parliament and of the Council of 27 April 2016 on the protection of natural persons with regard to the processing of personal data and on the free movement of such data O.J. L 119, 4 May 2016, 1–88. Directive (EU) 2019/790 of the European Parliament and of the Council of 17 April 2019 on copyright and related rights in the Digital Single Market and amending Directives 96/9/EC and 2009/29/EC, O.J. L 130, 17 May 2019, 92–125. *Regulation (EU) 2015/2120 Laying Down Measures Concerning Open Internet Access and Mending Directive 2002/22/EC on Universal Service and Users' Rights Relating to Electronic Communications Networks and Services and Regulation (EU) No 531/2012 on Roaming on Public Mobile Communications Networks within the Union. Directive (EU) 2018/1972 Establishing the European Electronic Communications Code,* https://eur-lex.europa.eu/legal-content/ EN/TXT/ PDF/?uri=CELEX:32018L1972&rid=2 Proposal for a Regulation of the European Parliament and of the Council concerning the respect for private life and the protection of personal data in electronic communications and repealing Directive 2002/58/EC (Regulation on Privacy and Electronic Communications) – COM/2017/03 (COD). *Directive 2000/31/EC of the European Parliament and of the Council of 8 June 2000 on Certain Legal Aspects of Information Society Services, in particular Electronic Commerce, in the Internal Market (Directive on Electronic Commerce). Commission Recommendation of 1 March 2018 on Measures to Effectively Tackle Illegal Content (C(2018) 1177 final). Directive (EU) 2015/2366 of the European Parliament and of the Council of 25 November 2015 on Payment Services in the Internal Market, Amending Directives 2002/65/EC, 2009/110/EC and 2013/36/EU and Regulation (EU) No 1093/2010, and Repealing Directive 2007/64/EC (PSD2).*

the market and not creating monopolies that are so complex and even harder to unwind. This is an area of ongoing study.

5.4 United Kingdom

The UK was, at the conclusion of 2020, continuing to implement the EU framework, as highlighted earlier. Even though the EU and UK had agreed on a Brexit Agreement by 31 December 2020, it was not conclusive, and there was not enough information available to categorically determine or otherwise any future changes to MA laws for UK businesses. Nonetheless, the additional layer to the EU framework from the UK perspective is the Takeover and Mergers Code (the 'Code')[109] which enables supervision and regulates takeovers, amongst others. It has been designated as the supervisory authority to carry out certain regulatory functions in relation to takeovers pursuant to the Directive on Takeover Bids 2004/25/EC. Its statutory functions are set out under Chapter 1 of Part 28 of the Companies Act 2006, as amended by the Companies Act 2006 (Amendment of Schedule 2) (No 2) Order 2009. It established a panel of 36 members, and a committee and reports to the Panel of the establishment of rules within the Code. It sets our rules for the takeovers, such as 30% rule for a partial takeover.[110] It further acknowledges that schemes of arrangement can also be used to facilitate a merger. Nonetheless, it is out of scope to comprehensively compare the Code with other jurisdictions. Although, practitioners will need to be vigilant on post Brexit for any changes in this area. For instance, the UK has begun to address the foreign investment rules, to take into account more of their own sovereign needs.

5.4.1 Foreign Purchasing Rule

It has been highlighted throughout the book, that the UK has left the EU. While not specifically stated, as a result of Brexit, in November 2020, the National Security and Investment Bill (the Bill) was introduced into the national Parliament.[111] At the time of writing the book the UK by and large followed the EU framework for foreign investment, this new Bill strengthens their sovereign arrangements surrounding the need to set the future direction for investment, security and national identity. In December 2020, the Bill was due to be read for the third time, however, a date had not been set. In our view, the Bill begins to bring the UK into a similar position to that of Australia, by allowing specific investment decisions to be based on their own needs and not that of anyone else.

109 Takeovers and Mergers Code (2016), https://www.thetakeoverpanel.org.uk/wp-content/uploads/2008/11/code.pdf?v=7Nov2019.

110 Ibid, rule 36.

111 National Security and Investment Bill 2019–21, https://publications.parliament.uk/pa/bills/cbill/58-01/0210/20210.pdf.

The Bill will allow the relevant Secretary to issue a notice where it is believed that the UK need to establish mechanism to protect the national interest and security of the state. The proposed framework will establish what they have termed as a trigger event to qualifying entity or qualifying asset on grounds of national security.[112] The proposal aims to be retrospective, because it will allow for a notice to be issued on the same grounds for any arrangements that are in progress or being contemplated. Arguably, the question arises about what constitutes a trigger event. Therefore, a trigger event, under the current proposal, will arise where a person gains control of a qualifying entity, as set out in Sections 8 or 5 or a person gains control of a qualifying asset, as set out in Section 9.[113]

Most noteworthy is proposed Section 7. It has many similarities to that of the EU and to a lesser extent Australia. Proposed Section 7 clarifies two key elements of foreign investment to the UK. The first is the qualifying entity, and the second is qualifying asset. A 'qualifying entity' is any entity, whether or not a legal person, that is not an individual and includes a company, a limited liability partnership, any other body corporate, a partnership, an unincorporated association and a trust. An entity which is formed or recognised under the law of a country or territory outside the UK is a 'qualifying entity' only if it carries on activities in the UK, or supplies goods or services to persons in the UK.[114] On the other hand, a qualifying asset constitutes land, tangible (or, in Scotland, corporeal) moveable property, ideas, information or techniques which have industrial, commercial or other economic value.

Tangible property also covers trade secrets, databases, source code, algorithms, formulae, designs, plans, drawings and specifications, and software.[115] This list is broad and arguably covers many industry sectors that are paramount to the security of the UK. In our view, the proposal has a strong focus on technology and the future digital economy when classifying databases, source code, algorithms and formulae. This arguably covers area such as the systems and infrastructure that will be used across most, if not all, of the economy from engineering, health, education, defence, law enforcement and environment. More pervasively, however, different to Australia, the UK has proposed to classify 'land or moveable property to not only include both on or in the UK itself, but also extended to where this land or moveable property is located outside the UK or the 30-territorial sea'.[116]

In addition to this, but unlike the other jurisdictions discuss in this chapter, the UK is proposing to opt for a threshold that will, in accordance with Section 8, place controls over entities at three specific stages. In other words, a person gains control of a qualifying entity if the person acquires a right or interest in, or in relation to, the entity and as a result one or more of the cases described in this Section

112 Ibid, Chapter 1.
113 Ibid, Chapter 2.
114 Ibid, Section 7.
115 Ibid.
116 Ibid.

arises. For shares, this equates to a person holding 'from 25% or less to more than 25%, 2), from 50% or less to more than 50%, or 3), from less than 75% to 75% or more'.[117] A similar threshold has been proposed for voting rights.

Central to controlling ownership of foreign investments, is the level of control or otherwise afforded to asset. Therefore, the control of assets proposed Section 9, will provide that:

> a person gains control of a qualifying asset if the person acquires a right or interest in, or in relation to, the asset and as a result the person is able to use the asset, or use it to a greater extent than prior to the acquisition, or to direct or control how the asset is used, or direct or control how it is 45 used to a greater extent than prior to the acquisition.[118]

Moreover, the proposed Bill has a comprehensive administrative component to assessing, reviewing, granting and denying the approval of an investment. However, it is out of scope of this Section to discuss the procedural steps. Based on the proposal, it is our view that the UK is wanting to ensure their future sovereign needs are protected from investment predators. While they classify land as important, they have not specified the type of land such as Australia has in relation to agriculture. Agriculture may not be as problematic to the UK as it is to Australia. Nonetheless, their productive capacity, in our view, would warrant specific protection in the future.

5.5 Conclusion

Mergers and acquisitions provide an alternative to insolvency. This chapter has demonstrated the fine line that needs to be balanced by jurisdictions in relation to restructuring through MA. It is a complex, overlapping and competing area of law. On the one hand, MA are often the preferred form of investment to gain entry into a foreign market, particularly in markets which – for one reason or another

117 Ibid, Section 8. The reference to holding a percentage of shares is (i) in the case of an entity that has a share capital, to holding shares comprised in the issued share capital of the entity of a nominal value (in aggregate) of that percentage of the share capital, (ii) in the case of an entity that does not have a share capital, to holding a 5% right to a share of that percentage of the capital or profits of the entity, (iii) in the case of a limited liability partnership, to holding a right to a share of that percentage of any surplus assets of the partnership on a winding up. Also note Section 10, holding and acquiring interests and rights: supplementary. Schedule 1 provides for particular cases in which a person is to be treated for the purposes of this Act as holding an interest or right.

118 Ibid, Section 11. However, this is subject to Section 11 that provides for the purposes of this Act a person is not to be regarded as gaining control of a qualifying asset by reason of an acquisition made by an individual for purposes that are wholly or mainly outside the individual's trade, business or craft.

– present high entry barriers.[119] These barriers vary across sectors and often apply to all new entrants, whether foreign or domestic.

In oligopolistic industries for example, firms might erect barriers to entry for new competitors, or these barriers might arise from the nature of the industry itself where distribution channels are few and selective or where consumer tastes are idiosyncratic.[120] Often the regulatory environment discourages new entrants, either because of its opacity or because of outright restrictions on entry such as a temporary prohibition on new banking licences.[121] It is this competition in the market and for the market that creates competing outcomes. There is no better example today than has been seen throughout the onset of technology. It is largely dominated by a few as a very high level, who have established monopolies through acquiring smaller rivals.

Central to the development and implementation of MA law by the jurisdictions compared earlier, is the common approach to restrict the development of monopolies. Additionally, there have been calls by some that Australia should consider following EU law, particularly in relation to competition issues arising from MA. This is a matter for Australia to resolve. However, and keeping with the main argument of this book to internationalise areas of cross-border insolvency and restructuring, at this stage, and due to the divergent approach to foreign investment rules, achieving any form of legal convergence and harmonisation will be complex and very difficult. Thus, we do not call for any harmonisation of MA foreign investment law or rules. Rather we put forward that nation states should consider developing a set of international principles to ensure an even level playing field for foreign investment. However, even this proposal is problematic, because it would go against globalisation, and potentially, drive into even more protectionist law and rules.

An additional layer added to an already multi-layered problem as a result of ongoing financial stress from the pandemic and other economic and geopolitical impact, is for government to lower standards for MA. Arguably, should the decision be taken by government to dilute, or in other words, lower the standards of MA requirements and the eschewing threshold tests, it goes against controlling monopolies. While COVID-19 has, in part, contributed to this revised approach, jurisdictions had been reviewing and strengthening their national interest requirements for some time before 2020. Put simply, the impact of COVID-19 has had a significant economic impact across the world. This is further compounded by the conflict in the Ukraine. In some countries, more than other countries, it has placed individuals and entities involved in cross-border trade into a high level of financial stress. That said, the pandemic at the time of concluding this book in 2021, was

119 Organisation for Economic Cooperation and Development, *Economic and other Impacts of Foreign Corporate Takeovers in OECD Countries* (2007), 67. https://www.oecd.org/daf/inv/investment-policy/40476100.pdf.

120 Ibid, 67.

121 Ibid.

far from over, and the full financial impact will not be understood for some time. It might be not until 2025 or 2026 that the full extent of financial stress from the worldwide pandemic is able to be calculated, with a high level of accuracy.

Nonetheless, there is a general shift by jurisdictions, as part of looking inwards, to consider broader sectors outside of the tradition defence industries to be classified as in the national interest – national security. While internationalising foreign investment is a stretch too far and unlikely to ever be realised. However, in our view, and going forward, an alternative approach would extend national security to, environmental matters, money laundering, and illegal migration. In some states this does already occur, although it is achieved under certain parameters, which has been outside the scope of this chapter to explore. It could and should be also tied to ethic development, deployment and use of current and future artificial intelligence, biohazards, pests and diseases. Doing so, is what they define as soft diplomacy to achieve a convergence of approaches.

5

RESTRUCTURING: MERGERS AND ACQUISITIONS PART 2

5.1 United States [US]

The US is both the world's largest foreign direct investor and the largest beneficiary of foreign direct investment.[1] Like every sovereign country, the US has sought to temper its embrace of open markets with the protection of its national security interests. However, achieving this balance, which has shifted over time, has meant 'placing certain limitations on overseas investment in strategically sensitive sectors of the US economy',[2] which has become increasingly evident since 2018.

Nonetheless, the control of foreign investment in the US dates back to the 1890s.[3] The US Congress passed the first antitrust law, the Sherman Act in 1890, as a 'comprehensive charter of economic liberty aimed at preserving free and unfettered competition as the rule of trade'.[4] In 1914, the Congress passed two additional antitrust laws, the Federal Trade Commission (FTC) Act, which created the FT Commission itself, and the Clayton Act[5]. The Clayton Act has played an important role in protecting trade and commerce against unlawful restraints and monopolies. Centrally, the antitrust laws proscribe unlawful mergers and business practices in general terms, leaving courts to decide which ones are illegal based on the facts of each case.

1 Johnathan Masters, James McBride, Foreign Investment and U.S. National Security, *Council on Foreign Relations* (2016), 1.

2 Ibid.

3 Tania Pantazi, The Legal Framework for Mergers and Acquisitions in the European union and the United States, in A. Bitzenis (ed), *Mergers and Acquisitions as the Pillar of Foreign Direct Investment*, Springer (2012), Chapter 11. 2000–2010.

4 Federal Trade Commission, https://www.ftc.gov/tips-advice/competition-guidance/guide-antitrust-laws/antitrust-laws Sherman Antitrust Act, 15 U.S.C. §§ 1–7

5 Clayton Act 15 U.S.C. §§ 12–27.

DOI: 10.4324/9781003311874-8

The Sherman Act makes it clear that competition will be regulated through contractual arrangements. It is limited in its scope and does not identify the conduct of relevant parties. This has been reaffirmed by the US Supreme Court, which stated that:

> The Sherman Act, unlike most traditional criminal statutes, does not, in clear and categorical terms, precisely identify the conduct which it proscribes. Both civil remedies and criminal sanctions are authorized with regard to the same generalized definitions of the conduct. . . . Nor has judicial elaboration of the Act always yielded the clear and definitive rules of conduct which the statute omits; instead open- ended and fact-specific standards . . . have been applied to broad classes of conduct falling within the purview of the Act's general provisions.[6]

It further states that:
'Every contract, combination in the form of trust or otherwise, or conspiracy, in restraint of trade or commerce among the several States, or with foreign nations, is declared to be illegal. Every person who shall make any contract or engage in any combination or conspiracy hereby declared to be illegal shall be deemed guilty of a felony, and, on conviction thereof, shall be punished by fine not exceeding $100,000,000 if a corporation, or, if any other person $1,000,000, or by imprisonment not exceeding 10 years, or by both said punishments, in the discretion of the court'.[7]

In addition, the Act goes onto restrict the ability of individuals and entities to create monopolies. Although, in practice monopolies across the US are evident. Section 2 goes onto provide that: 'every person who shall monopolize, or attempt to monopolize, or combine or conspire with any other person or persons, to monopolize any part of the trade or commerce among the several States, or, with foreign nations, shall be deemed guilty of a felony, and, on conviction thereof, shall be punished by fine not exceeding $100,000,000 if a corporation, or, if any other person, $1,000,000, or by imprisonment not exceeding 10 years, or by both said punishments, in the discretion of the court'.[8] Interestingly, it does not go onto provide specific threshold(s) for investment. It does, however, specify that sections 1–7 do not apply to conduct involving trade or commerce other than import trade and commerce with foreign nationals unless the conduct has a substantial and reasonably foreseeable effect on trade or commerce[9].

Additionally Clayton Act (CA) addresses specific practices that the Sherman Act does not clearly prohibit, such as mergers and interlocking directorates (that is,

6 *US v United States Gypsum Co*, 438 US 422 (1978).
7 Sherman Act § 1, 15. U.S.C. § 1.
8 Ibid, § 2.
9 Foreign Investment Risk Review Modernization Act of 2018, which provides for further thresholds.

the same person making business decisions for competing companies).[10] The CA also discourages any level of price discrimination by making it 'unlawful for any person engaged in commerce, in the course of such commerce, either directly or indirectly, to discriminate in price between different purchasers of commodities of like grade and quality, where either or any of the purchases involved in such discrimination are in commerce, or where such commodities are sold for use, consumption, or resale within the United States or any Territory'.[11] More importantly, Section 7 prohibits:

> a person to engage in commerce where they acquire, directly or indirectly, the whole or any part of the stock or other share capital and no person subject to the jurisdiction of the Federal Trade Commission shall acquire the whole or any part of the assets of another person engaged also in commerce to create a monopoly.[12]

On this basis, no person shall acquire, directly or indirectly, the whole or any part of the stock or other share capital and no person subject to the jurisdiction of the Federal Trade Commission shall acquire the whole or any part of the assets to create a monopoly. However, this Section shall not apply to person purchasing such stock solely for investment and not using the same by voting or otherwise to bring about, or in attempting to bring about, the substantial lessening of competition'.[13] Again, there is no upper or lower limit threshold that has been set under the CA to determine how such a monopoly would become an actual or perceived monopoly. The question arises – will this cause a material issue overall to any current or future foreign investment? This is a question for the US to consider. Yet, in our view, and as nation states continue to look further inwards since the pandemic had been declared, countries are looking more closely at foreign investment proposals.

A more problematic issue has recently emerged from the mergers, acquisitions and takeovers in the development and growth in the technology sector. On the one side, there is the fully established competitor that is viewed by another entity to acquire in order to push them out of the market. On the other side, David Emanuelson and Danielle Drory make the point that Section 7 of the Clayton Act becomes challenging because, when the acquired firm is not a fully-fledged competitor, but could be, the analysis is more challenging. The acquired firm might be considered a 'potential competitor', which is distinguished from an 'actual competitor',[14] from

10 Federal Trade Commission, https://www.ftc.gov/tips-advice/competition-guidance/guide-antitrust-laws/antitrust-laws.

11 Clayton Act § 2, 15 U.S.C. § 13.

12 Ibid, § 7.

13 Ibid.

14 David Emanuelson, Danielle Drory, *The Potential Chilling Effects of Lowering Standards for Tech M&A Enforcement*, American Bar Association (2020), 1–7.

the proposed merger. In unpacking this proposition, it is easy to understand that any merger (if not regulated) could result in a fully blown competitive edge being created that would result in a high level of monopolisation. The authors go onto say that this is specifically the case for the technology sector, whereby the Federal Trade Commission has challenged and even blocked acquisitions and mergers. This is because of the stage at which the company either acquiring another entity, or merging with another entity and taking over it in part or in full.[15] It could be that the acquisition is based on the potential that the entity will be a challenger in the future. Such a scenario is arguably playing out in many jurisdictions. The Merger Guidelines noted by Emanuelson and Drory have attempted to address this issue, whereby Section 2.1.5 states that 'if one of the merging firms has a strong incumbency position and the other merging firm threatens to disrupt market conditions with a new technology or business model, their merger can involve the loss of actual or potential competition'.[16] It remains under review and in particular relating to start-ups, in and across the technology sector. Even though, this issue does not directly relate to cross-border insolvency, it highlights the emerging variables associated with mergers and acquisitions more broadly, when a more powerful entity is restructuring and wanting to dominate a market.

Central to the merger procedures are the Horizontal Merger Guidelines, issued jointly by the Division and the Federal Trade Commission (FTC) on August 19, 2010.[17] The Horizontal Merger Guidelines are designed to outline the Division's standards for determining whether to oppose mergers or acquisitions with a horizontal overlap under Section 7 of the Clayton Act. The Non- Horizontal Merger Guidelines from Section 4 of the 1984 Merger Guidelines remain in effect for nonhorizontal mergers (ie, vertical mergers; mergers that eliminate potential competitors), although they do not describe the full range of potential anti-competitive effects of nonhorizontal mergers.[18]

The Horizontal Merger Guidelines,[19] in part, set out the threshold test for evaluating various mergers, such as 'consumptive mergers, direct comparisons based on experience, market shares and concentration in a relevant market, substantial head-to-head competition, and disruptive role of a merging party'.[20] While it is out of scope to examine each of these areas, they guide the decision maker to determine where there is or will be an unfair competitive advantage created by the proposed

15 Ibid, 1–5.
16 Ibid, 4–7.
17 United States Justice Department, Ant-Trust Division, https://www.justice.gov/atr/file/761131/download
18 Ibid.
19 The Horizontal Merger Guidelines, https://www.justice.gov/sites/default/files/atr/legacy/2010/08/19/hmg-2010.pdf. The relevant statutory provisions include Section 7 of the Clayton Act, 15 U.S.C. § 18, Sections 1 and 2 of the Sherman Act, 15 U.S.C. §§ 1, 2, and Section 5 of the Federal Trade Commission Act, 15 U.S.C. § 45.
20 Ibid.

merger. Any substantial threshold test can be found under market concentration, whereby agencies generally classify markets into three types of unconcentrated Markets: HHI below 1500, moderately Concentrated Markets; HHI between 1500 and 2500, highly Concentrated Markets; and HHI above 2500.[21]

Furthermore, and in addition to this, the US has adopted a sectorial approach to the administration of different industry sectors, such as primary industries and banking will be further regulated under specific legislation, including the Bank Merger Act, 12 U.S.C. § 1828(c). This creates a special procedure under which bank merger reviews are conducted by the appropriate banking agency. Therefore,

> all merger applications involving a bank or savings association (including an application to acquire assets or assume liabilities) are to be forwarded to the Attorney General.[22]

The sectorial approach is further compounded by the Federal Trade Commission Act, whereby it does in part in accordance with Section 5, aggregate specific conduct to the federal level. Section 5(a) of the Federal Trade Commission Act (FTC) (15 USC §45) prohibits unfair or deceptive acts or practices in affecting commerce. This prohibition applies to all persons, including foreign nationals, engaged in commerce, including banks. Furthermore, Section 5 is procedural and does not establish any threshold levels for evaluating deceptive conduct. Thus, it is out of scope to examine the FTC any further in this chapter.

Notwithstanding this, financially stressed entities can apply for reorganisation in accordance with Chapter 11 of the Bankruptcy Code. The bankruptcy regimes in many jurisdictions are still not well adapted to regulate mergers and acquisition transactions. Consequently, for companies in financial difficulty with some connection to the US, the commencement of a Chapter 11 case in the US may be the most effective method of attempting to reorganise.[23] In reinforcing the operation

21 Ibid, 18. The Agencies employ the following general standards for the relevant markets they have defined: *Small Change in Concentration:* Mergers involving an increase in the HHI of less than 100 points are unlikely to have adverse competitive effects and ordinarily require no further analysis. *Unconcentrated Markets:* Mergers resulting in unconcentrated markets are unlikely to have adverse competitive effects and ordinarily require no further analysis. *Moderately Concentrated Markets:* Mergers resulting in moderately concentrated markets that involve an increase in the HHI of more than 100 points potentially raise significant competitive concerns and often warrant scrutiny. *Highly Concentrated Markets:* Mergers resulting in highly concentrated markets that involve an increase in the HHI of between 100 points and 200 points potentially raise significant competitive concerns and often warrant scrutiny. Mergers resulting in highly concentrated markets that involve an increase in the HHI of more than 200 points will be presumed to be likely to enhance market power. The presumption may be rebutted by persuasive evidence showing that the merger is unlikely to enhance market power.

22 Bank Merger Act, 12 U.S.C. § 1828(c).

23 Sandor E. Schick, Mergers and Acquisitions of Foreign Debtors under Chapter 11 of the US Bankruptcy Code, *Business Law International,* Vol. 6, No. 1 (2005), 2–12.

of Chapter 11, the following discussion briefly highlights a merger in May 2018 by McDermott who combined with Chicago Bridge & Iron Company N.V. It was a downstream provider of onshore petrochemical, refining, power, gasification and gas processing technology as a collective (combination). As a result of this merger, McDermott became a fully integrated, onshore-offshore company.[24] The merger presented a unique opportunity for McDermott's to win new projects and offer more expansive services. Brought certain challenges for the combined enterprise. At the same time, the debtors were working to address the losses, which the debtors believed would be replicated in future projects. The debtors were winning new projects at a high rate, as was reflected in McDermott's record project backlog, which now exceeds $19 billion.[25] With this success, though, the resulting effect saw an increase in the near-term financial obligations. In addition to front-end capital investment, each of these projects required new letters of credit to support the debtors' performance obligations under the applicable project contracts. However, the debtors had reached the limit of their existing letter of credit capacity and were unlikely to be able to secure access to new letters of credit on any terms, much less favourable terms. The debtors' efforts to mitigate the financial strain brought on by adverse market conditions through non-core asset divestitures and operational 'rightsizing', were heightened. The debtors' liquidity position also remained strained and was projected to be insufficient over the long-term to fund the capital-intensive nature of the business and to service its highly leveraged capital structure.[26]

In addressing Chapter 11, it was stated that concluding the Restructuring Support Agreement was a significant achievement for the debtors. In addition, the Agreement made provision for compromises and settlements. That sought to preserve value by enabling the debtors to avoid protracted, value-destructive litigation over potential recoveries and other causes of action that could delay the debtors' emergence from Chapter 11. The core terms of the Restructuring Support Agreement were to be implemented through a Chapter 11 plan of reorganisation – namely, a Plan.[27] In relation to the merger, the Court stated: 'the actions to implement the Restructuring Transactions may include the execution and delivery of appropriate agreements or other documents of merger, amalgamation, consolidation and restructuring'.[28] The Court had to decide on the solicitation of votes to accept or reject the Reorganisation Plan in accordance with Sections 1125–1126 of the Bankruptcy Code which required the disclosure of the Joint Pre-packaged

24 In the United States Bankruptcy Court for The Southern District of Texas Houston Division, Disclosure Statement for the Joint Prepackaged Chapter 11 Plan of Reorganisation of McDermott International, Inc. and its Debtor Affiliates, January 2020, https://www.sec.gov/Archives/edgar/data/708819/000119312520010618/d858406dex992.htm.

25 Ibid, 1–2.

26 Ibid.

27 Ibid, 1–3.

28 Ibid, 29.

Chapter 11 Plan of Reorganization of McDermott International, Inc. and its debtor affiliates. Therefore, each debtor's board of directors, member, or manager, approved the transactions contemplated by the Reorganisation Plan and outlined in the disclosure statement.

Viewed this way, the US has taken a multi-layered approach to corporate mergers and acquisitions, whether under financial stress or otherwise. In our view they are leaders in providing alternatives to full blown insolvency. They encourage the preventative approach, whereby they would rather an entity negotiate a way out of financial stress. What has emerged, is that jurisdictions are viewing insolvency as a last resort. Nevertheless, such mergers are subject to the foreign investment rules of the state.

5.1.1 Foreign Purchasing Rule

The US, similar to the other jurisdictions compared, had at the time of writing this book embarked on its own review of foreign investment rules. This has, in part, been due to concerns with foreign transactions that are typically associated with mergers, acquisitions, and takeovers of established domestic firms rather than new investments, known as greenfields.[29] US lawmakers, much like their peers around the globe, have passed legislation that restricts or reviews foreign deals that could cause the loss of sensitive technologies, significant outsourcing of jobs, or impairment of various sectors of critical infrastructure. In recent years, many nations have reassessed their laws in light of fears associated with international terrorism, global investments by state-owned enterprises (foreign government controlled companies) and sovereign wealth funds, many of which suffer from lack of transparency and accountability.[30] Moreover, a merger, acquisition or takeover of an existing American business, is subject to review by the United States Committee on Foreign Investment. This is an agency consisting of high-level government officials, which may be prohibited or suspended by the President if he determines that it threatens to impair the national security of the US.[31]

In 2018, the US undertook a significant reform on the implementation of the Foreign Investment Risk Review Modernization Act of 2018 (FIRRM).[32] Section 201 became important by defining specific terms that need to be understood by practitioners and legal scholars. The definitions vary from other jurisdictions

29 Johnathan Masters, James McBride, Foreign Investment and U.S. National Security, *Council on Foreign Relations* (2016), 2.

30 Ibid.

31 Fred Morrison, The Protection of Foreign Investment in the United States of America, *The American Journal of Comparative Law*, Vol. 58 (2010), Supplement: Welcoming the World: U. S. National Reports to the XVIIIth International Congress of Comparative Law (2010), 437–453.

32 Foreign Investment Risk Review Modernization Act of 2018, https://www.congress.gov/115/crpt/hrpt784/CRPT-115hrpt784.pdf.

compared in this chapter. Firstly, control means the power, direct or indirect, whether or not exercised, to determine, direct, or decide important matters affecting an entity, subject to regulations prescribed by the Committee. Secondly, a covered transaction constitutes any transaction that is proposed, pending, or completed on or after the date of the enactment of the Foreign Investment Risk Review Modernization Act of 2018. Importantly, this is similar to the UK proposal, in that it allows for certain transactions to be scrutinised retrospectively.

More pervasively, the US has gone a step further in comparison to the other jurisdictions, whereby it has classified countries by defining them as a national or a government of, or a foreign entity organised under the laws of, a country of special concern.[33] The categories extend to AA or BB. AA constitutes control that is exercised or exercisable by a national or a government of, or by a foreign entity organised under the laws of, a country of special concern. On the other side, BB relates to control exercised by the government of a country of special concern or an entity organized under its laws. An AA classified national or government must have a substantial interest and as a result of the transaction, could obtain sensitive personal data as defined by regulations prescribed by the Committee of United States Citizens, and that data could be exploited in a manner that threatens national security. For a BB government of a country of special concern, the issue relates to where that government could have an influence over substantive decision making of the US business regarding the use, development, acquisition, or release of critical technologies.[34] While the FIRRM does not specifically state what countries are classified as AA or BB, it does however allow the Committee on Foreign Investment (CoFI) in the US to review sensitive non-controlling investments involving countries of special concern, including China, Russia, Venezuela and state sponsors of terrorism.[35]

The threshold test can be found at Section 308. By and large, it relates to the Defense Production Act 1950. Arguably, defence is the highest priority for the US, in national security terms. It provides the ability for the US Government to acquire or maintain the equipment and systems that are necessary for defence, intelligence, or other national security functions. It further requires that there be limited cumulative control of any one type of critical infrastructure, energy asset, material or critical technology by a foreign person.[36] Noteworthy too, is the requirement whereby any foreign person that would acquire control of a US business as a result of the covered transaction has a history of complying with US laws and regulations and prior adherence. This is on the basis that it is applicable, to any agreement or condition, and adhering to contracts or other agreements with entities of the US Government. Further thresholds include, but are not limited to, the release of

33 Ibid, Section 201.
34 Ibid.
35 Ibid, Section 581.
36 Ibid, Section 308.

sensitive personal data of a US citizen, where cybersecurity can be compromised or exacerbated by the exposure of sensitive personal national security information. The FIRRM also amended the Export Control Reform Act 2018 and the Anti-Boycott Act of 2018. However, it is out of scope to explore the reforms to these Act in this chapter.

The FIRRM goes one step further than the other laws examined in this chapter. Specifically, it provides CoFI with additional jurisdiction to have oversight of foreign investments by foreign persons. Similar to Australia and the UK, it provides CoFI with the authority to undertake a review of a lease or purchase of land that forms part of an air or maritime port, within close proximity to a US military installation, allowing a foreign person to collect intelligence, expose national security activities and meet other requirements set out by the committee (regulations).[37] More importantly, it allows for the CoFI to monitor incremental acquisitions of a non-controlling investment, by a foreign person who has received approval for a prior controlling investment.[38] This is something that other jurisdictions studied do not provide for within their respective laws. In addition to this requirement, is the required review and monitoring of partners to investments in which:

> limited partners may qualify as passive investors, provided the conditions are met, including: (i) the fund is managed by a U.S. general partner or an equivalent; and (ii) restrictions on the limited partner to impact certain investment decisions whether through a committee, advisory board, or another form of authority.[39]

With the increasing trade, economic, technological and military advancements and competition around the world, it is evident from the US laws that they have a priority focus on maintaining the US's status as a world leader and super power. In the words of the US President in December 2020, on the reforms that the FIRRM provides:

> This new authority will enhance our ability to protect cutting-edge American technology and intellectual property vital to our national security. You've all been reading that intellectual property and all sorts of different things of that nature are being stolen from us by other countries. It's going to be very hard for them to do that. We're putting a lot of safeguards in, and we're doing a lot of things against foreign acquisition of property, and especially where they're near sensitive military installations. So this was a very big deal. This was a very important deal. And the people in this room are the people that

37 It is out of scope to examine the CoFI regulations.

38 STA Law firm, Foreign Investment Risk Review Modernization Act, 2018-USA, https://www.mondaq.com/terrorism-homeland-security-defence/989118/foreign-investment-risk-review-modernization-act-2018-usa.

39 Ibid.

> really were most instrumental in wanting it and getting it passed. Because of our incredible achievements, other nations seek to steal, copy, or control American intellectual property. And we had very, very little safeguards up. We had, in many cases, I would say, Marco, no safeguards. And now we have probably the best there is in the world. We'll see if that's good enough, and if it's not, then we will keep adding on to it. This weakens our economy when they steal, destroys our jobs, and threatens the security of our country. I'm pleased this new legislation provides the Committee on Foreign Investment in the United States greater authority when it comes to reviewing foreign ownership of American firms with critical technology and intellectual property[40].

Even though the US reforms extended beyond the impact of COVID-19, they do, in part, resemble the thinking and policy direction that some states are taking towards others that will significantly impact the traditional form of MA. In comparing the US with the EU, the US has established a similar framework to Australia that is consumer based. In other words, the framework has been designed to maximise the protections to the consumer. The EU's framework uses different terminology, but the purpose is to achieve a similar outcome to the US. Significantly, the US reforms have also significantly raised the profile of nationalism in foreign investment, through national security requirements.

5.2 Singapore

The Singapore Government is heavily involved in the economy as a regulator and as a market participant through its government departments, statutory bodies and ownership or control of commercial entities. Thus, the issue of foreign competition is one of importance for the jurisdiction.[41] The Competition Act, Chapter 50B of Singapore (CA), prohibits mergers, acquisitions of control and certain joint ventures that have resulted, or may be expected to result, in a substantial lessening of competition within any market (or market segment) across Singapore. The Competition Act is directed at the conduct of 'undertakings', which means that it applies to individuals or entities carrying on business, unless they are exempt under its provisions. The prohibitions cover fairly standard competition law areas of horizontal agreements, the abuse of market dominance, and mergers.[42] Horizontal agreements are prohibited if they have the object or effect of preventing competition within Singapore. Agreements which fix prices or trading conditions, limit or

40 Remarks by President Trump at a Roundtable on the Foreign Investment Risk Review Modernization Act, December 2020, https://www.whitehouse.gov/briefings-statements/remarks-president-trump-roundtable-foreign-investment-risk-review-modernization-act-firrma/.

41 Deborah Healey, Application of Competition Laws to Government in Asia: The Singapore Story, *KLRI Journal of Law and Legislation*, Vol. 2 (2012), 65–78.

42 Ibid, 65–72.

control production, technical development or investment, share markets or sources of supply or impose supplementary obligations fall within the prohibition. The Law is based on the UK Competition Act 1998 as derived from the pre-2004 EU competition law provisions. For Debra Healy, the Act draws on European concepts of markets, dominance and market power, although it does not slavishly follow the UK Competition Act or other EU laws. Section 54 details how a merger can eventuate. It states that a merger occurs if:

> 2 or more undertakings, previously independent of one another, merge; one or more persons or other undertakings acquire direct or indirect control of the whole or part of one or more other undertakings; or the result of an acquisition by one undertaking (the first undertaking) of the assets (including goodwill), or a substantial part of the assets, of another undertaking (the second undertaking) is to place the first undertaking in a position to replace or substantially replace the second undertaking in the business or, as appropriate, the part concerned of the business in which that undertaking was engaged immediately before the acquisition.[43]

Particular emphasis has been placed on the level of control another entity obtains from the merger. That is, Section 54(3) describes the threshold for control to be:

> rights, contracts or any other means, and extended to ownership of, or the right to use all or part of, the assets of an undertaking; or rights or contracts which enable decisive influence to be exercised with regard to the composition, voting or decisions of the organs of an undertaking.[44]

Furthermore, control is and can be:

> acquired by any person or other undertaking if he or it becomes a holder of the rights or contracts, or entitled to use the other means, referred to in subsection (3); or although not becoming such a holder or entitled to use those other means, acquires the power to exercise the rights derived therefrom.[45]

However, based on this, a merger will not be realised where the person acquiring control is a receiver or liquidator acting as such or is an underwriter. This has subtle but important ramifications for cross-border restructuring to be undertaken as a result of cross-border insolvency, in order to achieve a merger in Singapore. Nonetheless, the merger acquisition is limited to where a receiver, liquidator or underwriter would assume control. In addition, a merger will not be realised where

43 Competition Act Cap 50B, 2004, Section 54.
44 Ibid, Section 54(3).
45 Ibid, Section 54(4).

all of the undertakings involved in the merger are, directly or indirectly, under the control of the same undertaking; and where control is acquired solely as a result of a testamentary disposition, intestacy or the right of survivorship under a joint tenancy.[46] The remaining Sections, which are out of scope of this chapter, provide for procedural steps pertaining to notification of a merger or anticipated merger, along with notification requirements and any decision by the Commission on the merger. There is power within the CA for regulations to be made, so as to assist in the facilitation of mergers. However, they will not be examined in this Section.

Nontheless, Singapore has adopted a similar structure to that of the UK, with the Code on Take-overs and Mergers (the Code).[47] The Code:

> applies to both take-overs and mergers. It applies to corporations with a primary listing of their equity securities, business trusts with a primary listing of their units in Singapore. While the Code is drafted with listed public companies, listed registered business trusts in mind, unlisted public companies and unlisted registered business trusts with more than 50 shareholders or unitholders, as the case may be, and net tangible assets of $5 million or more must also observe the letter and spirit of the General Principles and Rules, wherever this is possible and appropriate. The Code does not apply to take-overs or mergers of other unlisted public companies and unlisted business trusts, or private companies.[48]

Additionally, corporations and business trusts with a primary listing in Singapore, public companies and registered business trusts with a primary listing overseas, as well as unlisted public companies and unlisted registered business trusts with more than 50 shareholders, or unitholders, as the case may be, and net tangible assets of $5 million or more may apply to the Council to waive the application of the Code. In considering such applications, the Council takes into account, amongst others: 'the number of Singapore shareholders or unitholders and the extent of trading in Singapore; and the existence of protection available to Singapore shareholders or unitholders provided under any statute or code regulating take-overs and mergers outside Singapore'.[49]

46 Ibid, or control is acquired by an undertaking referred to in subsection (8) in the circumstances specified in subsection (9).

47 Code on Take-overs and Mergers, https://www.mas.gov.sg/-/media/MAS/resource/sic/The_Singapore_Code_on_Take_Overs_and_Merger_24-January-2019.pdf?la=en&hash=8DCB4A29BF6DDA17527EC7E54A8CB5CFEDDAEE7D.

48 Ibid, 1.

49 Ibid, 3.

A central feature of the Code is that:

> [it] is not concerned with the financial or commercial advantages or disadvantages of a take-over or merger; such matters should be decided by the company and its shareholders. The Code represents the collective public opinion on the standard of conduct to be observed in general, and how fairness can be achieved in particular, in a take-over or merger transaction. A fundamental requirement is that shareholders in the company subject to a take-over offer must be given sufficient information, advice and time to consider and decide on the offer.[50]

For acquisitions, a foreign purchaser may acquire a Singapore business by one of two possible methods. First, the purchaser acquires the issued shares of the Singapore company that carries on the business (Share Sale). Second, the purchaser acquires the business (assets and liabilities) of the Singapore company (Business Sale).[51] Thus, in summary the Code is enforceable, and sets out additional procedural steps to be undertaken, pre, during and after a merger or takeover. As noted by the Takeover Code, it does not have the 'force of law and does not give rise to criminal proceedings, and its breach may result in the imposition of sanctions by the Securities Industry Council (SIC)'.[52] Sanctions that the SIC may impose include private reprimands, public censure. Further action may be taken when the breach is flagrant, to deprive the offender temporarily or permanently of its ability to enjoy the facilities of the securities market. SIC may also order compensation to be paid to shareholders or former shareholders by persons who have contravened certain provisions of the Takeover Code.[53]

5.2.1 Foreign Purchasing Rule

Singapore does not have a law on foreign investment or an economy-wide investment law governing both domestic and foreign investment. Instead, investment is governed by laws of general application, for example, the common law of contract and the Singapore Companies Act, and sector-specific legislation.[54] In general, there is no difference between the treatment of foreign investment and domestic investment in the Island state, except insofar as differences in treatment are

50 Ibid, 1.

51 Ibid, 5.

52 Wai Yee Wan, Mergers and Acquisitions, in *Reading Law in Singapore*, Research Collection School of Law (2014), Chapter 7, 65–67.

53 Ibid, 66–67.

54 Jonathan Bonnitcha, *Investment Laws of ASEAN Countries: A Comparative Review,* The International Institute for Sustainable Development, 2017, https://www.iisd.org/system/files/publications/investment-laws-asean-countries.pdf.

authorised by a specific law.[55] As a Southeast Asian economic, legal and technology hub, the island state has built a strong reputation in the region for its finance, business, legal, research and development expertise. While it is well understood that the country relies on expatriates to fill the gap in the local workforce and economy, the state arguably has one of the highest educated workforces in the world. It prides itself on maintaining the rule of law and ensuring a high level of transparency, to provides confidence and certainty in business investment. This is underpinned by a number of policy incentives, such as very attractive tax rates for both the employee and employer.

However, Singapore restricts some foreign investment in several sectors, including telecommunications, media, banking and land ownership. Restrictions on foreign investment are found in relevant sectoral legislation, for example, under the Newspaper and Printing Presses Act 1975[56] imposing restrictions on foreign control of newspaper companies. In practice, these limitations on foreign investment are implemented by the relevant regulatory government authority. In another, the Monetary Authority of Singapore regulates foreign investment in the banking sector through the system of licensing established by Section 7 of the Banking Act 1971. Section 7 provides that:

> a company which desires authority to carry on banking business in Singapore shall apply in writing to the Authority for a licence under this Section and shall supply a copy of the memorandum of association and articles of association or other instrument under which the company is incorporated, duly verified by a statutory declaration made by a senior officer of the company; a copy of the latest balance-sheet of the company; such other information as may be called for by the Authority.[57]

The overall threshold test to obtain a banking license in accordance with Section 9. This Section provides that a company must not be granted a licence unless its paid-up capital is not less than $1,500 million and its head office capital funds are not less than the equivalent of $200 million. Noteworthy too, is that the requirements are largely capital based. They do not require a threshold test that includes national security or public interest. For example, money laundering through banks and financial institutions are by and large regulated through separate criminal laws and are not determining factors in order to secure a licence. In addition, foreign nationals (including both individuals and foreign-owned Singapore companies) must seek government approval before acquiring landed residential property.

Compared to the other jurisdictions discussed in this chapter, arguably, Singapore's regulations depict it as the most liberal and open to foreign investment. These

55 Ibid, 19.

56 Newspaper and Printing Presses Act 1975, Section 8.

57 Ibid, Section 7.

regulations have been instrumental in leading trade and investment throughout the Asia region for more than four decades. Singapore is open to foreign investment and offers tax benefits that businesses can enjoy following registration.[58] The government is continuously supplying the 'national economy with public investments, for instance, transportation infrastructure projects (such as the high-speed train line between the city-state and Kuala Lumpur) or programs encouraging the transfer towards the future economy'.[59] Even so, at the time of finalising this book, this rail project had been cancelled by the respective governments.[60] However, the challenge lies in the fact that the country continues to hold a monopoly on certain key sectors, such as financial services, professional services, media, telecommunications. Furthermore, government-related enterprises play a dominant role in the domestic economy and, in turn, in investment.[61] The monopoly on these sectors is justified by the fact that Singapore has no natural resources to rely on, unlike Australia, US and other countries that have relied on them for decades. Singapore has had been adaptable to new and emerging technologies that have transcended the way in which its home spun industries have managed to build well-earned reputations for leading their sectors. The next section examines mergers and acquisitions in India.

5.3 India

Mergers and acquisitions in India are regulated by the Companies Act 1956. Sections 390 through 391 provide for the administrative and procedural arrangement for amalgamations and mergers to develop and establish a compromise or scheme of amalgamation. The expansion of foreign direct investment from India has, in a sense, been led by MAs abroad. This is on the backdrop that the internationalisation of firms from India is also reflected in the growing number with foreign affiliates.[62] Increasingly, India is seen by many nation states as the next frontier for foreign investment.

However, an important feature of MA activities in India is its sectoral composition.[63] It is interesting to note that firms in the service sector were the pioneers to

58 United Nations Conference on Trade and Development, *World Investment Report 2020*, https://unctad.org/system/files/official-document/wir2020_en.pdf.

59 Nordea, https://www.nordeatrade.com/en/explore-new-market/singapore/investment.

60 Malaysia Pays SG$102 Million in Compensation for Termination for KL-Singapore HSR Project, https://www.channelnewsasia.com/news/singapore/malaysia-singapore-compensation-high-speed-rail-14517142.

61 Ibid.

62 Deepak Nayyar, *The Internationalisation of Firms from India: Investment, Mergers and Acquisitions*, University of Oxford, Department of International Development SLPTMD Working Paper Series No. 004, 5. https://ora.ox.ac.uk/objects/uuid:5170c1fd-2e8c-40b7-9d2b-e84d84a8b2bf/download_file?file_format=pdf&safe_filename=SLPTMD004-Nayya.pdf&type_of_work=Working+paper.

63 Vidhisha Vyas, Krishnan Narayanan, A. Ramanathan, Determinants of Mergers and Acquisitions in Indian Pharmaceutical Industry, *Eurasian Journal of Business and Economics*, Vol. 5, No. 9 (2012), 79–102.

undertake MA as a means of expansion globally as well as domestically, later being joined by Indian manufacturing firms. On the international level, the success of the service sectors had strong positive spill-over effect on the pharmaceutical sector.[64] For example, Indian drugs firms have led the MA wave to strengthen their position in the regulated overseas markets like the US, Germany and the UK. The pharmaceutical sector has also became a major player in MA activity. The successful adoption of MAs by software and pharmaceutical firms has had all-round effects on Indian firms in other sectors like chemicals, automotive, steel, etc.[65]

While out of scope of this chapter, the language used under Indian law is quite different to its common law counter parts. Its Sections do not establish an overall threshold beyond providing for two entities being merged into a single entity. Furthermore, Section 581ZN sets out the requirements for a company going through an amalgamation, merger or division on the transfer of assets and liabilities. Nevertheless, for cross-border foreign investments that would include mergers and acquisitions, India has established a comprehensive set of rules on which foreign entities can enter the Indian market and in which specific sectors (see later).

In addition, India has also developed a similar framework to that of the other jurisdictions compared in this chapter, whereby a central element of managing MA is to balance the economic needs of the state with anti-competition behaviour and the formation of monopolies. Therefore, the Competition Act 2002 aims to minimise anti-competitive actions, whereby, under Section 5, a threshold level is established. Section 5 states:

> [T]he acquisition of one or more enterprises by one or more persons or merger or amalgamation of enterprises shall be a combination of such enterprises and persons or enterprises, if any acquisition where the parties to the acquisition, being the acquirer and the enterprise, whose control, shares, voting rights or assets have been acquired or are being acquired jointly have, either, in India, the assets of the value of more than rupees one thousand crores or turnover more than rupees three thousand crores; or in India or outside India, in aggregate, the assets of the value of more than five hundred million US dollars, including at least rupees five hundred crores in India, or turnover more than fifteen hundred million US dollars, including at least rupees fifteen hundred crores in India.[66]

In addition:

> [T]he group, to which the enterprise whose control, shares, assets or voting rights have been acquired or are being acquired, would belong after the

64 Ibid, 80–100.
65 Ibid, 80–102.
66 Competition Act 2002, Section 5.

> acquisition, jointly have or would jointly have, a) either in India, the assets of the value of more than rupees four thou sand crores or turnover more than rupees twelve thousand crores; *[in India or outside India, in aggregate, the assets of the value of more than two billion US dollars, including at least rupees five hundred crores in India, or turnover more than six billion US dollars, including at least rupees fifteen hundred crores in India]*; or, b) acquiring of control by a person over an enterprise when such person has already direct or indirect control over another enterprise engaged in production, distribution or trading of a similar or identical or substitutable goods or provision of a similar or identical or substitutable service.[67]

In reinforcing this position, it has been argued that it is sufficiently clear that the merger regulation under Competition law is essential to balance the positive and negative effects of mergers.[68] Moreover, competition regulations provide further procedural requirements that will not be examined in this Section. The authors go on to say that competition law has direct bearings upon MAs. Accordingly, they maintain that MAs are to be treated as a 'gating issue', to be considered as a hurdle to be cleared prior to entering into them.[69] This is not only the case for India, but also other jurisdictions examined in this chapter. That is, competition law is a direct by-product of mergers and acquisitions law, directed at minimising the potential for monopolies to be created.

5.3.1 Foreign Purchasing Rule

India, is another common law country along with Australia, UK, US and Singapore, that has much to offer to the Central Asian Region. Like several other major economies, the Indian economy has been adversely affected by the lockdowns and market disruptions caused by the COVID-19 pandemic. In these circumstances, valuations and stock prices of Indian companies have witnessed precipitous declines. Similar to the other jurisdictions compared in this chapter, foreign investments have played a pivotal role in India to supplement the low level of domestic investment.[70]

Nevertheless, more recently, the government of India revised the Indian investment laws to maintain a high level of control over 'opportunistic takeovers/

67 Ibid, Section 5.

68 Sivani KMS, Critical Analysis of the Effects of Regulations under Competition Law on Mergers and Acquisitions: A Comparison of the India, EU, US and UK Laws, *Journal of Corporate Governance & International Business Law*, Vol. 1, No. 2 (2019), 2.

69 Ibid, 8.

70 Dr. Jasbir Singh, Sumita Chadha, Dr. Anupama Sharma, Role of Foreign Direct Investment in India: An Analytical Study, *International Journal of Engineering and Science ISSN: 2278–4721*, Vol. 1, No. 5 (October 2012), 38.

acquisitions' of Indian companies.[71] The Revised Rules [Foreign Exchange Management (Non-debt Instruments) Rules, 2019], relate to any 'investing entity that belongs to/is incorporated in; or that is beneficially owned by a citizen of or a person situated in, a country sharing a land border with India must obtain the Government's approval prior to making its investment'.[72] Interestingly, India has been very specific in the new rules of 2019, limiting the investment controls to its transborder states. Under the 2019 rules, the Indian government is now required to provide a high level of approval for the direct acquisition of a stake in an Indian entity. The broad scope of this requirement includes any Indian entity. The threshold test does not appear to limit an acquisition to a particular state, for instance, 25% or more in an entity, or to a Rupia amount. It does however include a similar process to that of the US, whereby an indirect acquisition that can result in the investor becoming the beneficial owner of an Indian entity, will be assessed. What has emerged in some states is how control can be obtained incrementally by foreign individuals, companies and state-owned enterprises. Additionally, prior Government approval must also be obtained for any transfers of existing foreign investments, which would result in an Affected Investor securing beneficial ownership of an Indian company.[73]

Importantly, the 2020 Foreign Direct Investment Policy[74] of India sets out the overall framework for foreign investment rules. Interestingly, it is only a Policy and not formally transcribed into national law. A person constitutes an 'individual, a Hindu undivided family, a company, a firm, an association of persons or a body of individuals whether incorporated or not, every artificial juridical person, or any agency, office, or branch owned or controlled by such person'.[75] Foreign Investment means any 'investment made by a person resident outside India on a repatriable basis in capital instruments of an Indian company or to the capital of a LLP'.[76]

A Non-Resident Indian (NRI) can invest in the capital of a firm or a proprietary concern in India on non-repatriation basis, provided that the '(a) amount is invested by inward remittance or out of NRE/FCNR(B)/NRO account maintained with Authorized Dealers/Authorized banks[;] (b) The firm or proprietary concern is not engaged in any agricultural/plantation or real estate business or print media sector[; and] (c) Amount invested shall not be eligible for repatriation outside India'.[77]

However, foreign investment in sectors/activities under the government approval route can be achieved where an Indian company is being established by

71 Gibson & Dunn, *New Foreign Investment Restrictions Imposed by India,* https://www.gibsondunn.com/new-foreign-investment-restrictions-imposed-by-india/.

72 Ibid.

73 Ibid.

74 Foreign Direct Investment Policy, https://static.investindia.gov.in/2020-10/FDI-PolicyCircular-2020.pdf.

75 Ibid, 2.1.40.

76 Ibid, 2.1.17.

77 Ibid, 3.4.1.

that investment and is not owned by a resident entity or an Indian company and is not controlled by a resident entity. Additionally:

> [t]he control of an existing Indian company, currently owned or controlled by resident Indian citizens and Indian companies, which are owned or controlled by resident Indian citizens, will be/is being transferred/passed on to a non-resident entity as a consequence of transfer of shares and/or fresh issue of shares to non-resident entities through amalgamation, merger/demerger, acquisition.[78]

Furthermore, approval will need to be obtained where the:

> owner ship of an existing Indian company, currently owned or controlled by resident Indian citizens and Indian companies, which are owned or controlled by resident Indian citizens, will be/is being transferred/passed on to a non-resident entity as a consequence of transfer of shares and/or fresh issue of shares to non-resident entities through amalgamation, merger/demerger, acquisition.[79]

Notwithstanding this, India has, similar to the US, adopted the approach of totally excluding certain industry sectors. These include lottery business including government and private lottery, online lotteries, gambling and betting including casinos, chit funds, Nidhi company, trading in transferable development rights, real estate business or construction of farm houses.[80] Included in the prohibited industry sectors is the manufacturing of cigars, cheroots, cigarillos and cigarettes, and tobacco or of tobacco substitutes. Sectors that are not open to private sector investment extend to atomic energy and railway operations, along with foreign technology collaboration in any form including licensing for franchise, trademark, brand name, and management contract.[81]

Apart from this, one of the most sensitive areas of national protection for India, similar to Australia, is primary production. No FDI is allowed in 'floriculture,

78 Ibid, 3.4.2.

79 Ibid. It is clarified that foreign investment shall include all types of foreign investments, direct and indirect, regardless of whether the said investments have been made under Schedule I (FDI), II (FPI), III (NRI), VI (LLPs), VII (FVCI), VIII (Investment Vehicles) and IX (DRs) of Foreign Exchange Management (Non-Debt Instruments) Rules, 2019. FCCBs and DRs with underlying instruments can be issued under Schedule IX, being in the nature of debt, shall not be treated as foreign investment. Investment by NRIs under Schedule IV of Foreign Exchange Management (Non-Debt Instruments) Rules, 2019 will be deemed to be domestic investment at par with the investment made by residents. A company, trust and partnership firm incorporated outside India and owned and controlled by non-resident Indians will be eligible for investments under Schedule IV of Foreign Exchange Management (Non-Debt Instruments) Rules, 2019 and such investment will also be deemed domestic investment at par with the investment made by residents.

80 Ibid, Chapter 5, 'Real estate business' shall not include development of townships, construction of residential /commercial premises, roads or bridges and Real Estate Investment Trusts (REITs) registered and regulated under the SEBI (REITs) Regulations 2014.

81 Ibid.

horticulture and cultivation of vegetables and mushrooms under controlled conditions; development and production of seeds and planting material; animal husbandry (including breeding of dogs), pisciculture, aquaculture, apiculture; and services related to allied sectors'.[82] The threshold for agriculture production includes a level of under-controlled conditions, notably, the cultivation under controlled conditions' for the categories of floriculture, horticulture, cultivation of vegetables and mushrooms, is the practice of cultivation wherein rainfall, temperature, solar radiation, air humidity and culture medium are controlled artificially. Control within these parameters may be affected by protected cultivation within green houses, net houses, poly houses or any other improved infrastructure facilities where micro-climatic conditions are regulated anthropogenically.[83] More specifically, none of the other jurisdictions examined throughout this book have extended prohibitions to the plantation sector, namely coffee, rubber, cardamom, palm oil tree or olive oil plantations.[84] Mining and exploration of metal and non-metal ores including diamond, gold, silver and precious ores, but excluding titanium bearing minerals and its ores, are subject to the Mines and Minerals (Development & Regulation) Act 1957.[85] Exploration activities, such as oil, petroleum products and natural gas, LNG Regasification infrastructure, market study and formulation and petroleum refining in the private sector, are also limited.[86] Similar to the US, other defence industries are also restricted. The defence industry is subject to an industrial license under the Industries (Development & Regulation) Act, 1951 and the Arms Act, 1959.[87] Furthermore, there are limitations on technology, air-services, airports, construction-infrastructure, industrial parks, satellite, print media and media more generally, amongst others. Nonetheless, the broader threshold requirements extend to FDI in which up to 74%, operating under an automatic route, shall be permitted to companies seeking new industrial licenses.[88] Arguably, India has established

82 Ibid, 5.2.1.
83 Ibid, 5.2.1.1.
84 Ibid, 5.2.2.
85 Ibid, 5.2.3.1.
86 Ibid, 5.2.4.1.
87 Ibid, 5.2.6.
88 Ibid, 5.2.6.2, '(ii) Infusion of fresh foreign investment up to 49%, in accompany not seeking industrial license or which already has Government approval for FDI in Defence, shall require mandatory submission of a declaration with the Ministry of Defence in case change in equity /shareholding pattern or transfer of stake by existing investor to new foreign investor for FDI up to 49%, within 30 days of such change. Proposal for raising FDI beyond 49% from such companies will require Government approval. (iii) Licence applications will be considered by the Department for Promotion of Industry and Internal Trade, Ministry of Commerce & Industry, in consultation with Ministry of Defence and Ministry of External Affairs. (iv) Foreign investment in the sector is subject to security clearance by the Ministry of Home Affairs and as per guidelines of the Ministry of Defence. (v) Investee company should be structured to be self-sufficient in the areas of product design and development. The investee/joint venture company along with the manufacturing facility, should also have maintenance and life cycle support facility of the product being manufactured in India. (vi) Foreign Investments in the Defence Sector shall be subject to scrutiny on grounds of National

through its National Policy one of the most comprehensive and specific areas of FDI control compared to any other jurisdictions.

Central to the implementation of the earlier National Policy is the National Foreign Exchange Management Act 1999 (FEMA). The FEMA, in accordance with Section 2, defines:

> foreign security to mean any security, in the form of shares, stocks, bonds, debentures or any other instrument denominated or expressed in foreign currency and includes securities expressed in foreign currency, but where redemption or any form of return such as interest or dividends is payable in Indian currency.[89]

It is a broad definition largely focusing on key economic investment activity within the state. In other words, the FEMA facilitates transnational investment particularly foreign currency exchanges. It sets a level of controls for the Reserve Bank to have particular oversight of the export of goods.

Section 7 provides that every exporter of goods shall:

> furnish to the Reserve Bank or to such other authority a declaration in such form and in such manner as may be specified, containing true and correct material particulars, including the amount representing the full export value or, if the full export value of the goods is not ascertainable at the time of export, the value which the exporter, having regard to the prevailing market conditions, expects to receive on the sale of the goods in a market outside India.[90]

Most noteworthy is the threshold processes pertaining to authorised persons dealing in foreign exchanges. That is, the powers of the Reserve Bank extend to the oversea dealings in foreign exchanges by issuing specific authorisation.[91] Any authorisation provided can be revoked at any-time on public interest grounds, or where the authorised person has failed to comply with the conditions of the authorisation. The FEMA is specific to foreign exchange investments and is largely administrative by stablishing a framework for monitoring such investments by the Indian Reserve Bank. Thus, it is out of scope of this chapter to examine the FEMA any further. No different to the other states examined earlier, the globalisation of Indian business has been one of the major strategies adopted by Indian firms to withstand global competition.[92]

Security and Government reserves the right to review any foreign investment in the Defence Sector that affects or may affect national security'.

89 Foreign Exchange Management Act 1999, Section 2.

90 Ibid, Section 7.

91 Ibid, Section 10.

92 Beena Saraswathy. *The Globalisation of Indian Business: Cross-Border Mergers and Acquisitions in Indian Manufacturing*, Routledge (2018), 1.

5.4 Conclusion

This chapter has highlighted the significant influence foreign investment rules are having on current and future mergers and acquisitions (takeovers), as an alternative to cross-border insolvency. Centrally, there is a continued push to implement the universalist approach to cross-border insolvency, and as a by-product, cross-border restructuring has benefited from this transnational model.

The respective mergers and acquisitions laws are generally similar. All jurisdictions treat MA as a form of anti-competitive behaviour, and therefore, have imposed multi-layered approaches to assessing whether an MA will be approved or otherwise.

More pervasively, states have made continual attempts to regulate foreign investment in the framework of the broader cross-border regime, for example the old Treaties of Friendship, Commerce and Navigation.[93] What is more challenging is the fact that such efforts have largely failed. This continued dilemma is that the regulation of foreign investment within the international trade legal framework is still located very much on the peripheral. Carlos Espluhues argues that foreign investment has long been a subject of controversy and conflicting approaches, and are treated as peripheral.[94] The response by states, even before COVID-19 outbreak and a direct consequence of the pandemic, is a heightened sense of controversy and concern. Espluhues makes the point that, as a matter of principle, provision for access to foreign investment cannot be fully developed if states shy away from dependence on it.[95]

Importantly, what has emerged is states placing greater emphasis on the achievement of certain legitimate domestic policy objectives. States are increasingly concerned about the risk of international investment law placing undue constraints on their sovereign regulatory powers, and have attempted to respond to this situation in various ways.[96] These concerns have given way to changes in the level of protection imposed on cross-border MA. The preservation of the host state's 'public order', 'public security', 'national essential security interests' or similar notions are gaining importance.[97] For Espluhues, the spread of foreign investment screening raises complex but well justified concerns. Firstly, from an economic standpoint, in the long term, their increasing popularity will most likely affect the freedom to invest. Increasingly, as states look inwards, the freedom to invest will be curtailed. Secondly, this approach today demonstrates a winding back of the liberal approach to foreign investment in recent decades. Third, the increasingly inward and nationalist approach to foreign investment threatens to undermine the ability

93 Carlos Espluhues, *Foreign Investment, Strategic Assets and National Security*, Inertia (2018), 24–27.
94 Ibid.
95 Ibid.
96 Ibid, 25.
97 Ibid, 63.

for entities to embrace an alternative to cross-border insolvency, through cross-border restructuring.

Conversely, the balance of policy objectives by states in response to a major pandemic and rising global inflation, is warranted to ensure that individuals and entities are not subject to predatory investment activities leading to a convergence of investment capital in elite hands. Thus, the ongoing challenge for states is to balance the international investment landscape, not so much with a legal framework that allows for MA, but by foreign investment rules that shape what and who can invest transnationally.

The decline in economic activity economic, political, social and human shocks globally, is likely to result in governments further tightening foreign investment rules. Therefore, the current rule, particularly the concept of national security, could be expanded to include such areas as the environment, migration, biochemicals, amongst others.

6

CLOSE-OUT NETTING (ARRANGEMENTS) PART 1

Close-out netting provisions have become a quiet achiever and not often discussed due to their functioning primarily through agreements between parties with limited statutory regulation and oversight. However, close-out netting is being added to the already comprehensive insolvency (cross-border) and risk management legal frameworks, particularly in the area of international finance. This chapter will examine the characteristics of close-out netting, and the regulatory approach adopted by the jurisdictions examined throughout this book. The chapter also stresses the need to develop a more uniform model of close-out netting.

Close-out netting already plays a vital role in minimising the risk of losing billions, and even trillions of dollars in cross-border transactions. They are not new and have been used in large financial contacts for many years. However, they have grown in importance and in 2013, the International Institute for the Unification of Private Law (UNIDROIT)established its Principles on Close-out netting. These Principles have since been reinforced by the International Swaps and Derivatives Association[1] and the Financial Stability Board.[2]

This chapter will examine the 2013 UNIDROIT Principles on close out netting provisions, and key areas of divergence among jurisdictions in adopting them. The chapter will also propose further transnational reform directed at greater harmonisation.

1 The legal enforceability of the close-out netting provisions of the ISDA Master Agreement and their consequences for netting on financial statements, International Swaps and Derivatives Association. See Appendix 1 for a comprehensive overview of the role close-out netting provisions have within ISDA Master Agreements.

2 EBF Response to FSB Consultation: Solvent Wind-down of Derivatives and Trading Portfolios, https://www.fsb.org/wp-content/uploads/EBF-2.pdf.

DOI: 10.4324/9781003311874-9

6.1 Introduction

Close-out netting provisions are a relatively new addition to the finance regulatory framework.[3] However, close-out netting practices, as legal mechanisms and tools of insolvency, date back to the beginning of commercial relations and property rights.[4] They are also, effective tools in times of economic and geopolitical instability arising such global health hazards.

The early history of insolvency law provides some fundamental implications that netting and setoff can have in promoting efficiency in today's financial markets.[5] For the purposes of this chapter, close-out netting provisions is referred to as netting, netting arrangements or netting provisions. In essence, close-out netting is a process for reducing exposure to risk on an open contract, should one party declares insolvency. A close-out netting agreement does not ordinarily apply to restructuring. In effect, such contracts are often entered into in financial markets through agreements that require the parties to account for their losses and profits and to pay compensation to the extent of that net loss to the party or parties who would otherwise sustain that loss.

Such close-out netting agreements have provided a level of legal harmonisation and convergence in the law of international finance, based on a patchwork of informal regulatory networks that comprise both public and private entities. International bodies, such as the International Organization of Securities Commissions (IOSCO), the Basel Committee on Banking Regulation, Financial Stability Board, the International Association of Insurance Supervisor (IAIS), the International Accounting Standards Board (IASB), and the International Swaps and Derivatives Association (ISDA) promulgate best practices and standards as informal means of regulating netting arrangements.[6] While not often discussed, their importance in providing effective resolution to parties under financial stress, makes a significant contribution to stabilising a critical sector of the global economy.

3 Robert Walters, Leon Trakman, The Fragmented Approach toward Close-Out Netting Provisions in Australia, Indonesia, Malaysia and Singapore Compared, *Journal of Banking Regulation* (2019), 1. This chapter draws upon the earlier work of Robert Walters and Leon Trakman related to close-out netting provisions. Robert Walters, *Close-out netting Provisions – Their Current Value in a Time of International Uncertainty,* International Company and Commercial Law Review – Sweet & Maxwell (2020).

4 William Bergman, Robert Bliss, Christian Johnson, George Kaufman Netting, *Financial Contracts, and Banks: The Economic Implications, Research in Financial Services,* Federal Reserve Bank of Chicago, WP 2004–02 (2003), 4.

5 Ibid.

6 See Abraham Newman, David Bach, The European Union as Hardening Agent: Soft Law and the Diffusion of Global Financial Regulation, *Journal of European Public Policy*, Vol. 21, No. 3 (2014), 430–452. This soft law regime is striking in its thin degree of institutionalization and widespread reliance on voluntary compliance. Nevertheless, such soft law standards have diffused widely and are shaping market dynamics.

Most noteworthy are the various types of netting arrangements that have been accepted and adopted by the financial and related sectors. They have created a structure within which a mutual settlement can be arranged between debtors and creditors. The reality is that many netting agreements provide that, once a net balance has been determined under the close-out netting provision, that 'net amount is available for contractual set-off by the non-defaulting party against other amounts due between the parties that are outside the scope of the netting agreement'.[7] Such netting arrangements are separate from and subsequent to the operation of the close-out netting provision within a general contract.[8] Nevertheless, the term netting is used generally and somewhat lazily, to 'refer to all forms of the concepts below, as well as to collateral enforceability'.[9] These different 'formulations should be regarded as loose financial vernacular'.[10] Put another way, at its most central point, netting involves the contractual cancellation of rights and obligations and their replacement with a single amount. The result has been the development of a number of different netting instruments, including payment netting[11] (in some states referred to as settlement netting[12]), netting by novation,[13] balance-sheet netting,[14] market-to-market,[15] and finally a pricing or valuing of interest rate

7 ISDA – 2018, *ISDA Model Netting Act and Guide*, file:///C:/Users/ROB/Documents/Books%20-%20Journals/2018-isda-model-netting-act-and-guide-7237164-readkong-com.pdf, 12.
8 Ibid.
9 Akber Datoo, *Legal Data for Banking: Business Optimization and Regulatory Compliance*, Wiley, Chichester, United Kingdom (2019), 105.
10 ISDA – 2018, *ISDA Model Netting Act and Guide,* file:///C:/Users/ROB/Documents/Books%20-%20Journals/2018-isda-model-netting-act-and-guide-7237164-readkong-com.pdf, 12.
11 See id, Payment Netting is often referred to as settlement netting. Under this type of netting, contracting parties undertake to accept the net performance of the other(s). It generally only applies to amounts (or deliveries) due on the same date and only if the payments are in the same currency (or the deliveries are of the same asset).
12 Aib's Memorandum of Law in Opposition to Citibank, N.A.'s Motion to Strike Aib's Demand for Trial by Jury, *ALLIED IRISH BANKS, P.L.C., Plaintiff, v. BANK OF AMERICA, N.A. and Citibank, N.A., Defendants. Bank of America, N.A. and Citibank, N.A., Counterclaim and Third-Party Plaintiffs, v. Allied Irish Banks, P.L.C., Counterclaim Defendant, and M&T Bank Corporation and Manufacturers and Traders Trust Company, Third-Party Defendants.* No. 03 Civ. 3478 (DAB) (GWG). 2012, 16.
13 Akber Datoo, *Legal Data for Banking: Business Optimization and Regulatory Compliance*, Chichester, Wiley, West Sussex, United Kingdom (2019), 101. Novation Netting is a contractual mechanism under which the contracting parties agree that all contracts between them shall be consolidated into a single contract as soon as each new contract is entered into. Each new contract is effectively combined with the existing contract.
14 Ibid, 101. Balance sheet netting, refers to the offsetting of financial liabilities and assets in the balance sheet if the criteria for offsetting have been met. On-balance-sheet netting can also apply in relation to repo transactions and securities, or commodities lending or borrowing transactions.
15 Ibid, 103. The market-to-market value of a contract defines the net value of all future payments and/or deliveries involved in that contract. It is therefore the amount that would have to be paid, or which would be received, if the contract were terminated and replaced with an equivalent contract, involving identical rights and obligations for the period remaining outstanding at current market rates.

swap.[16] However, close-out netting should be distinguished from payment netting.[17] Payment netting takes place during the normal business of a solvent firm: it involves combining off-setting cash flow obligations between two parties on a given day in a given currency into a single net payable or receivable. Two of the most common types of netting provisions that are used include bilateral and multilateral netting arrangements.

On the one side, bilateral arrangements relate to financial contracts concluded between two counterparties.[18] The process of closing out, along with settlement netting, is equally important in both bilateral and centrally interposed scenarios. Under such arrangements, the 'bilateral process interposes the central entity between the parties to every financial contract'.[19] It further allows for the calculation of exposure. In other words, the net risk exposure is calculated on a bilateral basis, so that each participant's exposure exists exclusively against the central entity. This applies to both regular business scenarios (settlement netting mechanisms), and to the default situation, where close-out netting arrangements can be implemented to manage and minimise financial risk. Thus, from a legal point of view, central clearing remains strictly bilateral, and considerations in respect of bilateral settlement generally apply to central clearing.[20]

On the other side, multibranch netting becomes important where the parties have several branches in jurisdictions other than at their head office. Therefore, a netting agreement may extend to the entirety of financial contracts entered into (with the same counterparty) by the head office and its foreign branches.[21] Branches, as opposed to subsidiaries, are not legally independent from the head office, but form part of the same legal entity. As long as a multi-branch entity is not insolvent, 'multi-branch netting would be recognised in the same extent as is netting generally'.[22] What is significant under these netting arrangements is the fact that, as soon as a 'multi-branch party becomes insolvent, everything will depend on whether there is a single insolvency proceeding, or, whether there are separate proceedings over some

16 Ibid, 104. Bank A has 5,000 trades with Bank B. Some may be of positive value to Bank A ('in-the-money' – Bank A would need to pay a third party to replace Bank B on the other side), whereas the others are negative in value to Bank A ('out-of-the-money' – a third party would pay Bank A to replace Bank B on the other side). If Bank B is not performing (is failing to make payments due under the various trades), then we will usually want to replace them. Typically, we want to close out all of our transactions with them and make a claim on our counterparty's estate for what is owed.

17 ISDA – 2018, *ISDA Model Netting Act and Guide*, file:///C:/Users/ROB/Documents/Books%20-%20Journals/2018-isda-model-netting-act-and-guide-7237164-readkong-com.pdf, 1.3, 1.

18 Philipp Paech, *The Need for an International Instrument on the Enforceability of Close-out Netting in General and in the Context of Bank Resolution*, UNIDROIT Study Group on principles and rules on the netting of financial instruments, UNIDROIT 2011 S78C – Doc. 2 Original: English, March 2011, First Meeting Rome, 18–21 April 2011, 14–15.

19 Ibid.

20 Ibid.

21 Ibid.

22 Ibid.

or all the branches'.[23] However, a third element to netting is what is commonly referred to as multilateral. Importantly, the distinction between multibranch and multilateral is how these netting arrangements deal with a specific situation.

While not often understood, a 'multibranch arrangement can be applied to payment systems in which a number of independent financial market participants compute their mutual exposure on a multilateral basis, employing functionalities similar to those used in close-out netting, capped by a system of mutual cross-assignments'.[24]

The problem with this is that parties can use a 'multilateral approach to delineate the exposure of one market participant in relation to a multitude of others'.[25] More problematic are the contractual and legal complexities associated with these netting arrangements. In particular, 'the contractual agreement is highly complex, using a system of mutual cross-assignments and cross-guarantees'.[26] Secondly, the recognition of a multilateral netting agreement by the applicable insolvency law depends on whether netting in general and multilateral netting in particular are legally recognised. Thirdly, to the extent that cross-assignments are only agreed to on an ad hoc basis in the event of default of one party, the insolvency administrator may subsequently avoid these agreements.[27] Fourthly, in a cross-border situation, the 'applicable insolvency laws may exacerbate the aforementioned difficulties'.[28] However, and more problematic is the ability to enforce and the enforcement approach that is available under these arrangements. Thus, the enforceability of netting arrangements is fundamentally important to prevent parties from circumventing their legal requirements, particularly when the insolvency of one party is involved. More specifically, determining the scope of a multilateral netting agreement depends on whether and how netting in general and multilateral netting in particular are recognised under the insolvency law of different jurisdictions. An international regime that regulates close-out netting arrangements that is not recognised and enforced under the law in which one party to insolvency proceedings is located, renders the application of that arrangement ineffective. What is necessary is a multilateral legal

23 Ibid. see also United Nations Commission on International trade Law [UNCITRAL] Model Law on Cross-Border Insolvency, in particular Article 20.

24 Philipp Paech, *The Need for an International Instrument on the Enforceability of Close-out Netting in General and in the Context of Bank Resolution*, UNIDROIT Study Group on principles and rules on the netting of financial instruments, UNIDROIT 2011 S78C – Doc. 2 Original: English, March 2011, First Meeting Rome, 18–21 April 2011, 16. Paech highlights the following example of multilateral netting in operation. A-Bank, B-Bank and C-Bank conclude a multilateral netting agreement under which claims existing on a bilateral basis are replaced by net claims calculated on a multilateral basis. At a given point in time, A owes EUR 20 to B; B owes EUR 60 to C; and C owes EUR 40 to A. Following their agreement and after cross-assignment and computation, these claims are to be settled by A paying nothing, B paying EUR 40 to C, and C paying EUR 20 to A.

25 Ibid, 16.

26 Ibid.

27 Ibid.

28 Ibid.

regime that transcends legal divergence among state laws in regulating and enforcing multilateral netting arrangements. Multibranch netting arrangements need to be dealt according to the specific rules governing their enforceability in the applicable jurisdiction and according to the ISDA Master Agreement. This is primarily required where a branch of a bank is located in different countries and has entered into more than one transaction.

6.2 Harmonising Multilateral Netting Arrangements

As mentioned earlier in this chapter, there has been a recent shift towards international harmonisation in relation to close-out netting provisions. This has successfully been achieved by the implementation of the UNIDROIT establishing Principles on the Operation of Close-out netting Provisions.[29] Central to understanding the history and operation of the UNIDROIT Principles is to trace them back to their origins. They originated 'a decade ago in which the General Assembly of UNIDROIT approved the work programme for the development of an international instrument on netting'.[30] In 2011, a paper was released highlighting the need for an international instrument on the enforceability of close-out netting.[31] That paper stressed the importance of netting arrangements and that an international regulatory approach was long overdue. In calling for greater harmonisation, the Report identified a major gap in the regulatory responses adopted by states to stabilise financial markets around the world. The Report argued that:

> There existed a significant difference between countries in their understanding of the concept of netting and also in devising concrete legal mechanism to protect the enforceability of netting arrangements in cases of insolvency. Incompatible laws enforcing netting among regulatory regimes can have a particularly destabilising effect on trans-border netting. The threat of states adopting different netting principles and mechanisms can potentially nullify the very operation of multinational netting arrangements. A satisfactory solution cannot be achieved merely by clarifying rules of private international law.[32]

29 UNIDROIT Principles on the Operation of Close-out Netting Provisions which were adopted by the UNIDROIT Governing Council at its 92nd session, Rome, 8–10 May 2013.

30 Ibid. 67th Session in Rome (1 December 2010).

31 Philipp Paech, *The Need for an International Instrument on the Enforceability of Close-out Netting in General and in the Context of Bank Resolution*, UNIDROIT Study Group on principles and rules on the netting of financial instruments, UNIDROIT 2011 S78C – Doc. 2 Original: English, March 2011, First Meeting Rome, 18–21 April 2011.

32 Ibid, 38–39.

The Report underscored the need for states to meet the international objective of ensuring legal convergence and harmonisation in regulating multilateral netting arrangements. This entailed a preliminary inquiry, namely, to determine whether there is any pre-existing consensus over the meaning of close-out netting.

As a general definition:

> close-out netting is a process intended to reduce exposures on open contracts should one party should become insolvent, or should a like event occur before the settlement date. Consistent with this definition, applicable agreement typically provides that, on an event of default in relation to one party, the other party can terminate all outstanding contracts between the parties, calculate the losses and gains on each contract, and then set them off, leaving only the outstanding balance owing. These losses and gains are usually the difference between the agreed price of each transaction in issue and the market price at termination, essentially being compensation for the termination calculated on damages principles. The contract ordinarily provides that the parties will account to each other for losses and gains. Such contracts are routinely provided for in financial markets and other related sectors.[33]

The notion of reducing an entity's exposure in open contracts is best summarised as a means of reducing or minimising financial risks to other parties, should one party become insolvent. The benefit of netting provisions in such agreements is twofold. First, they mitigate both 'counterparty risk on particular transactions' (credit risk) and 'systemic risk to the entire financial system' (systemic risk).[34] Second, in taking these benefits one step further, netting arrangements minimise 'exposures on open contracts if one party should become insolvent or a like event occurs before the settlement date'.[35] Thus, netting provisions provide parties with greater security to maximise their profits from such financial arrangements. In doing so, 'close-out netting is also conceived as expanding upon global wealth by both stabilising and increasing the volume of such transactions for the common good'.[36] However, the risk to netting parties and to public interests may be considerable because of estimates that netting arrangements reduce total credit

33 Ibid, 1.

34 Vincent Johnson, International Financial Law: The Case against Close-out Netting, *Boston University International Law Journal,* Vol. 33 (2015), 395–418. See also – Robert Bliss, George Kaufman, *Derivatives and Systemic Risk: Netting, Collateral, and Closeout*, Federal Reserve Bank Chicago, WP-2005–03 (2005), 3. Rizwaan J. Mokal, Liquidity, Systemic Risk, and the Bankruptcy Treatment of Financial Contracts, *Brooklyn Journal of Corporate, Financial & Commercial Law*, Vol. 10 (2015). Ole Böger, Close-out Netting Provisions in Private International Law and International Insolvency Law (Part II), *Uniform Law Review*, Vol. 18, No. 3–4 (December 2013), 532–563.

35 Ibid, 110–116.

36 Ibid.

risk by as much as 85%.[37] Viewed this way, the benefits of enforcing netting provisions by operation of law outweighs the absence of law which so provides. In the contemporary world, and in the absence of netting provisions, 'liquidity problems can lead to solvency problems [and a] relatively small shock can cause liquidity to dry up and create [a] financial cris[i]s'.[38] The point is that risk minimisation from the adoption and implementation of netting arrangements cannot be underestimated. While there is no concrete statistical data to demonstrate whether such arrangements reduce risk exposure by a specified percentage, Akber Atoo maintains that risk pertaining to OTC derivatives that rely on netting arrangements has been reduced by more than 85%.[39] His estimation is significant in reinforcing the argument that close-out netting arrangements are extremely significant in further stabilising the trans-border financial sector. However, further research is needed to more accurately understand the role that netting play in minimising risk contagion.

More pervasively, the study undertaken by Philipp Paech demonstrates that general domestic law, particularly in the areas of commercial and insolvency law, 'fails to provide sound and predictable legal results in cross-jurisdictional cases dealing with the enforceability of netting in insolvency'.[40] In so arguing, he highlights the areas in need of harmonisation, and more broadly, legal convergence:

1) 'the definition of netting;
2) the legal mechanism protecting netting in insolvency;
3) the lists of eligible parties and eligible financial contracts;
4) formal requirements; and finally; and
5) the relevant conflict-of-laws rules'.[41]

Therefore, this chapter will assess whether the jurisdictions studied have adopted these requirements in whole or part. The ensuing chapters will also recommend further possible reform at both national and international levels.

37 Ibid, 407. Netting arrangements enable parties to derivative contracts to avoid future fluctuations in value by closing out their positions when a counterparty becomes insolvent.

38 Ibid, Johnson further argues that systemic risk occurs where market participants are exposed to each other's failure in such a way that the inability of one financial market participant to meet its obligations due will cause other participants to fail to meet their obligations when due.

39 Akber Datoo, *Legal Data for Banking: Business Optimization and Regulatory Compliance*, Wiley, Chichester, West Sussex, United Kingdom (2019), 103.

40 Philipp Paech, *The Need for an International Instrument on the Enforceability of Close-out Netting in General and in the Context of Bank Resolution*, UNIDROIT Study Group on principles and rules on the netting of financial instruments, UNIDROIT 2011 S78C – Doc. 2 Original: English, March 2011, First Meeting Rome, 18–21 April 2011.

41 Ibid.

6.2.1 Definition

Beginning with the definition of close-out netting arrangements, Principle 2 of the UNIDROIT Principles on the Operation of Close-out netting Provision – defines close-out netting provisions:

> A 'Close-out netting provision' mean a contractual provision on the basis of which, upon the occurrence of an event predefined in the provision in relation to a party to the contract, the obligations owed by the parties to each other that are covered by the provision, whether or not they are at that time due and payable, are automatically or at the election of one of the parties reduced to or replaced by a single net obligation, whether by way of novation, termination or otherwise, representing the aggregate value of the combined obligations, which is thereupon due and payable by one party to the other.[42]

Central to this definition, close-out netting is very similar to a process known as insolvency set-off.[43] The rule of insolvency set-off provides that, before a company goes into liquidation, an account must be taken of what is due from each party to the other in respect of their mutual dealings, and that the sums due from one party must be set off against the sums due from the other, even if the sums are not yet due, are contingent or need to be ascertained.[44] Netting arrangements achieve the same or a very similar result. However, netting arrangements are based on a contract between the parties, whereas the insolvency set-off rule is determined by mandatory law.[45] Phillip Paech elaborates that, 'when a bank or other participant in the financial market takes a risk and expose themselves to counterparty's insolvency, and that risk materializes, netting arrangements perform an important function. They reduce the risk of a party being exposed to the insolvency of a counterparty'.[46] Secondly, the concept of termination becomes important in enabling a party to terminate a contract, while the risk of financial instability could still be regulated effective. Failure to do so could result in greater financial instability, not only for the parties, but also for the financial market in issue.

42 International Institute for Unification of Private Law, *Principles on the Operations of Close-out Netting*, https://www.unidroit.org/instruments/capital-markets/netting. Principle 2.

43 Philipp Paech, Close-out Netting, Insolvency Law and Conflict-of Laws, *Journal of Corporate Law Studies*, Vol. 14, No. 2 (October 2014), 419–452.

44 Ibid.

45 Ibid.

46 Philipp Paech, *The Need for an International Instrument on the Enforceability of Close-out Netting in General and in the Context of Bank Resolution*, UNIDROIT Study Group on principles and rules on the netting of financial instruments, UNIDROIT 2011 S78C – Doc. 2 Original: English, March 2011, First Meeting Rome, 18–21 April 2011.

In responding to related financial risks, the Basel Cross-Border Bank Resolution Group (BCBRG) maintained that unrestricted close-out netting enforced by a bank might, under certain circumstances, constitute a significant additional threat to the stability of the financial market.[47] Thus, automatic termination and close out of non-performed contracts upon the occurrence of an enforcing event potentially exacerbate the harm arising from market destabilisation. In addressing this concern, it was noted that acceleration, aggregation and valuation underpin the general definition of netting arrangements in relation to termination orders.[48] However, these arrangements can vary. Efforts to reconcile netting arrangements and termination orders can be undertaken by either a valuation of each obligation or the aggregation of all values, to constitute one net payment obligation. Doing so, can result in an accelerated net obligation or the creation of a new payment obligation representing the overall value. Therefore, it will be important to confirm whether the jurisdictions examined have designed their respective laws to accommodate these practical steps in accordance with the definition of close-out netting. Importantly, any divergence from the generally agreed international definition, regardless of the extent of that divergence, only continues to pose problems to the continued internationalisation of netting regulation and arrangement. This problem persists, even though in practice, the ISDA Master agreements have been adopted largely consistently.

6.2.2 Legal Mechanism Protecting Insolvency

The operation of close-out netting provisions in accordance with UNIDROIT Principle 6, encourages states to develop national laws in which netting provisions are enforceable. It also encourages that, 'in national law, more than one obligation is covered by netting arrangement; however if they are either invalid, unenforceable or ineligible, their operation should not be affected by those other obligation that are valid, enforceable and eligible'.[49] Additionally, the Principle 6 specifies that:

> The Principles do not render enforceable a close-out netting provision, or an eligible obligation, that would otherwise be unenforceable in whole or in part on grounds of fraud or conflict with other requirements of general application affecting the validity or enforceability of contracts.[50]

Furthermore, Principle 7 expands on the general approach taken earlier under Principle 6 by specifically accounting for insolvency. Therefore, central to the

47 Ibid, 40.

48 Ibid.

49 International Institute for Unification of Private Law, *Principles on the Operations of Close-out Netting* (2013), https://www.unidroit.org/instruments/capital-markets/netting, Principle 6.

50 Ibid.

issues surrounding the operation of insolvency, Principle 7 ensures that any netting arrangements which are present within agreements or contracts that are subject to insolvency are dealt with in a way that parties to the insolvency can resolve any matters. Under Principle 7(1), it is required that, subject to Principle 8 and in addition to Principle 6, the law of the implementing State should ensure that upon the commencement of an insolvency proceeding, or in the context of a resolution regime in relation to a party to a close-out netting provision:

(a) the operation of the close-out netting provision is not stayed;
(b) the insolvency administrator, court or resolution authority should not be allowed to demand from the other party performance of any of the obligations covered by the close-out netting provision while rejecting the performance of any obligation owed to the other party that is covered by the close-out netting provision;
(c) the mere entering into and operation of the close-out netting provision as such should not constitute grounds for the avoidance of the close-out netting provision on the basis that it is deemed inconsistent with the principle of equal treatment of creditors; and
(d) the operation of the close-out netting provision, and the inclusion of any obligation in the calculation of the single net obligation under the close-out netting provision, should not be restricted merely because the close-out netting provision was entered into, an obligation covered by the provision arose or the single net obligation under the close-out netting provision became due and payable during a prescribed period before, or on the day of but before, the commencement of the proceeding.[51]

This is a coercive yet cooperative provision that reinforces the importance of national laws, and captures the principles, concepts and elements that facilitate closing out under insolvency and resolution. It allows for insolvency proceedings to be administered so that the process provides a way forward. That said, Principle 7(2) goes on to provide that the 'overall principles themselves do not affect a partial or total restriction on the operation of a close-out netting provision under the insolvency law of the implementing State. In addition to those referred to in sub-paragraphs (c) and (d), it addresses such further factors as knowledge of a pending insolvency proceeding at the time the close-out netting provision was entered into or the obligation arose; the ranks categories of claims; and avoiding transaction that defraud creditors'.[52] Thus, the UNIDROIT Principles[53] have ensured that, in order to minimise instability in financial markets following an insolvency,

51 Ibid, Principle 7.
52 Ibid.
53 Ibid.

netting arrangements would not be restricted or limited in their use. In other words, they would continue to operate and allow a party to close out transactional and contractual arrangements. Moreover, insolvency proceedings under the UNIDROIT Principles encompass a combination of judicial or administrative proceedings, including an interim proceeding, in which the assets and affairs of the debtor are subject to control or supervision by a court. The UNIDROIT Principles also extend to judicial and administrative proceedings that cover both liquidation and reorganisation, as defined by the UNCITRAL Legislative Guide on Insolvency Law that provides for:

> Liquidation proceedings to sell and dispose of assets for distribution to creditors in accordance with the insolvency law; and 'reorganization' is the process by which the financial well-being and viability of a debtor's business can be restored and the business continue to operate, using various means, possibly including debt forgiveness, debt rescheduling, debt-equity conversions and sale of the business (or parts of it) as a going concern.[54]

Viewed this way, the UNCITRAL's reference to debt extends to cross-border insolvency matters. Of greater importance, the UNCITRAL 2004 Legislative Guide on Insolvency Law promotes the idea of sustaining relationships to avoid insolvency. It does so through the concept of reorganisation which constitutes the process by which the financial well-being and viability of a debtor's business can be restored and continue to operate. The UNCITRAL Guide on Insolvency Law proposes various means to accomplish these objectives, including debt forgiveness, debt rescheduling, debt-equity conversions and sale of the business (or parts of it) as a going concern. The Guide also proposes that a reorganisation plan be established, whereby the financial well-being and viability of the debtor's business can be restored.[55] What is not clear is whether this plan extends to restructuring. It is arguable that, a reorganisation plan could constitute a restructure in that restructuring is an important means of regulating insolvent parties, such as through mergers and acquisitions. Restructuring a debtor's business also reinforces the value of netting arrangements, as tools of contracts, in relation to insolvency. Therefore, the ability to control the ability for parties to cherry pick elements of the contract by debtors, is a process to ensure the contract continues to be read in its entirety. Principle 7(1)(b) of the UNIDROIT applies to cherry picking. It states:

> In an insolvency proceeding, the insolvency administrator or court may have the right to 'cherry pick' from the insolvent party's non-performed contracts.

54 Ibid, United Nations Commission on International Trade Law, 2004 Legislative Guide on Insolvency Law, Glossary (u) (kk) p. 6–7.
55 Ibid.

> This refers to the right to require any counterparty to perform those contracts that are favourable to the insolvent estate while rejecting those that are unfavourable to it. If it were possible to cherry pick among a netting set, the bundle of transactions would be disassembled and the solvent party would be required to perform its obligations under all the transactions that were unfavourable from its perspective, whereas the insolvency administrator would not perform the obligations under the favourable transactions – ultimately, the solvent party would be exposed to the full counterparty risk. Cherry picking is essentially contrary to the characteristics of a single relationship as set out supra (cf. key considerations in respect of Principle 4). Furthermore, cherry picking disproportionately increases the counterparty risk for the other party and should not, therefore, be available to the insolvency administrator.[56]

Notwithstanding this, a resolution agreement, as a means by which parties can plan for regulating debts through their contracts, arguably has distinct benefits. It enables the parties to regulate their relationships, including the repayment of debts to avert insolvency or participate in insolvency proceedings. It also enables the parties to avoid disputes over trans-border debts leading to, or following, insolvency. Failing that, it provides the parties with dispute resolution options, such as by resort to international commercial arbitration. This allows the parties to resolve their disputes through a process that sustains their business relationship. As an illustrated benefit, initiating a stay can enable a failing financial institution to continue with, or wind down its operations in an orderly fashion that mitigate risks of financial instability. This ability to stay proceedings is especially valuable in sustaining financial operations when there are large amounts of money involved in multiple transactions. That is often the case when multiple transactions are undertaken through ISDA Master Agreements.[57] While it is well understood that contractual arrangements, such as ISDA Master Agreements, are likely to render netting provisions enforceable, such enforceability is less clear in relation to insolvency due to the divergence among states enforceability.

Robert Bliss and George Kaufman highlight that enforceability in both netting (or more generally, set off) and as collateral are based on legal concepts with long histories in commercial and private property law.[58] They elaborate that legislation and common-law developments have enhanced these concepts, notably in applying them in derivative markets and payments systems. While cross jurisdictional

56 International Institute for Unification of Private Law, *Principles on the Operations of Close-out Netting* (2013), https://www.unidroit.org/instruments/capital-markets/netting, Principle 7(1)(b), paragraph, 125–127.

57 See Appendix I.

58 Robert Bliss, George Kaufman, Derivatives and Systemic Risk: Netting, Collateral, and Closeout, *Journal of Financial Stability* (2006), 55–70.

disparities remain in the treatment of netting and collateral by contracts, there is widespread consistency in the treatment of netting and collateral associated with derivative contracts in many jurisdictions.[59] More recently, close-out netting permits the immediate or at least early termination of contracts under certain conditions, such as under the ISDA Master Agreements. These provisions for early termination and enforcement play an important role in protecting, not only the financial parties to these agreements, but the financial markets that are directly impacted by such enforcement. That is, the contractual arrangements could involve hundreds of thousands or millions of dollars at any one time. Therefore, they form a component of these contracts that allow for the overall contract to be enforced. As a result, the conditions governing termination, such as under the ISDA Master Agreements, are critical to the efficient functioning of financial derivatives markets. They are also necessary to prevent the failure of any one or more large firms from extending to other firms, leading to a systemic breakdown of those impacted institutions.[60] However, and while there is a general consensus on a regulatory response, both nationally and internationally, the current approach is far from coherent.

In reinforcing this, netting arrangements play an important role prior to and during an insolvency. They are applied to a solvent party and generally will be enforceable. On the other side, when an insolvency has commenced, netting arrangements become even more important in reducing the counterparty's risk from materialising. Therefore, netting serve an important role in the early termination of relevant contracts between the parties. The result is to provide the basis for a single net amount to be agreed upon. Consequently, the contract can be closed out. Yet, from time to time, the central role of netting in insolvency is contrary to other aims attributed to insolvency procedure itself, such as equal ranking of creditors, equal treatment, and coordinated management of assets. Thus, the end result, from the application of netting arrangements is to minimise the opportunity for avoidance of these provisions, or cherry picking by insolvent estates, requiring that a counterparty perform those contracts that are favourable to it.

6.2.3 Eligible Parties and Eligible Financial Contracts

It is generally accepted that banks, as financial market participants, are eligible parties in relation to close-out netting provisions, including enforcement. However, in the development of the UNIDROIT Principles, it was not clear whether other participants were intended to be included as eligible parties.[61] This includes, but not limited to insurance companies, investment firms, partnerships, investment

59 Ibid, 56.

60 Ibid.

61 International Institute for Unification of Private Law, *Principles on the Operations of Close-out Netting* (2013), https://www.unidroit.org/instruments/capital-markets/netting, Principle 3.

funds, hedge funds, proprietary traders, pension funds, central banks, public authorities and international financial institutions. At the international level, to reconcile this dichotomy between contract and insolvency law, the UNIDROIT Principles provide a level of certainty on to the parties.[62] Thus, Principle 1, along with Principle 3, incorporates the concept of eligible party. Principle 1 states that these 'Principles deal with the operation of close-out netting provisions that are entered into by eligible parties in respect of eligible obligations'.[63] Principle 1(2) adds that, except as otherwise expressly indicated in these Principles, the 'operation' of close-out netting provisions include:

> all aspects [of the operation], from the creation, validity, enforceability, effectiveness against third parties and admissibility in evidence of a close-out netting provision. This is predicated on the notion that all these aspects of an 'operation', especially in insolvency, are covered by the UNIDROIT Principles. Where the Principles seek to ensure the enforceability of close-out netting provisions, this concerns all these aspects, which can be summed up as the operation of the close-out netting provision. The term 'operation' of a close-out netting provision is therefore used throughout the Principles as a functional, shorthand reference to the various aspects described above and replaces the need to refer to the more specific terms which are not necessarily defined sufficiently precisely in an international context.[64]

Principle 3 extends Principle 1. It establishes that an eligible party includes both a commercial and a public party. It defines an eligible party' in the commercial sector to be:

> a qualifying financial market participant, including a bank, investment firm, professional market maker in financial instruments or other financial institution which (in each case) is subject to regulation or prudential supervision; insurance or reinsurance company; and undertaking for collective investment or an investment fund. It also extends that eligible party to a central counterparty or a payment, clearing or settlement system, or the operator of such a system which (in each case) is subject to regulation, oversight or prudential supervision; and a corporation or other entity that, according to criteria determined by the implementing State, is authorised or supervised as an important participant in the implementing State's markets in contracts giving rise to eligible obligations.[65]

62 Ibid, paragraph 17.
63 Ibid.
64 Ibid, paragraph 15.
65 Ibid, Principle 1.

The definition of 'eligible party' is expansive, yet selective. It includes a public authority that is either a governmental or other public entity, central bank, or, the Bank for International Settlements, a multilateral development bank, the International Monetary Fund (IMF) or any similar entity.[66] While the Principles accommodate larger organisations as eligible parties, in our view, it is not sufficiently flexible to include smaller to medium financial organisations. This is potentially problematic as emerging financial sectors and hubs, such as in India and Indonesia, are increasingly involved in transnational financial contracts. Such emerging markets are also expansive in scope, in being cybercentric in growth and capable of attracting eligible parties globally.

A number of factors reinforce the potential to absorb eligible parties operating internationally into insolvency proceedings. In reinforcing this absorption the process of 'financial internationalisation, computer and telecommunication technology has made it possible to use integrated financial system and programs to conduct highly complex financial transactions'.[67] There has also been an explosion in the immediate and systemic exploitation of available information that may be relevant to financial operations and that opens the market to additional smaller and medium sized players. Expanding classes of eligible parties in this manner enables a wider range of contracts to be taken into account in aggregating losses and gains. This assists in establishing the 'net amount' in close-out netting arrangements. Alternatively phrased, a default or insolvency, the close-out netting agreement typically provides that the 'solvent or non-defaulting party can terminate all outstanding contracts between the parties, calculate the losses and gains on each contract, and then set them off so that only a balance is owing'.[68] If the 'net amount', is positive for the insolvent estate, the solvent party must pay the balance. Thus, utilising close-out netting arrangements differs from solvent (common) set-off. On the one hand, a solvent set-off traditionally applies only to obligations of the same kind which are already due. On the other hand, the close-out netting arrangements are 'designed to aggregate the values of a multitude of contracts including multiple parties, that are still open and have variable contents'.[69] The ability to achieve such a result enables these multiple contracts to be addressed through this process all at once. That, in and of itself, provides for greater expediency.

66 Ibid, Principle 3. Paragraph 53–55. The definition of 'eligible parties' determines and restricts the scope of the Principles, in conjunction with the definition of 'eligible obligation'. Therefore, the application of the Principles to a legal relationship between two parties depends on whether both are eligible parties, and whether the relevant legal relationship represents an eligible obligation.

67 I. Pak, International Finance and State Sovereignty: Global Governance in the International Tax Regime, *Annual Survey of International & Comparative Law,* Vol. 10, No. 1 (2004), Article 7.

68 Ibid.

69 Philipp Paech, Close-out Netting, Insolvency Law and Conflict-of Laws, *Journal of Corporate Law Studies*, Vol. 14, No. 2 (October 2014), 425–426.

Regarding eligible financial products that are not specifically covered in the UNIDROIT Principles, they include derivative contracts that relate to securities or commodities. Some jurisdictions also allow for the inclusion of security interests, including non-title transfer collateral agreements and title-transfer collateral agreements. Additionally, agreements regarding the maintenance of financial instruments in accounts (intermediated securities), along with the safekeeping of physical securities. It is arguable that eligible financial contracts are capable of being broadened to include smaller and medium sized participants in financial markets, so long as the applicable contracts fall within the scope of the Principles. Consistent with this view, Principle 4 maintains that an:

> eligible obligation includes those arising from a contract of any of the following kinds between eligible parties, at least one of which is a public authority or a qualifying financial market participant. Therefore, eligible obligations arise from financial agreements and instruments that extend to derivative (options, forwards, futures, swaps) contracts for differences and any other transaction in respect of an underlying or reference asset.[70]

Those contracts also encompass 'repurchase agreements, securities lending agreements and any other securities financing transaction, in each case in respect of securities, money market instruments or units in an undertaking for collective investment or an investment fund'.[71] It is these contracts that pervade the banking and financial sector, helping to facilitate millions and sometimes billions of dollars in international transactions daily and weekly. Without netting having a role in performing these contracts, regional and global financial sectors would be subject to even greater levels of vulnerability than prevails at present.

The UNIDROIT Principles have construed the provisions for eligible contracts further to those that:

> assist in facilitate the trade and transaction in collateral for the sale, purchase or delivery of securities, money market instruments, units in an undertaking for collective investment or an investment fund, currency of any country, territory or monetary union, gold, silver, platinum, palladium or other precious metals.[72]

70 International Institute for Unification of Private Law, *Principles on the Operations of Close-out Netting* (2013), https://www.unidroit.org/instruments/capital-markets/netting, Principle 4.

71 Ibid, Principle – Definition of Eligible Obligation.

72 Ibid, (b) an obligation of an eligible party (whether by way of surety or as principal debtor) to perform an obligation of another person which is an eligible obligation under sub-paragraph (a); (c) a single net obligation determined under a close-out netting provision entered into by the same parties in respect of obligations under sub-paragraph (a) or (b). (2) An implementing State may elect to broaden the scope of paragraph (1)(a) in one or both of the following ways: (a) by providing that it is

By and large, this broad provision for contracts embodied in Principle 4, cover most, if not all parties that deal with large scale investment transactions across multiple countries. In further support, these provisions have become central mechanisms in terminating a course of dealings between parties to general agreements, and ISDA Master Agreements (see Appendix 1).[73] Moreover, these provisions serve as key contractual means of accelerating obligations in closing-out future dealings between parties.[74] Specifically, these provisions provide that, on default by one contracting party, the time for the performance of obligations reverts to the time of default, leading to the conversion of non-cash obligations into debts, and to set-off obligations.[75] The flexibility of Principle 4, is also central to the UNIDROIT Principles on close-out netting in which banks and financial institutions are located in multiple jurisdictions. In many cases, these institutions have branches in many, if not all major economic and trading countries.

Arguably, contract law, at least in common and civil law systems, has largely converged to account for most, if not all contractual performance obligations and breach. A good example of such contracts is the ISDA Master Agreements that are based on a blend of common and civil law embodied in the UNIDROIT Principles. The relationship between the ISDA Master Agreements and the UNIDROIT Principles is reinforced by Paragraph (1)(c) of Principle 4. It provides that 'obligations arising as single net obligations under the close-out netting mechanism of a master agreement are likewise eligible obligations that allow close-out netting to take effect under master-master agreements. These include, among others, agreements under which there are several master agreements covered by another master agreement providing for the netting of the single net obligation arising under the covered master agreement'.[76] These types of obligations generally arise '(1)(c) only to the extent that the covered master agreements have been concluded by the same parties and in respect of obligations covered by paragraphs (1)(a) and (b) eligible obligations between eligible parties, at least one of which is a public authority or a qualifying financial market participant, or obligations assumed by eligible parties under a suretyship agreement as security for such an obligation'.[77] However, as netting arrangements continue to form essential clauses within financial contracts,

---

to extend to obligations arising under contracts between parties neither of whom is a public authority or a qualifying financial market participant; (b) by providing that it is to extend to obligations not limited to those listed in paragraph (1); subject, in either case, to such limitations or exceptions as the implementing State may specify.

73 Marco Giovanoli, Virtual Money and the Global Financial Market: Challenges for Lawyers, *Yearbook of International Financial and Economic Law* (1996), 16.

74 Vincent Johnson, International Financial Law: The Case against Close-out Netting, *Boston University International Law Journal,* Vol. 33 (2015), 101–125.

75 Ibid.

76 International Institute for Unification of Private Law, *Principles on the Operations of Close-out Netting* (2013), https://www.unidroit.org/instruments/capital-markets/netting, Principle 4. Paragraph 81.

77 Ibid.

further harmonisation across national legal systems is needed, as highlighted in the preceding chapters. In our view, apart from a consistent definition of close-out netting, another important area of the law in which harmonisation is most needed relates to the formal requirements associated with the conflict of laws.

6.2.4 Formal Requirements & Conflict-of-Laws Rules

Formal requirements,[78] such as prior notice or court approval, are common features of contracts, unless the parties agree otherwise. Formal requirements also include the registration of a netting agreement, or similar acts, with a pre-determined public, private or self-regulatory entity. However, these formal requirements differ among jurisdictions. In particular, the netting agreement must be governed by domestic law and/or must form part of a master agreement and cannot be customised. Importantly too, the master agreement must follow a model approved by an authority or self- regulatory body, allowing for no or only certain customised clauses to be included, which have been endorsed by a recognised trade association.[79] Arguably, the reference to the master agreement is to the internationally recognised ISDA Master Agreements. However, where compliance with formalities is required, those formalities often differ because each netting agreement is inextricably linked to its national regulatory architecture (ie, registration with one specific, national register). Failure to comply with the formal requirements, including divergent formal national law requirements, usually renders the netting agreement unenforceable. The flow on effect of an unenforceable agreement can have significant repercussions for the banking sector. It can reduce the availablility of liquidity in the financial system that would otherwise have flow on benefits in promoting and protecting cross-border investment and trade.

What followed in response to this divergence between formal national registers and international master agreements was the establishment of Principle 5. It provides for formal acts and reporting requirements, stipulating that the law of the implementing State should not make the operation of a close-out netting provision dependent on performance of any formal act, other than a requirement that a close-out netting provision be evidenced in writing or any legally equivalent form. The national laws should also not be dependent of the use of standardised terms of specific trade associations. That is, the law of the implementing State should not

78 Philipp Paech, *The Need for an International Instrument on the Enforceability of Close-out Netting in General and in the Context of Bank Resolution*, UNIDROIT Study Group on principles and rules on the netting of financial instruments, UNIDROIT 2011 S78C – Doc. 2 Original: English, March 2011, First Meeting Rome, 18–21 April 2011, 29.

79 Ibid. The master agreement must be a 'domestic' one; promoted by a domestic trade association, in the domestic language, etc. The operation of the netting agreement needs to be notified to a court or other authority. The operation of the netting agreement needs to be authorised by a court or other authority.

make the operation of a close-out netting provision and the obligations covered by the provision dependent on the compliance with any requirement to report data relating to those obligations to a trade repository or similar organisation for regulatory purposes.[80]

Importantly, formal requirements that impinge upon the legal enforceability of close-out netting provisions have considerable potential to create legal uncertainty in a cross-jurisdictional context. Accordingly, the operation of close-out netting provisions should not depend on such requirements as prior registration with a public register or notarisation. Confirming whether those jurisdictions that have established formal legislation or other legal mechanisms to implement Principle 5 will be more significant in demonstrating the virtue of international harmonisation upon the overall regulatory framework underlying netting arrangements.

Central to any international legal framework is having to deal with conflict of laws issues that can arise from transnational contracts and agreements. Even though the drafters of the UNIDROIT Principles understood that most, if not all, the conflict of laws matters were settled, doubts remained over the existence of a generally accepted conflict-of-laws principle.[81] Two areas of doubt emerged, namely, the application of conflict of laws to insolvency proceedings (*lex fori concursus*) and to netting agreements (*lex contractus*). Regarding the application of conflict of laws to insolvency, the choice of law was between the law of forum (*lex forum concursus*) and the law at the place (jurisdiction) at which the insolvent party had one or more branches. Therefore, where the principle of universality was applied, the law at the forum or branches were subject to a common proceeding, namely, the *lex forum concursus*.

The obstacles to states adopting uniform choices of jurisdiction and law are severalfold. The first obstacle is territorialism in which states adopt such choices based on the sovereign powers. Even if the jurisdiction of the central entity applies the principle of universality, it cannot prevent a foreign jurisdiction from taking a territorial approach to the insolvency of a branch in that foreign jurisdiction. The result of such territoriality is that different insolvency proceedings will be commenced under different laws in different jurisdictions.[82] Secondly, a netting agreement, whether a stand-alone contract or as part of a master agreement (ISDA Master Agreement), is considered to be a private contract. Therefore, the parties can choose the law applicable to the contract. The parties may also base those choices of law on those contained in the ISDA Master Agreements, namely, English

80 International Institute for Unification of Private Law, *Principles on the Operations of Close-out Netting* (2013), https://www.unidroit.org/instruments/capital-markets/netting, Principle 5.

81 Philipp Paech, *The Need for an International Instrument on the Enforceability of Close-out Netting in General and in the Context of Bank Resolution*, UNIDROIT Study Group on principles and rules on the netting of financial instruments, UNIDROIT 2011 S78C – Doc. 2 Original: English, March 2011, First Meeting Rome, 18–21 April 2011, 32–33.

82 Ibid.

law or New York Law (see Appendix 1). Once they choose that law, it will determine enforceability on insolvency; its determination will also bind the parties. As a result, the mandatory rules of *the lex forum concursus* might supersede the netting agreement to the extent of a conflict between that law and the netting agreement. Significantly, the UNIDROIT Principles do not address these concerns.

The development of the UNIDROIT Principles on close-out netting provisions has, arguably, set a clearer road map for jurisdictions to incorporate them into their national laws. However, for all the benefits that netting arrangements provide, five key areas have been identified where netting provisions are inadequate: (i) Excessive Externalisation of Risk,[83] (ii) Lack of Transparency,[84] (iii) Inconsistency and Opaqueness,[85] (iv) Disparate Treatment[86] and (v) Accelerated Insolvency and Systemic Risk.[87] A more pervasive criticism has also emerged, relating to the manner in which netting arrangements disproportionately favour large institutions. An overriding concern is that netting provisions can accelerate bankruptcy. They can contribute to the failure of indebted entities due in part to them being placed prematurely into insolvency proceedings even when those entities could have survived, such as through a restructuring plan. In addition, such failures potentially have a ripple effect by destabilising financial markets. As a result, netting provisions:

> pose a great risk of thrusting some financial institutions prematurely into bankruptcy. This not only endangers specific institutions, but also creates a risk of precipitating an adverse domino effect of firm failures throughout financial systems. Despite these dangers, the law in netting-friendly

83 Vincent Johnson, International Financial Law: The Case against Close-out Netting, *Boston University International Law Journal,* Vol. 33 (2015), 409. The strongest argument against close-out netting is that the process does little or nothing to minimize the risks that large-scale financial transactions create; rather, close-out netting merely shifts those risks to other persons who have no choice in the matter. See also Joanna Benjamin, *Financial Law*, Oxford University Press (2007).

84 Ibid, 411, Johnson notes that close-out netting arrangements lack transparency. Thus, without any meaningful consent on their part, general creditors are forced to bear a larger share of the losses that occur soon after a party that is protected by a close-out agreement defaults, cashes in its chips, and leaves the table, even as its counterparty fails.

85 Ibid, 412, Johnson further argues that the problems with close-out netting agreements are not merely their lack of transparency and nondisclosure of material information. Far worse, close-out netting agreements are framed to be both deliberately opaque and unpredictable in operation. Parties to close-out netting agreements are given a great deal of freedom to define their terms by specifying, for example, what constitutes a default sufficient to trigger the closing-out process. While this flexible arrangement can be praised as consistent with the ideal of 'private ordering', it means that the operation of financial and insolvency law is far from predictable. In some instances, an adverse credit event affecting an affiliated entity is sufficient to justify termination and acceleration of mutual obligations; in other cases, it is not. There is no way for affected third parties to know much about when they are likely to be drawn into a maelstrom of close-out netting which, by accelerating obligations between the parties, may thrust one of those parties into bankruptcy.

86 Ibid, 414.

87 Ibid, 416.

> jurisdictions insulates the financial institutions that assert their close-out rights from obligations under the law of insolvency. This is true regardless of the magnitude of the risks created by their activities and financial products.[88]

Bliss and Kaufman go further. They contend that, notwithstanding the frequent use of the combined term 'close-out netting', close-out and netting perform different economic functions, and both are tied to collateral in practice.[89] These legal mechanisms have evolved for purposes other than reducing systemic risks. These authors argue that market participants tend to be more concerned with their own welfare in their day-to-day business environments than with possible adverse externalities, including systemic market failure. They contend further that netting and collateral arrangements serve the needs of market participants, even when there is no systemic threat. Such arrangements, in turn, facilitate market risk and counterparty credit risk management. They also favour the expansion of dealer activities, enhancing the depth and liquidity of the derivatives markets.[90] The broad application of close-out netting does pose challenges at the international level because of their lack of legal convergence in domestic law systems. However, in our view, they play a major role in underpinning the rules-based system, by stabilising financial sectors of impacted domestic and trans-border economies.

David Mengle has adopted a countervailing rationale. He maintains that the objective of close-out netting is to protect non-defaulting counterparties from the consequences of a distressed counterparty's default.[91] However, he notes that, at times this objective comes into conflict with other statutes, such as insolvency laws that seek to preserve the assets of the defaulting party for the benefit of its stakeholders. This proposition of netting protecting non-defaulting counterparties, in and of itself, is problematic because Mengle argues further that such a conflict with other statutes is not inevitable. Most notably, in 'jurisdictions that follow English legal traditions, this conflict remains where the established law supports the right of creditors to pursue close-out netting processes following the insolvency of a counterparty'.[92]

Notwithstanding this, Principle 8 highlights where legal harmonisation is most needed. The core of Principle 8 states that it 'provides for "a without prejudice to a stay" or any other measure which the law of the implementing State, subject to appropriate safeguards, may provide for in the context of resolution regimes for

88 Ibid, 123.

89 Robert Bliss, George Kaufman, *Derivatives and Systemic Risk: Netting, Collateral, and Closeout*, Federal Reserve Bank Chicago, WP-2005–03 (2005), 3.

90 Ibid.

91 David Mengle, *Close-out Netting and Risk Management in over-the-Counter Derivatives,* International Swaps and Derivatives Association and Fordham University (2010), 4.

92 Ibid.

financial institutions'.[93] The UNIDROIT Principles, in establishing this provision, encourage implementing states to extend their 'resolution regimes' to include rules for netting for financial institutions in particular.[94] However, Principle 8 restricts the operation of close-out netting arrangements by ensuring that there are 'appropriate safeguards'.[95] Such measures extend to the protection and validation of interests of the counterparty in the financial institution that is being resolved,[96] while ensuring the latter's effective resolution. Central to the notion of 'appropriate safeguards' and support for a stay, is the requirement that, in order to exercise any contractual acceleration or early termination rights, 'the resolution authority should have the power to stay such rights temporarily where it arise by reason only of entry into resolution or in connection with the exercise of any resolution powers'.[97] In such circumstances, the stay itself should be limited to a period of two days; it should ensure that there is adequate protection of the integrity of financial contracts, and that it provides certainty to the counterparties. Additionally, the stay should also not affect the exercise of early termination rights of a counterparty against the firm being resolved in the case of any event of default not related to entry into resolution or the exercise of the relevant resolution power occurring before, during, or after the period of the stay – where there is a failure to make a payment or deliver or return collateral on a due date.[98]

In being constituted in this manner, netting arrangements are formidable legal mechanisms within an overall framework of global governance of financial markets. The UNIDROIT Principles provide further important functional rules for managing the parties involved in insolvency. As highlighted earlier, netting arrangements are applied upon default or insolvency of one party. The UNIDROIT Principles also reinforce the views of scholars and experts that netting arrangements should provide certainty and stability within and across the financial sector.[99] They have enabled parties using netting arrangements to enhance market stability, notably in volatile sectors in which market crashes can occur and inflict serious financial harm upon parties such as parties to over-the-counter (OTC) contracts.

The Principles when applied to defaults, they extend to the counterparty market participants, so as to enable the calculation of claims on a gross basis, rather than a

93 International Institute for Unification of Private Law, *Principles on the Operations of Close-out Netting* (2013), https://www.unidroit.org/instruments/capital-markets/netting, Principle 8, 64–66.

94 Ibid.

95 Ibid.

96 Ibid. The use of the term 'appropriate safeguards' is to be understood as a reference to the international standards with regard to special resolution regimes for financial institutions which are implemented under the various national resolution regimes and which include standards for the protection of close-out netting provisions in the context of such resolution regimes.

97 Ibid, 64–66.

98 Ibid.

99 International Institute for Unification of Private Law, *Principles on the Operations of Close-out Netting* (2013), https://www.unidroit.org/instruments/capital-markets/netting.

creditors basis, for the net amount only. Thus, once calculated under the netting arrangements, they act as a control mechanism when the inability of one participant to meet its obligations creates or increases financial difficulties for counterparties. Failure to apply netting arrangements or to adhere to the rules guiding their operation can result in a chain of failures of market participants (the contagion effect or result of systemic risk). Thus, the effect of contagion on the impacted market sector can have serious consequences for broader, national, regional and international economies, and for financial markets. At their extreme, the failure to adequately apply and use netting arrangements, can result in a massive economic and/or financial meltdown across market sectors that are both interrelated and interdependent.

Based on this, a central component of netting arrangements, arguably, are the contracts that support them, notably as facilitated by the ISDA Master Agreement as one of the most notable sources of contracts that uses close-out netting provisions. The next section discusses ISDA Master Agreement, while **Appendix 1** provides comprehensive detailed outline of the contents and operation of such an ISDA Master Agreement.

6.2.5 ISDA Master Agreements: Derivative Contracts

The International Swaps and Derivatives Association (ISDA) Master Agreement (the Master Agreement) serves as a standardised contract under which OTC derivatives transactions between counterparties take place (see Appendix I).[100] The ISDA Master Agreement has become a central legal instrument in facilitating and protecting millions of dollars (in multiple currencies) across the world. The agreements themselves are among the most widely used instruments to reduce credit risk.[101] A further key benefit of contracts derived from the ISDA Master Agreement is in providing a 'high level of legal certainty in an otherwise complex environment in which financial institutions transact large amounts of money continuously'.[102]

For more than a decade, the amount of money transacted by OTCs alone has been enormous. In June 2008, the notional value of all outstanding OTC financial contracts was in excess of $680 trillion, according to the Bank for International

100 Ibid.

101 Nina Hval, Credit Risk Reduction in the International over-the-Counter Derivatives Market: Collateralizing the Net Exposure with Support Agreements, *The International Lawyer*, Vol. 31, No. 3 (1997), 801–803.

102 Peter Werner, Close-out Netting and the World of Derivatives in Central and Eastern Europe and beyond: ISDA's Perspective, *Law in Transition* (2012), 48–55. As of 2012, ISDA has over 830 member institutions from 60 countries worldwide. These members include most of the world's major institutions that deal in privately negotiated derivatives, as well as many of the businesses, governmental entities and other end-users that rely on over-the-counter derivatives to efficiently manage the financial market risks inherent in their core economic activities.

Settlements.[103] In contrast, the value of all cleared derivatives traded by private regulated exchanges was below $20 trillion in notional value. The Bank of International Settlements highlighted how the 'notional estimated amount of OTC derivatives rose to $640 trillion by the end of June 2019. This was up from $544 trillion at end-2018 and the highest level reached since 2014'.[104] This growth was 'led by increases in Euro interest rate derivative contracts'.[105] What these upward trends highlight is how since the GFC, but prior to the financial impact of the coronavirus, the value of OTC contracts has grown significantly. Consequently, the protection they provide to contracting parties and financial markets becomes increasingly important.

COVID-19 presented another financial obstacle to the efficient use of close-out netting provisions. Early in the pandemic, Gita Gopinath, the IMF's chief economist, reported in April 2020 that COVID could reduce global GDP by $9 trillion (£7.2 trillion) over the then ensuing two years.[106] While out of scope of this book, it is difficult to confirm the number of OTC derivative contracts that would be impacted. Regardless of the longevity of COVID-19, prior to its acknowledgement in January 2020, the 'gross market value of OTC derivatives was estimated to be worth $12 trillion'.[107] That amount of money is significant no matter what country, countries or entities are involved in financial transacting. However, the gross market value of OTC Derivatives does not provide data on the average OTC transaction, or the amount protected by ISDA Master Agreements. Neither does it provide data on the respective netting arrangements in individual transactions. On the one side, these estimates can be viewed quite positively, because they highlight the significant amount of money being transacted, even though the world was in the midst of a pandemic. On the other side, is the challenge arising from the reduction in global investment and the significant amount of money that is still invested in international financing and subject to exposure to further market declines. This challenge can lead in a rise in transnational insolvencies.

However, it must be understood that there are subtle but important differences between set off and netting arrangements. Firstly, a set-off is legally complex and arises between two parties who owe each other a debt.[108] For example, a set-off

103 Gordon Rausser, William Balson, Reid Stevens, *Centralized Clearing for over-the-Counter Derivatives*, Department of Agricultural & Resource Economics, UCB CUDARE Working Papers (University of California, Berkeley) (2009), 2.

104 *Statistical Release: OTC Derivatives Statistics at End June 2019*, The Bank of International Settlements, https://www.bis.org/publ/otc_hy1911.pdf.

105 Ibid.

106 Szu Ping Chan, *Coronavirus: 'World Faces Worst Recession since Great Depression'*, April 2020, https://www.bbc.com/news/business-52273988.

107 Bank of International Settlements, https://www.bis.org/publ/otc_hy1911.htm, the BIS is owned by 62 central banks, representing countries from around the world that together account for about 95% of world GDP.

108 Set-off and Netting in Finance Transactions-Overview, https://www.lexisnexis.com/uk/lexispsl/bankingandfinance/document/391289/55KB-65S1-F185-X13T-00000-00/Set_off_and_netting_overview.

used within a contract will arise where it has been provided for within a specific contractual clause. It is used when contracting parties want to extend or limit set-off rights that are available in law generally, but cannot be used to alter the scope or operation of insolvency set-off which applies mandatorily regardless of any contractual agreement between the parties.[109] Set-off enables the parties to determine: how and when set-off should take effect; when to permit set-off of claims which are not mutual; and when to permit set-off of certain types of claims which are not necessarily eligible for set-off by other means, such as unmatured claims, unliquidated claims, and contingent claims. On the other hand, when applied or used in an insolvency, the set-off will be self-executing; it becomes automatic and is mandatory. Therefore, centrally, the parties cannot contract out of or waive the automatic and mandatory application of set-off. The mandated set-off takes precedence over any other form of set-off exercised before the liquidation, administration, or bankruptcy.[110] The resulting effect is that the parties have agreed to transact with each other and will not make individual cross claims against each other. Instead, at any time there will be only one amount owed by the party whose notional cross claim is worth less than its counterparty's cross claim.[111] More generally, set-off is usually defined by an agreement to mean 'set-off, offset, the combination of accounts, the right of retention or withholding, or a similar right or requirement to which the payer of an amount under Section 6 is entitled or subject (whether arising under this Agreement, another contract, applicable law or otherwise) that is exercised by, or imposed on, such payer'.[112] Put another way, a set off arrangement is any 'amount payable to one party (the payee) by the other party (the payer) where there is a defaulting party or one affected party in the case where a termination event has occurred'.[113] Therefore, the amount that can be set-off can

---

There are five types of set-off arrangements. These include independent set-off, transaction set-off, contractual set-off, insolvency set-off, banker's set-off.

109 Ibid.

110 Ibid.

111 Ibid.

112 ISDA International Swap Dealers Association, Inc. Master Agreement, dated as of September 26, 2007 COMERICA BANK, a Michigan banking corporation and RACKSPACE US, INC. a Delaware corporation have entered and/or anticipate entering into one or more transactions (each a "Transaction") that are or will be governed by this Master Agreement, which includes the schedule (the "Schedule"), and the documents and other confirming evidence (each a "Confirmation") exchanged between the parties confirming those Transactions. https://www.sec.gov/Archives/edgar/data/1107694/000119312508091225/dex1032.htm.

113 Ibid, paragraph d Part 5. 'X will give notice to the other party of any set-off effected under this paragraph. For this purpose, either the Early Termination Amount or the Other Agreement Amount (or the relevant portion of such amounts) may be converted by X into the currency in which the other is denominated at the rate of exchange at which such party would be able, acting in a reasonable manner and in good faith, to purchase the relevant amount of such currency. If an obligation is unascertained, X may in good faith estimate that obligation and set-off in respect of the estimate, subject to the relevant party accounting to the other when the obligation is ascertained. Nothing in this paragraph shall be effective to create a charge or other security interest. This paragraph shall be without prejudice and in addition to any right of set-off, combination of accounts, lien or other

be deducted from the amount payable by the payer to the payee. This is somewhat different to closing out in which netting arrangements relate to the amount due in accordance with the ISDA Master Agreement. On the other hand, set-off enables the amount payable to be reduced against a terminating factor. A terminating factor generally includes a failure to pay or deliver, breach of agreement, credit support default, misrepresentation or a default under a specified transaction.

6.2.6 Over-the-Counter (OTC) Derivatives

In OTCs, close-out netting is used only in the event of default by a counterparty. The counterparty will agree to use close-out netting in a master agreement to terminate and net all ongoing derivatives transactions across all value dates and across all currencies. OTC derivatives permit counterparties to offset gains or losses they may have on a number of transactions between them.[114] Applied to a credit support agreement, securities can be pledged as collateral against the net credit exposure resulting from the market-to-market valuation of all outstanding transactions.[115] As a result, a party with net credit exposure may reduce or eliminate his or her credit risk against a counterparty by receiving an interest in securities, the value of which is equal to its net credit exposure. 'In reaching this conclusion, netting is enforceable in the counterparties' jurisdictions and the counterparty, in receipt of securities, has complied with the applicable legal requirements to affect a transfer or to create a security interest in the securities, thereby guaranteeing a party's rights of enforcement in the event its counterparty defaults on its obligations'.[116]

Central to the ISDA Master Agreement are two forms of netting. In the first form of netting under ISDA Master Agreement 2002, payment netting takes place during the normal business of a solvent firm. It involves combining offsetting cash flow obligations between two parties on a given day in a given currency into a single net payable or receivable, whereby payment netting is essentially the same as set-off. The purpose of payment netting is to reduce both settlement risks and processing costs by reducing the number of separate payments to be made on a given day. In its second form, netting is limited to close-out netting in transactions between a defaulting party and non-defaulting party.[117] Therefore, close-out netting is a process involving termination of obligations under a contract with a

right to which any party is at any time otherwise entitled (whether by operation of law, contract or otherwise)'.

114 Nina Hval, Credit Risk Reduction in the International over-the-Counter Derivatives Market: Collateralizing the Net Exposure with Support Agreements, *The International Lawyer*, Vol. 31, No. 3 (1997), 801–803.

115 Ibid.

116 Ibid.

117 David Mengle, *Close-out Netting and Risk Management in Over-the-Counter Derivatives*, International Swaps and Derivatives Association and Fordham University (2010), 4.

defaulting party.[118] On the other hand, across the trading world, many entities aim to have a Master Agreement or other appropriate legal documentation in place prior to trade. In some cases, there may be a delay in completing the relevant legal processes, such as in dealings with less sophisticated clients or ones that lack internal legal expertise. In such cases, management decisions may be taken to execute a trade without completed documentation.[119]

Nonetheless, there are four methods used to collateralise net credit exposure in credit support agreements annexed to OTC derivatives master agreements:

(i) an English law set-off and transfer agreement,
(ii) a fixed charge under English or other common or civil law,
(iii) a Uniform Commercial Code (UCC) pledge under US law or
(iv) a Japanese loan and pledge agreement.[120] Credit support agreements governed by English law generally utilise the first two methods.

However, when deciding which collateralisation method to use, a counterparty should analyze the treatment of the various methods under both the law governing the credit support agreement and the insolvency laws of its counterparty.[121] On the other hand, branches of entities engaged in cross-border financial transactions are often located in different financial centres, given that the biggest users of and dealers in derivatives are international banks. In citing cross-border transactions in the US, Asia and Europe as examples, Nina Hval elaborates:

> When entering into a cross-border transaction, the counterparties must assess the laws of each relevant jurisdiction regarding the recognition of netting, the legal requirements to transfer or create a valid security interest in the securities representing the credit support, and the insolvency law treatment of those practices and interests. Legal risk involving the risk of loss always exists due to either an unexpected application of a law or an unenforceable contract.[122]

Nonetheless, in stressing the need to manage and reduce the risk of loss to parties, there is a need to also determine the counterparties' rights to the securities representing the credit support. Most parties respond to this risk by adhering to the conflicts of laws' *lex situs* rule. Moreover, in an era of immobilisation and dematerialisation, ownership and security interests are more frequently kept by electronic book entry, not by physical possession. The risk is that the liquidator of an insolvent counterparty will fail to recognise or enforce close-out netting provisions in

118 Ibid.

119 Nina Hval, Credit Risk Reduction in the International over-the-Counter Derivatives Market: Collateralizing the Net Exposure with Support Agreements, *The International Lawyer*, Vol. 31, No. 3 (1997), 801–803.

120 Ibid, 808.

121 Ibid.

122 Ibid, 801–803.

cross-border insolvency proceedings, contrary to master agreements that recognise the insolvency policies and practices at branch offices of a counterparty. This poses a challenge, not only when an insolvency proceeding relates to the transnational enforcement of close-out netting provisions, but also because a growing number of OTC derivative transactions take place across borders, and because the multibranch nature of many counterparties increases the risk. Often, counterparties will elect the multibranch party option in their master agreement, which allows parties to book transactions through any of the branches listed in the agreement.[123] However, each country where a branch is located is likely to adopt a distinct policy on the need for local proceedings to group branch assets incorporated into its insolvency laws, which may or may not recognise close-out netting.[124] The resulting effect is a legal disharmony across national insolvency laws and in their application.

Arguably, and as highlighted earlier, the conflict of laws issues that arise from transnational netting contracts is largely settled through the rules of private international law. Yet, what is problematic for netting arrangements is when the transnational dispute falls within the confines of insolvency. This is because the *lex fori concursus* requires that the mandatory law of the forum be applied, in addition to the application of the *lex contractus*. The *lex fori concursus* can override parts of the contract, where the insolvency laws have been breached. The result is an inherent conflict between the law of the forum and the foreign law governing the netting arrangement(s), particularly in multibranch netting arrangements. This can result in netting provisions being ineffective.

6.2.7 ISDA 2018 Model Netting Act

The Model Netting Act [MNA] was first established by the ISDA in 1996, some 17 years before the UNIDROIT Principles came into operation.[125] This section examines the definition, enforceability, termination, cherry picking and multibranch netting arrangements. It will demonstrate how the 2018 Model Law has influenced the development of the UNIDROIT Principles.

6.2.8 Definition

The Model Netting Law, rather than define close-out netting provision(s), has defined netting arrangement and netting in their own terms in Section 1 of Part I of the 2018 MNA as follows:

> netting agreement which covers master agreements and master-master netting agreements, as well as collateral arrangements related to these types of

123 Ibid.

124 Ibid.

125 International Swaps and Derivatives Association, 2018 ISDA Model Netting Act and Guide (2018).

> agreements. Netting agreement means an agreement between two persons that provides for netting, including, without limitation (a) an agreement that provides for the netting of amounts due under two or more netting agreements; and (b) a collateral arrangement relating to or forming part of a netting agreement.[126]

In addition, netting constitutes:

> the operation of a set of provisions in an agreement between two persons that may be commenced by notice given by one person to the other person upon the occurrence of an event of default with respect to the other person or other termination event or that may, in certain circumstances, occur automatically as specified in the agreement.[127]

While this definition of close-out netting is not consistent with the UNIDROIT Principles, it has evolved over a longer time period and has been applied extensively to netting contracts and ISDA Master Agreements in particular. The ISDA affirms this definition by highlighting the importance of close-out netting arrangement within ISDA Master Agreements. As highlighted earlier in this chapter, the ISDA Master Agreements have facilitated a growing number of transactions transnationally. Essentially, the ISDA Master Agreements enable a netting agreement to be terminated by notice, and valued to the current day market-to-market value. The resulting net balance is calculated as being equal to the difference between the aggregate mark-to-market value of terminated transactions 'in the money' to the non-defaulting party. Additionally, the calculation is based on the value of the aggregate market-to-market value of terminated transactions 'out of the money' to the non-defaulting party. However, if the first valuation exceeds the second, the net amount is paid to the non-defaulting party.

6.2.9 Enforcement and Termination

Legal mechanisms or tools are of little to no benefit if they are unable to be enforced. The 2018 MNA underscores the importance of national laws providing mechanisms to ensure that netting arrangements in specific contract clauses

126 Ibid, 11.

127 Ibid. The operation of a set of provisions in an agreement between two persons '(b) has the following effect: (i) the termination, liquidation and/or acceleration of any present or future payment or delivery rights or obligations arising under or in connection with one or more qualified financial contracts entered into under the agreement; (ii) the calculation or estimation of a close-out value, market value, liquidation value or replacement value in respect of each right and obligation or group of rights and obligations terminated, liquidated and/or accelerated under (i) and the conversion of each such value into a single currency; and (iii) the determination of the net balance of the values calculated under (ii), whether by operation of set-off or otherwise, giving rise to the obligation of one person to pay an amount equal to the net balance to the other person'.

are, by and large, legally enforceable. Section 4(a) of Part I of the 2018 MNA expressly confirms that the 'provisions of a netting agreement will be enforceable in accordance with the terms, even if the counterparty is subject to insolvency proceedings'.[128] However, the Model Law does not highlight what event will trigger a default or termination. The ISDA has left this area of law largely to national regulators. On this basis, it is necessary for enforcement to be provided outside of the insolvency rules.

Moreover, netting legislation should not require 'termination' of the netting agreement itself, since only transactions terminate. The netting agreement should survive so that its netting provisions can be performed effectively.[129] Section 4(i) of Part I of the 2018 MNA expressly states that a netting agreement should be enforceable even if this netting agreement contains transactions that are not qualified financial contracts. The pre-insolvency enforceability issue is dealt with in Section 3(b) of Part I of the 2018 MNA. It provides that the parties to a qualified financial contract cannot subsequently seek to repudiate it or avoid obligations arising under the qualified financial contract.[130]

The ISDA recognises that, national insolvency laws in many jurisdictions limit the effectiveness of early termination provisions in contracts that are triggered by the commencement of insolvency proceedings. Thus, the MNA goes beyond generally affirming the enforceability of netting agreements provided in Section 4(a) of Part I. It also provides in Section 4(g) that an 'insolvency practitioner shall not be able to prevent the termination of any qualified financial contracts or the acceleration of any payment owed under such qualified financial contracts'.[131] Therefore, most state laws provide for multibranch agreements and netting. Consequently, the ISDA promotes the need for national laws to accommodate both bilateral and multibranch netting contracts.

6.2.10 Multi-Branch Netting

Multibranch netting agreements are not uncommon. The 2018 ISDA MNA and Guideline state that netting legislation should 'permit netting under a netting agreement to be enforced against a multibranch party that has a head office in one jurisdiction and various branches in other jurisdictions'.[132] Optional Part II of the

128 Ibid.

129 Ibid, 15.

130 Ibid, 16. It is a normal feature of insolvency proceedings that one or more persons is appointed to administer the affairs of the insolvent party during the insolvency proceeding. Such a person may be referred to in English-speaking jurisdictions as an insolvency practitioner, an insolvency representative, an insolvency 'officeholder, a liquidator, an administrative receiver, a receiver, a trustee in bankruptcy, a conservator, an administrator or by some similar name.

131 Ibid, 18.

132 Ibid, 19. Note the general rules of private international law will apply, however, ringfencing may become an issue. That is, a netting agreement may cover both a bilateral and multi-branch netting

2018 MNA provides detailed provisions to ensure the effectiveness of multibranch netting in the event of the cross-border insolvency of a multibranch bank. However, those provisions do not apply to a local organised subsidiary of a foreign parent company, since that local subsidiary would be a separate legal entity and not a branch.[133] As highlighted earlier the ability to engage in multibranch netting is included to provide financial institutions with multiple branches in different jurisdictions the option to modify an ISDA Master Agreement in order to incorporate more than one branch in a single jurisdiction.

6.2.11 Cherry Picking

The aforementioned analysis highlights the dichotomy between contract and insolvency law. The 2018 MNA and its Guidelines respond to the long-standing problem that an insolvency practitioner often has the right to 'assume, affirm or require the continuation of contracts or transactions that are favourable to the insolvent party, coupled with the power to disclaim, reject or repudiate contracts or transactions that are not favourable to the insolvent party'.[134] This is often referred to as its cherry-picking power. The exercise of this power has significant ramifications for the solvent party. If an insolvency office holder is allowed to 'cherry pick' transactions under a netting agreement, then the solvent party would be forced to pay the full amount of any obligations owed under the affirmed transactions, while then being able to claim only as an unsecured creditor for the transactions.[135] Sections 1 and 6 of ISDA Master Agreements have dealt, in part, with this issue.[136]

Today, Section 1(c) of the ISDA Master Agreements makes it clear that the Master Agreement and all Transactions under it form a single agreement between the parties upon which they rely in concluding their contracts.[137] The single agreement nature of the ISDA 2002 Master Agreements is also reflected in the close-out netting provisions. Their Section 6(c)(ii) provides that no further obligations are owed in respect of terminated transactions, but without prejudice to the separate obligation arising under Section 6(e) to pay the early termination amount. However, in the event of insolvency proceedings, there are no individual 'cherries' to

---

contract. Multi-branch netting goes some way to reducing the problem of 'ring-fencing' under particular transactions allocated in different jurisdictions which may apply their own insolvency provisions.

133 Ibid.

134 Ibid, 17–19. The insolvency officeholder in such a case has the power to keep the 'good' cherries (contracts beneficial to the insolvent party) and to reject the 'bad' cherry (contracts burdensome to the insolvent party). Contractual close-out netting arrangements under netting agreements were originally developed in the mid-1980s precisely to overcome this problem.

135 Ibid.

136 Ibid, 17–19.

137 Ibid.

pick, but merely one net claim due under Section 6(e).[138] While the ISDA Master Agreements have largely addressed this issue, cherry picking remains an ongoing problem. In response, Section 4(d) of Part I of the MNA aims to impede any form of cherry picking from disrupting close-out netting.

6.2.12 Influence of ISDA Model Netting Act

A key question is whether and to what extent the ISDA MNA has influenced the development of the UNIDROIT Principles. In 2011, a UNIDROIT study group[139] evaluated whether then proposed Draft UNIDROIT Principles should be extended to protect underlying netting contracts and obligations that jeopardised both the netting agreement, contracts and obligations. Arguably, in part, this was a response to the already extensive number of netting contracts that were being used effectively in trans-border transactions across financial sectors. It also highlighted the importance that ISDA Master Agreements have had in and across financial sectors. It emphasised, too, that the fundamental principles of contract law relating to the formation, performance and termination of contracts should not be subject to selective modification, such as in enforcement proceedings in particular jurisdictions.

The 2011 Report of the UNIDROIT study group, motivated by Article 3 of the ISDA MNA of 2006, added that:

> A qualified financial contract shall not be and shall be deemed never to have been void or unenforceable [solely because mutuality was established by novation in a multilateral netting system], by reason of [legal provisions] relating to games, gaming, gambling, wagering or lotteries [or by being qualified as an insurance contract].[140]

Importantly, as was highlighted earlier, the enforceability of netting provisions in finance contracts are important because, in the absence of such enforceability, the contracts would be unable to redress debts precipitating into insolvency of the debtor. Thus, the Report advocated redrafting Principle 10 of the Draft UNIDROIT Principles to model Article 4 of the ISDA MNA, providing for the enforceability of netting provisions.[141]

138 Ibid.

139 International Institute for the Unification of Private Law, UNIDROIT Study Group on principles and rules on the netting of financial instruments, UNIDROIT 2011, Study LXXVIII C – Doc. 4 Original: English July 2011, First Meeting Rome, 18–21 April 2011.

140 UNIDROIT Study Group on Draft Principles and rules on the netting of financial instruments, Second Meeting, Rome, 13–15 September 2011, UNIDROIT 2011, Study LXXVIII C – Doc. 9 December 2011, 16–25.

141 Ibid.

The aforementioned analysis also confirms that the MNA has provided a significant part of the rationale for developing the UNIDROIT Principles. The 2011 UNIDROIT Report cautioned against broadening the scope of the Draft Principles in applying them to the underlying netting contracts and related obligations. The Report also recommended that the Principles should protect those contracts and obligations against certain, clearly defined obstacles, as identified earlier.

6.3 Conclusion

Close-out netting arrangements, in our view, have become an integral part of the overall legal framework for both the stabilisation and minimisation of risks or default on debt within and across financial markets. Today, close-out netting arrangements are considered formidable legal instruments in protecting parties to financial transactions from such risks arising before or during insolvency proceedings. These mechanisms provide an instrumental framework for ensuring a higher level of liquidity directed at averting or otherwise limiting the growth of debilitating debts that threaten financial arrangements and also markets that are exposed to those debts. Therefore, having a harmonised framework to regulate close-out netting arrangements within national legal systems adds a significant layer of certainty, and the liquidity, to avoid market destabilisation.

Commencing in 2012, the support for netting has become increasingly universal across financial sectors and upon national and international policymakers. More than 40 countries had enacted legislation that provides for the enforceability of close-out netting.[142] The current international legal framework, has contributed materially to facilitate the enforceability of netting agreements in derivative markets and payments systems. Even though cross jurisdictional differences persist, greater consistency and uniformity have evolved in the cross-border treatment of netting and collateral in relation to derivative contracts.

However, perfection is an illusion. The number of netting arrangements that have been developed vary; they take different forms and have different functions. Netting arrangements are bilateral or multilateral. They encompass netting by novation, balance-sheet netting, market-to-market, and pricing or valuing interest rate swaps. Furthermore, even jurisdictions that have embraced netting arrangements have diverged because netting provisions are subject to different substantive laws and inconsistent legal treatment across jurisdictions. As a result, providing for the choice of law by contract is increasingly essential to limit inconsistencies arising from divergent laws and procedures regulating the enforcement of close-out netting arrangements. In response to the lack of legal convergence and harmonisation in the regulation of netting arrangements, the 2013 UNIDROIT Principles on

142 Peter Werner, Close-out Netting and the World of Derivatives in Central and Eastern Europe and beyond: ISDA's Perspective, *Law in Transition* (2012), 48–55.

Close-out netting provisions came into effect. The areas of concern stress, then and now, how different laws and jurisdictions have defined and construed close-out netting provisions.[143] These concerns have extended to the legal mechanisms used to protect netting that is related to insolvency; the eligible parties and eligible financial contracts to such protection, and the formal requirements and conflict-of-laws rules to support those mechanisms and outcomes.

The normative value of close-out netting in redressing debt and insolvency is contestable. Opponents of close-out netting argue that close-out netting procedures lack transparency, operate inconsistently and have disparate impacts upon participants in financial transactions. They also magnify systemic risks by accelerating insolvency and impeding the rescue of troubled institutions. Furthermore, netting arrangements can lead to the excessive externalisation of risk and compound the lack of transparency, inconsistency, disparate treatment and opaqueness in close-out netting procedures. More pervasively, the normative value of close-out netting in redressing debt and insolvency is contestable. Viewed this way, there are obstacles to their use. On the contrary, and as demonstrated earlier, their role is allowing parties to manage and reduce the risk on millions, of dollars of loan contracts, often well outweighs their negative effects.

The formal and functional operation of close-out netting arrangements is different to that of set-off arrangements. As this chapter has demonstrated, a set-off price is an amount that can be used to reduce the overall price against the amount that will paid from the payee to the payer. A set-off arrangement can only be used under the terminating factors specified by the ISDA Master Agreement. On the other hand, close-out netting arrangement relate to the overall amount due under the entire ISDA Master Agreement.

Therefore, in our view, the adoption, use and application of close-out netting provisions, subject to the guidelines proposed earlier, far outweigh their potential limitations. As the financial sector has become increasingly internationalised, these provisions have the material ability to extend protection to parties to insolvency disputes, but also in contractual disputes more generally. Our further view is that the universalist approach towards close-out netting provisions enables regulators a in different jurisdictions to redress limitations in the application of those provisions by shared, not mutually exclusive-means. For the universalist approach to be fully adopted, the UNCITRAL and UNIDROIT should consider developing a project to confirm or otherwise whether it is time to further internationalise the universalist approach to cross-border insolvency, by raising the Principles to a Model Law. The incremental approach to internationalising commercial law is, in our view, the most viable option because states are unlikely to support comprehensive change instantaneously, by raising the Principles to convention status.

143 International Institute for Unification of Private Law, *Principles on the Operations of Close-out Netting* (2013), https://www.unidroit.org/instruments/capital-markets/netting.

Arguably, in our view developing a Model Law on Close-out netting Provisions, is a viable option to address these and other concerns. Doing so could also go some way to promote and encourage more nation states to adopt the current UNIDROIT Principles, were they to become a Model Law. The ensuing chapters will develop on this view in relation to selected legal systems and jurisdictions. These will include the law and practice in Australia, EU, India, Indonesia, Singapore, United Kingdom, United States and China. The chapters will evaluate, in particular, how these jurisdictions have adopted and implemented the UNIDROIT Principles on Close-out netting in defining and applying these netting mechanisms in regulating cross-border debt and insolvency.

6

JURISDICTIONAL COMPARISONS OF NETTING ARRANGEMENTS PART 2

6.1 Australia

Australia is a leading jurisdiction in adopting specific legislation for the administration, application and use of closeout netting provisions.[1] Australia established the Payment Systems and Netting Act (1998) [Netting Act – No. 83] that epitomises the absence of a definition of close-out netting in legislation. Being established in 1998, it had been operational for fifteen years before the UNIDROIT Principles were established. This operational history highlights the already long-standing function that netting arrangement have played within Australia's financial sector. It should be noted that Australia's Netting came into force a year after the 1997 Asian financial crisis which had a significant impact on Australia. However, the Netting Act only defines close-out netting contracts, to mean: (a) a contract under which, if a particular event happens: (i) particular obligations of the parties terminate or may be terminated; and (ii) the termination values of the obligations are calculated or may be calculated; and (iii) the termination values are netted, or may be netted, so that only a net cash amount (whether in Australian currency or some other currency) is payable; or

(b) a contract declared by the regulations to be a close-out netting contract for the purposes of this Act;

1 This chapter builds on the earlier work undertaken by the authors. However, given developments and divergence in close-out netting in some jurisdictions, the chapter extends that analysis to China and India. The discussion on these additional developments draws from practice management, ISDA Opinions, Clifford Chance, Germany. See further, Robert Walters, Leon Trakman, The Fragmented Approach toward Close-out Netting Provisions in Australia, Indonesia, Malaysia and Singapore Compared, *Journal of Banking Regulation* (2019), 1. See also Robert Walters, *Close-out netting Provisions – Their Current Value in a Time of International Uncertainty!* International Company and Commercial Law Review – Sweet & Maxwell (2020).

DOI: 10.4324/9781003311874-10

but does not include:

(c) a contract that constitutes, or is part of, an approved netting arrangement; or
(d) a contract in relation to which a declaration under section 15 is in force; or
(e) a contract declared by the regulations to not be a close-out netting contract for the purposes of this Act.[2]

The Netting Act also makes no reference to either the 1992 or 2002 ISDA Master Agreements, nor to the UNIDROIT Principles, nor to the definitions espoused in these instruments. It provides for payment systems and close-out netting of contracts on the occurrence of particular events.[3] In such cases, the obligations of the parties are terminated or may be terminated, and the value of the obligations are calculated or may be calculated. By ensuring that termination values is also netted, it provides a level of certainty to the market, whereby a net cash amount (whether in Australian currency or some other currency) is payable. Arguably, this becomes important to protecting parties to the contract.

Australia's Netting Act focuses directly on the contract and contractual arrangements between the parties, unlike the UNIDROIT Principles and the Model Law.[4] Furthermore, it identifies when a contract is declared by the regulations in the Netting Act as a close-out netting contract for the purposes of the Act. However, the Netting Act does not apply to a close-out netting contract that constitutes, or is part of, an approved netting arrangement.[5] Additionally, the Netting Act does not apply to a contract declared as being a close-out netting contract under Section 15 of that Act;[6] or a contract declared by the regulations not to be a close-out netting contract for the purposes of the Act.[7] In other words, the 'Reserve Bank of Australia has the power to declare in writing that Section 14 does not apply to a close-out netting contract if it is satisfied that systemic disruption in the financial system could result if a party to the contract went into external administration. It must be noted that in Australia, the Reserve Bank is a separate entity to the Australian government, and makes its decisions based on the public interest of the entire economy'.[8] The Reserve Bank plays a key role in stabilising and managing risk to the broader economy, not only the finance sector.

The significance of the definition of close-out netting provisions in a contract has been clarified by the courts. In *Re Opes Prime Stockbroking Ltd,*[9] the Australian

2 Payment Systems and Netting Act 1998 [Netting Act – No. 83], Section 5.
3 Ibid.
4 Ibid.
5 Payment Systems and Netting Act 1998, Section 15.
6 Ibid.
7 Ibid, Section 5.
8 Robert Walters, Leon Trakman, The Fragmented Approach toward Close-out Netting Provisions in Australia, Indonesia, Malaysia and Singapore Compared, *Journal of Banking Regulation* (2019), *supra* note 1. See also Robert Walters, *Close-out netting Provisions – Their Current Value in a Time of International Uncertainty!* International Company and Commercial Law Review – Sweet & Maxwell (2020)
9 (2008) 171 FCR 473.

Federal Court reinforced the definition of close-out netting contract in Section 5 of the Netting Act. It emphasised that this definition was directed at ensuring that close-out netting contracts used in a variety of financial market transactions are effective under Australian insolvency law.[10] It drew attention to the Explanatory Memorandum which accompanied the Act providing that: 'The definition is intended to operate broadly to encompass super – netting under a master netting contract'.[11] Therefore, the scope of a close-out netting under the Netting Act is portrayed as expansive in its nature and scope of application,[12] and in covering a range of different kinds of financial transactions.

In addition to this, subsections 14(2)(d) to (f) provide that:

> [O]bligations that are, or have been, netted or terminated under the close-out netting contract are to be disregarded in the external administration; any net obligation owed by the party under the close-out netting contract that has not been discharged is provable in the external administration; any net obligation owed to the party under the close-out netting contract that has not been discharged may be recovered by the external administrator for the benefit of creditors.[13]

Section 14(2)(g) provides that, 'relevantly, the netting or termination of obligations under the contract and a payment made by a party to discharge a net obligation under the contract are not to be void or voidable in the external administration of that party'. Thus, arguably, the protection afforded to close-out netting under the Netting Act applies despite:

> any disposal of rights that may be netted under the contract; or the creation of any encumbrance, or any other interest, in relation to those rights; or the operation of any encumbrance, or any other interest, in relation to those rights, in contravention of a prohibition in the contract or the security.[14]

The inclusion of this provision is intended to ensure that close-out netting that is applied to an external administration is not affected by the interests of third parties that arise in contravention of a prohibition in the contract, subject to any specified

10 Payment Systems and Netting Act 1998, Section 5.

11 Ibid, 37. The obligations referred to in the definition are intended to apply broadly to encompass monetary obligations arising under a financial contract such as an interest rate or currency swap, and to non-monetary obligations such as an obligation to deliver commodities under a commodities derivative contract or securities under a securities derivative contract. The obligations covered by the definition are also intended to cover contingent obligations.

12 Robert Walters, Leon Trakman, The Fragmented Approach toward Close-Out Netting Provisions in Australia, Indonesia, Malaysia and Singapore Compared, *Journal of Banking Regulation* (2019), 1.

13 Scott Farrel, Kings & Wood Malleson, Letter correspondence to International Swaps and Derivatives Association, https://www.isda.org/a/AogDE/august-8-2017-collateral-provider-blackline.pdf.

14 Ibid.

stay provision that applies to the contract.[15] It is intended to provide a level of security over financial property.[16]

Notwithstanding this, the enforcement of close-out netting provisions under the Netting Act is limited to Sections 141(ca) and 142(fa). A dilemma has arisen because the effectiveness of a close-out netting contract can only be substantiated when Australian law so determines and where the contract is enforceable by an Australian court.[17] On the other hand, it is the contract which determines when the obligations of the parties may be terminated, how the termination values may be calculated, and when the net amount owed may become payable. More importantly, the enforcement of close-out netting contract only applies when security for a party's contractual obligations is given over financial property, where such enforcement accords with the terms of that security, and where the terms of that security are evidenced in writing.[18] Therefore, 'the enforcement of such a contract encompasses security given over financial property in respect of obligations owed by party to that contract which may be enforced in accordance with the terms of the security that is evidenced in writing'.[19] Interestingly, the earlier provisions do not replicate each other but apply to different issues such as those covered by the Australian constitution and those that relate to the individual person in accordance with section 141 (ca).

However, by further unpacking Section 14, Section 14 2(fa) applies to a person who is, or has been, a party to a close-out netting contract and goes into external administration. Viewed this way, both the '1992 ISDA Master Agreement and the 2002 ISDA Master Agreement are close-out netting contracts for the purposes of the Netting Act, provided that in the case of the 1992 ISDA Master Agreement and the "Second Method" is chosen'.[20] The First and Second Method relate to the enforcement and application of ISDA Master agreements within the context of Australia's *Personal Property Securities Act 2009*[21] (Cth) and Netting Act. This is important because the definition of close-out netting contract requires that a net cash amount is payable. Under the circumstances where the First Method is chosen, it is limited to the net cash amount only payable under the 1992 ISDA Master Agreement. However, this can only occur if the payee in is the Non-defaulting Party under the 1992 ISDA Master Agreement, and therefore, would not satisfy the definition of closeout netting contract. On the other hand, in

15 2016 Explanatory Memorandum, [1.124], in Scott Kings & Farrel, Wood Malleson, Letter correspondence to International Swaps and Derivatives Association, https://www.isda.org/a/AogDE/august-8-2017-collateral-provider-blackline.pdf
16 Ibid, 18.
17 Ibid.
18 Payment Systems and Netting Act 1998, Section 14 1(ca).
19 Ibid, Section 14 2(fa).
20 Scott Farrel, Kings & Wood Malleson, Letter correspondence to International Swaps and Derivatives Association, https://www.isda.org/a/AogDE/august-8-2017-collateral-provider-blackline.pdf
21 Personal Property Securities Act 2009 regulates a security interest in personal property that has been derived from a transaction securing payment for that obligation.

reinforcing this result, in our view, Section 14 becomes one of the most important provisions within the Australian Netting Act. In dealing with close-out netting provisions, more broadly and in relation to contracts, it provides a level of certainty in managing financial security, thus further protecting its enforceability under the Netting Act.

In understanding the importance of Section 14, 'Australian law governs a close-out netting contract, and the contract is entered into in circumstances that are within Commonwealth constitutional reach'. In addition, subsections:

> 14(1)(d) and (e) are intended to clarify that netting will not be affected by the interests of third parties in the obligations being netted. Moreover, the relevance of section 14 to ISDA Master Agreement lies at section 14(1)(d), whereby, it deals specifically with the purported creation of interests in contravention of prohibitions like Section 7 of the Master Agreement.[22]

Noteworthy too, subsection 14(1)(e) goes further than 14(1)(d) by providing that the obligations owed to a party to which a third party may seek to attach an interest in the assets of the party on netting taking effect. As a result, the interests which purportedly attach to those assets will cease to exist. Given that subsection 14(1)(e) does not rely on the presence of any prohibition in the contract, it has a wider effect than subsection 14(1)(d).[23] Thus, it can be argued that, considering the combined effect of sections 14(1)(c) and (e), subsection 14(1)(d) is technically unnecessary.[24]

Furthermore in accordance with Section 14 of the Master Agreement, Section 14(3) of the Netting Act provides that Sections 14(1) and (2) have legal effect on a close-out netting contract 'despite any other law (including the specified provisions)', but subject to any specified stay provision that applies to the Master Agreement.[25] A specified stay provision applies to a close-out netting arrangement by preventing the contracting party or a counterparty from closing out transactions relating to the contract on the grounds discussed in the relevant specified stay provision. Yet, a specified stay provision does not prohibit a counterparty from closing out transactions under a Master Agreement for any other reason.[26]

In *Enron Australia Finance Pty Limited (in Liquidation) v. Integral Energy Australia,*[27] the Court raised concern about the proper construction of a particular clause in the ISDA Master Agreement ('the ISDA Master' or 'the umbrella agreement') which is part of a suite of agreements brought into existence by the International Swaps and Derivatives Association, Inc., formerly known as the International Swap

22 Payment Systems and Netting Act 1998, Section 14(1)(a)–(d).
23 Ibid.
24 Ibid.
25 Ibid, 11.
26 Ibid.
27 [2002] NSWSC 753.

Dealers Association, Inc.[28] A further concern raised by the Court was over a series of electricity swap contracts entered into between Enron and Integral under the ISDA (Australia) Master Agreement and the early termination provisions as they related to the operation of the market quotation. The swap contracts were for the sale of electricity. The facts were as follows:

> [The] dispute arose in circumstances where in reliance upon the appointment of the administrators as an Event of Default within the meaning of clause 5(a)(viii)(2) and (4), Integral designated 5 December 2001 as the Early Termination Date for all outstanding electricity swap contracts ('*outstanding transactions*') under the agreement. The dispute concerns the operation of the provisions governing the occurrence under the ISDA (Australia) of an Event of Default in terms of the determination of the amount, if any, payable by Enron to Integral under clause 6 (e) of the agreement.[29]

In reconciling these concerns, the Court noted the importance of these legal tools and stated:

> The ISDA Master Agreement is an important risk management tool that helps reduce documentation risk, promote legal certainty, and reduce credit risk through netting of contractual obligations. As the business has developed and grown, ISDA has expanded and updated the ISDA Master Agreement and its supporting documents, a process that continues today.[30]

Moreover, the Court reinforced the importance of ISDA Master Agreements to the international financial sector, arguing:

> The few scattered documents which went into evidence concerning agenda for meetings in relation to the ISDA documentation and the suggestion that possibly Enron holding company representatives or Enron Australian representatives may have attended and acquired certain knowledge of the workings of the overseas ISDA Master early termination practice fell light-years short of proving *what was necessary to be proved* by the defendant on this leg of its case. It is drawing a very long bow indeed to suggest that without calling clear direct evidence in this regard one can establish with any precision, let alone the necessary precision, that the parties by reference to previous dealings must be taken to have intended that a particular practice said to operate in terms of the ISDA Master in overseas electricity derivatives markets would have that same operation in relation to the ISDA (Australia).[31]

28 Ibid, 1.
29 Ibid, 6.
30 Ibid, 31.
31 Ibid, 80.

Nonetheless, and a year following the implementation of the Australian Netting Act in 1998, the Court in *Powercor Australia Ltd*[32] made the point that it:

> was required to consider the application of commodity derivate contracts in the electricity sector and how they were hedges against the risk under an ISDA Master Agreement. In this case the parties had entered into an ISDA Master Agreement on 21 November 1996 but was exchanged on or about 16 December 1996.[33]

One of the issues raised by the Court was the effect an ISDA Master Agreement had on trading between the parties.[34] In further recognition of the importance the agreements play in Australia, the Court emphasised that the ISDA Master Agreement is a standard document, devised by experts in future trading, that is used throughout the world in commodity and financial derivatives transactions. Additionally, the Court noted that the ISDA Master Agreement is the 'culmination of the efforts of those experienced in the derivative transaction markets to provide a standard contract to govern their [the parties'] trading relationship'.[35] The Court, in referring to Dr Alastair Hudson's 2013 book on the Law on Financial Derivatives,[36] stated:

> there is a drift towards market standards of documentation. The foremost in this field is the ISDA contract (produced by the International Swaps and Derivatives Association) which has slowly adapted to cover the breadth of derivatives contracts which are arranged between private counterparties on a bilateral basis. Most of these documents are based upon the English and American systems of law.[37]

In the only reference to netting, the Court highlighted Hudson's work on the ISDA Master Agreement:

> Derivatives documentation is structured by organising the way in which the parties will deal with one another across all applicable derivatives of products, under one master agreement. The ISDA structure has formed itself

32 *Powercor Australia Ltd v Pacific Power* [1999] VSC 110.

33 Ibid, 78. Pursuant to that agreement the parties agreed to enter into futures transactions in the New South Wales and Victorian electricity market on the terms and conditions contained therein. The terms of the Master Agreement form part of each transaction by reason of the fact that the parties provided that each futures transaction was to be an amendment to the Master Agreement.

34 Ibid, 143, 259, the court noted that according to the ISDA Master Agreement definitions 'Trade Date' means the date 'on which the parties enter into the transaction'. The confirmation is also dated the same date, but it was not signed and exchanged until 18 March 1997.

35 Ibid, 318.

36 2nd ed. (2013), 90,

37 Ibid, 319.

> into something close to an ideology: the master agreement provides that the master agreement together with all of the other documents entered into between the parties across all transactions are to be read as being a single agreement. (See cl.1(c)). The purpose behind this provision in the master agreement's terms is to seek to achieve netting across all payments made under all transactions between the parties. The master agreement contains all the central terms about what the parties are to do if one of them defaults, or if tax regulations change, or if there is a dispute as to the manner in which amounts owed reciprocally can be set off against one another, and so forth. . . . it sets the parameters for all derivatives transactions.[38]

However, the Court in *Powercor Australia Ltd* did not go any further to confirm the definition of netting according to domestic legislation. Still, it did take account of the role Master Agreements played in supporting netting arrangement in enabling obligations to be set off against one another so that payments between the parties could be made net rather than gross.[39]

Therefore, it can be demonstrated from the *Enron* and *Powercor* cases that Australian Courts not only recognised the importance of ISDA Master Agreements in providing greater stability within the financial sector. They highlighted the interconnectedness between the ISDA Master Agreements and netting arrangements. Yet, the Court in *Powercor Australia Ltd* stopped short of in making any reference to Australia's federal netting law and in particular the close-out netting provisions within the Netting Act. The cases also highlight how an ISDA Master Agreement can assume many forms, including even the governing Agreement that provides for the purchase and sale of electrical power. These Agreements are therefore, not limited to financial market transactions.

On the other hand, the Court in *Re Opes* went some way to explain and reconcile the tensions that had emerged within the Netting Act. It argued:

> The first question the administrators seek to have answered is whether the SLA is a 'close-out netting contract' as defined in section 5 of the Netting Act. The case highlighted how section 5, relevantly, defines a close-out netting contract as 'a contract under which, if a particular event happens: (i) particular obligations of the parties terminate or may be terminated; and (ii) the termination values of the obligations are calculated or may be calculated; and (iii) the termination values are netted, or may be netted, so that only a net cash amount (whether in Australian currency or some other currency) is payable. Section 14 provides that a close-out netting contract will be effective

38 Ibid, 320.

39 Ibid, 216–321. see Section 2(a)(ii) of the Master Agreement and netting; the process of setting off obligations under transactions one against the other was provided for in Section 2(c) of the Master Agreement.

> when the obligations the contract imposes, both outside external administration and in external administration, and despite any other law. The close-out netting contract is further explained in s 14(2).[40]

The case was very different to the aforementioned *Enron* and *Powercor* cases, in that *Re Opes* dealt with contracts to secure the borrowing of securities. The facts were that Opes Prime Stockbroking Limited (OPSL) and a related company, Leveraged Capital Pty Ltd (LCPL), were in administration. The second meeting of creditors for each company has been deferred pending the decision on the application in issue. At the meetings, the creditors were charged with deciding upon the legal status of the debtor Company.[41] There were three alternatives: that (i) the Company execute a deed of company arrangement, (ii) the Company be wound up or (iii) simply that the administration of the Company to be terminated. The administrators were required to investigate the affairs of each company and report to, and advise, the creditors on the options they should adopt. The administration was complicated and gave rise to difficult legal issues. The administrators sought information in determining how to advise creditors on some of the applicable issues. They also sought advice on how to estimate creditors' claims for voting purposes.

The issues in this case arose from the Securities Lending Agreements (SLAs) entered into between each of OPSL and LCPL and its respective clients. The SLA was based on the standard form Australian Master Securities Lending Agreement (AMSLA), published by the Australian Securities Lending Association. That Agreement was, in turn, an adaptation, for Australian purposes, of the standard form Overseas Securities Lending Agreement (now superseded by the Global Master Securities Lending Agreement) published by the International Securities Lending Association.[42] In relation to the netting arrangement, the Court articulated that a key feature of all 'standard-form share lending agreements, which is shared with other agreements in the financial market (e.g. sale and repurchase agreements, currency and interest rate swaps), is that they make provision for close-out netting in the event of default'.[43] While the netting arrangement was complete approximately five years before the publication of the UNIDROIT Principles on close-out netting, the Court determined that:

> close-out netting is the process by which contractual obligations are converted into money obligations which can then be set off against each other to arrive at a net amount payable by one party to the other. An important object

40 (2008) 171 FCR 473. Payment Systems and Netting Act 1998, Section 14(1), Section 14(2), Section 14(4).

41 Ibid, 1.

42 Ibid, 2.

43 Ibid, 3.

> of close-out netting is to reduce exposure in the event that one party to the agreement becomes insolvent prior to the completion date.[44]

Thus, the issue raised by the administrators in a summons for directions under s47D of the *Corporations Act 2001* (Cth) concerned the operation and effect, including the effectiveness, of the close-out netting clause.

In applying its reasoning above, several additional issues arise. One is the applicable jurisdiction when the parties in Australia have entered into one or the other Master Agreements (1992 or 2002), and when one party becomes insolvent. Another issue arises when the applicable currency is not in Australian dollars, but is used as part of the termination process. The currency chosen to enable closing out of the contract, varies with the parties and what has or has not been specified within the contract, including in the ISDA Master Agreement. Finally, in Australia, the approach towards ISDA Master Agreements is found in both the legislation and court decisions. However, the Australian regulatory approach towards netting arrangements had begun before the current international approach had been implemented.

6.1.2 Enforcement

Notwithstanding the uncertain scope of close-out netting provisions in Australia, the *Foreign Judgement Act 1991*[45] provides that foreign judgements are enforceable in Australia. The rationale underlying such enforceability applies, not only in the scenario identified in subsection 3.0, but to trans-border contracts more generally. In effect, a foreign judgement is enforceable when the contract is entered into between parties, one of whom is located in Australia and the other in another state, and when the contract provides for its enforcement including by a court outside Australia. This extraterritorial enforceability of contracts was discussed in *Who Ya Gonna Call Bark Busters Pty. Ltd. v. Brooke.*[46] In referring to the Transfer Agreement, the District Court of New South Wales observed:

> 1. Transfer Payment – 1.1 Brooke shall pay Licensor a Transfer Payment in the amount of $500,000 U.S. Dollars which represents 12.5% of the Redemption Proceeds received by Brooke from the Stock Redemption.
>
> 1.2 Licensee acknowledges that Brooke will receive the Redemption Proceeds in two separate transactions: (i) $3,000,000 on or about the date that Brooke tenders all of his Common Stock to Licensee ('Closing Date'), and (ii) $1,000,000

44 Ibid.

45 Foreign Judgements Act 1991, Part 2. However, a judgment given by a court of New Zealand is only registrable under the Foreign Judgments Act if it is given before 11 October 2013.

46 (2013) 16 DCLR (NSW) 366.

upon the payment by Licensee of the promissory note ('Promissory Note') issued to Brooke on the Closing Date.

1.3 Brooke shall tender the Transfer Payment as follows: a, $375,000 within 30 days of the Closing Date ('Initial Transfer Payment'), b. $ 125,000 within 30 days of Brooke's receipt of final payment under the Promissory Note ('Financed Transfer Payment').[47]

The Court elaborated that:

> the law of the agreement is governed by the substantive law of the State of New South Wales, Australia, without regard to its conflict of law rules. Less clearly articulated is whether an Australian court has the jurisdiction under Australian Law to award damages in a foreign currency. From this case, it is unclear when a court would do so, and what rate of exchange it would apply to that foreign currency.[48]

Nevertheless, it is well understood that under conflict of law rules in Australia, a foreign judgement relating to a contract with close-out netting provisions is enforceable in Australia. However, a challenge posed by Section 14 of the Netting Act and the enforceability for close-out netting provisions arises under subsection 14 A(5)(ii). That subsection states that the intermediary must not comply with instructions given by the grantor in relation to the financial property without seeking the consent of the secured person (or a person who has agreed to act on the instructions of the secured person). The operative word is 'consent', and the determinative requirement is 'seeking consent' of the secured person. A difficulty is in delineating the scope and application of such consent along a slippery slope between 'seeking consent' as required by Section 14 A(5)(ii) and securing that consent. A more material problem is the nature of the need for such 'consent' in the first place, as proposed by the Australian Financial Markets Association [AFMA].

The AFMA raised concerns over the meaning and application of section 14A(5). Their concern was that 'uncertainty in the drafting of that sub-section potentially undermines the effectiveness of the security given for contract obligations under the Netting Act, especially with regard to the right to consent in subsections 4 and 5'.[49] They explained that the confusion in interpreting the intention in drafting the section arises from Section 14A(5) being expressed as not limiting the scope of

47 Ibid, 6. In Robert Walters, Leon Trakman, The Fragmented Approach toward Close-out Netting Provisions in Australia, Indonesia, Malaysia and Singapore Compared, *Journal of Banking Regulation* (2019), 1.

48 Ibid, 67.

49 Australian Financial Markets Association, *Resilience and Collateral Protection Law Amendments* (2016), https://afma.com.au/policy/submissions/R01-16%20Treasury%20Collateral%20Bill.pdf. In Robert Walters, Leon Trakman, The Fragmented Approach toward Close-out Netting Provisions in Australia, Indonesia, Malaysia and Singapore Compared, *Journal of Banking Regulation* (2019), 1.

subsection 14A.1(b). Section 14A.1(b) applies to the enforcement of security over financial property, when the financial property is transferred or otherwise dealt with so as to be in the possession, or under the control of, the secured person or another person.

However, the AFMA argued that it is difficult to identify any other construction of subsection 14A(5). The AFMA concluded that difficulty is likely to lead to confusion in interpretation unless the legislative drafting intention is made clear.[50] The AFMA elaborated that 14A (5) states that paragraph 1(b) is taken not to be satisfied if Column 2 of the Table sets out a condition which is not satisfied. The conditions in subsections 4 and 5 state that the secured party must have the right to consent.[51] Nonetheless, these subsections contend that a condition of consent is neither necessary nor desirable; and that it is contrary to market practice. Of note, in the ISDA Credit Support Annexes under New York law, consent to substitution is not typically required by market participants, and the secured party's consent is not part of the procedure by which excess collateral is withdrawn.[52] The AFMA maintains further that the secured party is protected in respect of substitutions, as the substitute collateral must be received prior to release of the original collateral.[53] Additionally, the secured party may dispute any calculations under the Credit Support Annex, including in respect of return amounts.

Therefore, what remains unclear is the extent to which the enforceability of close-out netting provisions will extend within the Australian legal framework.[54] This lack of clarity is exacerbated by a lack of judicial jurisprudence in this area of Australian law. There is also the potential to overextend protection by providing for the consent of secured parties which is not required, nor recognised, nor clarified by the UNIDROIT Principles.

Australia provides the recognition and enforcement of foreign judgements under the Foreign Judgements Act 1991 [FJA]. The FJA provides for such enforcement, through registration of judgments rendered by the superior courts (and specified inferior courts) of those countries that are listed in the Foreign Judgments Regulations 1992.[55] These measures, directed at recognising and enforcing

50 Ibid.

51 Robert Walters, Leon Trakman, The Fragmented Approach towards Close-out netting Provisions in Australia, Indonesia, Malaysia and Singapore Compared, *Journal of Banking Regulation* (2020), 224–240, https://doi.org/10.1057/s41261-019-00109-w.

52 Ibid.

53 Ibid.

54 Ibid.

55 Foreign Judgements Act 1991 – Foreign Judgement Regulations 1992, The basis of such enforcement is 'substantial reciprocity' in the enforcement of judgments between Australia and each country. The statutory regime applies to the following jurisdictions: Bahamas, British Virgin Islands, Canada, Cayman Islands, Dominica, Falkland Islands, Fiji, France, Germany, Gibraltar, Grenada, Hong Kong, Israel, Italy, Japan, Korea, Malawi, Montserrat, PNG, Poland, St Kitts and Nevis, St Helena, St Vincent and the Grenadines, Seychelles, Singapore, Solomon Islands, Sri Lanka, Switzerland, Taiwan, Tonga, Tuvalu, United Kingdom, and Western Samoa.

foreign judgements such as in respect of close-out netting contracts, have a stabilising impact on international financial markets. However, that impact is blunted by restrictive construction of close-out netting contracts in some other jurisdictions, including in the enforcement of contracts and their provisions.

Nevertheless, in Australia, as highlighted earlier, close-out netting arrangements are effective. Australia provides for bilateral and multilateral netting reciprocally. That is, in arrangements between an Australian bank with a foreign bank branch and a foreign bank with an Australian bank branch. In addition, multibranch netting provisions will not be affected by a non-netting jurisdiction.[56] Nevertheless, additional clarification was required for the 2002 ISDA Master Agreement. It did so by inserting the following into the definition of 'Close-out Amount':

> A Close-out Amount is not required to be the market value of the Terminated Transaction or group of Terminated Transactions and the Determining Party is not obliged to use midmarket quotations or mid-market valuations in determining a Close-out Amount.[57]

However, in Australia to date, there has been no effect from the implementation of either the 2001 ISDA Cross-Bridge Agreement or the 2002 ISDA Energy Bridge Agreement (see Chapter 3).[58] Although the opinion does not cover statutory corporations, local counsel provides two options. Either the relevant statutory provisions would apply to validate the close-out and netting provisions of a Master Agreement in insolvency proceedings as affecting such a corporation, or the courts would enforce these provisions in accordance with the governing law of the Master Agreement, provided this is not contrary to Australian public policy.[59] There remains a significant risk that close-out netting will not be enforced against general insurers or life insurance companies where a judicial manager has been appointed. However, this restriction will not apply to Master Agreements entered into before 18 October 2008 and/or where the right to close out is based on an event other than the appointment of a judicial manager, even if a judicial manager has been appointed.[60] Australia has adopted the international legal framework to netting arrangements and Master Agreements. That action advances Australia's position in the Asia Pacific Region, as an economic and insolvency hub.

56 Fieldfisher, ISDA Master Agreement Legal Opinions on Close-out netting, Copyright Fieldfisher LLP (August 2016), 27–30. Thanks to Chance Clifford, Munich Office for providing the book on Legal Opinion.

57 Ibid, 27–30.

58 ISDA The 2002 Energy Bridge, which is based on the 2001 ISDA Cross-Agreement Bridge, https://www.isda.org/book/2002-energy-bridge-and-commentary/

59 Fieldfisher, *ISDA Master Agreement Legal Opinions on Close-out netting*, Copyright Fieldfisher LLP (August 2016), 27–30; Legal Opinions, provided to the authors by Chance Clifford, Munich Office.

60 Ibid.

6.2 Singapore

Singapore, similar to its regional neighbours, including Australia, has a complex history and has also adopted the common law of England. In 1997, Singapore's economy was not immune to the dislocation arising from the Asian economic crisis; and, since then, it has arguably been working hard with regional partners to establish legal frameworks and mechanisms to reduce risks to the financial sector.[61] A decade later, in 2003, Singapore implemented the Payment and Settlements Systems (Finality and Netting) Act[62] (Singapore Netting Act). The Singapore Netting Act does not adopt a specific definition of close-out netting provisions/clauses of contracts.

Walters and Trakman note that Section 13 of Singapore's Netting Act states that, notwithstanding any provision of the law of insolvency, if a court has made an order for bankruptcy or winding up of a participant in a designated system, or a resolution for the voluntary winding up of such participant had been passed, the operator of the designated system may affect the netting of all obligations owed to or by that participant.[63] The operator may net those obligations up to one business day after the Court has made the order for bankruptcy or winding up of the participant, or the resolution for the voluntary winding up of the participant had been passed. The obligations that are netted shall be disregarded in the bankruptcy or winding up proceedings. The Court added that 'any net obligation owed to, or, by the participant that has not been discharged – is payable to the participant'.[64] Additionally, it provided for the recovery for the benefit of creditors of any net obligation owed, or if that obligation is provable in the bankruptcy or winding up proceedings. Nevertheless, it stipulated that the netting made by the operator of the designated system and any payment made by the participant pursuant thereto shall not be voidable in the bankruptcy or in winding up proceedings.[65] Section 15 of Singapore's Netting Act therefore accords the creditor with a wide scope of protection thereafter.

In *Tan Poh Leng Stanley v. UBS AG*,[66] the High Court of Singapore highlighted several areas of dispute. At issue was the interpretation of the International Swap

61 Robert Walters, Leon Trakman, The Fragmented Approach towards Close-out netting Provisions in Australia, Indonesia, Malaysia and Singapore Compared, *Journal of Banking Regulation* Vol. 21 (2020), 224–240. https://doi.org/10.1057/s41261-019-00109-w.

62 Payment and Settlements Systems (Finality and Netting) Act 2003, Act 39 of 2002, Most recently amended by Act 4 of 2018 wef 06/06/2018.

63 Robert Walters, Leon Trakman, The Fragmented Approach towards Close-Out Netting Provisions in Australia, Indonesia, Malaysia and Singapore Compared, *Journal of Banking Regulation* (2020), 224–240, https://doi.org/10.1057/s41261-019-00109-w.

64 Ibid.

65 Ibid.

66 [2016] SGHC 17, at 7, The plaintiff, Stanley Tan Poh Leng ('ST'), was a private wealth client of the defendant, UBS AG ('the Bank'). Between October 2007 and August 2008, ST invested in 16 equity accumulators ('the Accumulators') on a margin trading basis. At one time, ST owned equity stocks with a combined market value in excess of S$100 million in his account with the Bank ('the Account').

Dealers Association Master Agreement. The main argument presented by Tan Poh Leng Stanley (ST) in these proceedings was that the bank, UBS, was obliged to give notice as stipulated under the 2006 version of the ISDA Master Agreement before it could lawfully terminate and unwind the accumulators. ST argued in the main that he would have had sufficient assets to salvage the shortfall in his account and preserve his positions in the accumulators. ST's claim was thus for damages for breach of the 2006 version of the ISDA Master Agreement (2006 ISDA). ST assessed his loss to be SG$33,778,163. The bulk of this figure was for the Unwinding Costs (SG$25,461,800).[67] The Court noted that the ISDA Master Agreement has to be interpreted in a manner that allows the parties to customise their rights by amending the relevant agreement or through separate agreements. This is often necessarily so, given that the ISDA Master Agreement forms part of a broader transaction relationship.[68] Moreover, the Court discussed the application of Section 6 of the ISDA Master Agreement whereby ST also alleged that UBS had breached Section 6(d)(i) of the ISDA Master Agreement because it had sent details of the unwind of the accumulators to ST by email.[69] Section 6(d)(i) provides that:

> On or as soon as reasonably practicable following the occurrence of an Early Termination Date, each party will make the calculations on its part, if any, contemplated by Section 6(e) and will provide to the other party a statement (1) showing, in reasonable detail, such calculations (including all relevant quotations and specifying any amount payable under Section 6(e)) and (2) giving details of the relevant account to which any amount payable to it is to be paid. In the absence of written confirmation from the source of a quotation obtained in determining a Market Quotation, the records of the party obtaining such quotation will be conclusive evidence of the existence and accuracy of such quotation.[70]

Based on the foregoing, the Court required UBS to provide a statement showing in reasonable detail the calculations it made following the occurrence of an Early Termination Date. Furthermore, it stipulated that Section 12(a) of the 2006 ISDA Master Agreement provides that such a statement may not be given by facsimile transmission or electronic messaging system. The Court went onto say that on its face, Section 6(d)(i) of the 2006 ISDA Master Agreement applies on the occurrence of an 'Early Termination Date'. Therefore, when the parties had agreed to unwind the Accumulators outside the ISDA Master Agreement, subsection 6(d)(i) was prima facie inapplicable, as an 'Early Termination Date' within the meaning of the Master Agreement had not occurred.[71] However, it maintained that,

67 Ibid, 3.
68 Ibid, 184(a).
69 Ibid, 236–237.
70 Ibid, 236.
71 Ibid, 240.

under subsection 12(a) of the 2006 ISDA Agreement, the Statement Clause may not be given 'by facsimile transmission or electronic messaging system'.[72] Assuming that the Termination Provisions are applicable, the UBS's e-mails to [YCB] on 23 and 24 October 2008 referred to earlier, and its e-mail to [YCB] on 2 December 2009, appear broadly to contain information that meets the requirements under Section 6(d) of each Master Agreement. The final determination is as much a commercial as a legal one (e.g. whether the information was provided in 'reasonable detail'). The emails sent by Clara to YCB on 23 October 2008 and 24 October 2008 after the unwinding of each batch of Accumulators do provide reasonable details required by the Statement of Calculations, given that they state the price at which the respective Accumulators were unwound and the Unwinding Costs.[73] The Court held that the unwinding of the accumulators was pursuant to a mutual agreement outside of Section 6(d)(i) of the ISDA Master Agreement and the notice provisions in the ISDA Master Agreement.[74] Nevertheless, the Court highlighted that it is trite that a term is only implied in the face of 'necessity' and not 'sensibility'.[75] In this regard, it was not necessary to imply a term that the Statement Clause should apply to the oral agreement between UBS and ST to unwind the Accumulators. Thus, in applying the necessity test, the Court[76] endorsed the Statement Clause in accordance with the determination in *Sembcorp Marine Ltd v. PPL Holdings*[77]. Yet, the Court did not address whether UBS was obliged to determine the termination amount in connection with the unwinding on the basis of subsection 6(e) of the ISDA Master Agreement.

Materially in issue was that UBS had not conducted the close out in a manner that was consistent with the exercise of reasonable care and did not provide the Claimant with calculation statements, as is required in the ISDA Master Agreement. A threshold question was whether UBS had a duty of care, owed in both contract and tort, to conduct the close out exercise promptly and with reasonable care.[78] The Court elaborated, by holding that the ISDA Master Agreement must be interpreted in a manner that allows the parties to customise their rights by amending the relevant agreement or by reaching a separate agreement. This determination is necessary, as the ISDA Master Agreement often forms part of a broader transactional relationship. The Court added that UBS and the Claimant were, not only counterparties in a derivatives transaction, but were also, among their other

72 The Statement Clause is the relevant portion of the ISDA Experts' Joint Report that deals directly with the application of that clause to the consent of the parties in this case.
73 Ibid, 237–238.
74 Ibid, 242–249.
75 Ibid, 243.
76 *Sembcorp Marine Ltd. v. PPL Holdings Pte. Ltd.* [2013] 4 SLR 193 at [101].
77 [2013] 4 SLR 193.
78 Robert Walters, Leon Trakman, The Fragmented Approach towards Close-out netting Provisions in Australia, Indonesia, Malaysia and Singapore Compared, *Journal of Banking Regulation,* Vol. 21 (2020), 224–240, https://doi.org/10.1057/s41261-019-00109-w.

functions, the Charger and Chargee in relation to the Charge Over Assets.[79] This is an important determination because Singapore's Netting Act does not expressly provide any direction or guidance on the enforcement of close-out netting provisions. Nonetheless, the Court noted that UBS, rather than relying on an ISDA Master Act, had in fact established a Credit Services Notice Letter (CSNL), relying on its Enforcement Procedure. The Court went further by highlighting that the CSNL Enforcement Procedure is consistent with the 2006 ISDA[80] However, the Court did not discuss the definition of close out, nor the content of the ISDA Master Agreement with regard to the governing law or jurisdiction.

Two years later in *Macquarie Bank Ltd*[81] at issue was whether Macquarie's USD 1.2 million was recoverable as a closed-out amount. The Court stated:

> Macquarie's case [is] that the Transaction was made in the course of certain emails in May 2014 and recorded in a Long Form Confirmation ('LFC') dated 6 June 2014 incorporating the standard 2002 International Swaps and Derivatives Association Inc. Master Agreement (the 'ISDA Form'); that Graceland wrongfully repudiated the Transaction thereby entitling Macquarie to terminate the Transaction as it did on 8 July 2014; and that the sum of US$1.2 million is recoverable by Macquarie as the 'Close-out Amount' (as defined in the ISDA Form).[82]

Accordingly, the Close-out Amount was allegedly USD 1.2 million, being the difference between USD 315 and USD 275 (ie, USD 40) multiplied by 30,000mts [make to stock].[83] The Court held:

> [When referring to the] calculation of the Close-out Amount, it was submitted that the definition of Close-out Amount in Clause 14 of the ISDA Form provided in material part as follows: 'Close-out Amount' means, with respect to each Terminated Transaction . . . and a Determining Party, the amount of the losses or costs of the Determining Party that are or would be incurred under then prevailing circumstances (expressed as a positive number) or gains of the Determining Party that are or would be realised under then prevailing circumstances (expressed as a negative number) in replacing, or in providing for the Determining Party the economic equivalent of, (a) the material terms of that Terminated Transaction . . . including the payments and deliveries by the parties under Section 2(a)(i) in respect of that Terminated Transaction . . . that would, but for the occurrence of the relevant Early Termination Date, have been required after that date (assuming satisfaction of the

79 *Tan Poh Leng Stanley v UBS AG* [2016] SGHC 17, 184.
80 Ibid, 189–200.
81 *Macquarie Bank Ltd. v. Graceland Industry Pte. Ltd.* [2018] SGHC(I) 5.
82 Ibid, 2.
83 Ibid, 103.

> conditions precedent in Section 2(a)(iii)) and (b) the option rights of the parties in respect of that Terminated Transaction.[84]

The definition of close out amount within the ISDA Master Agreement departs significantly from the definition of close-out netting within the Singapore Netting Act. This divergence is understandable because, in practice, this legal mechanism is to provide a process whereby the parties to the Master Agreement can terminate. There would be no practical requirement to define close-out netting in the ISDA Master Agreement(s). In reconciling the amount that will be afforded during a close out:

> it will be undertaken by the Determining Party (or its agent), which will act in good faith and use commercially reasonable procedures in order to produce a commercially reasonable result. . . . Each Close-out Amount will be determined as of the Early Termination Date or, if that would not be commercially reasonable, as of the date or dates following the Early Termination Date as would be commercially reasonable.[85]

In determining that Macquarie's termination was reasonable. The Court recognised that 'Clause 14, provided':

> Macquarie with the choice between identifying the losses or costs, or the gains which it would incur or realise in (i) replacing or (ii) in providing for itself the economic equivalent of, two items, viz, (i) the material terms of the Terminated Transaction (as defined) and (ii) the option rights of the parties in respect of the Terminated Transaction (as defined). It must be noted that, the dispute did not concern any option rights of the parties in respect of the Terminated Transaction.[86]

While the Court did not engage in further discussion of close out, netting, governing law or jurisdiction, the importance of the case is that it highlighted how close out provisions within the ISDA Master Agreement are used to calculate the close out amount. In that case the Court determined that Macquarie's calculation of the close out amount was commercially reasonable.

6.2.1 Enforcement

The enforcement of an ISDA Master Agreement and/or a contract, and close-out netting provisions in Singapore are comparable to the rules in Australia. That is, the enforcement of ISDA Master Agreements that contain close-out netting

84 Ibid, 134.
85 Ibid.
86 Ibid, 134(b).

arrangements follow the Australian netting process. Singapore's Netting Act and the judicial interpretation of it, articulate the nature and scope of netting clearly, as elaborated by the Court in *Tan Poh Leng Stanley v. UBS AG.*[87] Singapore law recognises choice of law provisions in netting contracts, subject to domestic public policy requirements, where Singapore is the forum. The overriding regulatory aim of Singapore law on the subject is to satisfy domestic business demands for creditor protection in the face of bankruptcy or winding up of a participant in a designated financial system. In our view, the close-out netting laws underpin the current national policy of Singapore to maintain and grow its status as a central business and finance hub in Southeast Asia.

Notwithstanding this, the position taken under Singapore law is that ISDA Master Agreements are effective and readily used. However, Early Termination, as of 2016, was not necessarily applicable. In other words, where automatic Early Termination is not selected, then there is a 'risk that the right of the Non-defaulting Party to designate an Early Termination Date and terminate the Transactions with notice after the onset of insolvency can be affected if the liquidator of the Defaulting Party has already exercised his right to disclaim any Transactions under Section 332 of the Companies Act'.[88] However, under this scenario, a liquidator cannot choose to disclaim only some (but not all) of the Transactions.

On the one hand, multibranch netting arrangements are effective between a Singapore bank with a foreign bank branch and vis-à-vis a foreign bank with a Singapore bank branch. On the other side, multibranch netting provisions are not affected by non-netting jurisdiction. The Monetary Authority of Singapore has powers in relation to banks, insurance companies and other financial institutions. However, these powers do not extend to the validity of the application of provisions of an ISDA Master Agreement. Rather, it would be left to the courts to decide on the validity or otherwise of the provisions of an ISDA Master Agreement. Noteworthy, too, an insurance company is only covered by transactions entered into under an ISDA Master Agreement that is attributable to the same insurance fund that is maintained by that company.[89] Similar to most other states, Singapore accepts the notion that multibranch netting arrangements are important parts of the overall netting framework where more than two banking institutions are involved in transacting. Arguably, this approach and more broadly, the acceptance of the use of netting arrangements and ISDA Master Agreements, underpin Singapore's policy direction in continuing to be a regional and international financial and legal hub in the future.

87 *Tan Poh Leng Stanley v. UBS AG* [2016] SGHC 17, [7].

88 Fieldfisher, *ISDA Master Agreement Legal Opinions on Close-out netting*, Copyright Fieldfisher LLP (August 2016), 22–203 Thanks to Chance Clifford, Munich Office for providing the book on Legal Opinion.

89 Ibid, 202.

6.3 India

In India, as distinct from Australia and Singapore, there is no uniform and explicit legislation governing close-out netting. Repeated attempts have been made to enact clear and comprehensive netting procedures for financial contracts in order to improve derivative market, to improve investor's confidence, and to expand the scope of credit default swaps. The government of India is planning to introduce a common netting law for all financial institutions and intermediaries,[90] specifically a law for netting of financial contracts.[91] Although India has limited provisions in existing legislation on the subject, inconsistency in provisions is a major concern. Repeated attempts over two decades have been made to establish bilateral netting procedures for financial contracts.[92] Currently, in the absence of bilateral netting, the regulations of the Reserve Bank of India [RBI] require the banks to measure credit exposure to a counterparty for over-the-counter (OTC) derivative contracts, based on gross market-to-market (MTM) exposure instead of net MTM exposure.[93]

A proposal for bilateral netting (close-out netting in mutual transactions in insolvency, winding up or liquidation) was presented in the Financial Resolution and Deposit Insurance (FRDI) Bill, was withdrawn in August 2018. The Bill proposed netting related amendments to the 1934 RBI Act.[94] Should this FRDI Bill be adopted into law, it could become significant in relation to close-out netting. Nonetheless, the Payment and Settlement Systems Act 2007 (PSS) is one of the Indian statutes that have been enacted to regulate and supervise the payment system in India. This statute provides a legal base for netting and settlement, providing for the regulation and supervision of Indian payment system. The RBI is empowered under the Act to operate and commence the payment and settlement systems in India. The PSS Act makes reference to netting procedure in a few of its provisions. The Supervision of Payment and Settlement Systems Regulations 2008 and the Payment and Settlement Systems Regulations 2008 are two important regulations under the PSS Act. Under subsection 7(v)[95], the scope for netting is provided in special circumstances. On the application made by any person seeking to commence the payment system, the RBI, after enquiring into the genuineness of the application, may issue authorisation for the payment system, considering various

90 Ashwin Manikandan, Gayatri Nayak, *Proposed Common Netting Law May Help Free Up Banks' Capital* (2019), https://economictimes.indiatimes.com/markets/stocks/news/proposed-common-netting-law-may-help-free-up-banks-capital/articleshow/71251951.cms?from=mdr.

91 FE Bureau, *Permitting Netting of Financial Contracts Positive Move for Credit Default Swaps Market*, February 2020, https://www.financialexpress.com/market/permitting-netting-of-financial-contracts-positive-move-for-credit-default-swaps-market/1855059/.

92 Ibid.

93 Ibid.

94 Reserve Bank, 1934.

95 The Payment and Settlement Systems Act 2007.

factors including netting as one option. Section 23[96] of the Act regulates payment obligations and the settlement system in accordance with gross or netting procedures, with the approval of the RBI.

Several specific provisions for netting were provided for in the Payment and Settlement Systems (Amendment) Bill 2018.[97] One inter-ministerial committee was set up by the Ministry of Finance, to re-examine and finalise the amendments to the Payment and Settlement Systems (PSS) Act 2007. That Committee recommended[98] that the law relating to payments be amended and consolidated. There were few provisions for netting in the proposed 2018 PSS Amendment Bill. Clause 2(1) v. defines 'netting' to mean:

> the determination by the system provider of the amount of money or securities, due or payable or deliverable, as a result of setting off or adjusting, the payment obligations or delivery obligations among the system participants, including the claims and obligations arising out of the termination by the system provider, on the insolvency or dissolution or winding up of any system participant or such other circumstances as may be provided in the bye-laws, in relation to the payment system, of the transactions admitted for settlement at a future date so that only a net claim be demanded or a net obligation be owned.[99]

Furthermore, should the 2018 PSS Amendment Bill be resurrected and adopted, Clause 60 could provide that a system provider shall disclose to the existing or potential system participants, the terms and conditions including the charges and the limitations of liability under the payment system. The amended PSS could also require that the system provider supply participants with copies of the byelaws governing the operation of the payment system, netting arrangements and other relevant documents as may be specified.[100] How this disclosure requirement would function in practice is not fully clear; however, it is assumed that the applicable provisions in the amended PSS would provide a layer of transparency which would make participants aware of the netting arrangements in place. Additionally, proposed Clause 62 would address the determination of the payment obligation and settlement instructions to be applied in the gross or netting procedure.[101]

In the Proposed PSS Bill, the payment obligations and settlement instructions among system participants would be determined in accordance with the applicable

96 Ibid.

97 Payment and Settlement Systems (Amendment) Bill 2018.

98 Report of the Inter-Ministerial Committee for Finalisation of Amendments to the PSS Act, 2007, https://dea.gov.in/sites/default/files/Payment%20and%20settlement.pdf.

99 The Payment and Settlement Systems Bill 2018, https://dea.gov.in/sites/default/files/Payment%20and%20settlement.pdf, at Preliminary Definitions.

100 Ibid.

101 The Payment and Settlement Systems Bill 2018.

gross or netting procedure, approved by the Payments Regulatory Board and applied by the Board issuing authorisation to a payment system under section 20, or through gross or netting settlement and netting procedures. The procedure adopted may be approved by the Board under any other provisions of the Act. Nevertheless, prior to the enactment of the PSS Act 2007, a working group submitted a report in 2003 on Rupee derivatives, where an attempt was made to extend netting procedure to OTC derivatives.[102] The working group recommended that, any legislation enacted on netting would be operationalised by novation for application to derivative markets. It also recommended that multilateral netting by novation for derivative markets may be operationalised by Clearing Corporation of India Limited (CCIL), with well-defined procedures for management credit and liquidity risks that specify the responsibilities of each of the CCIL participants. To implement the CCIL report, guidelines on netting by novation would need to be issued. Thus, India, at this stage, is considering making various options available for the regulation of netting provisions, so as not to restrict the market to a single netting mechanism.

The scope of netting is not limited to netting law. Netting is permissible in the winding up procedure under India's Companies Act 2013 and previous company laws. More specifically, the insolvency law of India also has scope for netting. In the liquidation process, when the liquidator forms the liquidation estate under Section 36 of the Insolvency and Bankruptcy Code 2016 (IB), the assets which are subject to netting and setting off in multilateral trading or clearing transactions are excluded.[103] Section 173 of the IB Code addresses mutual credit and set off, where the set off sums due from one party with sums due from another party is possible during the administration and distribution of the bankrupt estate.[104] During the corporate insolvency resolution process under the IB Code, claim form B for completion by operational creditors requires that claimants provide information relating to mutual credit, mutual debt, or other mutual benefits between the corporate debtor and creditors which can be set off against the claim.[105] Throughout the resolution process, netting between creditor and corporate debtor is possible.

There have been positive movements in India to establish a uniform law for close-out netting. In 2019, RBI report on 'Benchmarking India's Payment System' (RBI Report)[106] emphasised the value of a sound and appropriate legal framework to address issues of insolvency, electronic signature and netting for establishing an efficient payment system. The report represented a wide-ranging exercise and

102 Report of the Working Group on Rupee Derivatives, January 2003, https://rbidocs.rbi.org.in/rdocs/PublicationReport/Pdfs/34148.pdf, at recommendations 7.24–7.28.

103 The Insolvency and Bankruptcy Code, 2016.

104 Ibid.

105 The IBBI (Corporate Insolvency Resolution Process) 2016.

106 Benchmarking India's Payment System, Department of Payment and Settlement Systems Reserve Bank of India, https://rbidocs.rbi.org.in/rdocs/PublicationReport/Pdfs/BIPS04062019CE3C72-E9873244ED8BAAE9C8FC5955A8.PDF, 18–19.

included a comparative analysis of 21 countries from different continents, including advanced economy countries and some developing Central and South East Asian economies. In the 2019–2020 economic survey, the balance of opinion favoured bilateral netting to release bank capital.[107]

Raghuram Rajan[108] (former Governor of RBI) explained the requirement of netting in derivative contract and the future possibility of the netting by amendments to the 1934 RBI Act. However, the Indian Government may also reintroduce a Bill on bilateral netting.[109] Consistent with these developments in regulating netting, in September 2020 the Indian Lok Sabha (Parliament of India) approved the proposed Bilateral Netting of Qualified Financial Contracts Bill.[110] The next stage towards the adoption of the Bill is Presidential assent, followed by implementation. The Bill would help banks release a portion of their capital locked in transactions in the OTC derivatives market and spur lending. Arguably, the Bill is 'absolutely critical' for the country's financial stability.[111] Finance minister Nirmala Sitharaman is of the view that the absence of a bilateral netting law prevented banks from on-lending by as much as Rs 2.14 lakh crore during the financial years of 2017–2020, as they were forced to lock up higher capital against trades in the OTC market.[112]

Indian law permits the multilateral netting of OTC derivative financial contracts through the Clearing Corporation of India, but bilateral netting is not permitted because bilateral contracts do not have any firm legal basis there.[113] This could be problematic in future large-scale investment transactions. Nonetheless, the value of bilateral derivative contracts is estimated by the Clearing Corporation of India to be Rs 56,33,257 crore as of March 2018; as such, bilateral contracts constitute approximately 40% of total financial contracts.[114] On the other hand, it would not be unreasonable to expect India to follow the English law governing close-out netting. The practice of adopting English Law in trade, finance and investment law is consistent with India's position as a common law and commonwealth jurisdiction. This practice was evident in 2012 in a letter from the ISDA to the Deputy

107 Vishwanath Nair, *Economic Survey 2020: 'Bilateral Netting' to Help Release Bank Capital*, January 2020, https://www.bloombergquint.com/business/economic-survey-2020-bilateral-netting-to-help-release-bank-capital.

108 Raghuram Rajan: Strengthening Our Debt Markets Annual Day Address by Dr Raghuram Rajan, Governor of the Reserve Bank of India, to the Foreign Exchange Dealers Association of India, Mumbai, 26 August 2016.

109 Vishwanath Nair, *Economic Survey 2020: 'Bilateral Netting' to Help Release Bank Capital*, https://www.business-standard.com/article/economy-policy/govt-to-reintroduce-frdi-bill-timeline-not-decided-yet-says-fm-sitharaman-.

110 FE Bureau, *Netting Law to Help Banks Unlock Capital and Spur Lending, Says FM Nirmala Sitharaman*, https://www.financialexpress.com/industry/banking-finance/netting-law-to-help-banks-unlock-capital-spur-lending-says-fm-nirmala-sitharaman/2090384/.

111 Ibid.

112 Ibid. Note that one trillion rupees is equal to one lakh crore rupees.

113 Ibid.

114 Ibid.

Governor of Indian Reserve Bank. The letter noted that the collateral arrangement is best suited to India's legal system and regulatory regime as margining arrangements established with OTC derivative transactions generally follow the ISDA English law Credit Support Annex (English law CSA).[115] The letter also noted:

> It is relevant to notes that RBI has, in the context of the Indian CDS market, permitted to use of the English law CSA for either (i). Onshore INR CDS transactions only, or (ii). All onshore transactions including INR CDS transactions. From a legal standpoint, the English law CSA constitutes a confirmation of a transaction under the ISDA Master Agreement and is not a separate or security document as that term is commonly understood. The effectiveness and enforceability of the English law CSA therefore hinges upon close-out netting under the ISDA Master Agreement.[116]

However, page 4 of the letter did state further that the requisite English law may not meet the requirements of legal certainty for bilateral arrangements in the Indian contractual and legal context.[117]. On the one hand, and even in contractual matters operating outside of bankruptcy, the close-out netting provisions of the ISDA Master Agreement are effective in accordance with both English and New York law. What is unclear is whether the enforceability of close-out netting provisions under Indian insolvency law would be impeded, although this should not be so when the entity is incorporated under the Indian corporation's law that includes banks and other finance entities.[118] Adding to the lack of clarity is that the High Court of India, to date, has not presided over insolvency cases that have required it to consider the establishment, definition, application, or enforcement of close-out netting provisions. Individuals and entities interested in this area of the law will need to be vigilant as to how India respond, and what regulatory approach will be settled upon for close-out netting provisions, in the future.

India's transition towards internationalized norms is evident in recent judicial decisions there, particularly in relation to ISDA Master Agreements. In the Bombay High Court case of *Hdfc Bank Ltd. v. Rohan Dyes and Intermediates,*[119] the Court considered the effect of ISDA Master Agreements, entered into in 2007.[120] The facts were that:

> HDFC Bank Ltd. sought to winding up the Respondent Company – Rohan Dyes and Intermediates Ltd. on the ground that the Respondent Company

115 International Swaps and Derivatives Association (2012), https://www.isda.org/a/6QiDE/india-submission-oct-12.pdf, 4.
116 Ibid.
117 Ibid.
118 Ibid, 2.
119 *Company Petition NO. 320 OF 2013*, 19 July 2016, Bench: B.P. Colabawalla.
120 Ibid, paragraph 3 (d).

> is unable to pay its debts. It is the case of the Petitioner that the Respondent Company is indebted to the Petitioner in the sum of approximately Rs.8.74 Crores which comprises of a principal sum of Rs.8.19 Crores and simple interest of Rs.54.96 Lacs.[121]

Importantly the claim in the petition arose from certain derivative transactions that were entered into between the Petitioner Bank and the Respondent Company. The Court stressed that it was not in dispute that the Petitioner Bank was an authorised dealer in foreign exchange and listed as an authorised dealer in accordance with the RBI Guidelines. The Court also noted:

> Under this Agreement, CBOP and the Respondent Company agreed to enter into various derivative transactions each to be evidenced by a deal confirmation which would be supplemental to, a part of and subject to the ISDA Agreement and the Schedule thereto. Along with the ISDA Agreement, the Company also executed a Risk Disclosure Statement dated 15 November, 2007 in acceptance and acknowledgment of its understanding of the risks involved in entering into derivative transactions. It is not in dispute that the ISDA Agreement as well as the Risk Disclosure Statement were signed on behalf of the Respondent Company by persons who were authorized in that regard as per the board resolution dated 14 November, 2007.[122]

While there was no discussion or recognition of netting arrangements, the Court highlighted that one option to pursue was the use of net settlement. The Court argued:

> Be that as it may, as per the deal confirmation dated 26 June, 2008, on the expiry of the first option (i.e. on 27 June, 2012), since the US Dollar was trading above Rs.43.15 per Dollar, the first option was exercised by the Petitioner on the expiry date of the said option. As per the said option, the Company was obliged to sell US$800,000/- to the Petitioner at the pre – agreed USD/INR rate of Rs.43.15 (the strike price). Hence the Petitioner addressed an email dated 27 June, 2012 to the Company containing the details of the said option and called upon the Company to inform the Petitioner as regards utilization and/or net settlement of the said option so exercised by the Petitioner.[123]

121 Ibid, 1.
122 Ibid, paragraph 3 (c).
123 Ibid, paragraph 3 (n).

Against this backdrop, the Court identified the further requirement that it reconcile issues relating to the currency to be used in settling the contractual requirements. It determined:

> [U]nder the Master ISDA Agreement, the calculation agent is the Petitioner Bank, unless otherwise specified in the Deal Confirmation in relation to a particular transaction. In fact, even the Deal Confirmation dated 26 June, 2008 specifically states that the calculation agent shall be as per the signed Master ISDA Agreement which in term makes the Petitioner Bank the calculation agent. In each of the e-mails that have been sent by the Petitioner Bank to the Respondent Company on the expiry of the relevant options, a specific US Dollar rate has been mentioned by the Petitioner Bank.[124]

While the Court did not expressly recognise the enforcement of the ISDA Master Agreement, it did infer how Indian courts are likely to take into consideration these agreements as part of the wider insolvency issues that banks are to address in calculating the extent of the debt obligations.

Five years later in 2018, the Delhi High Court in *Transport Corporation of India v. Reserve Bank of India & Anr*[125] considered the transactions arrangements set out in contracts between the two entities. The Court highlighted how the:

> Transport Corporation sought a declaration of the transaction aforesaid as void on the ground of the same being unconscionable, in contravention of law and public policy including the Comprehensive Guidelines on Derivatives, the Master Circular on Interbank dealing and the Foreign Exchange Management (Foreign Exchange Derivative Contract) Regulations.[126]

In light of the transactional arrangements, the Court posed the following questions:

> whether there is accord and satisfaction achieved in respect of the transactions in issue or, discharge of the contract by virtue of performance of obligations undertaken therein or, by mutual agreement?[127] . . . Whether the transaction was conducted in pursuance to the ISDA agreement dated 06.09.2007 and the deal confirmation dated 20.09.2007? OPP 9. Relief.[128]

124 Ibid, [26].
125 *Transport Corporation of India v. Reserve Bank of India & Anr* Delhi High Court, 2 May 2018.
126 Ibid, 4.
127 Ibid.
128 Ibid, 4.7.

While the Court dismissed the case, it concluded that counsel for the plaintiff had drawn attention to paragraph 28 of the written statement. There the appellant/defendant had pleaded that, in terms of Guidelines and Directives issued by RBI:

> [the] appellant/defendant was under an obligation to enter into an exactly off-setting transaction and option deals with another person and that it covered the transaction with the plaintiff in entirety by entering into various transactions at the same time with another person and that the appellant/defendant in this process was able to comply with the RBI Mandate, while being able to service the plaintiff and that the bank benefited.[129]

Even though the Court gave little attention to the ISDA Master Agreements, it highlighted that they are extensively used in India. It further demonstrated that India, as an emerging economy, had embraced a universalist approach to contracts commonly used in the banking and finance sector. By default, it is arguable that India has adopted elements of netting arrangements, as is inferred from this case.

A year later in 2019, the Bombay High Court in *Kotak Mahindra Bank Ltd.*[130] exhibited a more significant signs of how Indian courts will approach the application and use of ISDA Master Agreements. It noted that the Writ Petitioner had invoked a remedy by filing an Application under Section 19 of the recovery of debts due to Banks and Financial Institutions Act 1993. Most noteworthy was how the Court had to respond to a sum amount that was to be payable in accordance with an ISDA Master Agreement. The Court noted that by:

> Decree in sum of ₹ 6,01,11,346.54 being amount due and payable as on 28.02.2010 with further default interest @ applicable under ISDA Agreement with effect from 01.03.2010 till realization was prayed for. It was prayed that such additional amounts as may become due and payable in respect of derivative transactions entered, be also decreed. It was stated in the claim that Defendant-Company had made profits out of derivative transactions executed with the writ petitioner to the tune of ₹ 4,94,76,370/-.[131]

In referencing the importance of the ISDA Master Agreement, the Court noted:

> [P]ursuant to the Sanction Letters, the Defendant Company executed the ISDA Agreement with the Applicant for entering into derivative transactions. The ISDA Agreement was executed by the Defendant Company

129 Ibid, 10.
130 *Kotak Mahindra Bank Ltd* vs Alps Industries Limited, Bombay High Court, 18 November 2019 1/14 202-wp-1583–10.doc. On jurisdiction also see Madras *High Court ICICI Bank Limited vs M/S. Fab N Fabrics* on 29 April 2011.
131 Ibid, 2.

> through its Chairman, Mr. K. K. Agarwal, pursuant board resolution dated 12 November 2005 whereby the Board of Directors of the Defendant Company duly authorized severally its Chairman and Managing Director to enter into ISDA Agreement for the purpose of executing derivative transactions for and on behalf of the Defendant Company with the Applicant. The Defendant Company later on also furnished Board Resolutions dated 29 December 2006 and 31 October 2007 for and on behalf of the Defendant Company whereby the authorised signatories mentioned therein were permitted to deal in derivative transactions at the 202-wp-1583–10.doc enhanced limits sanctioned and as set out in the respective Sanction Letters of the Applicant. The board resolutions dated 12th November 2005, 29 December, 2006 and 31 October 2007 are collectively referred to as the 'Board Resolutions'.[132]

The Court elaborated further:

> The ISDA Agreement sets out that each party would make payment or delivery specified in each confirmation to be made by it, subject to the other provisions of the ISDA Agreement. There are also detailed provisions in the ISDA Agreement as to the manner and time at which payment should be made by the Defendant Company. Clause 2(e) of the ISDA Agreement made provision for default interest in the event of a party defaulting in performance of any of its payment obligation. Through Clause 3(a)(ii) of the ISDA Agreement, the Defendant Company represented that it had the power to execute and deliver the agreement and other documents and had taken all necessary actions to authorize such execution, delivery and performance. The Defendant Company has under Clause 3(g) of the ISDA Agreement, as amended and supplemented by the Schedule represented that it has taken an independent decision to enter into the ISDA Agreement and Transactions thereto without placing reliance on any communication, whether written or oral, by the Applicant and that it is acting on a principal-to-principal basis. Under the clause 3(h) of the ISDA Agreement, as amended and supplemented by

132 Ibid, 4, 5.1.5. 'Hereto annexed and marked as Exhibit 'B-1 and B-2' (colly) are copies of the said ISDA Master Agreements dated as of 14th November 2005 and executed on 18th November 2005 and 25th July 2006 respectively and hereto annexed and marked as Exhibit 'C-1', C-2 and C-3 (colly) are copies of the aforementioned Board Resolutions dated 12 November 2005, 29th December 2006 and 31 October 2007 respectively. 5.1.6 Along with the ISDA Agreements, the Defendant Company also executed two separate Risk Disclosure Statement for Derivative Transactions dated 18th November 2005 and 19th November 2006 whereby Defendant Company, accepted and acknowledged that it not only understood the nature of and risks involved in derivative transactions but also was capable of assuming and assume the risks arising out of the derivative transactions. Hereto annexed and marked as Annexure 'D-1 and D-2' (colly) are copies of the Risk Disclosure Statement for Derivative Transactions dated 18th November 2005 and 19th November 2006'.

> the Schedule, the Defendant Company also represented that it was capable of assessing and understanding the Transactions whether on its own or through its independent advisers. Clause 5 of the said ISDA Agreement set out the Events of Default and the Termination Events. Failure to make payment in accordance with the ISDA Agreement or breach of the terms of the ISDA Agreement as provided under Clause 5 was expressly stated to be an Event of Default.[133]

On the issue of jurisdiction, the Court noted that the:

> Applicant is a banking company which extends various banking services and financial facilities to its customers as a scheduled commercial bank and authorised dealer. The Applicant is carrying on business from its office at Mumbai. The Defendant Company is a company registered under the Companies Act 1956 and its registered office is situated in Uttar Pradesh. The ISDA (International Swaps & Derivative Association) Agreement dated as of 14 November 2005 was executed on 18 November 2005 together with Schedule thereto and the subsequent ISDA Agreement together with Schedule dated as of 14 November 2005 was executed on 25th July 2006 (both the ISDA Agreements along with their respective Schedules collectively referred to as the 'ISDA Agreement/the said Agreement') between the Applicant and the Defendant Company at New Delhi. The transactions in question were executed and performed at Mumbai. The ISDA Agreement specifically provides for the exclusive jurisdiction of the Courts/Tribunals at Mumbai.[134]

The resulting outcome was that the writ petition was disposed of, setting aside the impugned Order. The importance of this case cannot be underestimated. The clear recognition by the courts of the role ISDA Master Agreements have in providing a framework and managing risks relating to Indian investments highlights the importance of those Agreements. In this case it was demonstrated how the Court drew upon specific provisions in the ISDA Master Agreement to determine the defaulting party and additionally where jurisdiction resided. However, it did not confirm how its provisions would be enforced. Furthermore, and while there was no mention of whether close-out netting provisions formed a component of the agreement, it highlights the need for India to adopt netting arrangements through legislation. Thus, what has emerged is an evolving and developing landscape in relation to the application of ISDA Master Agreements and netting provisions.

133 Ibid, 4, 5.1.8. At 5.1.9 Pursuant to the ISDA Agreement and Sanction Letters, Mr. Sandeep Agarwal, the Managing Director and Mr. K. K. Agarwal, the Chairman of the Defendant 202-wp-1583–10.doc Company jointly executed Deeds of Guarantees, more particularly personal guarantee dated 18 November 2005 pursuant to Sanction Letter dated 27 October 2005 and personal guarantee dated 2 January 2007 pursuant to Sanction Letter dated 29 December 2006.

134 Ibid, 5.

6.3.1 Enforcement

The enforcement of an ISDA Master Agreement and/or contract and close-out netting provisions falls within the Indian Contracts Act 1872 (the CA).[135] Firstly, Section 37 of the CA sets out the:

> obligations of the parties whereby the parties to a contract either perform, or offer to perform, their respective promises, unless such performance is dispensed with or excused under the provisions of this Act, or of any other law. Promises bind the representatives of the promisors in case of the death of such promisors before performance, unless a contrary intention appears from the contract.[136]

Secondly, the Act provides that the enforcement of a contractual obligation will be subject to the event that occurred. In effect, a contract that is subject to a contingent condition, such as the occurrence of an uncertain future event, cannot be voided unless and until that condition is satisfied. For example, until an unforeseen pandemic eventuates and renders performance impossible, the contingent condition providing for such an eventuality, remains unsatisfied and prevents the contract from being rendered unenforceable on that ground.[137] Thirdly, Section 226 of the CA extends the scope of the contracts arising through an agent and for obligations arising from the performance of that agent. The CA provides that the agent's acts may be enforced in the same manner, and with the same legal consequences, as if the contract had been entered into and the acts had been performed by the principal in person.[138]

Viewed this way, the law of contract in India will, in part, depend on the intention of the parties. This was evidenced in *M/s Gobindram v. Shamji K. & Co.86.*[139] There the Respondents agreed to sell 500 bales of African raw cotton to

135 The Indian Contract Act 1972, No. 9 of 18721.

136 Ibid, Section 37. In an example, in illustrations (a) A promises to deliver goods to B on a certain day on payment of Rs. 1,000. A dies before that day. A's representatives are bound to deliver the goods to B, and B is bound to pay the Rs. 1,000 to A's representatives. (b) A promises to paint a picture for B by a certain day, at a certain price. A dies before the day. The contract cannot be enforced either by A's representatives or by B.

137 Ibid, Sections 32–33 illustrate that: A makes a contract with B to buy B's horse if A survives C. This contract cannot be enforced by law unless and until C dies in A's lifetime. A makes a contract with B to sell a horse to B at a specified price, if C, to whom the horse has been offered, refuses to buy him. The contract cannot be enforced by law unless and until C refuses to buy the horse. A contract to pay B a sum of money when B marries C. C dies without being married to B. The contract becomes void.

138 Ibid, Section 226. A buys goods from B, knowing that he is an agent for their sale, but not knowing who is the principal. B's principal is the person entitled to claim from A the price of the goods, and A cannot, in a. suit by the principal, set-off against that claim a debt due to himself from B. (b) A, being B's agent with authority to receive money on his behalf, receives from C a sum of money due to B. C is discharged of his obligation to pay the sum in question to B.

139 *M/s Gobindram v. Shamji K. & Co.86* AIR 1961 SC 1285.

the appellants. Upon failure to perform the contract, the parties submitted their dispute to the Bombay High Court being the agreed forum under the contract.[140] The contract also included an arbitration clause, with India as the chosen venue for arbitration. On appeal, the Supreme Court ruled that the proper law to be applied is Indian law. The Court remarked:

> Whether the proper law is the *lex loci contractus or lex loci solutionis* is a matter of presumption; but there are accepted rules for determining which of them is applicable. Where the parties have expressed themselves, the intention so expressed overrides any presumption. Where there is no expressed intention then the rule to apply is to infer the intention from the terms and nature of the contract and from the general circumstances of the case'.[141]

In the case of State Bank of *Indict v. Ghamandi Ram*[142] the Court was called upon to resolve whether the liability of the Appellant (State Bank of India) to the Respondent (Ghamandi Ram) in India should be deemed to have been extinguished under the Pakistan Evacuee Property Ordinance. In effect, the Indian Court considered whether to defer to Pakistan law under a conflict of laws clause in which the parties chose the Law of Pakistan, in the review of an international arbitration award. In concluding that the Pakistan Ordinance was applicable, the Indian Court determined that the amount in dispute had become vested in the Custodian of Evacuee Property, Pakistan with effect from March 1, 1947. The Court so decided under the rule of private international law on the involuntary assignment of debts as applied by English courts to which the Court deferred.[143]

Indian courts have also ruled on the recognition of foreign judgements, notably in the judicial review by foreign courts of international commercial arbitration awards relating to cross-border insolvency disputes. In *Vtshwanathan v. Abdul Wtjid,*[144] the Court highlighted how a foreign court must be a court of competent jurisdiction. The Court acknowledged that the law relating to conclusiveness of the foreign judgement contained in Clauses (a) to (f) of Section 13 of the Code of Civil Procedure creates substantive not merely procedural rights. The Court further argued that: [The] conclusiveness in Section 13 refers to the final adjudication and not the reasons; the binding character of the judgement can be displaced only on the basis of the six grounds mentioned in the section; the question whether the principle of effectiveness'[145] formed the basis of conclusiveness of the foreign judgement is debatable. It added that 'conclusiveness referred to in Section 13 is

140 Ibid.
141 Ibid, [1294].
142 *State Bank of Indict v Ghamandi Ram* AIR 1969 SC 1330.
143 Lakshmi Jambholkar, *Conflict of Laws, Fifty Years of the Supreme Court,* 651–688, http://14.139.60.114:8080/jspui/bitstream/123456789/713/24/Conflict%20of%20Laws.pdf.
144 *Vtshwanathan v. Abdul Wtjid* AIR 1963 SC 1.
145 *Mobji Narsingh Rao v. Shankur Saran* AIR 1962 SC 1737.

different in its operation from the rule of res judicata envisaged in Section 11 as applicable to domestic judgements'.[146]

On the bases of these determinations, the Court in *Vtshwanathan* affirmed that the 'procedure governing the recognition and enforcement of foreign arbitration awards was subject to the Indian Arbitration and Conciliation Act 1996'.[147] Comparably, the Bombay High Court in *Gobindram,*[148] in upholding parties' choice of the Law of India, reasoned that 'such arbitration clauses in agreements, it has been said on more than one occasion that they lead to an inference that the parties have adopted the law of the country in which arbitration is to be made'.[149] Therefore, where an ISDA Arbitration clause has been provided for by contract and recognised under the applicable law, the general laws of international commercial arbitration will apply.

However, while India is a signatory to the New York Convention, issues have arisen over the 'commercial reservation' India made in becoming a signatory. In particular, India's 'commercial reservation' limits the enforcement of foreign arbitral awards to those which are considered to be commercial in nature. This commercial reservation is distinct from a 'reciprocity reservation which limits the enforcement of arbitral awards to those made by other New York Convention signatories.[150] Both reservations have found their way into Part II of the Indian Arbitration and Conciliation Act dealing with the enforcement of foreign arbitral awards, through the definition of what constitutes a 'foreign award'. Section 44 of the Act defines a 'foreign award' to be one that 'arises out of legal relationships, whether contractual or not, considered as commercial under the law in force in India; and is made in one of such territories as the Central Government of India, being satisfied that reciprocal provisions have been made, declares by notification in the Official Gazette to be a territory to which the New York Convention applies'.[151] Gehle and Kantaria maintain that, 'although the term 'commercial' has not been defined by the Act, the Indian Supreme Court has favoured a wide interpretation of this term and guidance can also be taken from the UNCITRAL Model Law which considers 'commercial representation or agency' and 'consulting' to be relationships of a commercial nature'.[152]

146 Lakshmi Jambholkar, *Conflict of Laws, Fifty Years of the Supreme Court*, 651–688, http://14.139.60.114:8080/jspui/bitstream/123456789/713/24/Conflict%20of%20Laws.pdf.

147 The Arbitration and Conciliation Act, 1996 No. 26, Part II.

148 *M/s Gobindram v. Shamji K. & Co.86* AIR 1961 SC 1295.

149 Ibid, paragraph 29.

150 Bjon Gehle, Saloni Kantaria, *The Enforcement of Arbitral Awards in India – The Elephant in the Room* (2011), https://www.claytonutz.com/knowledge/2011/february/the-enforcement-of-arbitral-awards-in-india-the-elephant-in-the-room.

151 The Arbitration and Conciliation Act 1996, Part II – Enforcement of Certain Foreign Awards Chapter I: New York Convention Awards, Section 44.

152 Bjon Gehle, Saloni Kantaria, *The Enforcement of Arbitral Awards in India – The Elephant in the Room* (2011), https://www.claytonutz.com/knowledge/2011/february/the-enforcement-of-arbitral-awards-in-india-the-elephant-in-the-room.

Drawing any salutary conclusion from this wide interpretation, the result could be greater uncertainty. That uncertainty could include that foreign awards relating to cross-border insolvency might not be enforced in India on wide grounds. However, to remedy this issue, particularly within the framework of ISDA Master Agreements, vigilance will be required in drafting these and other contracts that utilise close-out netting arrangements.

Noteworthy too, are obstacles India faces in regulating close-out netting in its emergence as a major democracy in central Asia. While close-out netting arrangements have legal effect since the ISDA Master Agreements of 2006, the 1987 ISDA Master Agreements are not covered by the 2006 Master Agreement.[153] Material, too, in regard to an Early Termination for non-bank entities, the relevant India state government may suspend rights under the ISDA Master Agreement, including those relating to close-out netting, for a period of up to 15 years.[154] In contrast, while 'multibranch netting arrangements are effective between Indian banks with foreign banks, Indian courts could refuse to recognise the retroactive effect of Automatic Early Termination in relation to the events listed in Section 5(a)(vii)(4) of the 2006 Master Agreement'.[155] Furthermore, it has been highlighted that India allows the liquidator to carve out from the ISDA Master Agreement transactions by or between the Indian branches of the solvent and insolvent party; but, local counsel believed that such an attempt by the liquidator would not easily succeed.[156] Nonetheless, under the law of the jurisdiction in which the head office of an Indian branch is incorporated, close-out netting is unenforceable, so that the Indian courts may refuse to apply close-out netting in such cases.[157]

A further challenge posed is that it is unclear whether close-out netting would be enforceable in the event of the bankruptcy of a state-owned insurance company, as the Indian government can direct how these proceedings are to be conducted. For a bank and non-bank entities there are subtle variables to be taken into account. On the one side, for banks, the Indian government (state or nationalised banks) or the Reserve Bank of India has discretion to direct the process of a bank's liquidation which could, in theory, override the netting provisions of an ISDA Master Agreement.

Noteworthy too, is where there are any discretionary powers exercised, the courts are likely to set such an exercise aside if they determine that they are arbitrary and/or unreasonable. However, in relation to non-bank entities, the Legal Opinion recommended that cross-default under 'section 5(a)(vi) should be specified as

153 Fieldfisher, *ISDA Master Agreement Legal Opinions on Close-out netting*, Copyright Fieldfisher LLP (August 2016), 121–124. Thanks to Chance Clifford, Munich Office for providing the book on Legal Opinion.
154 Ibid, 123.
155 Ibid, 123.
156 Ibid, 123–124.
157 Ibid, 124.

applying and that the definition of specified indebtedness should be reviewed so that it is appropriate for that entity's activities.'[158]

India is a rising and emerging economy in the Central Asia and Asian region with much to offer the global economy. Their economy is increasingly being aligned and intertwined with Indo-Pacific nations. It is well understood that India has embraced and follows the English common law. Arguably, adopting the UNIDROIT Principles on close-out netting provisions will go a long way in assisting India in further reinforcing its place in the international economy. Doing so will also place India regionally in a stronger position to assume a higher level of investment certainty, particularly across the financial sector.

6.4 Indonesia

Indonesia, like India, is a rising economy. Indonesia is emerging as an important trading and financial market throughout the Asia Pacific region. Indonesia is also Australia's closest neighbour among the jurisdictions compared throughout the book. Until the recent impact of the COVID-19 pandemic upon Indonesia's global markets, it enjoyed stable economic growth consistently for the past decade.[159] Following COVID-19, the World Bank identified Indonesia as having exhibited strong macroeconomic performance, but that its developmental needs remained significant.[160] This need for development in Indonesia's financial sector is significant, given the sector's important role in raising the social and economic standards of a large population dispersed over thousands of islands. In performing this role, Indonesia also needs to do more to stabilise its financial sector by fully adopting the international framework for close-out netting arrangements.[161]

A more specific problem is that Indonesia has no specific close-out netting laws.[162] Cross-Border transactions in Indonesia are governed instead by various laws. These include the Bank of Indonesia Regulations[163], along with the Act of the Republic of Indonesia Number 3 of 2011 Concerning Funds Transfer and the Law of the Republic of Indonesia on the Currency.[164] Neither of these laws define close-out netting provisions or provide for enforcement mechanisms.

Indonesia has recognised the need to regulate the use of standardised contracts in derivatives trading. Notably, the Bank of Indonesia has issued guidelines for the

158 Ibid, 123.

159 Robert Walters, Leon Trakman, The Fragmented Approach towards Close-out netting Provisions in Australia, Indonesia, Malaysia and Singapore Compared, *Journal of Banking Regulation,* Vol. 21 (2020), 224–240, https://doi.org/10.1057/s41261-019-00109-w

160 World Bank, *Financial Sector Assessment*, Republic of Indonesia (2017), http://documents.worldbank.org/curated/en/104191505745150824/pdf/Indonesia-FSAP-Update-FSA-07072017.pdf.

161 Robert Walters, Leon Trakman, The Fragmented Approach toward Close-out Netting Provisions in Australia, Indonesia, Malaysia and Singapore Compared, *Journal Banking Regulation* (2019), 1.

162 Ibid.

163 No. 14/15/PBI/2012.

164 Number 7. 2011.

use of standardised contracts by Indonesian parties, otherwise known as Perjanjian Induk Derivatif Indonesia[165] [PIDI] or as the Master Agreement for Indonesian derivatives transactions. Provisions in the PIDI are based primarily on the 2002 ISDA Master Agreement. The aim of the PIDI is to assist Indonesian banks in preparing certain contracts specific to derivatives. Nevertheless, the PIDI neither refers to, nor defines or provides a legal basis for the enforcement of close-out netting provisions. A further piece of the Indonesian jigsaw puzzle on netting is evident in Indonesian Law No. 7 of 2011 on the Currency [Law No. 7]. Articles 21 and 23 of the Law appear to contradict other areas of the PIDI. According to Article 21, 'the national currency, the Rupia should be used in every transaction, settlement obligation, where money is used, provided that the transaction is undertaken within the territory of Indonesia'.[166] On the one hand, where a transaction involves a foreign exchange deposit in an international financing transaction, Article 21 is not applicable. In other words, any currency other than the Rupia can be used in international transactions that operate in or outside of Indonesia.[167] Adding to the complication is Article 23 of the Law No. 7. It prohibits an entity from refusing to use the Rupiah as a currency of tender where the transfer is intended as payment or as the settlement obligations that must be fulfilled in Rupiah and/or in other transactions. On the other hand, the restricted use of a foreign currency is not applicable where the transaction has been agreed to in writing (by contract or other agreement) and specifies that another currency can be used. It remains to be seen whether this provision in Article 23 will be challenged before Indonesian courts. Furthermore, it is not conclusive whether Indonesian courts will settle the law based on a literal interpretation of Law No. 7 of the PIDI and Master Agreement; or whether they will resort to a more contextualised construction of that law. Regardless, the PIDI or Master Agreement permits parties to resort to arbitration to resolve any cross-border dispute. While Indonesia is an emerging economy,[168]

165 Bank Indonesia issued two Bank Indonesia Regulations regarding foreign exchange transactions against Rupiah: (i) Bank Indonesia Regulation No. 18/18/PBI/2016 on Foreign Exchange Transactions against Rupiah between Banks and Domestic Parties ('PBI 18/18') and (ii) Bank Indonesia Regulation No. 18/19/PBI/2016 on Foreign Exchange Transactions against Rupiah between Banks and Foreign Parties ('PBI 18/19'). As a general rule, to conduct a foreign exchange transaction against Rupiah, banks must satisfy the following requirements: those imposed by the banking authority(ies) under which only a certain category of bank is allowed to conduct foreign exchange transactions; implement risk management as required under the banking authority(ies) regulations on the implementation of risk management in banks; provide training on foreign exchange transactions against Rupiah to customers; and comply with the Bank Indonesia regulation on the mandatory use of Rupiah.

166 Ibid, Articles 21–23.

167 Robert Walters, Leon Trakman, The Fragmented Approach towards Close-out netting Provisions in Australia, Indonesia, Malaysia and Singapore Compared, *Journal of Banking Regulation,* Vol. 21 (2020), 224–240, https://doi.org/10.1057/s41261-019-00109-w.

168 Bank Indonesia Regulation No. 18/18/PBI/2016 on Foreign Exchange Transactions against Rupiah between Banks and Domestic Parties ('PBI 18/18') and (ii) Bank Indonesia Regulation

in our view, its recognition of ISDA Master agreements and therefore close-out netting, is comparable to its neighbours, Australia and Singapore.

Notwithstanding this, another widely used and effective instrument that is adopted across Indonesia is multibranch netting by which Indonesian banks enter into netting agreements with foreign banks and with foreign banks with Indonesian branches. However, provision for multibranch netting could be affected by non-netting jurisdictions. Moreover, and while early termination is not affected, early termination provisions (both automatic and by notice) are likely to be upheld in Indonesia. Even though there is no relevant Indonesian case law, it is possible that 'section 36 of the Bankruptcy Ordnance (giving the receiver in bankruptcy the ability to declare that he will perform a contract – if he performs, he must provide collateral for the obligations) may be mandatory'.[169] Noteworthy too, banks that are licensed in the state are only allowed to enter into derivative transactions whose value is a derivative of a foreign currency. The resulting effect is that an interest rate or a combination of an interest rate and an exchange rate, is not a structured product relating to foreign exchange transactions against the Rupiah.[170] As a result, those banks may not enter into equity derivative transactions. While there does not appear to be any restriction on the ability of banks to enter into credit derivative transactions, there is no specific authority on the point. More pervasively, there are restrictions on the ability of Indonesian banks to enter into foreign currency derivatives. Yet, to deal with this dichotomy, where a transaction falls outside the Indonesian party's capacity, a clause can be inserted into the ISDA Master Agreement which allows the Indonesian party to confirm its power to enter into Transactions, acknowledges corporate benefit and waives its right to claim that transactions are null and void.[171] In addition, it is argued that an Indonesian party should provide copies of constitutional documents and government licenses in order to verify its authority and capacity to so transact.[172]

A fundamental element of contract law in Indonesia, impacting on trading in foreign currency derivatives, is that the Indonesian language must be used. Article 31 (1) of Law No. 24 of 2009 on the National Flag, Language, Emblem and Anthem requires that the Indonesian language must be used in memoranda of understanding or agreements that involve state organs, government institutions of the Republic of Indonesia, private Indonesian entities, or individuals who are citizens of the Republic of Indonesia. However, as recently as 2019, Presidential Regulation (PR) No. 63 of 2019 on the Use of Bahasa Indonesia, dated 30

No. 18/19/PBI/2016 on Foreign Exchange Transactions against Rupiah between Banks and Foreign Parties ('PBI 18/19').

169 Fieldfisher, *ISDA Master Agreement Legal Opinions on Close-out netting*, Copyright Fieldfisher LLP (August 2016), 126. Thanks to Chance Clifford, Munich Office for providing the book on Legal Opinion.

170 Ibid, 127.

171 Ibid.

172 Ibid.

September 2019, implementing regulation of Law No. 24 of 2009 appears to have changed the foreign language requirements in relation to agreements between an Indonesian and a foreign party.[173] Article 26 of PR No. 63 first restates the provisions in Article 31 of Law No. 24 and then introduces two new paragraphs, which read as follows:

> Article 26 (3): *Bahasa nasional pihak asing dan/atau bahasa Inggris sebagaimana dimaksud pada ayat (2) digunakan sebagai padanan atau terjemahan Bahasa Indonesia untuk menyamakan pemahaman nota kesepahaman atau perjanjian dengan pihak asing.* **English Translation:** 'The national language of the foreign party and/or the English language referred to in paragraph (2) shall be used as an equivalent (*padanan*) or translation (*terjemahan*) of the Indonesian language to align understanding of the memorandum of understanding or agreement with the foreign party.
>
> Article 26 (4): *Dalam hal terjadi perbedaan penafsiran terhadap padanan atau terjemahan sebagaimana dimaksud pada ayat (3), bahasa yang digunakan ialah bahasa yang disepakati dalam nota kesepahaman atau perjanjian.* **English Translation:** 'In case of a difference in interpretation of the equivalent or translation referred to in paragraph (3), the language used shall be the language agreed in the memorandum of understanding or agreement.'[174]

This revised approach, embodied in Presidential Regulation No. 63 of 2019, is likely to have significant impact on the adoption and use of current ISDA Master Agreements under Indonesian Law. However, a risk assessment would, arguably, by undertaken on a case-by-case basis to ensure that any future ISDA Master Agreement is current and follows Indonesian law. Nonetheless prior to the declaration of this revised approach, the West Jakarta District Court issued a decision in 2013 which declared that a contract not drafted in the Indonesian language was null and void.[175] The Court argued that the absence of an Indonesian language version of the contract was a violation of Paragraph 1 of Article 31 of Law No. 24 of 2009 on the National Flag, Language, Emblem and Anthem. In other words, there was a formal requirement for the Indonesian language to be used in a memorandum, agreement or contract which involves Indonesian government institutions, Indonesian private entities or Indonesian citizens. The Court ruled that the contract was null and void in light of Article 1335 of the Indonesian Civil Code (ICC),

173 Herbert Smith Freehils, *Update on Indonesian Language Requirements for Contracts with Indonesian Parties* (2019), https://www.herbertsmithfreehills.com/latest-thinking/update-on-indonesian-language-requirements-for-contracts-with-indonesian-parties.

174 Translation verified by Sinta Dewi Rosadi, Associate Professor, Information Technology Law-Data Privacy Law, Fakultas Hukum Universitas Padjadaran, Indonesia.

175 The West Jakarta District Court Decision No. 451/Pdt.G/2012/PN. Jkt.Bar dated 10 July 2013. Translation verified by Sinta Dewi Rosadi, Associate Professor, Information Technology Law-Dat Privacy Law, Fakultas Hukum Universitas Padjadaran, Indonesia.

which provides that an agreement without reason, or which has been made on a false or forbidden reason, shall have no effect. Additionally, Article 1337 of the ICC, which provides that a cause is forbidden[176], if it is forbidden by the law, or if it is contrary to good morals or public order. Lastly, the Court considered that the *fiducia* security agreement, or for that matter any type of security agreement, was an accessory to a loan agreement. It then declared that the *fiducia* security agreement was null and void.

In addition, and in the same year, the West Jakarta District Court in the case of *Bangun Karya Pratama Lestari v. Nine AM Ltd.*, ruled that a loan agreement that was established between an Indonesian Borrower and a non-Indonesian lender was void under Article 31 of Law No. 24 of 2009.[177] While the Court did not rule on the validity of an ISDA Master Agreement, such loan agreements are generally drafted in the English language, due to the dominance of English as the working language of global commerce. The Court went onto rule that the mandatory requirement of Article 31 would not be compromised by the Minister's 2009 clarification that, the absence of the Indonesian language on a contract would not affect the validity of that contract.[178] However, it is material that the Court's decision in Indonesia, not having common law system, does not constitute a binding judicial precedent. As a result, a future court, arguably, could construe Article 31 as rendering the contract including ISDA Master Agreements, as being unenforceable, not unlike a common law court declaring a contract unenforceable due to force majeure.[179] Moreover, a future Indonesian court could declare that a loan agreement in English is valid and consistent with Article 31.

A cautious approach has evolved since 2016, directed at avoiding confusion over the language requirements set out in Law No 24 the law. The cautious proposal is to use 'the language of the foreign party or English' in addition to (but not in substitution for) Indonesian.[180] What remains an ongoing challenge is uncertainty over whether agreements not set out in Indonesian will be declared invalid or unenforceable. On the other hand, Law No. 24 of 2009 does not impose sanctions

176 Indonesia Civil Code, Article 1337, https://www.trans-lex.org/602560/_/indonesian-civil-code%C2%A0-/ Verified Professor Sinta Dewi, Assistant Professor of Information Technology Law/Data Privacy Law, Fakultas Hukum Universitas Padjadjaran, Indonesia.

177 Ibid. PT *Bangun Karya Pratama Lestari v Nine AM Ltd* (Decision Number 451/Pdt.G/2012/PN.Jkt Bar.)

178 Based on Article 1337, ICC, the release of Law 24, the Minister of Law and Human Rights of Indonesia released two letters clarifying that the absence of an Indonesian language version of a contract *would not affect the contract's validity*. The minister made reference to the principle of freedom of contract pursuant to which parties are free to determine the provisions of their contract, including selecting the language. The objective of this clarification was to give certainty to legal practitioners and foreign investors, although it raises more issues than it clarifies.

179 International Swaps Derivatives Association, https://www.isda.org/a/yDEDE/indonesia-submission.pdf

180 Fieldfisher, *ISDA Master Agreement Legal Opinions on Close-out netting*, Copyright Fieldfisher LLP (August 2016), 127. Thanks to Chance Clifford, Munich Office for providing the book on Legal Opinion.

for breach of Article 31. Therefore, it can be argued that a duplicated ISDA Master Agreement be provided in the Indonesian language.

The choice of arbitration under Indonesian Law is potentially significant in relation to the development of netting law and practice in Indonesia. Law No. 30 of 1999 concerning Arbitration and Alternative Dispute Resolution ('New Arbitration Law') implemented the New York Convention on the Recognition and Enforcement of Foreign Arbitral Awards.[181] In regulating the adoption of the International Swaps and Derivatives Association (ISDA) Master Agreements, the Central Jakarta District Court in *Bankers Trust Company & Bankers Trust International v. PT. Mayora Indah*[182] refused to enforce a London Court of International Arbitration [LCIA] award in favour of Bankers Trust [BT], because the South Jakarta District Court had issued a decision in favour of the Respondent, Mayora.[183] The underlying dispute related to derivatives trading between BT and Mayora under the ISDA Master Agreements, which contained an arbitration clause. Mayora defaulted on certain payment obligations under the Agreements. Subsequently, it filed a case before the South Jakarta District Court, 'seeking annulment of those agreements on the grounds that the agreements were contrary to Indonesian law or public policy. Mayora argued that these agreements dealt with swap trading, an activity similar to gambling, which was strictly prohibited under Indonesian law'.[184] In response, BT commenced LCIA arbitration proceedings against Mayora in London. BT obtained an arbitral award in its favour, while the South Jakarta District Court decided in favour of Mayora.

Against this backdrop, BT subsequently registered the arbitral award at the Central Jakarta District Court for its recognition and enforcement.[185] Soemartono noted that BT also appealed the decision of the South Jakarta District Court. It argued that the South Jakarta District Court did not have jurisdiction to hear the case because the parties had agreed to settle their disputes through arbitration. However, the Central Jakarta District Court refused to enforce the arbitral award and held that any enforcement of the arbitral award was contrary to the public interest, since the decision of the South Jakarta District Court had not yet become *res judicata*.[186] The Supreme Court of Indonesia affirmed the decision of the Central Jakarta District Court and declined to enforce the arbitral award.[187] The Supreme Court's decision might have been less contestable had the parties agreed to refer

181 Indonesia. Law No. 30 of 1999.

182 Decisions of the Central Jakarta District Court No. 001/Pdt/Arb.Int/1999/PN.JKT.PST, No. 002/Pdt/Arb.Int/1999/PN.JKT.PST, and No. 002/Pdt.P/2000/PN.JKT.PST issued on 3 February 2000. In G. Soemartono, Interpretation and Application of the New York Convention in Indonesia, in G. Bermann (ed), *Recognition and Enforcement of Foreign Arbitral Awards*. Ius Comparatum – Global Studies in Comparative Law, Vol. 23, Springer, Cham (2017), 495.

183 Ibid, 495–496.

184 Ibid.

185 Ibid.

186 Ibid.

187 Ibid.

any disputes to the courts of Malaysia. Yet, in this case, there was a written agreement to arbitrate which should have prevented the state court from entertaining the lawsuit.[188] Soemartono has argued that the:

> law in Indonesia does not expressly draw a distinction between international public policy and domestic public policy, even though Indonesian authors have made such a distinction. The New Arbitration Law simply states that a foreign arbitral award can only be enforced in Indonesia if the arbitral award is not contrary to public policy.[189]

In the more recent 2017 Indonesian case, *PT Monas Permata Persada*,[190] the Supreme Court of Indonesia considered multiple international arbitrations and disputes relating to ISDA Master Agreements and accompanying derivative agreements. The case involved a complex and elaborate investment scheme across multiple international jurisdictions, with millions of dollars at stake. There, the entity Pelawan was established, located in Indonesia and subject to Indonesian law. It was engaged in the wire industry and cables, and in trading shares on the Indonesia Stock Exchange; and the holder of 79,485,000 shares in PT Jembo Cable Company Tbk. Control over its and other shares are as follows:

> Pelawan, Terlawan's shares were also controlled by the general public through the Indonesia Stock Exchange as many as 14,896,700 shares of a total of 151,200,000 shares, or with a composition of 9.8%. Fujikura Ltd, domiciled in Japan, holder of 20,430,000 shares also participated in a total of 151,200,000 shares, or with a composition of 13.5% (thirteen point five percent), and Fujikura Asia Limited, domiciled in Singapore, holds 9,810,000 of the total shares 151,200,000 shares, or with a composition of 6.5%, as well as PT Indolife Pensiontama as the holder of 26,578,300 shares of the total 151,200,000 shares, or with a composition of 17.6%.[191]

The matter that was submitted to arbitration in 2011, was to be decided in accordance with the Rules of the Singapore International Arbitration Centre (SIAC).[192] In issue was a dispute over the application of the 2002 ISDA Master Agreement established in September 2012, and the signing of additional derivative agreements of other derivative documents by the counterparty. A further issue that arose, which

188 Ibid.

189 G. Soemartono, Interpretation and Application of the New York Convention in Indonesia, in G. Bermann (ed), *Recognition and Enforcement of Foreign Arbitral Awards*. Ius Comparatum – Global Studies in Comparative Law, Vol. 23, Springer, Cham (2017).

190 *PT Monas Permata Persada v. Standard Chartered Bank*, Supreme Court of the Republic of Indonesia, Number 101 PK / Pdt.Sus-Arbt / 2017.

191 Ibid, 2.

192 Ibid, 5, SIAC No 5.

was also challenged, was the signing of the derivative agreements and a determination of the law that was applicable to Pelawan, Indonesian Law under Article 61 (1) of Law Number 40 of 2007 concerning Limited Liability Companies. Article 61 (1) of the Law requires that: 'every shareholder has the right to fight back against the company to the District Court, if harmed due to actions companies deemed unfair and without reasonable reasons as a result resolutions of the GMS, Directors and/or Board of Commissioners'.[193] The Supreme Court noted that in order for the 2002 ISDA Master Agreement and derivative agreements to be signed, there must be some other agreement in place, for the derivative transaction agreement mentioned (underlying transaction).[194] The Court held further that the 'documents and ISDA Master Agreement being drafted in the English language, [which] was contrary to Bank Indonesia Regulation Number 11/26/PBI/2009, particularly Article 24 paragraph (2) and paragraph (3) and Article 27 paragraph (1) and paragraph (3). Furthermore, the proposition that, the 2002 ISDA Master Agreement and derivative documents were in fact based on bad faith'.[195]

A further accentuating issue that arose from the SIAC award[196] was whether the award could be executed in Indonesia. The first decision was rendered by the Chairman of the Central Jakarta District Court in April 2014 in which the Court had assumed jurisdiction to process the appeal request.[197]

In appeal, the Supreme Court further examined the background of the arbitration award and whether the Central Jakarta District Court decision was invalid and erred in processing the appeal request.[198] The Supreme Court ruled that the SIAC award could be implemented in Indonesia because it did not conflict with the public order of the country:

> After careful examination that the verdict The International Arbitration can be carried out in Indonesia because does not conflict with public order, in accordance with the provisions regulated in Article 63 juncto 62 paragraph (1) of Law Number 30 Year 1999 concerning Arbitration and Alternative

193 Ibid, 6.
194 Ibid, 12.1.2.
195 Ibid, 12.4.
196 See SIAC, Number 005 of 2011 23 September 2012 juncto Number 13 / Pdt / ARB-INT / 2013 / PN Jkt. Pst.,
197 2 April 2014, Number 28/2014.
198 *PT Monas Permata Persada v. Standard Chartered Bank*, Supreme Court of the Republic of Indonesia, Number 101 PK / Pdt.Sus-Arbt / 2017, 50. 'Considering, that the International-Singapore International Arbitration Award Arbitration Center (SIAC) Number 005 of 2011 dated 21 September 2012 has been registered / deported at the Registrar's Office of the District Court Central Jakarta on Tuesday, 11 June 2013, which are listed below Register Number 13 / Pdt / Arb-Int / 2013 / PN Jkt. Pst., In accordance with the provisions Articles 65 to Article 69 in conjunction with Article 67 paragraph (1) in conjunction with Law Number 30 of 1999 concerning Arbitration and Alternative Dispute Resolution: Considering, that prior to the execution of the International Arbitration Award'.

> Dispute Resolution; Considering, that based on what has been considered above, and after we pay attention to the Petitioner's petition along with other evidences attached, presumably a request Applicant (Terlawan) has fulfilled the requirements and is not contrary to the law.[199]

Thus, this case demonstrates that international arbitration in relation to ISDA Master Agreements is an accepted practice to resolve disputes between the parties. In our view, it is time for Indonesia to consider embracing the international framework on close-out netting provisions. They could adopt a similar position to that of the Netherlands, as they do, in part, follow Dutch law,[200] which would translate into adopting some of the EU approach.

6.5 Conclusion

The jurisdictions compared in this chapter have demonstrated how some states have recognised that close our netting provisions are highly important. Moreover, states, such as Australia and Singapore, had adopted netting laws well before the internationalisation of their importance by the UNIDROIT in 2013. On the other hand, India and Indonesia appear to be some way off from establishing specific legislation on netting provisions. Nonetheless, these latter countries are not as advanced economically as Australia or Singapore. Yet, an affirmative sign that they are embracing the internationalisation of close-out netting regulations is their use of ISDA Master agreements. The UNIDROIT Principles on close-out netting are also embedded in the international and, to different degrees, in some national legal frameworks. They act as a stabilising mechanism, to ensure large and complex (multi-million, multi-billion) contracts such as ISDA Master Agreements are equipped to deal with financial stress of an organisation or party. Put another way, states increasingly appreciate the importance of the internationalisation of close-out netting provisions in managing financial risks associated with insolvency. Allowing the parties to agree on a payment of a single net value as a result of insolvency provides their financial markets and related sectors with significant benefits. That benefit can be measured to some extent, by the level of contagion that has either been stopped or minimised by the effective use of close-out netting provisions in trans-border insolvency proceedings.

Problematic though, is the continued varied response by states that, while recognising the benefits of close-out netting provisions, have sometimes not treated them priority in emerging law. When coupled with ISDA Master Agreements,

199 *PT Monas Permata Persada v. Standard Chartered Bank*, Supreme Court of the Republic of Indonesia, Number 101 PK / Pdt.Sus-Arbt / 2017, 50.

200 Rudy, The Pathway of Civil Law Development in Indonesia: Laws on Land, in Y. Kaneko (ed), *Civil Law Reforms in Post-Colonial Asia*. Kobe University Monograph Series in Social Science Research, Springer, Singapore (2019), https://doi.org/10.1007/978-981-13-6203-3_4.

those states that regulate close-out netting provisions have largely defined what these provisions constitute. Generally, their definitions follow the internationally agreed definition provided by the UNIDROIT Principles on Close-out Netting Provisions. More pervasively, for netting arrangements to be truly internationalised, it is our view that more needs to be done by states to ensure there is a consistent approach adopted.

The current piecemeal approach does not bode well for the world financial markets or other sectors that rely on close-out netting provisions to safeguard multi-million/billion-dollar transactions. The continued adoption of a minimalist approach and not fully adopting the UNIDROIT Principles, will only further accentuate the risk(s) to the international community if and when the next financial crisis, epidemic, pandemic or environmental catastrophe occurs.

What has emerged is the need for growing economies in the Asia region to internationalise their respective national laws, specifically in relation to close-out netting arrangements. More specifically, if India and Indonesia are to assume a greater role in international investment through their banking and finance sectors, they need to fully adopt the UNIDROIT Principles. While they readily embrace the use of ISDA Master Agreements, they also need to advance further by incorporating netting arrangements into their respective laws, not unlike in Australia and Singapore.

Even though there are subtle but important differences between the common of contracts and the civil law of obligations, those differences are potentially reduced where the parties in both states have engaged in transnational trade and investment for a number of years. Thus, it is not a large hurdle to jump, for common and civil law jurisdictions to embrace and regulate close-out netting arrangements in a compatible manner. There are also alternative pathways to internationalisation, such as in a close-out netting case involving UK and Dutch parties in which the UK withdrew from the EU while the Netherlands remained an EU member.

Most noteworthy and in need of redressing is the continuing varied approach that states take to the enforcement of netting provisions in cross-border contracts, including ISDA Master Agreements. This chapter has demonstrated this divergence in the approaches of the states studied. Australia has replicated the obligations of enforcement and aligned this process to that of the UNIDROIT Principles, while India and Indonesia have invoked the law of contract to resolve such issues as enforcement. Singapore has aligned its enforcement approach to national insolvency laws. Of the states compared in this chapter, Indonesia is the only state that requires their contracts to be in their national language. While this may be viewed as problematic, in practice it does not add a particularly intrusive layer to the development of contracts that include close-out netting provisions.

Finally, while some states provide for netting arrangements in their insolvency, banking, bankruptcy or contracting laws, other states deal with netting through rules of enforcement embodied in their respective contract laws. ISDA Master

Agreements provide clearly for enforcement, including in domestic law. However, such enforcement is less clear when those Agreements are not adopted, or, if they are adopted, enforcement extends beyond ISDA Master Agreements. The next Part compares the remaining jurisdictions of the European Union, United Kingdom, United States and China.

6

JURISDICTIONAL COMPARISONS OF NETTING ARRANGEMENTS PART 3

6.1 European Union: United Kingdom

The EU in 2020, like many other jurisdictions around the world, is grappling with a complex array of policy and legal uncertainty.[1]

In 2013, the European Parliament released a policy relating to shadow banking.[2] Its purpose was to address two different spheres of legal issues surrounding collateral assets. These includes changes to insolvency law and providing a basic introduction into repos and securities lending. In addition, the policy was extended to close-out netting, risk management and capital requirements.

Importantly, the policy statement upheld the current international framework. arguing that close-out netting is the number one risk mitigation tool, alongside collateral, that is used across the entire financial wholesale market. In other words, the Policy Statement took the position that the international regulatory community, including the Financial Stability Board (FSB),[3] had agreed on these beneficial effects and had unanimously underlined its importance. However, the European Banking Federation (EBF) while recognising the benefit of netting provisions, takes a slightly different stance to that of the FSB. The EBF, goes further, arguing that:

> as regards the contractual recognition clauses mentioned as a means to mitigate the risk of financial contracts due to close-out, we believe it is necessary

1 Robert Walters, *Close-out netting Provisions – Their Current Value in a Time of International Uncertainty!* International Company and Commercial Law Review – Sweet & Maxwell (2020). This chapter builds on the earlier work undertaken by Robert Walters and Leon Trakman. The additional enforcements draw upon practice management ISDA Opinions from Clifford Chance Law Firm.

2 European Parliament, Directorate General for Internal Policies, Policy Department, *A: Economic and Scientific Policy, Shadow Banking: Legal Issues of Collateral Assets and Insolvency Law* (2013), 4.

3 Financial Stability Board, https://www.fsb.org.

DOI: 10.4324/9781003311874-11

> to recognise the limits of these recognition clauses: we, of course, agree that the close-out of positions upon initiation of resolution measures can negatively affect the resolution measures.[4]

The EBF highlights the need to strike a balance between parties over the manner in, and the extent to which, to rely on close-out netting provisions to mitigate their exposure to financial risk. In their view, that balance can be achieved through the use of temporary stay-powers, by drafting specific clauses to account for such stay powers.

The Directive of the European Commission on close-out netting arrangements is more specific when compared to Principle 6 of the UNIDROIT Principles.[5], For example, Article 4 of the Directive specifies the enforcement arrangements for collateral.[6] Article 7 places clear obligations on all EU member states. In contrast, the UNIDROIT Principles are not mandatory. Close-out netting is also part of the EU *acquis communautaire*.[7] Article 7 of the EU Directive provides that:

> Member States shall ensure that a close-out netting provision can take effect in accordance with its terms: (a) notwithstanding the commencement or continuation of winding-up proceedings or reorganisation measures in respect of the collateral provider and/or the collateral taker; and/or (b) notwithstanding any purported assignment, judicial or other attachment or other disposition of or in respect of such rights.[8]

Member States are also mandated to ensure that the operation of a close-out netting provision is not subject to any of the requirements identified in Article 4(4), unless the parties have agreed otherwise. One of the two EU Directives that provide for

4 European Baking Federation, 2019, 4–5, https://www.fsb.org/wp-content/uploads/EBF-2.pdf.

5 UNIDROIT Principles, Operation of Closeout Netting Provisions in General, Principle 6 (1) The law should ensure that a close-out netting provision is enforceable in accordance with its terms.

6 Directive 2002/47/EC on financial collateral arrangements, as amended ('Financial Collateral Directive') O.J. L 168, Article 4 Enforcement of financial collateral arrangements. 'Member States shall ensure that on the occurrence of an enforcement event, the collateral taker shall be able to realise in the following manners, any financial collateral provided under, and subject to the terms agreed in, a security financial collateral arrangement: (a) financial instruments by sale or appropriation and by setting off their value against, or applying their value in discharge of, the relevant financial obligations; (b) cash by setting off the amount against or applying it in discharge of the relevant financial obligations'.

7 European Parliament, Directorate General for Internal Policies, Policy Department, *A: Economic and Scientific Policy, Shadow Banking: Legal Issues of Collateral Assets and Insolvency Law* (2013), 4. Articles 7 and 8 Directive 2002/47/EC on financial collateral arrangements, as amended ('Financial Collateral Directive') O.J. L 168, 27.6.2002, p. 4.; Article 25 Directive 2001/24/EC on the reorganisation and winding up of credit institutions O.J. L 125, 5.5.2001, 15–23.

8 Ibid, Article 7.

netting arrangements, Directive 2002/47/EC, also defines close-out netting provisions as:

> a provision of a financial collateral arrangement, or of an arrangement of which a financial collateral arrangement forms part, or, in the absence of any such provision, any statutory rule by which, on the occurrence of an enforcement event, whether through the operation of netting or set-off or otherwise: (i) the obligations of the parties are accelerated so as to be immediately due and expressed as an obligation to pay an amount representing their estimated current value, or are terminated and replaced by an obligation to pay such an amount; and/or (ii) an account is taken of what is due from each party to the other in respect of such obligations, and a net sum equal to the balance of the account is payable by the party from whom the larger amount is due to the other party.[9]

While this definition departs from the UNIDROIT Principles on close-out netting, it goes some way to incorporate elements of the internationally agreed definition. It is noteworthy that this definition was established more than a decade before the UNIDROIT definition was established in 2013. Article 7 of the EU Directive requires Member States to ensure that a close-out netting provision can take effect in accordance with its terms:

> (a) notwithstanding the commencement or continuation of winding-up proceedings or reorganisation measures in respect of the collateral provider and/or the collateral taker; and/or (b) notwithstanding any purported assignment, judicial or other attachment or other disposition of or in respect of such rights.[10]

Additionally, Member States are to ensure that the operation of a close-out netting provision may not be subject to any of the requirements mentioned in Article 4(4) (Enforcement of financial collateral arrangements], unless otherwise agreed to by the parties. As noted by the EU, the reason for the broad definition of netting in Directive 2002/47/EC, compared to the UNIDROIT's Close-out netting Provisions,[11] is because netting in the EC Directive is not limited to financial collateral arrangement.

9 Ibid, Preamble (n).

10 Ibid, Article 7.

11 Council of the European Union, *UNIDROIT Draft Principles Regarding the Enforceability of Close-out Netting Provisions – Non-paper by the Services of the Commission,* Brussels, 25 January 2019, https://data.consilium.europa.eu/doc/document/ST-5710-2013-DCL-1/en/pdf.

The broader regulatory framework for close-out netting arrangements within the EU can also be found within Directive 2001/24/EC,[12] Regulation (EC) No 1346/2000[13] and the Commission Proposal of 6 June 2012 for a directive on crisis resolution for banks (COM (2012) 280 final).[14] Article 69 provides for:

> the protection for financial collateral, set off and netting agreements Member States shall ensure that there is appropriate protection for title transfer financial collateral arrangements and set-off and netting arrangements so as to prevent the transfer of some, but not all, of the rights and liabilities that are protected under a title transfer financial collateral arrangement, a set-off arrangement or a netting arrangement between the institution and another person and the modification or termination of rights and liabilities that are protected under such a title transfer financial collateral arrangement, a set-off arrangement or a netting arrangement through the use of ancillary powers.[15]

In contrast, Principle 4 of the UNIDROIT Principles provides for 'an eligible obligation, which means an obligation arising under one of the following contracts, such as, derivative instruments, meaning an option, forward, future, swap, contract for differences or other transaction in respect of a reference'.[16] Thus, when compared with Article 2 of the EC Directive, 'financial collateral arrangement' means 'a title transfer financial collateral arrangement or a security financial collateral arrangement whether or not these are covered by a master agreement or general

12 Directive 2001/24/EC of the European Parliament and of the Council of 4 April 2001 on the reorganisation and winding up of credit institutions O.J. L 125. It provides that netting agreements are governed solely by the law of the contract which governs such agreements, Article 25. Such agreements will therefore be upheld in insolvency if the parties chose a 'netting-friendly' law. See Regulation (EC) No 593/2008 on the law applicable to contractual obligations (Rome I) which grants the party the freedom to choose the law applicable to their contract, Article. 3.

13 Council Regulation (EC) No 1346/2000 of 29 May 2000 on insolvency proceedings O.J. L 160. Preamble (27) provides that there is also a need for special protection in the case of organisation of insolvency proceedings in the case of payment systems and financial markets. This applies exclusively to the legislation of Member States, for example to the position-closing agreements and netting where there are specific and substantiated reasons for the agreements to be found in such systems and for the Council to reserve the right to amend these Annexes on the sale of securities and guarantees provided, *in order to take account of any amendments to the domestic such transactions as governed in particular by Directive law of the Member States*. [Emphasis added]. See 98/26/EC of the European Parliament and of the Council of 19 May 1998 on settlement finality in payment and securities settlement systems.

14 Directive of the European Parliament and of the Council, establishing a framework for the recovery and resolution of credit institutions and investment firms and amending Council Directives 77/91/EEC and 82/891/EC, Directives 2001/24/EC, 2002/47/EC, 2004/25/EC, 2005/56/EC, 2007/36/EC and 2011/35/EC and Regulation (EU) No 1093/2010.

15 Ibid, Article 69.

16 UNIDROIT Principles, Operation of Closeout Netting Provisions in General, Principle 4.

terms and conditions'.[17] Most noteworthy too, is that the Directive is more specific than the UNIDROIT Principles, understandably, as member states are required to implement EU law.

As a further significant distinction, there is no specific reference in the UNIDROIT Principles to ISDA Master Agreements.[18] While this does not exclude the adoption of such Agreements under the law of states that rely on the UNIDROIT Principles, it does not resolve uncertainty over the regulatory scope of domestic law in relation to the application and scope of those ISDA Master Agreements.

In 2012 following four appeals, the court *Lomas*,[19] considered a series of questions in relation to derivatives in the form of interest rate swaps and forward freight agreements on the International Swaps and Derivatives Association Inc, based on the 1992 and 2002 Master Agreements.[20]

The first question was whether the obligations to make payments subsist after the party to whom payment is due has committed an Event of Default and, if so, for how long. Section 2(a)(i) of the Master Agreement provided for an obligation on each party to make the payment, followed by provisions in section 2(a)(ii) that such payment is to be made on the due date in the place specified in the Confirmation.[21]

More importantly, in the third and fourth appeals, the issues that arose were in relation to close-out netting provisions within the Master Agreement. The Court noted that the Master Agreement gave the Non-defaulting Party a right to terminate in certain circumstances upon an Event of Default. It provided further that the parties may opt for Automatic Early Termination ('AET') upon the occurrence of certain 'Bankruptcy Events of Default'. In the event of Termination, the Master Agreement prescribed a regime of 'close-out netting'.[22]

The fourth appeal raised a distinct point concerning the operation of the close-out netting provisions. It concerned the question 'whether, in certain circumstances,

17 Directive of the European Parliament and of the Council, establishing a framework for the recovery and resolution of credit institutions and investment firms and amending Council Directives 77/91/EEC and 82/891/EC, Directives 2001/24/EC, 2002/47/EC, 2004/25/EC, 2005/56/EC, 2007/36/EC and 2011/35/EC and Regulation (EU) No 1093/2010, Article 2.

18 UNIDROIT Principles, Operation of Closeout Netting Provisions in General. Principle 2, Explanatory and commentary, states that in relation to Principles 2, Definition, at 21. It provides that, in practice, a clause allowing for close-out netting between the parties may be included in standard master documentation, be part of a tailor-made framework agreement, or be an entirely self-standing agreement. The definition also covers contractual provisions that are not contained in the clauses of a single agreement, but in several interrelated arrangements, especially master-master agreements to the extent that the underlying obligations covered by the various master agreements are eligible obligations under Principle 4.

19 *Lomas & ORS (Together the Joint Administrators of Lehman Brothers International (Europe) and JFB Firth Rixson Inc. & ORS.* [2012] EWCA Civ 419, 2.

20 Ibid.

21 Ibid, 4–5.

22 Ibid, 8.

the close-out netting provisions require an assumption to be made that the Defaulting Party would in fact have satisfied the conditions precedent to its entitlement to receive payment from the Non-defaulting Party'.[23]

In the third appeal, the Court in analysing Flaux J.'s position on the application of the close-out netting provisions within the Master Agreement. It maintained that the Justice's position was not correct.[24] Flaux J. held that netting was not available to the Defaulting Party where the conditions contained in Section 2(a)(iii) of the Master Agreement had not satisfied in regard to the date for payment. However, this view was contrary to the position taken by Gloster J. in Pioneer Freight Futures Company Limited.[25] Gloster J. maintained there that the calculation of liability assumed that it was not required to give credit by way of netting under Section 2(c) for sums otherwise due during the period of default. The third appeal was granted, on the basis that the Master Agreement expressly recognised that there may be sums owing which are not the subject of close-out netting. Rather the sum payable was part of the set-off provisions within the Master Agreement.

In this fourth appeal, which it dismissed, the Court concentrated on specific words within the Master Agreement, specified in section 6, such as 'loss' and 'market quotation'.[26] The Court concluded that, focusing on loss and market quotation as they relate to close-out netting, within section of the Master Agreement, would provide a level of clarification of the operation of the netting arrangements. The Court maintained that the 'definition of loss is a method of calculating close-out positions irrespective of which party is in breach and it does not nor is it intended to produce a result equivalent to the common law measure of damages'.[27] The Court went further, stating that loss and market

23 Ibid, 9.

24 Ibid, 113. At paragraph 71, the question whether the non-defaulting party is obliged to give credit in this way against the gross liability of the Defaulting Party remains a live issue in the Cosco appeal in which netting under Section 2(c) was relied on by Pioneer as an alternative means of recovery to that provided for under Section 6 of the Master Agreement. The assumption was that all of the transactions (including the eight whose expiry dates occurred before the first Event of Default) were brought into account as Terminated Transactions under the wash-out provisions. At paragraph 72, in the case of Marine Trade SA, Flaux J held that netting under Section 2(c) was not available to the Defaulting Party where the conditions precedent contained in Section 2(a)(iii) were not satisfied as of the date for payment. He confirmed this view in his judgment in Cosco. The basis of his decision was that netting under Section 2(c) applies only where the amount due from the Non-defaulting Party "would otherwise be payable". In that event the obligations of each party in respect of the same transaction "to make payment" of the fixed or floating rates are discharged and replaced by an obligation upon the party not in the money to pay the net balance due.

25 Ibid, *Pioneer Freight Futures Company Limited v. TMT Asia Limited* [2011] EWHC 1888 ('TMT 2') [2011] 2 Lloyd's Rep. 565. Gloster J. considered that the overall scheme of the 1992 Master Agreement was to provide for netting off of the gross liability of each party at each payment date under Section 2(c) and for a wash-out calculation of a final net figure under Section 6(e)(4), following automatic termination of all outstanding transactions.

26 Ibid, 123.

27 Ibid, 133.

quotation did, by and large, achieve the same result. The application of close-out netting provisions within ISDA Master Agreement continue to be assessed on a case-by-case basis. This is largely due to the drafting of other clauses with the Master Agreement that provide for another mechanism to manage any default payments, such as, through sett-off. The Lomas case highlights the importance of well drafted ISDA Master Agreements, and that, where close-out netting provisions are intended to be used in the event of a default, they should not be clouded or obstructed by other clauses. It is therefore beneficial for the parties and to the courts that, when a dispute arises, the clauses are clear in how and when they are to apply.

In a final comparison between the UNIDROIT Principles and the EC Directive, Principle 9 provides that the private international law rules of the implementing State should determine the law that governs the operation of the closeout netting provision, taking into account to the extent permitted by the laws of the implementing State, any choice of the governing law by the parties.[28] More precisely, at paragraph (5):

> if insolvency proceedings have been commenced in respect of a party to the close-out netting provision [or a branch of that party] and under a law other than the law determined in accordance with paragraph (1), the implementing State may provide that the law governing the insolvency proceedings governs also: a) the determination of the scope of parties and obligations that are eligible for close-out netting for the purposes of the enforcement of the close-out netting provision in the context of insolvency proceedings before the courts of the relevant implementing State; and b) the avoidance of a close-out netting provision as a fraudulent transaction or as a preference that is detrimental to other creditors of the insolvent party.[29]

Given that the regulatory approach towards close-out netting arrangements in the EU has departed from the more general approach adopted by Australia and Singapore, it is not surprising that the EU has generally left ISDA Master Agreements to provide for close-out netting arrangements. The EU's approach has the advantage of establishing a direct correlation between netting and insolvency for the purpose of protecting creditors.

In two cases that were heard by Italian courts in 2012 and 2014, the ISDA Master Agreements were discussed in relation to the jurisdiction of the English courts. Close-out netting provisions were not an issue in either case. However, they are general provisions within these contractual arrangements. In *Municipality of Milan*[30]

28 Ibid, Principle 9.

29 Ibid, Principle 9(5).

30 *Municipality of Milan v. JP Morgan Chase Bank, UBS Italia SIM S.p.a., Dafka Bank PLC, Deutsche Bank A.G. and J.P. Morgan Securities Ltd.*, Italian Supreme Court, joint divisions, 27 February 2012, no. 2926. In Jones Day the Italian Supreme Court's Interpretation of the Jurisdiction Clause

(Milan) and *Municipality of Venice*[31] (Venice) the Italian Supreme Court considered the scope of the jurisdiction clauses that favoured English courts in ISDA Master Agreements. The central argument was whether Article 13 of the ISDA Master Agreement extended to both contractual and tort disputes. In the *Milan* case, there was a complex debt restructuring transaction that included collateral consultancy provided by the banks. They had been issued on a 30-year debenture loan, which began in 2005 for more than €1.6 billion. They encompassed four identical contracts, each including swap agreement and an interest rate swap collar. The swap agreement with each bank was governed by an ISDA Master Agreement and accompanying schedules and confirmations. In the same case, it was asserted that the 'municipality found that the entire transaction was fraudulently imbalanced in favour of the banks due to the existence of implicit costs incorporated in the swaps, in 2008'.[32] Article 13 of the ISDA Master Agreement contained jurisdiction clause that submitted to English courts.

In Venice, the municipality commenced proceedings against the banks due to the derivatives transactions governed by the ISDA Master Agreement providing unfavourable loan conditions that induced it to assume undeclared and unpredictable risks, which then resulted in serious losses. At issue was whether local Italian courts had jurisdiction to hear the case, claiming that the jurisdiction clause contained in Article 13 of the ISDA Master Agreement provided for jurisdiction of English courts. The Italian Supreme Court, in each case, concluded that Italian courts did have jurisdiction over the dispute. It rejected the defendants' position that the jurisdiction clause contained in Article 13 of the ISDA Master Agreement conferred jurisdiction on English courts.

Central to the Italian Supreme Court's interpretation of Article 13 of the ISDA Master Agreement was the jurisdiction of the Court. In construing how far Article 13 extended, the Court concluded that it relates to all disputes relating to this Agreement. Thus, the Court's interpretation of Article 13 under Italian law, did not mean that the jurisdiction of English courts, as described by the clause, were connected to the contractual implementation of derivatives governed by the ISDA general conditions.[33] The Court referred instead to the:

> Italian Civil Code principles on contract interpretation, including Article 13 of the Italian Civil Code, which provides that a contract must be interpreted with regard to the common intention and the behaviour of the parties, and not merely to the literal meaning of its wording, and with regard to Article 13,

Favoring English Courts Contained in ISDA Master Agreements, https://www.jonesday.com/en/insights/2015/01/the-italian-supreme-courts-interpretation-of-the-jurisdiction-clause-favoring-english-courts-contained-in-isda-master-agreements.

31 Ibid, *Municipality of Venice v. Merrill Lynch International Bank Ltd. and Fincon S.r.l. in liquidazione*, Italian Supreme Court, joint divisions, 18 September 2014, no. 19675.

32 Ibid.

33 Ibid.

> which provides that, even if the wording contained in a contract is general, a contract exclusively covers the objects on which the parties intended to contract.[34]

The Italian Supreme Court also referred to 'Article 13 of the Italian Civil Code, pursuant to which the clauses inserted in general conditions, in case of doubt, are interpreted in favour of the non-drafting party'.[35]

Furthermore, the Italian Supreme Court ruled that: 'Italian courts have jurisdiction under Article 5, no. 3 of the EU Regulation 44/2001, because Italy was the place where the harmful event caused by the defendants' wrongful behaviour occurred or may have occurred. Finally, the Court held that the jurisdiction clause in favour of English courts contained in ISDA Master Agreements, relating to disputes, did not extend to contractual claims'.[36] In effect, the Italian Supreme Court reinforced the use of ISDA Master Agreements and their importance in governing large-scale transnational financial transactions.

Three years later, in the case of *Deutsche Bank AG v. Commun di Savona*[37] in 2018, there was an appeal about two theoretically competing jurisdiction clauses. The clauses, in favour of the Italian and English courts respectively, were included in: '(i) a written agreement dated 22 March 2007 between Deutsche Bank AG and Comune di Savona; and (ii) a 1992 multicurrency ISDA Master Agreement dated 6 June 2007 agreed between the same parties'.[38] On 6 June 2007, the Bank and Savona entered into a 1992 multicurrency ISDA Master Agreement. Clause 13 of the Agreement provided that the governing law and jurisdiction would be construed in accordance with [English Law], and jurisdiction would vest in English courts.[39] The English Court argued that, it was necessary to consider Article 25 (ex-Article 23) of the revised Regulation (EU) No. 1215/2012. Article 25 provides for its application where the parties have agreed that a court has jurisdiction over 'disputes which have arisen . . . in connection with a particular legal relationship'.[40] In referring to the earlier 2015 judgement of the English Court of Appeal in *Deutsche Bank v. Petromena,*[41] the Court stated that:

> English law cannot, however, be decisive of the matter in the European context. It is important to note that Article 23 is itself confined to agreements

34 Alessandro Corno, Locke McMurray, Lamberto Schiona, Margherita Magillo, Harriet Territt, *Italy:* The Italian Supreme Court's Interpretation of the Jurisdiction Clause Favoring English Courts Contained in ISDA Master Agreements, 19 January 2015.

35 Ibid.

36 *Municipality of Venice v. Merrill Lynch International Bank Ltd. and Fincon S.r.l. in liquidazione*, Italian Supreme Court, joint divisions, 18 September 2014, no. 19675.

37 [2018] EWCA Civ 1740.

38 Ibid.

39 Ibid, 6.

40 Ibid.

41 [2015] 1 WLR 4225, at paragraph 85–86.

> to settle disputes 'which have arisen or which may arise in connection with a particular legal relationship'. The emphasis on the 'particular legal relationship' shows that a dispute arising from a second relationship is not likely to be included in an agreement for resolving disputes in an earlier, and different, relationship.[42]

The English Court of Appeal highlighted the importance of maintaining market stability and certainty, which is largely why ISDA Master Agreements have been successful. The Court concluded 'it would be startling if the bank's claims falling squarely under the swap contracts could not be brought in the forum selected by the parties through the jurisdiction clause under those agreements, namely that contained in the ISDA Master Agreement'.[43] The Court reaffirmed the importance that ISDA Master Agreements have been widely accepted across most jurisdictions to assist in managing debt.

More recently, in the case of England, *Alfred,*[44] the Court had to reconcile swap transactions that had been performed without challenge by either party, on the basis that notice was either provided by a contractual or by some other prescribed method, if at all. Alfred Street Properties Limited entered into facilities totalling £111.5 million with Anglo Irish Banking Corporation, together with five extendable interest rate swaps to hedge its interest rate exposure under those facilities. The National Asset Management Agency subsequently acquired the Bank's interests in the loans and the Swaps. A material issue was the absence of consideration given to netting clauses provided for in the ISDA Master Agreement. The Court argued that:

> whilst a strict approach, favouring clarity, certainty and predictability, is required in interpreting the terms of standard market agreements such as the ISDA master agreement or Definitions, the authorities recognise that those documents are in each case subject to the specific provisions in any agreed Schedule and that the terms of the specific confirmation must prevail in the event of any uncertainty.[45]

In sending a strong message, the Court concluded that the claim was opportunistic and based on a technical point as to the validity of contracts taken months after the contracts had been fully executed by both parties. More problematic was the overly pedantic nature of the claim and the unreasonable interpretation of commercial confirmations of the relevant contracts. Arguably, the claim should have been summarily dismissed.[46]

42 *Deutsche Bank AG v. Commun di Savona* [2018] EWCA Civ 1740, 85.
43 Ibid.
44 *Alfred Street Properties Ltd v National Asset Management Agency* [2020] EWHC 397.
45 Ibid, 46.
46 Ibid, 123.

Based on the brief analysis above, the permutations surrounding ISDA Master Agreement clauses alone have been debated in some courts, and arguably, may not yet be settled. A settled position may never be achieved when the drafters of such clauses, knowingly or to manage risk, cloud or obstruct one clause with another.

6.1.1 United Kingdom: Brexit

The UK, along with the US, has arguably been a leader in the areas of both ISDA Master Agreements and the application of close-out netting provisions. However, the legal framework for close-out netting arrangements and ISDA Master Agreements in the UK remained in place in early 2021, that is, directly following its exit from the EU.

Nonetheless, UK courts have presided over cases involving the use of ISDA Master Agreements and close-out netting provisions for more than a decade. In *Marine Trade,*[47] an issue arose as a result of a dramatic fall in the freight market in the fourth quarter of 2008. The Claimant ([Marine Trade] and the First Defendant [Pioneer] entered fourteen Forward Freight Agreements [FFAs] between May 2007 and September 2008. The 2007 Terms of the Forward Freight Agreement Brokers Association [FFABA] entered into between the parties on 16 April 2008, constituted a Master Agreement in terms of the 1992 International Swap Dealers Association (Multi-Currency-Cross-Border) Master Agreement as supplemented and amended by clause 9 of the FFABA 2007 Terms, under which each of the FFAs was a Transaction.[48]

One of the issues that emerged, in reading clauses 7, 8 and 9 of the FFABA 2007 Terms, together with Section 2 of the Master Agreement, was whether the obligation that came into existence when the Settlement Sum was calculated could be discharged in one of two ways: (1) by payment of the relevant Settlement Sum and (2) by netting coupled with payment of the resulting balance. That gave rise to the further question of whether netting payments was available under Section 2(c) when payment was due regardless of default, or subject to the condition precedent of the party not being in default under Section 2(a)(i).[49]

In analysing both Sections 2 and 9, the Court concluded that remedies are available and will be calculated accumulatively. However, when applying remedies in accord with both Sections, each Section must be read separately to allow for any netting arrangements to be made available. The effect of such non-compliance is merely to suspend the obligation to pay, so long as the condition precedent operates.[50] The Court elaborated: '[T]he effect of non-compliance with the conditions

47 *Marine Trade S.A. Claimant – and – (1) Pioneer Freight Futures Co Ltd BVI (2) Armarda (SINGAPORE) PTE LTD*, [2009] EWHC 2656.

48 Ibid.

49 Ibid, 20.

50 Ibid.

precedent in Section 2(a)(iii) is that the amounts have not become payable. That is only consistent with 'payable' meaning immediately due for payment.'[51]

Despite the Court not having to rule on jurisdiction of the choice law, it argued that, to recover the sum paid under protest in February 2009, Marine Trade must bring itself within one of the established categories which English law recognises as sufficient to make retention of the money by the other party unjust, specifically (since no other category is relied on) that the money was paid by mistake.[52]
It concluded that determining the commercial balance is insufficient to gainsay the clear meaning of Section 2(c). Notwithstanding considerable debate over and analysis of the provisions underpinning the ISDA Master Agreement, the Court reinforced that the purpose of meeting arrangements is to protect parties when another party defaults and becomes insolvent. As highlighted earlier, in Lamos, in considering provisions in ISDA Master Agreements, a court will construe them in light of a strict interpretation of the contract. It will decide based on its construction of specific clauses and provisions, to determine the validity or otherwise of a close-out netting provision.

A year later in 2011 in the case of *Belmont Park Investments PTY Limited,*[53] the Court noted that the credit default swap agreement ('the Swap Agreement') had been constituted by: (i) an ISDA Master Agreement, including the Schedule (and Credit Support Annex) between Dante and LBSF (to which the Issuer subsequently acceded); and (ii) a Swap Confirmation between LBSF and the relevant Issuer.[54]

The Court maintained that the contractual provisions were effective as a matter of English law[55] and, in particular, did not offend the anti-deprivation rule. More importantly, the Court decisively conveyed that 'all of the documents are expressly

51 Ibid, '[T]he word "payable" in Section 2(c) means "falling due for payment" (i.e. even if the obligation to pay has been suspended) and not "enforceable by payment", so that netting remains available even when the party seeking to do so is affected by an Event of Default. However, where Pioneer is affected by an Event of Default, as a consequence of Section 2(a)(iii), Marine Trade has no obligation to make payment to Pioneer at all. That "payable" connotes an immediately enforceable obligation to pay is also clear from the definition of "Unpaid Amounts" for the purposes of the calculation of the payment due on Early Termination. This refers to such unpaid amounts being "the amounts that became payable (or that would have become payable but for Section 2(a)(iii))" which demonstrates that the effect of non-compliance with the conditions precedent in Section 2(a)(iii) is that the amounts have not become payable. That is only consistent with "payable" meaning immediately due for payment and wholly inconsistent with Mr Tselentis' construction of "payable" as somehow covering a situation where the payment obligation has been suspended. Mr Tselentis accepted that if his construction of "payable" was wrong (which I do consider it to be), his argument on Issue 2 could not run' (21–24).

52 Ibid, 65.

53 *Belmont Park Investments PTY Limited (Respondent) v. BNY Corporate Trustee Services Limited and Lehman Brothers Special Financing Inc. (Appellant)* [2011] UKSC, 38.

54 Ibid.

55 Ibid, 32.

governed by English law, and consequently, the provisions are void and unenforceable under English law'.[56] Even in the absence of an expansive discussion of close-out netting arrangements, the Court noted that, following communications between the High Court in England and the Bankruptcy Court in New York, it was agreed that, in order to limit potential conflict between decisions in the two jurisdictions, relief would be limited to declaratory relief.[57] The Court did, however, refer to the previously mentioned case of *Lamos,*[58] highlighting the importance of analysing specific sections of the ISDA Master Agreement to determine what and how any netting arrangements should be interpreted.[59]

Based on a sample of cases decided by English courts before Brexit, it was well established that English law is widely applied in ISDA Master Agreements. Given this, it is likely that the influence of English law on the construction, and use, of ISDA Master Agreements, and indirectly netting arrangements, will likely continue well after post-Brexit.

The authority of English law related to the quantum of the claim, is evident in the 2015 case of *SwissMarine Corporation Limited*.[60] On 15 May 2015, SwissMarine Corporation Limited ('SwissMarine') applied for an anti-suit injunction against O W Supply & Trading A/S, a Danish company that had filed for bankruptcy in the Bankruptcy Court of Aalborg, Denmark on 7 November 2014. SwissMarine sought an order

> restraining OW Supply (i) from proceeding with an action that it had brought in the District Court in Lyngby, Denmark and (ii) from commencing any other or further proceedings in Denmark or elsewhere against SwissMarine directed to obtaining a 'disputed' sum claimed under an ISDA Master Agreement or any transaction thereunder.[61]

Regarding the regulation of netting arrangements, the Court had little to say, other than the Lyngby action was issued on 9 March 2015, and O W Supply by its trustees had lodged the claim that:

> SwissMarine 'be ordered to pay to [OW Supply] the countervalue of USD 2,552,083.33 plus statutory interest from the institution of these proceedings until payment is made'. It refers to the bankruptcy proceedings in the Aalborg court, and pleads that 'When OW [Supplies] went bankrupt

56 Ibid, 51.
57 Ibid. [33].
58 Ibid, *Lomas v. JFB Firth Rixson Inc.* [2010] EWHC 3372 (Ch).
59 Ibid, 175.
60 Case No: 2015–183 *SwissMarine Corporation Limited v. O.W. Supply & Trading A/S* (in bankruptcy) Neutral Citation Number: [2015] EWHC 1571 (Comm).
61 Ibid, 1.

> there were outstanding accounts between the parties under the derivatives agreement subject to [the ISDA Agreement] in the form of [the September transaction]', and that the 'close-netting out of the parties' accounts as at 7 November 2014 shows net outstanding accounts in [OW Supply's] favour of USD 2,552,083.33'. It goes on to plead that, in view of section 58(h) of the Danish Securities Trading etc Act, 'the term laid down in clause 2(a)(iii) of the [ISDA Agreement] must be deemed not to apply to a Danish estate in bankruptcy both as a consequence of the general insolvency law principles and as a consequence of the close-out netting laid down in the Danish Securities Trading etc Act'. OW Supply exhibited to the writ a legal opinion of Professor Ulrik Rammeskow Bang-Pedersen about the effect of section 58h: it explains that the section is by way of a derogation from the general rule in section 40(2) of the Danish Bankruptcy Act that close-out netting takes place as at the date of the issue of the bankruptcy order.[62]

In response, it became apparent that the use of ISDA Master Agreements by entities engaged in close-out netting in bankruptcy proceedings is generally supported by national insolvency or bankruptcy laws. The Court further confirm[ed] the status of the relevant jurisdiction and governing law, referring directly to the ISDA Master Agreement paragraph, 18. On this basis, the Court stated:

> The meaning and application of the jurisdiction agreement, and the starting point, of course, must be the wording of the contract. In pointing to the specific provisions of the ISDA Master Agreement, the Court noted that section 13 of the ISDA Agreement is headed 'Governing Law and Jurisdiction', and it provides (so far as is material) as follows: (a) *Governing Law*. It went onto make the point that this Agreement will be governed by and constituted in accordance with the law specified in the Schedule. (b) *Jurisdiction*. With respect to any suit, action or proceedings relating to any dispute arising out of or in connection with this Agreement ('Proceedings'), each party irrevocably: (i) submits: (1) if this Agreement is expressed to be governed by English law, to (A) the non-exclusive jurisdiction of the English courts if the Proceedings do not involve a Convention Court and (B) the exclusive jurisdiction of the English courts if the Proceedings do involve a Convention Court; or (2) if this Agreement is expressed to be governed by the laws of the State of New York, to the non-exclusive jurisdiction of the courts of the State of New York and the United States District Court located in the Borough of Manhattan in New York City.[63]

62 Ibid, 12.
63 Ibid, 18.

As a practical matter, the Court stressed that it cannot diverge from the provisions in the ISDA Master Agreements. More importantly, it arguably confirmed the status and contents of these Agreements that formed and had become integral parts of the international legal framework. The Court elaborated:

> When parties choose to use for a contract a standard wording such as the ISDA Master Agreement form, generally their own circumstances at the time of the contract will not affect the interpretation of the wording. By choosing standard wording, parties usually evince an intention that the wording as incorporated into their contract should be given its usual meaning.[64]

However, in reconciling the issues of whether an English Court was the appropriate jurisdiction, the Court asserted that:

> Where 'the Proceedings do involve a Convention Court', a court that is bound to apply to them either article 17 of the Brussels Convention or article 17 of the Lugano Convention. It went onto to explain the application of EU law, in this situation, whereby, Article 17 of the Brussels Convention provides that, if the parties, one or more of whom is domiciled in a Contracting State, have agreed that a court or the courts of a Contracting State are to have jurisdiction to settle any disputes which have arisen or which may arise in connection with a particular legal relationship, that court or those courts shall have exclusive jurisdiction. Article 17 of the Lugano Convention is to similar effect.[65]

Finally, in addressing the alleged breach of jurisdiction within the ISDA Master Agreement, the Court referred to Dicey, Morris & Collins[66] stating that, subject to the provisions of the Brussels I Regulation and the Lugano Convention, an English court may restrain a party over whom it has personal jurisdiction from the institution or continuance of proceedings in a foreign court where it is necessary in the interest of justice.[67] To conclude, the Court took the position that the insolvency and bankruptcy proceedings derived from factors that were closely connected to and within the scope of Article 2 of the Brussels Regulation.[68] This approach demonstrates that the courts, when dealing with entities that are not full members of the EU but members of the EEA, will examine the ISDA Master Agreement to identify close-out netting provisions, the governing law and jurisdiction; but, where appropriate, they will apply EU Law.

64 Ibid, 27.

65 Ibid, 31.

66 Ibid, The Conflict of Laws (15th ed., 2014) at rule 38(5), at paragraph 15.

67 Case No: 2015–183 *SwissMarine Corporation Limited v. O.W. Supply & Trading A/S* (in bankruptcy) Neutral Citation Number: [2015] EWHC 1571 (Comm).

68 Ibid, 15–46–47.

6.1.2 Brexit

Notwithstanding this, between 2012 and 2018, there were a number of cases where the UK Courts considered close-out netting and ISDA Master Agreements. While some developments will eventuate since August 2021 when research for the book was completed, it is important to understand the complex arrangements that had ensured both pre- and post-Brexit.

Importantly, the fluid nature of Brexit has highlighted many unresolved issues, even though the withdrawal required some continuity, particularly for ISDA Master Agreements, and for the netting arrangements they provided. The alternative was the risk of a potentially catastrophic economic impact upon billions of dollars. Given these destabilisation threats to the global economy, Scott O'Malia emphasised in 2018 that there would be little change to the administration and application of law of ISDA Master Agreements. Due to the uncertainty that was playing out politically, he stated that:

> As it currently stands, virtually all of the ISDA Master Agreements entered into between counterparties based in the EU or EEA are governed by English law. Counterparties typically also submit to the jurisdiction of the English courts. Because the UK is part of the EU and EEA, it means any English court judgement is automatically recognized and enforced across those member states. Without some type of deal that replicates the effects of EU/EEA membership, English law would become a third-country law after Brexit. One of the consequences is that English court judgements would not be automatically recognized in EU/EEA countries. To be clear, this doesn't mean an English court judgement *won't* be recognized and enforced by an EU court after Brexit, and it doesn't mean an English law agreement becomes less 'valid' or that EU/EEA counterparties won't be able to continue to use English law Master Agreements. It does potentially mean more expense, more uncertainty and more red tape. Say an Italian and French counterparty are trading under an English law agreement with English court jurisdiction after Brexit; there's a dispute and the English court makes a judgement in favour of the Italian counterparty. The Italian counterparty would need to get that English court judgement recognized by a French court in order to get it enforced – it's an extra step in the process that could take years or, worse, result in another court deciding to reopen parts of the case.[69]

Viewed post-Brexit, the resulting impact that the withdrawal will have upon courts in England and Wales, remains unclear. In the absence of a determinative roadmap,

69 Ibid.

the parameters of English law influence over trans-border insolvency remains somewhat speculative. However, the 2002 ISDA Master Agreement provides that, if a proceeding relating to an ISDA Master Agreement involves a Convention Court (as defined in the 2002 ISDA Master), English courts have non-exclusive jurisdiction. If the proceeding does not involve a Convention Court, English courts have exclusive jurisdiction.[70] The Convention Court definition also includes an exclusive jurisdiction clause for ISDA Master Agreements governed by English law that are entered into between EU counterparties and reciprocal recognition across the EU of the judicial decisions in member states. However, more recently, in March 2020, the International Swaps and Derivatives Association (ISDA), released a template amendment agreement which allows the parties to an ISDA Master Agreement governed by English Law to convert that amendment agreement to an equivalent of the Irish or French law version.[71] Thus, as the UK officially exited from the EU, triggering Article 50 on the Treatyon EU[72] on 31 January 2020, this has led to a rethinking of what relevant law will govern ISDA Master Agreements.

Still, the jurisdictional road ahead is not as simple as switching the light switch off to the recognition and use of English law, and for entities to adopt either French or Irish law as alternatives. Arguably, due to the long-held leadership position of English law in the use of ISDA Master Agreements, decoupling those Agreements from English Law may prove difficult. The ISDA reinforces this point by stating that, beyond practical and commercial considerations, the continued use of English law to govern ISDA Master Agreements is likely to remain attractive, particularly until the future relationship between the UK and EU becomes clear.[73] Across the EU, the Rome I Regulation (**Rome I**) lays down the rules on the applicable law governing contractual obligations. Rome II Regulation (**Rome II**) lays down

70 See for example – Section 13 – Governing Law and Jurisdiction, (a) *Governing Law*. This Agreement will be governed by and construed in accordance with the law specified in the Schedule. (b) *Jurisdiction*. With respect to any suit, action or proceedings relating to any dispute arising out of or in connection with this Agreement ('Proceedings'), each party irrevocably; (i) submits: (1) if this Agreement is expressed to be governed by English law, to (A) the non-exclusive jurisdiction of the English courts if the Proceedings do not involve a Convention Court and (B) the exclusive jurisdiction of the English courts if the Proceedings do involve a Convention Court; or (2) if this Agreement is expressed to be governed by the laws of the State of New York, to the non-exclusive jurisdiction of the courts of the State of New York and the United States District Court located in the Borough of Manhattan in New York City, at, https://www.sec.gov/Archives/edgar/data/1065696/000119312511118050/dex101.htm.

71 Over to EU: ISDA Publishes Template Amendment to Convert Legacy English Law Governed Agreements to French or Irish Law, *Eversheds-Sutherland*, https://www.eversheds-sutherland.com/global/en/what/articles/index.page?ArticleID=en/Financial_services/isda-publishes-amendment_130320, note the information was not taken from the ISDA website due to the need to purchase the original paper.

72 Treaty on European Union, Official Journal of the European Union c326/1.

73 Over to EU: ISDA Publishes Template Amendment to Convert Legacy English Law Governed Agreements to French or Irish Law, *Eversheds-Sutherland*, https://www.eversheds-sutherland.com/global/en/what/articles/index.page?ArticleID=en/Financial_services/isda-publishes-amendment_130320.

the rules on the applicable law governing non-contractual obligations. In general terms, both Rome I and II will give effect to the choice of governing law made by an EU counterparty, subject to the passing of a Rome III. If and until a Rome III eventuates, the choice of English law by EU counterparties will continue to be recognised by the courts of EU Member States.[74]

Considered transitionally, therefore, the cross-border enforceability of English law has remained where insolvency proceedings commenced before the end of the transitional or implementation period. As a result, an English judgment obtained pursuant to those proceedings would be recognised and enforceable in any EU Member State under the Brussels I Recast Regulation.[75] However, following the expiry of the transitional or implementation period, the ISDA have noted that 'this position is not clear and it may still be possible for judgments of an English court made in under an English ISDA Master Agreement are no longer be recognised and enforceable in EU member states'.[76] At the time of writing, that position has remained unclear.

Also pertinent is how an EU bank counterparty that enters into an English-law-governed ISDA Master Agreement with a 'counterparty that is established in a third country may be required to include certain provisions in that ISDA Master Agreement in order to satisfy requirements under the EU Bank Recovery and Resolution Directive'.[77] While exploring that development is outside the scope of this Section, it is likely to have a significant future impact on the regulation of ISDA Master Agreements.

Another important area in need of clarification relates to jurisdiction. While this appears to be a major hurdle to overcome, the Lugano Convention,[78] which already applies in Iceland, Norway and Switzerland, if adopted and acceded by the UK would provide some clarification. According to Article 1.2, the Convention would 'not apply to the status or legal capacity of natural persons, rights in property arising out of a matrimonial relationship, wills and succession; or bankruptcy, proceedings relating to the winding-up of insolvent companies or other legal persons,

74 Ibid.

75 Ibid.

76 Ibid, English court judgments will only be recognised in EU Member States if either: (i) 2005 Hague Convention on Choice of Court Agreements (Hague Convention) is applicable; or (ii) the local position of an individual EU Member State is such that foreign judgments are respected and enforced. Some EU Member States currently do not recognise judgments from third countries, meaning enforcement may not be possible in these jurisdictions if the Hague Convention does not apply.

77 Directive 2014/59/EU of the European Parliament and of the Council of 15 May 2014 establishing a framework for the recovery and resolution of credit institutions and investment firms and amending Council Directive 82/891/EEC, and Directives 2001/24/EC, 2002/47/EC, 2004/25/EC, 2005/56/EC, 2007/36/EC, 2011/35/EU, 2012/30/EU and 2013/36/EU, and Regulations (EU) No 1093/2010 and (EU) No 648/2012, of the European Parliament and of the Council, Official Journal of the European Union L 173/191.

78 Convention on jurisdiction and the recognition and enforcement of judgments in civil and commercial matters, Official Journal of the European Union L 339/3.

judicial arrangements, compositions and analogous proceedings'.[79] However, jurisdiction will only apply to civil and commercial matters, regardless of the ISDA Master Agreement and the commercial matters it governs.

Even so, a more problematic issue that will need to be reconciled is how terminations clauses will be dealt with post-Brexit. One potential contractual implication of Brexit on ISDA Master Agreements, the ISDA noted, relates to how different jurisdictions will respond to provisions dealing with Illegality Termination, Force Majeure, Termination Event or Impossibility Termination Event,[80] On the surface, this appears to be a benign issue, but not so on more serious reflection. At the time of writing, this issue was as yet unresolved.

A starting point in seeking answers to these questions, in our view, is to acknowledge divergence between the 1992 and 2002 ISDA Master Agreements and their applicability post-Brexit. Firstly, the ISDA provided, prior to Brexit, that an illegality Termination Event under the 1992 ISDA Master Agreement is triggered by an adoption or change in the applicable law. As a result, it became unlawful for a party to make/receive any payment or delivery or to comply with any other material provision of the ISDA Master Agreement in relation to the Termination in questions. Secondly, there is uncertainty over whether the applicable law governing the application of the ISDA Master Agreement will have changed following the Brexit Deal, in relation to EU proceedings involving a UK party, or UK proceedings involving an EU party.[81] Thirdly, an intertwined issue is whether the removal of passporting rights for EU citizens under UK law is likely to constitute a change in the law.[82] Arguendo, a similar outcome is likely to eventuate under the 2002 ISDA Master Agreement, as under the 1992 ISDA Agreement.[83] A terminating event would not require a change in the applicable law.

Seeking relief from performance on account of a terminating event could be undertaken in accordance with the 2002 ISDA Master Agreement, Force Majeure provision. Evaluating the termination arrangements in light of the difference between the 1992 and 2002 ISDA Master Agreements, could be problematic post-Brexit. More specifically, the Force Majeure provision in the 2002 ISDA Master Agreement provides that, where there is an event that is an act of the state, it constitutes a Terminating Event. It is arguable that further consideration will need to be undertaken when drafting ISDA Master Agreements and close-out netting clauses post Brexit, at least through between 2021 and 2023, to ensure that the parties remain clear on issues that are related to dispute and default provisions. While this is not likely to

79 Ibid.

80 International Swaps, Derivatives Association, Brexit Version 8, 2020, https://www.isda.org/2020/07/21/Brexit-faq/.

81 Ibid.

82 Ibid, note, as this stage there is no specific opinion of legal advice provided to the ISDA.

83 Ibid, This Termination Event provides greater clarity as to the scope of applicable law, which includes the law of any country in which payment, delivery or compliance is required by either party.

be a practical challenge, it nevertheless reflects the need for wider consideration of drafting these important contractual arrangements during a time of political change.

In further developments, on 17 December 2020 and directly before Brexit, the UK released a Protocol for Dispute Resolution (UK PPD).[84] which varied from the 2013 ISDA Protocol.[85] The December 2020 Protocol provided for its application to in-scope UK financial and non-financial counterparties where those counterparties trade with EU or other third-country counterparties. Thus, where counterparties adhere to the UK Protocol, it has the effect of amending any ISDA Master Agreement entered between them on or before the date to which the later counterparty adheres. The UK Protocol therefore applies to existing relationships between counterparties and stipulates the methods by which those counterparties comply with the UK PDD Requirements.[86] However, counterparties can also specify other agreements to be covered by the Protocol. Non-ISDA members can also agree that the Protocol should govern their relationship for the purpose of the UK PDD Requirements. On the point of jurisdiction and jurisdictional clauses during the Brexit transition period, the Hague Convention on Choice of Court Agreements requires that, where the parties have agreed upon an exclusive jurisdiction clause, contracting states must give effect to that clause where it purports to give exclusive jurisdiction to the courts of a contracting state.[87] It must be noted that, from the time when the UK acceded to the Hague Convention,[88] which became effective on 1 January 2021, the UK became a signatory in its own right. However, the Hague Convention only gives effect to clauses agreed to from the effective date of accession of the state of the chosen courts. As a result, exclusive jurisdiction clauses in favour of UK courts which were agreed prior to 1 January 2021 may not be given effect under the Hague Convention. This does not mean that such clauses are unenforceable, but rather that their enforcement will be determined in accordance with local law.[89]

As demonstrated earlier, English law has had a major impact upon the construction of ISDA Master Agreements to date, including in the EU. That situation is

84 ISDA 2020 UK EMIR Portfolio Reconciliation, Dispute Resolution and Disclosure Protocol, http://assets.isda.org/media/11dbf4df/7ebef173-pdf/.

85 Travis Smith, *Post-Brexit Checklist for UK and EU/EEA Users of Derivatives*, January 2021, https://www.traverssmith.com/media/6648/post-Brexit-checklist-for-uk-and-eueea-users-of-derivatives.pdf.

86 Ibid.

87 Ibid, 13.

88 Hague Conference on International Private Law (2020), https://www.hcch.net/en/instruments/conventions/status-table/notifications/?csid=1318&disp=resdn, In the event that the Withdrawal Agreement is signed, ratified and approved by the United Kingdom and the European Union and enters into force on 30 March 2019, the United Kingdom will withdraw the Instrument of Accession which it has today deposited. In that case, for the duration of the transition period as provided for in the Withdrawal Agreement as stated earlier, the United Kingdom will be treated as a Member State of the European Union and the 2005 Hague Convention will continue to have effect accordingly.

89 Travis Smith, *Post-Brexit Checklist for UK and EU/EEA Users of Derivatives*, January 2021, https://www.traverssmith.com/media/6648/post-Brexit-checklist-for-uk-and-eueea-users-of-derivatives.pdf

unlikely to change radically post-Brexit, given the commercial value of maintaining consistent and predictable regulations to govern the choices of the contracting parties. Specifically, too, the parties need to draft their variants of netting arrangements and ISDA Master Agreements carefully to express their expectations and default options including in light of the applicable law.

6.2 United States

The US has for many years played a pivotal role in being a global leader in the banking and finance sector. The role of its derivatives market is largely unmatched across the world. Therefore, counterparties not only need to understand the operation of ISDA Master Agreements, but also the benefits or otherwise of close-out netting arrangements. The Federal Bankruptcy Code[90] (the Code) governing most corporations is generally pro-debtor, with some exceptions. The Code will stay or pre-empt rights under state laws that are inconsistent with its provisions. However, in the absence of such pre-emption, the Code will generally enforce a party's contractual rights under state law. Furthermore, there is no general right of setoffs, or netting, of obligations provided for under the Code, although federal bankruptcy law recognises the right of set-off as (but only if) provided for by the state law governing the contracts involved. Insolvency of an insured financial institution is governed by the Federal Deposit Insurance Act (FDIA).[91] Noteworthy too, both the FDIA and the Federal Deposit Insurance Corporation Improvement Act of 1991(FDICIA) have a role in regulating close-out netting arrangements.

The Federal Deposit Insurance Corporation[92] (FDIC) has stated its view in connection with a proposed rulemaking that FDICIA does not preclude the FDIC's exercise of authority under Section 11(e) of the FDIA (12 USC §1821(e)). That exercise of authority includes the FDIC acting as a receiver or conservator of Insured Institutions, to override any contractual right a counterparty might otherwise have to terminate and close out its contracts by reason of the appointment of the FDIC as a receiver or conservator.[93] The FDIC also stated that the 'exercise of the FDIC's authority would be limited to those circumstances where

90 Title 11 – United States Bankruptcy, Title I, §101, 6 November 1978, 92 Stat. 2549. https://www.govinfo.gov/content/pkg/USCODE-2017-title11/pdf/USCODE-2017-title11.pdf. See also, Robert Walters, *Close-out netting Provisions – Their Current Value in a Time of International Uncertainty!* International Company and Commercial Law Review – Sweet & Maxwell (2020).

91 William Bergman, Robert Bliss, Christian Johnson, George Kaufman, *Netting, Financial Contracts, and Banks: The Economic Implications, Research in Financial Services,* Federal Reserve Bank of Chicago, WP 2004–02 (2003), 13, amended by the Financial Institutions Reform, Recovery, and Enforcement Act (FIRREA).

92 Federal Deposit Insurance Corporation, https://www.fdic.gov.

93 Clifford Chance Roger &Wells LLP, NYC -1/38197/09 100664/00005, 16 February 2000. https://www.sifma.org/wp-content/uploads/2017/08/Cross-Product_CPMA-2000-Legal-Opinion-Clifford-Chance-Rogers-and-Wells-LLP-%E2%80%93-Enforceability-of-the-Netting-Provisions-FDIC-Improvement-Act.pdf.

(a) as a receiver it seeks to transfer a failed institution's contracts to another Insured Institution for performance (a so-called purchase and assumption transaction) or (b) as a conservator it enforces the performance of the contracts'.[94] The FDIC has acknowledged that the FDIA requires it, as receiver or conservator for an Insured Institution, to transfer all or none of such failed institution's qualifying financial contracts with a single counterparty to a single Insured Institution.[95] No different to netting regulations in other states compared throughout this chapters, the regulatory framework on netting in the US is to ensure there are appropriate controls in relation to minimising risk.

Additionally, the FDICIA[96] also regulates the treatment of certain derivative contracts upon insolvency. Subtitle A of Title IV of FDICIA provides special treatment to certain netting contracts in relation to the insolvency of a qualifying counterparty. Most noteworthy, the FDICIA provides that a 'netting contract' between two 'financial institutions' will be enforceable, notwithstanding that a financial institution may be a 'failed financial institution'.[97] The FDICIA further provides that no stay, injunction, avoidance, moratorium or similar proceeding or order, whether issued or granted by a court, administrative agency or otherwise shall limit or delay the application of otherwise enforceable netting contracts.

The foregoing provisions apply if the netting contract is governed by the laws of the United States, any State thereof, or any political subdivision of any State.[98] The netting contract is defined as a contract which provides for netting present or future payment obligations or payment entitlements (including liquidation or close-out values relating to the obligations or entitlements) between parties to the contract. The term netting contract cannot apply to any contract that is invalid under, or precluded by, the Federal laws of the United States.[99] The FDICIA's provision for statutory pro-

94 Ibid.

95 Ibid, Fed. Reg. 37726, 37730 (25 July 1994). Under Section 11(e)(9) of the FDIA, the FDIC is required to transfer to one depository institution (i) all QFCs and claims under such contracts between any person or any affiliate of such person and the depository institution in default or (ii) none of such QFCs and claims. 12 U.S.C. § 1821(e)(9). It is our view that a similar result obtains under FDICIA in respect of a netting contract, whether or not the netting contract includes QFCs. That is, the FDIC as receiver of an Insured Institution would be required to assign an Agreement which meets the requirements of FDICIA and all Principal Agreements which are covered by its terms to the same Insured Institution or else assign none of such contracts. To do otherwise would be to negate Section 403(a) of FDICIA which requires that the 'covered contractual payment obligations and the covered contractual payment entitlements between any two financial institutions' (i.e., the Settlement Amounts determined under the Principal Agreements) be 'netted in accordance with, and subject to the conditions of, the terms of any applicable netting contract'. 12 U.S.C. § 4403(a). Under Section 403(e) this requirement applies 'notwithstanding that a financial institution is a failed financial institution'. 12 U.S.C. § 4403(e).

96 Federal Deposit Insurance Corporation Improvement Act of 1991, Public Law 102–242 102d Congress, TITLE IV – MISCELLANEOUS PROVISIONS Subtitle A – Payment System Risk Reduction, https://fraser.stlouisfed.org/files/docs/historical/congressional/pl102_242.pdf.

97 Ibid.

98 Ibid, 12 U.S.C. §§ 4401–4407.

99 Ibid, 12 U.S.C. § 4402(14).

tections still apply notwithstanding that a financial institution is a failed financial institution. A failed financial institution is defined as a financial institution that: (a) fails to satisfy a covered contractual payment obligation when due; (b) has commenced or had commenced against insolvency, liquidation, reorganisation, receivership (including the appointment of a receiver), conservatorship, or similar proceedings (Insolvency Proceedings); or (c) has generally ceased to meet its obligations when due.[100]

Nevertheless, and in light of the foregoing, the FDIA is also supplemented by the National Bank Act in the case of national banks, and by a state's banking laws for a state-chartered bank. Creditors cannot force a bank into bankruptcy since banks are specifically exempted from the Code.[101]

Notwithstanding this, the Code does not specifically define the term close-out netting. Rather at section 38A, it defines the term master netting agreement to mean:

> An agreement providing for the exercise of rights, including rights of netting, setoff, liquidation, termination, acceleration, or close out, under or in connection with one or more contracts that are described in any one or more of paragraphs (1) through (5) of section 561(a), or any security agreement or arrangement or other credit enhancement related to one or more of the foregoing, including any guarantee or reimbursement obligation related to 1 or more of the foregoing; and if the agreement contains provisions relating to agreements or transactions that are not contracts described in paragraphs (1) through (5) of section 561(a), shall be deemed to be a master netting agreement only with respect to those agreements or transactions that are described in any one or more of paragraphs (1) through (5) of section 561(a).[102]

The reference to master netting agreement was made, following the 2008/2009 GFC in *Lehman Brothers Holding.*[103] There, a challenge arose from a complex financial structure that included an added layer of complexity due to the pendency of parallel and potentially conflicting legal proceedings in the United States Bankruptcy Court. One of the areas of concern was the language and structure of the ISDA Master Agreement. The ISDA Master Agreement was not a standalone agreement, but formed a central part of the Swap Agreement. Importantly, paragraph 9(c) of each ISDA Master Agreement expressly provided that the obligations of the parties under the relevant Swap Agreement shall survive the termination of

100 Ibid, 12 U.S.C. § 4402(7).

101 William Bergman, Robert Bliss, Christian Johnson, George Kaufman, *Netting, Financial Contracts, and Banks: The Economic Implications, Research in Financial Services,* Federal Reserve Bank of Chicago, WP 2004–02 (2003), 13–14.

102 Bankruptcy Code, § 38A-(B). (38B) The term 'master netting agreement participant' means an entity that, at any time before the date of the filing of the petition, is a party to an outstanding master netting agreement with the debtor.

103 In re *Lehman Brothers Holdings Inc., et al., Debtors. Lehman Brothers Special Financing Inc., Plaintiff, v. BNY Corporate Trustee Services Limited, Defendant.* No. 08–13555 (JMP). Adversary No. 09–01242 (JMP) (12 May 2011).

any transaction.[104] Given that all obligations of the parties under the ISDA Master Agreement remained outstanding, the failure of either party to complete performance constituted a material breach excusing the performance of the other. In addition, each of LBSF and BNY Corporate Trustee Services had unsatisfied contractual obligations to make various payments. Therefore, what, if any influence or impact netting arrangements would have in this case were minor. Rather, the case revolved around the overall contractual arrangements that had been established by both parties. As highlighted in the aforementioned, both the ISDA Master Agreement and Swap Agreement had to be performed.

Significant too, the case neither determined jurisdiction, choice of law nor close-out netting. However, the Court went to some length to highlight the important provisions of the Bankruptcy Code of 1978. It highlighted that the Bankruptcy Code effected a change in the treatment of contract or lease clauses that would seek to modify the relationships of contracting parties due to the filing of a bankruptcy petition.[105] Moreover, the Court noted how the 'safe harbour provisions of Section 560 of the Bankruptcy Code protect a non-defaulting swap participant's contractual rights to (i) liquidate, terminate or accelerate one or more swap agreements because of condition of the kind specified in Section 365(e)(1)' or (ii) 'of the Bankruptcy Code offset or net out any termination values or payment amounts arising under or in connection with the termination, liquidation, or acceleration of one or more swap agreements in Section 11 U.S.C. § 560'.[106] These provisions specifically permit termination solely 'because of a condition of the kind specified in Section 365(e)(1) that is, the insolvency or financial condition of the debtor and the commencement of a bankruptcy case. 11 U.S.C. §§ 560, 561'.[107]

Thus, as the *Lehman Brothers* case highlighted, Section 560 of the US Bankruptcy Code is arguably one of the important provisions related to insolvency and the ability to close out under netting arrangements. This is because Section 560 provides the contractual right to liquidate, terminate, or accelerate a swap agreement. It states that:

> [T]he exercise of any contractual right of any swap participant or financial participant to cause the liquidation, termination, or acceleration of one or more swap agreements because of a condition of the kind specified in section 365(e)(1) of this title or to offset or net out any termination values or payment amounts arising under or in connection with the termination, liquidation, or acceleration of one or more swap agreements shall not be stayed,

104 *LBSF Br [Lehman Brothers Special Financing Inc.*, Supp. Ex. E § 9(c); Ex. F § 9(c)
105 In re *Lehman Brothers Holdings Inc., et al., Debtors. Lehman Brothers Special Financing Inc., Plaintiff, v. BNY Corporate Trustee Services Limited, Defendant.* No. 08–13555 (JMP). Adversary No. 09–01242 (JMP) (12 May 2011).
106 Ibid.
107 Ibid.

> avoided, or otherwise limited by operation of any provision of this title or by order of a court or administrative agency in any proceeding under this title.[108]

The ability to net out allows for the contract to be terminated on grounds of being able to pay out the amount, or amounts, arising from termination, liquidation or swap agreement. Section 561 also provides for parties a contractual right to terminate, liquidate, accelerate or offset under a master netting agreement and across contracts in proceedings under Chapter 15.[109] In addition, Chapter 15[110] becomes important when dealing with cross-border insolvency matters.

In the case of *Bank One Corporation,*[111] the US Tax Court confirmed the current day legal framework for close-out netting provisions, stating:

> In 1990, Congress amended then 11U.S.C. section 362(b)(14), now section 362(b)17)(2000), and added to the Bankruptcy Code 11 U.S.C section 560 to limit a bankruptcy trustee's avoidance powers. These sections exempted swap agreements from the automatic stay and permitted swap participants to net positions in the setting of a bankruptcy. Congress passed the Federal Deposit Insurance Corporation Improvement Act of 1991 (FDICIA), Pub.L. 102–242, 105 Stat. 2286, 1 year later. Under 12U.S.C sections 4401–4407 (2000), which were enacted as part of the FDICIA, netting provisions are viewed by the CFTC as designed to assure the enforceability of netting among specified financial institutions and among members of clearing organizations for CFTC-regulated exchanges. By enacting the FDICIA, and the Financial Institutions Reform, Recovery, and Enforcement Act of 1989, each applying to failed depository institutions, Congress reduced systemic risk by providing a high degree of legal certainty that netting provisions would be upheld in insolvency proceedings in the United States.[112]

108 Ibid.

109 Bankruptcy Code, (a) Subject to subsection (b), the exercise of any contractual right, because of a condition of the kind specified in Section 365(e)(1), to cause the termination, liquidation, or acceleration of or to offset or net termination values, payment amounts, or other transfer obligations arising under or in connection with one or more (or the termination, liquidation, or acceleration of one or more) – (1) securities contracts, as defined in Section 741(7); (2) commodity contracts, as defined in Section 761(4);

110 Ibid, a prior chapter 15, consisting of Sections 1501 to 151326, related to a pilot program for a United States trustee system, prior to repeal by Pub. L. 99–554, title II, §231, 27 October 1986, 100 Stat. 3103. §1501. Purpose and scope of application (a) The purpose of this chapter is to incorporate the Model Law on Cross-Border Insolvency so as to provide effective mechanisms for dealing with cases of cross-border insolvency.

111 United States Tax Court *BANK ONE CORPORATION (Successor in Interest to First Chicago NBD Corporation, Formerly NBD Bancorp, Inc, Successor in Interest to First Chicago Corporation) and Affiliated Corporations, Petitioner v. Commissioner of Internal Revenue,* Respondent Nos. 5759–95, 5956–97. 2 May 2003.

112 Ibid, E.1.3.

The case arose from the application of a 1992 ISDA Master Agreement, where the agreement itself allowed for two methods of ascertaining the close-out netting settlement amount. The first 'method was the 'Market Quotation' method. The second method was the 'Loss' method. Neither method provided specifically that the settlement amount should take into account the credit risk of the counterparty or administrative costs'.[113] The Court went further by highlighting the need to account for more than a single transaction, and at times, multiple transactions,[114] for the purpose of managing these types of contracts. The Court elaborated, that in the case of a foreign entity counterparty, netting was not always enforceable. Of the 488 swaps at issue in 1993, 173 were with foreign counterparties. Of those 173, 119 were with counterparties located in countries which, according to the G-30 Report, had enforceable netting arrangements. Of the remaining 54 swaps (173–119), 9 were with counterparties that did not ultimately come from a G-10 or EU country. The G-30 and G-10 have important roles in providing a deepening understanding of global economic and financial issues, and to explore the international repercussions of decisions taken in the public and private sectors.[115] However, there was no discussion, confirmation or otherwise, on the governing law or jurisdiction set out in the ISDA Master Agreement. These areas of the law are arguably well settled once they have been established under the ISDA Master Agreement.

In a US District Court case of *Signal Hill Service*,[116] the Plaintiff's, Signal Hill Service, Inc. and Carpenteria Offshore Project Partnership (collectively, 'Signal Hill') commenced an action on February 22, 2011, alleging claims arising from a financing contract with defendant, Macquarie Bank Limited ('MBL'). While there was little reference to close-out netting provisions and their operation in the case, the Court noted that and 'MBL had agreed, that requiring a bond was warranted. Neither party disputed that Signal Hill owed MBL at least $7.5 million, even if MBL's designation of an Early Termination Date was improper and even if it was not entitled to close out the remaining hedge transactions and calculate an amount

113 Ibid, E.1.b-c.

114 Ibid, b. *Single Transaction Netting* – The ISDA form agreements provided that payments in the same currency and with respect to the same swap were automatically netted. This type of netting is known as single transaction netting. c. *Multiple Transaction Netting* –The ISDA form agreements provided that the parties could in certain circumstances elect a net amount that would be payable for two or more transactions. This type of netting is known as multiple transaction netting. Multiple transaction netting applied where the payments on more than one swap with the same counterparty were due on the same day and in the same currency.

115 Group of Thirty, Consultative Group on International Economic and Monetary Affairs, Inc, https://group30.org/about.

116 2011 WL 13220305 United States District Court, C.D. California. *SIGNAL HILL SERVICE, INC., a California Corporation, Carpinteria Offshore Project Partnership, a California Limited Partnership, Plaintiffs, v. Macquarie Bank Limited, an Australian Limited Liability Company*, Defendant. Case No. CV 11–01539 MMM (JEMx) Signed 06/29/2011.

due based on the market value of the hedged oil volumes as of that date'.[117] The Court limited its discussion and analysis of the parties obligations under the ISDA Master Agreement, and concluded that, under Section 5(a)(i) of the ISDA Agreement, Signal Hill's failure to make a settlement payment constituted an Event of Default. Paragraph 6 of the ISDA Agreement governed the 'Right to Terminate Following Event of Default'. The Court noted that the ISDS Agreement provided that in:

> the 'Event of Default . . . the Non-defaulting Party may . . . designate a day . . . as an Early Termination Date in respect of all outstanding Transactions. On the Early Termination Date, MBL is entitled to close out the remaining hedge transactions, and calculate the sum due and owing based on the market value of the hedged oil volumes on the date termination is affected. On February 22, 2011, MBL designated February 23, 2011 as the Early Termination Date. On February 24, 2011, it notified Signal Hill that the total amount due and owing under the ISDA was $25,737,896.16. In addition, (3) Taking any action to enforce any and all provisional remedies set forth in the 2002 ISDA Master Agreement, the ISDA Schedule to the 2002 ISDA Master Agreement, and/or the transaction Confirmations issued thereunder (collectively, the 'Project Financing Agreement'), under any documents that are in any way related to or connected with the Project Financing Agreement, and/or under applicable law.[118]

The right to close out under netting arrangements were afforded to either party in accordance with Section 6 of the ISDA Master Agreement. That is as far as the Court went, otherwise confirming that the issue centred largely around the granting of an injunction. The Court concluded by granting Signal Hill's motion for a preliminary injunction and denying MBL's motion for the appointment of a receiver. Signal Hill's *ex parte* application for a temporary restraining order was denied as moot. The Court specified was to take effect when Signal Hill's had posted a $7.5 million bond.

6.2.1 Safe Harbour

A key feature of the US framework is the adoption of the 'safe harbour' concept. That is, in addition to the requirements outlined earlier, the Bankruptcy Code has, for some time, established a safe harbour, which requires the satisfaction of two preconditions. First, the contracts must fit within the Bankruptcy Code's

117 Ibid, 24. At 5, it was noted that the court, on the Early Termination Date, MBL is entitled to close out the remaining hedge transactions, and calculate the sum due and owing based on the market value of the hedged oil volumes on the date termination is effected.

118 Ibid, 22.

definition of 'commodity contract', 'forward contract', 'securities contract', 'swap agreement', 'repurchase agreement' or 'master netting agreement'. Second, the party must qualify as a 'commodity broker', 'forward contract merchant,' swap participant', 'financial participant', 'repo participant' or 'master netting agreement participant'.[119] The principal safe harbour from the automatic stay that benefits swaps are

> §362(b)(17, 560 and 561 of the Bankruptcy Code. § 362(b)(17) provides that the filing of a bankruptcy petition: does not operate as a stay . . . of the set off by a swap participant or financial participant of a mutual debt and claim under or in connection with one or more swap agreements that constitutes the set off of a claim against the debtor for any payment or other transfer of property due from the debtor under or in connection with any swap agreement against any payment due to the debtor from the swap participant or financial participant under or in connection with any swap agreement or against cash, securities, or other property held by, pledged to, under the control of, or due from such swap participant or financial participant to margin, guarantee, secure, or settle any swap agreement. § 560 is a safe harbor from the automatic stay for swap agreements.[120]

The safe harbour provides as follows:

> [t]he exercise of any contractual right of any swap participant or financial participant to cause the liquidation, termination, or acceleration of one or more swap agreements because of a condition of the kind specified in §365(e)(1)of this title or to off-set or net out any termination values or payment amounts arising under or in connection with the termination, liquidation, or acceleration of one or more swap agreements shall not be stayed, avoided, or otherwise limited by operation of any provision of this title or by order of a court or administrative agency in any proceeding under this title.[121]

These provisions in the Bankruptcy Code protect the rights of non-defaulting counterparties to set – off mutual claims against an entity that has filed a bankruptcy petition and to exercise contractual rights that otherwise would have been automatically stayed upon the filing of such a petition.[122] As highlighted earlier in

119 Stephen Moller Partner, Anthony Nolan, Howard Goldwasser, Section 2(a)(iii) of the ISDA Master Agreement and Emerging Swaps Jurisprudence in the Shadow of Lehman Brothers, *Journal of International Banking Law and Regulation* (2011), 314–315.

120 §362(b)(17), 560 and 561 of the Bankruptcy Code.

121 Ibid, §365(e)(1).

122 Stephen Moller Partner, Anthony Nolan, Howard Goldwasser, Section 2(a)(iii) of the ISDA Master Agreement and Emerging Swaps Jurisprudence in the Shadow of Lehman Brothers, *Journal of International Banking Law and Regulation* (2011), 314–315.

Appendix – 1, as exemplified in in the 2002 ISDA Master Agreement between Bank of America and LKQ Corporations, safe harbour provisions are generally included in US Master Agreements.

6.2.2 Enforceability

The enforceability of netting provisions can be achieved under the FDICIA.[123] Centrally, the provisions contained in the Agreement by which a closing-out party may close out all principal agreements upon the occurrence of a close-out event to arrive at a single net payment obligation (if any) which is owed by one Party to the other. This would be enforceable in respect of a closed-out party, notwithstanding that insolvency proceedings have been commenced against the closed-out party.[124] Therefore, Section 403 of FDICIA provides that payment obligations which are 'covered' by a netting contract shall be netted in accordance with the terms thereof and the only obligation or entitlement that either Party to the netting contract shall have (including a failed financial institution) is the net obligation or net entitlement as determined by the netting contract.[125]

On the one side, and highlighted earlier, close-out netting arrangements along with ISDA Master Agreements are effective in the US, although automatic Early Termination is not necessary.[126] Multibranch netting arrangement, while complex, have arguably become common place. In the US, multibranch netting is effective and can be undertaken between a US bank with a foreign branch, and vis-à-vis, a foreign branch with a US bank. However, with respect to a foreign branch of a nationally chartered bank, the relevant US authority has taken the position that, in appropriate circumstances, such a branch should be treated as a separate entity from the US head office following a 'sovereign risk event'.[127] Moreover, in relation to a foreign branch of a federally insured New York State chartered bank, there are limits on the bank's liability (i) if a bank organised under the laws of that foreign country would not be liable under an equivalent contract and (ii) if an unrecognised government of that foreign country seizes assets of a foreign bank.[128]

Noteworthy too, is the position of multibranch netting. A New York branch requires the derivative transaction to be a 'qualified financial contract' under the

123 Clifford Chance Roger &Wells LLP, NYC -1/38197/09 100664/00005, 16 February 2000. https://www.sifma.org/wp-content/uploads/2017/08/Cross-Product_CPMA-2000-Legal-Opinion-Clifford-Chance-Rogers-and-Wells-LLP-%E2%80%93-Enforceability-of-the-Netting-Provisions-FDIC-Improvement-Act.pdf

124 Ibid.

125 Ibid, 12 U.S.C. § 4403.

126 Fieldfisher, *ISDA Master Agreement Legal Opinions on Close-out netting*, Copyright Fieldfisher LLP (August 2016), 239 Thanks to Chance Clifford, Munich Office for providing the book on Legal Opinion.

127 Ibid, 242–243.

128 Ibid.

New York Bankruptcy Law. Thus, 'most derivatives commonly documented under ISDA Master Agreements should be within this definition but that "more unusual" transactions should be checked with the New York Office of the Superintendent'.[129] Therefore, it is argued that, netting of amounts due will be calculated under both a global and a New York only basis, with the lesser of the two being payable to the counterparty. However, in the case of a federal branch, it is unclear if multibranch close-out netting provisions would be enforced, or if close-out netting would only apply to transactions entered into through that branch, or, only for transactions entered into through any US branch.[130] On the other side, it is necessary for individuals involved in the preparation of ISDA Master Agreements in the US to apply the correct national-law approach, and ensure that when they are dealing with insurance entities, they refer to the correct state. In conclusion, it is 'important to further note that where a non-netting jurisdiction is involved, local counsel state that there are some narrow factual scenarios where the outcome would be different from that for multibranch netting involving netting jurisdictions'.[131] Where required in the US, the adoption of an arbitration clause within an ISDA Master Agreement could provide the parties with an effective arbitral process for resolving disputes.

Despite the extensive law and court decisions in the US, other British Commonwealth states, such as Singapore, Australia and India, discussed in the previous chapter, have arguably looked to English decisions for guidance. Noteworthy, Indonesia is largely adopting the international framework and is using close-out netting arrangements and ISDA Master Agreements. At the end of the day, the application of ISDA Master Agreements will be construed as contracts and therefore close-out netting provisions will be interpreted in light of the broader contractual clauses. On the other hand, China, while not formally part of the ISDA, has generally adopted its own variant of the international approach, as will be highlighted later.

6.3 China

Similar to India, China is another state that, as of 2021, has had no specific regulation on netting arrangements. Zhao Sheng makes the point that there is a market perception that a non-defaulting party's right to terminate transactions and net their termination values (close-out netting) under a derivatives master agreement

129 Ibid.
130 Ibid, 243.
131 Ibid.

may be unenforceable when a Mainland China counterparty is subject to bankruptcy proceedings.[132] Sheng goes onto say:

> A non-defaulting party can always rely on the automatic early termination (AET) provisions of the derivatives master agreement which usually provide that, if not terminated earlier, all the transactions will terminate 'automatically' upon the occurrence of a specific event before the commencement of bankruptcy proceedings as specified by the parties. To this end, the right to close-out netting of the nondefaulting party under any derivatives agreement has been much fortified by the use of AET provisions. Significantly, in line with Basel capital rules and international developments, the China Banking and Insurance Regulatory Commission, the banking and insurance regulator, has promulgated the Rules for the Measurement of Default Risk Assets of Counterparties in the Trading of Derivatives (effective January 2019), which enable commercial banks in Mainland China to calculate risk capital for derivative transactions on a net basis. Accordingly, it is evident that market demand for the use of close-out netting to mitigate credit risks in the burgeoning derivatives market in Mainland China coincides with the expectations and policy of regulators.[133]

In support of this, 'close-out netting against a party before its bankruptcy is supported by China's Contract Law' and conflict of law principles.[134] Specifically, at the time of writing this book, close-out netting can be invoked under Chinese Law against a defendant at, or after, its bankruptcy. Therefore, and as Sheng highlights,

> the right to close-out – the right of a non-defaulting party to terminate transactions would be subject to a stay upon the commencement of the

132 Zhao Sheng, *China Netting*, March 2020, https://e.linklaters.com/62/961/downloads/linklaters-publication-china-netting-march-2020.pdf. The authors of this book are not proficient in the national language of China and have thus drawn upon material interpreted by individuals such as Zhao Sheng's and King & Wood Malleson's work to provide an overview of netting arrangements across China. Due to the lack of specific netting legislation in Mainland China, the authors recognize that a non-defaulting party's right to terminate transactions and net their termination values (close-out netting) under a derivatives master agreement may be unenforceable when a Mainland China counterparty is subject to bankruptcy proceedings.

133 Ibid, 1.

134 Article 113 of the Chinese Contract Law provides: 'Where one of the parties does not perform a contractual obligation, or does not perform a contractual obligation as agreed, resulting in losses to the other party, the total compensatory amount shall be equivalent to the total losses sustained by the other party due to the breach of contract, including benefits that the other party would have been able to obtain upon the contract being performed, but this amount shall not exceed the total losses that the breaching party, at the time of concluding the contract, foresaw or should have foreseen to probably result from breach of contract,' at 54. In King & Wood Malleson, *Whitepaper China's Derivatives Market and Judicial Trends* (2018), https://www.isda.org/a/9pREE/Chinese-Derivatives-Market-and-Legal-Trends.pdf, 54–56.

> bankruptcy of the mainland Chinese entity (which is the acceptance of the bankruptcy petition of the entity by the court).[135]

The parties face material choices in deciding whether and how to use an Automatic Early Termination (AET) provision. On the one hand, the

> parties are entitled to agree on an AET provision designating an event before the commencement of the bankruptcy proceeding (such as the approval of the regulator for bankruptcy petition, the submission of the bankruptcy petition or the registration of the petition with the court, each of which precedes the acceptance of the petition by the court) as the event that triggers AET, which provision would be enforceable in the bankruptcy of the mainland entity.[136]

On the other hand, parties are advised not to use a 'retroactive' AET provision where a termination is triggered upon the making of a bankruptcy order, but where the termination operates retroactively from (or backdated to) the time of submission of the bankruptcy petition. Any concerns

> over 'frivolous' bankruptcy petitions may be addressed through designating an event, such as approval by the regulator of the bankruptcy petition or the registration of the petition with the court as the trigger for AET, since any frivolous and vexatious petition would likely have been filtered out by the regulator or the court.[137]

Thus, the right to have an insolvency set-off enforced in net termination proceedings under China's Bankruptcy Law might have value in China.[138]

Moreover, in another sign that the Chinese judiciary has considered embracing the international framework in relation to close-out netting provisions, the Shanghai Pudong People's Court has considered the standards and practices adopted by the international derivatives market when dealing with derivatives disputes. For example, the Shanghai Pudong People's Court has published its opinion that, in addition to the Chinese Contract Law provisions, 'Chinese courts should also consider prevailing industry standards and practices in the international derivatives market when dealing with derivatives disputes'.[139] There is also evidence that

135 Ibid.
136 Ibid.
137 Ibid.
138 Ibid.
139 The Shanghai Pudong People's Court published 10 financial cases relating to Free Trade Zone, in King & Wood Malleson, *Whitepaper China's Derivatives Market and Judicial Trends* (2018), https://www.isda.org/a/9pREE/Chinese-Derivatives-Market-and-Legal-Trends.pdf, Section 1(c) of the ISDA Master Agreement provides that the Master Agreement and all confirmations documenting

Chinese courts accept a "single agreement" concept in relation to close out netting termination transactions. In particular, 'the case of the Golden Globe demonstrates the support of Chinese courts for the 'single agreement' concept in the context of a close-out termination of a master derivative contract between a bank and a counterparty'.[140] Citi (China) entered into a master derivative contract with the Shanghai Golden Globe International Trading Co. Ltd. (Golden Globe) whereby there were up to five separate transactions relating to copper traded on the London Metals Exchange. Citi (China) requested Golden Globe to pay the required margin and to enter into an account pledge agreement. Golden Globe failed to do so, thereby triggering a termination event under the master derivative contract. Citi (China) delivered an early termination notice, specifying a date upon which all outstanding transactions would be deemed to be early terminated. Citi (China) later informed Golden Globe of the early termination amount that it failed to pay. The Court held that:

> The derivative contract was an industry prescribed form and upheld the validity and effectiveness of its early termination provisions (including the close-out mechanism in respect of all outstanding transactions following an event of default or termination event). The court implicitly recognized and accepted the single agreement clause in the master derivative contract and applied a close-out netting process.[141]

The importance of this case cannot be underestimated since the proceedings and consideration by the Court of a contractual dispute sat outside Chinese Enterprise Bankruptcy Law. Although the Golden Globe case involved a contractual dispute over transactions entered into under a master derivative contract without consideration of the Chinese Enterprise Bankruptcy Law. It confirmed the support for the single agreement concept in the context of a master derivative contract in China.[142]

In the same case, the Chinese Court expressly upheld the close-out netting and payment netting provisions as a matter of contract law. That is, Citi (China) and

the underlying transactions form a single agreement between the parties. This principle is also common across other derivative documents, such as the NAFMII Agreement, the SAC Agreement and some mini-master agreements. If the 'single agreement' concept is recognized in the bankruptcy proceedings of a counterparty, the administrator can either continue to perform, or terminate, all outstanding transactions, rather than 'cherry pick' the performance of specific Transactions. Whilst the 'single agreement' concept is not expressly provided for in Chinese legislation, nor has it been specifically examined in a bankruptcy proceeding in Chinese courts, the latest regulatory developments and judicial views tend to endorse the 'single agreement' concept as a reflection of the contracting parties' 'freedom to contract.

140 Ibid, 79. *Citibank (China) Co., Ltd. v Shanghai Golden Globe International Trading Co., Ltd.* S2958, 2015. 花旗银行(中国)有限公司诉上海金环球国际贸易有限公司等金融衍生品交易纠纷案【上海市浦东新区人民法院，2015）浦民六（商）初字第s2958号】

141 See earlier, King & Wood Malleson, *Whitepaper China's Derivatives Market and Judicial Trends* (2018), https://www.isda.org/a/9pREE/Chinese-Derivatives-Market-and-Legal-Trends.pdf, 51.

142 Ibid.

Golden Globe entered five LME copper swaps under a master derivative contract in the period from September to December 2014. The first transaction expired on 22 December 2014, but the company failed to pay the settlement amount. In December 2014, Golden Globe failed to sign an Agreement of Pledge over Account and did not post the required margin to Citi (China). In addition, a loan advanced by Citi (China) Shanghai branch to Golden Globe was accelerated in late 2014. Those performance failures constituted events of default under the mini-master agreement and Citi (China) served an early termination notice to close out four outstanding transactions, designating December 24, 2014 as the early termination date for the outstanding transactions.[143] Citi (China) determined the 'close-out amount' in respect of each early terminated transaction. Citi (China) was 'in-the-money' in respect of three transactions and the 'out-of the-money' for the fourth transaction. When determining each close-out amount, Citi (China) adopted quotations from a third party.[144]

Another demonstration that Chinese courts are accepting close-out netting provisions is Citi (China) and Yingda Life Electric (Zhongshan) Co., Ltd. (Yingda) (*Yingda*).[145] The case involving a dispute over a mini-master agreement. The parties entered into a USD/RMB forward. They were scheduled to exchange US dollar and renminbi amounts on five different settlement dates. However, before the occurrence of any settlement date, the defendant, Yingda, defaulted.[146] Citi (China), calculated and determined the close-out amount based on the amount of losses or costs it would incur or gains it could realise in replacing or in providing the economic equivalent of the material terms of the terminated transaction. This 'close-out amount'/'replacement transaction' calculation method was upheld by the Shanghai Pudong New Area People's Court. Therefore, the absence of

143 Ibid, 52.

144 Ibid, Citi (China) calculated a single net amount by setting off the four close-out amounts and the unpaid settlement amount in respect of the first transaction. The calculation was upheld by the Shanghai court. The court was satisfied that the calculation of the early termination amount was made in good faith and in a commercially reasonable manner, and based on the fair market value of the terminated transactions. Also note, a Chinese bankruptcy case against GITIC involved a dispute over a cross-border swap transaction documented under the 1987 version of an ISDA master derivative agreement. The case was heard by the Guangdong People's High Court pursuant to the Interim Version of the Chinese Enterprise Bankruptcy Law as of 1986. Although the Chinese court and the bankruptcy committee did not challenge the effect of an automatic early termination of the master derivative agreement, the dispute involved only one transaction entered into under the master derivative agreement, and that the foreign counterparty's claim for the settlement amount calculated pursuant to such agreement was rejected by the court.

145 *Citibank (China) Co., Ltd. v. Yingda Life Electric (Zhongshan) Co., Ltd.* S3800, 2014, 花旗银行(中国)有限公司诉樱达生活电器(中山)有限公司等金融衍生品种交易纠纷案上海市浦东 新区人民法院，(2014)浦民六(商)初字第S3800号In King & Wood Malleson, *Whitepaper China's Derivatives Market and Judicial Trends* (2018), https://www.isda.org/a/9pREE/Chinese-Derivatives-Market-and-Legal-Trends.pdf.

146 Ibid, 52–52.

close-out netting provisions within a single agreement will be taken into consideration, where there is no proceeding of bankruptcy that has been commenced.[147]

The lack of specific close-out netting legislation is nevertheless problematic, although not distinctive to China. This gap will continue to pose significant challenges, because of the reliance on Article 113 of the Chinese Contract Law. As noted by King, Wood and Mallesons, a counterparty may argue that a close-out amount is in the nature of compensation for losses, which should not be awarded if there is no proof of the actual loss suffered by the non-defaulting counterparty.[148] The need to address this balance is reflected in Article 113 of the Chinese Contract Law provides:

> Where one of the parties does not perform a contractual obligation, or does not perform a contractual obligation as agreed, resulting in losses to the other party, the total compensatory amount shall be equivalent to the total losses sustained by the other party due to the breach of contract, including benefits that the other party would have been able to obtain upon the contract being performed, but this amount shall not exceed the total losses that the breaching party, at the time of concluding the contract, foresaw or should have foreseen to probably result from breach of contract. Where business operators engage in fraudulent behaviour with respect to consumers in the provision of goods or services, they shall be liable to provide compensatory amount in accordance with the provisions of the Law of the People's Republic of China on the Protection of the Rights and Interests of Consumers.[149]

Despite the fact that close-out netting provisions appear, in part, to be accommodated for within the current Chinese regulatory framework, there is a significant amount of work to be undertaken by the state to protect and ensure the long-term stability of their financial markets as, and if it chooses, to further integrate international investment. Thus, there have been calls for overseas investors to adopt the ISDA Master Agreements in China.[150] That is, as China continues to rise as a major economy, it is promoting the adoption of the international framework that has been successfully used globally across the investment sector. Furthermore, in a sign of further adopting the current internationally agreed framework, future investors will be afforded a choice between signing an ISDA Master Agreement or local master agreements offered by the National Association of Financial Market Institutional Investors and the Securities Association of China. Nevertheless, and while there are calls for a more coherent approach to be adopted, there has been acknowledgement of the use of ISDA Master Agreement(s) where they have been

147 Ibid, 53.

148 Ibid.

149 Ibid.

150 Chang Geng Lai, BNP Paribas China, Yicai (2020), https://www.yicaiglobal.com/news/isda-deal-to-attract-more-overseas-investment-in-china-bnp-china-chief-says.

governed by Chinese law. This positive sign further demonstrates the interconnectedness of financial markets and of entities operating across jurisdictions globally.

In the 2017, the China International Economic and Trade Arbitration Commission (CIETAC) Beijing Arbitration decision, the defaulting party to an ISDA 2002 Master Agreement governed by Chinese law alleged that the early termination amount calculated under Section 6 of the ISDA Master Agreement constituted liquidated damages for the purpose of Article 114 of the Chinese Contract Law. The defaulting party subsequently alleged that the amount was 'excessively greater than the losses caused' as a result of a breach of that agreement and petitioned the relevant arbitral tribunal to reduce the liquidated damages. However, the tribunal did not accept this position. It held that any obligation that has not been performed does not need to be performed. The non-defaulting party was obliged to adopt measures to prevent any increase in the losses suffered.[151]

In reinforcing this, there are cases in which Chinese arbitrators, even though they are applying Chinese law to ISDA Master Agreements, calculate compensation for losses in a manner that is comparable, in part, to the practice adopted in jurisdictions that recognise and enforce those Agreements. Notably, in a 2016 CIETAC Shanghai Arbitration decision, the Tribunal held that, the early termination provision governed by ISDA Master Agreement was valid in providing a method for calculating the amount of compensation for losses under Chinese Contract Law.[152] The Tribunal held that:

> [I]n determining the early termination amount, the bank had a contractual right to reference market quotations or to rely on its actual unwind price. The bank only used the actual unwind price to calculate the early termination amount. The tribunal held, however, that the bank should rely on the more objective market quotation prices (rather than the actual unwind prices) to determine the early termination amount. The tribunal therefore made minor reductions to the calculation of the early termination amount. However, there have been cases and awards where the courts and arbitration tribunals adjusted the early termination amount due to gaps or flaws in a bank's evidence supporting its calculation of the early termination amount. A bank should therefore collate all its supporting evidence in obtaining third-party

151 Ibid, 55–56. Under Articles 97 and 119 of the Chinese Contract Law: After a contract has been discharged, the performance of any obligations that have not been performed is terminated. Where obligations have already been performed, depending on the status of performance and the nature of the contract, a party may demand to be put in the position as if no contract were entered into or resort to other remedies, and a party may also demand compensation for any losses sustained; and the non-defaulting party must take measures to prevent any increase in the losses sustained, failing which it may not demand compensation for any increase in the losses sustained.

152 Ibid, 59.

price quotations when determining the close-out amount(s) to demonstrate the calculation is undertaken in a commercially reasonable manner.[153]

Despite the governance of ISDA Master Agreements by Chinese national contract law, liquidated damages (the compensatory amount for losses) should be substantially equivalent to the actual losses suffered by the non-defaulting party, and that party bears the burden of establishing the quantum of its losses.[154] Nevertheless, to date, close-out netting is not a formal regulated legal concept expressly recognised under Chinese law, nor is it expressly addressed under the Chinese Enterprise Bankruptcy Law. That said, and even before the call for greater recognition of ISDA Master Agreements, Chinese Courts and Arbitration Centers[155] have understood the importance of ISDA Master Agreements to the overall financial sector and in managing potential-actual defaulting party.

The next step for China it to consider the formal regulation of close-out netting provisions in light of the law and practice in other states examined earlier, such as Australia. The potential shared benefit of doing so, will be to provide greater legal certainty and stability to financial markets in the Asia region and beyond. It will also provide greater policy, legal and commercial certainty to investors and states by demonstrating that China is willing to further open its financial and banking sectors globally. In part, China has gone some way in regulating close-out netting provisions, by showing its willingness to adopt the transnational ISDA Master Agreement framework, of which netting arrangements form an integral part. By and large, China has adopted the internationally agreed contractual framework and law of contract that has gone someway to building its investment and financial sectors. While this policy direction is for China to determine in its national interests, it can demonstrate international leadership by enhancing commercial and economic development based on a sound rules-based framework that underpins the rule of law.

In support of this development, international arbitration in China has been growing under the extended rules and jurisdiction of such Chinese arbitration associations as the China Economic and Trade Arbitration Commission (CIETAC). Similar to the other states compared in this chapter, China understands the importance of having choice law provisions within contracts to resolve cross-border disputes. Article 18 of the Law of the Application of Laws for Foreign-related Civil Relations of the People's Republic of China allows parties to an agreement to choose an applicable law for arbitration. The Civil Procedure Law of the People's Republic of China also provides for arbitration. Finally, China is a signatory to the

153 Ibid.

154 Ibid, 56.

155 *Arbitration Law of the People's Republic of China 1994.* This provides that an arbitration agreement come in the form of arbitration clauses contained in the underlying contract or other forms of written agreements for arbitration reached before or after the dispute arises, under Article 16.

New York Convention on the Recognition and Enforcement of Foreign Arbitral Awards 1958.

6.4 Conclusion

The importance of close-out netting provisions to the world economy cannot be underestimated. It has been demonstrated that, while close-out netting is a comparatively recent means of internationalisation and harmonisation of transnational, finance, investment and insolvency law, it is being increased embraced internationally. At the same time, it has not been embraced across nation states. This chapter has briefly compared the regulation and use close-out netting in select states. A comparison across a larger number of states is needed to identify how and to what extent nation states have adopted, or are contemplating adopting, close-out netting in their national legal systems.

The recognition, use and application of ISDA Master Agreements that, more often than not, contain close-out netting provisions have become the contractual choice across the international finance sector. Despite the extensive law and judicial decisions in the US and UK, other states, such as Singapore India, Singapore and Australia, have adopted the common law model originating in the UK. Significantly, as will be highlighted in ensuing chapters, China, while not formally part of the ISDA, has generally adopted an approach that is comparable, in part, to the ISDA modelling in the West.

Arguably, a theme is emerging, reinforced by global financial hubs in London and New York that have rendered ISDA Master Agreements more effective and sustainable. Reinforcing this is the enhancement and acceptance of ISDA Master Agreement by Chinese courts in calculating the level of compensation for losses. This is illustrated by the 2016 CIETAC Shanghai Arbitration decision discussed earlier, declaring valid an early termination provision under an ISDA Master Agreement, albeit governed by Chinese Law. In our view, this is a strong sign that China well appreciates the importance of using effective legal mechanisms and tools in order to maximise upon the stability of industry sectors, such as banking and finance, both domestically and internationally. The chapter has also demonstrated that China has for some time embraced the transnational approach such as by adopting and using ISDA Master Agreements. By default, China has accepted the application, in part, of English and New York law as the predominant law used by these agreements. Yet, and while we are advocating for the further adoption of netting provisions in national laws and their additional internationalisation from Principles to a Model Law, a high-level layer of internationalisation has already been achieved by adopting close-out netting provisions into ISDA Master Agreements. Problematic though, in making this assumption is that all ISDA Master Agreement adopt close-out netting provisions, is the absence of adequate information available to confirm that this is the case. Further research is therefore necessary.

An uncertainty in the current regulatory and legal regulation of netting and ISDA Master Agreements is a result of Brexit. While not resolved at the time of writing, England's regulatory choices remain open. EU member states continue to revert to Rome I and II, with established and distinctive rules governing ISDA Master Agreements. In issue is whether, despite the EU and UK reaching a Brexit Deal, whether the UK will follow a different course to the EU Specifically, the Force Majeure provision in the 2002 ISDA Master Agreement provides that, where there constitutes an event that constitutes an act of the state, it constitutes a Terminating Event. Brexit is not a force majeure event, in not being unforeseen or beyond the reasonable control of the UK and EU. However, the 2020 Brexit deal is a Terminating Event in being a termination agreement concluded by these two Parties. However, in our view, this agreement does not constitute the UK's exit from the ISDA. On the contrary, it provides the opportunity for the UK to strengthen its global position as an investment hub and to reinforce the importance of ISDA Master Agreements and the need for including carefully drafted netting arrangements in such agreements.

As highlighted in this chapter, drafting close-out netting clauses is very important to maintain sustainable cross-border financial dealings. Care is therefore required when drafting other clauses that may act as an obstacle or totally override netting provisions, particularly when the intention was not to do so. The understanding of close-out netting versus set-off arrangements needs to be carefully managed to avoid courts being embroiled in confusion over which provision applies.

However, to internationalise close-out netting arrangements, states need to provide explicitly for them. Doing so will go a long way to stabilising billions of dollars in investment transnationally under the various contractual arrangements that are transacted daily use. A harmonised global close- out netting regime, in our view, will go some way to ensuring that, in the next post-COVID-19 global disaster. Doing so will ensure that contractual clauses are prepared, confidently and transparently, to prevent and minimise the risk of enlarging financial stress and ensuing loss. This arguably has to be a priority in the global economy that has becomes increasingly precipitous, even as it appears to be restabilising.

INDEX

www.ingramcontent.com/pod-product-compliance
Ingram Content Group UK Ltd.
Pitfield, Milton Keynes, MK11 3LW, UK
UKHW020156200926
475702UK00016B/2736
9781032318813